AF835599

CSCW '92

SHARING PERSPECTIVES

Proceedings of the Conference on Computer-Supported Cooperative Work

October 31 to November 4, 1992   Toronto, Canada

SPONSORED BY ACM SIGCHI & SIGOIS

Jon Turner and Robert Kraut, eds.

The Association for Computing Machinery
1515 Broadway
New York, New York 10036

Copyright © 1992 by the Association for Computing Machinery, Inc. Copying without fee is permitted provided that the copies are not made or distributed for direct commercial advantage, and credit to the source is given. Abstracting with credit is permitted. For other copying of articles that carry a code at the bottom of the first page, copying is permitted provided that the per-copy fee indicated in the code is paid through the Copyright Clearance Center, 27 Congress Street, Salem, MA 01970. For permission to republish write to: Director of Publications, Association for Computing Machinery. To copy otherwise, or republish, requires a fee and/or specific permission.

Soft Cover ISBN: 0-89791-542-9
Series Hard Cover ISBN: 0-89791-543-7

Additional copies may be ordered prepaid from:

ACM Order Department
P.O. Box 64145
Baltimore, MD 21264

1-800 342-6626
1-410 528-4261 (Outside US, MD and AK)

ACM Order Number: 612920

From the Conference Chairs

Marilyn Mantei

Department of Computer Science and
Faculty of Library and Information Science
University of Toronto
Toronto, Ontario
Canada M5S 1A1
mantei@dgp.utoronto.ca

Ron Baecker

Department of Computer Science and
Computer Systems Research Institute
University of Toronto
Toronto, Ontario
Canada M5S 1A1
baecker@dgp.utoronto.ca

It is our pleasure to welcome you to the 1992 Conference on Computer Supported Cooperative Work. Since the first such conference held in Austin, Texas, in 1986, the conference has grown and the CSCW field taken on shape and form. As chairs of the conference we have had the great privilege bestowed upon us of being able to help in the shaping of the field and the generation of future paths to follow. We owe thanks to the original visionaries who began these conferences a short six years ago and established the foundations and perspectives for us to follow. We have tried to preserve and also build upon these foundations in order to accommodate the growth of the field, the stresses associated with this growth, the influx of new researchers into the field and the widely diverse disciplines that form it.

Our conference theme, appropriately, is *sharing perspectives.* It reflects the many different facets of CSCW and the efforts we have made to accomodate the diversity. The conference artwork embodies the conference theme. Integrated into a single face is time, technology, humans, work and a map of the conference location.

It is our belief that continuing to bring the multiple disciplines of the field together is the only way to establish a thriving research field. We feel it is important that systems people steeped in their paradigms of remote procedure calls and hash tables and human behavior people worried about contingency theory and Cronbach's alpha reliability take the time to listen to each others' research talks, attend their panel sessions and find centers of mutual understanding.

We also find that industry is becoming excited about groupware products and beginning to search for examples and methodologies to help build such products. Although it is not our intent to lose the research nature of the conference, we felt we needed to do a better job of building bridges to and *sharing perspectives* with those engaged in building, delivering, and supporting products.

Growth, alone, has created difficulties. The CSCW community is no longer the small intimate collection of researchers that can be accomodated in a one track conference of three days. To accomodate the increased interest in CSCW, we had to rethink our conference publications and our schedules, and add new activities.

Tutorials now provide research dissemination both for practitioners and for researchers needing to learn about distant paradigms. Workshops provide the intimacy and the chance for small similarly focused researchers to get together for a day. Videos provide a set of examples of new systems and system design techniques. As part of the SIGGRAPH video review, they also provide a new and accessible conference archive for the CSCW community.

Growth has forced us to make our proceedings papers shorter and doubled the number of paper tracks in the conference. In conjunction with our theme of *sharing perspectives*, we have organized the tracks so that no attendee can follow only their specific research interests.

A conference is built not only upon its frazzled chairs trying to hold the pieces together but upon its abundant source of incredibly energetic, enthusiatic and well-organized volunteers. We list this wonderful crowd of unselfish people on the next page. Our heartfelt thanks goes out to them.

A very special note of thanks goes to one member of the committee, our conference administrator, Barbara Whitmer. It is not just her endless hours of work and creative solutions, but her cool head that kept the conference on track.

We also wish to thank our industrial sponsors who gave us the financial backing to allow this conference to take place, The Information Technology Research Centre for the Province of Ontario, Lotus Development Corporation, Intel Corporation and Xerox Palo Alto Research Center.

Our thanks also go to our two sponsors, ACM SIGCHI and SIGOIS who have not only been supportive financially but also in sharing their long years of experience in running conferences.

Conference committee

Conference Chairs
Marilyn Mantei and Ron Baecker, University of Toronto

Technical Program
Robert Kraut, Bellcore

Panels
Sara Bly, Xerox PARC

Tutorials
Lee Sproull, Boston University

Demonstrations
Michael Muller and Aita Salasoo, Bellcore

Workshops
Ray Panko, University of Hawaii

Videos
Saul Greenberg, University of Calgary

Treasurer and Assistant Chair
Paul Brennan, Northern Telecom

Publications
Joan Cherry, University of Toronto

Proceedings
Jon Turner, New York University

Local Arrangements
Rhona Charron and Elyse Hayden, Ontario Institute for Studies in Education

Student Volunteers
Steve Portigal, University of Guelph
Mark Benthin, Bell-Northern Research

Publicity
Wendy Cukier, Ryerson Polytechnic Institute

Registration
Steve Anderson, Lawrence Livermore National Laboratory

Book Exhibits
Scott Ambler, University of Toronto

Cruise Director
Tim Hill, Sirius Solutions

Audio / Visual
Beverly Harrison, University of Toronto
Tammy TeWinkel, University of Guelph

Computer Support
Gifford Louie and Russell Owen, University of Toronto

Industrial Liaison
Peter Orbeton, Lotus Development Corporation

Protocol
Gale Moore, University of Toronto

SIGCHI Liaison
Lisa Neal, EDS Center for Advanced Research

SIGOIS Liaison
Carson Woo, University of British Columbia

Conference Support
Barbara Whitmer, University of Toronto

Conference Advisor
Bill Buxton, University of Toronto and Xerox PARC

Review committees

Workshops
Ray Panko (Chair), University of Hawaii
Laku Chidambaram, University of Hawaii
Philip Johnson, University of Hawaii

Demonstrations
Michael Muller (Chair), Bellcore
Aita Salasoo (Chair), Bellcore
Hiroshi Ishii, NTT Human Interface Laboratories
Gary Olson, University of Michigan

Videos
Saul Greenberg (Chair), University of Calgary
Stephen Hayne, University of Calgary
Allan McLean, Rank Xerox EuroPARC
Catherine Plaisant, University of Maryland
John Tang, Sun Microsystems
Christian Heath, Rank Xerox EuroPARC
Paul Luff, Rank Xerox EuroPARC
Mark Roseman,University of Calgary

Contents

Video spaces

Building real-time groupware

Innovations in e-mail

The power of simple shared workspaces

Ethnographically-informed design

Collaborative writing

Conversational props

Consistency in collaborative systems

Emerging technologies for cooperative work

Field studies in coordination

Collaboration in the real world

Organizational influences on CSCW success

Domain specific collaborative tools

From the Program Chair

Robert Kraut

Bellcore
445 South Street
Morristown, NJ 08962
kraut@bellcore.com

Welcome to CSCW 92, the fourth international research conference on Computer Supported Cooperative Work. The conference is committed to presenting the best of new research in the behavioral, computer and engineering sciences on the fit between groups and the technology that might allow them to work better.

Yet the phrase *Computer Supported Cooperative Work* is a misnomer and implies a more limited field of study than the diverse collection of research that will be presented at the conference. A glance at previous conference proceedings shows that the phrase refers to the study of group and organizational work practices and the application of communications and computing -- information technology generally -- to support work, education and occasionally play in groups varying in size, permanence, and structure.

The papers to be presented at CSCW 92 reflect the interdisciplinary perspective that has been evident from the first of these conferences in 1986. Contributions come from social scientists, attempting to understand the requirements that real groups impose on applications and to evaluate the impact of technology on group performance, computer scientists and electrical engineers trying to provide new concepts and facilities for creating computer and communication applications, application builders, whose interest is in creating useful tools for groups, and practitioners dedicated to making good use of this knowledge and these tools. This cross-fertilization has made the field a vibrant one.

In selecting papers, panels and plenary speakers, the program committee attempted both to identify leading edge research and thinking about the role of information technology in supporting groups and to maintain a balance among the different groups who contribute to the field. The program reflects both the technological and the social aspects of the field. Over a third of the presentations come from outside of North America

While the program committee attempted to consider the concept of technological support for groups broadly, the focus this year, as in the past, is on white-collar work. For some reason we do not receive many papers on robots on the assembly line or distributed learning environments.

The large number of good paper and panel submissions forced us to abandon the single-track format common to the prior CSCW conferences. The program committee selected 48 of the 191 papers and three of the 12 panels submitted to the conference. Even so, we were forced to turn down many good papers and panels, for reasons of space.

Our two plenary speakers provide some of the "big picture" that is often missing from detailed research reports. Shumpei Kumon presents a theory about the role that computer networks play in the shift from an industrial to a post-industrial age. Joseph McGrath presents an empirical critique of the literature on CSCW and group performance.

In addition to the papers and panels, the program will include pre-conference workshops, videos, and demonstrations. These alternate approaches to experiencing the CSCW domain should help make the research content come alive for many attendees.

Both the program committee and our ad hoc reviewers deserve tremendous thanks for the hours they donated to evaluating submissions and shaping the final program. Each submission was evaluated by at least two reviewers, and most were reviewed by three. Under tight time constraints, members of the program committee and the reviewers wrote over 500 evaluations, attempting simultaneously to judge whether submissions were of sufficient quality and breadth to warrant presentation to the highly diverse CSCW audience and to provide helpful comments to the authors.

I hope that you enjoy the CSCW 92 program, that you learn from it, and that you use the opportunity of this conference to meet with your colleagues, to exchange ideas, and that the result of this activity will be to xkeep the field as vibrant and intellectually exciting as it as been in the past.

Program committee

Sid Ahuja
AT&T Bell Labs

Prasun Dewan
Purdue University

Irene Greif
Lotus Development Corp.

Saul Greenberg
University of Calgary

Jonathan Grudin
University of California at Irvine

Starr Roxanne Hiltz
New Jersey Institute of Technology

Hiroshi Ishii
NTT Human Interface Laboratories

Robert Johansen
Institute for the Future

Sara Kiesler
Carnegie-Mellon University

John L. King
University of California at Irvine

Robert Kraut
Bellcore (Technical program chair)

Thomas Malone
Sloan School of Management

Chris Neuwirth
Carnegie Mellon University

Judith Olson
University of Michigan

Stephen Reder
Northwest Regional Educational Laboratory

Michael Robinson
University of Amsterdam

John B. Smith
University of North Carolina

Norbert Streitz
GMD-Integrated Publication and Information Systems Institute

Lucy Suchman
Xerox PARC

Andy Whinston
University of Texas at Austin

Ilze Zigurs
College of Business and Administration

Sara Bly
Xerox PARC (Panel chair)

AD HOC REVIEWERS

Mark Abel
Mark Ackerman
Vinod Anupam
Murali Aravamudan
Laurel Austin
Liam Bannon
Nick Belkin
Steve Benford
Tom Brink
Bonnie Buckland
Jeff Buterfield
Rajiv Choudhary
David Constant
Coleen Cool
Kevin Crowston
Wayne Dyksen
Robert Ensor
Robert Fish
Jolene Galegher
Louis Gomez
Sylvia Hart-Landsberg
Jim Herbsleb
Ralph Hill
John Hoxmeier
John Hughes
Simon Kaplan
Kenneth Kozar
Balachander Krishnamurthy
Jintae Lee
Carlyn Lowery
Paul Luff
Carolyn Nguyen
Gary Olson
Wanda Orlikowski
John Patterson
Colleen L. Phillips
P. Venkat Rangan
Sukumar Rathnam
Paul Resnick
Doug Riecken
John Riedl
Tom Rodden
Andrei Roussakov
Kjeld Schmidt
Robert G. Schwab
Eugene Spafford
Marianne Storrosten
David Stotts
Susan Straus
Toshihiko Yamakam
Raj Yavatkar

From wealth to wisdom: A change in the social paradigm

Shumpei Kumon

Center for Global Communications
International University of Japan
5-2-32 Minami Azabu, Minato-ku
Tokyo, 106 Japan
E-mail: shumpei@twics.co.jp

Modern Civilization is about to enter its third phase, accompanied by a shift from the paradigms of an industrial society to the paradigms of an information society. The first phase was characterized by militarization and state-formation, while the second was characterized by industrialization and enterprise-formation. In the first phase a competitive social game, the prestige game, was played by the sovereign states. In the second phase another game, the wealth game played by industrial enterprises was added to and eventually replaced the prestige game.

In contrast, in the third phase of Modern Civilization, *informatization* and *intelprise*-formation will take place. Informatization is the process of rapid and continuous technological innovation in the sphere of information processing. It will lead to the emergence and spread of a new type of social actor, that is, intelprises who become players of what might be called the wisdom game.

During this third phase a number of new elements of Modern Civilization will emerge. One of values that sustains the Modern Civilization is active instrumentalism. The individual actors use various means to influence the world in order to attain goals that they regard as desirable. Acts that are designed to control the acts and states of other actors are political acts. Threats and coercion were widely used as the basic means and goals for the prestige game; these shifted to exchange and exploitation as the means and goals of the wealth game. As the third phase of modernization emerges, we expect a gradual increase in the use of persuasion and inducement as the basic means and goals of the wisdom game.

The wisdom game will differ from the wealth game in a number of other respects. In the wealth game, entrepreneurs produce individual and specific goods in factories and sell them as commodities. By selling their goods successfully, entrepreneurs demonstrate the social usefulness of their products and gain rewards in the form of wealth, thereby acquiring the abstract and general power to trade. In this sense, the market is also an arena in which the social usefulness of entrepreneurs' activities is evaluated.

Similarly, the intelpreneurs who participate in the wisdom game produce individual and specific information in offices and seek to share it with others. By successfully sharing their information, they demonstrate the value of the individual pieces of information that they have supplied in terms of the social values of truth, goodness and beauty. Their reward is wisdom, which is the abstract and general ability to persuade or exert intellectual influence. In other words, many people will be prepared to heed the words of an intelpreneur who has gained a social reputation as a person of wisdom.

Since, in the third phase, worth is based on sharing information, information rights, rather than sovereignty or property rights, will be the basic value on the basis of which the wisdom game will be built. Its players, the intelprises, will compete in the global "intelplace" to acquire and display wisdom as a general and abstract means of persuasion and inducement.

Technological breakthroughs such as the Internet form the basis of the intelprises' abilities to participate in the intelplace. Indeed, one can view the burgeoning volume of news groups on the USENET as an early form of a global intelplace,

The transition to the third phase of Modern Civilization will be neither automatic or without conflict. The roles of individuals, of enterprises, of sovereign states, and of supra-national actors all need to be negotiated. The talk ends with some speculations about how the transition might come about.

Groups Interacting with Technology: The Complex and Dynamic Fit of Group, Task, Technology, and Time

Joseph E. McGrath

Department of Psychology
University of Illinois
Champaign, IL 61820
jmcgrath@s.psych.uiuc.edu

A review of research on the use of technology for collaborative work in groups, and a launching of an empirical research program in that area, has led us to several important conclusions:

1. That the extant body of research literature on this topic contains many interesting ideas and some empirical evidence; but that the empirical base is meager, and, unsystematic in coverage of all of the relevant factors and their interplay.

Specifically, the literature as a whole shows a major multi-way confound of a) research "lab" or locale at which a study was done, b) type of technology studied, c) type of group task and group composition studied, d) dependent variables studied, and e) research strategy used. Each "lab" studies its own technology factors, using its own group types and task types, and its own preferred research strategy, and even studies its own preferred subset of dependent variables. Thus, bodies of work generated from different labs or research locales are not comparable. They are not studies of "the same thing" in any of several senses. And the body of work done in each "lab", while interesting and useful, lacks a broader verification that can come only from testing of the same issues in other contexts.

2. That both the theoretical ideas in this area and the available empirical evidence suggests that the effects of technology on collaborative work in groups involve very complex interactions of features of technology with: attributes of members, features of group structure, type and characteristics of group tasks, and attributes of the context within which the group is working.

Specifically, the effectiveness of any given technology appears to be a complex and complicated function of the "fit" of four panels of attributes: member and group; task; technology; and context.

3. Moreover, that "fit" is not only complex, it is also dynamic. The optimum fit varies over time. But two quite different effects are a function of time, and they work in opposing directions:

a. Time as Medium for Accrual of Experience: In general, continued experience -- with the same group membership, with the same task, with the same technology, and/or in the same operating context -- tends to have a routinizing effect on group interaction and task performance.

b. Time as Medium for Change: In general, changes - in group membership, task type and conditions, technology, and/or operating conditions -- tends to have a perturbing effect on group interaction and task performance.

The talk will be an effort to lay out as much of that complex puzzle as possible, supporting the assertions where possible with references to the existing literature, reports of our own studies, and/or putatively compelling conceptual formulations.

CSCW '92 Workshops

Raymond Panko

College of Business Administration
University of Hawaii
Honolulu, HI 96822
Panko@DScience.CBA.Hawaii.edu

Workshops provide an opportunity for conference attendees to devote an entire day to a specific research focus and to work closely with a small group of associates discussing their specific research interests. Many of the conference workshops proposed to outline or structure the issues facing the subdiscipline.

The range of workshop topics at CSCW'92 reflects the diversity of the field and its maturing into subdisciplines. The application of ethnographic studies to computer systems design contrasts with a workshop on CSCW tools and implementation techniques. Education issues are featured in a workshop that discusses how collaborative problem solving can be supported by CSCW techniques whereas another workshop considers the invasion of privacy that the new CSCW technologies might bring.

A capsule summary of each workshop that took place at the conference is presented in the sections which follow.

ETHNOGRAPHIC STUDIES OF WORK AND CSCW SYSTEM DESIGN

John Hughes, Lancaster University
Dave Randall, Lancaster University
Graham Button, Plymouth Polytechnic and Rank Xerox EuroPARC

A major cause of systems failure is a mismatch between system functionality and the realities of its work context. One way to study work contexts is through the use of ethnography.

While ethnography is a well-established tradition in sociology and psychology, systems design is a new context with many new methodological issues. For instance, whereas systems designers tend to decompose tasks and activities, ethnographers tend to view things in terms of socially organized collectivities. Another problem is organizing ethnographic materials in a form that is easily communicable to developers.

The workshop provided a forum in which social researchers and system designers met to discuss ethnomethodologies in practice and the refinements that are needed for CSCW design.

REAL TIME GROUP DRAWING AND WRITING TOOLS

Saul Greenberg, University of Calgary
Stephen Hayne, University of Calgary

Participants at meetings often share physical work with one another: notes documents, plans, slides, and drawings, as well as a common work space that allows people to annotate, draw, brainstorm, record, and convey ideas. New technology may be able to enhance this type of sharing. Unfortunately, there appears to be a great deal of replication and overlap. The time is now ripe to proceed toward empiricism, in which lessons are drawn from experience.

Workshop attendees discussed the human and technical issues surrounding shared drawing/writing tools, bringing together the human factors, technical factors and innovations, and empirical validation of experiences with people using shared work spaces.

UNDERSTANDING AND SUPPORTING SUCESSFUL GROUP WORK IN SOFTWARE DESIGN

John Bennett, IBM Almaden Research Center
John Karat, IBM Watson Research Center

Experienced practitioners and reflective researchers met to discuss how to improve group activity in software design. The emphasis was on the types of supports and interventions needed to increase the probability of system success. The outcome resulted in a set of collected techniques and an understanding of how to apply these techniques to both group processes in software design and development and to the use of such software in meetings.

Topics included what characterizes successful groups in terms of group memberships and group tasks, and how changes can be made to the way groups work so that future group work is more productive. The discussion focussed on useful group management techniques including both the technology-based techniques and techniques that had their foundations in human skills (such as facilitation).

CSCW TOOLS AND IMPLEMENTATION

Simon Kaplan, University of Illinois
Prasun Dewan, Purdue University
Tom Rodden, Lancaster University
Steve Benford, Nottingham University
Philip Johnson, University of Hawaii

This workshop served as a forum for developers of CSCW tools and technologies enabling them to share ideas, problems, and proposed solutions. Issues addressed included such things as architectures and abstractions to support CSCW applications, sharing, concurrency control, access control, and undo/redo models for CSCW applications; incorporating multimedia in CSCW applications; techniques for allowing high degrees of tailoring and flexibility; impact of CSCW on existing applications; facilitating cooperation among CSCW applications; and sharing of organizational information and resources among applications.

TECHNOLOGY AND PEDAGOGY FOR COLLABORATIVE PROBLEM SOLVING

Denis Newman, Bolt, Beranek and Newman
Timothy Koschmann, Southern Illinois University

A large part of the current school reform movement centers around changing the nature of the educational activity in schools from teacher-led lessons on subject matter content to project-based work in which students are active problem-solvers and theorists while the teacher plays more of a coaching role. Very often, the complexity of the projects invites collaborative work as a way to bring multiple perspectives on the problem and for students to learn from each other. Collaborative problem solving in schools is making use of computer tools for analysis, simulation, display and communication. The workshop investigated ways to mold both the technology and the pedagogy to take best advantage of student collaboration.

Attendees focussed on two distinct domains of work: (1) Wide area work groups which involve teachers, researchers and developers exchanging information across wide area networks and (2) Local area work groups in which teachers, researchers and developers work within indivdual classrooms to develop collaborative techniques.

This workshop was jointly sponsored by CSCW'92 and the Ontario Institute for Studies in Education.

INTERDISCIPLINARY THEORY FOR CSCW DESIGN

Dan Shapiro, Lancaster University
Yvonne Waern, University of Stockholm
Thomas Schael, Instituto RSO

Domain issues in CSCW design have become too complex to attack on the basis of common sense or a single discipline. We need to improve the ways in which practitioners and researchers in various fields can make their work useful and intelligible to one another.

The workshop focused on the following questions. What are the key goals, methods, and characteristics of the different disciplines? What are the key terms and concepts, and to what extent are they reconcilable or in conflict? What real examples exist of disciplinary contributions making a real difference in practical design? What practical experience is there in interdisciplinary collaboration in CSCW design, and what lessons have emerged?

PRIVACY CONSIDERATIONS IN CSCW

Andrew Clement, University of Toronto

CSCW tools often provide new ways to collect massive amounts of data about individuals. These databases and new tools for keeping track of people, such as media spaces and active badges, create the possibilities of unwelcome interruption and exposure.

The workshop consisted of a group of researchers and practitioners who have an ongoing interest in the privacy implications of CSCW technology. It focused on identifying the major privacy issues in CSCW, particularly in relation to paradigmatic applications (e.g., email, media spaces), and proposed a framework to guide CSCW developers and implementers in creating applications that are sensitive to privacy concerns.

CSCW '92 Tutorials

Lee Sproull

School of Management
Boston University
Boston, MA 02215

As we learn more about CSCW, education and professional development can help leverage our knowledge and experience. CSCW '92 tutorials provide a key to this leverage. They cover some of the most important topics in CSCW today in formats designed for managers, practitioners, educators and researchers.

1. CSCW AND GROUPWARE: OVERVIEW OF BEHAVIOURAL ISSUES AND SURVEY OF SYSTEMS

Jonathan Grudin, Information and Computer Science Dept., UC Irvine

Steven Poltrock, Boeing Computer Services

Objective: To survey the definition and scope of the field; the current state of research and development in several application areas; design and evaluation issues, including problems and promising approaches.

Content: How do we ensure that changes in communication and coordination enhance productivity and job satisfaction? Specific challenges that have led to groupware failures and research and development approaches that address them are described. Application areas are illustrated through descriptions and videotapes of existing prototype and commercial systems.

Instructors: Steven Poltrock is an AI Specialist at Boeing's Advanced Technology Center, where he leads a project supporting collaborative engineering. Jonathan Grudin has worked as developer, researcher, and consultant before joining the faculty at UC Irvine.

2. COMPUTER-SUPPORTED MEETING ROOMS

Lisa Neal, EDS Center for Advanced Research

Objective: To present an overview of the state of the art of computer-supported meeting rooms.

Content: Computer-supported meeting rooms are an increasingly important focus of CSCW. The number of rooms is increasing as companies try to make meetings more efficient and effective. Existing rooms are surveyed including hardware platforms and software tools, how rooms have been used, and their benefits and disadvantages. Both research and marketing results are covered.

Instructor: Lisa Neal is a senior research engineer at the EDS Center for Advanced Research, where she leads a CSCW project.

3. BUILDING CSCW INTERFACES

Alan Wexelblat, Bull Information Systems

Objective: To give engineers/designers confidence and understanding to actually go out and implement CSCW systems and to give decision-makers trade-offs and decision criteria for making better decisions involving CSCW systems.

Content: This course covers the issues and tradeoffs in building a system for more than one user. These include representing multiple peoples' work (for example, by multiple cursors) and implementing additional communications channels. An overview of example existing systems is given, with demonstrations and videotapes highlighting important interface issues in each system. Detailed examples showing the different challenges posed by graphics and text are also given, including distribution of source code for two simple CSCW systems so that students can see down to the code level the effects of design and construction decisions on the final system.

Instructor: Alan Wexelblat is an engineer involved in the design and construction of user interfaces.

4. ETHNOGRAPHY AND SYSTEM DEVELOPMENT: BOUNDING THE INTERSECTION

Dave Randall, Sociology Dept., Lancaster University

Richard Bentley, Computing Dept., Lancaster Univ.

Objective: To develop an appreciation for the need to analyze the social setting in which work takes place when deriving requirements for co-operative systems. Participants will learn the relevance of ethnographic analysis for capturing social complexity and its relationship to other social investigation methods for CSCW systems development.

Content: Part I concentrates on the need for social analysis in CSCW systems development and the relevance of ethnography. Part II addresses specific problems in integrating ethnography with requirements formulation and show how some of these can be eased when an interactive model of development is applied. Part III is a practical session and discussion examining the ways in which the nature of a task is changed using different interfaces.

Instructors: David Randall and Richard Bentley are researchers in CSCW at Lancaster University, UK. They are currently investigating electronic information display in the domain of UK Air Traffic Control.

5. MIME: ENHANCED INTERNET MAIL STANDARD AS APPLICATION BASE FOR CSCW

Nathaniel S. Borenstein, Bellcore

Objective: To present a technical overview of MIME (Multipurpose Internet Mail Extensions), the new proposed standard format for Internet mail messages, which has the potential to vastly extend the functionality of electronic mail and its usefulness for CSCW applications. By the end of the tutorial, attendees will have a clear idea of what MIME can be used for and enough technical information to begin designing MIME-based applications.

Content: The tutorial covers the philosophy behind MIME, the basic structure of email data in MIME format, the specific data types that are predefined by MIME, and the mechanisms and procedures for extending MIME to include new types of data. All of this is made concrete through the presentation of numerous examples of MIME messages and MIME-compliant mail-readers in operation.

Instructor: Nathaniel S. Borenstein has been a researcher in the area of electronic messaging and CSCW for ten years. He is one of the primary authors of the Andrew Message system. He is the author of the recent book, *Programming As If People Mattered*, and is one of the primary authors of the MIME standard.

6. THE ROLE OF HYPERMEDIA FOR CSCW APPLICATIONS

Norbert A. Streitz, Integrated Publication and Information Systems Institute

Objective: To provide an understanding of the innovative potential of hypertext and hypermedia for CSCW applications. The tutorial covers the concepts of hypertext/hypermedia, a range of examples of selected hyperdocuments and hypermedia systems supporting cooperation, and how to evaluate the opportunities offered by hypermedia in CSCW situations.

Content: The tutorial addresses the following issues: the necessity of non-linearity for coordination and collaboration, implications of multi-person authoring results for the usefulness of hypertext, the relationship between hypertext as a communication medium and other multi-media means, and the usefulness of hypermedia for asynchronous interaction and real-time work.

Instructor: Norbert A. Streitz is the Vice Director of the Integrated Publication and Information Systems Institute of the National Research Center for Computer Science and Information Technology of the Federal Government of Germany.

7. VIDEO/AUDIO NETWORKS FOR COLLABORATION

Rob Fish and Bob Kraut, Bellcore

Objective: To provide a grounding in the fundamentals of video/audio conferencing and current trends.

Content: The tutorial surveys station equipment, networks, networking options, compression technology, and multipoint systems. It addresses use and usability issues such as formal and informal communication, visual and audio quality, privacy, and integration with shared computer tools as well as the benefits and pitfalls of using these systems.

Instructors: The instructors have worked for the last several years on a number of projects involving the creation of useful video/audio networks for collaborative use. These projects have included the VideoWindow large-screen telepresence system and the CRUISER™ desktop teleconferencing system.

8. STRATEGIES FOR ENCOURAGING ADOPTION OF GROUP TECHNOLOGIES

Susan E. Rudman, US West

Ellen Francik, Pacific Bell

Objective: To provide detailed practical advice for introducing innovative communication systems into organizations.

Content: The tutorial covers: (1) challenges in design and adoption; (2) resulting interdependence between development, human factors, marketing, sales support and customer groups; (3) strategies for accurate, productive placement of systems; (4) interviewing techniques that can be used during product design, early testing, and implementation in customer sites; (5) use of interview data for market redefinition and system redesign. We use historical examples and case studies to illustrate the early problems of currently successful products as well as adoption problems faced by today's groupware systems.

Instructors: Susan E. Rudman is responsible for designing user interfaces for multi-media applications at US West. Ellen Francik is in Pacific Bell's Human Factors Engineering Laboratory and works on the design of group support systems and messaging products.

CSCW '92 Formal Video Program

Saul Greenberg

Department of Computer Science
University of Calgary
Calgary, Alberta
Canada T2N 1N4
saul@cpsc.ucalgary.ca

Much of the experimental work in CSCW involves highly interactive systems and complex group interactions. While paper can convey the academic details of CSCW work, video is far more appropriate for capturing the true flavor and details of interactions. The CSCW conference has recognized the importance of video by creating its first refereed formal video program, published as a videotape in the SIGGRAPH Video Review series. Tapes can be purchased from:

SIGGRAPH Video Review Order Department
c/o First Priority
PO Box 576
Itasca IL USA 60143-0576
Phone: (within USA) 1-800-523-5503
(outside USA) +1-708-250-0807
Fax: +1-708-250-0038

The sections below give a capsule summary of each video, followed by a list of references to related publications. As you will see, the formal video program is varied. Its contents cover enabling technologies, groupware prototypes, scenarios of real-life groupware use, and laboratory tools for analyzing group interaction.

THE CONVERSATION BOARD
Tom Brinck, Bellcore

The CONVERSATION BOARD is a prototype multi-user drawing application built to be used by people who are conversing over a distance, using a phone or a video phone system [2]. It was built in RENDEZVOUS™, an experimental language and tool kit designed at Bellcore for constructing multi-user applications. The CONVERSATION BOARD is a structured graphics editor that provides "drawing" tools such as markers, lines, circles, rectangles, text, connectors, and images. Users can draw simultaneously and have telepointers, so their gestures are visible to each other. Images can be made "sticky", so that when a user draws onto an image, the drawing becomes grouped with the image. The video describes the first version of the CONVERSATION BOARD, and presents a scenario of one person giving directions to another by annotating a map.

RUBBER ROCKS
Larry Koved, IBM

The *Veridical User Environments* project is developing a Virtual Laboratory that brings together user interface technology, computational modeling of physical and non-physical phenomena, and visualization. Virtual worlds technology provides human-computer interfaces to computational simulation and visualization systems. One challenge is in providing a means to allow people to collaborate on a computational model through its virtual worlds interface. The video demonstrates Rubber Rocks, a prototype multi-user virtual world that supports real-time conferencing. The application is a real-time simulation of objects modeled as point masses and springs. Through a hierarchically organized dialog manager, the single-user version of Rubber Rocks was easily transformed into a multi-user system [8].

DELFT-WIT: RESEARCH ISSUES AND METHODS FOR BEHAVIORAL ANALYSIS
Jeroen van der Velden, Delft University

Delft WIT-lab is a research environment for studying both human-computer interaction and CSCW [1]. The video describes a first series of experiments studying distributed group work, focusing on the experimental setup and the tools used to capture and analyze interaction data. In the experiment, small task teams played a management game under various interaction conditions for a period of ten weeks [9]. Data capture is through a computer-controlled video recorder that can record and play simultaneously on two or more tapes. A program developed at NPL-London allows video incidents to be indexed, retrieved, and edited. The video also shows a tool that registers the speech frequency and computer use of each group member during the experiment. With this tool, information can be derived of the group interaction – the participation of each group member, their speech duration, and the speech sequences.

ENHANCED FACTORY COMMUNICATION
Burke Magee and Glenna Cox, Boeing

Capturing and conveying visual information is the most significant communication need of today's factory.

Technologies now available on standard workstations can increase the quality and ease of visual communication within the factory and between the factory and companies around the world. With multimedia mail, text, photos, pictures, and motion video can be electronically mailed to remote locations. With real time information transmission, face to face meetings can be held between remotely located personnel within the factory. The video shows an example of how multimedia mail and computer-based conferencing can provide direct communication between a Boeing factory, its suppliers and its customers, thereby reducing communication flow time and the need for travel.

COUPLING THE USER INTERFACES OF A MULTI-USER PROGRAM

Prasun Dewan, Purdue University

An important question in the design, implementation, and use of multi-user programs is what should be the coupling between the user interfaces of a multi-user program? In other words, which objects should be shared among the users of a program and when should changes made by a user to a shared object be communicated to other users sharing it? The authors have developed a coupling model that allows users to control the coupling between their interfaces [3]. The model is based on a generalized multi-user editing interaction model, where multiple users view programs as active data that can be concurrently edited. The coupling model is implemented within SUITE, a framework that supports multi-user programs. The video uses a SUITE example to motivate and illustrate the main principles in the design of the coupling model.

TOWARD SEAMLESS COLLABORATION MEDIA: FROM TEAMWORKSTATION TO CLEARBOARD

Hiroshii Ishii, Kazuho Arita and Minuro Kobayashi, NTT Human Interface Laboratories

This video presents the evolution of collaboration media design activities at NTT Human Interface Laboratories. "Seamlessness" has been a key concept of their evolving media design. The authors show the progression of their design from TEAMWORKSTATION to CLEARFACE to CLEARBOARD. TEAMWORKSTATION provides distributed users with a seamless shared workspace [6]. Each user can still use their favorite application programs or desktop tools, so there is only a minor cognitive seam between the individual and shared workspaces. CLEARBOARD permits coworkers in two different locations to draw with color markers or electronic pen while maintaining direct eye contact, gaze awareness, and the use of natural gestures [7].

THE PANDORA MULTIMEDIA SYSTEM

Andy Hopper, Olivetti

The PANDORA system makes available networked multimedia workstations to users in the Cambridge (UK) area [5]. The design is optimized for handling multiple audio and video streams with maximum flexibility. Many applications using both live and stored streams have been evaluated. Applications are integrated with an ACTIVE BADGE system that provides location information of personnel. The system has been in use for two years and the most popular facilities are video-phone and video-mail.

GROUPSKETCH

Saul Greenberg and Ralph Bohnet
University of Calgary

GROUPSKETCH allows a small geographically-distributed group to list, draw, and gesture simultaneously in a communal work surface, supporting interactions similar to those occurring in the face-to-face drawing process [4]. It is a simple group sketching tool that allows its users to draw on a virtual piece of paper (the screen). GROUPSKETCH facilitates collaboration by: a) allowing gestural expression through large unique cursors visible on all displays; b) conveying the process of expressing ideas by transmitting small granular changes of user activity with minimum time delay; c) intermixing gestural, textual, and graphical expression modelessly; and d) providing simultaneous access to a common view of the work surface area, where any person can do any action at any time. The video illustrates several scenarios of GROUPSKETCH in action.

REFERENCES

1. Andriessen, J.H.T.H. and van der Velden, J.M. (1972) Back to process with synchoronous communication. Dept of Work and Organizational Psychology, Delft University, Delft, The Netherlands.
2. Brinck, T. and Gomez, L.M. (1992). A collaborative medium for the support of conversational props In *Proc Conderence on Computer-Supported Cooperative Work*, Toronto, Canada, November 1–4, ACM Press.
3. Dewan, P. and Choudhary, R. (1991) Flexible user interace coupling in collaborative systems. In *Proc CHI'91 Human Factors in Computing Systems*, Monteray, CA, April 27–May 2, p41–49, ACM Press.
4. Greenberg, S. and Bohnet, R. (1991) "GroupSketch: A multi-user sketchpad for geographically-distributed small groups." In *Proc Graphics Interface '91*, Calgary, Alberta, June 5-7, p207–215.
5. Hopper, A. (1992) Improving Communications at the Desktop. In *Communications after 2000AD: Report of the Royal Society Discussion Meeting*, Chapman and Hall, March 18–19. In press.
6. Ishii, H. and Miyake, N. (1991) Toward an open shared workspace: Computer and video fusion approach of TeamWorkStation. Comm ACM **34**:12, December.
7. Ishii, H., Kobayashi, M. and Grudin, J., (1992) Integration of inter-personal space and shared workspace: ClearBoard design and experiments. In *Proc Conference on Computer-Supported Cooperative Work*, Toronto, Canada, November 1–4, ACM Press.
8. Koved, L., Codella, C., Jalili, R., Lewis, J.B., Long, D.T., Lipscomb, J.S., Rabenhorst, D.A., and Wang, C.P. (1992) Dialog manager support For real-time conferencing. In *Virtual Worlds*, Research Report RC17968, IBM Research, P.O. Box 218, Yorktown Heights, NY 10598, April.

CSCW'92 Demonstrations*

Michael J. Muller

Bellcore
Room RRC-1H229
444 Hoes Lane
Piscataway NJ 08854 US
michael@bellcore.com

Aita Salasoo

Bellcore
Room RRC-1P293
444 Hoes Lane
Piscataway NJ 08854 US
aita@ctt.bellcore.com

Demonstrations are coming into their own as a first-rank medium for direct communication of CSCW achievements. This year's demonstrations program includes a broader range of the activities that, together, make up the emerging discipline of CSCW—not only technologies, but also methodologies for research and practice. We also see the emergence of infrastructures and toolkits to support and integrate the next generation of CSCW applications, and the maturation of CSCW technologies and practices into significant products. Finally, we see the continuing development of important projects and products, and significant new work.

MULTIPOINT, MULTIMEDIA GROUPWARE SERVICES

John Bell, IIS Technologies

Group TeleCommunications Software (GTCS) is an application for real-time multimedia, multipoint, visual conferencing using industry-standard personal computers. The system supports shared views of documents, viewgraphs, photographs, and computer-generated images, with shared gestures and annotations, through an intelligent data bridge that executes at a single workstation to interconnect the others over a variety of standard communication interfaces. The product will be available in a meeting room for practical use by interested groups. The author will be available to serve as facilitator and trainer.

THE “WORK IN PREPARATION” (PREP) EDITOR

Ravinder Chandhok, James Morris, Paul Erion, David S. Kaufer, Christine M. Neuwirth, and Dale Miller, Carnegie Mellon University

The "work in preparation," or PREP Editor, is a prototype writing environment intended to support the collaborative authoring, reviewing, commenting, and editing associated with work "in preparation." The PREP Editor allows participants to create "margins," called columns, in which they can interact, and allows each user to add, delete, hide, show, move, and resize margins with direct manipulation. The system creates a kind of "text spreadsheet" that allows for easy reorganization of a document.

SUITE: A HIGH-LEVEL AND FLEXIBLE SYSTEM FOR IMPLEMENTING MULTI-USER PROGRAMS

Prasun Dewan, Purdue University

Suite is a research system developed to support the implementation of multi-user programs. It supports a generic collaboration model, which allows the users to view all multi-user programs as active data that can be concurrently edited by multiple users, using generic models for sharing, undo/redo, and access control. These models are parameterized by a large number of collaboration parameters, which can be dynamically defined by a group of users to define the interface to the program. Suite provides a simple and powerful inheritance model for specifying default values of these parameters. The demonstration will illustrate the various components of Suite by showing how a novel and complex multi-user program is built using the system.

GROUPSKETCH

Saul Greenberg, University of Calgary

Ralph Bohnet, MPR TelTech Ltd.

GroupSketch allows a small geographically-distributed group to list, draw, and gesture simultaneously in a communal work surface, supporting interactions similar to those occurring in the face-to-face drawing process. The authors will show how GroupSketch facilitates collaboration by: (a) allowing gestural expression through large unique cursors visible on all displays; (b) conveying the process of expressing ideas by transmitting small granular changes of user activity with minimal time delay; (c) intermixing gestural, textual, and graphical expression modelessly; and (d) providing simultaneous access to a common view of the work surface area.

---

* These descriptions are based on longer abstracts submitted by the authors, which have been shortened to fit these pages by the Demonstrations Committee.

Aspects is a trademark of Group Technologies. Macintosh is a trademark of Apple Computer. RENDEZVOUS is a trademark of Bellcore. X-Windows is a trademark of MIT.

OVAL: A RADICALLY TAILORABLE TOOL FOR COOPERATIVE WORK

Robert Halperin, Christopher Fry, and Thomas W. Malone, Massachusetts Institute of Technology

Oval is a "radically tailorable" tool for cooperative work. Four kinds of building blocks — objects, views, agents, and links — can provide most of the functionality of many multi-user systems. Progressive, incremental modification of systems based on these building blocks involves user actions to define new objects, new attributes, new views, and new relationships among objects, leading to an elementary "tailoring language." Following a formal presentation, attendees will be invited to use these basic resources to create multi-user applications in a kind of "Oval clinic."

WINCOLL — COLLABORATION EXPERIMENTS USING EXISTING X-WINDOWS APPLICATIONS

Ming C. Hao, IBM Palo Alto Scientific Center

WinColl is an X-Windows™ based application that creates a collaborative computing environment by allowing for controlled shared access to existing X-Windows applications, and by providing tools for communication with colleagues — with no changes to existing applications, minimal impact upon the system, and the execution of WinColl at only *one* of the workstations involved in the collaboration. Key features include: communication protocol structured by collaboration metaphor; floor control policies; and tools such as chalk, eraser, beeper, marker, and telepointer.

REAL-TIME GROUP TOOLS

Stephen C. Hayne, University of Calgary

Mark Pendergast, University of Florida

Participants at conventional real-time meetings often share physical work with each other, include notes, documents, plans, slides, drawings, and some common work space that allows each person to annotate, draw, brainstorm, record, and convey ideas during the meeting's progress. This demonstration focuses on technology that provides face-to-face or geographically distributed groups with concurrent real-time access to shared spaces. The authors will show a family of tools that support simultaneous shared views with individual perspectives, gestural communication, and linked views, supported by replicated data at each workstation and a variety of interaction models, including structured and unstructured, locking and optimistic models.

CONVERSATIONAL PROPS AND THE RENDEZVOUS™ LANGUAGE AND ARCHITECTURE

Ralph D. Hill, Tom Brinck, Wayne T. Wilner, John F. Patterson, Steve L. Rohall, and Louis M. Gomez, Bellcore

The RENDEZVOUS system, language, and architecture are designed to build multi-user applications for conversational settings — i.e., *conversational props*, or artifacts that facilitate or augment conversations. The architecture is based on a centralized *abstraction* — a collection of information that is common to all users — and individualized *views* — manipulable presentations of the information in the abstraction. The authors will demonstrate a number of applications that have been implemented in the system, including Card Table and Conversation Board.

SUPPORT FOR HUMAN COLLABORATION: APPLE OPEN COLLABORATION ENVIRONMENT

Patrick A. Holleran and Gursharan S. Sidhu, Apple Computer, Inc.

Apple's Open Collaboration Environment is designed to provide a computing architecture and environment that supports collaboration. By providing resources such as directory services, store-and-forward messaging, collaborative toolkits and programming interfaces for developers, security features, and connectivity to other collaborative or communication protocols and services, it is hoped that a new generation of innovative and powerful collaborative applications will be possible. The authors will meet with attendees at published times in order to present their architecture and environment.

CONVERSATIONBUILDER: FLEXIBLE, ACTIVE SUPPORT FOR COLLABORATIVE WORK

Simon M. Kaplan, University of Illinois at Urbana-Champaign

ConversationBuilder (CB) is an *open architecture* for collaborative work. CB is *open* in two senses: (a) it provides a rich set of mechanisms, tailorable for domain-specific support policies; and (b) it can be tailored by the introduction of new tools, adapting itself to existing user cultures and user needs. Attendees will be invited to experience existing CB applications, and to experiment with the system themselves, based on scenarios drawn from the authors' work in developing and using the system.

DISTEDIT TOOLKIT FOR GROUP EDITING

Michael J. Knister and Atul Prakash, University of Michigan

The DistEdit toolkit allows conversion of standard text editors to group editors with minimal change to their code. The authors will demonstrate several capabilities: (a) support for different editors in the same session; (b) *undo* for user's and well as group actions; (c) fault-tolerance against node crashes; (d) concurrency protocols for good response time.

THE KNOWLEDGENET WITH THE COLLABORATIVE DESKTOP INTERFACE — AN ENVIRONMENT FOR DISTRIBUTED DESIGN

Hans Marmolin, Yngve Sundblad, Konrad Tollmar, Royal Institute of Technology

Anneli Avatare and Hans Eriksson, Swedish Institute for Computer Science

The KnowledgeNet with the Collaborative Desktop interface is a CSCW environment for distributed design work, which is under continuous development within the Swedish MultiG research program on multimedia application in high-speed networks. Supported by a slowly-changing common database that contains *shared information about who knows what*, team members are treated as *primary objects*, meeting in a tool-oriented *room metaphor* or an *electronic hallway*, using integrated communications media (text, graphics, sound, video). Example applications include team maps, connection exchange, answering machines, bulletin boards, and common whiteboards.

COLLABORATIVE COMPUTING IN A GROUP ENVIRONMENT: THE SMART 2000 CONFERENCING SYSTEM

David A. Martin, SMART Technologies, Inc.

The SMART 2000 Conferencing System integrates a touch-sensitive display board for group presentations with modem-networked personal computers running conventional applications for local or geographically distributed meetings. The product will be available in a meeting room for practical use by interested groups. The author will be available to serve as facilitator and trainer.

TELEPICTIVE, A PROTOTYPE TOOL FOR COLLABORATIVE GUI DESIGN

David S. Miller, Michael J. Muller, John G. Smith, Ellen A. White, and Daniel M. Wildman, Bellcore

TelePICTIVE is an experimental prototype that provides an interface for designers of diverse expertise to cooperate in the design of a graphical user interface (GUI). It uses the abstraction-link-view paradigm of the RENDEZVOUS system to provide shared access to a design space of computer analogs to paper-and-pencil objects. TelePICTIVE supports inter-user awareness through telepointers and linked views. The authors will provide a demonstration and an environment for attendees to explore first-hand groupwarefor GUI design.

THE PICTIVE APPROACH TO COLLABORATIVE DESIGN

Michael J. Muller, Ellen A. White, and Daniel M. Wildman, Bellcore

PICTIVE is a *method for collaborative participatory design* of computer systems, supported by a detailed set of models: an "equal opportunity" *object model* of low-tech design objects; a *process model* emphasizing mutual education, validation, and responsibility; and a *participation model* that attempts to enfranchise all of the stakeholders in a software system (users, developers, writers, marketers, etc.). The authors will facilitate attendees' participation in PICTIVE group design sessions, using either design problems provided by the authors or problems brought by attendees.

ASPECTS™ REAL-TIME CONFERENCING SOFTWARE

Derick E. Naef, David K. Stokely, and Andrew M. Lewis, Group Technologies, Inc.

Aspects is a commercial Macintosh™ application that lets two to sixteen users on a network or modem link work together on a document at the same time and see each other's changes as they happen. Document contents include text, drawing, and bit-mapped painting. The product will be available in a meeting room for practical use by interested groups. The authors will be available to serve as facilitators and trainers.

SASSE: A COLLABORATIVE WRITING TOOL

Dimitrios Nastos and Ron Baecker, University of Toronto

Documents are created through a number of activities, including brainstorming, outlining, writing, editing, and reviewing. SASSE, the Synchronous Asynchronous Structured Shared Editor, supports the different requirements of each of these activities, as well as smooth transitions among these activities (in any order). Synchronous work is aided by color-coding of participants and their selections, views that enhance collaboration awareness, and the use of sound. Asynchronous work is aided by automatically-generated change descriptions and by writer-inserted annotations.

VANNA: A SYSTEM FOR ANALYZING AND ANNOTATING VIDEO RECORDS

Russell Owen, Beverly Harrison, and Ron Baecker, University of Toronto

VANNA is a video annotation system that supports a method for analyzing and "coding" video data of collaborative activities. The system uses a computer with touch screen and on-screen video to make notes about a video tape while it plays, thus reducing analysis time by narrowing the focus of the coder's concentration. Visualization tools for providing overviews of the annotated video tape and identifying possible areas of interest will also be demonstrated.

TELEPHONE-BASED CSCW APPLICATIONS WITH HYPERVOICE

Paul Resnick, Massachusetts Institute of Technology

Telephones are the most ubiquitous, best-networked, and simplest computer terminals available today. They are thus an attractive platform for cooperative work applications such as event calendars, issue discussions, task tracking, and question-and-answer gathering applications — especially those in which local area network connection of all users cannot be assumed. HyperVoice is an application-generator for telephone-based applications, including a new telephone interface called Skip and Scan that opens up the possibility of complex telephone-based applications. The author will demonstrate the Skip and Scan interaction style and a number of telephone applications that have supported a variety of user activities in the field.

CSILE: A COLLABORATIVE HYPERMEDIA SYSTEM FOR EDUCATION

Peter Rowley, Ontario Institute for Studies in Education

The goal of the Computer-Supported Intentional Learning Environment (CSILE) Project at OISE is to build (a) an instructional theory driven by cognitive science research into collaborative learning processes and expert knowledge organization, and (b) a collaborative educational hypermedia system. The system has been used in classrooms for the past six years, supporting learning for students in grades one to thirteen as well as adults. CSILE supports deep understanding through (a) a cognitively reflective model of learning; (b) encouragement of students to contribute to the social construction of each others' knowledge; (c) knowledge-building environments that facilitate incremental integration of a student's existing knowledge with new information via connective frameworks; and (d) support for teachers to monitor the evolution of students' knowledge in the database. The authors will provide a guided tour of the system, illustrating the social conventions that they have created for effective use, and highlighting points of success and remaining problems.

Controversies About Privacy and Open Information in CSCW

Moderator: Rob Kling, University of California at Irvine

Panelists: Andy Hopper, Olivetti Research Laboratory and University of Cambridge Computer Laboratory
James Katz, Bellcore
Additional panelist(s) to be announced

The field of computer-supported cooperative work must be particularly sensitive to the effect of technologies on individual and group privacy rights. These technologies are often designed to provide access to people or collect (and thus make available) potentially-sensitive information about participants. Thus CSCW technologies are not only media for intentional communication between consenting parties; their use often creates a documentary history which can be shared with third parties or moved well beyond the original interactional context and mutual understandings in which it was constructed.

The panelists will present general issues of privacy, especially with respect to social control and technology use in workplaces. Panelist perspectives are grounded in specific technological examples from their own experiences, using both existing and research technologies as a means of discussing their specific impacts on privacy. A focus of the panel will be to grapple with the question of how we go from understanding the issues of privacy to taking action in our own research, development, and use of CSCW technologies.

The panel is intended to stimulate thought and discussion in a way that brings out the seriousness and complexity of the issues while exploring constructive ways to incorporate such issues in CSCW work. Privacy issues arise out of a fundamental tension at the heart of CSCW technologies—namely the widening spread of increasingly fine-grained information about individual behavior as technologies emerge with the intent of supporting individual connection and work collaboration. Privacy concerns are not confined to a relatively few extreme situations or overly sensitive individuals. These are complicated and provocative issues that often engender discussions that easily degenerate into heat instead of light. The key is to think about just how serious and complex the issues are; a serious consideration of the value conflicts and social choices involved. We want to get a breadth of perspective on what constitutes privacy issues and to push ourselves on how we could be incorporating these perspectives and concerns into our research/design/development of new CSCW technologies.

The specific focus of the panel will be to address the question:

How do conflicts between collaborative technologies and individual privacy arise in the use of various CSCW technologies? How commonplace are such tensions? How important are privacy issues in the context of other competing values? Do we have a responsibility to take action in our work or are these matters for "others" to solve—managers, workers, legislators, and newspaper columnists?

In addressing the question of the inevitability of conflicts between CSCW technologies and individual privacy, the following issues should be considered:

- How does one assess the social risk involved in new technologies?
- Given that cooperative work inherently means some loss of control over personal information, is the concept of "privacy" meaningful? Are there other terms about the construction and control of information which help us better express the key tensions and their possible resolutions?
- Do technologies that identify people to a wide variety of often unknown "others," such as caller ID and active badges, pose an inherent social conflict or tradeoff between personal privacy and freedom of information?
- Who will use information resulting from CSCW technologies and for what purpose?
- What is the nature and extent of privacy rights in the workplace?
- What responsibility do we have as members of the CSCW community in understanding and addressing privacy issues?
- What mechanisms should we have for dealing with the questions concerning privacy that developing CSCW technologies raise?
- Are there specific features that should be avoided or built into technologies (e.g. caller ID or active badges) for addressing privacy issues, or do these concerns belong exclusively to the social realm?
- If you are in charge of a program where privacy issues could be very significant such as a caller ID or an active badge R&D program, what research or analyses would you do to understand potential social consequences of the technology? What recommendations would you make to organiztions that are likely to use these technologies?
- How do we go from understanding the issues involved to taking action in our own work?

Problem or Solution? CSCW and the Paradox of Stalled Productivity

Moderator: Sara Kiesler, Social Sciences and Social Psychology, Carnegie-Mellon University

Panelists: Paul Attewell, Sociology, The Graduate School and University Center of the City University of New York

John King, Information and Computer Science and School of Management, University of California at Irvine

James Morris, Computer Science, Carnegie-Mellon University, and Maya Design Group

In 20th century dreams and nightmares of computing, computers build cars and win battles, and robots take jobs. According to research, the reality is both mundane and paradoxical. Whereas computers can process information faster and better than ever before, the productivity payoffs for organizations have (apparently) been negligable or worse. Some experts even fault computers that "help" people work together. (If people are busy talking, they don't get their real work done, according to this argument.) Others claim we haven't built the right CSCW technologies—those that will link individual workers and information to organizational needs.

In this panel we look at evidence for the paradox and reasons it may exist. Then we air different views of how to think about CSCW and organizational productivity. And we suggest how design might be targeted at productivity.

Commercial Products for CSCW

Moderator: Esther Dyson, Editor, Release 1.0, EDventure Holdings, Inc.

Panelists: Charles Digate, President, Beyond, Inc.

Irene Greif, Director, Workgroup Technologies, Lotus Development Corporation

Terry Winograd, Founder, Action Technologies, Inc., and Professor, Stanford University

Michael Zisman, President and CEO, SoftSwitch

This panel continues the discussion started two years ago at CSCW '90 on "Commercial CSCW or How to Get Group Software out of the Labs and into Real Use." At that time we found very few CSCW products in use. Email was still the main communications software outside research labs. A few organizations like Price-Waterhouse had adopted Lotus Notes. A panelist from Price-Waterhouse explained how they were deploying Notes and the panel debated whether groupware required that kind of corporate-wide installation or could be implemented on a one-at-a-time basis. An overview of a product based on the Information Lens (an MIT research project led by Professor Tom Malone) led to some discussion of the distance to be covered when taking ideas from research prototype to product.

This year, we look at what's changed since then. We find that many of the same issues are still unresolved. Some of the questions are:

- Why is it taking so long for CSCW software to get to market?
- What is happening with current CSCW products that are on the market
- Is CSCW research having impact on product design and deployment?
- What happened to Coordinator?
- What else is happening with Email? Lotus Notes?
- What will be the next breakthrough product?

The panelists all have commercial affiliations and some link to research. Their product experiences give each a unique perspective on topics that include the process of transforming research ideas into product, the importance of *group-enabling* of conventional desktop products, the potential of workflow technology in products, and the role of large electronic mail networks in groupware implementation.

The Affordances of Media Spaces for Collaboration

William W. Gaver

Rank Xerox Cambridge EuroPARC
61 Regent Street
Cambridge CB2 1AB, U.K.
+44 223 341 527
gaver@europarc.xerox.com

ABSTRACT
In this paper, I discuss the affordances offered by media spaces for collaboration, contrasting their properties with those of the everyday medium and exploring the implications for perception and interaction. Collaboration is situated in a physical environment which supports or constrains the various forms social interactions might take. An analysis of the affordances of the environment – the properties that offer actions and interactions to those within it – thus complements analyses which emphasize social and cultural factors. Examining the "physics" of media space systems is helpful both in understanding how people use them to collaborate and in suggesting possibilities for design.

KEYWORDS
Video, mediaspaces, affordances, ecological approaches

INTRODUCTION
Recently there has been increasing interest in "media spaces" – computer-controllable networks of audio and video equipment used to support synchronous collaboration (e.g., 7, 16, 3, 17, 19, 21). Because they allow simultaneous, two-way transmission of visual and auditory information, these systems are often thought to simulate the everyday medium within which we collaborate. In fact, a number of analogies to the everyday world have arisen to describe the experience with such systems. The term "media space" itself indicates an analogy to the everyday space; they are said to support "virtual copresence," to act as "tailorable office-spaces," "meeting rooms," or "hallways."

These metaphors are useful in indicating some of the intended functions of media spaces, but they may well be misleading in suggesting that media spaces are like the everyday medium for interaction. In the everyday world, collaboration is situated within a shared, encompassing space, one which is rich with perceptual information about objects and events that can be explored and manipulated. The "space" created by current audio-video technologies, on the other hand, has very different properties for perception and interaction. By comparing these properties with those of the everyday medium, we can better understand the nature of these systems and the challenges and opportunities for their design.

Permission to copy without fee all or part of this material is granted provided that the copies are not made or distributed for direct commercial advantage, the ACM copyright notice and the title of the publication and its date appear, and notice is given that copying is by permission of the Association for Computing Machinery. To copy otherwise, or to republish, requires a fee and/or specific permission.

© 1992 ACM 0-89791-543-7/92/0010/0017...$1.50

An Ecological Approach To Understanding Media
In this paper, I discuss the *affordances* offered by media space systems for perception and interaction. Affordances are properties of the environment that offer actions to appropriate organisms (8). They are defined with respect to both the environment and the interacting organism, and thus provide physical analyses that can complement sociological perspectives on situated action. In addition, because they focus on relevant physical properties of the environment, analyses of affordances can directly suggest implications for design (6).

An examination of the affordances of media spaces for collaboration is a useful complement to analyses which emphasize social and cultural influences. Social activities are *situated* in their environment (22): if collaboration depends on complex, subtle social relations, it also depends on a medium in which these relations can work. From this point of view, an important aspect of understanding collaboration is understanding the environment in which it takes place. Because the concept of affordances focuses directly on the relations between properties of the environment and possibilities for (inter)action, it is a particularly valuable tool for succinctly describing situational factors relevant for collaboration.

In considering the affordances of audio-video technologies, I am inspired by Gibson's (8) discussion of the affordances of the everyday medium. According to this approach, the everyday medium is characterized by a number of properties and corresponding affordances. Gibson lists six. In his account, the medium:

- transmits light, affording vision,
- transmits vibrations, affording hearing,
- offers little resistance, affording motion,
- allows chemical diffusion, affording smell,

- contains oxygen, affording breathing,
- has an intrinsic up and down, affording orientation.

Clearly this analysis is too coarsely grained to serve as a basis for a comparison with media spaces. But it is useful in suggesting that the properties of the everyday medium can be directly related to the actions it affords – the fact that it transmits light, for instance, allows vision, the fact that it offers little resistance allows motion, and so on. This is the essence of affordances: they point to the relationship between properties of the environment and the possibilities for action it allows.

THE AFFORDANCES OF MEDIA SPACES

Typical media spaces have different properties from those of the everyday medium and thus provide different possibilities for action. They use computer-controlled links to transmit perceptual information to and from nodes incorporating one or more cameras, microphones, monitors and speakers (see Figure 1). Thus people are not surrounded by information in media spaces, they cannot move within them, and communication within them is constrained by the limited bandwidth they offer. In fact, the "space" created by these technologies is both discontinuous and arbitrary. These properties of the audio-video medium shape how we collaborate using it just as the everyday medium shapes our interactions within it. In further exploring these properties, then, we can better understand how people interact in media spaces.

Moreover, because an analysis of media spaces' affordances focuses on the physical attributes of the medium, it highlights possibilities for design. Neither media spaces nor their component technologies – video, audio, or computer – are stable artifacts. With changes in the technologies come changes in their affordances; creating or emphasizing affordances is, in fact, a useful way to characterize the purpose of design (8).

In order to stress possibilities for design, this account focuses on properties of media spaces which constrain various forms of perception and interaction. I take this stance not to damn media spaces, however, but to understand them. In the end, some of the constraints of media spaces can be put to good use. Many of the truly limiting aspects can be improved. And some offer entirely

Figure 1. A typical media space node: a video monitor with a nearby camera, microphone, and speaker.

new possibilities: Above all, audio-video technologies have an important affordance that the everyday medium does not:

> *Media spaces convey visual and auditory information between arbitrary points, and thus afford remote collaboration.*

In the following discussion, I explore several of the properties of audio-video systems that shape their affordances for perception and interaction. I start with an account of vision, audition, and movement in media spaces as a way of describing the environment within which action and collaboration is situated. Using this as a foundation, I turn from affordances for obtaining perceptual information to an explicit consideration of collaboration, and consider the ways that the audio-video medium shapes our interaction within it.

AFFORDANCES FOR VISION

Simple awareness of one's colleagues is a strong predictor of their collaboration (19). Because media spaces provide visual information about remote sites, we might expect to maintain awareness of events in media space much as we do local events. For example, Figure 2 shows an image taken from the video camera in a colleague's office. This view makes visual information available that supports the video equivalent of face-to-face interaction, and is more generally useful for maintaining awareness of activities in her office. However, awareness of the scene is significantly constrained by the video technologies employed. For instance, is she looking at her computer, at the camera, or at my image on her monitor? Is there somebody else in her office, perhaps standing just to the left of the view? What's that paper on the table? Clearly, the properties of current video technologies shape their affordances for vision.

Field of View and Resolution

> *Video provides a restricted field of view on remote sites. This limits peripheral vision and constrains perceptual exploration.*

Unless we are standing next to an obstacle, we usually have access to a spherical field of optical information. Even if the head and eyes are kept motionless, our natural range of vision is almost hemispherical. Video cameras, in contrast, have a much narrower field of view; typically well less than a quarter and often closer to an eighth of their surroundings. This is compounded by the fact that video monitors are often relatively small, taking up only a fraction of one's normal field of view. When we look at video images, then, we only have access to a constrained view of the remote site. In addition, peripheral awareness of activities in such scenes is limited, both in the sense that remote information is not available to the entire visual field and in the sense that remote events often go unnoticed when the monitor is on the periphery of the visual field.

The resolution of video limits detailed inspection.

In the everyday medium, constraints on visual acuity come from our visual systems rather than from the nature of the medium itself. The level of detail that is made available by video images, in contrast, is always fixed at pixel size. In addition, to the extent that pixels are sharply defined, spurious high-frequency visual information is added which further masks details (1). The result is that close scrutiny of video images reveals the structure of the medium itself rather than details of a remote scene. We can't read remote partners' computer screens, nor share a detailed drawing with them. Our ability to inspect remote scenes is limited by the technology, not our visual systems.

Design Implications

Because of the limited resolution of current video technologies, there is a tradeoff between the field of view offered and the ability to focus on details. The effects of this tradeoff can be seen in the image shown in Figure 2: the camera is positioned against a corner of the room to view an appreciable amount of the scene, and this limits our access to distant objects. Wide-angle lenses can make more of the ambient information at a distant site available, but imply a loss of detail (especially at the edges of displays). Wall-sized video displays or eye-covering displays can make video information more encompassing, but again as the image grows visually the lack of resolution becomes more apparent. This tradeoff can only be overcome by the development of video with resolution greater than our eyes can register, by the integration of multiple video images, or – as I will discuss below – by allowing movement in remote scenes.

Information for Three Dimensions

Video conveys a limited amount of information about the three-dimensional structure of remote scenes, and thus limits exploration, inspection, and peripheral awareness.

Light provides a great deal of visual information about the three-dimensional structure of the everyday world. Much of this information is lost using current video technologies. Clearly, stereopsis and convergence are impossible given the single image presented by current video displays. Less obviously, but equally important, both motion parallax – changes in the scene caused by movement independent from the observer – and especially movement parallax – changes in the scene produced by self-induced movement around a fixation point – are also lost. Only occlusion, texture gradients, and movement in the scene itself provide information about a space within media spaces – and this is countered by information about the flatness of the monitor screen itself. This interferes with our ability to discriminate and attend to people and things on the basis of their distance. It also means that awareness of colleagues and events on the periphery is often disrupted: movements in the remote space are largely two-dimensional and do not seem to impinge on the local scene. The "space" created by video is hardly a space at all, and is certainly not one that extends continuously from the local environment.

Figure 2: A framegrabbed image from a colleague's video node. Is she looking at her computer, at the camera, or at my image on her monitor? Is there somebody else in her office, perhaps standing just to the left of the view? What's that paper on the table? This is a reduced and reproduced image, but the same limitations hold for full-sized video.

Design Implications

Information for three-dimensional structure can be increased in several ways. Stereopsis and convergence can be made available by various technologies that allow different images to be presented to each eye (see, e.g., 18, 11). The best-known systems require that viewers wear equipment over their eyes: either small monitors such as used in virtual reality research, polarized or red-green glasses, or spectacles which use rapidly-switched liquid crystal lenses to occlude the view to alternating eyes. Such systems create a convincing experience of depth, but are intrusive both in requiring viewers to wear special equipment and in interfering with the view of the local scene. More interesting are passive displays, which present different views to each eye without requiring spectacles. These include systems which collimate the light emitted by a conventional screen into narrow parallel beams which are swept through the azimuth (24), lenticular lens systems, and Visidep systems (15) which rapidly alternate the view from two vertically-mounted cameras. As yet, such systems have not been employed in media-space research; the incorporation of stereoscopic information in such systems is an interesting possibility for further exploration.

AFFORDANCES FOR LISTENING

Just as the everyday medium surrounds us with light, so we are enveloped in a rich, reverberating field of structured sound, one created by the coupling between vibrating surfaces and air. In media spaces, the situation is very different: sound is transmitted in limited ways by constrained channels. This has several implications for listening in such environments.

Audio equipment is usually monophonic, impeding localization and conveying a biased sample of remote audio information.

Because we are surrounded by the everyday medium, sounds reach us from every direction, allowing us to localize their sources. Most media spaces, in contrast, use only a single microphone to capture sounds, drastically reducing cues for localization. Not only does this interfere with orientation to individual speakers, but also with attention to a single "stream" of sound in a noisy environment (2). Localization helps us *ignore* undesirable sounds – we can hold a conversation in a crowded room, for instance, by attending to a single stream of sound. When localization is reduced as it is in video systems, unwanted noises intrude on desirable signals.

Sounds are altered by the electronic medium, biasing the auditory information made available.

Most sounds are produced by a coupling between sources and the air, and thus are all conveyed with roughly the same efficiency. In most media spaces, on the other hand, microphones are usually attached to some solid object which itself may vibrate. The effect is similar to placing ones head against a vibrating surface: the sounds of the object overwhelm those conveyed by air. In addition, microphones pick up a disproportionate amount of airborne mechanical noise from locations near where they are mounted – noise from nearby machines, footsteps and so forth. Finally, microphones, cables, amplifiers and speakers all shape audio signals as well. The result is that remote colleagues may be difficult to understand, and all are likely to be readily distinguished from those in the local environment.

Design Implications

These observations have obvious implications for design. Localization can be aided by using stereo audio equipment. Microphones can be hung freely or mounted on damped supports, just as our ears are supported by a highly-damped material, to reduce biases caused by mechanical coupling. Finally, attention to the fidelity of audio equipment is of paramount importance if remote events are to sound like local ones, or to be interpretable at all.

AFFORDANCES FOR MOVEMENT

So far this discussion has concerned static perception of remote scenes – the differences between viewing a remote scene via a video image and being present but motionless, sitting in a chair with an unmoving head. However, perception is seldom static. Instead, we explore our environment to discover new perceptual information. In media space, we cannot do this: the effect is as if we were paralyzed at the remote location, unable to move or even shift our eyes.

Cameras and microphones are stationary or only moved remotely, preventing perceptual exploration.

As Gibson (8, 9) stressed, the visual system consists of movable eyes in a movable head on a movable body. Movement allows us to achieve panoramic vision from a single station point by bending over, turning around, and so forth. We can view a shared workplace from different angles by moving around it, we can inspect the details of a shared work object by moving closer, or achieve a more encompassing field of view by moving further away. Moreover, movement allows us to obtain a great deal of information about the three-dimensional layout of a scene; as we move, the visual flow fields corresponding to different depths shift at different rates.

Similarly, movement allows listeners to orient to each other, to avoid locations which are particularly noisy and so forth. We can lean towards an interesting conversation, or away from an obtrusive one, or walk over to an entirely different group of people. In general, movement is crucial for perception and collaboration.

But exploratory movement is not supported by typical media space systems. Cameras are usually mounted at stationary vantage points meant to provide satisfactory views and are often left at a wide angle of focus to give maximum contextual information. Microphones are usually placed at a location near cameras, and are usually omnidirectional. Cameras and microphones are moved or camera foci changed only by people at the distant location – producing an experience more like watching a home movie than like that of self-generated perceptual exploration.

Design Implications

In general, providing remote controlled movement in media spaces has the potential to compensate for many of the limitations of still video cameras and monitors. For instance, using multiple cameras at each remote location to provide access from various angles and distances provides a partial solution to the tradeoff between field of view and resolution. This approach might be extended, for instance by the development of a synchronous version of video mosaic techniques (12) which allow the progressive unfolding of detail in a video image to approximate the ability to focus more or less narrowly on a scene. Finally, remotely controlled pan-tilt-zoom units, already used in many commercial teleconferencing systems, can provide an even richer degree of self initiated movement.

Similarly, user controlled mixing of the signals from multiple remote microphones would not only allow a more representative sample of ambient audio information, but produce an effect similar to moving between the microphones' remote locations. In this case, microphones should be well spaced and speakers separated, since the purpose is to capture a more representative sample of the remote audio information rather than to create a stereo image.

But systems might also be designed which allow true exploratory movement in remote spaces. Possibilities include mounting cameras and microphones on remotely-controllable robot arms or vehicles. For instance, at EuroPARC we have experimented with a camera mounted on a radio-controlled model car; though impractical for everyday usage, the device allows true exploration of remote spaces and is remarkably easy to control.

The development of such systems is promising, but emphasizes issues concerning the control of movement. Successful systems must *afford* movement – more than making it possible, they must make it easy to initiate and control. Pan-tilt-zoom units used in teleconferencing systems are often very slow and awkward to use; cameras mounted on radio-controlled cars are fun, but impractical. Unless the cost of gaining additional information is low enough, it will not seem worth the additional effort.

But systems can be designed that rely on natural exploratory movement. For instance, the intuitive experience of looking through a window into a remote space, with the ability to move with respect to the scene, has been simulated by using a head-tracking device to control remote camera movement (18). This system follows head movement quickly and accurately enough to create true movement parallax, and thus three-dimensional exploration of remote scenes is possible. With controls such as these, systems allowing remote movement present exciting possibilities for future media space research.

AFFORDANCES FOR INTERACTIVE MOVEMENT

Understanding the effects of the medium offered by current media-space technologies on perception and action provides a good foundation for understanding their effects on collaboration. Collaboration is situated in a medium for perception and action; what we can see and do in this medium has profound effects on how we can communicate and interact. If the properties of audio-video technologies have implications for perception of remote spaces, they combine to produce even more pronounced effects on interaction.

For instance, Heath and Luff (10) have observed that certain kinds of communicative gestures seem to be relatively ineffective over video. Trying to capture a remote person's attention, for example, one may begin by making relatively subtle gestures. These are often overlooked, and increasingly large movements result, sometimes ending in a humorous display of waving, face-making, etc. The effect is that we sometimes seem not only to be paralyzed in media space, but invisible as well.

> *Media spaces are often discontinuous, reducing the ability to create communicative gestures and to control conversational access.*

In the everyday medium, we can move with respect to one another in a variety of ways. We can reach into other peoples' views, almost literally grasping their attention and directing it to oneself or to a relevant direction. We can manipulate other people's access to our conversations through control of the audibility of speech, the visibility of facial expressions, and so forth. Movement affords a smooth transition between privacy and accessibility: people may subtly gesture their willingness to converse, bend and talk with their neighbors, or straighten and address an entire assembly.

In current media spaces, these abilities are often limited. One can't gesture within a shared space because of the barrier presented by monitor screens. Peripheral vision is limited by constrained camera views and screen sizes, and also because video emits light rather than reflecting it, so that people and objects in a video scene appear more similar to each other than to those in the surrounding local environment. The paucity of information about the three-dimensionality of remote scenes produces further discontinuities between local and remote spaces. The result is that gesturing is limited both because it is not always noticed and because there is not a mutual space for gesturing but instead two separated territories.

Control over conversational access is also constrained by current audio-video systems (4). Media space systems usually allow only one video and audio signal to be broadcast from a given location to all others; this does away with any possibility of speaking privately with a subset of members. Even when addressing one person in a group, the loss of visual and auditory cues produces confusion. In general, because media spaces are not shared, we cannot move within them, but only gesture and talk from one side of a barrier to all other spaces that may be connected to it.

Design Implications

Gesturing can be facilitated simply by using larger monitors, thus making movement more salient (10). But the perceived distance of a person in the remote scene often conflicts with that of the monitor itself. This leads to the problem that increasing monitor size enough to make others noticeable can make the monitor itself overwhelming. A more demanding but potentially more effective solution is to increase the sense of shared space in media spaces, providing greater information for three-dimensionality either through stereopsis or movement. This would allow gestures to move towards and perhaps even "into" the space surrounding remote colleagues. Media space would thus become a much more encompassing and fluid medium, capable of supporting more natural interaction.

Conversational access can be re-established by using multiple cameras and microphones (20), or by using voice-tracking to determine which of several possible speakers is displayed on a screen (4). This sort of approach is relatively new, but extremely promising in overcoming limitations in conversational control.

AFFORDANCES FOR PREDICTABLE INTERACTION

Considering the affordances of the everyday medium is helpful in highlighting the affordances of the audio-video medium. But considering the affordances of media spaces can also highlight those of air, including affordances so taken for granted as to be easily overlooked. For instance, *isotropism* is a term used in physics to refer to a material which has characteristics that are the same when measured along any axis.

> *Media spaces are often anisotropic, making prediction difficult.*

Air is isotropic with respect to light and – unless it is moving – with respect to sound as well. This means that air affords reciprocal communication, that people can predict what their partners will see and hear by what they themselves see and hear. Many of the social conventions which surround interaction rely on this property of the medium; without it, they are problematic.

Media spaces, in contrast, are often functionally anisotropic. Because of the independence and separation of cameras and monitors, microphones and speakers, the effect is that light and sound travel differently between different points (see Figure 3). This interferes with the foundation of predictability that lies behind many social conventions of interaction. For instance, if I can see your eyes in the everyday medium, then you can see mine (unless I'm wearing sunglasses). This is often not the case for video.

The anisotropism of media spaces is as crucial for social interaction as immobility is for perception. Here I discuss just two implications of anisotropism; there are many more which might be considered.

> *Video is anisotropic, interfering with the design of communicative gesture and with gaze awareness.*

One of the reasons communicative gesturing is often

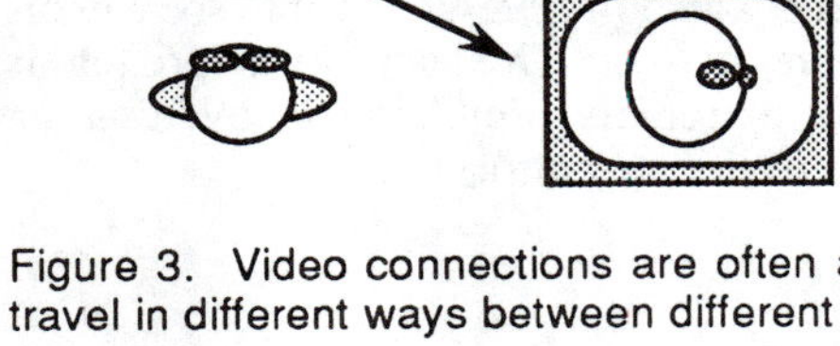

Figure 3. Video connections are often anisotropic: views travel in different ways between different nodes.

ineffective in media spaces is that there is no shared space between conversational participants. But the anisotropism of video as a medium further interferes with gesturing because the affordance of predictability is weakened. Gesturing not only requires a shared space in which to move, but the ability to design a gesture within that space for the desired impact. The loss of predictability in media spaces undermines affordances for communicative gesture (cf. 10).

Gaze awareness also relies on a predictable shared space to be effective. Gaze is used a great deal in conversations to facilitate turn-taking, indicate interest, and reflect social relations (16). The anisotropic nature of video disrupts gaze just as it does gesture. Not only does it prevent true eye contact, but it constrains the perception of gaze direction. For instance, because monitors are usually smaller than the scenes they portray, looking from one side of a video scene to another results in relatively small eye movements.

Design Implications

Two broad classes of solution to this problem have emerged: one technical, the other social. On the one hand, the loss of eye-contact has prompted the development of "video tunnels" which employ half-silvered mirrors to allow cameras to view a scene as if mounted directly in front of a monitor (3). Similarly, the ClearBoard system (14) merges video tunnel technology with that used to create VideoDraw (23) to produce the illusion of drawing on, and looking through, a pane of glass. Not only does this allow eye contact, but participants can see what their partners are looking at. Both these systems represent technological solutions to the problem of gaze awareness, though at the expense of affordances such as movability of the equipment itself.

On the other hand, a social solution has also evolved to compensate for the loss of reciprocity in looking. Experienced inhabitants of EuroPARC's media space sometimes choose to look at their cameras instead of their monitors while engaged in conversations – giving up visual access to their partner in order to create the illusion of access for communicative purposes. This is an interesting example of a social custom being reshaped to fit the physical properties of the medium in which it is situated. More generally, this example highlights the complementary nature of ecological and social explanations of interaction. On the one hand, the physics of the environment, understood at an ecological level, constrains possibilities for social patterns. On the other hand, society and culture shape our experience of the environment and guide our actions within it. These sorts of issues become particularly clear when considering technologies such as media spaces, which involve the design of physical artifacts that affect social relations.

Media space is anisotropic, affording "spying," but also unobtrusive "glances" and "office shares."

Because air is an isotropic medium, finding an observation point which allows access to a scene without allowing visual access to oneself is difficult. Video, in contrast, affords one-way viewing and listening to a far greater degree. In the everyday medium, to obtain visual information is usually to make information available; in media spaces, making information available is an independent act from obtaining it.

There are both positive and negative aspects to the affordance for asymmetrical access offered by media spaces. These technologies afford spying: we don't need to let people know that we're watching or listening to them. But they also afford unobtrusive awareness: we don't have to interrupt people to find out if they're around or busy.

Design Implications

Attempts to change media spaces' affordances for asymmetrical access must find a balance in the tension between privacy and intrusion. One might reduce the ability to hide by enforcing "symmetry," so that if I can see or hear you then you can see or hear me. But symmetry is introduced at the expense of unobtrusive awareness. Because cameras and monitors are usually kept in fixed locations, there is no way to differentiate an appearance on them that is meant to be unobtrusive from one meant to capture attention: symmetry implies interruption.

A different approach to the problem is to provide control over who can access one's camera, allowing privacy to be maintained without interruption (5). In addition, another channel of feedback (e.g., notifications on the workstation, nonspeech audio cues) may be provided to indicate when someone is tapping the signal from one's camera. The combination of these two approaches seems to recreate the mixture of unobtrusive but knowable access found in the everyday world (7). But these sorts of solutions are post hoc additions to media space systems; asymmetrical access seems an enduring feature of media space technologies.

CONCLUSIONS

Although I have only touched on a few of the properties of media spaces and their implications for perception and interaction, it is evident from this analysis that the "space" created by audio-video technologies is significantly different from spaces as found in hallways, offices or meeting rooms. Compared to the everyday medium, the audio-video medium conveys a limited subset of visual and auditory information, prevents movement and exploration, and is often arbitrary and discontinuous. These properties shape the possibilities media spaces offer for collaboration.

Of course, saying that media spaces have different affordances than the everyday medium does not imply that collaboration is always "worse" in media spaces, merely that it is different. For instance, the ability to make one-way video connections has been useful in allowing unobtrusive "glances" into remote spaces. Similarly, the fact that audio from remote sites is shaped by the technology and thus easily distinguishable can be useful in allowing remote office mates to ignore conversations that do not concern them. Comparisons to the everyday world are useful in emphasizing the potential richness of interactions in media spaces. But an appreciation of the everyday should not interfere with an understanding of the new affordances offered by audio-video technologies. For as applications such as ClearBoard (14) demonstrate, media space technologies can potentially allow us to go "beyond being there" (13).

From this point of view, comparing media spaces to the everyday medium represents a first step towards understanding the unique affordances of media spaces. But it is a step that is useful in understanding collaboration using these technologies. Such an analysis is valuable in complementing those which stress social and cultural influences on interaction over media spaces. Because it emphasizes the relations between the "physics" of media spaces and the interactions they support, it highlights the fact that these social and cultural effects are situated, that they take place using a group of technologies that can be designed and changed, and points directly to relevant changes that might be made. For as I have hoped to make clear in this discussion, there are not only a number of differences between media spaces and the everyday medium, but a wealth of possibilities for the design of systems allowing richer, more intuitive forms of interaction and collaboration.

ACKNOWLEDGEMENTS

My thanks to Wendy Mackay, Allan Maclean, Don Norman, and Anne Schlottmann for their many helpful comments on this paper. I also thank Victoria Bellotti, Sara Bly, Paul Dourish, Steve Harrison, and Christian Heath for fruitful discussions about these ideas.

REFERENCES

1. Berry, D., Baron, R., Kean, K., and Misovich, S. (1991). Meaning-in-motion: Acquiring social knowledge from dynamic events. In Studies in Perception and Action: Posters presented at the 6th International Conference on Event Perception and Action. Beek, P., Bootsma, R., and van Wieringen, P. (eds). Rodopi, Amsterdam.

2. Bregman, A. (1990). Auditory scene analysis: The perceptual organization of sound. MIT Press.

3. Buxton, W., and Moran, T. (1990). EuroPARC's integrated interactive intermedia facility (iiif): Early experiences. In Proceedings of the IFIP WG8.4 Conference on Multi-User Interfaces and Applications (Herakleion, Crete, September 1990).

4. Buxton, W. & Sellen, A. (1992). Interfaces for multiparty videoconferencing. Technical Report No.

EPC-92-129, Rank Xerox EuroPARC, Cambridge U.K.

5. Dourish, P. (1991). Godard: A flexible architecture for AV services in a media space. Technical Report No. EPC-91-134, Rank Xerox EuroPARC, Cambridge U.K.

6. Gaver, W. (1991). Technology affordances. In proceedings of CHI, 1991 (New Orleans, Louisiana, April 28 - May 2, 1991) ACM, New York, pp. 79 - 84.

7. Gaver, W., Moran, T., MacLean, A., Lövstrand, L., Dourish, P., Carter, K., and Buxton, W. (1992). Realizing a video environment: EuroPARC's RAVE system. In proceedings of CHI, 1992 (Monterey, California, May 3 - 7, 1992) ACM, New York, pp. 27 - 35.

8. Gibson, J. J. (1979). The ecological approach to visual perception. Houghton Mifflin, New York.

9. Gibson, J. J. (1966). The senses considered as perceptual systems. Allen and Unwin, Ltd., London.

10. Heath, C. and Luff, P. (1991). Disembodied conduct: Communication through video in a multi-media office environment. In proceedings of CHI, 1991 (New Orleans, Louisiana, April 28 - May 2, 1991) ACM, New York, 1991. pp. 99 - 103.

11. Hodges, L., and McAllister, D. (1987). True three-dimensional CRT-based displays. Information Display.

12. Hodges, M. (1986, May). The visual database project – Navigation. Internal Technical Report, Educational Services, Digital Equipment Corporation.

13. Hollan, J., & Stornetta, S. (1992). Beyond being there. In proceedings of CHI, 1992 (Monterey, California, May 3 - 7, 1992) ACM, New York, pp. 119 - 125.

14. Ishii, H., & Kobayashi, M. (1992). Clearboard: A seamless medium for shared drawing and conversation with eye contact. In proceedings of CHI, 1992 (Monterey, California, May 3 - 7, 1992) ACM, New York, pp. 525 - 532.

15. Jones, E., McLaurin, A., and Cathey, L. (1984). Visidep: Visual image depth enhancement by parallax induction. SPIE Advances in Technology, 457, 16 - 19.

16. Mantei, M., Baecker, R., Sellen, A., Buxton, W., Milligan, T., and Wellman, B. (1991). Experiences in the use of a media space. In proceedings of CHI, 1991 (New Orleans, Louisiana, April 28 - May 2, 1991) ACM, New York, 1991. pp. 203 - 208.

17. Moran, T. P. and Anderson, R. J. (1990). The workaday world as a paradigm for CSCW design. In Proceedings of CSCW'90 (Los Angeles, California, October 1990). ACM, New York.

18. Overbeeke, C., and Stratmann, M. (1988) Space through movement. Non-published doctoral thesis, TU Delft, The Netherlands.

19. Root, R. W. (1988). Design of a multi-media vehicle for social browsing. In proceedings of CSCW'88 (Portland, Oregon, September 1988) ACM, New York. pp. 25-38.

20. Sellen, A., Buxton, W. & Arnotte, J. (1992). Using spatial cues to improve desktop video conferencing. 8 minute videotape presented at CHI'92 (Monterey, CA., May 2 - 7, 1992).

21. Stults, R. (1986). Media space. Xerox PARC technical report.

22. Suchman, L. (1987). *Plans and situated actions: The problem of human machine communication.* Cambridge University Press, Cambridge, U.K.

23. Tang, J., & Minneman, S. (1990). VideoDraw: A video interface for collaborative drawing. In proceedings of CHI, 1990 (Seattle, Washington, April 1 - 5, 1990) ACM, New York, pp. 313 - 320.

24. Travis, A., & Lang, S. (1991). The design and evaluation of a crt-based autostereoscopic 3-D display. In Proceedings of SID, Vol. 32/4.

Iterative Design of Video Communication Systems

C. Cool

Rutgers University
New Brunswick, NJ 08903
cool@zodiac.rutgers.edu

R.S. Fish, R.E. Kraut, C.M. Lowery

Bellcore
445 South Street,
Morristown, NJ 07962
robf@bellcore.com
kraut@bellcore.com
lowery@thumper.bellcore.com

ABSTRACT
This paper reviews the design and implementation of several video telephony systems at Bellcore as a case study in iterative design. In contrast to single user compuer applications, communication systems consists of both the interconnection technology and the people who are interconnected. From a user's point of view, the capabilities provided by the system, the rules for its use, and its reaction to their actions depend jointly on what its developers implemented and how other users behave. This fact has wide-ranging implications for system design, use, and evaluation. In reviewing our design experience, we identify four dilemmas for iterative design that flow from the inherently social nature of communication systems. We conclude with methodological and theoretical suggestions to supplement conventional iterative design principles as applied to communications systems.

KEYWORDS
Human-computer interaction, Computer-supported-cooperative-work, Design, Software engineering, Evaluation, Video, Group work, Groupware, Collaboration, Videophone.

Permission to copy without fee all or part of this material is granted provided that the copies are not made or distributed for direct commercial advantage, the ACM copyright notice and the title of the publication and its date appear, and notice is given that copying is by permission of the Association for Computing Machinery. To copy otherwise, or to republish, requires a fee and/or specific permission.

© 1992 ACM 0-89791-543-7/92/0010/0025...$1.50

OUR CYCLE OF DESIGN
During the past three years, we have prototyped several video telephony systems, one of which is now serving about 125 users on a daily basis. Our goal has been to devise new telecommunication systems to support collaboration among members of geographically distributed work groups. A subgoal of these systems has been to support the type of informal communication common among people who are physically co-located. Our experience has demonstrated that iterative design is extremely useful for developing communications applications. Yet in some significant ways, design of communications technology differs from design of typical office automation and single user applications. While it may be obvious that applications in different domains require different design approaches, this phenomenon nevertheless created some unforeseen difficulties for us.

The design process that we use in the Interpersonal Communications Research Group at Bellcore combines behavioral and social science data collection with prototyping of communication systems and software. To assess needs for telecommunications systems, we have conducted national surveys, telephone interviews, and field observations in what we considered to be diagnostic work settings. We prototyped, deployed, and evaluated three iterations of video telecommunication systems. Our evaluation techniques included both quantitative and qualitative methods to understand how the systems were being used and how to change them.

The current paper describes this research program. During the course of iteration, we made improvements in supporting collaboration and balancing the tensions between privacy and accessibility. But in building these systems we discovered some limitations on iterative design principles as they apply to video telephony systems in particular and communications systems in general. These limitations are described in terms of four challenges to applying iterative design principles. We examine why these challenges exist from a theoretical viewpoint and suggest some pragmatic steps to supplement conventional iterative design procedures.

Empirical studies of communication needs

We began with empirical research to understand the communication needs of distributed work groups. We studied two application domains that typified the problems of distributed work: telecommuting (e.g., Kraut, 1989) and small-group scientific research collaboration (e.g,, Kraut, Egido, & Galegher, 1990). We concluded from these studies, as well as from detailed observations of how spontaneous conversations come about (Kraut, Fish, Root, & Chalfonte, 1989), that in the aggregate, spontaneous communication is useful. Although inefficient, it is a crucially important method that organizations use to accomplish work, transmit organizational culture and knowledge, and maintain the loyalty and good will of their members. On the other hand, almost any particular spontaneous conversation is expendable. Participants typically neither seek them out nor willingly incur costs to have them; rather they opportunistically exploit them when they come about by chance. Our research also highlighted the importance of the visual channel in enabling informal communication. Without it, smooth, negotiated entry into spontaneous conversation is difficult to achieve.

The VideoWindow system

The VideoWindow experimental prototype -- a large-screen video teleconferencing system with full-duplex audio (Bellcore, 1990; Fish, Kraut & Chalfonte, 1990) -- was our first attempt to use video to support informal, spontaneous communication. To encourage spontaneous communication we installed it as a link between two lounge areas in a single building, operating 24 hours per day for a 3-month trial. While the VideoWindow system made possible, spontaneous conversation across distance, the rate of spontaneous interaction across the VideoWindow was less than half of that for comparable face-to-face opportunities. Two types of problems led to this difference. The first, typical of a problem that can be fixed by traditional iterative design, was that the system did not support reciprocity as well as did face-to-face communication. Because cameras and microphones have a narrower field of view than projection screens and loudspeakers, people were often misled by seeing and hearing their partners into thinking they could be seen and heard. A second problem was less amenable to technological redesign. The centralized nature of the VideoWindow system resulted in a *critical mass* problem: potential encounters were limited to the set of people who occupied VideoWindow system's extended space at the same time. This led to lowered use because the technology was not placed within the situations in which people normally had a need to communicate. We believe this critical mass problem to be a general one and we will return to it below.

Initial *Cruiser* Implementations

As a next step, we moved away from the centralized VideoWindow to a distributed, desktop video telephony system called the *Cruiser*™[1] system (Root, 1988 Fish, 1989). This put the enabling technology in offices, where people in our organization spend about half of their workdays. In addition, we included features that actively encouraged informal conversations and allowed a greater degree of privacy control.

The first iteration of the *Cruiser* system was intended to give users the impression of taking a walk down a virtual "hallway," viewing others as they worked in their offices, and taking advantage of chance meetings to have conversations (Fish, Kraut, Root, and Rice, 1992). We provided three novel calling methods to encourage spontaneous conversation:

• *Cruises,* which consisted of one or a series of audio/video calls. When the caller issued the command, the system opened an immediate audio and video connection to the called party, which timed out after about three seconds unless one party explicitly continued it by issuing a "Visit" command. A list of people could also be called. If users issued a Cruise command without arguments, the system initiated a series connections to randomly selected users.

• *Glances*, which were one second video-only connections to one or a series of other people's offices. If users issued a Glance command without arguments, the system initiated a series of glances of randomly selected users.

• *Autocruises*, in which the system itself initiated calls between users at random times. Except for initiation, the protocol was the same as a Cruise. The intended analogy for the Autocruise was wandering in a corridor and randomly seeing other people, with whom one could speak.

The system included two privacy features. First, users could issue a *private* command, which notified callers that calls were not being accepted. Second, a *reciprocity rule* was imposed. Users were assured that if someone else could see and hear them, they could see and hear that person. The privacy command was not used much, both because it was designed with a poor user interface -- it was a typed command and provided no feedback about its current state -- and because users often didn't trust software-based privacy controls. Instead, when users wanted privacy, they exited the system or even disconnected their camera and microphone. While the reciprocity rule assured people they weren't being spied upon, as we describe below, it was one

---

[1] *Cruiser* is a trademark and service mark of Bellcore

of the factors that made non-obligatory opportunities for conversation difficult to achieve.

The *Cruiser* system was substantially more successful than the VideoWindow system, in the degree to which it was used and in its ability to support informal interaction. During one trial, people used the *Cruiser* system virtually to the exclusion of the telephone for communication among the group that had it. Individuals used it almost as frequently as typical staff members used the telephone, even though it provided access to far fewer parties. Because it was on people's desks, like the telephone, it was also used far more than special-purpose teleconferencing locations like the VideoWindow.

Moreover, even through the most frequent use of the system was to execute a point-to-point call to a single, named recipient, like the telephone, some of its features had the intended effect of providing users with greater awareness of others and increasing the frequency of spontaneous and informal interaction. For example, in one trial, 18% of calls were Glances, whose sole purpose was to provide information about others' availability. In one-fifth of these Glances, users let the system select parties to call. Glances rather than Cruises were used to find out this information because users perceived that it was quicker and less intrusive and therefore provided a better balance between convenience to themselves and disturbance of others. This concern on the part of users about how they are perceived by others is a major system design concern that we will return to later.

While the Glance feature improved informal interaction and organizational awareness, the Autocruise did not. As discussed previously, it did not provide a sufficiently subtle method for negotiating the start of conversations.

The system also fostered spontaneous interaction in ways we had not anticipated. In one example that we term the virtual shared office, pairs of people connected their offices for an extended period, without engaging in sustained conversation. Rather, the pair would work relatively independently, occasionally starting conversation to ask a question, to get help on a problem, brainstorm, or even tell a joke. Through this facility, people re-engineered their social environment to lower the barriers for conversation with a particular other and thus increased the spontaneity of interaction with that other person. In the course of these sustained calls, when others would enter one end of a virtual office, they would generally acknowledge and often engage in conversation with the remote office mate at the other end. In this case, the *Cruiser* system was being used similarly to the VideoWindow system described earlier; it provided a continual link to a remote social environment.

While the *Cruiser* system did foster spontaneous communication, informal chats were not often converted into intense, work-oriented meetings they way they often are in collocated workplaces. This early version of the system did not support shared data and tools for sustained work.

Cruiser redesign

Our initial experiences with the *Cruiser* system led to redesign last year. We enhanced the software in the areas of awareness and information services, support for small groups within the larger community, privacy controls and shared computing tools.

Awareness and information services can help provide a virtual workplace, with information about other people as well as places for people to meet. To provide awareness of others with minimal effort and as a side effect of other actions, we designed two awareness features: an awareness server and a virtual auditorium.

The *awareness server*, based in part on work by Borning and Travers (1990), enables people to obtain still images of their environment, including their coworkers' offices, and to have those pictures automatically updated. The *virtual auditorium* allows people to attend events "together". The events are network-based information sources, such as live lectures, television shows, and pre-recorded videos. Attendees watch such an event, while having a workstation window with slowly updated pictures of the other attendees. They may easily start side conversations with these others.

Support for smaller groups within the community and privacy controls became more important as the size of the user community grew. In the previous version of the *Cruiser* system, many people found it desirable for the system to automatically accept calls on their behalf without any action on their parts. However, more selective privacy controls were desirable once more people were on the network. The *Cruiser* system now includes named groups, both for directory listings and specification of permissions. In addition to global settings, preferences may be specified for particular individuals, so people may, for example, automatically accept calls from their closest colleagues, but require notification with explicit acceptance for other calls.

CHALLENGES IN APPLYING ITERATIVE DESIGN TO COMMUNICATION SYSTEMS

As the description above indicates, the communications systems we have prototyped have evolved through a process of iterative design. We studied the literature, collected data to understand human communication needs, prototyped systems, asked users about their reactions, gathered both qualitative and quantitative evaluation data, and then prototyped again. Many of the details of the user interface and even fundamental capabilities were improved through the iteration of the type recommended by Nielsen (1992) and Gould and Lewis (1983). To support spontaneous conversation, the reciprocity rule was relaxed, and the intrusive Autocruise was transformed into the more passive awareness server. While our initial goal was to support collaboration by enhancing informal interaction, observations of system use indicated that shared computing tools to jointly view and manipulate data were also crucial, and such tools have been added to the system.

Despite this testimonial for the value of iterative design, we have learned that communication systems are fundamentally different from computer systems intended for individual use, and as a result, the design process differs. Our conclusions parallel and extend those of Grudin (1989).

The most basic difference between single-user computer systems and communication systems is that in the case of communications, the system is jointly defined by the technology and the people it connects. To say that technological systems have a social component is not new (Trist, 1981, Johnson & Rice, 1984, Poole & DeSanctis, 1990). But in communication systems the social element is an integral property of the system, not an accidental one. From a user's point of view, the capabilities provided by the system, the rules for its use, and the reaction of the system to users' actions depend jointly on what the system developers implemented and how other users behave.

To see how social norms supplement technical capabilities to form system behavior, consider the fundamental design goal of the communication systems we have previously described -- to foster spontaneous, informal interaction. Some of the difficulties we encountered in achieving this goal resulted from traditional human factors problems; as we have discussed, the onset of communication opportunities over video were more sudden, intrusive and demanding of acknowledgment than in face-to-face communication. One can attempt to resolve these human factors problems by modifying the technology. We responded to the intrusion problems identified in the earlier prototype by converting the rich connections that characterized Autocruises-- high resolution, real-time, and interactive audio and video -- to more impoverished ones in the awareness server-- non-interactive, delayed, bitmapped images.

Nevertheless, interviews with users revealed that even the earliest versions of the *Cruiser* sytem fostered spontaneous interaction, without sophisticated awareness services. This came about partially because the user community developed norms allowing nonparticipants to enter into on-going conversations. They used the *Cruiser* sytem to negotiate entree into conversations, much as they would negotiate entering an on-going discussion in an office or hallway. As one interviewee reported, "When I'm talking on the phone, nobody would come in, but when I'm talking on *Cruiser*, people feel free to come in and interrupt. ... I would do the same thing. I would walk into somebody's office if they were on a *Cruiser* call. It's much more expansive, it's inclusive." Not only do visitors enter into *Cruiser* system calls, but the reverse also happens. That is, a caller happening upon a face-to-face conversation is often invited to join.

This behavior pattern of dropping into others' conversations is dependent on technological capabilities, to be sure, but people exploited the capabilities to produce outcomes they judged to be both useful and polite. For example, in the *Cruiser* system, we learned the lessons of reciprocity failures from the VideoWindow and tried to provide appropriate technical capabilities -- video cameras with wide angle lens coupled with a public monitor to provide mechanisms for a caller to see who already was in an office and to be seen. Office occupants explicitly harnessed these capabilities, by pointing their cameras to provide as much context information for callers as possible, and they supplemented this technological arrangement by announcing when another party was in their room, but out of the view of the camera.

This fundamental phenomenon about communication systems -- that others' behavior is an integral part of the system for every user -- has wide-ranging implications for system design, use, and evaluation. We have classified the consequent design challenges into four categories:

• System drift, in which system behavior changes as social norms change.

• User concern about the perceptions of others, in which individuals shape their use of the technology based on their beliefs about how others will evaluation them.

• Conflicting social goals, in which the different roles that the same users play may impede the achievement of group goals.

• Critical mass, in which the requirement to have a sufficient number of people using a system places constraints on the rapidity of iteration.

Autonomous system drift

If it is true that from a user's vantage point, the communication system consists of the actions of the technology combined with the actions of other users, then it follows that the communication system can change even though the technology does not. This phenomenon of what might be termed autonomous system drift is an anomaly for traditional iterative system design, where changes to the system are initiated by and controlled by system designers and implementers.

The impact of change in social norms makes system design problematic. When a system or feature is initially introduced, behavioral norms are likely to be inchoate and highly subject to change. With communication systems, as with most new technology, people's use and evaluations are based both on their direct experience with the technology and on their observations of others' experiences and views. The second-hand formation of opinions is especially likely in the case of communication systems. By definition, communication behavior is public. It is practiced in the presence of others who are often in the process of forming opinions about the technology. As a result, the behavior is often observed, is a source of inference about others' attitudes, and easily becomes a topic of conversation.

This social influence on system definition was the case with the *Cruiser* system. For example, some early users had experienced system errors, in which they were bridged into a conversation they had not intended to join. Not only did these experiences cause the initial victims to distrust the system, but their communication partners soon also adopted their attitudes. Members of this group became more likely than other users to invoke the system-provided privacy controls and to place lens caps on their cameras when not conversing.

As we observed, even apocryphal stories -- for example, that someone was viewed changing trousers -- may change a community's trust in a system and as a result, the privacy-related behavior they exhibit.

Exogenous events can also influence some users' behavior in ways that change the fundamental nature of the system for all of them. For instance, the *Cruiser* system allows users to connect to broadcast video sources. During the Persian Gulf war of 1991, many users connected to a television news station to stay abreast of developments. However, the system allowed users to be in only one call at a time. This meant that once a substantial number of users were watching television, use of the system for interpersonal communication went down; callers got busy signals whenever they tried to reach other people. Because of a feature that worked perfectly well from an individual's perspective, the *Cruiser* system was transformed from a interpersonal medium supporting pairwise communication to a broadcast medium.[2] This transformation reversed itself once the war was over, but it shows how the system can change radically, simply because of people's behavior.

All changes to the system are not triggered by identifiable events. As mentioned above, an individual's behavior is partially governed by social norms, and these norms drift over time. As one informant reported, "In lots of ways it's like walking into somebody's office. In lots of other ways it's like telephoning. If I telephone somebody, I don't know if someone else is in the office. Part of the time I find myself following telephone etiquette. When I call somebody, I ask, 'Are you busy, can you talk now?' Other times when I'm talking, somebody else walks in and gets involved in the conversation, so that's like walking-into-somebody-else's-office etiquette."

That other people's responses are an integral part of the communication system means that the system's response to any user's action is far more uncertain than it would be for a single-user computer system. In a very practical and unavoidable sense, the system is non-deterministic. Even the success of the most primitive action in a telecommunications system -- placing a call -- depends on whether people on the other end deign to answer it. The *Cruiser* system, for example, has several policies of call acceptance, one of which accepts calls by default, so that callers get information about a called party (e.g., an empty office), even if no one is available to answer a call. Success of call placement depends upon individual and normative decisions about how these call acceptance policies are set, as well as on many seemingly random factors such as whether the called parties are out of their offices or engaged in other activities, and whether they have turned on their workstations.

Concern for the perception of others

People use the video telephony systems we describe here, as they use most information technology, to pursue instrumental goals. They communicate to get work done, maintain personal relationships, or keep up with organizational gossip.

But in using the system and developing norms of use, people are trying to achieve other goals as well. The goal of maintaining their own and others' self-images -- what Goffman, (1967) calls "face work" -- is something that we believe is a major influence on the use and evaluation of video telephony systems. Goffman argues that concern for face exists in both mediated and direct interaction, yet research has shown that the degree of face work decreases as bandwidth narrows. Hiltz and Turoff (1978), for example, found little evidence of face work in computer conferencing. However, in a study of teleconferencing, Hiemstra (1982) discovered a high concern for face, along with the development of new politeness strategies that seemed to form around the teleconference.

We have found that symbolic interactionism (e.g., Blumer, 1969; Goffman, 1967; Mead, 1934) provides a useful theoretical framework from which to understand and evaluate this aspect of the behavior of communication systems. It sensitizes us to the fundamental fact that since these systems are trying to facilitate social interaction, an essential object of study is the rules that govern all social interactions. It directs our attention to the social matrix within which behavior takes place and to the larger framework of rules and social norms which define the self and regulate behavior.

One of the main premises of symbolic interactionism is that people "will act toward things on the basis of the meanings that the things have for them" (Blumer, 1969:2). *Cruiser* system users are continually developing usage norms. The meaning of these norms and their usage patterns can be understood by looking at their existence within a larger framework of regulatory rules governing all social interactions. Of particular interest is the tension that arises when the perceived norms of *Cruiser* system use seem to violate the commonly held beliefs about norms of proper interactive conduct.

---

2 This problem, once we became aware of it, had a technological fix. Users were given the ability to have more than one connection at a time and could designate a given connection as a "background" connection that was automatically interrupted when other calls came in.

For example, some early users described the *Cruiser* system as "intrusive". Further investigation revealed that this is a complicated phenomenon. What is salient to many people is not only that an incoming *Cruiser* system call has the potential for intrusiveness, but also that the awareness of the *Cruiser* system's capacity for intrusion into the personal space of others creates a heightened sensitivity to the social riskiness of using the system. In our interviews, people discuss the discomfort they feel about not knowing the availability of others they wish to Cruise. People are every bit as sensitive to the possibility of committing a socially offensive act - of intruding - as they are about being intruded upon.

In this sense, making a *Cruiser* system call is riskier than walking down the hall and determining the availability of another before initiating conversation. When people pass each other in the corridor or pass by another's office, they have subtle, but well-practiced mechanisms to assess or signal readiness for communication and to manage the transitions between lack of engagement to engagement and from engagement to disengagement (Goffman, 1963, Kendon & Ferber, 1973, Knapp, 1978). They do not have the same negotiated control when using a video telephony system. Sometimes, this results in reluctance to use the system. As one user said, "[You] have to learn to feel other people out. You wonder if you are going to cruise somebody if they don't want to be disturbed. I have cruised somebody when somebody was in their office and they said 'I'll have to talk to you later.'...If I had walked past her office, I would have looked in and I would have seen that she was talking to somebody and I wouldn't have bothered her." Similarly, another user said, "The other day I cruised my boss and he was on the telephone, and had I walked past his office and seen him on the phone, I wouldn't have gone in."

People are concerned with implicit communication as well as explicit communication. An example of the impact of this behavior can be seen in our experience after finding that an early version of the *Cruiser* system was viewed as potentially privacy-invasive. In response, we provided some privacy features. However, some people are reluctant to invoke these features because they fear that they will be viewed as being impolite in rejecting callers. As one person said, "[R]efusing [a] call is actually a pretty big thing. It seems like a major rejection of the other person." This sort of behavior means it is very difficult for system designers to determine how to help people tread the line between the needs for both accessibility and privacy.

Conflicting social goals

In designing any technological system, resolution of conflicting design goals is difficult, and it is particularly difficult in the case of groupware. As Grudin (1989) notes, conflicts in design goals come about because different groups of users often have conflicting interests in who bears the costs and who gets the benefits from a system. In communication systems the conflict is more unavoidable, because the same people play the conflicting roles. Our early empirical research demonstrated the value of spontaneous, informal communication for individuals, groups, and organizations. Yet, to gain these benefits, individuals playing one role need to incur costs when in other roles.

The asymmetrical nature of privacy judgments is a case in point. Previous research evaluating the *Cruiser* system showed that people perceive the video system as more privacy invasive than face-to-face communication when they receive calls but not when they initiate them. We see a similar conflict of interest when distributing information about why calls were not completed. Whereas the person refusing a call may prefer that the caller not know that the call was explicitly rejected, the caller typically wants to know exactly why the call was rejected, and when the callee will be available. For example one person commented, "You cruise someone and the interface says 'no one available' and that's kind of frustrating. I don't know if it's because they are in the middle of a cruise call ... Should I try calling back in a minute?" Yet people are quite sensitive to the message that is sent when they refuse a call. Rather than rejecting a call, many people use the automatic time-out feature to achieve the same result; as explained by one person, "No, I don't reject [a call]. I let it time out. There's some politeness in this ... I just prefer to have them think I'm not in my office rather than that I'm explicitly rejecting their call."

More generally, individuals have motives that are in the aggregate inconsistent: they want to be able to easily contact every other person in their network, yet maintain full control of others' ability to contact them. The trade-offs between policies that grant accessibility, privacy, and solitude are difficult to manage. Having access to other people at a convenient time often violates their solitude. Even to view others as a prelude to initiating contact potentially violates their privacy. It is possible to get the balance right, and many organizations do. We should note that the introduction of the telephone created a demand for answering machines and open offices increased demand for private secretaries, suggesting that solutions may not be stable. In cases like these, optimization can only be achieved at the level of the group.

One difficult problem from the standpoint of iterative design is that few users take the group perspective. That is, even though the value of informal communication is great in the aggregate, the benefits of a particular spontaneous interaction are difficult to discern, and the disruption of on-going effort is immediately felt. Therefore, individuals may not want to incur the costs of increased disruption and privacy reduction to gain what for them is the putative benefit of informal communication. One consequence for a system designer is that the typical tool used in iterative design -- users' feedback -- may not be an adequate gauge of how well a system is meeting the design objectives of supporting the group as a whole.

Critical mass

While in communications systems it is possible to discover interface and other flaws through rapid prototyping and thorough testing, assessing the value of a service requires that the system be exposed to a critical mass of users. Ideally, this means that when a user wants to contact someone else, that person is on the system. Critical mass varies from situation to situation; for example, a system designed for departmental communication needs to have most members of the department as users in order to attain critical mass. Unfortunately, this requirement for critical mass in testing a communications system conflicts with the iterative design technique of building something quickly and then throwing it away. The cost and scale of building a communications system that can support a critical mass makes it difficult to quickly iterate its features or to justify throwing it out and starting from scratch.

For example, reliability needs to be greater than in the typical research prototype, in order to get meaningful results. If the system fails often, people tend to not run it, and when fewer people are available, usage declines. With our current version of the *Cruiser* system, we knew we had attained an important milestone when people began to consider the *Cruiser* system nearly as much a part of the laboratory infrastructure as the local area network. A message advising people of an upcoming demonstration and asking them not to stress the system resulted in the joking reply: "Digital video demo in 1 minute. please do not use lab ethernet."

Crucial to the method of iterative design is users' feedback to designers. In the case of single-user systems, this feedback cycle can be rapid because the utility or usability of a feature becomes apparent to the designer as soon as a few users try it out and fail or complain in some way. In the case of a communication system, the time frame in which a designer should look for feedback is longer. As the Persian Gulf war example illustrated, the social (as opposed to personal) consequences of a system feature may only become obvious when its use becomes widespread.

A critical mass of users is also necessary for effective evaluation of communication systems because, as we have discussed above, usage norms change over time, and to some extent respond to changes in the user community. When *Cruiser* system use was confined to a small and homogeneous community, users were able to develop common understandings about how it was being used by others and were able to develop norms of used based on these observations. For example, in an early *Cruiser* system trial, when one person disconnected his camera in order to see others without being seen, this behavior was noted and censured by others in the community. However, as the user group becomes larger, more heterogeneous, and more anonymous, new usage norms must be established to guide behavior with the system in this expanded circle. We have seen in our research that the degree of comfort in using the *Cruiser* system is related to the social distance among interactants; that within a single work group there is often a common group norm about privacy settings and expected availability. Within some work groups there is a tacit understanding that it is permissible for group members to use the *Cruiser* system to interrupt one another, yet many of these same users hesitate to use the *Cruiser* system to contact someone outside of their group, or status level, because of uncertainty about the possibility of being intrusive.

IMPLICATIONS FOR ITERATIVE DESIGN METHODOLOGY

In summary, we have identified four dilemmas for iterative design that flow from the inherently social nature of communication systems. The unpredictability of the system's reaction to identical actions and the autonomous drift of the system over time mean that it is difficult to determine what the ultimate behavior of the system will be and, therefore, what modifications are needed to meet design goals. The critical mass of users needed before system use and perceived value stabilize means that rapid prototyping and quick iteration cycles are difficult to achieve. The conflicting interests of different individuals, of a single individual playing different roles, and of individuals and the group as a whole means that the traditional focus on optimizing individual performance and preference should be supplemented with a more social orientation. It also means that the typical reliance on individual informant's reactions should be supplemented with data focused on collective outcomes. Similarly, the fact that user behavior is influenced by the anticipated perceptions of others means that sociological analysis is critical. Because system behavior depends upon social norms and users' actions, modifying the system requires both social and technological engineering.

To gain the benefits of iterative design for communication systems requires changes from traditional iterative design methodology (Gould, Boies & Lewis, 1991). While the basic cycle of build-study-redesign is still valid, the implementation should be more complete and robust, and the study should extend over a longer time period before one trusts conclusions about the ultimate value of a new communications system. Changes need to be evaluated in the context of system use, rather than in the laboratory. And the need for interdisciplinary development teams consisting of computer scientists, engineers, and social scientists is even more important than is the case in general application design. Finally, the standard cognitive theory underlying most human-computer interaction research should be supplemented by a better understanding of social interaction. As Norman (1991:89) says, "there is no way that a system can work well with people, especially collaborative groups, without a deep, fundamental understanding of people and groups."

REFERENCES

1. Bellcore, (1990) *The VideoWindow Teleconferencing Service Model. Special Report SR-ARH-001424*. Morristown, NJ: Bell Communications Research.

3. Blumer, H. (1969). *Symbolic Interactionism.* Englewood Cliffs, N.J.: Prentice Hall.

4. Borning, A. & Travers, M. (1991) Two approaches to casual interaction over computer and video networks. In *Proceedings of CHI '91, Conference on Human Factors in Computing Systems.* Association for Computing Machinery, New York.

5. Fish, R. S., Kraut, R. E., Root, R. W. & Rice, R. E (1992). Evaluating Video as a Technology for Informal Communication. In *Proceedings of CHI '92, Conference on Human Factors in Computing Systems.* Association for Computing Machinery, New York.

7. Fish, R.S. (1989). *Cruiser*: A Multimedia System for Social Browsing. *SIGGRAPH Video Review,* Issue 45, Item 6.

8. Fish, R.S., Kraut, R.E., & Chalfonte, B.L. (1990). The Video Window system in informal communication. In *Proceedings of CSCW'90, Conference on Computer-Supported Cooperative Work* .Association for Computing Machinery, New York.

9. Goffman, E. (1963). *Behavior in public places.* New York: The Free Press.

10. Goffman, E. (1967) *Interaction Ritual.* Garden City, N.Y.: Anchor Books, Doubleday & Co., Inc.

11. Gould, J. D., Boies, S. J., & Lewis, C. (1991). Making usable, useful, productivity- enhancing computer applications. *Communications of the ACM, 349* (1), 59-73.

12. Gould, J.D., and Lewis, C. (1983). Designing for usability: Key principles and what designers think. In *Proceedings of CHI '83, Conference on Human Factors in Computing Systems.* Association for Computing Machinery, New York, 50-53.

13. Grudin, J (1989). Why groupware applications fail: Problems in design and evaluation. *Office: Technology and People, 4*(3), 245-264.

14. Hiemstra, G. E. (1982). Teleconferencing, concern for face, and organizational culture. in Michael Burgoon, (Ed.). *Communication Yearbook 6.* Beverly Hills, CA: Sage. 874-904.

15. Hiltz, S.R. & Turoff, M. (1978). *The Network Nation: Human Communication via Computer.* Readington, MA: Addison-Wesley.

16. Johnson, B., & Rice, R. (1984). Reinvention in the innovation process. In R. Rice (Ed.), *The New Media: Communication, Research, and Technology.* Beverly Hills: Sage Publications, p. 157-184.

17. Kendon, A. & Ferber, A. (1973). A description of some human greetings. In R. Michael & J. Crook (Eds.), *Comparative ecology and behavior of primates.* London : Academic Press.

18. Knapp, Mark L. (1978). *Social intercourse: From greeting to goodbye.* Boston: Allyn & Bacon.

19. Kraut, R. E., Egido, C., & Galegher, J. (1990). Patterns of contact and communication in scientific research collaboration. In J. Galegher, R. Kraut, & C. Egido. (Eds.), *Intellectual teamwork: Social and technological bases of cooperative work.* Hills dale, NJ: Lawrence Erlbaum Associates. Pp. 149-171.

20. Kraut, R.E., Fish, R.S., Root, R.W., & Chalfonte, B.L. (1990). Informal communication in organizations: Form, function, and technology. In S. Oskamp & S. Spacapan (Eds)., *Human Reactions to Technology: The Claremont Symposium on Applied Social Psychology.* Beverly Hills, CA: Sage Publications. Pp 145-199.

21. Mead, G.H. (1934) *Mind, Self and Society.* Chicago: University of Chicago Press.

22. Nielsen, J. (1992, March). The Usability Engineering Life Cycle. *IEEE Computer, 25*, 3.

23. Norman, Donald A. (1991). Collaborative computing: Collaboration first, computing second. *Communications of the ACM, 34* (12), 88- 90.

24. Poole, M. Scoot & DeSanctis, G. (1990). Understanding the use of group decision support systems: The theory of adaptive structuration. In J. Fulk & C. Steinfield (Eds.), *Organizations and communication technology.* Newbury Park, CA: Sage Publications.

25. Root, R.W. (1988) Design of a multi-media system for social browsing. In *Proceedings of CSCW'88, Conference on Computer-Supported Cooperative Work* .Association for Computing Machinery, New York., 25-38.

26. Trist, E.L. (1981) The sociotechnical perspective. In Van de Ven, A. & Joyce, W. F. (Eds.), *Perspectives on organization, design and behavior.* New York: John Wiley & Sons.

Integration of Inter-Personal Space and Shared Workspace: ClearBoard Design and Experiments

Hiroshi Ishii*, Minoru Kobayashi*, and Jonathan Grudin**

* NTT Human Interface Laboratories
1-2356 Take, Yokosuka-Shi, Kanagawa, 238-03 Japan
ishii@ntthif.ntt.jp (or ishii.chi@xerox.com), minoru@aether.ntt.jp

** Department of Information and Computer Science
University of California, Irvine, CA, 92717, U.S.A.
grudin@ics.uci.edu

ABSTRACT

This paper describes the evolution of a novel shared drawing medium that permits co-workers in two different locations to draw with color markers or with electronic pens and software tools while maintaining direct eye contact and the ability to employ natural gestures. We describe the evolution from ClearBoard-1 (based on a video drawing technique) to ClearBoard-2 (which incorporates TeamPaint, a multi-user paint editor). Initial observations based on use and experimentation are reported. Further experiments are conducted with ClearBoard-0 (a simple mockup), with ClearBoard-1, and with an actual desktop as a control. These experiments verify the increase of eye contact and awareness of collaborator's gaze direction in ClearBoard environments where workspace and co-worker images compete for attention.

KEYWORDS

ClearBoard, TeamPaint, shared drawing, groupware, video conference, eye contact, gaze awareness

INTRODUCTION

One major focus of groupware development has been the creation of virtual *"shared workspaces (SWS)"* in distributed computer environments. Some groupware definitions take this workspace-oriented view, such as:

> *"Groupware... the computer-based systems that support groups of people engaged in a common task (or goal) and that provide an interface to a shared environment."* (Ellis et al. [7])

Whiteboards and overhead projections of transparencies are examples of shared workspaces in face-to-face meetings. Participants can see, point to, or draw on a whiteboard simultaneously. An overhead projector makes hand-written or computer-generated documents visible to all participants in a room, while permitting the speaker to point or draw. SWS activities include sharing information, pointing to specific items, marking, annotating, and editing. In a distributed, real-time collaboration, these activities can be supported by computer-based groupware, including shared screen systems such as Timbuktu [8], shared window system [20], and multi-user editors such as Cognoter [10], GROVE [7], Commune [3], CaveDraw [21], Aspects [14], GroupSketch [13], GroupDraw [13], and TeamPaint (described later). Use of hand gestures in a SWS can be supported by shared video drawing media such as VideoDraw [27] and TeamWorkStation [16, 18].

© 1992 ACM 0-89791-543-7/92/0010/0033...$1.50
Permission to copy without use all or part of this material is granted provided that the copies are not made or distributed for commercial advantage, the ACM copyright notice and the title of the publication and its date appear, and notice is given that copying is by permission of the Association for Computing Machinery. To copy otherwise, or to republish, requires a fee and/or specific permission.

In face-to-face meetings, we speak, make eye contact, and observe each other's facial expressions and gestures. These verbal and non-verbal channels are important in building confidence and establishing trust [2, 5, 22]. A focus of tele-communication technologies such as the videophone and the video conferencing has been the creation of *"inter-personal spaces (IPS)"* that maintain a sense of "tele-presence" through the visibility of gestures and facial expressions of distributed group members. Media Space [26, 15], CRUISER [25], and VideoWindow [9] are examples of such technologies. Figure 1 illustrates these concepts and identifies relevant technical support[1].

LIMITATIONS OF EXISTING SUPPORT TECHNOLOGIES

Both SWS and IPS are present in ordinary face-to-face meetings and may be essential for remote, real-time collaboration. Several media space[2] technologies support both SWS and IPS.

---

1 This framework was developed through a discussion with William Buxton who pointed out the importance of a smooth transition between what he calls "shared task space" and "person space" [5].

2 "Media space," originally the name of a specific system [26, 15], is used here in the sense of Mantei et al. [22] as a general term to represent computer-controlled video environments.

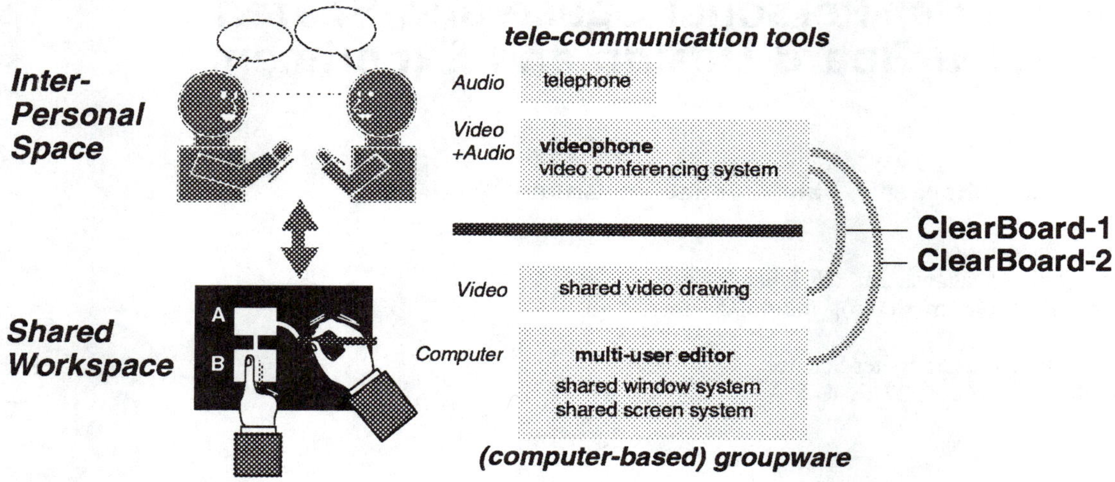

Figure 1. Inter-Personal Space, Shared Workspace, and Support Technologies in Real-Time, Remote Collaboration

Figure 2 illustrates three typical display arrangements of media spaces. In (a), a display providing a live video image of the partner's face is alongside a display for shared work. The ARKola simulation [11] in the IIIF environment [4], and some nodes of CAVECAT [22] adopted this arrangement. In (b), the displays are repositioned to resemble the situation of interacting across a table. VideoDraw [27] and Commune [3, 23] experiments adopted this arrangement. In (c), the live video images and the shared workspaces are incorporated into different windows of a single screen. TeamWorkStation [16-18], PMTC [29], MERMAID [30] and some CAVECAT nodes employed this desktop-video technology.

Although positive steps, these designs share a major

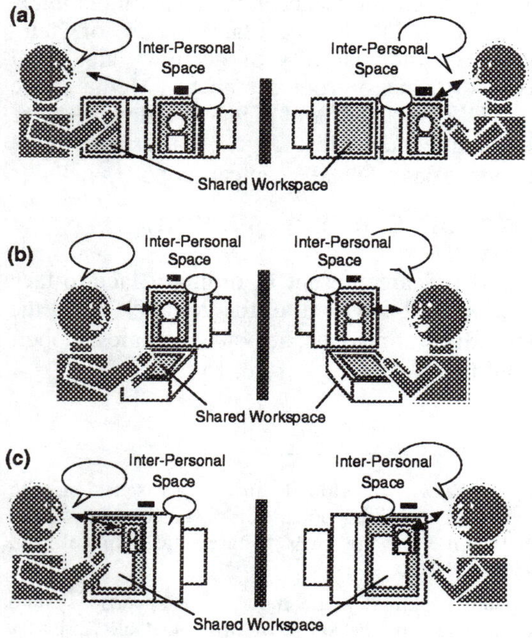

Figure 2. Typical Screen Arrangements in Media Space

limitation, an arbitrary *seam* between SWS and IPS. Experiments on TeamWorkStation proved that the problem is not entirely the superficial physical discontinuity between spatially separated windows. Users experience an undesirable *seam*, a gap between the two functional spaces, SWS and IPS. Absent are the *cues* that would enable a smooth shift of focus between these two spaces. Camera positioning prevents one person from knowing the direction of the other's gaze: It could be directed toward the face image, toward objects in the shared workspace window, or elsewhere. A shift in focus is not apparent until accompanied by a visible gesture, a mouse movement, or an audible remark. Mutual eye contact is impossible.

In a face-to-face design meeting, while using a whiteboard or drawing surface we frequently switch our focus between IPS and SWS. Even when drawing, we briefly glance at our partner's face to attract attention or to gauge comprehension. Similarly, our partner's head turning eye movement and gestures also attract our attention and trigger our focus shift. This dynamic and interactive focus switching between SWS and IPS is made possible by the presence of a variety of *non-verbal cues*.

Current media space technologies do not provide these cues. Spaces created by these technologies are discontinuous and arbitrary [12]. Users cannot switch their focus between the two spaces *naturally* and *smoothly*. ClearBoard is designed for pairs of users and overcomes these limitations by seamlessly connecting IPS and SWS (Figure 1). ClearBoard allows users to shift easily between IPS and SWS using familiar everyday cues such as the partner's gestures, head movements, eye contact, and gaze direction.

In the next section of this paper, we introduce the metaphor of ClearBoard: *looking through and drawing on a glass board.* We then introduce the architecture of ClearBoard-1, a prototype that supports remote collaboration through shared video drawing. Next we describe ClearBoard-2, which utilizes computer-based shared drawing to overcome the limitations of ClearBoard-1. Finally, we outline the experimental use of these prototypes[3]. These consist of both informal use and formal experiments, the latter designed to explore the feature of "gaze-awareness."

GLASS BOARD METAPHOR OF CLEARBOARD

Our first step was to consider metaphors that might allow us to create a medium that allows people to use everyday skills without requiring a special training.

In September 1990, Kobayashi and Ishii came up with the metaphor of "looking *through* and drawing *on* a big glass board" and gave it the name "ClearBoard" [19]. Figure 3 shows "ClearBoard-0" which is the simple mockup of this ClearBoard concept for co-located pair of users. ClearBoard-0 consists of a glass board positioned between the partners on which they draw or post objects. This prototype represents the best possible case for visual clarity. In addition to reinforcing the actual physical separation of the partners, ClearBoard requires *less eye and head movement* to switch focus between the drawing surface and the partner's face than would a whiteboard or desktop surface. A real glass board has the problem that written text appears reversed to one's partner; we were able to solve this problem by mirror-reversing a video image in ClearBoard-1 and 2 as described below.

Figure 3. ClearBoard-0: A Simple Mockup

The existing systems most similar to ClearBoard are VideoWhiteboard [28] and LookingGlass [6]. VideoWhiteboard utilizes the users' shadows to convey their gestures during shared drawing activity. VideoWhiteboard looks like a *frosted* glass board, in contrast to the *transparent* glass board that ClearBoard represents conceptually. VideoWhiteboard merges elements of IPS and SWS; however, the shadow images do not convey facial expressions, eye movement, or eye contact, all of which are present with ClearBoard.

LookingGlass displays the full-screen window of ROCOCO sketchpad (shared drawing software) over a full-screen video image of a remote partner. Using the the half mirror, LookingGlass supports eye-contact. However, the use of indirect drawing devices (mouse, digitizer) separates hand movements on a desktop from cursor movement on the computer screens, and users can not see the actual hand gesture behind the cursor movement. Another drawback is users can not place their hands close to marks on the computer screen surface because of the half mirror angled backwards at 45 degrees in front of the vertical screen surface. ClearBoard overcomes these limitations by allowing users to draw and gesture directly on the screen surface.

THE DESIGN OF CLEARBOARD-1

In order to implement the remote version of ClearBoard, we identified the following three design requirements.

(1) direct drawing on the display screen surface must be supported,

(2) the video image of user must be taken through the screen surface to achieve eye contact, and

(3) a common drawing orientation must be provided.

We devised the system architecture illustrated in Figure 4 to satisfy all these three requirements with simple technologies. We call this architecture "drafter-mirror" because it looks like a "drafter" (a desk for architectural drawing) and it uses a half mirror technique to satisfy requirement (2).

Kobayashi implemented the first prototype of ClearBoard-1 in November, 1990. Each terminal is equipped with a tilted screen, a video projector, and a video camera. The screen is angled backwards at about 45 degrees, and is composed of a projection screen, a polarizing film, and a half-silvered mirror. Video feedback between the two cameras and screen pairs is prevented by the polarizing filter placed over each camera lens and a nearly orthogonal polarizing filter that covers the surface of each screen. Users can write and draw on the surface of the screen using color paint markers and cloth erasers.

The video camera located above the screen captures the drawing marks on the screen surface and the image of the user reflected by the half mirror as a continuous video image. This image is sent to the other terminal through a video network, and projected onto the partner's screen from the rear. The partner can draw directly over this transmitted video image[4]. The image of the partner and his or her drawing is mirror-reversed so that ClearBoard-1 provides both users with a common drawing orientation on their screens. Since the user's image is also mirror-reversed, a right-handed partner will appear to be left-handed.

Results of ClearBoard-1 Experiments

Figure 5 shows snapshots of the ClearBoard-1 prototype in an experimental session described later. In summary, we observed effortless focus switching between the task and the partner. Users could read their partner's facial expression, achieve eye contact, and utilize their awareness of the direction of their partner's gaze (we call it "gaze awareness"

---

[3] Jonathan Grudin participated in this experimental and observational phase of the ClearBoard research.

[4] This shared video drawing technique, which allows remote partners to draw directly over the video image of their coworkers' drawing surface, was originally demonstrated in VideoDraw [27].

[19]). These last two features are novel aspects of ClearBoard prototypes and their importance is discussed later.

The drafter-mirror architecture results in the video camera capturing two images of the hand as it draws—one directly and the other reflected by the half-mirror, as shown in Figure 5. Most users did not notice this. Some users, however, reported an initial period of discomfort. No subjects reported difficulty with the mirror-reversal of the partner. This may be because our own images are reversed in mirrors.

An interesting and less critical confusion manifested itself when users directly drew over their partner's image, playfully adding a crown or mustache, for example. Clearly they had a "WYSIWIS" (what you see is what I see) expectation, not realizing that although the drawing is shared, the facial images are not, with each person seeing only the other's image. Thus, the metaphor of the ClearBoard is not always entirely assimilated.

We also encountered problems in using ClearBoard-1: The most serious problem of ClearBoard-1 was that video images on the screen are darker and less clear than is desirable. This is because i) the brightness of the projected video image is reduced by the use of half-mirrors and polarizing films, with more than half of the light lost; ii) the tilt of the screen places the bottom edge about 40 cm further from the camera than the top, making it hard to keep the entire drawing surface (and user's face) in sharp focus; iii) the video resolution was limited to the liquid crystal video projector's 90,000 pixels (in contrast to the approximately 400,000 pixels of the CCD camera).

The lack of video resolution forced the use of thick color paint markers; drawing with them is not precise and quickly uses up the available display space (50 cm x 55 cm). This problem is exacerbated by the difficulty of recording the resulting drawings. (We mainly used Polaroid™ cameras or video printers.) In addition, an inherent limitation of shared video drawing is that a user cannot erase the partner's drawing [27]. Marks drawn by each user exist only on their respective screen surfaces, and users often hesitate to ask each other to erase marks or are embarrassed by requests to erase their own marks. Moreover, the cloth erase is somewhat ineffective, especially after the color paint has dried.

These problems were a major motivation to develop our next prototype, ClearBoard-2, with its pen-based computer input technology which permits the direct recording of work. It would be desirable to be able to bring both (a) computer files and (b) printed materials directly into the ClearBoard shared drawing space, much as was accomplished in TeamWorkStation. The first limitation is addressed by ClearBoard-2; the second is not easy to solve if we stick to direct drawing. If user A puts a sheet of paper on his/her ClearBoard surface and marks it, user B can see it, but subsequent marks by B will not be seen by A because the paper blocks the rear-projected image.

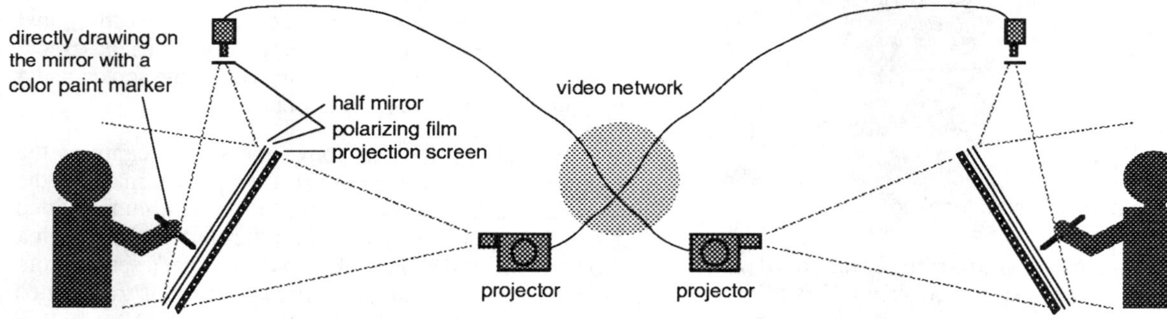

Figure 4. System Architecture of ClearBoard-1

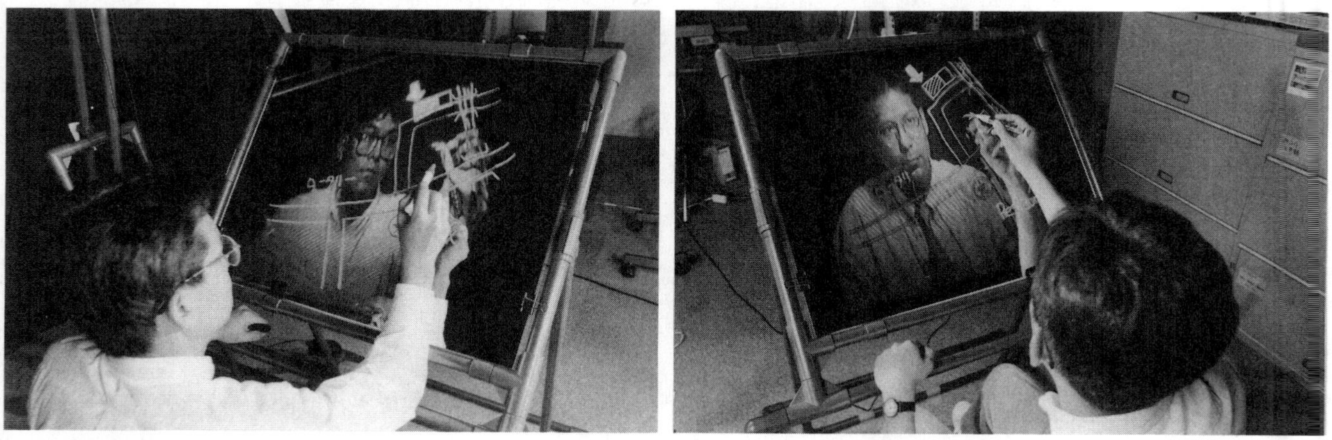

Figure 5. ClearBoard-1 in Use

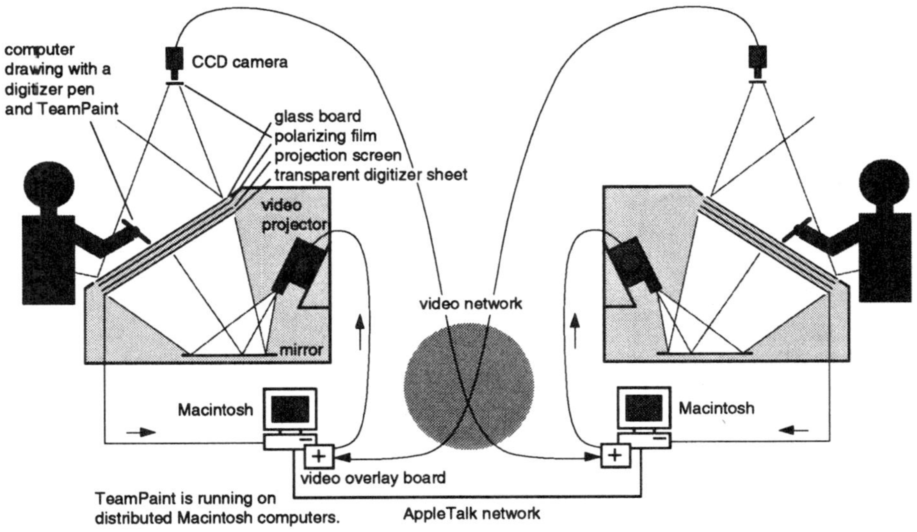

Figure 6. System Architecture of ClearBoard-2

THE DESIGN OF CLEARBOARD-2 WITH TEAMPAINT

To overcome many of the problems of ClearBoard-1, we designed a new computer-based prototype, ClearBoard-2. Instead of video drawing with color paint markers, ClearBoard-2 provides users with TeamPaint, a multiuser computer-based paint editor running on networked Macintosh™ computers, and digitizer pens. To improve the clarity of the screen image, we used a CRT-based rear projection display with a transparent digitizer sheet. The digitizer is mounted to the surface of a flat panel display. The screen size is 80 cm x 60 cm, 1.7 times bigger than that of ClearBoard-1.

Figure 6 illustrates the system architecture of ClearBoard-2. Although ClearBoard-2 is based on the same "drafter-mirror" architecture as ClearBoard-1, the digitizer pen and TeamPaint added the following new functions: (a) collaboratively created drawings can be saved in computer files and re-accessed later; (b) documents created with other editors can be imported, and (c) editing and erasing marks are easy. The shared drawing image (RGB video) is overlaid onto the video image of the partner (NTSC) using a special video overlay board and the mixed RGB video image is projected onto the screen by a video projector. Chroma-keying in the overlay sharpens the drawing image against the image of the co-worker.

TeamPaint: A Multiuser Paint Editor

TeamPaint is not a special component of ClearBoard-2, it is a groupware application that runs on AppleTalk™-networked Macintosh™ computers without any special hardware. It can be used by any number of users simultaneously, with some drop-off in performance. A mouse or tablet can be used for indirect drawing; the digitizer-screen supports direct drawing. Figure 7 shows an example of a TeamPaint screen. TeamPaint was designed based on the following principles.

(1) *A simple human interface .*
TeamPaint provides an intuitive interface based on the metaphor of drawing on a sketch pad with a color pencil and an eraser. Scissors provide the functions of cutting, copying and moving marks. To maximize transparency, it is a simple bit-map paint editor, not an object-oriented draw editor.

(2) *Replicated architecture.*
To be usable in time-pressured design sessions, TeamPaint was implemented so as to maximize run-time performance by employing replicated architecture [20]. It does not require a central server.

(3) *Multi-layer structure.*
Each user is provided with *individual layers* and can, by default, draw on only their own layers. All members see the composite of all layers. It is also possible to share one's layer, allowing another user or all other users to draw and erase the layer's image. Members normally use different colors to distinguish the ownership of marks. Because each layer is isolated from the others, *no access control* is necessary. *No floor control* mechanisms are needed to enable simultaneous gesturing and drawing by multiple users.

(4) *Gesture and process awareness.*
Gestures, in the form of cursor movements, and through them the drawing process, are visually shared by all members. This feature is important in enhancing the sense of a distributed group process[5].

---

[5] Awareness based on such a tele-pointer may have limitations. Actual hand gestures have much more power of expression, and with ClearBoard-2, the real hand and pen gesture images that lie behind the tele-pointer augment the awareness provided by TeamPaint. This video-augmented computer-drawing technique was originally demonstrated in VideoCom presented by Minneman and Bly at CHI '91. In VideoCom, however, partner's hand image and face image are separated in different displays (see (b) of Figure 2).

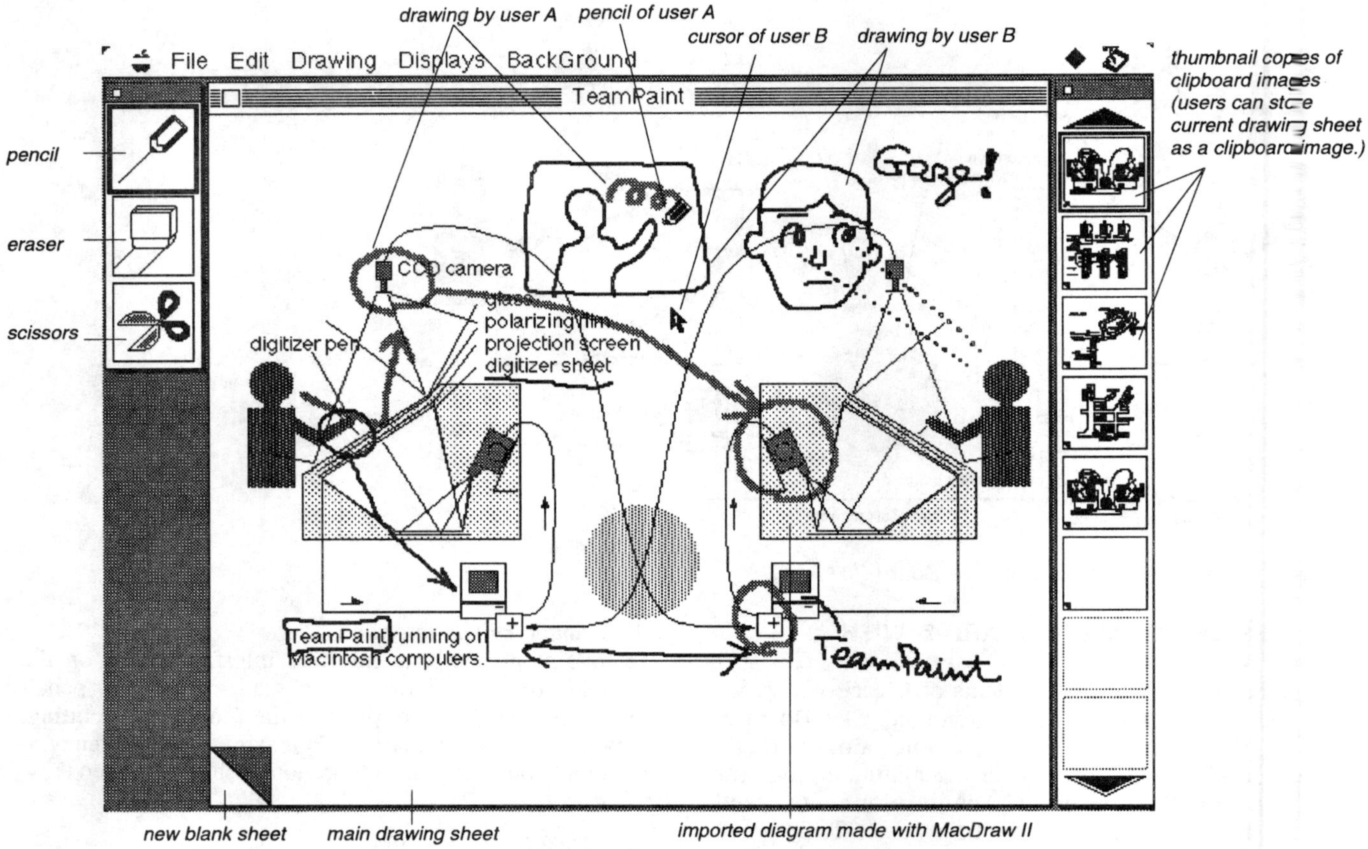

Figure 7. An Example of TeamPaint Screen

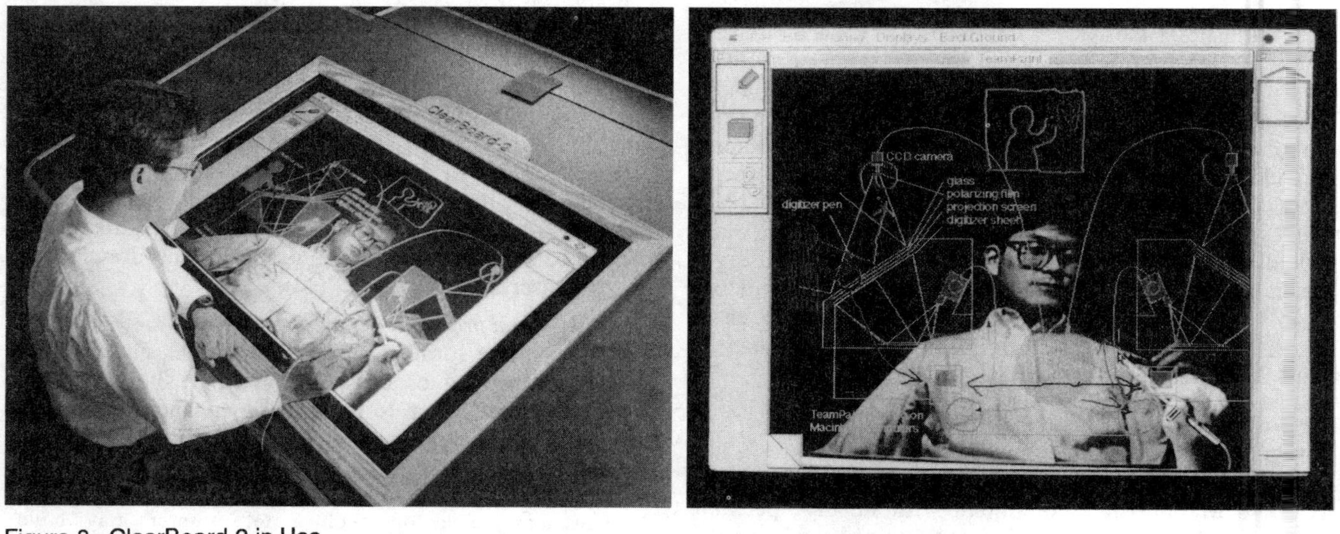

Figure 8. ClearBoard-2 in Use

(5) *Data exchange via standard format file.*
TeamPaint can store the results of shared drawing in the PICT file format which can be read by standard Macintosh™ programs. TeamPaint can also read PICT files created by other editors.

Initial ClearBoard-2 Experience
We finished an implementation of ClearBoard-2 in February 1992 and have used it for several sessions. The capability of recording results and reusing the data made in previous sessions or any other application programs promises to add tremendous value to an already practical tool. The use of

RGB video and the chroma-keying overlay technique do increase the clarity. Since the partner's video image is seen in the background of the TeamPaint groupware running in a Macintosh™ window, one has the feeling of interacting with one's partner through a window instead of through a big glass board.

The change of screen angle (45 degrees in ClearBoard-1, and 35 degrees in ClearBoard-2) decreased arm fatigue, but created more of an impression that the partner is *under* the screen, rather than *behind* it as in ClearBoard-1. Furthermore, it prevents users from covering the screen with their body and hindering the camera view.

Since ClearBoard-2 provides a precise shared drawing surface through the use of TeamPaint software, we found its video calibration need not be as strict as that required by ClearBoard-1.

It was often observed that the user's gaze follows the partner's pen movements. We confirmed that *gaze awareness* is as well supported as it is in ClearBoard-1. A user can know what object in the TeamPaint screen the partner is looking at.

The most serious problem of the current prototype is that drawing is sometimes halted because of the poor sensitivity of the switch at the digitizer pen tip. Users complained about the situation using the expression "out of ink".

EMPIRICAL RESEARCH USING CLEARBOARD PROTOTYPES

We have used the ClearBoard prototypes in work or work-like situations and in tasks constructed to explore certain aspects of the technology. In some cases we ourselves have been the users, in others the users were people not involved in the development of the technology. This section outlines some of the purposes of these studies and gives examples of the results.

One purpose was to obtain a quick first impression of the usability of the prototypes and of any obvious technical or behavioral problems. Many of the ClearBoard-1 problems and resulting ClearBoard-2 requirements described earlier were discovered through such use.

A second purpose of our experiments was to explore in more detail the way that users react to the new aspects and capabilities of the technology. More careful study is needed to see how people react to overlaid images and to collaborating remotely yet with eye contact and awareness of gaze direction, for example.

A third purpose was to gain increased understanding of how people work together and how technology might ideally support this. There are basic research questions that must be addressed before we can understand how our technologies affect or could affect collaboration.

Results from informal studies of use

The authors and six colleagues not involved in this research used the ClearBoard-1 prototype in conceptual design exercises (the limited marker resolution prevented the detail required by complicated electronic circuit diagrams, for example).

We found that users easily and frequently glanced at each other's face and achieved eye-contact both while conversing and while drawing. Switching focus from the drawing to the partner's face required almost no head movement. The effect seemed to be an increased feeling of intimacy and co-presence. These impressions were addressed more quantitatively in experiments described later.

Ishii and Arita found that users of ClearFace [17] hesitated to draw over the image of the partner's face, where the partner's image was in a translucent small window that appeared to be superimposed on a larger drawing image. In ClearBoard, users did seem to see the partner as *behind* the drawing and thus were not reticent in drawing on the board *in front of* the partner. This may be attributable to the transparent glass metaphor and to the relatively large size of the partner's image and head movements. Even with overlapping images, users did not report having trouble distinguishing drawing marks from the video background.

The importance of eye-contact is often discussed in the context of communication tools [1]. However, we found that even more important may be the more general capability that we call "gaze awareness," the ability to monitor the direction of a partner's gaze and thus his or her focus of attention [19]. More easily than is possible in an ordinary meeting environment with a whiteboard, a ClearBoard user can tell what screen objects the partner is gazing at during a conversation.

Experimental tasks

Further observations were carried out on ClearBoard-1 using a collaborative problem solving paradigm with a sharply delineated spatial element, the "river crossing problem." Through these experiments, described in [19], we confirmed the ability of users to recognize the direction of their partner's gaze and the utility of this information in understanding and guiding the partner.

More extensive experiments were carried out by videotaping "backgammon instruction" on a modified game board using ClearBoard-0, ClearBoard-1, and an ordinary table top as a control. The backgammon positions were laid out in a square as shown in the photographs from a ClearBoard-0 session in Figure 9. By confining the instructional activity to the periphery, we could differentiate patterns of visual attention to the workspace and to the partner, as seen in Figure 9. The backgammon game succeeded in engaging the subjects, and motivated them to focus on the task.

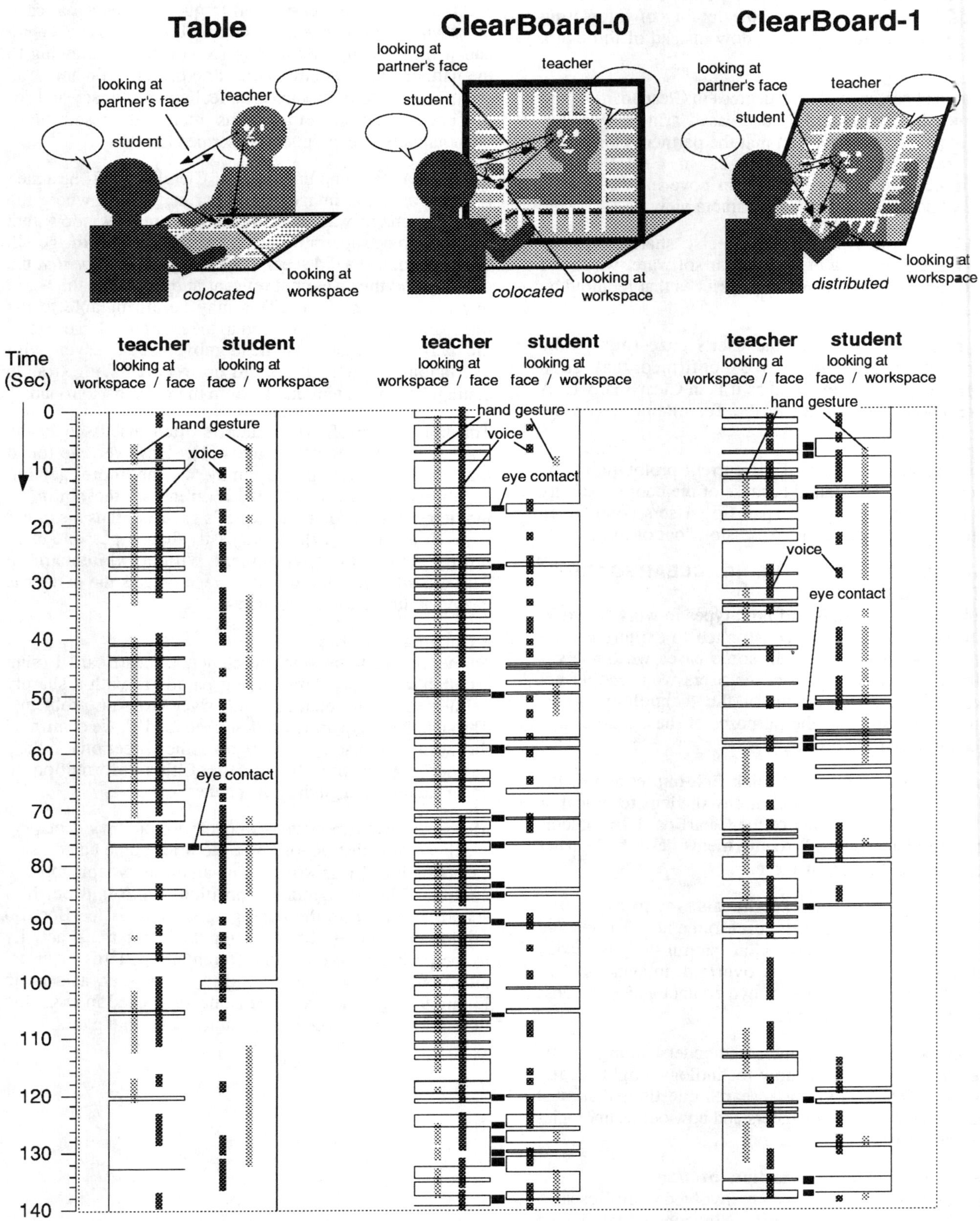

Figure 10. Time Chart of Gaze, Gesture and Speaking Pattern in Teaching Phase

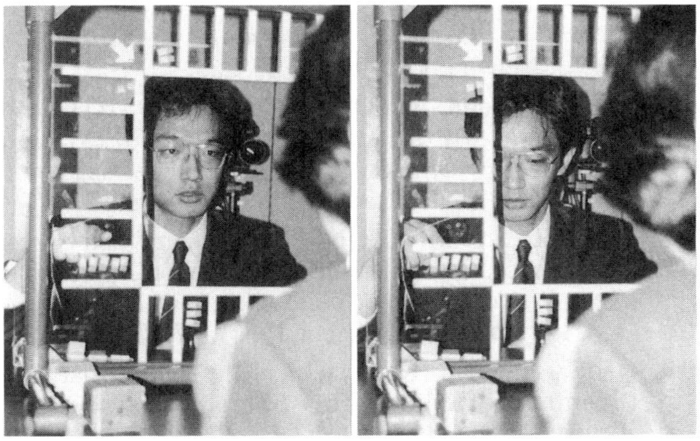

Figure 9. Gaze awareness in backgammon instruction with ClearBoard-0

We used the same student-teacher pair (neither of them involved in the research effort) in three settings. The teacher, a backgammon expert, instructed the student in different backgammon tactics in three settings (table, ClearBoard-0, and ClearBoard-1). Each session took about 20 minutes, with the first half mainly being used for teaching the rules and tactics and the latter half spent playing a game using the knowledge that the student acquired. In the game playing phase, both teacher and student were often absorbed in the game, and rarely looked at each other's face in any of the settings. In the teaching phase, however, we found a big difference in the patterns of focus shifting. We analyzed the patterns of gaze, gesture and speaking in 140 second segments from the middle of each of the three teaching phases. As can be seen in the coded transcript of the patterns of conversation, gesture and gaze shown in Figure 10, there was considerably more shifting of focus between shared workspace and inter-personal space in ClearBoard-0 and 1 settings than when using the table.

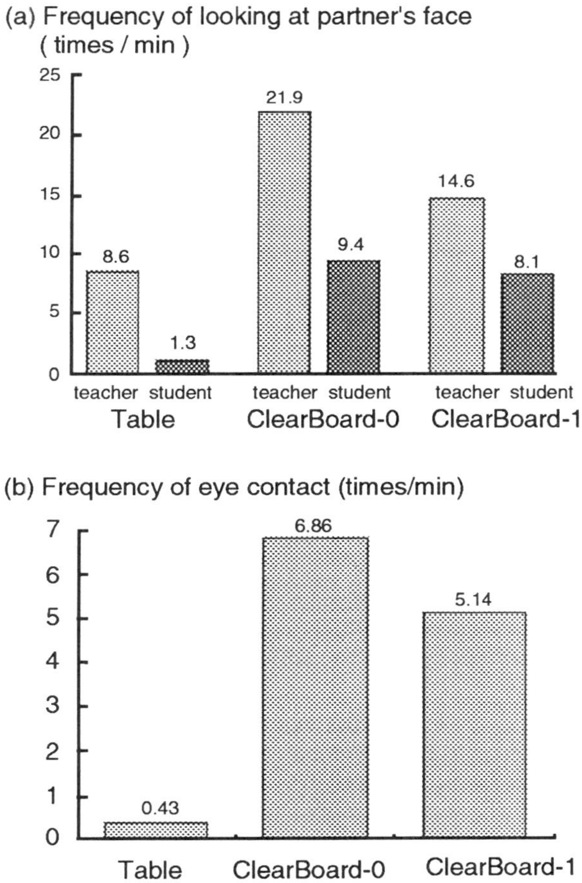

Figure 11. Frequency of Looking At Partner's Face and Eye Contact

The results of these experiments are summarized in Figure 11. They provide evidence that the participants do have a greater incidence of eye contact and focus shifts between SWS and IPS with the ClearBoard technologies. There is a decrease with ClearBoard-1 because of its lower resolution video, but the incidence is still considerably greater than the tabletop, where the separation of workspace and inter-personal space is greater.

CONCLUSION

We have described the designs of shared drawing media ClearBoard-1 and 2 which permit smooth transitions between shared workspace and inter-personal space. ClearBoard-2, in particular, can be seen as a bridge between two different technology streams: groupware technology and video conferencing technology. We expect that the seamless integration of computer-based groupware and video communication will realize the next generation of collaboration media.

Our studies suggest that users can make effective use of the ability to shift focus, making eye contact and monitoring a partner's direction of gaze. *Gaze awareness* may be crucial to the next generation of shared drawing media, a potentially useful capability that CSCW technology can greatly enhance. ClearBoard is the first system to provide distributed users with this capability.

In addition to refining the prototype systems, we plan to study visual behavior further in the context of overlaid images. Existing work on the roles of visual attention and eye contact (e.g., [2], [24]) will have to be supplemented with further research to explore the effects of the facilitated eye contact and gaze awareness provided by these technologies. We expect ClearBoard to be useful both as a collaboration medium and as a vehicle to investigate the nature of dynamic human interaction.

ACKNOWLEDGMENT

Ishii thanks William Buxton at University of Toronto for stimulating discussions on the SWS/IPS framework. We thank Naomi Miyake at Chukyo University for her insightful comments on the role of gaze in the experiments on ClearBoard. Thanks are also due to A. Sasaki and Y. Hanamoto for their collaboration in developing TeamPaint software, and to Takaya Endo for supporting this research and Grudin's visit to NTT Human Interface Labs in November 1991.

REFERENCES

1. Acker, S., and Levitt, S. Designing Videoconference Facilities for Improved Eye Contact. *Journal of Broadcasting & Electronic Media, 31, 2* (Spring 1987), 181-191.
2. Argyle, M. *Bodily Communication.* Methuen & Co. Ltd., London, 1975.
3. Bly, S.A., and Minneman, S.L. Commune: A Shared Drawing Surface. *Proceedings of COIS '90,* ACM, New York, 1990, pp. 184-192.
4. Buxton, W. and Moran, T. EuroPARC's Integrated Interactive Intermedia Facility (IIIF): Early Experiences. *Proceedings of the IFIP WG8.4 Conference on Multi-User Interfaces and Applications,* North-Holland, Amsterdam, 1990, pp. 11-34.
5. Buxton, W. Telepresence: integrating shared task and person spaces. *Proceedings of Graphics Interface '92,* Morgan Kaufmann Publishing, Los Altos, 1992, pp. 123-129.
6. Clark, S., and Scrivener, S. The ROCOCO Sketchpad Distributed Shared Drawing Surface. LUTCHI Report No. 92/C/LUTCHI/0150. LUTCHI Research Centre, Loughborough University of Technology, UK, 1992.
7. Ellis, C.A., Gibbs, S.J., and Rein, G.L. Groupware: Some Issues and Experiences. *Communications of the ACM, Vol. 34, No. 1* (January 1991), 39-58.
8. Farallon Computing Inc. *Timbuktu 4.0 User's Guide,* Falallon Computing Inc., Emeryville, CA, 1991.
9. Fish, R.S., Kraut, R.E., and Chalfonte, B.L. The VideoWindow System in Informal Communications. *Proceedings of CSCW '90,* ACM, New York, 1990, pp. 1-11.
10. Foster, G., and Stefik, M. Cognoter, Theory and Practice of a Colab-orative Tool. *Proceedings of CSCW '86,* ACM, New York, 1986, pp. 7-15.
11. Gaver, W., Smith, R., and O'Shea, T. Effective Sounds in Complex Systems: The ARKola Simulation. *Proceedings of CHI '91,* ACM, New York, 1991, pp. 85-90.
12. Gaver, W. The Affordance of Media Spaces for Collaboration. *Proceedings of CSCW '92,* ACM, New York, 1992 (to appear).
13. Greenberg, S., Roseman, M., Webster, D., and Bohnet, R. Issues and Experiences Designing and Implementing Two Group Drawing Tools. *Proceedings of HICSS '92,* IEEE Computer Society, Los Alamitos, CA, 1992, pp. 139-150.
14. Group Technologies, Inc. Aspects: The First Simultaneous Conference Software For The Macintosh. *Aspects User's Manual,* Group Technologies, Inc., Arlington, VA, 1990.
15. Harrison, S., Minneman, S., Stults, R. and Weber, K. Video: A Design Medium. *SIGCHI Bulletin,* January 1990, pp. 86-90.
16. Ishii, H. TeamWorkStation: Towards a Seamless Shared Workspace. *Proceedings of CSCW '90,* ACM, New York, 1990, pp. 13-26.
17. Ishii, H., and Arita, K. ClearFace: Translucent Multiuser Interface for TeamWorkStation. *Proceedings of ECSCW '91,* Kluwer Academic, Dordrecht, The Netherlands, 1991, pp. 163-174.
18. Ishii, H., and Miyake, N. Toward An Open Shared Workspace: Computer and Video Fusion Approach of TeamWorkStation. *Communications of the ACM Vol. 34, No. 12* (December 1991), 37-50.
19. Ishii, H., and Kobayashi, M. ClearBoard: A Seamless Medium for Shared Drawing and Conversation with Eye Contact. *Proceedings of CHI '92,* ACM, New York, 1992, pp. 525-532.
20. Lauwers, J.C., Joseph, T.A., Lantz, K.A., and Romanow, A.L. Replicated Architectures for Shared Window Systems: A Critique. *Proceedings of COIS '90,* ACM, New York, 1990, pp. 249-260.
21. Lu, I., and Mantei, M. Idea Management In a Shared Drawing Tool. *Proceedings of ECSCW '91,* Kluwer Academic, Dordrecht, The Netherlands, 1991, pp. 97-112.
22. Mantei, M., Baecker, R., Sellen, A., Buxton, W., and Milligan, T. Experiences in the Use of a Media Space. *Proceedings of CHI '91,* ACM, New York, 1991, pp. 203-208.
23. Minneman, S.L., and Bly, S.A. Managing a trois: a study of a multi-user drawing tool in distributed design work. *Proceedings of CHI '91,* ACM, New York, 1991, pp. 217-224.
24. Neisser, U., and Becklen, R. Selective Looking: Attending to Visually Specified events. *Cognitive Psychology, 7* (1975), 480-494.
25. Root, R.W. Design of a Multi-Media Vehicle for Social Browsing. *Proceedings of CSCW '88,* ACM, New York, 1988, pp. 25-38.
26. Stults, R. Experimental Uses of Video to Support Design Activities. *Technical Report of Xerox Palo Alto Research Center,* 1988.
27. Tang, J.C., and Minneman, S.L. VideoDraw: A Video Interface for Collaborative Drawing. *Proceedings of CHI '90,* ACM, New York, 1990, pp. 313-320.
28. Tang, J.C., and Minneman, S.L. VideoWhiteboard: Video Shadows to Support Remote Collaboration. *Proceedings of CHI '91,* ACM, New York, 1991, pp. 315-322.
29. Tanigawa, H., Arikawa, T., Masaki, S., and Shimamura, K. Personal Multimedia-Multipoint Teleconference System. *Proceedings of INFOCOM '91,* IEEE Communications Society, 1991, pp. 1127-1134.
30. Watabe, K., Sakata, S., Maeno, K., Fukuoka, H., and Ohmori, T. Distributed Multiparty Desktop Conferencing System: MERMAID. *Proceedings of CSCW '90,* ACM, New York, 1990, pp. 27-38.

GROUPKIT
A Groupware Toolkit for Building Real-Time Conferencing Applications

Mark Roseman
Saul Greenberg

Department of Computer Science
University of Calgary
Calgary, Alberta, Canada T2N 1N4
(403) 220-6015 roseman@cpsc.ucalgary.ca

ABSTRACT
This paper presents our approach to the design of groupware toolkits for real-time work, and how the design is instantiated in our toolkit, GROUPKIT. The design is based on both the technical underpinnings necessary for real-time groupware, and on user-centered features identified by existing CSCW human factors work. We also present three strategies for building GROUPKIT's components. First, an extendible, object-oriented *run-time architecture* supports managing distributed processes and the communication between them. Second, *transparent overlays* offer a convenient method for adding general components to various groupware applications, for example supporting gestures via multiple cursors and annotation via sketching. Third, *open protocols* allow the groupware designer to create a wide range of interface and interaction policies, accommodating group differences in areas such as conference registration and floor control.

KEYWORDS
real-time groupware, toolkit, development tools

INTRODUCTION
Real-time computer conferencing applications have been a major focus of groupware development efforts. Often motivated by CSCW research, we have recently seen the creation of numerous systems, such as shared text editors [23], freehand sketching systems [13,22], structured drawing programs [15], and group support systems [24]. Yet construction of these applications is fraught with difficulties. Besides all the normal problems of building single-user applications, the groupware developer must be concerned with technical issues such as synchronization, concurrency, communications, registration and more. The developer must also understand and incorporate the fundamental CSCW human factors issues identified for effective group work. *Groupware toolkits* are now emerging that address some of these issues. By providing the key components for common groupware needs, the toolkits can reduce development effort, enable rapid prototyping, and increase product quality of multi-user applications.

Permission to copy without fee all or part of this material is granted provided that the copies are not made or distributed for direct commercial advantage, the ACM copyright notice and the title of the publication and its date appear, and notice is given that copying is by permission of the Association for Computing Machinery. To copy otherwise, or to republish, requires a fee and/or specific permission.

© 1992 ACM 0-89791-543-7/92/0010/0043...$1.50

Of course, there are many potential groupware applications, and no one toolkit could cover all possibilities. In our case, we are concerned with toolkits that assist in constructing real-time *work surfaces* — shared visual environments where one user's actions are made immediately visible to other users [11]. These work surfaces are useful in both face to face and geographically distributed meetings. At its simplest, a work surface is a "What You See Is What I See" (WYSIWIS) space [27] that conference participants use for creating, importing, displaying, and interacting with their artifacts — usually text and graphics of some sort. Thus work surfaces include generic applications such as shared windows, whiteboards, structured drawing systems, and shared editors. But work surfaces can be far more powerful and specialized than that. For example, WYSIWIS could be relaxed so that people could view the work surface from different perspectives; an example would be a competitive card game [26]. Specialized applications could expand the notion of work surface to include tools for voting, brainstorming, organizing ideas, and so on.

This paper discusses our toolkit design philosophy, as embodied in GROUPKIT. We begin by listing a preliminary set of requirements for groupware toolkits, derived from both human factors work and technical innovations in CSCW. The following section presents an overview of GROUPKIT, with a detailed description of its technical architecture. Examples of three strategies for designing toolkit component are then given.

TOOLKIT DESIGN REQUIREMENTS

In this section we propose and defend some of the underlying design requirements we feel are important for a real-time conferencing toolkit. We do not believe this list is complete, nor will every item be necessary for every groupware application. However, we do feel the requirements listed will apply to a wide range of real time conferencing applications, and that they provide a reasonable starting point for discussion. Requirements listed in the first section are human-centered, and those in the second are programmer-centered.

Human-centered design requirements

Supporting multi-user actions over a visual work surface.
We believe there are several general but critical activities that people do over a shared work surface, regardless of its contents. Two of these, gesturing and annotation, are described below.

a) Provide support for gesturing. Researchers at Xerox PARC studied the use of conventional drawing surfaces by small groups [28]. A critical finding was that participants frequently gesture over the drawing surface: to enact ideas, to signal turn-taking, to focus the attention of the group, and to reference objects on the surface. Several recent computer systems emulating group drawing surfaces support gesturing with multiple cursors appearing on all displays [13,2,15], and their usability studies confirm the ubiquity of gesturing. We believe that gesturing can enhance communication in many diverse types of conferences, and should be supported at the toolkit level.

b) Provide support for graphical annotation. The Xerox studies also noticed many instances of annotations made to existing drawings, serving both as gestures (eg underlining text while saying "this one here") and as meta-level notes. Several systems now incorporate graphical annotations of their objects. FREESTYLE users, for example, can verbally and graphically annotate bitmap snapshots; the results can be mailed to others who can then play back the transcript [9]. Both PROOF-MARKS in *vmacs* [18], and the commercial MARKUP application allow comments and markup symbols to be added to written documents. As with gesturing, we believe that real-time group graphical annotation over a work surface is useful in many situations and should be supported by the toolkit.

Structuring group processes during a meeting
Some researchers believe that groupware should impose a social model of interaction on the group. This is an explicit attempt, based on management theory, to provide methods for keeping the group on task, enforcing roles and commitments, and making the group more efficient and productive. There is certainly controversy between those who believe that social protocol should be determined only by the group members (eg [7]), by the software (eg [24]), and somewhere in between (eg [16,14]). We believe that some group process primitives should be provided by the toolkit, accommodating groupware that wishes to control meeting structure. The list below discusses only a few group process requirements.

c) Provide various floor control policies. Floor control or turn-taking mechanisms provide a way to mediate access to shared work items. Lauwers [19] and Greenberg [14] recommend that systems should "support a broad range of [floor control] policies" to suit the users' needs. Systems such as SHAREDX [10] and ASPECTS (from Group Technologies) support a few different policies, while SHARE [14] strives to provide complete flexibility. Floor control can be important in many situations, such as shared screens allowing only serial interaction, or systems following strict interaction models, such as a teacher controlling which students can access the work surface.

d) Support different registration methods. Another part of group process controls who is allowed to join the meeting. For some meetings, anyone may be allowed to join. For others only a select group can participate, or perhaps new users must be "sponsored" by an existing user. Sometimes more spontaneous creation of conferences is desired [17] while other situations require a central facilitator to handle registration [24]. Toolkits should provide the flexibility to support any reasonable registration process.

e) Support latecomers to the conference. A consequence of spontaneous conferences is that all users will not join the conference at the start. Provisions should exist allowing newcomers to join at any time, as well as allowing existing members to leave. Strategies must also be supported to assist the newcomers in "getting up to speed." This may involve simply sending the current conference state to the new user [15] or providing summary information on how the conference has progressed over its lifetime.

Integration with conventional ways of doing work.
Groupware should not impose a barrier between "individual" and "group" ways of working. For example, the system should provide group members with ready access to their individual work, and allow them to import it to a conference. Additionally, all normal communication channels (eg telephone, email) should be readily available.

f) Integrate other forms of communication. Voice communication is an important factor in most conferences [4], and given the ubiquity of telephones, we should assume that a voice channel is available. While many real-time conferencing systems assume a voice channel is present, they do not explicitly support creating voice links. Ideally, there should be a mechanism in the conferencing system to establish voice conferencing — perhaps automatically when a data conference is started. Similar arguments hold for other channels that may be available such as video links.

g) Allow use of single-user applications. Soon, most computer applications may be designed to support multiple users. Unfortunately, most of today's applications support single users only. There are several reasons why single-user programs should be available in multi-user conference settings. Groupware counterparts to single-user programs may not exist; a person's work may be accessible only through a particular application; people are skilled on particular applications. Conference users should be able to view and interact with single-user systems through shared screen or shared windows eg SHARE [12] and SHAREDX [10]. The toolkit should provide shared windows or the means to incorporate other shared window systems.

Programmer-centered design requirements

Technical support of multiple and distributed processes.
Most groupware, especially for geographically distributed conferences, will require an architecture where multiple (perhaps distributed) processes can communicate with each other. While most operating systems provide process control and inter-process communication, the programmer's job of initiating, maintaining and tearing down processes and their communication channels is a tedious one. As well, state information about sessions may need to survive beyond the lifetime of a single process or meeting.

h) Provide processes for basic conference management. Groupware applications must oversee all conference management, which include activities such as participant registration, initiation and teardown of meeting processes, communications, and so on. Groupware toolkits have placed much emphasis in providing capabilities for conference management eg LIZA [11], CONFERENCE TOOLKIT [3], and MMCONF [5]. We too believe that the basic run-time infrastructure for conference management must be supplied by the toolkit.

i) Provide a robust communications infrastructure. Any groupware toolkit must provide the communications facilities on which to build conferencing components. At the very least, it must be possible for any process to send messages to specific processes owned by conference users, and it is preferable if a multi-cast facility is available to broadcast a single message to all. Of course, the communications demands will depend heavily on the way the process architecture is determined. The trade-offs between centralized and replicated architectures are well-documented [20], with centralized architectures simplifying concurrency control and replicated architectures being more efficient and robust to machine failure.

j) Provide support for persistent sessions. Often computer conferences will span more than a single session, for example decision support meetings [24]. It is desirable to maintain session state information over the full duration of the conference. There should exist a general mechanism whereby conference objects can be made persistent.

Technical support of a graphics model.
A visual work surface will require graphical and textual primitives. Yet shared graphics require several capabilities that are not present in single user systems.

k) Provide primitives to a shared graphics library. Many groupware applications require graphical library primitives for creating multi-user objects such as shared lines, rectangles, circles and text. Greenberg, Roseman et al's discussion of GROUPDRAW [15] describes technical issues of a shared object-oriented drawing package, and provides their design of an abstract drawing object that can be sub-classed into concrete objects such as shared lines [15]. Similarly, the fine-grained editing of simple graphics and text objects in Bier and Freeman's MMM system gives insight into how shared objects should behave [1]. Similar extendible graphics libraries should be provided by toolkits, so that programmers can easily create shared interactive graphical objects on the display.

l) Provide object concurrency control. Many groupware conferencing systems support access to some type of shared object, be it structured graphics or a text buffer. Concurrency control is often needed to mediate access to the object, for example, two people trying to manipulate the same point on a line. In fact several concurrency schemes have already been implemented in groupware toolkits [25,26,11]. Concurrency can be achieved through simple locking, transaction mechanisms, or numerous other schemes [8]. In addition, the degree of concurrency and access to shared objects can be specified through the notion of flexible coupling [6].

m) Separate the view of an object from its underlying representation. Many single-user graphical systems separate the properties of an object from its view on the screen. Patterson argues that this separation is critical in groupware [25,26], and that abstractions should be used to create an interface-independent representation of data. As a consequence, users can have multiple perspectives on the same data.

GROUPKIT
GROUPKIT is a toolkit a programmer can use to develop real-time computer conferencing applications for geographically distributed or face to face meetings. It provides not only support for basic connectivity, but also support for higher-level human factors concerns. As it is still being developed, we have not yet incorporated all our design principles. However components are provided for flexible policy conference registration, communications support, flexible floor control, and gestural and annotative communication.

GROUPKIT is written in C++, on top of the INTERVIEWS toolkit [21]. Applications built using GROUPKIT will run on any machine supporting INTERVIEWS, that is, Unix workstations running X-Windows. GROUPKIT relies on the INTERVIEWS glyph mechanism for its user interface constructs. Glyphs are lightweight objects (similar to widgets in other toolkits) that are composed to make interfaces. The INTERVIEWS Dispatch library — a front end to normal Unix sockets — is used for communications.

Process and Communications Run-Time Support

GROUPKIT's technical infrastructure is based upon a replicated architecture and communications support, as illustrated in Figure 1. The infrastructure supports conference registration and the subsequent communication between processes owned by conference participants. This is comparable to the communications support in RENDEZVOUS [25] and the CONFERENCE TOOLKIT [3]. The remainder of this section describes the infrastructure components by walking through an example scenario.

Registration. Suppose a user wants to create a shared drawing surface, perhaps to discuss a design problem with a remotely located colleague. On initiating the GROUPKIT-based program, the user must first create a conference. This is done through the *Registrar Client*, which provides an interface to the central *Registrar*.

The Registrar allows the user to create, join or leave one or more conferences. The Registrar Client is responsible for implementing particular registration policies, eg deciding who enters the conference, how they do so, and what the interface looks like. While GROUPKIT allows new Clients to be programmed, it also provides a library of predefined Registrar Clients implementing particular registration policies and user interfaces. One novel aspect of this scheme is that it allows group members to use different Registrar Clients to enter a single conference.

The Registrar is an independent process (invisible to the user) that maintains a list of all conferences and their users. One central Registrar would exist at each installation. The Registrar itself is *policy-free*, and leaves it to the Registrar Clients to implement a particular registration policy and to present a reasonable interface to the user. This allows different policies and interfaces to be implemented in order to accommodate group differences.

Conference Initiation. In our scenario, the user has just requested a new conference through the Registrar Client, which in turn passes the request on to the Registrar. Next, the Registrar Client asks the *Coordinator* to create a new *Conference* object. The Coordinator acts as an intermediary between the Registrar Client and application Conferences, permitting multiple conferences (eg sketching and editing applications) to share a common registration mechanism. Its main duties are to create Conferences at the request of the Registrar Client, and to direct requests from the Client to the appropriate Conference.

The Coordinator then spawns a new process which instantiates a Conference object. It is the Conference object that actually runs the specific groupware application. GROUPKIT provides a generic Conference object, which the developer may subclass to provide extra functionality required by the application. In this case, the generic

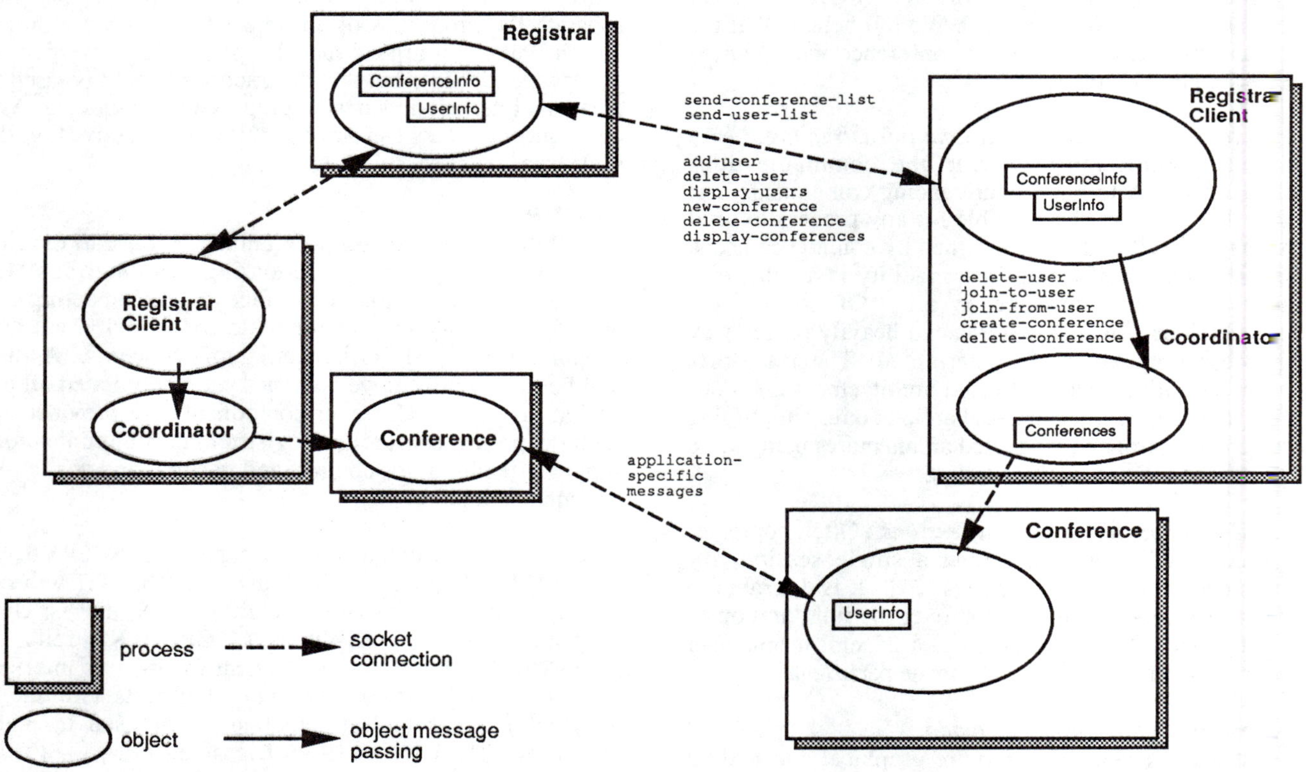

Figure 1. Communications infrastructure of GROUPKIT, showing message passing between objects. Here, objects owned by one user (rightmost Registrar Client, Coordinator, and Conference) interact with objects owned by another user, as well as the central Registrar. Small font text indicates the message passing protocol.

Conference object is used, along with a programmer-defined glyph (graphical interface) supporting a shared drawing surface.

Conference Maintenance. Other users can also create Conference objects. As each Conference locates the meeting participants via the Registrar, communications channels will be opened between all Conference objects. Facilities in the generic Conference are provided for exchanging messages with other user processes.

Communications between distributed processes are maintained by *messaging objects*. The two types of messaging objects ("Writer" and "Reader") provide a convenient method of communicating with processes owned by remote conference participants. These objects, derived from the INTERVIEWS Dispatch library, provide a primitive Remote Procedure Call (RPC) facility. Writer objects specify messages they can send, while Reader objects provide functions to be called when messages are received.

Conference Leaving and Termination. As with initiation, conference leaving and termination is handled through the Registrar Client. If a user wishes to leave the conference without terminating it, their Registrar Client sends the `delete-user` message (Figure 1) to the Registrar. Some Clients may permit explicit conference termination, allowing any user to terminate the conference, while more typically the Registrar Client for the last user to leave will terminate the conference. This is done by sending a `delete-conference` message to the Registrar, which will be rebroadcast to any remaining users' Registrar Clients.

Overlays

GROUPKIT provides components that may be included in any Conference object through an *overlay* strategy. Overlays are transparent "windows" placed on top of the main application graphics shown by the Conference object. Currently, overlay components have been implemented for gestural communication (via multiple cursors over a surface) and annotative communication (via freehand drawing over a surface). The motivation is that such components could be useful for a variety of groupware applications, as mentioned earlier.

Figure 2 provides a conceptual picture of adding an overlay for displaying multiple cursors on an existing application graphic. The transparent cursor overlay is written as an INTERVIEWS glyph that overlays any other glyph. Neither the cursor glyph nor the main application glyph need any knowledge of the other. Input events are received by the cursor glyph, which updates cursors as necessary. The event (eg cursor motion) is then passed to the application glyph, to use as needed. The application glyph need not even know the event went through the cursor glyph. As with single-cursor window systems, event-driven drawing operations are performed normally by the application glyph, based on these events, with the cursor glyph sketching the cursors on top of the normal graphics.

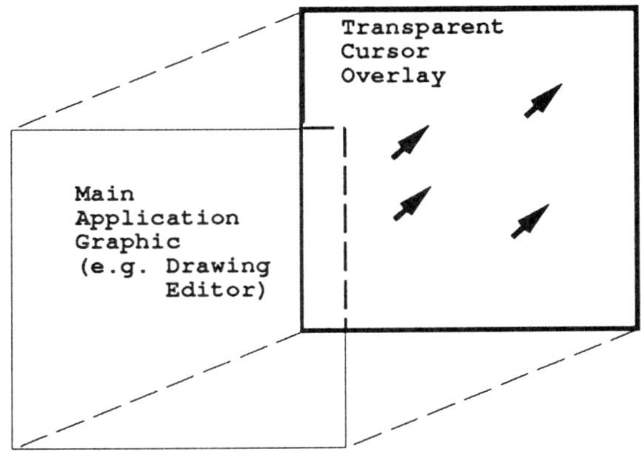

Figure 2. Adding a multiple cursor overlay.

To incorporate the multiple cursor overlay into an application, the programmer instantiates a CursorOverlay which surrounds the application's graphic. Code in the overlay's constructor allows the CursorOverlay to communicate with remote conference objects and inquire about new conference users.

This technique, also used to implement the freehand sketching overlay, seems very promising. Through the composition mechanism, adding overlay components to applications is extremely straightforward. As well, the overlays are kept separate — conceptually and in the code — from the underlying applications. Its strength is that the overlay does not interfere with the underlying graphics of the application, even if those graphics are changing. Because of this, it is a trivial matter to add, for example, annotation capabilities on top of a "live" shared terminal application. Unlike other systems that only allow annotation of screen snapshots (eg MMCONF [5]), the underlying application can be fully active. It is expected that further research will suggest other components that could be transparently added to a variety of conferences.

Open Protocols

One design requirement for GROUPKIT is to provide flexible policies where appropriate, allowing group processes to be structured during a meeting, and to accommodate group differences. *Open protocols* provide a means of implementing this flexibility. They have three components: a controlled object, a controller object, and a protocol describing how the two communicate. The controlled object's behavior does not incorporate any policy determining how its state can be manipulated. Instead, a protocol is defined, and the object will obey any external requests made to it to change its state. The controller is just an external object that implements a particular policy by the requests it sends to the controlled object.

Currently, two components have been implemented using open protocols, a floor control module and a registration module. We concentrate here on the registration module. Figure 3 shows the message protocol (beside the arrows) between the Registrar (the controlled object) and its Clients (the controllers). Here, the Registrar responds to *any* request from its clients, allowing any client to ask the Registrar to create a new conference, or conceivably even to delete any user out of any conference. While this does make it possible to create a "super-user" version of the Client, it also provides the flexibility to create any number of other Clients interfacing to the Registrar, without making any changes to the Registrar itself. As examples of this, the implementations of both a *free* and a *restricted* registration policy are now described. Under a free registration policy, new users may join any existing conference. The implementation here is straightforward. The Registrar Client sends an `add-user` message to the Registrar, which is broadcast to the other Registrar Clients in the selected conference. The Registrar Client also requests the Coordinator to create a new application Conference. The Conference makes connections with the other users, and the interaction proceeds normally.

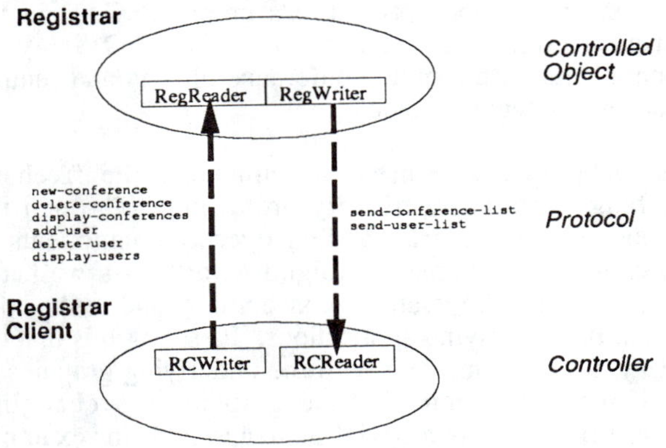

Figure 3. Registration Protocol.

In contrast, a restricted registration policy does not permit new users to join an existing conference unless "sponsored" by an existing conference participant. Here, the Registrar Client again sends an `add-user` message, which is rebroadcast to the other users. At this point, the local Registrar Client does *not* ask the Coordinator to create a new conference. The remote users are asked by their Registrar Clients if the new user should be accepted. A remote user can accept the new user, and sends them a message, prompting the new user to create the conference as before. If rejected (either explicitly or by timeout), the `delete-user` message is sent to the Registrar.

Floor control policies are handled similarly [14]. Each user has a flag, specifying if their actions should affect the conference or not. Any user can examine or change any other user's flag. A preemptive floor control scheme for serial interaction, where a user can immediately seize control from the current floor holder, can be implemented by setting the local flag to `write` and setting all others to `no-write`. The end result is that the local user gains control of the floor until preempted by another user. A ring-passing policy, where the floor may be seized only if it is free (ie the previous floor holder has released it), is implemented by setting the local flag to `write` only if all others are currently set to `no-write`. MMCONF [5] uses a similar strategy for floor control, but manipulates only a single token, thus allowing less flexibility in protocols.

Again, this strategy seems useful in general. By providing a simple protocol to change states, building new policies becomes a simple matter of expressing the policy's semantics in the language of the protocol.

BUILDING AN EXAMPLE APPLICATION

This section describes the steps necessary to build applications using GROUPKIT. The steps include specifying the application-specific graphical presentation and interaction, initializing objects to send and receive application messages, selecting an application Conference object, and initializing a Coordinator object.

As an illustration, we describe the construction of a simple multi-user freehand sketching program using the multiple cursor overlay. The interface is similar to GROUPSKETCH [13]: multiple cursors are always visible, any user can draw at any time, and fine-grained actions are immediately visible on all displays. Note that although GROUPKIT provides a sketching overlay, for illustration we will not use it.

Graphical presentation

The application needs one or more INTERVIEWS glyphs to manage the graphical presentation and user interaction aspects of the interface, as well as any internal data structures. For a freehand sketching application, this involves creating a glyph holding a bitmap, and providing tools (pencil and eraser) that respond to mouse events for changing the bitmap. To incorporate the cursor overlay, the bitmap glyph is "composed within" the cursor glyph.

Designing this part of the sketching application is comparable to designing a single user version of the group application. There are some general conventions that are helpful to follow, such as separating event handling (cause) and the result of events (effect) into different routines. This facilitates use of common routines for local and remote invocations [15].

Messaging objects

Writer and Reader objects are used to send and receive application-specific messages. The routines in Writer objects are invoked as a result of local actions, for example, transmitting coordinates of a drawn line segment to the other replicated applications. Callbacks in the Reader objects interpret these messages, usually calling routines in the graphical presentation object to handle requests. In the example, the Reader instructs the sketchpad glyph to draw the line specified in the message. The standard objects must be initialized to include the required callbacks.

Coordinator

The Coordinator connects the registration mechanism (via the Registrar Client) to the application Conference objects running as separate processes. Available conference types must be specified to the Coordinator, using the standard X resource mechanisms (ie .XDefaults).

Application Conference

The application Conference maintains communications channels with other distributed applications. In our example, the generic GroupKit conference has sufficient functionality. The main program instantiates this object, and "attaches" to it the bitmap glyph described earlier, so that the glyph can send and receive messages.

The Conference is notified when users join or leave. Routines in the base Conference class manage the low-level socket connections between users. However, other classes may be notified when new users join or leave, to manipulate application data structures maintained for each conference user. For example, the cursor overlay uses this information to add or remove cursors as users join or leave.

FUTURE WORK

The work presented here should be seen as an initial attempt to formalize the design and implementation of general groupware conferencing toolkits. The design requirements emphasize the important abstractions needed in real-time CSCW applications, and provide a basis for generalizing existing application or toolkit features. The three strategies presented — a run-time process and communication architecture, overlays and flexible policies — should be seen as general strategies that can be used to implement certain design features. It is expected that further design principles and strategies will evolve.

GROUPKIT has proven to be a flexible platform for testing our ideas. We have already built prototype drawing programs and shared terminals, and we will be constructing more elaborate and robust applications shortly. Currently, several of the design principles have not yet been embodied in the toolkit. Our immediate plans are to address the concurrency control issues, building a layer of support for generic shared graphical objects, that follow ideas presented in [15]. Ideally, a framework for building domain-specific group graphical editors could be created, drawn from the ideas in Unidraw [29].

Some other work has focussed on blurring the distinction between synchronous and asynchronous groupware, by providing a system that determines the appropriate means of conferencing (synchronous or asynchronous) and makes available various communication channels (text, voice, video). The choices offered the user depend on environmental information (ie who is currently around, what communication channels are available). The registration mechanisms in GROUPKIT provide the flexibility to implement such a scheme.

Groupware toolkits still have a long way to go to catch up to their single-user counterparts. We look forward to the day when all toolkits will incorporate multi-user features, and its interface components (such as control panels and editing widgets) have multi-user capabilities built into them. When that day comes, the artificial distinction between single and multi-user systems will disappear.

Note: GROUPKIT will be available for anonymous ftp by conference time, from the Department of Computer Science, University of Calgary (`cpsc.ucalgary.ca`).

REFERENCES

1. Bier, E.A. and Freeman, S. MMM: A User Interface Architecture for Shared Editors on a Single Screen. In *User Interface Software and Technology (UIST '91)*, Nov. 11–13 1991, pp. 79-86.

2. Bly, S.A. and Minneman, S.L. Commune: A shared drawing surface. In *Proceedings of the Conference on Office Information Systems (COIS '90)*, Apr. 25–27 1990, pp. 184-192.

3. Bonfiglio, A., Malatesa, G., and Tisato, F. Conference Toolkit: A framework for real-time conferencing. In *Proceedings of the 1st European Conference on Computer Supported Cooperative Work (EC-CSCW '89)*, Sept. 1989.

4. Chapanis, A. Interactive human communication. *Scientific American 232*, 3 (1975), 36-42.

5. Crowley, T., Baker, E., Forsdick, H., Milazzo, P., and Tomlinson, R. MMConf: An infrastructure for building shared applications. In *Proceedings of the Conference on Computer-Supported Cooperative Work (CSCW '90)*, Oct. 7–10 1990.

6. Dewan, P. Flexible user interface coupling in collaborative systems. In *Proceedings of the ACM CHI'91 Conference on Human Factors in Computing Systems*, Apr. 27–May 2, 1991, pp. 41-48.

7. Dykstra, E.A. and Carasik, R.P. Structure and support in cooperative environments: The Amsterdam Conversation Environment. *IJMMS 34*, 3 (Mar. 1991), pp. 419–434.

8. Ellis, C.A., Gibbs, S.J., and Rein, G.L. Groupware: Some issues and experiences. *Comm. ACM 34*, 1 (1991).

9. Francik, E., Rudman, S.E., Cooper, D., and Levine, S. Putting innovation to work: Adoption strategies for multimedia communication systems. *Comm. ACM 34*, 12 (Dec. 1991), pp. 37–63.

10. Garfinkel, D., Gust, P., Lemon, M., and Lowder, S., "The SharedX multi-user interface user's guide, version 2.0," , HP Research report, no. STL-TM-89-07, Palo Alto, California, 1989.

11. Gibbs, S.J. LIZA: An Extensible Groupware Toolkit. In *Proceedings of the ACM CHI'89 Conference on Human Factors in Computing Systems*, Apr. 30–May 4 1989, pp. 29-35.

12. Greenberg, S. Sharing views and interactions with single-user applications. In *Proceedings of the Conference on Office Information Systems (COIS '90)*, Apr. 25–27 1990, pp. 227–237.

13. Greenberg, S. and Bohnet, R. GroupSketch: A multi-user sketchpad for geographically-distributed small groups. In *Proc. Graphics Interface (1991).*

14. Greenberg, S. Personalizable groupware: Accomodating individual roles and group differences. In *Proceedings of the 2nd European Conference on Computer Supported Cooperative Work (EC-CSCW '91)*, Sept. 1991.

15. Greenberg, S., Roseman, M., Webster, D., and Bohnet, R. Human and technical factors of distributed group drawing tools. In *Interacting with Computers (Special Edition on CSCW, in press).*

16. Johnson-Lenz, P. and Johnson-Lenz, T. Post-mechanistic groupware primitives: rhythms, boundaries and containers. *IJMMS 34*, 3 (Mar. 1991), pp. 385–418.

17. Kraut, R.E., Egido, C., and Galegher, J. Patterns of contact and communication in scientific research collaborations. In *Intellectual Teamwork: Social Foundations of Cooperative Work*. Lawrence Erlbaum Associates, pp. 149–172, 1990.

18. Lakin, F. Visual languages for cooperation: A performing medium approach to systems for cooperative work. In *Intellectual Teamwork: Social Foundations of Cooperative Work*. Lawrence Erlbaum Associates, pp. 453–488, 1990.

19. Lauwers, J.C. *Collaboration transparency in desktop teleconferencing environments*, Ph.D. dissertation, Technical Report CSL-TR-990-435, Stanford University, Computer Systems Lab, CA, 1990.

20. Lauwers, J.C., Joseph, T.A., Lantz, K.A., and Romanow, A.L. Replicated architectures for shared window systems: A critique. In *Proceedings of the Conference on Office Information Systems (COIS '90)*, Apr. 25–27 1990, pp. 249-260.

21. Linton, M.A., Calder, P.R., Interrante, J.A., Tang, S., and Vlissides, J.M., *InterViews Reference Manual*, Stanford University, Sept. 1991.

22. Minneman, S.L. and Bly, S.A. Managing a trois: A study of a multi-user drawing tool in distributed design work. In *Proceedings of the ACM CHI'91 Conference on Human Factors in Computing Systems*, Apr. 27–May 2 1991, pp. 217-224.

23. Neuwirth, C.M., Kaufer, D.S., Chandhok, R., and Morris, J.H. Issues in the Design of Computer Support for Co-Authoring and Commenting. In *Proc. of the Conference on Computer-Supported Cooperative Work (CSCW '90)*, Oct. 7–10 1990.

24. Nunamaker, J.F., Dennis, A.R., Valacich, J.S., Vogel, D.R., and George, J.F. Electronic meeting systems to support group work. *Communications of the ACM 34*, 7 (July 1991), pp. 40-61.

25. Patterson, J.F., Hill, R.D., Rohall, S.L. and Meeks, W.S. Rendezvous: An architecture for synchronous multi-user applications. In *Proc. of the Conference on Computer-Supported Cooperative Work (CSCW '90)*, Oct. 7–10 1990.

26. Patterson, J.F. Comparing the programming demands of single-user and multi-user applications. In *Proc. User Interface Software and Technology (UIST '91)*, Nov. 11–13 1991, pp. 87-91.

27. Stefik, M., Bobrow, D.G., Foster, G., Lanning, S., and Tatar, D. WYSIWIS revised: Early experiences with multiuser interfaces. *ACM Trans. on Office Information Systems 5*, 2 (1987), pp. 147–167.

28. Tang, J.C. Findings from observational studies of collaborative work. *IJMMS 34*, 2 (1991), pp. 143–160.

29. Vlissides, J.M. and Linton, M.A. Unidraw: A Framework for Building Domain-Specific Graphical Editors. In *Proc. of User Interface Software and Technology*, Oct. 1989.

Access Control for Collaborative Environments

HongHai Shen and Prasun Dewan

Department of Computer Sciences
Purdue University
West Lafayette, IN 47907
hhs@cs.purdue.edu and pd@cs.purdue.edu

ABSTRACT

Access control is an indispensable part of any information sharing system. Collaborative environments introduce new requirements for access control, which cannot be met by using existing models developed for non-collaborative domains. We have developed a new access control model for meeting these requirements. The model is based on a generalized editing model of collaboration, which assumes that users interact with a collaborative application by concurrently editing its data structures. It associates fine-grained data displayed by a collaborative application with a set of collaboration rights and provides programmers and users a multi-dimensional, inheritance-based scheme for specifying these rights. The collaboration rights include traditional read and write rights and several new rights such as viewing rights and coupling rights. The inheritance-based scheme groups subjects, protected objects, and access rights; allows each component of an access specification to refer to both groups and individual members; and allows a specific access definition to override a more general one.

KEYWORDS

CSCW, groupware, access control, protection, security, user interface.

1 INTRODUCTION

Recently, there has been much research done in computer applications for facilitating collaboration among multiple, distributed users. However, there has been relatively little work done in controlling access to the collaboration. Most collaborative systems give all collaborators the same rights to all objects and expect access to be controlled by social protocol. Thus, they do not provide computer support for preventing mistakes, conflicting changes, or unauthorized access. The major exception known to us is the GROVE outline editor [5]. A major reason for the lack of access control in collaborative applications is the absence of a generic access control model for collaborative systems that meets the requirements of collaborative systems.

Although generic access control models have been studied extensively in non-collaborative domains, none of them meets the requirements of collaborative environments. We have designed a new access control model to meet these requirements. The model is based on a generalized editing model of collaboration, which assumes that users interact with a collaborative application by concurrently editing its data structures. It associates fine-grained data displayed by a collaborative application with a set of collaboration rights and provides programmers and users with a multi-dimensional, inheritance-based scheme for specifying these rights. The collaboration rights include traditional access rights such as read and write rights and several new rights such as the right to change the shared view of a displayed object and the right to couple with other users [3]. The inheritance-based scheme groups subjects, protected objects, and access rights; allows each component of an access specification (subject, object, right) to refer to both groups and individual members; and allows a more specific definition to override a more general one. We have implemented the model as part of the Suite generic framework for supporting editor-based collaborative applications.

In this paper, we use the concrete example of Suite to describe our access model. Section 2 describes the new requirements for access control raised by collaborative systems. Section 3 gives an overview of our approach for meeting these requirements. Section 4 briefly outlines the Suite multi-user framework used as the basis of our access model. Section 5 gives the details of the model, showing how we have extended the conventional access control model to meet our requirements. Finally, Section 6 compares our work with

[1] This research was supported, in part, by a grant from the Software Engineering Research Center at Purdue University, a National Science Foundation Industry/University Cooperative Research Center (NSF Grant ECD-8913133), and by National Science Foundation Grant IRI-9015442.

Permission to copy without fee all or part of this material is granted provided that the copies are not made or distributed for direct commercial advantage, the ACM copyright notice and the title of the publication and its date appear, and notice is given that copying is by permission of the Association for Computing Machinery. To copy otherwise, or to republish, requires a fee and/or specific permission.

© 1992 ACM 0-89791-543-7/92/0010/0051...$1.50

related work, gives conclusions, and presents directions for future work.

2 ACCESS REQUIREMENTS

We have identified several requirements that a generic access control model for collaborative environments should support:

Multiple, dynamic user roles: The model should allow users' access rights to be inferred from their roles [9]. Moreover, it should allow users to take multiple roles simultaneously and change these roles dynamically during different phases of collaboration.

Collaboration rights: Besides traditional operations such as read and write, all other operations whose results can affect multiple users should be protected by collaboration rights.

Flexibility: The system should support fine-grained subjects, objects, and access rights, that is, it should allow independent specification of each access right of each user on each object. For instance, it should allow independent protection of each line in a multi-user code viewer.

Easy specification: Users should be able to specify access definitions easily.

Efficient storage and evaluation: The storage of access definitions and evaluation of the access checking rule should be efficient.

Automation: The model should make it easy to implement access control in multi-user applications.

These requirements are motivated in more detail in the following sections along with our approach for meeting them.

3 OVERVIEW OF APPROACH

The classic access matrix model proposed by Lampson [8] and refined by Graham and Denning [7] provides the basic framework to describe protection systems. Conceptually, the model describes what a protection state is and how state transitions occur. A protection state is defined by the triple (S, O, A), where S is a set of *subjects* (entities wishing to access data), O is a set of *objects* (units of data that may be accessed), and A is a matrix with rows representing subjects, columns representing objects and A[s,o] denoting the *access rights* (privileges that are needed to do certain operations on objects) a subject s has over an object o. The model includes an access checking rule which ensures that a request for accessing object o by subject s is denied if A[s,o] does not contain the requisite right. The rule assumes that the subject requesting access is uniquely identified from the running process [1]. The model also contains a set of commands specifying how to make state transitions, i.e., to change (S, O, A).

The above model does not specify the exact nature of the subjects, objects or access rights supported by the system. Moreover, it does not require a particular mechanism to specify elements of the access matrix and has been used, for instance, to support specifications based on both capability lists and access lists. However, it is not sufficient for meeting the collaboration requirement of (i) multiple user roles, since a process is always associated with a unique subject at any moment; (ii) easy specification, since it does not address specification of access rights, (iii) automation since it does not offer an application mechanisms for managing and specifying the access matrix, and implementing the state transition commands and the access checking rule.

We have extended the conventional model in several ways to overcome these limitations of it:

1. Collaboration Rights: We define a new set of access rights designed for the Suite generic collaboration model.

2. Negative Rights: We support the notion of *negative rights* to allow explicit denial of access.

3. Inheritance-based Specification. We support an extended access matrix that supports not only individual subjects, objects, and rights but also groups of these entities. The value of an element of the access matrix does not have to be specified directly and can be inferred from values of other elements of the matrix.

4. Automation: Our model includes mechanisms that relieve an application of the task of implementing the details of access control. These mechanisms are based on the Suite multi-user framework, which relieves an application of the task of implementing the details of the Suite collaboration model.

We have implemented these extensions in Suite. In the following sections, we use the example of Suite to motivate, describe, and illustrate our access control model and compare it with related works.

4 SUITE MULTI-USER FRAMEWORK

As discussed above, our access control model is based on the Suite multi-user framework. The framework allows all interaction with the system to be modeled as concurrent editing of fine-grained data structures called *active variables*. Each active variable is associated with a set of *attributes*, which determine various interactive properties of the variable such as its format and which properties of it are shared among users. A system-provided structure editor called a dialogue manager handles a user's interaction with the system. The framework is described in more detail in [4].

To illustrate the framework, consider the example of a Suite application called Ctool, which allows multiple users to edit and test C functions. The active variables of Ctool are C programs, functions, and lines. Figure 1 shows two users, `rxc` and `hhs`, interacting with the tool. In this session, the users have set the `ValueCoupled` and `ViewCoupled` attributes [3] of the active variables to `True`, thereby sharing both their values and views. As a result, when user `rxc` changed the view of the `minit` procedure by "eliding" it[2], the result was shared by both users, as shown in the figure.

The model described above does not include access control. It allows, for instance, user `rxc` to elide arbitrary pro-

[2]elide is an operation used to condense the visual representation of a data structure.

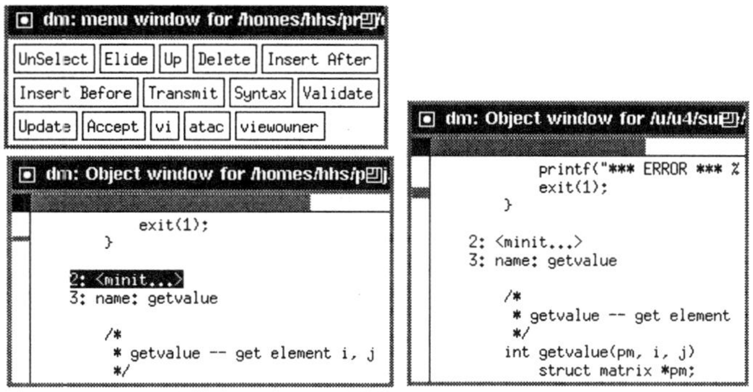

Figure 1: Two users in a collaborative editing session: when `rxc` (left) elides a function `minit` by pressing the `elide` button, `hhs`'s view is affected (right).

cedures being viewed by user `hhs`, which is not desirable if the former is required only to play the role of an "observer". It even allows `rxc` to change or delete arbitrary functions inserted by `hhs`. The model described in the next section overcomes this problem.

5 THE SUITE ACCESS MODEL

5.1 Positive and Negative Rights

Like conventional systems, Suite supports positive rights, that is, allows explicit granting of a right. In addition, it also supports negative rights, that is, explicit denial of a right. This notion is borrowed from a previous work on access control for database systems [10]. In this work, it was used along with the notion of strong and weak authorization to facilitate the access specification in the presence of a large set of data objects, which also applies to our environment. To illustrate this use of negative rights, assume a user is to be denied read access to one line of a 1000-line-long program. Instead of granting him the positive read right over 999 other lines, it is simpler to grant him a (weak) positive read right over the program and a (strong) negative read right over the line. We have found that negative rights can also be used to ease the specification task for CSCW applications supporting dynamic roles. To illustrate this use, consider the scenario where a user `hhs` wants to grant the read access of a private comment line to all users taking the `suite` role except `rxc`. Supporting only positive rights would require that `hhs` identify all `suite` users and explicitly grant each one of them except `rxc` the positive read right. This approach, however, suffers from two related disadvantages. First, it is painful for `hhs` to specify this definition if the list of `suite` members is long. Second, since users may take and relinquish the `suite` role dynamically, the above specification may become invalid later. With the notion of negative rights, the above can be achieved by granting a positive read right to `suite` and a negative read right to `rxc`. The use of negative rights can also reduce the time required to search the inheritance space, as discussed in section 5.6.

5.2 Protection State

The Suite protection state is represented by a 4-tuple (S,O,A,F), where S is the set of subjects consisting of both individual users and their groups, O is is the set of objects consisting of individual objects and their groups, A is the extended matrix with A[s,o] representing *explicitly* specified rights subject s has over object o, and F is an inference function allowing inference of rights that have not been explicitly specified. F takes as arguments a (subject, object, right, A) tuple and returns the value {`True`, `False`, `Undecided`}. Our access checking rule is the following modification of the conventional access rule:

Access Checking Rule: *To check the access privilege r of subject s over object o, A[s,o] is first consulted. If A[s,o] contains a positive or negative r, then access is granted or denied, respectively. Otherwise access is granted only if F(s,o,r,A) evaluates to true.*

Sections 5.3,5.4 and 5.5 describe the three dimensions of the extended access matrix and the associated inference rules in detail.

5.3 Object Dimension

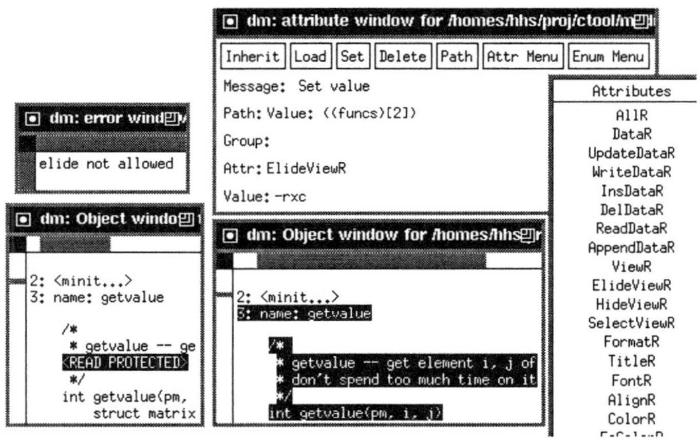

Figure 2: Fine grained specification: user `hhs` (right windows) denies `rxc` the elide right to the function `getvalue`. Thus, `rxc` (left windows) gets an error message when he tries eliding. The figure also shows an even finer-grained specification: `hhs` protects a comment line from being read by `rxc`.

Suite supports protection of fine-grained active variables. Continuing with the example of Figure 1, it allows user `hhs` to prevent user `rxc` from eliding a procedure he is currently working on (Figure 2). To specify this access definition, `hhs` first selects the function `getvalue` from the object window; presses the `Path` button in the attribute window, which fills out the `Path` field of the selected object in the window; selects the `ElideViewR` right from the menu; fills the `Value` field with "-rxc" and presses the `Set` button, which enters the access definition into the matrix. The figure also shows the result of a finer-grained specification, which disallows user `rxc` from reading a comment line.

Fine-grained specification requires users to specify and the system to store an access specification for each active variable, which is tedious and inefficient for most applications. To illustrate, assume that the user `hhs` does not want `rxc` to delete any line in a procedure he has just added. In this situation, he would have to specify an access definition for each of these lines and the system would have to store all of these definitions.

Therefore, Suite allows a user to specify an access definition for a group of active variables called value groups, and allows a specific definition to override a more general definition. Values are grouped on the basis of several properties including their structural parents and types. Because an active variable can belong to multiple value groups, an inheritance directive is associated with each active variable defining from which of these groups the specification should be inherited and the order in which they should be searched. This approach was first proposed for specifying display formats and other attributes of active variables by Dewan [2] and is described in detail there. We use this approach in the following inheritance rule for the object dimension:

Object Inheritance and Conflict Resolution Rules: *A right r of subject s on object o is inherited from the value groups containing o that are chosen by the inheritance directive, i.e.,* $F(s, V(o,r), r, A) \rightarrow F(s, o, r, A)$ *where V(o,r) are the value groups specified by the inheritance directive associated with o and r. In case of conflicts, the access definition in the first value group chosen by the inheritance directive is used.*

To illustrate this rule, assume that user `hhs` wants to disallow user `rxc` from deleting any line of the function `getvalue`. He can achieve this control by granting `rxc` a negative delete right on the function `getvalue`, which causes any line within the function to inherit this definition. In this example, access rights were structurally inherited. They can also be inherited from types. For instance, if `hhs` denies `rxc` the eliding right to type `function`, all objects of this type (that is, all functions) inherit this access specification.

5.4 Access Dimension

The Suite coupling model allows users to share the results of all operations on an active variable [3]. To meet the requirement of collaboration rights, our access model associates each of these operations with its own access right. For example, it defines the `ElideViewR` right, which determines whether a user can elide a variable; the `ColorR` right, which determines whether a user can change the color of a variable ; the `RawListenR` right, which determines whether a user can receive raw changes to a variable made by another user; the `ParsedListenR` right, which determines whether a user can receive syntactically checked changes to a variable made by another user; the `RawTransmitR` right, which determines whether a user can transmit raw changes to a variable to another user; the `ValueCoupledR` right, which determines whether a user can share value changes to a variable with another user; the `FormatCoupledR` right, which determines whether a subject can share formatting properties of a variable with another user, and so on. In all, Suite currently supports over 50 rights. We call these *individual rights* as opposed to the right groups described below.

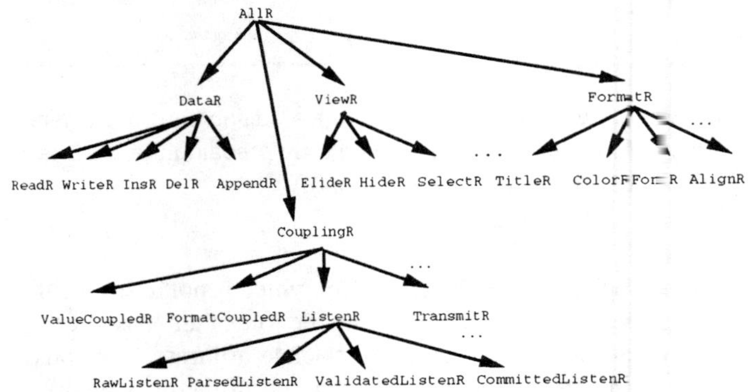

Figure 3: *Include* relationship among access rights

Introducing a large set of rights brings the associated problems of specification and storage of rights. To solve the problem, we introduce the notion of *right groups*, which are defined by classifying the individual rights into logical categories. Figure 3 gives part of the tree hierarchy of the grouping of rights where a transitive relationship *include* is defined. For example, `RawListenR` and `ParsedListenR` are included in the right group `ListenR`, `RawTransmitR` and `ParsedTransmitR` are included in the right group `TransmitR`, and `ListenR` and `TransmitR` are included in the right group `CouplingR`. Note that unlike an individual right, a right group does not correspond to any specific operation on an object.

The inheritance rule below defines the semantics of the *include* relationship.

Right Inheritance Rule 1: *A positive or negative right r of subject s on object o is inherited from the right groups it belongs, i.e.* $F(s, o, R, A) \rightarrow F(s, o, r, A)$ *and* $F(s, o, -R, A) \rightarrow F(s, o, -r, A)$ *where R includes r.*

Continuing with the example, assume that after some collaboration, `hhs` thinks he can trust `rxc` with several rights including the `DeleteR`, `InsertR`, `ElideR`, and `HideR` rights, but he still wants to restrict the coupling rights of `rxc`. He only has to grant `rxc` the corresponding right groups `DataR` and `ViewR`. Now `rxc` can invoke the insert, delete, elide, etc., operations. But he still cannot change the coupling. Fine-grained access rights together with right groups gives users fine-control over collaboration while relieving him from the task of tediously specifying all the rights.

We motivated and described above a relationship called *include* for grouping rights. This relationship alone is not sufficient for supporting easy specification of and maintaining consistency among access rights. Consider the following scenario. A new user abc joins the serc role and is not familiar with the system. To ensure security, hhs denies abc the data rights on the function he just created. Also assume that after some time, hhs decides that it is now safe to allow abc to insert new lines into the function though he still does not want him to delete anything in it. Naturally, this implies that abc should get the right to read the function. In some systems such as Unix, hhs has to grant the read right to abc explicitly, which is unnecessary. In our model, however, hhs does not have to do so explicitly since read is implied automatically by insert. This is an example of the *imply* relationship over individual access types, which is used to model the fact that the right to do a more powerful operation guarantees the right to do a less powerful one. It is similar to the *include* relationship in that it is also used to infer rights. The differences between the *include* and *imply* relationships are as follows: The *include* relationship is defined over individual rights as well as right groups while the *imply* relationship is defined only over individual rights. Moreover, unlike the *include* relationship, only positive authorizations are inherited from the *imply* relationship while negative authorizations are not. For example, write implies read, but negative write does not imply negative read, although negative read does imply negative write. Fernandez et al [6] suggested this approach for database systems and identified *imply* relationships among traditional access rights. We believe this approach is crucial for the more complex collaborative systems for two reasons. First, it reduces the problem of specifying the large number of rights necessary in a collaborative system. Second, in a collaborative system, users are prone to specifying conflicting rights because they have to specify, often dynamically, a large number of access rights. The *imply* relationship can be used by the system to detect these conflicts automatically. For example, if a write right is to be granted to a user who has been previously denied the read right explicitly, the system can detect the conflict because negative read implies negative write.

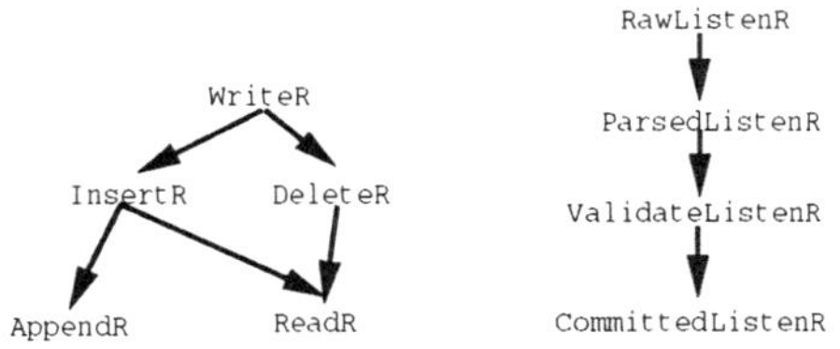

Figure 4: Some *imply* relationships among individual access rights

Therefore, we support the notion of implication of rights and have identified and implemented the *imply* relationships among the Suite access rights. Figure 4 gives some of these relationships. These relationships allow, for instance, the RawListenR to imply the ParsedListenR since a user in Suite listening for raw values of active variables can also listen for parsed values [3].

The following inheritance rule summarize the above discussion:

Right Inheritance Rule 2: *A right r of subject s on object o, if undecided, is inherited from the rights that imply r, i.e.,* $F(s, o, rx, A) \rightarrow F(s, o, r, A)$ *where rx implies r.*

Supporting both the *include* and *imply* inheritances allows an access right to be inherited from multiple sources. To illustrate, consider the situation above where user abc was granted a negative data right and a positive insert right. We have a conflict since the negative read right can be inferred from the first definition while the positive read right from the latter. In such situations, the *imply* relationship is used first. This is because the *imply* relationships are defined over the individual rights and exist even if right groups are not defined. From another perspective, right groups can be regarded as mere macro conventions. Furthermore, the *imply* relationship is introduced for both easy specification and right consistency, while the *include* relationship only for easy specification. Thus, rights are more tightly related by the *imply* relationship than the *include* relationship. Thus, in the scenario above, the imply relation is used to grant abc the read right. Our conflict resolution rule is summarized below:

Right Conflict Resolution Rule: *The imply relationship is used in preference to the include relationship in case of conflicts.*

5.5 Subject Dimension

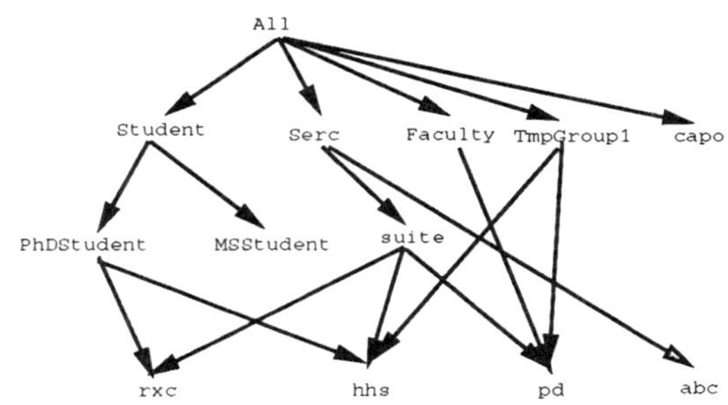

Figure 5: *Take*: inherit all rights of a role

Like conventional systems, Suite allows a subject to be a specific user. In addition, it allows a subject to be a *role* and allows a user or role to "take" a role. A subject takes a role if a *take* mapping is defined between the subject and the role, which can be changed dynamically. A subject can take multiple roles simultaneously. Moreover, multiple subjects can take a role. As a result, the notion of a role includes the concept of a user-group supported by traditional systems.

The take relationship allows a subject to inherit the rights of its roles according to the following inheritance rule:

Subject Inheritance Rule 1: *Subjects inherit both positive and negative rights from the take relationship, i.e., if s takes the role of S, then* $F(S, o, r, A) \rightarrow F(s, o, r, A)$ *and* $F(S, o, -r, A) \rightarrow F(s, o, -r, A)$.

Continuing with the Ctool example, if we allow the `faculty` role to insert new functions into the program but explicitly deny the `student` role from doing so, then `pd` gets the right by taking the `faculty` role while `rxc` is denied the right by taking the `student` role.

We also support another inheritance relationship among subjects which is useful in maintaining access privileges. There are certain inheritance relationships among subjects which take only a subset of the positive access rights (privileges) of others. We define a relationship *have*, which treats positive access rights as privileges and supports inheritance of selected privileges. Formally, *have* is defined as a mapping from $S \times R \times S$ to { *true, false*} where S is the domain of subjects and R is the domain of positive rights. Figure 6 illustrates some *have* relationships of Ctool, which allow a `PhDStudent` to have all the data rights of `MSStudent` and `pd` (manager) to have all the data rights of `rxc` and `hhs` (employees). We support inheritance of selected rights rather than all the rights because it reflects the "least privilege" principle [11] more faithfully. The following inheritance rule reflects the semantics of *have*:

Subject Inheritance Rule 2: *If subject s1 has right r of subject s2, i.e., have(s1,r,s2)=true, then* $F(s2, r, o, A) \rightarrow F(s1, r, o, A)$ *where r is a positive right.*

Allowing a user to take multiple roles in the above manner introduces potential conflicts. Continuing with the Cool example, if `serc` is granted the positive right and `student` is granted the negative right for some data object, how should we decide the right for `rxc` who takes the role of both `student` and `serc`?

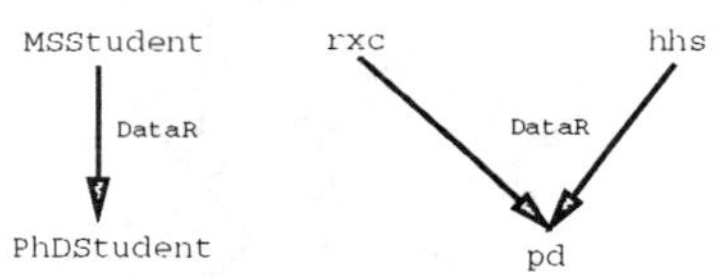

Figure 6: *Have*: inherit selected privileges

One approach to resolve this problem is to check the consistency of all of the access definitions and disallow any conflicts. However, this approach is inappropriate in a collaborative environment where the set of access objects can be very large and dynamic, and a user may take dynamic, multiple roles. Whenever a new role is assigned, or a *take* or *have* relationship is changed, or there is a change of explicit access rights of a role to an object, potential conflicts could result. Checking all these conflicts is costly and sometimes even unnecessary when a particular user may need to access only a very small part of a large set of objects. Thus, it is not only too rigid, but also computationally expensive to adopt the approach of simply disallowing conflicts.

To illustrate our solution, let us turn to some more examples. First, we observe that the *take* relationship actually defines an inheritance hierarchy which decides which role is more "specific". For instance, if `rxc` is checked against the access list `(+all-student+PhDStudent)`, although he takes all of the three roles in the list, he should be granted the right because `PhDStudent` is the most specific role he takes in the list. Thus, we derive our first rule in resolving conflict:

Subject Conflict Resolution Rule 1: *A more specific role defined by the take relationship should be used first.*

However, there are cases when it is impossible to decide which role is more specific as in the case of the access list `+serc-student` where there is no *take* relationship between the two roles, and the effects of `+serc-student` on subjects taking both roles can be interpreted as either positive or negative. In this situation, we interpret the access list to be "position sensitive", which corresponds to the heuristic of "putting important things first". According to this rule, `-student+serc` will grant negative rights to those taking both roles while `+serc-student` positive rights. This is our second rule in resolving conflict:

Subject Conflict Resolution Rule 2: *In case of conflicts, the access definition that appears earliest in the access list is chosen.*

By adopting the above rules, our approach provides a simple but flexible solution to this conflict problem. In one extreme case, all the negative definitions can be put before the positive ones to ensure maximal security `(-student-capo+faculty+serc)`. In the other extreme case, all the positive ones can be put before negative ones to ensure maximal sharing `(+faculty+serc-student-capo)`. Between these two extremes, users can adjust their needs by putting subjects at different positions. In conventional systems such as Unix and [10], a user is given the union of the rights that all of his roles can have. In Multics [11], a user is asked to supply upon login which role and compartment he will take and his rights in the session is subsequently checked against the `(individual, project, compartment)` triple. This approach, however, actually does not allow multiple roles of a user in a session.

The above two rules specify how to resolve conflicts due to the *take* relationship. Conflicts can also arise when a negative right is inferred from the *take* relationship and a positive right is inferred from the *have* relationship. In the algorithm we use, the *take* relationship is used in preference to the *have* relationship because of the following reasons. First, the *take* relationship can infer both positive and negative rights, which is safer than the *have* relationship as the latter can only infer positive rights. Second, the *take* relationship infers rights a user inherits *directly* from the roles he takes, while the *have* relationship infers rights a user gets *indirectly* from other users or roles which he may not take. Therefore, we define the following rule:

Subject Conflict Resolution Rule 3: *The take relationship is used in preference to the have relationship in case of conflicts.*

5.6 Multi-dimensional Inheritance and Extended Access Lists

In the above sections, we have described multiple inheritances in the object, type, and subject dimensions. There is yet another important question we have to answer: in which order are the inheritances in the three dimensions used when calculating a right? The answer determines both the semantics of the access model and the efficiency of the lookup. It is not currently clear to us which conflict resolution method is the most semantically meaningful. Therefore, we choose the method based on the efficiency considerations, which are related to the access data structures used to represent the access matrix. Traditionally, two main data structures have been chosen to represent the access matrix: capability lists and access lists. The first stores the matrix by rows, i.e., each subject is associated with a list of pairs (object, rights) called capabilities. The second approach stores the matrix by columns, i.e., each object is associated with a list of pairs (subject, rights) [7]. If we use the capability list mechanism, we should start the search from the subject dimension because it is the most efficient way to search the underlying data structures. If we use the access list mechanism, we should start the search from the object dimension for the same reason.

We did not choose the capability list mechanism because we found it difficult to devise a simple way using the capability mechanism to resolve conflicts arising from supporting multiple roles. Consider the `+serc-student` example again in the preceding section. Assume that the capability approach is adopted. Also assume the `serc` role has positive rights to procedure f1 and f2 and the `student` role has negative rights to them. Further assume that if conflicts arise we want the positive `serc` role to win in the case of f1 and the negative `student` role to win in the case of f2. According to this requirement, the capability list of the `serc` role must be used when the protection object is f1, while the capability list of the `student` role must be used when the object is f2. Thus, which capability list should be used depends on the object being accessed. This suggests that the information for the choice should be attached to objects, which can be more straightforwardly supported by an access list approach.

We have used an extended form of access list in our implementation of the model. In our approach, an object is associated with a list of pairs (r, u-list), where r is a right and u-list is a string of the form $(\omega_1 U_1 \omega_2 U_2 ... \omega_i U_i)$. Here, ω_j can be either + or - indicating a positive or negative right, and U_j is a subject, where $1 \leq j \leq i$. When a subject s is checked against the access rights r on object o, we first search the access list associated with o to get the (r, u-list) pair. The u-list, which is sorted according to the topology of the *take* relationship, is then used for inheritance in the subject space. If no definite right can be calculated from the subject space, inheritance in the rights dimension is used. If no definite right can be inferred based on the access list associated with the object, we use inheritance in the object dimension to infer the right. Finally, if we still do not find a definition for the right, we infer a negative right.

As shown above, the notion of negative rights makes the inheritance scheme more complicated. Nevertheless, we support negative rights for two related reasons. First, introducing negative rights can make access specification much easier, as discussed above. Second, negative rights help short-circuiting the search space since it is not necessary to do an exhaustive search of the inheritance space to infer denial of access.

5.7 Automation

The various aspects of the access control model described above allow end-users to easily and flexibly specify access rights but make it difficult for programmers of collaborative applications to implement access control. It requires implementation of the user interface for specifying access definitions, the extended access lists, and the various rules given above. We have automated this tedious process by implementing access control completely in Suite dialogue managers, which are provided by the system and which control all interactions between users and applications. As a result, the access awareness in an application such as Ctool is kept low since it is responsible only for specifying access control and not implementing it.

6 CONCLUSIONS AND FUTURE WORK

In this paper, we have identified access control requirements for a collaborative environment and presented a new access control model for meeting these requirements.

The main components of our model are:

1. A generic set of collaboration rights.
2. Fine-grained specification of access rights.
3. Multiple, dynamic user roles.
4. A set of inheritance rules in the subject, object, access right dimensions.
5. A set of conflict resolution rules in the multiple dimensions.

Some of the ideas in the model are based on a variety of previous works. The idea of *imply* relationship among access rights has been suggested in [6] which is extended by us to support collaboration rights. The concept of the *include* relationship among rights has not been discussed in other works to the best of our knowledge. Inheritance among objects takes its origin from the work in this area to support flexible displays and flexible coupling [3, 2], which has not been used before for access control. The idea of inheritance among subjects has been proposed by database researchers[6, 10]. We have extended their work by providing two kinds of inheritances: *take* according to user roles and *have* according to user privileges, and comparing these two relationships for inheriting access rights. By allowing inheritance of *have* to be based on a selected subset of rights, the "least privilege" principle is reflected more faithfully in our model. We have also developed rules for resolving role conflicts that employ the "position first" rule to resolve conflicts.

Our model in its complete form is complex. We believe any flexible model for collaborative systems will have this property. However, we have provided several methods for incrementally using and learning it. In particular, we have provided multiple dimensions of inheritance, which can be learned and used independently, as illustrated by our examples.

It has been observed in [5] that "Groupware's requirements can lead to complex access models, a complexity that must be managed, ..., there must be lightweight access control mechanisms that allow end-users to easily specify changes. User interfaces should smoothly mesh the access model with the user's conceptual model of the system. Changing an object's access permissions should, for example, be as easy as dragging the object from one container to another". Our access control model is a first-cut effort at meeting this goal. It is important to mention that while our model is designed for a collaborative environment, parts of it are also suitable for non-collaborative domains in which the set of objects, subjects, and rights are large.

A current limitation of our model is that its set of protected objects includes only active variables. We are investigating mechanisms for protecting other shared objects such as windows, sessions and subjects. We are also investigating policies for using our model. We plan to devise rules for checking consistency of access requirements based on these policies.

Acknowledgments: Discussions with Rajiv Choudhary, John Riedl and Tim Korb have been helpful in developing the model.

References

[1] D.E. Denning. *Cryptography and Data Security.* Addison-Wesley Publishing company, 1982.

[2] Prasun Dewan. An inheritance model for supporting flexible displays of data structures. *Software – Practice and Experience*, 21(7):719–738, July 1991.

[3] Prasun Dewan and Rajiv Choudhary. Flexible user interface coupling in collaborative systems. In *Proc. of ACM CHI'91 Conf.*, pages 41–49, April 1991.

[4] Prasun Dewan and Rajiv Choudhary. Primitives for programming multi-user interfaces. *Proc. of the 4th ACM SIGGRAPH Symp. on User Interface Software and Technology*, pages 69–78, November 1991.

[5] Clarence A. Ellis, Simon J. Gibbs, and Gail L. Rein. Groupware: Some issues and experiences. *CACM*, 34(1):38–58, January 1991.

[6] E. B. Fernandez, R. C. Summers, and C. Wood. *Database Security and Integrity.* Addison-Wesley, 1981.

[7] G.S. Graham and P.J. Denning. Protection – principles and practice. *Proc. Spring Jt. Computer Conf.*, 40:417–429, 1972.

[8] B.W. Lampson. Protection. *ACM Oper. Syst. Rev.*,, 8(1):18–24, 1974.

[9] John F. Patterson. Comparing the programming demands of single-user and multi-user applications. In *Proc. of the 4th ACM SIGRAPH Conf. on User Interface Software and Technology*, pages 79–86, November 1991.

[10] Fausto Rabitti, Elisa Bertino, Won Kim, and Darrell Woelk. A model of authorization for next-generation database systems. *ACM TODS*, 1(16):88–131, March 1991.

[11] J.H. Saltzer. Protection and the control of information sharing in multics. *CACM*, 17(7):388–402, July 1974.

Relational Views as a Model for Automatic Distributed Implementation of Multi-User Applications

T.C. Nicholas Graham

GMD Forschungsstelle an der Universität Karlsruhe
Vincenz-Prießnitz-Str. 1
D-7500 Karlsruhe 1, Germany
graham@karlsruhe.gmd.de

Tore Urnes

Division of Computer Science and Telematics
Norwegian Institute of Technology (NTH)
N-7034 Trondheim, Norway
urnes@idt.unit.no

ABSTRACT

Multi-user applications support multiple users performing a related task in a distributed context. This paper describes*Weasel*, a system for implementing multi-user applications. *Weasel* is based on the *relational view model*, in which user interfaces are specified as relations between program data structures and views on a display. These relations are specified in *RVL*, a high-level, declarative language. Under this model, an application program and a set of *RVL* specifications are used to generate a multi-user application in which all issues of network communication, concurrency, synchronization, and view customization are handled automatically. These programs have a scalable distribution property, where adding new participants to a session does not greatly degrade over-all system performance. *Weasel* has been implemented, and was used to generate all examples in this paper.

KEYWORDS

Implementation, Groupware, Multi-User Applications

INTRODUCTION

Multi-user applications support multiple users performing some related task in a distributed context. Examples of multi-user applications include groupware systems, which provide computer support to group activities [3]. Multi-user applications are hard to implement due to a competing set of requirements [2,3,7,11,12]:

- *Evolutionary design:* user interfaces supporting cooperative work must evolve based on experimentation;
- *Customizability:* Users should also be able to customize shared views without modifying those of other participants;

Permission to copy without fee all or part of this material is granted provided that the copies are not made or distributed for direct commercial advantage, the ACM copyright notice and the title of the publication and its date appear, and notice is given that copying is by permission of the Association for Computing Machinery. To copy otherwise, or to republish, requires a fee and/or specific permission.

© 1992 ACM 0-89791-543-7/92/0010/0059...$1.50

- *Mixed Control:* Sometimes one or more users should control the session; sometimes the application should take charge; sometimes both should execute concurrently;
- *Distributed Implementation:* Applications must run efficiently in a distributed context; they should be *scalable* so that new participants joining a session do not significantly slow down over all performance.

In the *Weasel* system, we have developed tool and language support for creating multi-user applications that moves a significant distance toward meeting these goals. *Weasel* allows the automatic distributed implementation of multi-user applications: the programmer must provide a central application program, written in a traditional imperative programming language, and a set of view specifications, written in the declarative language *RVL*. From these specifications, the *Weasel* system creates a distributed implementation, where issues of network communication, concurrency, synchronization, and customization are handled automatically. This automation simplifies the programming of multi-user applications, making them easier to prototype and evolve. *Weasel* supports a wide range of direct manipulation user interfaces based on buttons, menus and dynamic layout of display objects. *Weasel* has been implemented to run on a network of Unix workstations, and was used to produce all examples in this paper.

One of the main advantages of *Weasel* over earlier systems for producing multi-user applications (e.g.[12]) is that systems generated by *Weasel* have a *scalable distribution* property -- that is, that adding new participants into a session does not significantly slow down the performance of the system as a whole. Timing results have demonstrated that a participant in 10-person session waits only 40% longer for updates than a participant in a single-person session Applications generated by *Weasel* are fast enough to use, but not yet not fast enough for a production environment. Many optimizations are planned, but in the meantime *Weasel* is a useful tool for rapid prototyping.

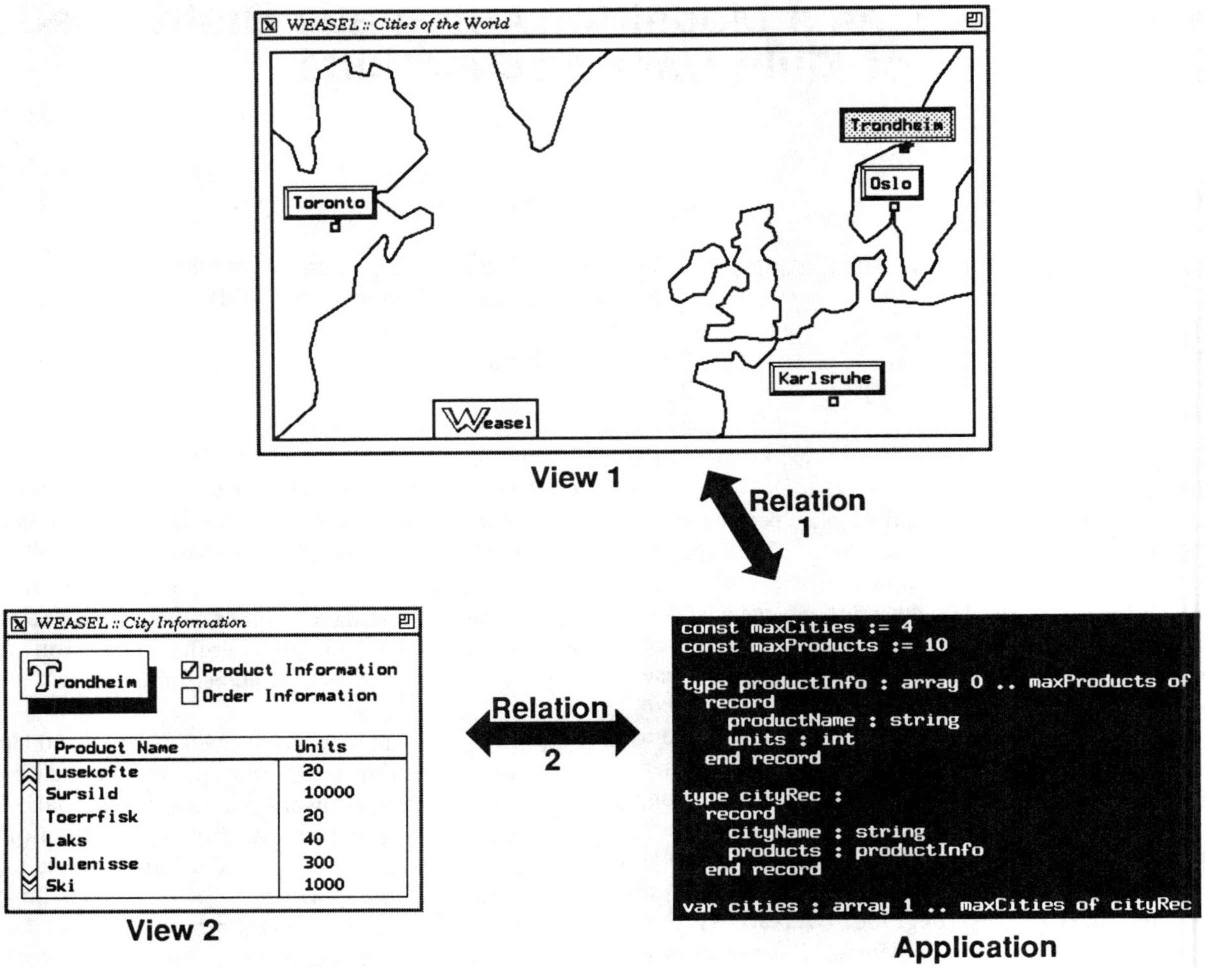

Figure 1. An inventory program as a pair of relational views. Users may click on a city, and view or modify product and order information for that city.

The paper is organized in two major sections. The next section introduces the relational view model (upon which *Weasel* is based), and the *relational view language* that is used to specify views. Section 3 then describes the mapping of relational views onto a network of workstations, and empirically evaluates the performance of systems generated by *Weasel*.

2 THE RELATIONAL VIEW MODEL

The motivation behind the relational view model of user interface construction is that user interfaces should be specified completely separately from application programs. The main advantage of such an approach is that user interfaces can evolve over time without impacting an operational application program. This strict separation brings the side-benefit that user interfaces can be easily distributed over a network, forming the basis of the *Weasel* implementation.

Under the relational view model, application programs are written in a traditional imperative language (in our case, Turing [8], a modular, Pascal-like language). The user interface consists of a set of *views*, graphical displays of data, which the user can manipulate directly using various input devices such as a mouse and keyboard. Every view is bound to the application program via a *relation*: whenever the program data changes, the picture is automatically updated to reflect the change, and whenever the user modifies the view through direct manipulation, the program data is automatically updated to reflect the change. These relations are specified in a special language called *RVL*, the Relational View Language, as described in section 2.1.

The paper contains two examples of relational views. Figure 1 shows an inventory program, where users at various sites can access order and inventory information by clicking a city on a map. The two views are specified by

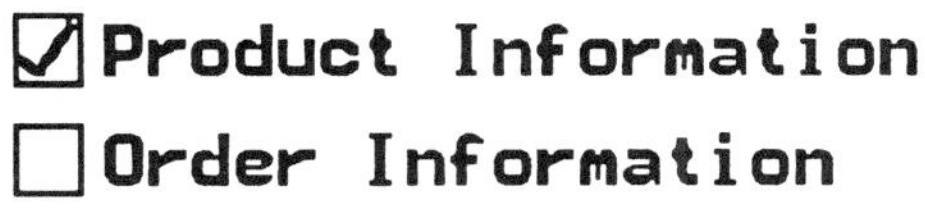

Figure 2. The toggle box from figure 1.

two different relations, each bound to the same data structure in the program. Each user receives the same views, but *customized*, so that if one user clicks on a different city, the other users' views do not change.

Figure 5 shows a tic-tac-toe game for two players. A strict turn sequence is observed, and both players view the current version of the board. The tic-tac-toe board is a *WYSIWIS* (What You See Is What I See) view [14], where a modification to the board by one player causes a modification to the other player's view.

The following sections describe the relational view language, and how relations are customized in a multi-user context.

2.1 The Relational View Language

Relational views are specified in the *Relational View Language (RVL)*, a version of the *GVL* output language [1], extended to handle input. *RVL* specifications are functions from data structures in the application to display views. These functions can be annotated with Garnet-style interactors [9] to allow input. *RVL* is a powerful functional language based on a small set of primitive functions such as lines, arrows, boxes, circles and text, and providing abstraction through function definitions. The language supports limited geometric constraints, and automatic tree and graph layout. Since programmers do not have to worry about state, control flow, or layout, *RVL* has a specificational flavour.

As an example to be specified in *RVL*, consider a toggle box view taken from the inventory program of figure 1. As shown in figure 2, the toggle box selects between two projections of information: either *Product Information*, giving inventory information for that city, or *Order Information*, showing outstanding orders between two cities. The current selection is indicated with a checkmark. Clicking the mouse anywhere on the checkboxes or text changes from one view to the other.

Figure 3 shows an *RVL* specification for the toggle box. In this example we use a visual syntax for *RVL*, as defined in [1,4]. It is our long-term hope that *RVL* specifications can be programmed directly in this notation using a graphical editor; for the time being, a textual version is used.

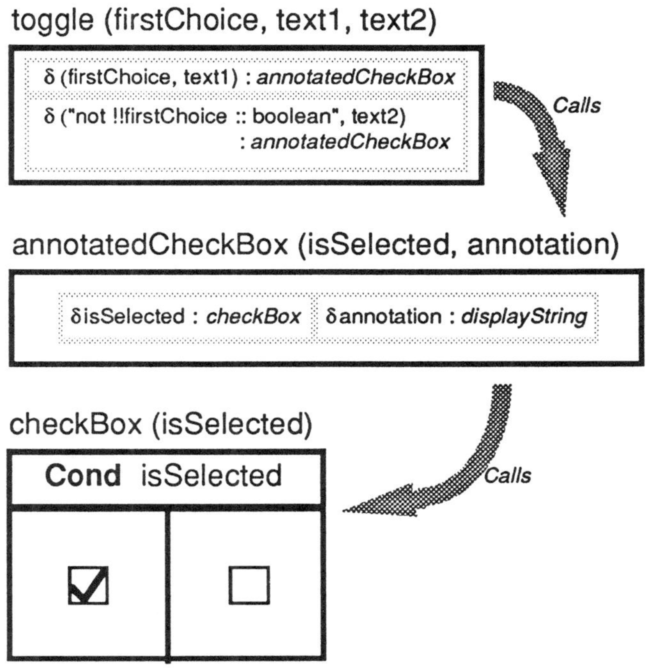

Figure 3. A *Relational View Language* specification of the toggle box from figure 2.

In figure 3, the togglebox is specified as a set of three functions that map the current state of the application to a picture on the display, where the correct projection is checked. The checkbox itself is specified with the function *checkBox*, which takes a single parameter *isSelected*. This parameter is a boolean value from the application that determines whether this box should be checked or not. The function is programmed using a *cond* construct: if *isSelected* is true, the picture on the left (a checked box) is displayed, and if false, the picture on the right (a box without a checkmark) is displayed.

To place a text label beside a checkbox, the function *annotatedCheckBox* is used. This function takes two parameters, *isSelected* to determine whether this box should be checked or not, and *annotation* which is the text label. The checkbox is drawn by applying the *checkBox* function to the parameter *isSelected*: this is accomplished with the syntax:

δ isSelected : *checkBox*

which can be read as: "display *isSelected* as a checkBox". The text label is displayed with the built-in function *displayString*. The grey boxes surrounding function calls indicate where the resulting picture is to be placed; these boxes are sized to fit, so in this case, the text label appears immediately to the right of the checkbox.

The full toggle box is then specified with the *toggle* function. The parameters to *toggle* indicate whether the first or second choice is to be used, and specify the two text annotations. The two lines are displayed one above the other, using the *annotatedCheckBox* function. In the upper line, the *firstChoice* parameter is used to indicate whether the box is to be checked or not. In the lower line, *firstChoice* is negated, so that the lower line is checked whenever the upper line is not. This shows how specifications can make use of expressions in the underlying programming language (in this case Turing): the expression

"**not** !!firstChoice :: boolean"

is to be evaluated as a Turing expression. The " :: *boolean*" part is the type of the expression; the "!!*firstChoice*" notation allows the embedding of an *RVL* parameter in a Turing expression.

2.1.1 Turning Views into Relations

The *toggle* function is a general function independent of any data structure in the application program. This generality provides the power of *RVL*: graphical techniques can be encapsulated in functions that are completely independent of any context. To use the functions, they must be applied to some data structure. The product/order information toggle box is displayed with the following application of the *toggle* function:

δ ("productDisplaySelected :: boolean",
"Order Information",
"Product Information") : *toggle* **button**

Here, *productDisplaySelected* is an application variable indicating whether the user has selected the product or order display. The function call is annotated with the *button* directive: this states that the result of the function, that is the graphical representation of the toggle box, should be defined as a button. The button is implicitly bound to the first parameter of the function call the application variable *productDisplaySelected.* Whenever the button is clicked, the sense of productDisplaySelected is changed: i.e., if the variable has the value *true*, it becomes *false*, and vice versa. Whenever the value of *productDisplaySelected* changes because of a button click, the view is automatically regenerated, causing the check mark to move to the other box.

Thus, *toggle* by itself is only a function from the data state of the application to the display state. Through the *button* interactor, *toggle* becomes a relation: direct manipulation of the screen image of the toggle box can effect changes in the data state, just as changes in the data state can effect changes in the display view.

There are a series of such annotations to allow input, inspired by the interactor concept of *Garnet* [9,10]. The *interactive* interactor allows direct editing of text or numeric data on the display. The *count* interactor is another kind of button that increments (or decrements) an integer counter every time it is clicked. The *signature* interactor is another kind of button; when clicked, it writes an integer guaranteed to be unique to this view into an integer variable.

2.2 Customization of Views

Customization is required in multi-user applications for two purposes. First, as in the inventory program of figure 1, different users may see the same view, but wish to specialize them locally. In the inventory example, all users' views are maintained by the same *city* relation (figure 4), but should be able to view different cities. We call this form *transparent customization*, since it is performed automatically through the mechanism of binding views to application programs. Secondly, relations may be bound to the central data structure differently according to who the user is. In the tic-tac-toe game, this allows two users to see the same board, but to receive different messages indicating whether it is their turn or not (figure 5). This form is called *signature* customization, meaning that the relation is implicitly parameterized by the signature (or name) of the particular client.

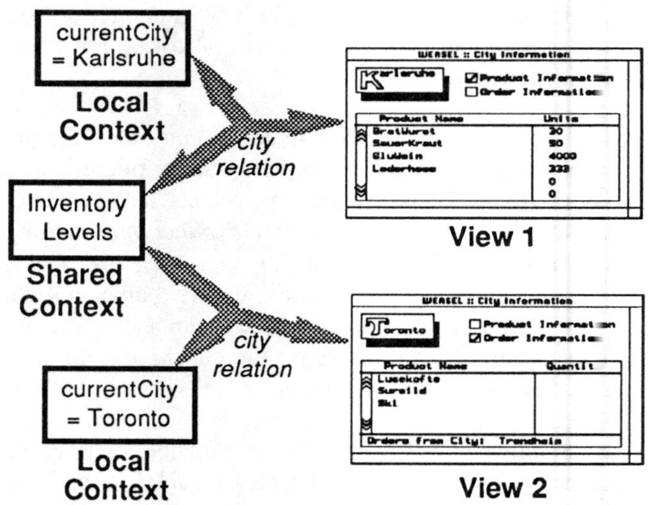

Figure 4. The same relation can be used to generate two different views by parameterizing each relation by a local context.

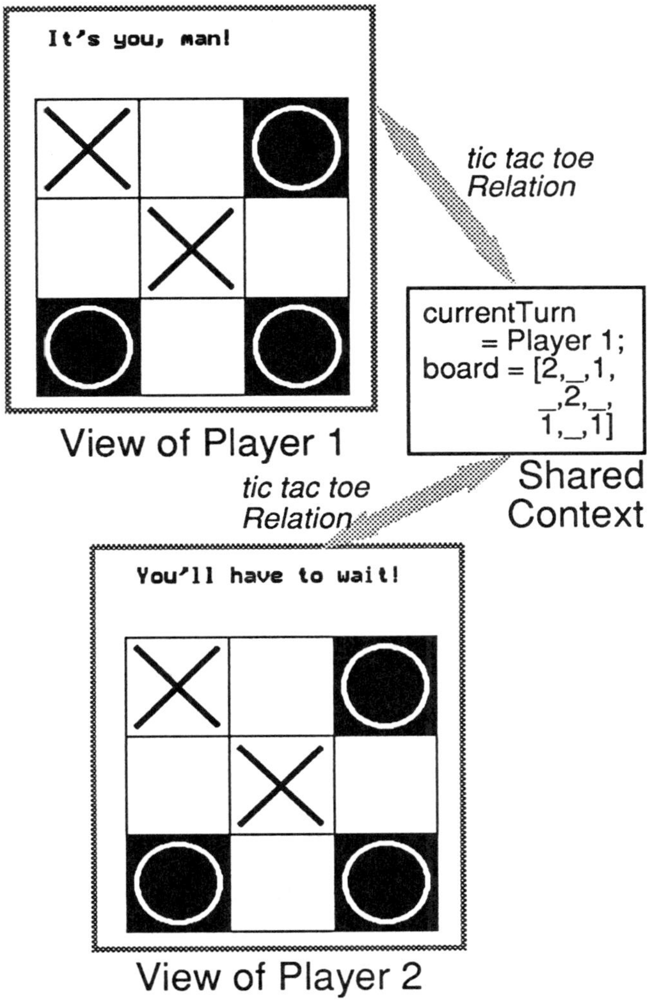

Figure 5. A Tic-tac-toe game as a relational view.

2.2.1 Signature Customization

Figure 5 shows a tic-tac-toe game as a relational view. Here, players take turns clicking on squares to indicate their moves. The underlying data structure is a 3 X 3 array representing the board state, and a variable representing whose turn it is. In this game, each player's view is customized in three ways, depending on whose turn it is: firstly, each player receives a message telling him/her either to make a move or to wait for the other player; secondly, the view of the active player is sensitive to input, whereas that of the waiting player is not; thirdly, when player one clicks on a square, an "O" is to be displayed, whereas player two's actions generate an "X" All this customization is to be achieved even though the same specification is used for both players.

One simple *RVL* mechanism accomplishes all three of these tasks, as shown in figure 6. This function draws one square of the board, displaying either an "X", an "O", or a blank square as appropriate. The parameter *pos* indicates which element of the underlying data structure is to be used to draw the position.

To make a square sensitive to input, it is tagged with the *signature* interactor:

δ pos : *item* **signature**

This displays the position *pos* as an *item* (i.e., a square with an "X", "O", or blank), and states that when the square is clicked, the *signature* of this user is to be written into *pos*. Each instantiation of a view (i.e., each player) automatically receives a unique integer signature, thus providing a means of recording which player clicked which square, even though the same *RVL* specification is used for all players.

This signature is also available for use in expressions. To test whether it is this player's turn or not, the expression:

cond "turn = signature :: boolean"

is used. Here, *turn* is an application variable indicating whose turn it is, and *signature* is a predefined parameter whose value is the unique signature of this view. This *cond* construct therefore chooses whether or not to apply the *signature* interactor to this square, depending on whether it is this player's turn. A similar *cond* expression is used to notify the player whether he/she should play or wait.

3 DISTRIBUTED IMPLEMENTATION OF RELATIONAL VIEWS

In a network of workstations, *Weasel* programs are organized following a client/server model (figure 7). The application program runs on a central workstation called the *server*. Each user works on a *client* workstation, which communicates with the server to access and modify application data.

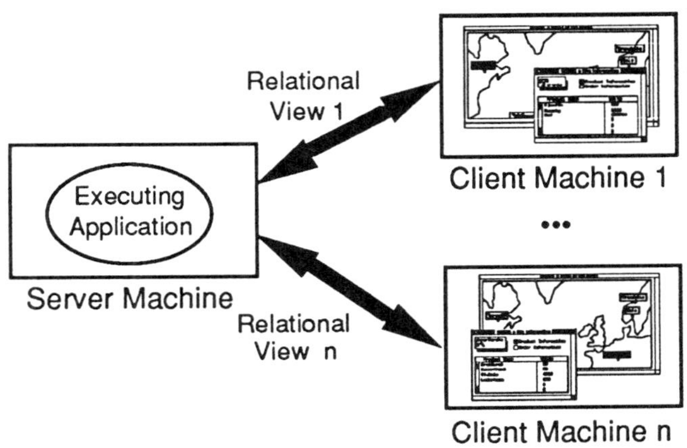

Figure 7. Distributed Organization of Relational Views.

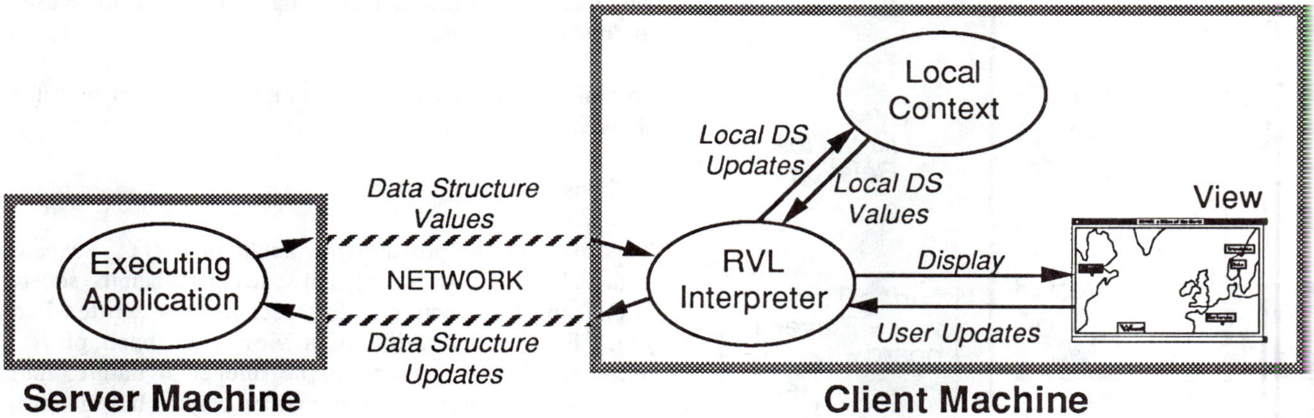

Figure 8. Distributed computation of a relational view.

Two goals form the key to this distributed implementation:

• Put as much useful computation as possible on the client machines;

• Keep the network traffic to a minimum.

The bottleneck of a client/server organization is that adding new clients increases the load on the server and the network. Eventually, the server or network becomes overloaded, and performance degrades unacceptably for all clients. By putting more computation on the client machines, scalability is aided, since each added client takes away from the total work to be done. It is also critical to keep network traffic low, since network communication is slow; too much reliance on the network can lead to a system that is scalable, but too slow to be useable.

Figure 8 shows how the computation is split between client and server. The application program itself executes on the server, while the entirety of the view computation occurs on the client. The heart of the client computation is the *RVL* interpreter. Given an *RVL* specification, this maps the current version of the application data state to a display view. The interface between the client and server is on the level of expression evaluation: whenever a Turing expression is reached in the *RVL* specification, a message is sent to the server, asking for the value of the expression. The expression value is returned, and interpretation of the *RVL* specification can continue.

Typical *RVL* specifications contain few expressions, so this interface requires little network communication. The cost of adding new clients is also small: since the entire user interface computation occurs on the client, the only cost that a new client introduces is an increased traffic of expressions to be evaluated. Since this number of expressions is small, large numbers of clients execute only minimally slower than smaller ones (section 3.1).

As an optimization, all data state used only in view computation is represented locally on the clients (figure 8). We call this data state the *local context*. This optimization allows many views to be computed without reference to the server whatsoever. As an additional optimization, the *RVL* interpreter performs expression caching so that the same expression does not get evaluated over the network twice in one view generation. We are examining extending expression caching to to the local context, so that re-evaluation would not occur between view generations either.

The main disadvantage of *Weasel*'s interface between client and server is that communication is synchronous: that is, whenever a client requests an expression, it must wait for a response before continuing. There are various possible optimizations to turn much of this synchronous communication into an asynchronous form, where computation can continue once a message has been sent. For example, most of the expressions used in an *RVL* specification are intermediate values that are used in the computation of other expressions, but are not directly required for the display. Communication could be saved by maintaining the result of such computations in the server a client would only have to make an asynchronous request to compute the expression, and save it with a name that can be used in computing later expressions.

The current *Weasel* implementation has some rough edges, and therefore cannot yet be considered to be production quality. Some aspects of *RVL* need improvement: true second-order functions would simplify many specifications, and the syntax of the language is sometimes awkward. Additionally, we have not yet implemented the full static analysis required to distribute *RVL* specifications completely automatically. The programmer must currently insert cues to indicate which expressions can be computed locally, and which must be done by the server. The *Weasel* implementation is described in detail in [4,16].

3.1 Evaluation of Implementation

In order to determine whether our means of distribution is effective or not, we performed some simple timings on a network of Sun workstations at the GMD Karlsruhe. These tests are described in detail in [16]. We used a Sparc II workstation with 32MB memory as the *Weasel* server, and a collection of 19 Sparc I and II stations as clients. Our testing was intended to determine the cost of bringing new users into a group session: specifically, it was hoped that bringing in new users would only minimally slow down the performance of the users already taking part in the session.

Using a modified version of the inventory program from figure 1, we found that the time per client to update views does rise as new clients are increased, but that the increase is modest: in a 10 client session, clients take approximately 1.4 times as long to make updates as in a 1 client session; in a 19 client session, this number increases to approximately 2.1 times longer.

In terms of absolute speed, the current *Weasel* implementation is fast enough to be usable, but not fast enough to be production quality (in this example, a full screen update takes about one second). The optimizations listed in this section show promise for achieving sufficient speedup without sacrificing scalability.

4 RELATED WORK

The relational view model builds from earlier work in the *conceptual view model* of output [5]. The output component of *RVL* is based on the *GVL* language [1], extended with interactors motivated by the Garnet system [10].

Several other systems [7,10,17] use constraints to achieve the same effect as *Weasel*'s relational views. In these systems, certain objects are predefined as being display objects. Display objects can be related to data in the application using explicit logical constraints. The constraints must always be maintained, so modifications in either the application or the display data automatically trigger updates in the other. Constraints are a much more general system than relational views: any constraint may be written over any data value of any object. Relational views make a clear separation between display maintainence (as accomplished by the *RVL* specifications), and the application program. It is this clear separation that makes it possible to create an effective distributed implementation.

The Trip-2 system [15] is also a realization of the relational view model. In this system, relations are specified in Prolog rather than *RVL*. Prolog is far more general than *RVL*, but the authors report severe performance difficulties. The RENDEZVOUS system [7,11,12] also provides high-level support for creating groupware and multi-user applications, and was perhaps the single biggest influence on our work. This system provides declarative support for output, implicit concurrency through Garnet-style constraints, and distribution based on the X Window System [13]. One problem noted by the authors is that the distribution does not scale, since view generation is performed entirely on their server machine. This was substantiated by our own measurements [16].

5 CONCLUSIONS

The computer support of cooperative work involves the programming of multi-user applications which aid a group of people in working together on some task. Such programs are difficult to create because of the conflicting demands of rapid prototyping, concurrency and distribution.

This paper has presented *Weasel*, a system for programming multi-user applications. Through declarative view specifications in the *Relational View Language*, normal, imperative application programs can be turned automatically into programs that run in a distributed environment. The paper showed how issues of concurrency, synchronization, and customization of views are handled automatically in *Weasel*. Timing results demonstrated that the implementations generated by *Weasel* have a scalable distribution property, where adding new users to a session does not severely impact the performance of the system as a whole.

Much future work remains with *Weasel*, in terms of optimizing the implementation, and increasing the flexibility and functionality of the *RVL* specification language. One interesting line we are persuing now is how to automatically distribute parts of the application program itself to the clients, so that communication is further reduced.

ACKNOWLEDGEMENTS

This work benefitted from many discussions with our *Weasel* compatriots in the great white north, James R. Cordy and Kevin Schneider. The presentation of this paper was also aided by the comments of three anonymous referees. The Weasel implementation was performed by the authors, James R. Cordy, and Stefan Hügel. We would also like to thank Holt Software Associates for making available the Turing Plus compiler. This work was partially funded by ESPRIT Basic Research Action 3147 (the Phoenix project), and by a student exchange scholarship from the NTH, Norway.

REFERENCES

1. James R. Cordy and T.C. Nicholas Graham. GVL: Visual Specification of graphical output. *Journal of Visual Languages and Computing*, 3:25-47, 1992.

2. Prasun Dewan and Rajiv Choudhary. Primitives for Programming Multi-User Interfaces. In *Proceedings of the Fourth Annual Symposium on User Interface Software and Technology*, pages 69-78. November 1991.

3. Clarence A. Ellis, Simon J. Gibbs, and Gail L. Rein. Groupware: Some Issues and Experiences. *Communications of the ACM*, 34(1):38-58, January 1991.

4. T.C. Nicholas Graham. Conceptual Views of Data Structures as a Programming Aid. Technical Report 88-225, Department of Computing and Information Science, Queen's University at Kingston, August 1988.

5. T.C. Nicholas Graham and James R. Cordy. Conceptual Views of Data Structures as a Model of Output in Programming Languages. In *Proceedings of the Twenty-Second Annual Hawaii International Conference on System Sciences*, January 1991.

6. H. Rex Hartson and Deborah Hix. Human Computer Interface Development: Concepts and Systems. *ACM Computing Surveys*, 21(1):5-92, March 1989.

7. Ralph D. Hill. Languages for Construction of Multi-User, Multi-Media Synchronous (MUMMS) Applications. In Brad A. Myers, editor, *Languages for Developing User Interfaces*. Jones and Bartlett, 1992.

8. Richard C. Holt and James R. Cordy. The Turing Programming Language. *Communications of the ACM*, 31(12):1410-1423, December 1988.

9. Brad A. Myers. Ideas from Garnet for Future User Interface Programming Languages. In Brad A. Myers, editor, *Languages for Developing User Interfaces*. Jones and Bartlett, 1992.

10. Brad A. Myers, Dario A. Giuse, Roger B. Dannenberg, Brad Vander Zanden, David S. Kosbie, Edward Pervin, Andrew Mickish, and Philippe Marchal. Garnet: Comprehensive Support for Graphical, Highly Interactive User Interfaces. *IEEE Computer*, pages 71-85, November 1990.

11. John F. Patterson. Comparing the Demands of Single and Multi-User Applications. In *Proceedings of the Fourth Annual Symposium on User Interface Software and Technology*, pages 87-9, November 1991.

12. John F. Patterson, Ralph D. Hill, Steven L. Rohall, and W. Scott Meeks. Rendezvous: An Architecture for Synchronous Multi-User Applications. In *Proceedings of the Third Conference on Computer Supported Cooperative Work*, pages 317-328. October 1990.

13. Robert W. Scheifler and Jim Gettys. The X Window System. *ACM Transactions on Graphics*, 5(2):79-109, 1986.

14. Mark Stefik, Gregg Foster, Daniel G. Bobrow, Kenneth Kahn, Stan Lenning, and Lucy Suchman. Beyond the Chalkboard: Computer Support for Collaboration and Problem Solving in Meetings. *Communications of the ACM*, 30(1):32-47, January 1987.

15. Shin Takahashi, Satoshi Matsuoka, Akinora Yonezawa, and Tomisha Kamada. A General Framework for Bi-Directional Translation Between Abstract and Pictorial Data. In *Proceedings of the ACM Symposium on User Interface Software and Technology*, November 1991.

16. Tore Urnes. A Relational Model for Programming Concurrent and Distributed User Interfaces. Technical Report Arbeitspapier 643, GMD Karlsruhe, May 1992.

17. Bradley T. Vander Zanden, Brad A. Myers, Dario Giuse and Pedro Szekely. The Importance of Pointer Variables in Constraint Models. In *Proceedings of the Fourth Annual Symposium on User Interface Software and Technology*, pages 155-164. November 1991.

Computational Mail as Network Infrastructure for Computer-Supported Cooperative Work

Nathaniel S. Borenstein

Bellcore
Room MRE 2D-296
445 South Street
Morristown, NJ 07962-1910
+01 201 829 4270
nsb@bellcore.com

ABSTRACT

Computational email -- the embedding of programs within electronic mail messages -- is proposed as a technology that may help to solve some of the key problems in deploying successful applications for computer-supported cooperative work. In particular, computational email promises to alleviate the problem of remote installation at separately-administered sites, the problem of getting users to "buy in" to new applications, and the problem of extremely heterogeneous user interaction environments. In order for computational email to be practical, however, key problems of security and portability must be addressed, problems for which this research offers new solutions. This paper outlines the promise of this new technology, the solutions to the key technical problems, and the areas where further work and application development are needed.

KEYWORDS

Electronic mail, Active mail, Security, Portability, CSCW Infratructure.

THE GOAL: DISTRIBUTED COMPUTER-SUPPORTED COOPERATIVE WORK

In recent years, increasing attention has been focused on the problem of computer-supported cooperative work (CSCW). This work, broadly defined, is the attempt to provide computer-based solutions to the problems that arise when two or more people attempt to cooperate to perform a task or solve a problem.

Permission to copy without fee all or part of this material is granted provided that the copies are not made or distributed for direct commercial advantage, the ACM copyright notice and the title of the publication and its date appear, and notice is given that copying is by permission of the Association for Computing Machinery. To copy otherwise, or to republish, requires a fee and/or specific permission.

© 1992 ACM 0-89791-543-7/92/0010/0067...$1.50

The simplest CSCW systems, from an architectural perspective, are those in which the cooperating individuals share a computerized application on a single machine, perhaps even using a single process. In such systems, many problems of coordination and communication can be avoided. However, such systems are increasingly implausible for solving the problems of real-world users, who may be widely separated geographically and may have significant amounts of computing power on their individual desks. Truly distributed applications seem natural in the face of a high ratio of computing power to available communications bandwidth. For many cooperative applications, distributed solutions seem inevitable, and indeed a growing number of CSCW prototypes are implemented in a distributed manner.

Unfortunately, the practical success of such systems to date has been extremely limited. This paper begins with a discussion of three key problems that have inhibited the widespread use of distributed applications for CSCW. Following this, the paper offers a description of a new technology, "computational electronic mail (email)", that offers a potential solution to these problems. Problems that have, in the past, rendered computational email impractical are discussed, along with proposed solutions to these problems. Following this is a discussion of the author's particular realization of these solutions, a language designed specifically for the unusual requirements of computational email. The design of this language and its prototype implementation are presented as a "proof-of-concept" for the practicality of computational email. The preliminary results of that implementation, and its implication for future systems, are discussed briefly at the end of the paper.

THE PRACTICAL DIFFICULTY OF WIDELY-DISTRIBUTED USER-ORIENTED COMPUTATION

When building a user-oriented distributed application, the programmer faces a special set of constraints above and beyond the usual substantial hurdles entailed in every new user interface. In particular, he or she must solve at least three problems that are not generally faced by single-user or single-machine applications:

THE PROBLEM OF REMOTE INSTALLATION

In order for an application to be used by multiple users at multiple sites, it must, perforce, be installed at all such sites. This is not a problem for applications in which all of the potential users are eager and knowledgeable participants, in which case they can be counted on either to install the software themselves or request such installation by the local authorities. However, this is by no means the normal situation for distributed applications. In many distributed systems, as noted by Grudin [8], there is a substantial imbalance between the motivations of the various particpants. A common scenario, for example, involves one user asking a question of a group of users. In such a situation, it is much more reasonable to expect the questioner to ensure the local installation of some CSCW software than to expect it of the people being asked.

In short, the participants in a cooperative application often have widely differing degrees of motivation, and are therefore likely to exert similarly varying degrees of persistence and effort in order to ensure that the software for that application is locally installed. Almost inevitably, this leads to a situation in which the highly-motivated individuals find themselves wheedling, cajoling, or even begging the less motivated individuals to install the software on their systems. Without extreme persistence, CSCW applications can fail without ever really being tried, simply because a sufficient installed user base was never created.

THE PROBLEM OF USER BUY-IN

Related to the problem of getting software installed at widely distributed sites is the problem of getting people to actually use the software once it is installed. Because of the differing motivations of the participants, it is likely that some users are far more likely than others to actually *run* the software. As Grudin has noted, the users who are most crucial to the success of a CSCW application often have the least personal stake in using it. For example, in any system that seeks to help novices get information from experts, the experts who know the answers have relatively little motivation to provide it. Some systems, such as the Answer Garden of Malone and Ackerman [1] rely on the good will (and memory) of the experts to periodically run a program to see if anyone needs help. Since the necessary combination of good will, reliability, and memory are relatively rare, this requirement can be crippling to the practical success of a system.

THE PROBLEM OF HETEROGENEOUS USER ENVIRONMENTS

For better or worse, there are a wide variety of user interaction environments in use today, and this seems unlikely to change in the foreseeable future. Potential participants in a cooperative application may be running on dumb terminals, Macintoshes, personal computers running MS-DOS with or without MS-Windows, OS/2 with Presentation Manager, UNIX with X11, SunTools, NeWS, or various other environments. It is unlikely, to say the least, that the purveyors of a cooperative application will be able to dictate, to all potential users of the system, a single interaction environment. (Malone and Ackerman's Answer Garden was an exception in this regard: they were able to assume that all users were running X11, for the simple reason that their application domain was questions and answers about the X11 system itself.)

In order for a distributed application to see widespread use and acceptance, it will have to run on a very wide variety of platforms, probably including all the ones just mentioned. But, as programmers well know, getting any piece of software to work on such a variety of platforms is a major task in itself, above and beyond the main thrust of the cooperative application.

NEEDED: A PLATFORM ON WHICH TO BUILD

If all of these problems afflict a wide variety of cooperative applications, it seems natural to seek a mechanism to solve them for the entire class of applications, rather than for each application individually. What is really needed is a *platform* on which distributed applications can be built without concern for the problems of distribution, user buy-in, and heterogeneous interaction environment.

If a computational engine can be defined in such a way as to support the requirements of many cooperative applications, yet without commitment to a particular user interaction technology, and if that single engine can somehow overcome the first problem, the problem of remote installation, then neither the problem of remote installation nor the problem of heterogeneous user environments will afflict applications that are built on top of such an engine. This leaves the problem of user buy-in: assuming such an engine were defined and widely implemented and installed, how could users be persuaded to use it regularly? One solution is to "piggyback" the engine on top of a technology that is already at the fingertips of most computer users today, electronic mail.

THE CASE FOR COMPUTATIONAL EMAIL

The basic idea of computational email is very simple: Instead of sending plain text, or even multimedia information, in a mail message, what is sent instead is a computer program in a well-defined language. At the recipient's end, the mail-reading software recognizes (via a well-defined mechanism) that the mail message is intended to be executed rather than read, and (accordingly) executes it. Thus, when the recipient reads a mail message, the message might first show him some introductory text, and then engage him in a question/answer dialogue. For example, it might ask him to select which of ten proposed dates and times he can make it to a meeting. The program might then mail the answers back to a network server that was collecting such answers from several such people, in order to find a meeting time suitable to all of them.

The greatest appeal in the idea of embedding applications within email is the simple way it solves the problem of user buy-in. Because nearly everyone who uses a networked computer nowadays is likely to be a regular reader of email, an application that is delivered to a user in the form of email requires no special effort or feat of memory, on the part of the recipient, in order to run it. Most important, remote users of a distributed application can, by embedding computation in email, solicit information or participation from a user who does not yet know that his participation is required.

While the idea of embedding computation in email suffers no less than any other application from the problems of distributing the initial software and devising an interaction mechanism that works regardless of interaction environment, it can be designed in such a way that the solution of the problem for computational email makes the problem simply nonexistent for applications built on a platform of computational email. In other words, solving the remote installation once, for a computational email infrastructure, will solve it for a whole class of follow-on applications.

PRIOR ART

The idea of computational or "active" mail is sufficiently simple as to have been mentioned, in the research literature, at least fifteen years ago, in a paper by Anderson and Gillogly [2], who discussed the concept without implementing it. Several researchers have implemented computational email, or "active messaging," including Vittal [15], Hogg [10], Borenstein and Hansen [5, 9], and Shepherd [12]. Each of these systems demonstrated facilities for embedding computation and email, and several offered convincing evidence for the general utility of such a facility.

Nonetheless, all of the prior work has suffered from at least two of four crucial flaws, which have prevented a generalized facility for computational email from becoming widely available:

1. Lack of generality. Some systems, notably the Andrew system without Ness [5], offered only highly specialized facilities for active messages, such as special-purpose "voting" messages. Though useful, such facilities do not provide a platform on which larger applications can be built.

2. Lack of conformity to the standard email transport model. Some systems, notably Imail [10], did not use asynchronous store-and-forward delivery, and thus might arguably not be called electronic mail. In particular, Imail provided a very powerful active messaging language, but could only be used to exchange messages between authenticated users of a single machine. Since most email crosses insecure network connections, such mechanisms do not generalize well to the real world.

3. Lack of security. Some systems, such as R2D2 [15] and Andrew with Ness [9], provided general-purpose mechanisms that were exceedingly dangerous. In such systems, a user is typically asked a question such as "There is a program here. Do you want to try running it?" If the user answers in the affirmative, he may have risked the destruction of all his files. This is probably unacceptable to most users in the real world.

4. Lack of portability. Computational mail that provides a rich user interface mechanism, such as Andrew with Ness [9], or Strudel [12], has typically been extremely non-portable with regard to user interaction environments. With Andrew messages, for example, the interaction mechanisms only worked properly if the recipient read his mail using the Andrew Messages program, under the X11 or WM window systems. In a highly heterogeneous world, such restrictions are not acceptable to many communities.

Thus, although the existing literature amply documents the continuing fascination that computational email holds for email researchers, it fails to provide a practical model for making computational email a part of the general shared infrastructure of a large, diverse, and not entirely trusting network community. This is the starting point for the research reported here.

PORTABILITY ACROSS USER ENVIRONMENTS

Stated in the most general and ambitious manner, the goal of making user interfaces entirely portable between a wide range of user interface environments is probably impossible. However, a lesser goal will suffice for computational email.

A significant number of applications can be built using user interface primitives that require only textual input and output, and that are specified in a manner that assume nothing about the capabilities of the user interaction environment. Examples of such primitives might include:

1. Get text (a string) from the user.

2. Get a number from the user.

3. Ask the user a multiple choice question.

4. Fill in the blanks in a form.

5. Display a chunk of text to the user.

As long as the language primitives refer only to the information that must be given to or obtained from the user, and make no reference to the technologies by which that information is to be given or obtained, and as long as the information can be expressed as simple text, such primitives can be implemented in virtually any interaction environment. For example, a multiple choice question might produce a dialog box for a user running in a graphical environment, while it might produce a numbered list on a teletype, with a request to "choose a number from 1 to 7."

What matters, in such primitives, is that the mechanism by which the information is conveyed is left unspecified by the definition of the primitive. Given that fact, a user can expect to compose and test a program in one environment, secure in the knowledge that it will behave well even in a very different environment, where the interpreter understands the same language, even though it might interact with the user rather differently.

SECURITY OF COMPUTATIONAL EMAIL

The security of a computational email message is an area where virtually no compromise is acceptable. This might not have been true a few years ago, but well-publicized episodes such as the Internet Worm [13] have made most computer users highly conscious of, and concerned about, the security of their computer systems.

However, despite such concerns, it must be explicitly recognized that certain risks are routinely accepted by the general computing public. Conventional electronic mail, for example, is not without risks. The most common risk in current mail systems is resource deprivation. For example, by repeatedly sending large mail messages, any network user can often fill the disk of another, depriving him (at least temporarily) of the use of that disk. This can often be done completely anonymously, and can be a minor nuisance or a major problem, depending on what else shares the disk. Similarly, a program that uses mail protocols on a network can, by playing "cat and mouse" with someone else's mail transport agent, effectively tie up much of the bandwidth available on a network, or even a substantial portion of the computational power of the remote processor.

Beyond resource deprivation, an even more insidious risk in mail systems is that they are vulnerable to intruders using essentially non-technical means. Recently, many users on the Internet were told, via official looking mail, that they had to change their passwords to "SYSTEST01" immediately; apparently more than a few complied. The infamous "Christmas Exec" virus that afflicted the IBM networks a few years back was entirely based on social engineering: Users received mail that appeared to come from someone they knew, saying "here's a neat program that will make an animated Christmas Tree on your screen." When executed, the program did exactly that, thus avoiding suspicion, but it also sent copies of itself to all of the users' regular correspondents.

Finally, existing mail systems, like all network software, are vulnerable to security problems through bugs. The Internet worm, for example, exploited a bug in a mail transport program as one of several mechanisms for transporting itself.

The point of the foregoing discussion is not to frighten the reader out of ever using email again, but rather to point out that a "risk free" solution is chimerical. A more realistic security goal for computational email might be characterized as follows: Computational email should entail no security problems that are worse, either in kind or in degree, than the problems that afflict ordinary (textual) email. Given such a goal, we may begin by characterizing the potential risks into three broad categories: destruction of resources (such as files), theft of resources (such as private files), and deprivation of resources (such as filling up a disk or tying up a CPU).

The key to the solution of this problem is the observation that nothing inherent in any computational language is dangerous; danger is posed only insofar as the effects of executing statements in a language include "side-effects" in the external world. (An exception to this claim is that such a program can still tie up the CPU, virtual memory, or swap space on a machine by going into an infinite loop; this can be handled via resource limitations.)

More concretely, if one starts with a conventional programming language, such as LISP [14], and removes all input and output from the language (including not only input and output to and from the user, but also to and from files, other processes, and arbitrary memory locations which might be connected with physical devices), one is left with a language without "wires" to the outside world. No matter what can be *expressed* in such a language, it can do no harm to the outside world.

Unfortunately, though it can do no harm, it can do little good, either. So the task of devising a secure language for computational email reduces, in practice, to the construction of a secure input/output mechanism for a conventional language. Devising such a mechanism is really just a matter of judicious trade-offs. For example, one can specify that the language has no general-purpose access to the file system, but has a limited form of access to a subset of the file system. In the system to be described below, programs have access only to a restricted subdirectory of the user's files, and the interpreter is expected to ensure that no "tricks" (such as, in UNIX, the use of ".." or symbolic links) can be used to access files outside that area. Within that restricted area, programs are additionally restricted in their ability to overwrite existing files, and in the number and size of the files they can create. In such a way, the potential harm to the file system that is caused by computational email is not greater than the disk-filling potential of textual email. Similar restrictions are applied to other input/output processes, including sending mail. Some security constraints also apply to user interaction: for example, in order to prevent subversion through the clever exploitation of "intelligent" terminals, input and output is restricted to printable characters.

HETEROGENEOUS MAIL READING SOFTWARE

A major impediment to any enhancements to electronic mail systems is the tyranny of the lowest common denominator. Multimedia mail systems such as Andrew [5] and Diamond [7] have long suffered from the fact that, in the absence of widely accepted standards for multimedia mail formats, most email traffic will necessarily be plain text, even for users of multimedia systems, because most of their correspondents will not be users of compatible systems.

The same problem affects any attempt to promote the use of computational email. In order for such a system to be widely used, it must not require the use of a special mail-reading tool. Instead, a mechanism is needed whereby a wide variety of mail-reading tools can easily be given the capability to handle computational email.

Such a mechanism has been prototyped by the author, and is described elsewhere [6]. Its essence, however, is simple. Each mail-reading user interface is modified in a small but crucial way: it is modified so that, whenever a user requests to see the body of a message, the software first checks to see whether or not the message is plain text. (In Internet mail, this is done by checking the Content-type header field.) If it is not plain text, then the body is not directly displayed; instead, an external program called *metamail* is invoked. The metamail program is a simple switch that compares the content-type of the current message to a configuration file (*mailcap* file) that tells how various types of mail can be handled at the local site. If a handler is found for the current message type, the message is passed off to that handler for presentation to the user. Otherwise the user is informed about the unrecognized data, rather than shown the (probably incomprehensible) raw data stream.

Given this mechanism, it is easy to integrate computational email into a wide variety of mail-reading agents. Once those agents have been modified to use the metamail software, as described above, it is simply a matter of installing an interpreter for the computation mail language, and adding an appropriate line to the local mailcap file.

ATOMICMAIL: A PRACTICAL SYSTEM FOR COMPUTATIONAL EMAIL

In accordance with the ideas described above, the author has designed a language suitable for embedding computation in electronic mail, known as ATOMICMAIL. The ATOMICMAIL software is designed to provide a secure and portable language for distributed applications that use electronic mail as a transport mechanism, or implement what might be called "User to User Remote Procedure Call."

ATOMICMAIL LANGUAGE DEFINITION

ATOMICMAIL uses LISP [14] as its basic language model. There is nothing essential about LISP for this purpose, although it is a very clean interpreted language, which eases the validation of the security mechanisms. (It would be considerably harder to be sure about the security of a compiled language, and particularly one like C [11] that includes mechanisms (e.g. pointers) for accessing arbitrary memory locations.) Of course, LISP is just a starting point. As mentioned before, all input and output facilities were removed from the basic language and replaced with input and output mechanisms that did not compromise security and that were portable to virtually any user interaction environment.

Thus, for example, LISP's READ primitive is gone, but new primitives such as GETSTRING and GETBOOLEAN are defined. Similarly, new file system primitives permit a strictly limited access to a circumscribed local file system.

A complete specification of the ATOMICMAIL language is too lengthy and detailed to be included here. The language is, however, rigorously specified in [4]. Figure 1 shows part of a small ATOMICMAIL program.

```
(handle-survey
  "nsb" NIL "Re: test"
   '((survey-complex-form "Please answer the
following questions to help us with our
research:"
    (("How many email messages do you receive
each day?" "integer")
      ("How many email messages do you send
each day?" "integer")
     ("Does email enhance your productivity,
overall?" "boolean")
       ("Do you use email for non-business
purposes?" "boolean")))))
```

Figure 1. Part of a simple ATOMICMAIL program

THE BELLCORE PROTOTYPE ATOMICMAIL INTERPRETER

Although a computational email language should be designed for portability and abstraction of user interface, an implementation (interpreter) must inevitably be grounded in some particular user interaction environment. Based on the realities of the heterogeneous environment at Bellcore, the initial ATOMICMAIL interpreter was written to use the curses library [3] for its user interface. The prototype interpreter will, therefore, run on any machine that is (or can emulate) a UNIX terminal. Under window systems such as X11, a terminal emulator window is used. This architecture clearly sacrifices a good deal of potential usability, but it ensures that the facilities of computational email will be available to the widest possible number of users. A graphical (X11) interpreter for the same ATOMICMAIL language is also being implemented, and should be operational soon. The prototype ATOMICMAIL interpreter uses, as its basic LISP engine, the Embedded LISP Interpreter (ELI) from the Andrew Message System [5].

Like any network service, the implementation of a computational email system may be less secure than its specification. A great deal of attention has been paid, in the design of ATOMICMAIL, to ensure that there would be no serious security problems in a hypothetical perfect implementation. No claims are made, however, that the prototype is such a perfect implementation. It seems likely that an ATOMICMAIL implementation is neither more nor less likely to contain unexpected and accidental security risks than any other network service software.

Figures 2 and 3 show the prototype ATOMICMAIL interpreter at work.

As of September, 1991, the ATOMICMAIL software has been deployed in at least four different laboratories at Bellcore. It is available to universities with a royalty-free license for non-commercial use.

INITIAL USES OF ATOMICMAIL

The initial deployment of ATOMICMAIL has demonstrated that computational email can be made to work portably and securely. It has not, however, proven that such a mechanism is worthwhile. Before such a claim can be made, it is necessary to have one or more substantial applications that are highly valued by the user community. While it is too early to evaluate their overall utility, six applications have been prototyped at Bellcore: a survey generator, a meeting scheduler, a document distributor, an information finder, an activist alert mechanism, and a distributed mail-based game.

The survey generator is a tool for generating simple surveys with ATOMICMAIL. With this tool, the user simply enters a set of questions (fill in the blank, multiple choice, etc.) and the mail addresses to which he wants the questions sent. The recipients are surveyed interactively by an ATOMICMAIL message, which then sends the response back as normal electronic mail, or (optionally) sends it to a process which collates the results and sends back only a high-level summary.

The meeting scheduler allows the person calling a meeting to specify the purpose of the meeting, a list of participants, and a set of possible dates and times for the meeting. Each participant is surveyed via ATOMICMAIL, and the results are collected and returned to the originator as a summary that quickly shows which times, if any, everyone can make it.

The document distributor is a tool that makes it easy for someone who is distributing documents to generate an ATOMICMAIL message that offers recipients a scrollable list of document titles. When a recipient selects a title, he is shown an abstract of the document and asked whether he wants to order it. Orders are sent to a designated "fulfillment" address via normal electronic mail.

The information finder is an application that maintains a database of expertise within an organization. Users are encouraged to send questions on any topic to the information finder, which will use ATOMICMAIL to ask the question of one or more relevant experts. If the experts don't know the answers, they are asked to suggest other experts, who are then surveyed in turn. This process continues, spreading out to more specialized and possibly more distant experts, until an answer is obtained that satisfies the user.

The activist alert mechanism is a program that shows its recipient a brief text explaining a "hot" political issue. It then asks if the user wants to lobby his or her elected officials on this topic. If the user assents, the program verifies the names of the user's elected representatives and either generates a paper copy of a letter to those representatives or sends a fax to them directly. Finally, it asks the user if there are any other people to whom the alert should be redistributed.

The "Name That Tune" game is an ATOMICMAIL version of the familiar game show. All of the "bidding" steps in the game are conducted via ATOMICMAIL. In the final step of the game, a multipart message, including both audio and ATOMICMAIL, is used to play the tune and ask the user to name it.

Earlier, ATOMICMAIL was also used to prototype another mail-related service, dynamic mailing lists. In this service, a message to a mailing list contained, in addition to its normal text, an ATOMICMAIL component that asked people whether or not they wanted to take part in further discussions on the same topic. In this case, although ATOMICMAIL facilitated a quick prototype, it soon became obvious that the functionality was better accomplished by modifying the message reading software so that even plain text messages could be the start of new dynamic mailing lists.

FUTURE WORK

There are many directions for the future of ATOMICMAIL. Beyond additional and enhanced ATOMICMAIL application services, there are several other promising directions for future work. A graphical interpreter for the current ATOMICMAIL language would both further demonstrate the interface-independence of the language and make the execution of ATOMICMAIL programs much more pleasant for those who could use it. By incorporating cryptographic techniques and digital signatures, it should be possible to extend ATOMICMAIL's capabilities to allow users to permit more dangerous actions to be executed when the mail is authenticated as coming from a trusted source. Another direction for extension would be to relax somewhat the assumptions about user interface environments. For example, an ATOMICMAIL-like language that presumed the presence of a bitmap display might permit substantially more interesting applications to be developed. Overall, there is no shortage of promising new directions for research on computational electronic mail.

ACKNOWLEDGEMENTS

The ATOMICMAIL project has been made possible by the enlightened management with which Bellcore is generally blessed. The development of the language and the prototype software has benefited greatly from the many clever people who have helped me with useful suggestions and encouragement, including Bob Kraut, Al Buzzard, Jonathan Rosenberg, Louis Gomez, John Patterson, Steve Rohall, Ralph Hill, Will Leland, Peter Clitherow, Shoshana Hardt-Kornacki, Steve Uhler, Mike Bianchi, Scott Stornetta, Michael Littman, Ron Underwood, Mike O'Dell, Nat Howard, Dana Chee, Mark Segal, Steve Butera, Dave Sincoskie, Mark Donadio, Laurence Brothers, and, no doubt, others whom I have inadvertently omitted.

REFERENCES

1. Ackerman, M. and Malone, T., "Answer Garden: A Tool for Growing Organizational Memory", Proceedings of the Conference on Office Information Systems, Cambridge, Massachusetts, 1990]

2. Anderson, R. H., and J. J. Gillogly, "Rand Intelligent Terminal Agent (RITA): Design Philosophy", Rand Corporation Technical Memorandum R-1809-ARPA, February, 1976.

3. Arnold, Kenneth C. R. C., "Screen Updating and Cursor Movement Optimization: A Library Package", *UNIX Programmer's Manual Supplementary Documents*, USENIX Association, 1984.

4. Borenstein, Nathaniel S., "MAGICMAIL Language Reference Manual", Bellcore Technical Memorandum.

5. Borenstein, Nathaniel S., and Chris A. Thyberg, "Power, Ease of Use, and Cooperative Work in a Practical Multimedia Message System", *International Journal of Man-Machine Studies*, April, 1991.

6. Borenstein, Nathaniel S., "Multimedia Electronic Mail: Will the Dream Become Reality?", *Communications of the ACM*, April, 1991.

7. Forsdick, H.C., Thomas, R.H., Robertson, G. G., and Travers, V. M., "Initial Experience with Multimedia Documents in Diamond", *Computer Message Service*, Proceedings IFIP 6.5 Working Conference, IFIP, 1984.

8. Grudin, J., "Seven plus one challenges for Groupware Developers", Rev. of DAIMI PB 323 Aarhus University Computer Science Department.

9. Hansen, W. Fred, "Enhancing Documents with Embedded Programs: How Ness Extends Insets in the Andrew Toolkit", *Proceedings of IEEE Computer Society 1990 International Conference on Computer Languages*, New Orleans, 1990.

10. Hogg, John, "Intelligent Message Systems", in *Office Automation*, D. Tsichritzis, editor, Springer-Verlag, 1985.

11. Kernighan, Brian W., and Dennis M. Ritchie, *The C Programming Language*, Prentice-Hall, 1978.

12. Shepherd, Allan, Niels Mayer, and Allan Kuchinsky, "Strudel -- An Extensible Electronic Conversation Toolkit", *Proceedings of CSCW '90*, October, 1990.

13. Spafford, Eugene H., "The Internet Worm: Crisis and Aftermath," *Communications of the ACM*, June, 1989.

14. Steele, Guy L., *Common Lisp: The Language*, Second Edition, Digital Press, 1990.

15. Vittal, John, "Active Message Processing: Messages as Messengers", in *Computer Message Systems*, R. P. Uhlig, editor, North-Holland Publishing Company, 1981.

Figure 2. The ATOMICMAIL help screen with the Curses-based interface

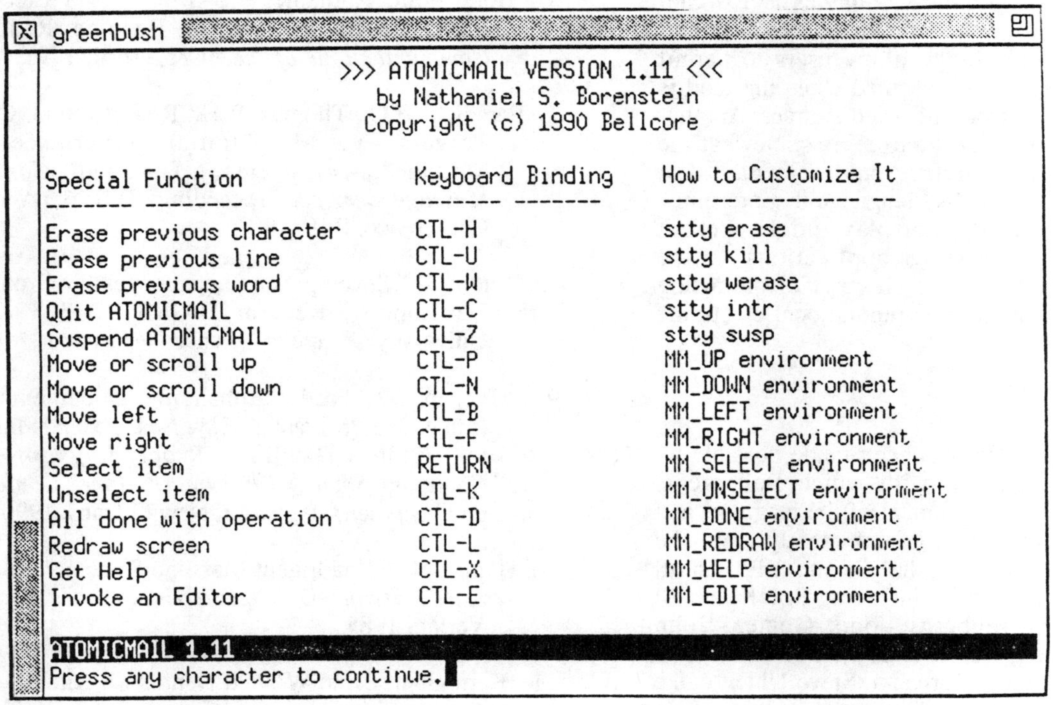

Figure 3. An ATOMICMAIL survey being run with the Curses-based interface

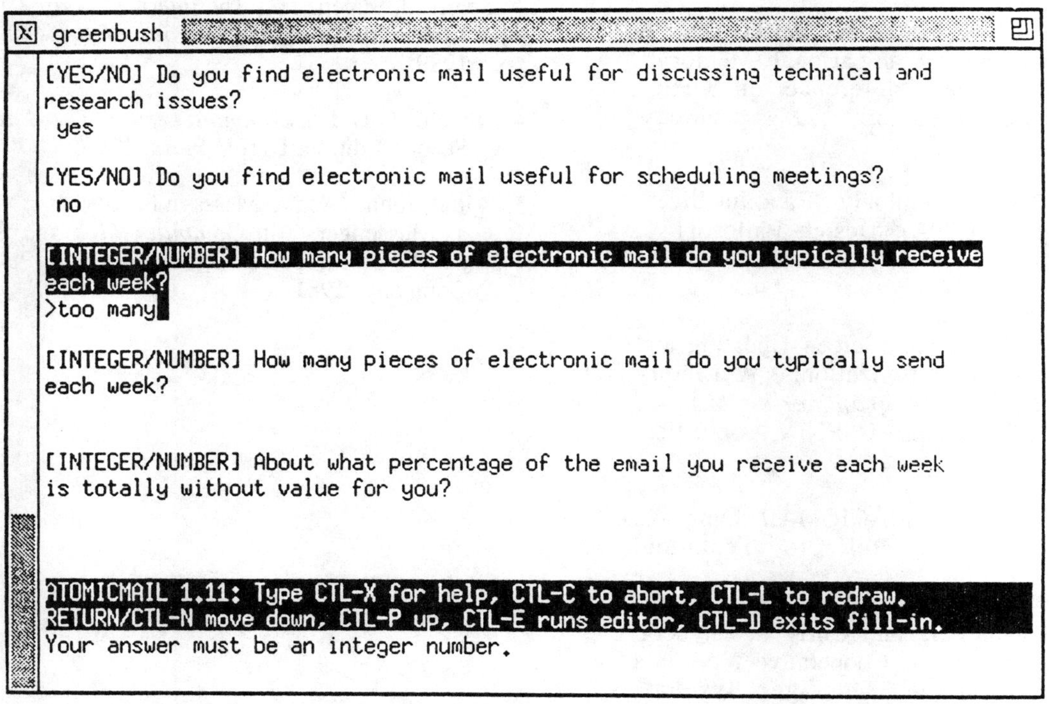

Active Mail—A Framework for Implementing Groupware

Yaron Goldberg, Marilyn Safran, and Ehud Shapiro
{gyaron, marilyn, udi}@wisdom.weizmann.ac.il
Department of Applied Mathematics and Computer Science
The Weizmann Institute of Science, Rehovot 76100, Israel

ABSTRACT

Most existing groupware products are either too passive or very intrusive. They either passively wait for user action or actively interfere with normal workstation activity by intruding on the user's screen; they are one-sided push or pull mechanisms.

A system for computer-mediated interaction, Active Mail obviates the dilemma with a protocol which enables a groupware application to involve a new user in a way that is non-intrusive, tolerates delayed response, and requires little effort on the user's part.

Active Mail piggybacks on ordinary electronic mail, retaining all the features that have made it so successful. Active Mail messages are used to establish persistent interactive connections among a group of users. Receivers of Active Mail messages can interact with the sender, with future recipients, and with remote, distributed multi-user applications. Groupware applications realized within the Active Mail framework include a text conversation tool, a collaborative writing facility with a floor passing protocol and revision control management, an interactive meeting scheduler, and some distributed multi-user interactive games.

In this paper we describe the architecture of Active Mail, present some of its applications, and discuss our preliminary experience with it.

KEYWORDS

groupware, electronic mail, active messages, shared editing, meeting scheduling

1 INTRODUCTION

Active Mail is a framework for implementing groupware, designed to support more effective computer-mediated interaction. Active Mail extends ordinary electronic mail with *active messages*, entities that contain communication ports. An active message, manifested as a window on the user's screen, contains facilities that allow communication and cooperation with other users. In particular, it allows its receiver to interact with its sender, with other users to whom a copy of the message was sent, as well as with remote, distributed multi-user applications connected to a communication port in the message.

Active Mail is an abstract architecture, within which many groupware applications can be realized. We have implemented this architecture and, within it, a few basic groupware applications.

Active Mail preserves the spirit of electronic mail in that in its degenerate form, the functionality as well as the "look-and-feel" of Active Mail reduces to that of ordinary electronic mail. We find this aspect of Active Mail important for two reasons: First, it provides some confidence that Active Mail preserves the features that have made electronic mail so successful. Second, it gives a smooth migration path for ordinary electronic mail users.

This paper reports on the architecture of Active Mail, its implementation, and some applications we have realized within it. Section 2 introduces the Active Mail concept via an example. The example uses the basic groupware applications we have already implemented — a text-based conversation tool, a collaborative writing tool, and a meeting scheduler. Section 3 presents the Active Mail abstract architecture. Section 4 presents the following views of Active Mail: As an extension of ordinary electronic mail, Active Mail employs active messages rather than static, passive ones. As a groupware protocol, it allows multi-user applications to involve a new user in an application in a way which is non-intrusive, tolerates delayed response, and requires little effort. And as a user-interface mechanism, it allows a user to organize and maintain a large collection of persistent connections to interactive multi-user applications. Section 5 describes the internal architecture of the Active Mail applications introduced in Section 2. The closing part of the paper reports on our experience with Active Mail, briefly describes our implementation effort, and discusses future work.

Permission to copy without fee all or part of this material is granted provided that the copies are not made or distributed for direct commercial advantage, the ACM copyright notice and the title of the publication and its date appear, and notice is given that copying is by permission of the Association for Computing Machinery. To copy otherwise, or to republish, requires a fee and/or specific permission.

© 1992 ACM 0-89791-543-7/92/0010/0075...$1.50

2 ACTIVE MAIL: AN EXAMPLE

We introduce the concept of Active Mail via an example, taken from a typical business situation in which a supervisor asks a subordinate to do a specific task. *(We use italics for commentary.)*

Using Active Mail instead of ordinary electronic mail, Renee initiates a conversation, and sends it to Wendel, wherein she asks him to write a document. *(Figure*

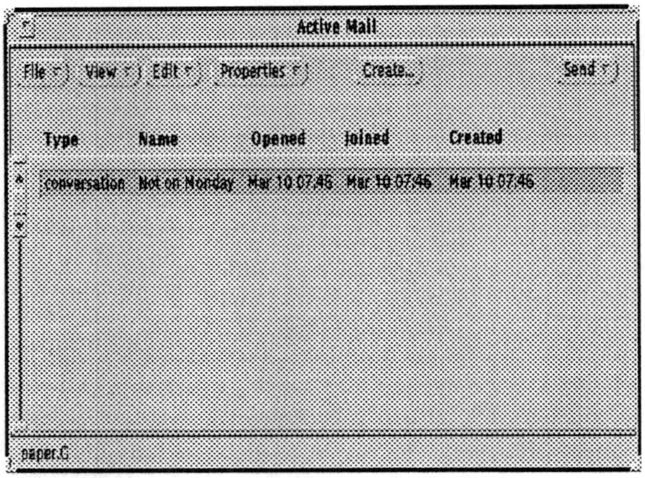

Figure 1: An Active Mail folder

1 shows Renee's Active Mail folder after she used the **Create** *button to create the conversation. As shown in Figure 2, she then types her contribution in the private subwindow and* **Publishes** *it into the shared conversation log, shown in the bottom subwindow. She then uses the* **Send** *button to send the conversation to Wendel.)* Wendel received the Active Mail "conversation"

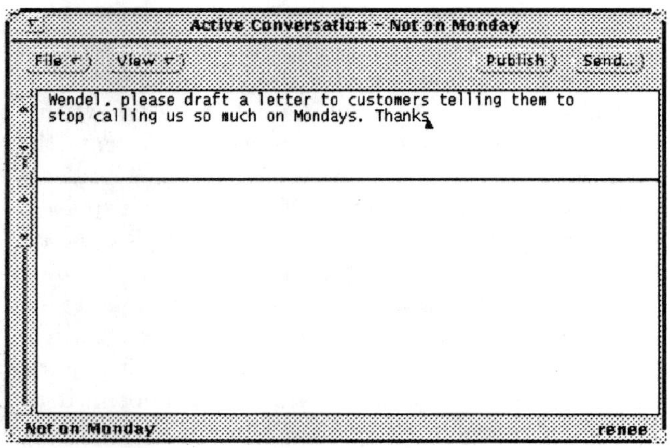

Figure 2: An Active Mail Conversation Window

message in his own Active Mail input folder, responds to Renee, and creates an initial version of the document, shown in Figure 3. *(The texts of the initial and final*

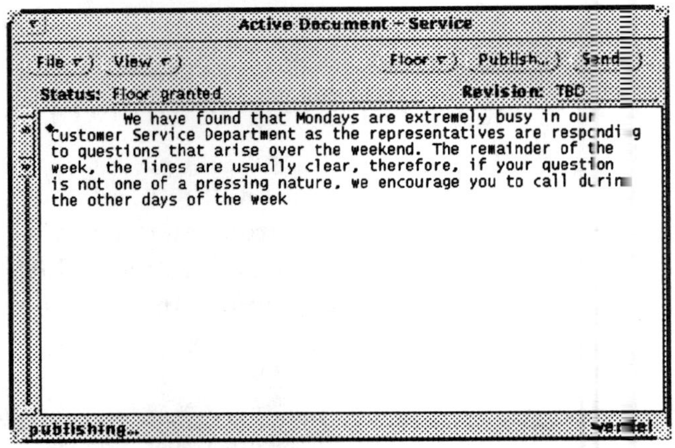

Figure 3: An Active Mail Shared Document Window

versions of the memo were taken from [25].)

(To edit a shared document, a participant must obtain the floor, using the **Floor** *button. Once obtaining the floor a participant may edit the document, publish the modifications and/or release the floor. Publishing the document makes it available to all current participants. Sending it to another user allows that user to become a participant. Note that publishing and sending can be done in either order.)*

When Wendel is happy with his initial draft, he publishes it, and sends the document to Renee. *(Now both Renee and Wendel share the conversation initiated by Renee and the document created by Wendel.)*

Knowing his boss, Wendel releases the floor so that Renee can edit his version. True to form, Renee comments on the draft and publishes her update. *(The modified document appears automatically on all participants' windows.)* Wendel's updated document window is shown in Figure 4 along with Renee's caustic comments in the conversation window in Figure 5. Real-

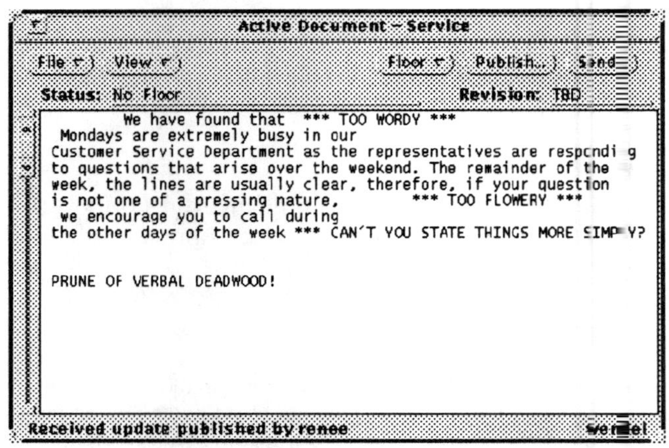

Figure 4: An Active Mail Shared Document Window

izing that he is in trouble, Wendel sends both the document and the conversation to Richard and asks for help.

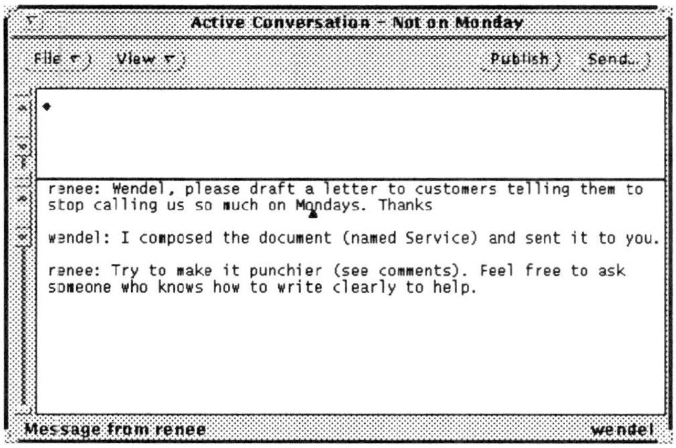

Figure 5: An Active Mail Conversation Window

Both active messages appear as entries in Richard's input folder.

Richard opens the conversation and responds positively. He opens the document as well, then requests and is granted the floor to the document.

At this time, if Renee is monitoring the participants in either of the items, she will see Richard's name appear in a participants window as shown in Figure 6.

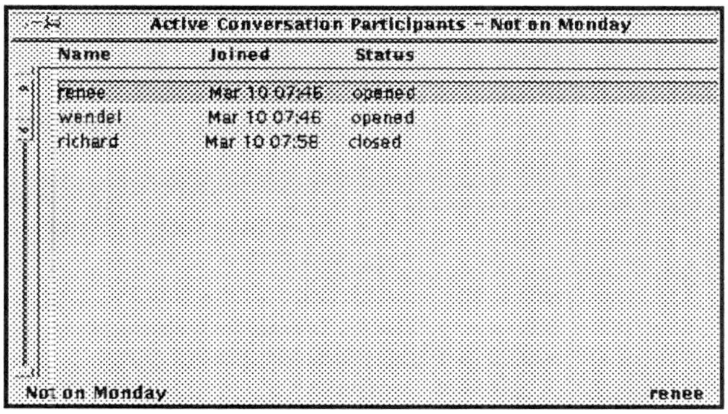

Figure 6: An Active Mail Participants Window

(Every Active Mail application has an associated Participants Window, which shows the current set of participants and dates for when they joined the application.)

When Richard completes his editing, he publishes the polished version, shown in Figure 7. To inspect the history of changes to the document, Wendel uses the window shown in Figure 8. *(The shared document is maintained under the RCS source control system. Using the underlying RCS system we can view previous versions, compare different versions, and view the document update history.)* Wendel and Renee see the new version appear on their screens and breathe sighs of relief.

To continue our example, Renee decides that Wendel's poor writing was just the catalyst she needed to call a long overdue meeting on effective writing. She sends a meeting scheduling message to Wendel, Richard,

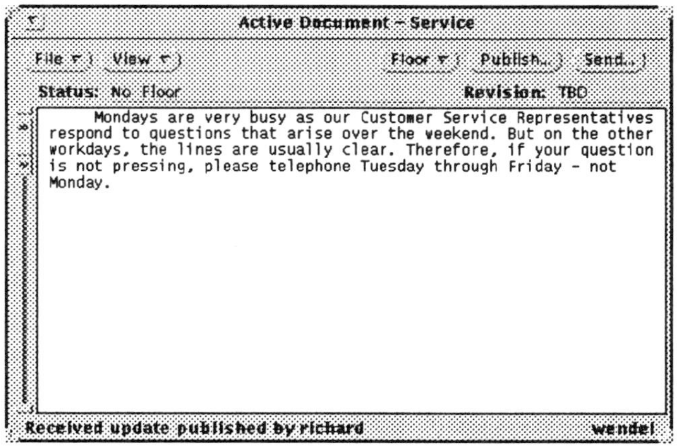

Figure 7: An Active Mail Shared Document Window

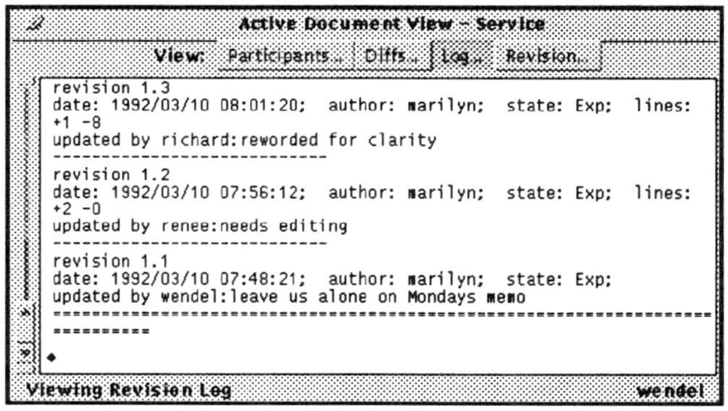

Figure 8: A Shared Document View Window

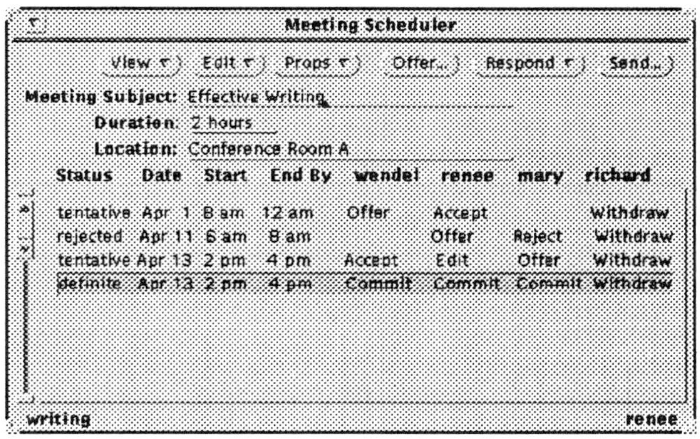

Figure 9: A Meeting Scheduler

and Mary (another mediocre writer). Figure 9 shows a summary of their go-arounds and final convergence on date and time.

The meeting scheduler is an application designed to find an available meeting time for a group of people. A user who wishes to schedule a multi-person meeting creates an Active Mail meeting scheduling agent. When the window appears on the screen, the user specifies the subject of the meeting, its expected duration, and its proposed location, and sends a copy of this window to all intended meeting participants. Each participant interacts with the meeting scheduler by making offers for a meeting time and by responding to other participants' offers.

3 ACTIVE MAIL ARCHITECTURE

We describe informally the abstract architecture of Active Mail, which underlies the previous example.

An Active Mail *configuration* consists of *agents*, interconnected via two-ported bidirectional *communication channels*. There are two types of agents: *users* and *applications*. An example of an Active Mail configuration is given in Figure 10. The icons used in this figure are explained in Figure 11. We say that a user is a *participant* in an application if there exists a port connecting it to the application. Figure 10 shows two users, *User A* and *User B*, participating in two applications *Application 1* and *Application 2*. *User B* participates in an additional application, not shown in the figure, and *Application 2* has an additional participant, also not shown in the figure.

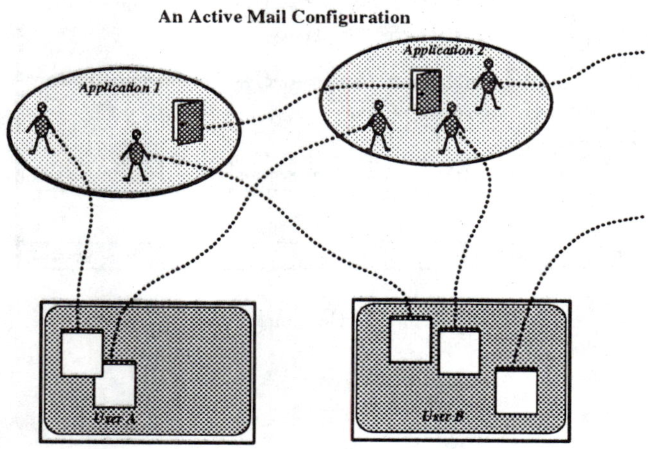

Figure 10: An Active Mail Configuration

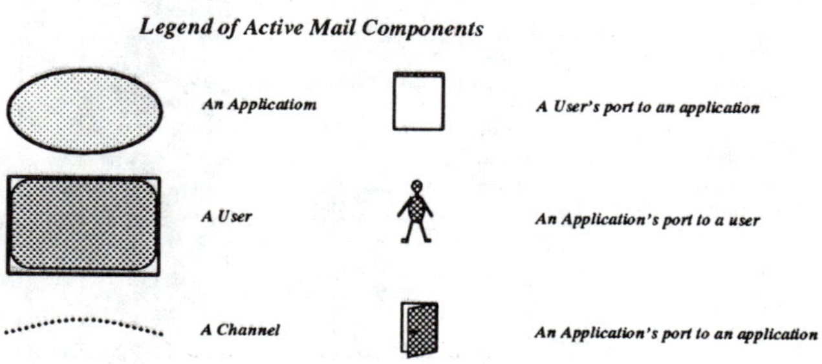

Figure 11: Legend of Active Mail Components

An Active Mail agent with a given set of ports may change its environment (the configuration it is in) using the following operations:

- Create a new application agent.
- Send a copy of one of its ports to a user.
- Discard one of its ports.

The effect of each of these operations is demonstrated in Figure 12.

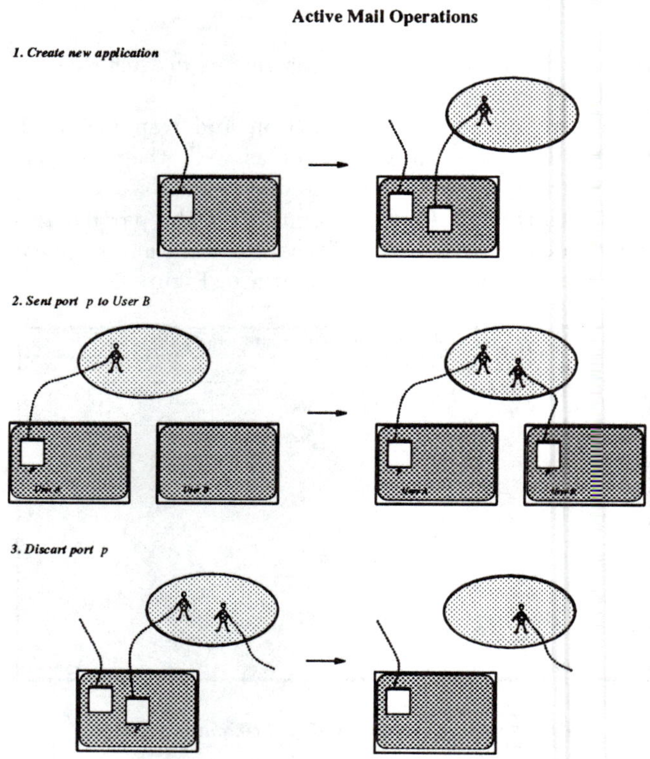

Figure 12: Active Mail Operations

In addition, an Active Mail agent may send messages to, and receive messages from, any of its ports.

A participant in an application (*i.e.*, a user with a port p to an application) may involve another user in the application by sending that user a copy of its port p. A user can leave an application by discarding its port to it.

Similarly, an application A having a port to some other application B may initiate an interaction between a user and the application B by sending to the user a copy of its port to B.

Abstractly, users interact with applications via a bidirectional communication port. The examples in Section 2 show how this abstraction is realized, via windows on the user's screen. Each application comes with one or more application-specific windows, which support the capabilities offered by the application. In addition, each application supports a uniform way to view and interact with the participants in the application.

Users are provided with an interface that allows them to spawn new application agents, as well as with a folder system, discussed in Section 4, to manage their application ports. One folder, the *Input* folder, is designated as the place where ports sent to the user arrive.

4 DIFFERENT VIEWS OF ACTIVE MAIL

Active Mail as an Extension to Ordinary Email

The Challenge

In his book on the Internet [5], Douglas Comer states that the main question driving current research on internetworking is:

> "How can we make substantial improvements in electronic communication while retaining all the features that have made electronic mail so successful?"

Electronic mail is so convenient for human interaction because of its non-intrusive, informal nature, its ability to support both asynchronous and rather immediate communication needs, and its ability to interoperate with other computer-based tools (such as text and graphics editors, and spreadsheets). Furthermore, it assumes no predefined roles for its users, both sender and receiver gain from using it, and no rigid format is required [10]. Hence, electronic mail has long ago reached the critical mass required for effective usage and has since acquired worldwide clientele.

The universal nature of electronic mail is the source of its power, but also prevents it from supporting the specific needs of the two main modes of interaction it is used for: computer-mediated conversations, and documents exchange.

When electronic mail is used for computer-mediated conversation, users often find it hard to maintain dialogue continuity: To which message does the current message respond? What was the sequence of messages exchanged on a particular topic? When participants join the conversation, how can they be brought up to date?

When electronic mail is used for exchanging documents, users often find it hard to maintain document consistency: What is the most recent version of the document? How can I distribute an update and ensure that all copies of previous versions are discarded? And, if the document is authored collaboratively, how are multiple authors coordinated?

An alternative to exchanging documents via electronic mail is placing them in a shared file system accessible to all group members, and performing version management with a source control system like RCS or SCCS, or editing them using collaborative writing tools. Source control systems lack the flexibility and interactive nature of electronic mail. All users must have access to a particular file system. No mechanism is provided for tracking the users interested in knowing that the file was modified, in automatically receiving updates, and/or in further editing the file. If such information is known to the user updating a file, that user could send an ordinary electronic mail message to all interested parties, notifying them of the update. A user receiving such a message would have to perform some operations to get a local copy of the updated file and/or to lock it.

Many collaborative writing tools exist [6, 12, 13, 15, 18]. However, as far as we know, they solve only the last problem of coordinating multiple authors. To participate in collaborative editing, a user must be notified by some other mechanism (e.g. electronic mail) that a shared document was set up, and which command should be used to access it. Once users leave the interactive editing session, there is no automatic mechanism of informing them that the document was modified.

From Passive to Active Messages

The path from passive electronic mail messages to truly active ones leads through several electronic mail extensions. One of the first is MIT's *Object Lens* [14]. Its underlying principle is augmenting electronic mail with more attributes (apart from the obvious "Subject:" and "Cc:") that classify messages into categories. Object Lens provides an object oriented class hierarchy of templates, each providing more attributes to fill in.

This scheme is extended to provide a template database by having templates of *persons*, *meetings*, *seminars* etc. Embedding such templates in other templates can provide hypertext-like documents.

While Lens is much more than electronic mail, it remains within electronic mail's concept of message sending. Lens's building block is still a letter. No online discussion can take place, and no active application such as decision support tools can be run.

The *Coordinator* system [7] employs Winograd and Flores's adaptation of *speech act theory* by structuring electronic mail correspondence. The Coordinator structures the electronic conversation by providing a universal state transition diagram of possible action-reply messages. For example, a cycle could start by "Requesting" action, replying by "Promising" to complete the action or "Declining" the request and so on until some end is reached.

Some find the universality of speech act theory questionable [4], and it is further doubted by us whether human beings *want* to formalize their statements in such ways.

The *Andrew Message System* [2] can be regarded as an extension and integration of electronic mail and bulletin board systems like the Usenet [5]. Operating at the Carnegie Mellon campus, the Andrew Message System is a collection of bulletin boards that enables the sending of messages which contain text, pictures, equations and hierarchical drawings.

Andrew also provides a rudimentary version of "active" messages. Certain types of messages activate a menu from which the message recipient can choose, and the choice is transparently mailed back. Such is a *vote message* which returns votes. This scheme was an *ad hoc* extension to Andrew and, as Borenstein himself states (1991) [3]:

> "...when one is implementing a fifth special case of active messaging, one begins to look for general mechanisms that might replace all the special cases"

Borenstein's general mechanism is a new language named *ATOMICMAIL* [3]. ATOMICMAIL's active message is actually an application whose code is sent via ordinary electronic mail. Special preceding keywords cause the application to execute itself.

There is a major difference between ATOMICMAIL's messages and Active Mail messages. While the former are batch-programs as far as the sending side is concerned, our scheme supports ongoing interactions between sender, receiver, and future participants through direct (non-e-mail) communication channels.

Active Mail as a Protocol for Computer-Initiated Interaction

We all know how to initiate an interaction with a computer; we issue an appropriate command, and the computer responds. We do not have a similarly obvious way for a computer to initiate an interaction with a user. Popping up a window on the user's screen, blocking input until some appropriate response is given, placing a message on the virtual console, and beeping, are all rather crude and intrusive solutions adopted by programs that require the user's attention.

We believe that the problem of computer-initiated interaction is of fundamental importance to groupware, and that the design of any groupware application must provide an answer to the following question:

> *How can a multi-user application cause a new user to "get on board" in a way which is non-intrusive, tolerates delayed response, and requires little effort on the user's part?*

Active Mail offers a protocol and a user interface to achieve just that.

For example, how can the user who wishes to schedule a meeting cause the meeting scheduler window to appear on each of the participants' screens? The answer Active Mail offers was demonstrated in the example above. The user sends an active message. The message is placed in the recipient's input folder. When the recipient chooses to open the message, the appropriate window will appear on the screen.

The same approach can be followed by any multi-user interactive application to involve new users in the application, as long as the application conforms to the Active Mail interface protocols.

Active Mail as a Tool for Maintaining Persistent Interactive Connections

When handling passive messages in electronic mail, two kinds of storage facilities are involved: the user mail-spool (sometimes referred to as the *in-tray*) where incoming mail resides, and the local file system, where old messages are saved in *folders*. Both forms are persistent, in that they survive logging out or computer shutdown.

Maintaining active messages is more of a challenge, since the messages can still communicate with the outside world. Active Mail provides an Active Folder hierarchy in which the user's persistent *active* connections are maintained. Thus users may hold multiple connections to various agents in their private folders and yet not lose them when logging out. Each user's folder system consists of two components: the Input folder, where incoming active messages are placed, with a functionality similar to the user's ordinary mail-spool, and a folder hierarchy which functions like a private file system hierarchy. Subfolders can be created and the folder system structure can be altered much the same way as users can create subdirectories and move files within a hierarchical file system.

In contrast to electronic-mail, active messages *change*, and the user has to be alerted about those changes (e.g., a new contribution to a conversation has arrived, the user's opponent in a chess game has moved etc.). Hence the Active Folder system incorporates a *notification mechanism* [17]. When an agent whose window is closed gets *notified* that a modification has occurred, its icon changes, and an audio sound is generated. A folder becomes notified if any of its member agents (including subfolders) is notified. Thus the modification of an agent may reach the root folder (and hence change the Active Mail icon if it is closed). Notification also manifests itself on open windows via changed fields and beeping.

5 INTERNALS OF SOME ACTIVE MAIL APPLICATION AGENTS

We describe briefly the internal architecture of the Active Mail application agents presented above: the conversation agent, the shared document agent, and the meeting scheduler.

The Conversation Agent

The conversation agent we describe is quite straightforward. One can easily envision more sophisticated conversation agents, which support real-time multi-media interaction [19, 22, 16]. Active Mail can accommodate such agents as long as they conform to its basic architecture.

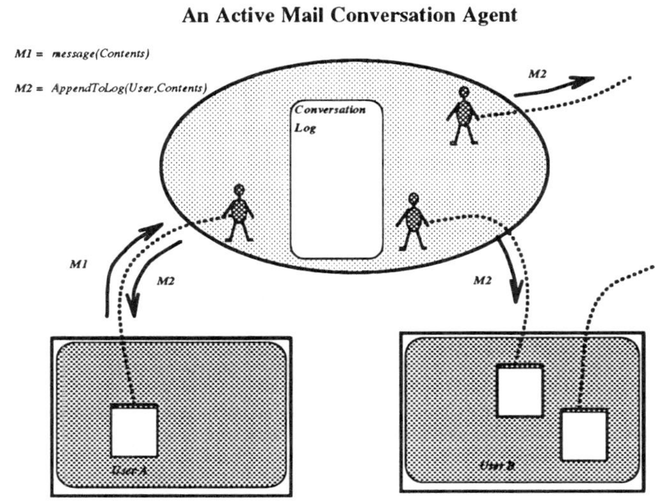

Figure 13: Active Mail Conversation

The conversation agent described in Section 2 supports an ongoing asynchronous conversation among a dynamically changing group of users. Its basic components are depicted in Figure 13.

The conversation agent maintains a conversation log. When the agent receives a contribution from a participant, it appends the data to the log and sends a message containing the contribution and the name of the contributor to all participants. When a new participant joins the conversation it receives a copy of the current conversation log.

The Shared-Document Agent

The shared-document agent we describe is simpler than many state-of-the-art collaborative writing tools [6, 12, 13, 15, 18]. Any of these more advanced tools can be integrated into Active Mail, by adapting their interfaces to conform to the Active Mail architecture.

The shared-document agent allows a dynamically changing group of users to operate on a shared document. Its basic components are depicted in Figure 14. Its user interface was shown in Figure 3 above.

The document agent maintains an updated copy of the document, a *Floor Status*, which may be free or contain the name of the user currently holding the floor, and a queue of pending floor requests.

Initially the document and the queue are empty and the floor is free. When a new participant joins in, the document agent sends it a message with the current floor status and a copy of the document.

When the agent receives a request for the floor, it appends the request to the queue. When the floor is free and the queue is nonempty, the agent grants the first request in the queue. A participant that holds the floor may publish an updated version of the document

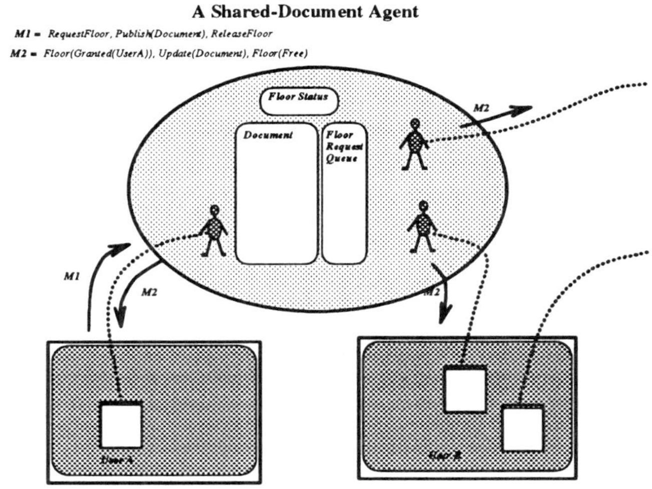

Figure 14: An Active Mail Shared Document

and/or release the floor. The document agent informs all participants when the document gets updated and/or the floor status is changed.

This basic agent has an additional functionality, derived from the RCS source control system. Rather than extending the basic document agent, we allow it to interoperate with an RCS agent; some if its capabilities were shown in our earlier example.

The Meeting Scheduler

One of the main criticisms [10] of existing meeting schedulers (*cf.* [1] and references therein) is that they require all participants to maintain their schedule on-line using the same tool, and let various algorithms search through their calendars for vacant slots. Many consider this to be a breach of privacy, quite bothersome, and of little benefit to anyone but the meeting coordinator.

In contrast, our meeting scheduler is not based on on-line calendars. Rather, it mimics the usual human meeting scheduling process by supporting an interactive negotiation between the expected meeting participants.

The steps of creating a meeting scheduler, specifying the meeting subject and location, sending a copy of the scheduler to all participants, as well as making offers and responding to them were discussed above.

Although the meeting scheduler does not depend on the existence of an on-line calendar, it can consult such a calendar, with the user's permission, when it exists. This is demonstrated in Figure 15, where the scheduler negotiates directly with *User A*, but negotiates with the on-line calendar agent of *User B*, rather than with *B*.

We say that an offer is *tentative* if no participant has rejected it but not all participants have responded yet; that an offer is *definite* if all participants have either accepted it or committed to it; and that an offer is *committed* if all participants have committed to it.

Participants interact with the meeting scheduler as

Figure 15: A Meeting Scheduler

follows. (The protocol is enforced using the standard technique of disabling options when they are illegal.) If there is no definite offer, each participant can make an offer. If there is a tentative offer, each participant must accept or reject it before making an additional offer. If there is a definite offer, each participant must either commit or reject it.

Two levels of agreement (*Accept* and *Commit*) are needed. The time to reach consensus could be long due to delayed responses; hence, we must allow a user to agree tentatively to attend several meetings within the same time slot, and commit to attending a meeting only when the offer becomes definite.

6 CONCLUSIONS

Implementation

Active Mail is implemented under the Logix [23] distributed programming environment in a subset of the concurrent logic programming language FCP [21, 24] which employs directed logic variables [11].

The main aspect of Active Mail that requires support from the underlying programming language is the ability of communication ports to migrate. Concurrent logic languages are particularly suitable for supporting dynamic port migration [20], and the Directed Logic Variables algorithm described in [11] provides a practical implementation of this capability over the datagram communication protocol of the Internet [5].

FCP has been provided with an interface to the X window system using the XView library (conforming to the OpenLook standard). An FCP transformer was also built to convert the output of an interface design tool (Sun Microsystems's dev-guide) to FCP, enabling easy creation of new interfaces.

In principle, Active Mail can span wide-area networks and have multiple distributed servers. The runtime architecture of the current implementation consists of a single server and a number of clients, which could be anywhere on the Internet. The server maintains all the Active Mail applications agents as well as the folder structure of each registered user. Clients are responsible for interacting with users and windows.

To log into Active Mail, the user creates an Active Mail client process that connects to the user's root folder, which resides on the server. From the root folder users can reach all their other folders, including their Input folders.

The server is persistent, in that it checkpoints its state periodically and can recover from failure. Client processes that run the user interfaces are not persistent. If a client process crashes, the user loses its windows – but upon logging in to Active Mail, all applications with ports in the user's folders are accessible, and the user can resume interaction with any of them.

The implementation code consists of two components: an application-independent kernel and the applications. Each application consists of two modules: the agent module and the user interface module.

Experience

We have been using Active Mail within our group for a few months and successfully maintain shared documents and enjoy playing chess. We appreciate its recoverability aspect, a feature that gets exercised quite often. We are currently working on improving the notification mechanism and interoperating with ordinary electronic mail.

Future Directions

Active Mail can accommodate a wide range of applications. We are planning to refine the currently available applications and provide additional ones.

The implementation of Active Mail is based on a single server. Although the Directed Logic Variables algorithm [11] may support a multi-server implementation, the lack of a recovery protocol that can sustain server failure prevents us from using it. We are currently working on such a recovery protocol, following ideas from [8].

The Active Mail architecture provides a powerful generalization of electronic mail, but does not provide a similar generalization of shared file systems. Its folders are private, and it has not notion of public, or shared, folders. We are currently working on a more general abstract architecture which supports such a notion of sharing.

References

[1] Beard D. et al., *A Visual Calendar For Scheduling Group Meetings*, CSCW Conference Proceedings, ACM SIGCHI and SIGOIS, Los Angeles, pp. 279-290, 1990.

[2] Borenstein N. S., Thyberg C.A., *Cooperative Work in the Andrew Message System*, CSCW Conference Pro-

ceedings, ACM SIGCHI and SIGOIS, Portland Oregon, pp. 306-323, 1988.

[3] Borenstein N. S., *Secure and Portable Active Messaging: A New Platform for Distributed Applications and Cooperative Work*, Unpublished paper, October 1991.

[4] Bowers W., Churcher J., *Local and Global Structuring of Computer Mediated Communication: Developing Linguistic Perspectives On CSCW in COSMOS*, CSCW Conference Proceedings, ACM SIGCHI and SIGOIS, Portland Oregon, pp. 125-138, 1988.

[5] Comer D., *Internetworking with TCP/IP*, Prentice-Hall, second edition, 1991, pp. 434-435.

[6] Ellis C. A., Gibbs S. J., Rein G. L., *Groupware - Some Issues and Experiences*, Communications of the ACM, Vol 34, No 1, January 1991.

[7] Flores F., Graves M., Hartfield B., Winograd T., *Computer Systems and the design of organizational interaction*, ACM Trans. Off. Inf. Syst, 6, 2, Apr 1988, pp. 153-172.

[8] Gaifman, H., Maher, M.J., and Shapiro, E., Replay, Recovery, Replication, and Snapshots of Nondeterministic Concurrent Programs, *Proc. ACM Conference on Principles of Distributed Computing*, ACM,1991.

[9] Goldberg Y., *Active Mail: A Framework for Implementing Groupware*, M.Sc. Thesis, The Weizmann Institute of Science, November 1991.

[10] Grudin J., *Seven Plus One Challenges in Understanding Social Dynamics for Groupware Developers*, CHI Conference, Tutorial Notes, 11, 1991.

[11] Kleinman A., Moscowitz, Y., Pnueli, A., Shapiro. E., *Communication with Directed Logic Variables*, In ACM conference of Principles of Programming Languages, 1991.

[12] Knister, M.J., Prakash, A., *DistEdit: A distributed toolkit for supporting multiple group editors*, Proc. CSCW'90 Conference on Computer-Supported Cooperative Work, October, Los Angeles.

[13] Koszarek, J.L., Lindstrom, T.L., Ensor, J.R. and Ahuja, S.R., *A multi-user document review tool*, Proceedings of the IFIP WG8.4 Conference on Multi-User Interfaces and Applications, Crete, 1990.

[14] Lay K.Y., Malone T.W., *Object Lens: A "Spreadsheet" for Cooperative Work*, CSCW Conference Proceedings, ACM SIGCHI and SIGOIS, Portland Oregon, pp. 115-124, 1988.

[15] Leland, M.D.P., Fish, R.S. and Kraut, R.E., *Collaborative document production using Quilt*, Proc. CSCW'88 Conference on Computer-Supported Cooperative Work, September, Portland, pp. 206-215.

[16] McCarthy J. C. et al, *An Experimental Study of Common Ground in Text-Based Communication*, CHI Conference Proceedings, ACM, New Orleans Louisiana, pp. 209-215, 1991.

[17] McCarthy J. C. et al, *Four Generic Communication Tasks Which Must Be Supported in Electronic Conferencing*, To appear in acm/SIGCHI Bulletin, January 1991.

[18] Neuwirth, C.M., Kaufer, D.S., Chandhok, R. and Morris, J.H., *Issues in the design of computer support for co-authoring and commenting*, Proc. CSCW'90 Conference on Computer-Supported Cooperative Work, October, Los Angeles, pp. 183-195.

[19] Nunamaker J. F. et al., *Electronic Meeting Systems to Support Group Work*, Communications of the ACM, pp. 40-61, July 1991.

[20] Shapiro, E., The Family of Concurrent Logic Programming Languages, *ACM Computing Surveys* 21(3), pp. 412–510, 1989.

[21] Shapiro, E. (Editor), *Concurrent Prolog: Collected Papers*, Vols. 1 and 2, MIT Press, 1987.

[22] Shepard, A., Mayer, N. and Kuchinsky, A., *Strudel - An extensible electronic conversation toolkit*, Proc. CSCW'90 Conference on Computer-Supported Cooperative Work, October, Los Angeles, pp. 93-104.

[23] Silverman W., Hirsch M., Houri A., Shapiro E., *The Logix System User Manual, Version 1.21*, in Concurrent Prolog: Collected Papers, Vol 2, Chapter 21, MIT press, 1987.

[24] Yardeni, E., Kliger, S., and Shapiro, E., The Languages FCP(:) and FCP(:,?), *Journal of New Generation Computing* **7**, 89–107, 1990. An earlier version appeared in *Proceedings of the International Conference on Fifth Generation Computer Systems*, pp. 763–773, Tokyo, 1988.

[25] Trenner R., *The Bell Labs Writer*, Bell Telephone Laboratories, Incorporated, 1985 Page 11.

[26] Woitass, M., *Coordination of intelligent office agents - applied to meeting scheduling*, Proceedings of the IFIP WG8.4 Conference on Multi-User Interfaces and Applications, Crete, 1990.

SUPPORTING INFORMAL COMMUNICATION VIA EPHEMERAL INTEREST GROUPS

Laurence Brothers,
Jim Hollan, Jakob Nielsen, Scott Stornetta,
Steve Abney, George Furnas, and Michael Littman

Bellcore
445 South St.
Morristown, NJ 07962-1910
{quasar, hollan, nielsen, stornetta, abney, gwf, mlittman}@bellcore.com

ABSTRACT
In this paper, we introduce ephemeral interest groups for supporting informal communication. Ephemeral interest groups are electronic discussion groups that, in contrast to bulletin boards and the like, are short-lived and ad hoc. They are designed as a medium for informal discussions of items broadcast to a wider community. We have implemented a prototype system to explore ephemeral interest groups. We discuss the goals of the system, characterize its evolution over the last ten months of deployment, and sketch our plans for future developments.

KEYWORDS
Ephemeral interest groups, informal communication, discussions, hypertext, bulletin boards, email, information filters, critical mass of users, measures of informality.

EPHEMERAL INTEREST GROUPS

In a recent paper [3], we view support for informal communication in terms of needs, media, and mechanisms. There are underlying needs served by communication, and different media enable different mechanisms for meeting those needs. Our approach is to exploit the distinctive mechanisms of the computational medium, as opposed to imitating the mechanisms of traditional interaction. In our earlier paper we sketched a series of projects to elaborate this position. In this paper we provide empirical details of one of those efforts: supporting informal communication via *ephemeral interest groups*. Ephemeral interest groups are short-lived, ad hoc electronic discussion groups spawned from items from a more widely-broadcast information source.

Permission to copy without fee all or part of this material is granted provided that the copies are not made or distributed for direct commercial advantage, the ACM copyright notice and the title of the publication and its date appear, and notice is given that copying is by permission of the Association for Computing Machinery. To copy otherwise, or to republish, requires a fee and/or specific permission.

© 1992 ACM 0-89791-543-7/92/0010/0084...$1.50

Electronic mail and other forms of electronic communication are increasingly being used for informal discussion. Most of these discussions are mediated by e-mail mailing lists or by bulletin boards. At Bellcore a simple bulletin board provides a forum for discussion of issues of interest to the general community. The majority of users access it through a Unix®* program, *msgs*. While originally intended for announcements about the system that are "short pieces of information suitable to be read once by most users of the system," it has come to be used more broadly to exchange information, make queries and requests, and discuss topics of general interest.

Based on our earlier proposal for supporting informal communication [3], we began to explore changes to the *msgs* system that would make it more useful for the community. We decided that any changes we made should be non-obtrusive, so that people who so desired could continue to use the system exactly as they had before. We understood that this greatly constrained the changes we could make, but we wanted to avoid any disruption to our colleagues.

A common complaint about *msgs* is that it contains too much irrelevant information. One might argue that a bulletin board consisting of multiple interest groups would better support users, because people could subscribe to or browse only those groups that interest them. However, we question this alternative for a number of reasons. First, there are many benefits of having a channel of communication that is read by virtually everyone in our community. In addition, it is difficult to generate a good set of categories for articles,

* Unix is a registered trademark of Unix System Laboratories, Inc.

and the burden of selecting an appropriate category is placed on the sender of each article. Studies of hypertext [1][2][4][5] have demonstrated that usability problems arise if systems require users to structure information prematurely. For these reasons, we felt that a hierarchical bulletin board system would not be useful for managing the kind of wide-ranging and short-lived discussions that are typical of *msgs*.

This led us to propose ephemeral interest groups. Unlike bulletin boards, netnews groups, and mailing lists, ephemeral interest groups can be created at virtually no transaction cost to users or to system administrators. The groups can be thought of as disposable, intended to last only days or hours.

We created a system, called *topics*, which almost invisibly supports ephemeral interest groups through *msgs*. In keeping with our design constraint, *msgs* continues on the surface as it has always been. But after reading an article, users now have the alternative of *joining* the article before going on to the next one. In the *topics* model, every article represents a potential topic of discussion, of interest to some subset of the community, and by joining an article, the user expresses interest in the topic. Joining an article adds the user to the ephemeral interest group associated with the article, creating it automatically, if necessary. The user receives a copy of the article in his or her regular e-mail along with a copy of discussion that has already taken place. To post to the ephemeral interest group, users need only reply within their normal mail reading program to any of the articles in the discussion. Thus, *topics* is similar to a traditional mailing list, but the procedure for creating the list is automatic and instantaneous.

An important consequence is that follow-ups can easily be sent to those people who have expressed an interest in a topic, rather than to the whole community. In this way, we expected to decrease follow-up activity on *msgs*. At the same time, we expected that there would be more discussions overall, and that discussions within ephemeral interest groups would have more follow-ups than they would have had on *msgs*, since participants know that they are addressing only those who have expressed interest in the topic, not the whole community. We also expected this awareness to influence the character of discussions; in particular, to make them more informal and personal.

Analysis of Prior Msgs System Usage

Before we made any changes to the *msgs* system, we analyzed the content of a collection of *msgs* articles and interviewed users of the *msgs* system. We classified about 700 articles from the period April 8 to May 24, 1991 into five mutually-exclusive categories:

- Information (249 articles, or 36%) The posting's main intent was to provide information to the community of *msgs* readers.
- Question (134, or 19%) The posting asked a question that could be answered by an e-mail response, or some other simple action from one's computer or telephone.
- Request (79 articles, or 11%) A request differs from a question in that responding to a request involves an action that cannot be handled from one's computer or phone; for example, giving a ride home from work.
- Offer (68 articles, or 10%) An offer differs from information in that taking advantage of an offer requires one to do more than just read it. An example of an offer is a posting that a book is available to the first person who picks it up.
- Scheduled Event (168 articles, or 24%) The posting announces a talk or other event taking place at a specific time.

We also marked articles with three optional codes, orthogonal to the five categories above:

- Leisure (119 articles, or 17%) Postings which seemed to have no direct bearing on work or work-related activities.
- Follow-up (194 articles, or 28%) Postings which were clearly following in the thread of a previous posting. Of these, 125 were classified as discussions, as opposed to repeated talk announcements.
- Groups (180, or 26%) Postings which were clearly intended for a definable subset of the *msgs* community.

From this analysis, we looked for opportunities to move traffic from *msgs* into ephemeral interest groups. For example, the analysis indicates that follow-ups to questions are often posted back to the entire community, presumably because the author believes people other than the requester are interested in the response, but has no way of determining precisely who might be interested. If an ephemeral interest group were attached to the query, and interested parties expressed their interest by joining the group, follow-ups could be posted to the ephemeral interest group rather than to the entire community. Similarly, many of the scheduled event announcements are second and third reminders. We conjectured that users would prefer to receive follow-up notices only if they had at least a slight interest in the talk to begin with, something that they could judge when they read the first talk announcement. Through ephemeral interest groups, a user could express interest in the first announcement, and follow-ups could be limited to interested parties. We also expected that some of the postings classified as groups would have been addressed to only the relevant individuals, if ephemeral interest groups had been available. In short, the postings that might not have appeared on *msgs*, had ephemeral interest groups been available, were the follow-up postings and group postings. Together, they make up 49% (343 postings) of the volume of traffic on *msgs*. The prospect of reducing *msgs* traffic by half seemed attractive.

We also did a series of informal interviews of a stratified sample of the user community. Those interviews confirmed our intuitions. *Msgs* is widely used in the community; it is

```
Message 10071:
From suri@polya.bellcore.com Mon Jan 13 13:28:47 1992
Subject: Lab 212 Seminar, Thursday 01/16/92
(16 lines) More? [ynq]
```

Figure 1 *Msgs* Prompt.

viewed as essential for obtaining a variety of work related information; and it is perceived to contain too much irrelevant information.

Modifications to Msgs to Support Ephemeral Interest Groups

Because we wanted to evaluate our ideas about ephemeral interest groups in the existing large community of *msgs* users, we had to work within the limits of the *msgs* system. *Msgs* users are predominantly Bellcore researchers, but also include some administrative and managerial staff. We recognized that, while many might be interested in using new features we created, we had to leave the system essentially unchanged for those who did not wish to participate. Because of the primitive nature of the *msgs* interface, this proved to be a significant constraint. However, we viewed the opportunity to experiment with a large user community as offsetting that limitation.

Most users read *msgs* articles using the *msgs* program, but a minority use a reader in GNU Emacs, the Andrew Mail System, or various netnews readers. Though we were not able to modify the netnews readers, by modifying *msgs*, and making minor changes to the Emacs and Andrew readers, we were able to provide the ephemeral interest group functionality to the large majority of users, with fairly minor modifications to the three systems.

Before settling on our final approach, we considered two other mechanisms for exploring ephemeral interest groups. First, we considered creating a special program to attach ephemeral interest groups only to announcements of talks, but rejected that because its success required all users to change their established behavior for announcing talks. Next, we implemented the system using an early version of dynamic mail objects. Several trial users complained of disruption to their normal mail activity. Finally we decided to implement ephemeral interest groups through ordinary electronic mail, making only minimal changes to the *msgs* program. Only interest group creation and subscription would be handled through *msgs*. Figure 1 depicts the basic prompt of the existing *msgs* bulletin board system. The user is presented with the sender, subject, date, and size of an article, and has the choice of reading it, skipping to the next article, or quitting the application. There are a number of additional features, though most users are unaware of them. These include saving the article to a file, entering a mailer, or jumping to a specific article. The system has no on-line command-lists or help.

The only visible modification we made was the addition of a fourth alternative to the command prompt: instead of `[ynq]`, the new prompt is `[ynqj]`. The effect of the 'j' command is to join the user to the ephemeral interest group associated with the current *msgs* article.

Most of the ephemeral interest group functionality is provided by a separate program, called *topics*. When a user types 'j' in response to a *msgs* article, the article is sent by electronic mail to the *topics* program. *Topics* looks in a central archive for an ephemeral interest group corresponding to the given msgs article, creating a new group if none already exists. It adds the user to the subscriber list for the group, and sends a digest of current discussion to the user via electronic mail. If the user replies to the digest, or to any other mail distributed by *topics*, the reply goes to *topics*, not *msgs*. *Topics* redistributes such replies only to subscribers of the ephemeral interest group, not to the entire *msgs* community.

In addition to handling requests generated by the 'j' key, and redistributing subsequent ephemeral interest group postings, the *topics* program responds to explicit commands sent via electronic mail. For a given group, users can request a list of subscribers or a digest of all postings. They can unsubscribe from the group, subscribe to other existing groups, or create new groups. A 'help' command is also provided.

EPHEMERAL INTEREST GROUP USAGE

In this section, we examine how ephemeral interest groups have been used, particularly, whether they have been used as we expected, and what weaknesses should be addressed in the next iteration of the system. The major results are: that ephemeral interest groups require a fairly large user community to function well; that ephemeral interest groups are good information filters; that discussions in ephemeral interest groups are indeed more informal and personal than discussions on msgs; and that ephemeral interest groups have been perhaps too unobtrusive, resulting in less usage than there might have been.avenues

Trends in Ephemeral Interest Group Formation

Use of the *topics* system began in August 1991. As of July, 1992 1279 ephemeral interest groups have been formed, and there have been 713 follow-up postings to groups. 3[illegible]7 people have joined at least one group; 172 have joined at least three groups.

The number of functioning ephemeral interest groups created in each of the first 46 weeks after the introduction of the 'j' command is shown in Figure 2. For the purposes of this figure, a *functioning* ephemeral interest group is one

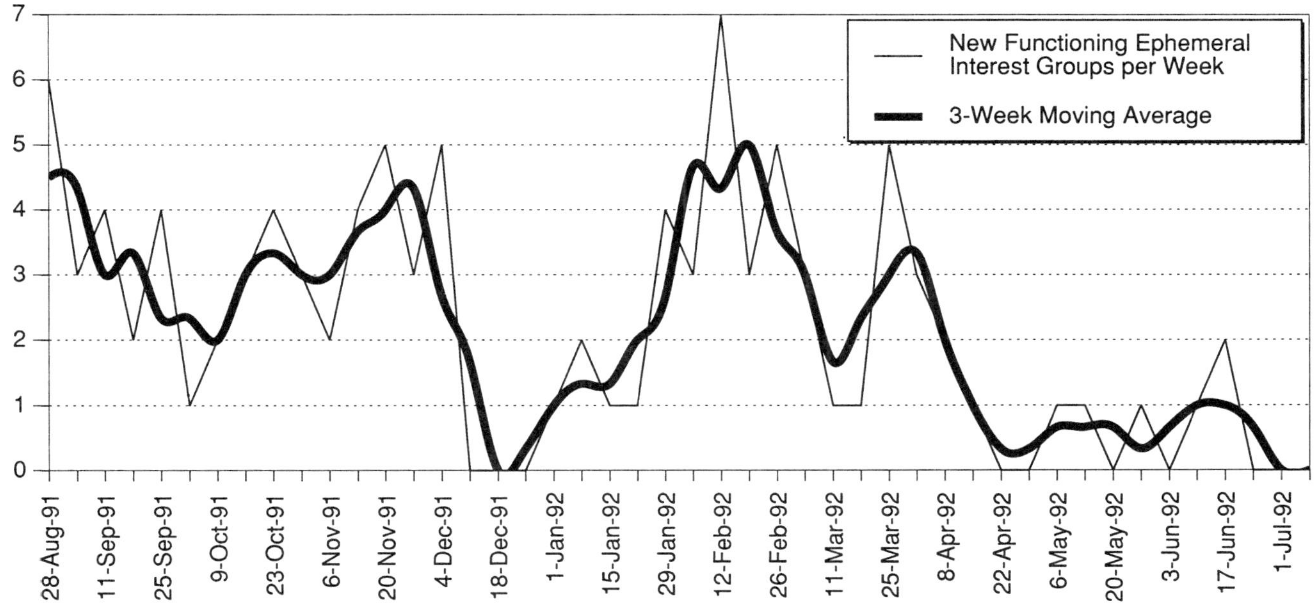

Figure 2 Number of functioning ephemeral interest groups for the first 46 weeks. Only groups with at least three postings and at least three subscribers are counted.

with at least three postings (the original *msgs* article and at least two follow-ups) and at least three subscribers. Obviously, there are major random fluctuations in interest group formation from week to week. The long-term trends do show some interesting patterns, however. After an initial flurry of activity, as users tried out the new feature, interest group creation declined to about two new functioning groups per week in early October 1991. Usage increased slowly until mid-November 1991, when a fairly steady level of about four new functioning groups per week was achieved. This result confirms that new technology is often slow to achieve full penetration of a large user environment.

One dramatic effect in the figure is the severe reduction of interest group creation in the last half of December. In fact, the laboratory was only closed for a few days around Christmas, but a fairly large number of users were gone for extended periods of time throughout December. The elimination of functioning interest group creation during the holiday season can be ascribed to the need for a critical mass of users. Our laboratory may not be large enough to sustain ephemeral interest groups unless almost everybody is present.

In addition to the downturn in interest group creation during the holidays, the figure shows that interest group formation took almost the whole month of January to regain its former level of about four new functioning groups per week. *Topics* usage was probably so slow to recover because users had effectively forgotten about it, and the 'j' in the *msgs* prompt was not enough to remind them of its availability. In short, our attempt to be unobtrusive may have been *too* successful. We return to this point below.

Usage remained fairly steady in February and March, with between two and four new functioning ephemeral interest groups created each week. Starting with the week of April 1st, however, usage declined almost to zero and has remained very low ever since. The week of April 1st saw an extensive discussion carried out on the main *msgs* board with a large number of practical, humorous, political, and "flaming" postings, all on the topic of nesting geese in the parking lot. We hypothesize that this high-visibility discussion made it acceptable again to post follow-up messages to the main *msgs* system which reemerged as the forum for electronic discussions in our lab.

Ephemeral Interest Groups as Information Filters

To assess how effective ephemeral interest groups were at directing information only to interested parties, we conducted a user survey in late February and early March of 1992. This period corresponded to the 25th through 27th week of the use of the *topics* system. We surveyed two different kinds of *msgs* users: those who subscribed to ephemeral interest groups, and those who did not. We counted as subscribers only those users that subscribed to at least three groups, of which at least two were within the last 90 days. People who subscribed to fewer groups were considered not to be *topics* users.

We collected every follow-up article posted to either the general *msgs* bulletin board or to a discussion group during the survey period. We sent each follow-up article to a randomly chosen *topics* user and to a randomly chosen non-user. We also sent each *topics* follow-up posting to a random member of the interest group it had been posted to. We classified interest group participants as being either the originator of the *msgs* article that spawned the group, or as

	No. Queried	Respondents	Resp. Rate	Relevance
Originators rating follow-ups to the ephemeral interest group they started	11	7	64%	4.9
Subscribers rating follow-ups to a subscribed ephemeral interest group	14	14	100%	3.9
Subscribers to ephemeral interest groups rating follow-ups to *other* groups	36	24	67%	2.7
Subscribers to ephemeral interest groups rating follow-ups posted to *msgs*	31	23	74%	3.0
Non-subscribers rating follow-ups to an ephemeral interest group	43	21	49%	3.0
Non-subscribers rating follow-ups posted to the *msgs* board	40	19	48%	2.7

Table 1 Rated relevance of follow-up articles posted either to an ephemeral interest group or to the general msgs bulletin board. The difference in ratings given by the originators and subscribers to the group to which a follow-up article was posted is significant at the $p<.05$ level. The difference in ratings given by subscribers to the group to which a follow-up article was posted and subscribers to other groups is significant at the $p<.01$ level. The differences in ratings between the bottom four lines in the table are not statistically significant. The difference in response rates between the subscribers and non-subscribers is significant at the $p<.01$ level. Relevance was rated on a 1–5 rating scale, with 1 indicating a completely irrelevant article and 5 indicating a very relevant article.

being a regular subscriber. For postings to interest groups, every posting after the initial seed article was considered to be a follow-up article. For postings to *msgs*, we made a subjective decision as to whether the article was a follow-up to a previous *msgs* article.

Each survey respondent was asked to assess how relevant the specific follow-up article was to him or her personally. The concept of "relevance" was described to the respondents as including both job-related need-to-know and more personal interest in the contents of the article. Relevance was rated on a 1–5 scale, with 1 indicating a completely irrelevant article and 5 indicating a very relevant article.

The results of the survey are reported in Table 1. One major result is that those who subscribed to a given discussion group considered follow-up articles posted to that group quite relevant to their interests (average score 3.9 on the 1–5 scale), in contrast to non-subscribers, who rated the same articles as less relevant to their interests (about 3 on the 1–5 scale). Discussion group originators considered follow-ups posted to their discussion groups as even more relevant to their interests (4.9). The higher rating of discussion group follow-ups by discussion group members cannot be ascribed to discussion group follow-ups being of higher "quality" than *msgs* follow-ups. The table shows that those who did not subscribe to a given group considered postings to that group to be no more or less relevant than postings to *msgs*. (None of the differences in the last four lines of the table are statistically significant.)

We conclude that ephemeral interest groups can successfully direct information to those who view it as most relevant to their interests. Given the information overload faced by most of our users, this filtering function is an important benefit of ephemeral interest groups.

The Tone of Discussions on Msgs and Topics

In order to get an idea whether *topics* discussions were more informal and personal than *msgs* discussions, we compared the frequency of personal pronoun use in each. Our assumption is that personal pronouns, specifically "I" and "you", are used more extensively in personal communications than in formal communications.

We analyzed a six week period (10/10/91–11/20/91) in detail, for both *msgs* and *topics*. During that period, there were 659 *msgs* postings, of which about a fifth (128) were "joined" to create topics. About a third of these (47) actually generated follow-up *topics* discussions, with a total of 107 follow-up articles (an average of 2.2 follow-ups each). During the same period *msgs* continued to be a forum for follow-ups as well, there being almost as many articles of a follow-up nature (95) posted there. We note that the average audience for discussion in these two media is quite different. *Msgs* discussions are read by all 250+ readers, whereas discussions in the ephemeral interest groups are read only by those who expressed interest in the topic (8–9 on average).

Msgs articles were categorized into three groups:

- *Msgs* articles that generated no follow-up *msgs* discussions
- *Msgs* articles that did generate follow-up *msgs* discussions
- *Msgs* articles that were themselves follow-ups to previous *msgs* articles

An analogous classification of *topics* articles yielded:

- *Topics* articles that generated no follow-up postings to the interest group (although by definition, people had "joined" such an article in hopes of future discussion)
- *Topics* articles that did generate follow-up postings
- *Topics* articles that were posted as follow-ups to a previous posting to the interest group

Note that only the last one of these involves articles that were mailed directly to the interest group; the first two involve articles that originally appeared on *msgs*.

For calibration purposes, we also examined electronic mail. The electronic mail data was more recent and was taken from 12 users who volunteered to run the word-counting

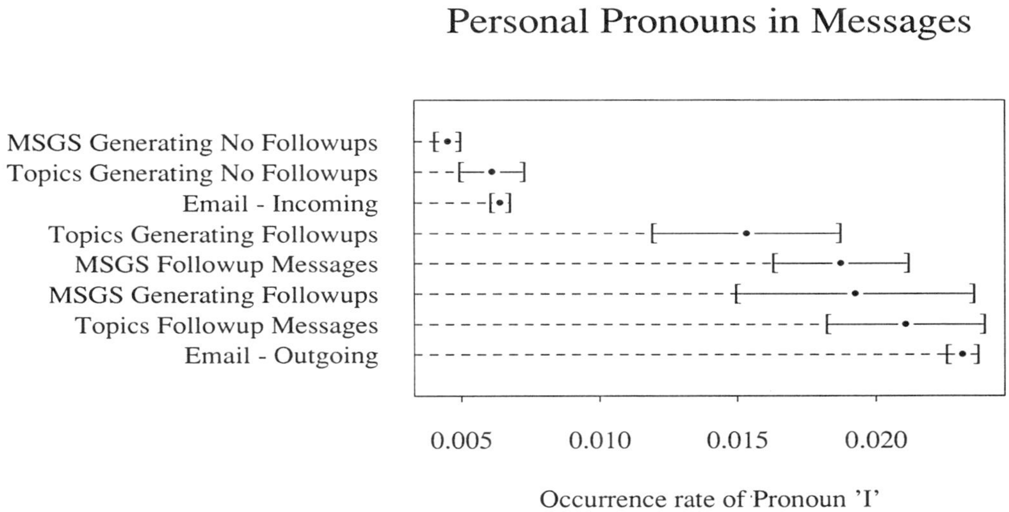

Figure 3 Analysis of the occurrence of the pronoun "I" in articles of different types. The plotted points indicate the estimated probability that a random word drawn from such messages is the pronoun "I". Brackets show 95% confidence intervals on the estimates.

scripts over their mail files. The two categories of mail examined were:

- incoming electronic mail – unfiltered collection of incoming e-mail articles received by the user
- outgoing electronic mail – unfiltered archives of outgoing e-mail articles sent by the user

We assume that outgoing mail is more personal on average than incoming mail, since the latter includes mass mailings. Put another way, outgoing mail counts articles before mail alias expansion multiplies their impact, whereas incoming mail is after alias expansion. Thus incoming mail includes proportionally more material written for bigger audiences. These two mail categories thus give some reference points for gauging the other categories of articles.

Figure 3 shows the proportion of the pronoun "I" in these different categories of articles. The first point to notice is that the proportions differ dramatically, with "I" being over four times more common in outgoing electronic mail than in articles that called forth no discussion (this difference is well over 10 standard errors).

There are several other notable patterns in these data. First articles that started discussions, either within *msgs* or *topics*, contained 2-3 times as many occurrences of "I" on average as those that did not; the follow-ups themselves had similar rates of occurrence of "I". In all, the rates for *topics* discussions were almost 75% of the rate for outgoing electronic mail. This result seems to indicate that articles in an informal style are more likely to spark discussion, and further that the discussion is more likely to be informal. The same rule seems to distinguish even the two categories of articles without follow-ups: the *msgs* articles that at least became topics by being "joined" (even if no discussion ensued) use "I" significantly more often, on average, than *msgs* articles that did not become topics. To summarize, ephemeral interest group postings are more informal than typical *msgs* articles, as we anticipated; but we did not find that ephemeral interest group discussions were significantly more informal than *discussions* taking place on *msgs*.

Increasing the Visibility of Ongoing Discussion Groups

One of our original expectations had been that the *topics* system would decrease follow-up traffic on *msgs*, while increasing the total number of follow-ups, by providing a more appropriate forum for informal discussion. When we compare the counts of follow-up articles in our study of pre-*topics* usage (April–May 1991) to the counts in the more recent study just described (October–November 1991), we see that the total amount of discussion did increase, but that there are only modest indications of a decrease in the follow-up traffic on *msgs* (p~.05). It appears that *topics*, though an attractive forum for many, is not attractive enough an alternative to draw a large proportion of follow-ups off of *msgs*.

We have already suggested part of an explanation: users had almost no reminder of the existence of topics. Indeed, a survey of *topics* users undertaken in mid-November 1991 showed that most of them were bothered by not knowing what interesting discussions they might be missing by not having joined the original posting on *msgs*. A week later, we conducted a small experiment to assess the extent to which a reminder facility would enable people to learn about important interest groups.

On November 25th an interest group was created to discuss issues related to a new set of management procedures at Bellcore. This group quickly gathered a large number of postings and subscribers, and thus seemed to be one that people might not have wanted to miss. Therefore, we posted

```
Message 10545:
From mlittman Fri Feb 14 08:52:25 1992
Subject: radio programming: coincidence or conspiracy?
(15 lines) #!topic:736 has 3 postings and 6 subscribers. [ynqj?]
```

Figure 4 Extension to *msgs*: Sample Prompt.

a reminder to the general *msgs* board the next day (November 26th) stating that a good discussion on this topic was underway and restating the instructions for how to join it. At the time of the posting of the reminder, the discussion group had 67 subscribers and 11 articles. Later we surveyed 41 of the users who joined the discussion group after the posting of this reminder to find out how they had joined the discussion. 23 users replied, giving a response rate of 56%. Of these 23 late joiners, only three had joined the discussion on the basis of the original article, indicating that the life-span of a *msgs* posting for attracting new interest group subscribers can at times be less than a day. Twenty subscribers joined in response to the reminder, though one stated that he had intended to go back to the original posting to join, but came across the reminder article first, and joined it instead. Thus 19 of the 23 respondents joined solely because of the reminder article, corresponding to 83% of the responding late joiners. Given that there were 65 late joiners in total, we can estimate that 54 joined because of the reminder article. In total, the ephemeral interest group ended up having 132 subscribers, so the posting of the reminder increased the membership by about 69% over what it would otherwise have been.

This indicates that *topics* usage would be greater if users could easily find out about ongoing discussions. In fairness, a few of the late joiners stated that they had joined because they respected the opinions of the person posting the reminder, so we should not expect that increasing *topics* visibility will necessarily cause as dramatic an increase in subscription as we saw in our experiment -- but it is clear nonetheless that the invisibility of discussions is a shortcoming of the current *topics* system.

SUMMARY AND FUTURE DIRECTIONS

We have introduced the notion of *ephemeral interest groups* and described the results of a first experiment in making them available to a large user community. Our findings show that such groups can be supported with minimal modification to a simple bulletin board system; that they appear to require a moderately large user community to be viable; that they can serve as a novel and effective form of information filtering; and that ephemeral interest group discussions are significantly more informal and personal than typical postings to *msgs*. Judging by an overall increase in follow-up traffic, ephemeral interest groups appear to have facilitated discussions that would not have taken place on *msgs*. However, not as much follow-up traffic as we had hoped has migrated off *msgs* into ephemeral interest groups. We believe the invisibility of ephemeral interest groups within *msgs* is an important factor influencing their ability to draw discussion traffic off of *msgs*, and one of our experiments supports that intuition.

We are currently experimenting with successors to *topics* that address the visibility problem and other shortcomings. One experimental system involves only slightly more obtrusive modifications to *msgs*. If a *msgs* article has already spawned an ephemeral interest group, that information is included in the *msgs* prompt (see Figure 4). In addition, users can directly access a list of current groups, their subscription lists, and their digests, directly from the *msgs* interface. These additional commands are not advertised in the prompt, but are described if the user type '?' for help. The modifications, though more substantial than our original modifications, still do not disturb the original *msgs* functionality for users uninterested in our innovations.

In a second experimental system, called Lynx, we abandon the *msgs* program altogether. A primary goal of Lynx is not only to address usability problems in the *msgs* program, but also to generalize the use of ephemeral interest groups to information sources other than *msgs*. Lynx provides a uniform, network-transparent browser to make information sources in our local environment more easily accessible, and to permit ephemeral interest groups to be spawned from items from any of those sources. In addition to the *msgs* information source, Lynx includes the Associated Press newswire, a calendar of events automatically extracted from *msgs*, and Unix man pages. Lynx provides facilities for browsing active and archived ephemeral interest groups. Finally, it also draws on local information sources to generate profiles of fellow group participants, including their pictures, locations, organizational affiliations, technical reports, etc., so that one can easily get to know other members of the community.

REFERENCES

1. Conklin, J., and Begeman, M. L. (1988). gIBIS: A hypertext tool for exploratory policy discussion. *ACM Trans. Office Information Systems* **6**, 4 (October 1988), pp. 303–331. Also in *Proc. 2nd Conf. Computer-Supported Cooperative Work* (Portland, OR, 26–28 September), pp. 140–152.
2. Halasz, F. G. (1988). Reflections on NoteCards: Seven issues for the next generation of hypermedia systems. *Communications of the ACM* **31**, 7 (July), pp. 835–852.
3. Hollan, J. D., and Stornetta, W. S. (1992). Beyond Being There. *ACM CHI'92 Proceedings*, pp. 119–125.
4. Monty, M. L. (1986). Temporal context and memory for notes stored in the computer. *ACM SIGCHI Bulletin* **18**, 2 (October), pp. 50–51.
5. Nielsen, J. (1990). *Hypertext and Hypermedia*. Academic Press, San Diego, CA.

How a Group-Editor Changes the Character of a Design Meeting as well as its Outcome

Judith S. Olson, Gary M. Olson, Marianne Storrøsten, Mark Carter

Cognitive Science and Machine Intelligence Laboratory
The University of Michigan
701 Tappan Street
Ann Arbor, MI 48109-1234
(313) 747-4948 olsons@csmil.umich.edu

ABSTRACT

This study reports how the introduction of a simple collaborative tool changed the way groups of people did an interesting problem solving task, the design of an automatic post office. The designs produced by the groups supported with this tool were of higher quality than those who worked with conventional whiteboard and paper and pencil. They liked the process a little less, probably because it was a new tool. But, more surprising was the fact that those supported with the tool did *less* extensive exploration of the design space. Our expectation was just the opposite. It appears that the tool helped the supported group keep more focused on the *core* issues in the emerging design, to waste less time on less important topics, and to capture what was said as they went.

KEYWORDS

Group support system, face-to-face work, concurrent editing, small group behavior

INTRODUCTION

Since the heart of the work in companies is done in groups, many people are designing a variety of new technologies to support it. The new technologies range from group decision rooms to asynchronous conferencing systems that help participants coordinate work across time and space. In our research, we are concentrating on the kind of group work that happens in small groups, such as project teams or task forces. We are looking for ways to support the "meeting" part of this work with various kinds of technology, initially for those meetings that take place face-to-face.

Our research strategy began by understanding group work in the field [13, 15] where we noted important baseline features of group work and gathered ideas about how various kinds of technology can help. We have now moved to the laboratory to study specific phenomena, such as how technologies change the flow of activities in meetings or affect the quality of the work. From these laboratory studies, we will move back to the field, assessing the use of these new technologies in the full organizational context. This strategy has the benefit that we are informed by actual practice and can eventually test ideas in the field, but also puts the burden on us to construct laboratory situations that mirror the field in important ways. This paper reports a laboratory study that fits into this overall research strategy.

Others have looked at various kinds of technology to support groups in face-to-face meetings, finding mixed results [7, 10]. One of the reasons the results are mixed is the difficulty of running a large number of intact groups. Most studies involve only a small number of such groups, and some resort to artificial groups whose members are new to each other. One goal of our research is to invest the time to run enough groups so that reliable effects can be determined above the noise of inherent between-group variation.

A second difficulty in comparing results from these studies is that they differ widely in both the tasks presented to the group and the kind of technology offered to them. For example, the groups in many studies are led by a facilitator who structures the discussion into phases of brainstorming, commenting, and voting, with various electronic support tools for each phase [4, 12]. Other studies use technology that is more free form [21] where the group organizes their activities on their own, using the tools whenever they seem appropriate. There is no general answer to whether technology helps or hinders these groups. It depends on the *tasks* the groups are engaged in, and it depends on what the *technology* does [17].

This paper reports how one kind of technology, a group editor, changes the face-to-face work of small groups of people working in the laboratory on a design task. We examined the meetings of 38 existing groups of people using either conventional meeting tools or a new group editor that allows all participants to see and edit the same document at the same time. We use a detailed analysis of their moment-by-moment talking and typing to study the *process* of group work. Since they are doing a standard

Permission to copy without fee all or part of this material is granted provided that the copies are not made or distributed for direct commercial advantage, the ACM copyright notice and the title of the publication and its date appear, and notice is given that copying is by permission of the Association for Computing Machinery. To copy otherwise, or to republish, requires a fee and/or specific permission.

© 1992 ACM 0-89791-543-7/92/0010/0091...$1.50

task, we can measure the quality of the *outcome* of their work, and through questionnaires can measure their *satisfaction* with their work.

METHOD

Subjects

The subjects were 38 existing groups of three professionals. Most of the groups consisted of three MBAs[1] each enrolled in the Michigan Business School, with a few consisting of one MBA and two of that person's work cohorts. In all groups, the members had worked together before in class or work projects and all knew at least one Macintosh application.

Setting

The group members were seated in a meeting room called the Collaboration Technology Suite (CTS) [14] in which workstation units make up a conference table, with the monitors recessed in the table top so as not to interfere with normal eye contact. One wall of the room has two large panels of whiteboard, which all groups were allowed to use. In practice, all but two unsupported groups used it for collecting their ideas, typically in lists; only one supported group used it, for a quick drawing of the proposed layout. All the sessions were video-taped.

Task

We chose to study the task of group design, that of early requirements definition, because it is both important and interesting. The early stages of design are probably the most important in the development of useful, usable, maintainable software [1, 3] And, the early stage of design is interesting because it is a classic example of an ill-structured problem [20].

In terms of McGrath's [8] task taxonomy, this activity is a blend of Planning, Creativity, Decision-Making and Cognitive Conflict. Our observations of design in the field show a seemingly erratic sequence of these subtasks, with associations, implications and evaluations taking the group from one topic to the next and back. But by categorizing details of the activity in the episodes into core design activities and coordination activities, we found interesting, systematic patterns of behavior [16]. In particular, groups engaged in periods of design activity, punctuated by coordination episodes. The behavior within each kind of activity showed strong regularities, and there was little intermixing. Once designing, the group designed; when they needed coordination, they did that for a time, and then jumped back into the regular design pattern.

In this study, all groups were instructed to draft the initial requirements definition for an Automatic Post Office (APO), a collection of postal services offered through a stand-alone device similar to an ATM for which a prototype could be built by their fictitious company of 30 people in a year. They were instructed to determine the core services they would offer, some of the required equipment, the rough cost/benefit analysis, and a list of things they would like to investigate before the next time they would (hypothetically) meet. They were given 1-1/2 hours to complete the assignment, producing meeting notes that could be read by a (fictitious) additional group member who could not attend that day's meeting.

Technology Support

The technology used here was one we designed and built called "ShrEdit," which stands for *Sh*ared *Edit*or [9] Its features were motivated from an analysis of the ways in which groups work in the field with conventional tools [15]. This analysis suggested that a number of observed difficulties would be alleviated by having a shared, editable display of their current work object. Since the design task is a small-group, free flowing task, we did not embed any particular design methodology or require a facilitator. ShrEdit is a simple text editor which allows all participants to view and change the same simple text document, with all participants being able to type simultaneously within one character position of each other. Although the individuals' views of the document are normally independent (each can scroll to a different part of the document or arrange the windows on the screen in a unique way), the views can also be locked together if the discussion calls for it.

Procedure

The subjects came to the CTS for a single three-hour period, broken into two 1-1/2 hour portions with a 15 minute break in between. In the first half, the subjects filled out background questionnaires and permission forms, and solved two small problems. These tasks served both to allow the subjects to warm up to the task situation and, for those in the supported condition, to learn the software and adjust to the software's capability for simultaneous editing. Those taught the technology were instructed in a 20 minute period before the two small problems. The instructions demonstrated the system's capabilities and how to control them, but did not prescribe how to use these features to support work. Those in the control condition were encouraged to use paper and pencil or whiteboard as is natural for their group. Following a 15 minute break, the groups did the APO task in a single 1-1/2 hour sitting. All groups filled out the questionnaire on satisfaction after the session. The unsupported groups were taught the software and given a 10 minute group task after the questionnaire.

Study Design

Groups were recruited en masse through various MBA classes, and encouraged to sign up at convenient times, either morning, afternoon, or evening sessions for three hours. The groups were assigned to conditions at random as they came in with the proviso that at the end of each week the conditions were balanced for time of day.

[1]Ninety percent of the MBAs at Michigan have significant work experience before coming back to school. These are professionals with practical group experience.

Measures

Our goal was to assess three things: the quality of the product, the participants' satisfaction with the process, and the process of design and coordination.

Outcome.

We assessed how the technology affected the *outcomes* of the meetings, the quality of the design as reflected in the final document of each group. In order to allow fair comparisons, the unsupported groups' written outputs were typed in the same style as the supported groups' output.

We developed a quality measure after extensive discussion with both designers and researchers of design. Three major aspects of the groups' output were scored: how completely the output covered all the aspects of the assigned task, the ease of understanding of the ideas reported in the document, and the judged quality of the post office design, including the feasibility of producing a prototype of the suggested post office within the stated time and manpower constraints, the coherence of the ideas, and the judged success of the ideas if marketed. Each aspect was then detailed further and a rating form constructed. Six researchers then coded the output from the same six meetings. The average pairwise correlation between raters was .85. Since this was well above acceptable range for reliability of measures, one researcher then coded the quality of the remaining 32 meetings' outputs using the same instrument. Out of a possible score of 80 points, the quality of the meetings ranged from 29-78.

Satisfaction.

To assess satisfaction, we constructed a post-session questionnaire that asked the participants to a) rate their satisfaction with the *process* that they used (adapted from [5, 6]) as well as with the design *result* [6], b) assess the evenness of the participants' contributions [6] and c) identify a leader if one emerged.

Process.

The transcripts of the meetings were coded for what kinds of activity were taking place at each moment, using the categories devised and tested in our study of field design meetings [15] The measures on various key aspects of activity related to design itself, with origins in the Design Rationale literature [11]. We also catalogued the time it took the group to organize themselves (an activity we call "meeting management"), to clarify their ideas, talk through difficulties with the technology, or engage in side digressions. The division of activity into task and process management was inspired by work in the literature [19, 22].

Several new categories were required to account for the work associated with producing the output: times when they would plan the organization and wording or dictate the words, called Plan and Write. In the supported groups, we required yet another two categories: times when they were confused about something having to do with the technology, and other comments about the placing of their work into the windows on the screen. We called these Technology Confusion and Technology Management, respectively.

Inter-rater reliability of the core 22 categories were measured in two ways. A strict measure shows the correspondence of categorization, second by second; our inter-rater reliability is .68%, with a Cohen's K = .64. If we look at the summary measures used, the correlation between the two raters' summary statistics on time in category is .97.

We also analyzed the groups for the breadth and depth of their discussions. To do this, we coded the transcripts not only for the type of activity, but noted which particular topic they were discussing at each moment. That is, we constructed a Design Rationale diagram, which connects the topic, the alternative solutions to the question posed, and the evaluative comments raised both for and against each proposed solution, independent of *when* each event occurred, or how many times the same alternative was mentioned. The notation is similar to that developed by researchers who advocate the use of a notation scheme to capture the aspects of design while it is happening. We use it instead to code the development of natural design activity. An example of part of a connected issue, alternative set, and associated criterial comments are shown in Figure 1.

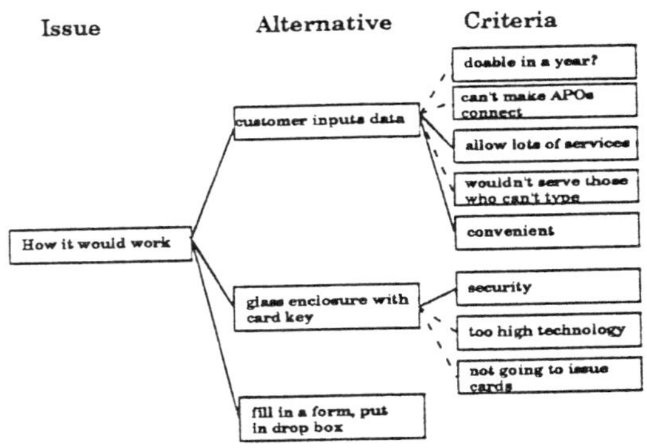

Figure 1. Portion of a Design Rationale.

RESULTS

The results are organized by the major classes of measures as described above: outcome, satisfaction, and process. But first, since this laboratory work was motivated by work in the field and we wish to generalize back to the field, we examine the correspondence between the measures of process in the field and that found in our *unsupported* laboratory condition.

Comparison of Unsupported Work in the Laboratory and the Field

The laboratory situation we chose was intended to be similar to early requirements tasks we examined in the field [15]. It differed from the field in that the participants met only once, were not concerned with their performance for career advancement, and did not have to spend the company's money to make the post office they designed. However, the task did require an examination of features to offer the user, how the device could work, and assessment of feasibility in terms of resources and benefit to the client. To assess the correspondence, we compared the behavior of our groups in the unsupported laboratory condition with that of the field groups on two key measures: the amount of time they spent doing various aspects of design versus managing their group process, and the breadth and depth of their discussions.

In general we found that the time spent in the laboratory task matched that in the field, with a few explainable exceptions. There was virtually no time spent doing project management in the lab, since the groups met only once, and they spent less time in clarifying the ideas in the lab study, presumably because the participants were solving a problem for which they have nearly equal expertise. And, since the lab groups were required to write up a document, they spent a significant portion of their time doing this, about 12%. The correlation between the lab and field groups for 22 base categories of activity is 0.62, using figures that exclude laboratory groups' writing time; with "project management" and all "clarification" time removed, the correlation rises to .69. They explored the issues more broadly in the laboratory, with 7 alternatives raised per issue in the lab and only 2.5 in the field. Since the nature of the task in the lab had people generate *lists* of features, benefits, and costs, it is reasonable that they would consider more such ideas. They raised about the same number of issues per hour in the two situations, and made similar kind of evaluative arguments. We are thus satisfied that the problem solving aspects of these two tasks are roughly comparable, and whatever we find in the lab in terms of effects of technology on group process has a chance of relating back to the field.

Outcome differences

Two key measures of the output of the session are shown in Table 1: the quality, as described above, and the length of the document. The average judged quality of the groups supported by ShrEdit was significantly higher than that for conventional groups ($t(36) = 2.32$, $p<.03$). Interestingly, the distribution of unsupported groups was far wider than the supported groups ($F(18,18) = 2.86$, $p<.05$). Something about the technology not only added to the average quality, but significantly raised the tail of the distribution.

Table 1.
Analysis of features of groups' output

	Quality	Length
Supported Groups	64.0	711 words
Unsupported Groups	55.5	391 words

On average, the groups using ShrEdit produced final documents that were twice as long ($t(36)=2.78$, $p<.01$). For the people with ShrEdit, the text explanation of their ideas was either in sentence form or more fully fleshed out, whereas the output from unsupported meetings consisted mainly of bullet lists. Overall, however, there was no correlation between length of document and quality ($r(37)= .29$, $p > .05$), nor within each of the conditions (unsupported $r(18)= .12$, $p > .05$, supported $r(18) = .27$, $p > .05$).

Satisfaction

Analysis of the questionnaires on satisfaction revealed very few differences between the two groups. In general both groups were satisfied with the process they used in generating, discussing and deciding on their design, and they liked their final post office design. However, the unsupported groups were marginally more satisfied with the discussion quality ($t(36) = 2.74$, $p < .01$) and they rated the problem solving process to be more even and fair ($t(36) = 2.24$, $p < 0.03$). However, both kinds of groups rated their groups equally when indicating whether one individual influenced the outcome more than others.

Process differences

What is it that produced the quality differences? We now look at how the groups spent their time, how they moved among activities in the course of design, and the breadth and depth of their discussions.

One way in which these groups differed was the amount of time spent on each of the subactivities. We coded the transcripts of the spoken parts of the meetings, noting the kinds of activities they engaged in, and then summarized how much total time was spent in each activity as well as the flow between activities. Figure 2 shows a view of the flow of activities, the unsupported groups on the left, the supported ones on the right. Comparable pictures of the times and transitions for field design groups can be found in [15]. Each category of activity is represented by a circle, the area of which represents the total time the group spent in that activity, aggregated over the whole meeting. White portions of the circle represent the direct introduction of the idea; the black wedges represent the time spent clarifying that topic. The arrows denote the transitions between them, the width of which reflects the likelihood of going from one category to the next.[2]

Most categories of activity are very similar across the supported and unsupported groups. Of interest, about the same amount of time (4%) is spent in managing the flow of meetings in both conditions, and they plan the writing for about the same amount of time (11% and 9% for supported and unsupported, respectively). The ShrEdit groups spend 7% of their time asking each other questions about the technology because they are unsure or confused.

Groups in these two conditions, however, differ in several striking ways. There is a clear tradeoff between the amount of time spent in discussing the design itself (the alternatives and their evaluative criteria) and the amount of

[2]To make this diagram less "busy," we include here only those transitions that occurred 1% of time or more.

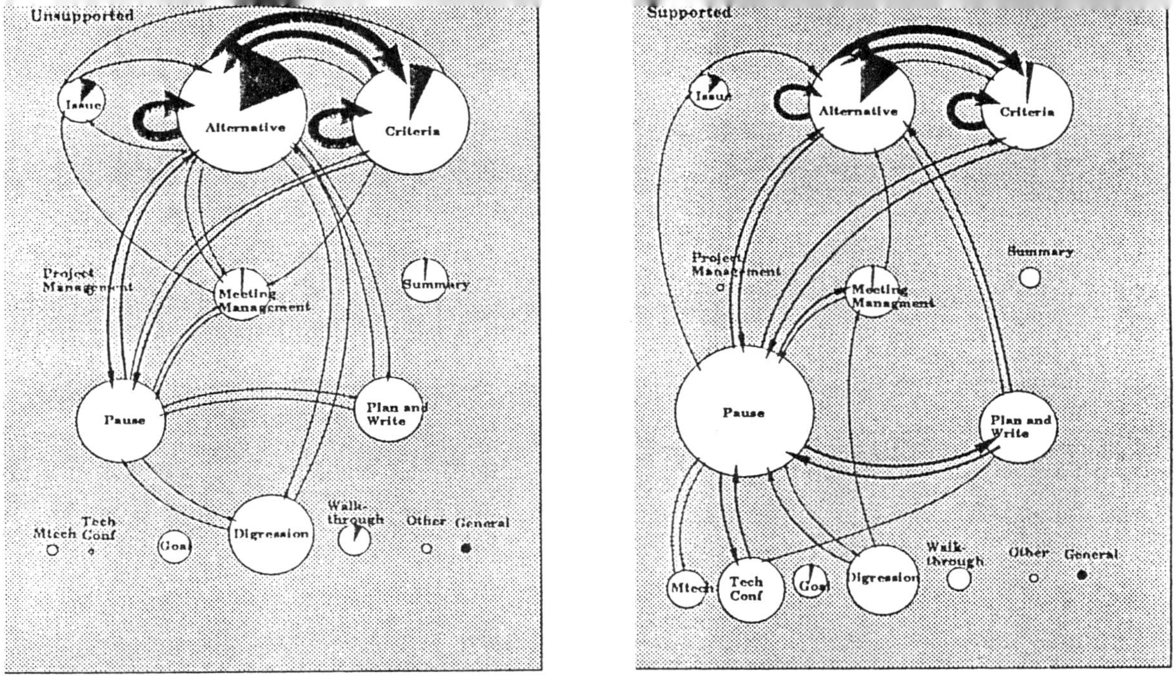

Figure 2. The timing and flow of activities in each category

time dictating and writing.[3] People supported with ShrEdit spent less time than the unsupported groups in direct discussion of issues, alternatives, and criteria (34% vs 53% for supported vs unsupported, respectively, $t(36) = 5.33$, $p<.001$). They spent much more time writing down their design (at least the amount that occurs during pauses) than the unsupported groups did (28% vs 13%, $t(36)=4.09$ $p<.001$).

Of note here is the activity in and out of pause, which occurred four times as many times in the supported groups compared to unsupported. In the supported groups, the writing of the ideas (which occurs primarily in the pauses) is much more interspersed than in the unsupported groups, and the average time spent writing is shorter for the supported groups (5 sec. per episode on average vs 10 sec for supported vs unsupported). In unsupported meetings the discussion of alternatives occurs with some note-taking on the board while they talk and *then* write their final reports.

We next coded the content of the discussion using Design Rationale notation, described earlier. Using this kind of analysis, we can compare these unsupported and supported groups for how many issues were raised, how many alternative solutions were raised for each issue, and how extensive the discussion was to evaluate each alternative raised.

[3]There was more writing than indicated here. This is the writing that is done when no one is speaking, or when someone is dictating word for word. It does not include time when someone wrote *while* other talking was going on. This is particularly important in interpreting the category "Digression," which often occurred between two people while a third wrote, in both conditions.

Table 2 shows the distribution of issues, alternatives, and criteria raised. Some striking differences appear. The unsupported groups covered more issues, and raised more alternatives than the supported groups did ($t(18)=3.11$, $p<.004$; $t(18)=2.24$, $p>.03$). Looking more closely, however, it turns out that the groups covered an equivalent proportion of the *core* topics[4] but the unsupported groups raised and discussed twice as many *ancillary* issues (8 vs. 4; $t(36)=3.08$, $p<.005$), each with on average 3 alternatives and only one evaluative statement. So, some of the extra time these unsupported groups spent on design is on less central topics.

Table 2.
Details of the depth and breadth of design discussion

	Average Numbers of Issues	Alternatives	Criteria
Supported	13.3	120.8	128.5
Unsupported	17.9	144.6	169.5

Also, the unsupported groups spent on average significantly more time per unique alternative than the supported groups (6.6 sec vs 8.3 sec, $t(36)=2.39$, $p<.02$). Observation shows that rather than this time being spent in explaining or elaborating the idea, it is spent merely repeating the ideas at various delays. Taken together, it appears that although the supported groups are spending more time "on design," they are not necessarily designing more.

[4]Core topics were the ten that the problem statement prompted them to talk about. Ancillary ones were topics the group brought up that were beyond the core ten.

There is one more difference that the technology affords. We compared the ideas (issues/alternatives/criteria) that were spoken some time during the meeting with those that appeared in the final document. Table 3 shows the comparisons between what appears in the final document and what is spoken for the groups in the two conditions, and the number of ideas that appear in the documents that were *never* spoken, called "extra."

Table 3
Ideas spoken, captured, and written without speech.

	Spoken	Captured	Extra
Supported	120.8	35.8	18.4
Unsupported	133.6	39.1	12.6

Two things are of interest here. First, many more ideas are spoken than appear in the final document. Some, of course, are ideas that are discussed and rejected. Most groups generate harebrained ideas (e.g., teleconferencing facility in an ATM-like post office station) as well as reasonable ones that they decide to eliminate (e.g., an address/zip code data base that serves marketing needs as well). But some are merely forgotten. Both kinds of groups captured about the same proportion of the alternatives raised (30% and 27% for supported and unsupported), and almost none of the criteria (2.6% and 1.7% respectivley).

But also of interest is the number of "extra" ideas written in both conditions. There are some ideas that appear on the final document that were never discussed. Both groups add these extra ideas. It appears that the one who "holds the pen" has some license. In the supported groups, however, *all* hold the pen, and all can see the extra items if they choose. Except for one unsupported group who passed the paper version of their output around to the other group members for checking, none of the unsupported groups' members saw the final output except its author.

So it appears from the analysis that there are differences in the way the groups approach the problem. The unsupported groups discuss more alternatives and evaluate them more, then write them down en masse at the end. The supported groups capture their ideas in the final document as they go (they have five times as many writing episodes, each half the length of those from the unsupported groups). Both groups add to the final document items that were never talked about, but in supported groups there is a chance that the other group members will read them and object if they disagree.

What correlates with quality?

Since all groups in this study were solving the same problem, we had a chance not only to look at the aggregate differences between the two support conditions and quality, but also to look within conditions for relationships among our process measures and quality. We examined whether quality was related to the time spent on writing, on raising alternatives, or on evaluating with various criteria, as well the number of issues and alternatives raised, and the number of criteria generated.

For supported groups *none* of the variables were significantly correlated with quality, likely because the variance among the quality scores was relatively small (from 49 to 78 on an 80 point scale, with a large number clustered very near the mean of 65). For the unsupported groups, which had a wider variance, an interesting pattern emerged, fitting with the major pattern of differences between groups. Interestingly, the *less* time spent on design (issues, alternatives, criteria and their clarifications), the higher the quality; the more time on writing (which includes "pauses" and "digressions" which cover occasions when one person is writing and the others are having a side conversation) the higher the quality ($r(18)=.44$, $p<.06$ for design; $r(18)=.58$, $p<.01$ for writing). Unsupported groups were better when they spent *less* time per alternative ($r(18)=.43$, $p<.07$). Quality was better also when there were *fewer* issues covered, and when core issues had more alternatives explored ($r(18)=.58$, $p<.02$).

The Use of ShrEdit

How much of the time is the technology being used? Do people ever type simultaneously? What do they do when typing simultaneously? Note that in teaching the groups ShrEdit we introduced them to the features, but we did not tell them how to use them to support various aspects of the meeting's work.

To answer these questions, we catalogued the timing of the keystrokes for each person individually and noted overlap. Since a keystroke is an instantaneous event, we assumed that a person's attention was paid to typing both a second before each keystroke and a second after. Using this technique, we found that, on average, simultaneous typing occurred 10% of the time. Figure 3 shows the timeline of typing and talking activity for one group[18]. The top twelve lines show the typing activity of three people in each of three windows, as well as their activity in private windows. The next three lines show aggregate talking by each of the three participants.

Looking at the transcript for these episodes, we note that in the earlier bursts, the group is typically brainstorming for features the post office should have. The second burst is typically what we call "divide and conquer," where group members take various sections of their emerging document and flesh it out. In several groups, for example, one wrote the introduction, while others expanded on the costs and benefits of this particular design.

In contrast, the unsupported groups use the white board to capture ideas as they occur, one at a time. They then stop their discussion early to begin the slow job of getting the ideas down on paper. This is typically done by one person

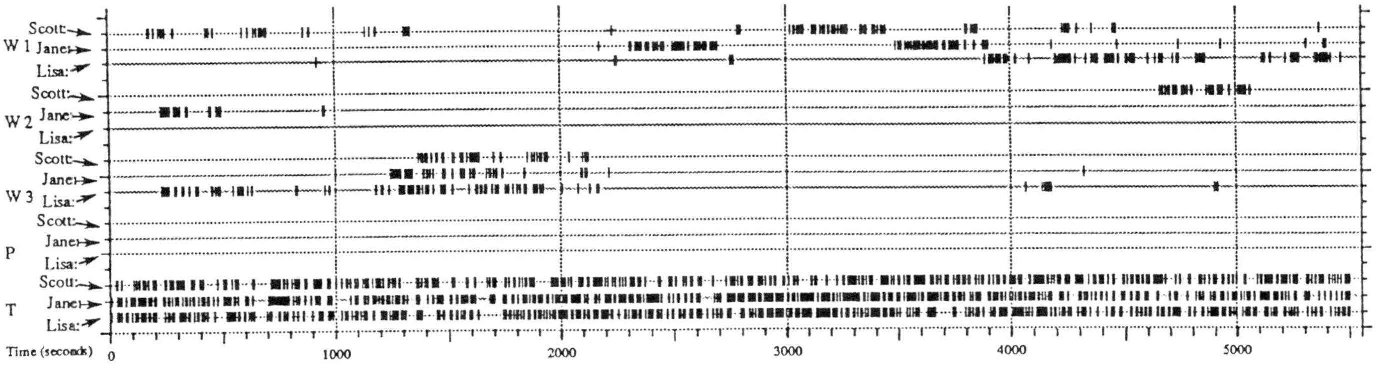

Figure 3. The pattern of typing activity in various windows by the three participants, and the general talking activity.

who "dictates" the ideas out loud for the others to confirm and/or question.

CONCLUSIONS

We gave subjects who were doing an interesting problem solving task (i.e., design) a simple collaborative tool to assist them in their face-to-face work. The tool provided no particular process support or structure to their work. They were free to organize their activities as they wished. By the time they did our target design task they had had about an hour's practice in using the new electronic workspace tool.

Yet this simple tool and this limited experience had a profound effect on their work. The designs they produced were of higher quality than those of the control groups who worked in a more traditional fashion. They liked the process a little less, perhaps not surprising given the use of a new technology. But most surprising of all was the way in which they worked. They actually did a less extensive exploration of the design space than the traditional, unsupported groups, contrary to our expectations. Instead of encouraging a more exhaustive look at design ideas, something about the technology led them to a more selective examination of what turned out to be better ideas. They seemed to focus more on the core issues, and captured and examined by reading what they were thinking *while they worked,* rather than in two stages-- once on the whiteboard and once on paper while those other than the scribe talked about other things.

We can only speculate about a lot of things that might have produced the effect: shared access to an easily editable workspace that permitted parallel work when appropriate; an easier blending of the activities of idea generation, idea selection, and report generation; early capture of good ideas that led to a quicker consensus about a sensible design; a mixed mode of participation (talking and typing) that favored consensus development as opposed to unfettered exploration of fringe design ideas. All of these are plausible, and so far our analyses have not pushed deeply enough to sort them out.

The technology had other direct effects on the behavior of the supported groups. They spent a large amount of their time (7%) trying to figure out the technology itself. On average they spent 10% of their time doing parallel work, though as we showed, in general this tended to be concentrated at specific stages of their work. They used the technology to capture ideas that they never felt compelled to talk about, since everyone could see the ideas as they emerged and comment if they disagreed.

Our overall impression is that the simple group editor we gave these subjects was a functional and useful tool. This was true despite its shortcomings of functionality and interface that were revealed by the subjects' use and comments [2]. On the basis of relatively little experience the subjects were able to organize their work with the aid of this tool.

In the final analysis, both the significant and non-significant results are interesting. Some confirm our notions of what makes a good meeting; some tell us that prescriptions we hold about good meetings (e.g., that discussing more alternatives is better) may not be widely true. To our knowledge, no one has ever before run this complete an analysis of technology's effect on work--run enough groups to overcome variability, analyzed the process in such detail, and had the opportunity to ferret out the relationship between process and quality of outcome.

ACKNOWLEDGEMENTS

This work has been supported by the National Science Foundation (Grant No. IRI-8902930), by the Center for Strategic Technology Research (CSTaR) at Andersen Consulting, by Arthur Andersen & Co., by Apple Computer, and by Steelcase, Inc.. Many people have participated in the collection and analysis of the data reported here, including Stacey Donahue, Alex Eulenberg, Barb Gamm, Jim Herbsleb, Robin Lampert, Mary Jane T. Lu, Brenda Montgomery, Max Rahder, Meredith Reitman, Adrienne Royce, Henry Rueter, Sue Schuon, Michael Walker, Rodney Walker, Garrick Wang, and Corinne Weirich.

REFERENCES

1. Curtis, B., Krasner, H., and Iscoe, N. (1988) A field study of the software design process for large systems. *CACM,* 31, 1268-1287.

2. Dourish, P, and Bellotti, V. (1992) Awareness and coordination in shared workspaces. *Proceedings of the Conference on Computer Supported Cooperative Work.*

3. Dunn, R. (1984) *Software defect removal.* NY: McGraw-Hill.

4. Gallupe, R., DeSanctis, G., and Dickson, G. (1988) Computer-based support for group problem solving: An experimental investigation. *MISQ,* 12, 277-296.

5. Gouran, D. S., Brown, C., and Henry, D. R. (1978) Behavioral correlates of perceptions of quality in decision-making discussions. *Communication Monographs.* 45(1), March, 51-63.

6. Green, S. G., and Taber, T. D. (1980) The effects of three social decision schemes on decision group process. *Organizational Behavior and Human Performance.* 25, 97-106.

7. Hollingshead, A. B., and McGrath, J. E., (in press) The whole is less than the sum of its parts: A critical review of research on computer-assisted groups. In R. Guzzo (Ed.) *Team Decision Making in Organizations.* San Francisco: Jossey-Bass.

8. McGrath, J. E. (1984) *Groups: Interaction and performance.* Englewood Cliffs, NJ: Prentice-Hall.

9. McGuffin, L., and Olson, G. M. (1992) ShrEdit: A shared electronic workspace. CSMIL Technical Report, The University of Michigan.

10. McLeod, P. L. (1992) An assessment of the experimental literature on electronic support of group work. *Human Computer Interaction.*

11. Moran, T. and Carroll, J., (Eds.) (in preparation) *Design Rationale.*

12. Nunamaker, J. F., Dennis, A. R., Valacich, J. S., Vogel, D. R. and George, J. F. (1991) Electronic meeting systems to support group work. *CACM,* 34(7) 43-61.

13. Olson, G. M. and Olson, J. S. (1991) User-centered design of collaboration technology. *Journal of Organizational Computing,* 1, 61-83.

14. Olson, G. M., Olson, J. S., Killey, L., Mack, L. A., Cornell, P., and Luchetti, R. (in press) Flexible facilities for electronic meetings. In S. Kinney, R. Bostrom, and R. Watson, (Eds) *Computer Augmented Teamwork: A Guided Tour.* Van Nostrand Reinhold.

15. Olson, G. M., Olson, J. S., Carter, M., and Storrøsten, M. (1992) Small group design meetings: An analysis of collaboration. *Human Computer Interaction.*

16. Olson, G. M., Olson, J. S., Storrøsten, M, Carter, M., Herbsleb, J., and Rueter, H. (in press) The structure of activity during design meetings. In T. Moran and J. Carroll (Eds.) *Design Rationale.*

17. Olson, J. S., Olson, G. M., Mack, L. A., and Wellner, P. (1990) Concurrent editing: The group's interface. In D. Diaper et al (Eds.) *Human-computer interaction INTERACT'90,* Elsevier, North-Holland.

18. Olson, J. S., and Storrøsten, M. (1990) Finding the golden thread: Representations of the analysis of videotaped group work. *CSMIL Technical Report, University of Michigan.*

19. Putnam, L. L. (1983) Small group work climates: A lag-sequential analysis of group interaction. *Small Group Behavior,* 14(4), 465-494.

20. Reitman, W. R. (1965) *Cognition and Thought* New York: Wiley.

21. Stefik, M., Foster, G., Bobrow, D. G., Kahn, K., Lanning, S. and Suchman, L.A. (1987) Beyond the chalkboard: Computer support for collaboration and problem solving meetings. *CACM,* 30(1), 32-47.

22. Zigurs, I., Poole, M. S., and DeSanctis, G. L. (1988) A study of influence in computer-mediated group decision making. *MISQ,* 12, 645-665.

Unblocking Brainstorming Through the Use of a Simple Group Editor

Charles McLaughlin Hymes, Gary M. Olson

Cognitive Science and Machine Intelligence Laboratory
University of Michigan
701 Tappan Street
Ann Arbor, Michigan, 48109-1234

Internet: chymes@csmil.umich.edu,gmo@csmil.umich.edu
Telephone: (313)-747-4948

ABSTRACT

Earlier studies of computerized brainstorming showed that by restructuring group processes, groups can overcome well known performance deficits that groups suffer relative to nominal groups. These earlier tools are essentially computerized versions of Nominal Group Technique. We examined the ability of a simple, unstructured parallel editor to facilitate idea generation in face to face groups. Our results showed that parallel interacting groups outperformed serial interacting groups, and parallel interacting groups did not differ significantly from nominal, non interacting groups. Thus, an informal tool that allows parallel work is an effective way to increase idea generation in real interacting groups.

KEYWORDS

Parallel Communication, Brainstorming, ShrEdit, Shared Editor

INTRODUCTION

A critical question for new emerging CSCW technologies is what their effect is on the work of groups and organizations who use them. As recent reviews [1, 2] have shown, a very mixed picture is emerging from the experimental literature. For instance, McLeod [2] concluded on the basis of a meta-analysis of published studies on group support systems that the technologies increased decision quality, equality of participation, and degree of task focus, but decreased consensus and satisfaction and increased the time needed to reach a decision. Thus, it already seems clear that the answer to questions about the effects of CSCW technologies is going to be quite complex, and will require a concerted empirical attack. What is required is separating component activities and looking at various features of tools and their effects on each activity. This paper does just this. We look at a simple, unstructured tool being used for one phase of problem solving, idea generation.

Permission to copy without fee all or part of this material is granted provided that the copies are not made or distributed for direct commercial advantage, the ACM copyright notice and the title of the publication and its date appear, and notice is given that copying is by permission of the Association for Computing Machinery. To copy otherwise, or to republish, requires a fee and/or specific permission.

© 1992 ACM 0-89791-543-7/92/0010/0099...$1.50

Many collaborative tasks involve problem solving, and as a result a number of CSCW technologies are emerging to support the problem-solving activities of groups. Problem solving has many stages, ranging from problem identification, idea generation, idea structuring, idea selection or decision making, and implementation. One approach to supporting these many stages is to create suites of tools, each tailored to a specific stage (e.g., Arizona's Plexus system, [3] Minnesota's SAMM system, [4]) As we will see below, these structured tools have shown some early promise in supporting group idea generation. We now need to know what specific features of these tools enhance productivity, and whether simpler, unstructured tools can support this phase of problem solving as well.

Idea generation is a critical component of many problem solving tasks. Everyone's intuitions are that to generate many ideas one ought to convene a group of people and brainstorm [5]. However, thirty years of research on brainstorming have led to a very clear and surprising outcome: For a given set of individuals, one can get both more ideas and more quality ideas by having them work by themselves and pooling their ideas (the so-called nominal group) than by working together as an interacting group [6].

There are many possible reasons for this [6, 7]. Among the most commonly discussed ones are:

- **evaluation apprehension** -- working in a group makes one's contributions visible to others, and despite the usual brainstorming instructions not to evaluate others' ideas, the members of a group can still be reticent to contribute their ideas

- **free riding** -- individual members of a group might not expend the effort since other members of the group are contributing ideas
- limited air time -- when only one person can speak at a time, there is limited time for each individual to contribute
- **production blocking** -- because of limited air time, individuals often have to hold on to their contributions until they get a chance to report them, and as a result they might forget them, or they might decide not to offer them; in either case, the act of holding on to them will prevent them from thinking of other ideas
- **cognitive inertia** -- at each moment only one line of ideas is being generated, since they are reported serially; groups will therefore tend to pursue fewer different kinds of ideas

In general, while all of these factors might play some role, it looks as if production blocking (and its associated factor, air time) is the dominant reason for the reduced productivity of real interacting groups relative to nominal ones [6].

Given the key role of production blocking, one obvious strategy is to allow interacting groups to report their ideas in parallel. Nominal Group Technique (or NGT; [8]) is a formal method for giving interacting groups the advantages of a nominal group. NGT has people generate their ideas in parallel on paper, and then exchange them with each other as a way of stimulating the flow of ideas that should be the advantage of groups. Madsen and Finger [9] followed this procedure by redistributing the groups' ideas at regular intervals. through written lists The groups using this technique were forbidden to communicate with each other except through the exchange of lists of ideas. In this sense they were quite similar to nominal groups in that ordinary conversation was absent. They found that the group using this procedure performed at a level close to the nominal groups, though not superior to them.

Another way of introducing parallelism is to allow brainstorming groups to use a computer-based tool that permits simultaneous entry of ideas yet still allows sharing of ideas among the group members (Electronic Brainstorming). The most extensive body of research on this is from the University of Arizona group [7,10,11,12] Their decision support system incorporates a brainstorming tool that is based on NGT. A moderator starts the session off by sending the topic to each individual in the group, who then enters an idea. The individual's contribution is sent into a central pool, and an idea from this central pool is picked at random and sent to the individual, who in turn can use this as a seed for generating another idea. All contributions are anonymous, to prevent evaluation apprehension. The sharing of ideas through the process of sampling and sending from the growing central pool is a guard against cognitive inertia. The fact that everyone can be entering ideas concurrently overcomes air time and production blocking problems.

Some findings of the Arizona group are quite encouraging. While they have reported a large number of studies of brainstorming, only a few have involved laboratory studies where both the Electronic Brainstorming groups and the individual members of the nominal groups all used computer-based tools. In all of our following discussion of this research we will confine our attention to studies which use computers for both kinds of groups. In these cases, they have found that for groups ranging from 9 to 18 members more ideas are produced using the Electronic Brainstorming tool than the pooled ideas of corresponding nominal groups [10,11].

There are some limitations with these findings, however. First, not all investigators have found Electronic Brainstorming advantages when compared to nominal groups. Gallupe, Bastianutti & Cooper [12], using the Arizona tool but in a different set-up at Queen's University and using different tasks, found no advantage for Electronic Brainstorming groups over true nominal groups when both were using the computer to generate their ideas. They looked at groups of four.

Second, the groups using the Arizona Electronic Brainstorming tool are for all practical purposes using Nominal Group Technique, in that they are following a very strict procedure without any normal group interaction. Individuals sit at their own terminal and are not allowed to talk to each other. There are of course some differences between the paper-and-pencil version of NGT [9] and the electronic one. For the electronic version the "work individually" segment is reduced to the time it takes to produce a single idea, and the ideas are instantly transmitted to other group members via computer instead of by carbon paper. But the groups are only allowed to interact through the computer, and only see a single idea at a time that is sampled from the pool of ideas being maintained by the computer system.

It is also difficult to know how to relate these Electronic Brainstorming studies to the traditional literature since they never compare an interacting group using a computer tool without group facilitation features, to an interacting group with a computer tool that does support group activity. Computerized reporting in and of itself seems to be an enhancer for individuals, whether or not they are in a group. Gallupe et al [13] found significant effects for Electronic Brainstorming groups compared to non computer groups regardless of whether the groups were nominal or interacting. Having computers was more important than being in a group. Because research on computer supported brainstorming is new, it is important to verify that the traditional findings still occur with computer reporting so we can be assured that we are addressing the same issues. Previous work has not done this. For instance, in the Gallupe et al. [13] study, in a non Electronic Brainstorming pair of conditions they did not replicate the standard advantage of nominal groups over interacting groups, even when both nominal and interacting groups were not using computers. (though, as a further problem, when testing for an Electronic Brainstorming effect, they confounded reporting techniques across the interacting group).

We were interested in how groups working under more normal circumstances with a simple shared editor would perform if given a tool that allowed parallel entry of ideas. Our subjects used ShrEdit [14], a shared text editor that allows fully parallel entry and editing of information in a file but provides minimal further structure to the activity of the group. The groups worked in a facility where the computer displays were embedded in a special table and they were facing each other in a reasonably normal arrangement with normal sight lines for group work. They were allowed to talk and interact in any way they wanted.

So as not to confound method of reporting, we compared these interacting groups with a nominal group that used a single-user version of ShrEdit called UnShrEdit. This had exactly the same editing functions as ShrEdit, but all of the multi-user functionality was removed.

To be sure that our computer-based way of collecting ideas still produced the standard finding in the literature, namely, that nominal groups produce more ideas than ordinary interacting groups, we included a replication of the standard nominal group versus interacting group condition. We did this by including a face-to-face interacting group that reported their ideas though our one-person-at-a-time editor, UnShrEdit In these groups UnShrEdit was run on a single computer, with four keyboards, mice, and screens attached to that computer. All the members of the group could see the display on their own screen and enter information through their own keyboard and mouse. However, in contrast to the groups using ShrEdit, there was only one channel into the shared document. Similar to a group of people all trying to talk at once, if one subject tried to enter text at the same time as another subject, their typed characters would be merged together, resulting in a useless jumble. These groups developed a social protocol much like ordinary conversation to avoid such problems.

In sum, our study contained three conditions:

1. ***Interacting Serial***: face-to-face interacting groups with serial recording of ideas. These groups were free to talk and interact, but they were asked to record their ideas using the electronic editor, and although all group members had access to the technology only one could type at a time.
2. ***Nominal***: isolated individuals pooled into nominal groups . These groups were composed of the output of individuals who used the electronic editor to record their ideas.
3. ***Interacting Parallel***: face-to-face interacting groups with parallel recording of ideas. These groups were free to talk and interact, and were able to enter their ideas in the electronic editor in parallel, whenever they wanted. They also could see the input of others immediately on their display screen if they wanted.

Since all three groups used the same editor, there is no confounding of reporting medium.

This design allows for a series of direct and important comparisons. By comparing the Interacting Serial with the Nominal groups, we can see if we replicated the standard brainstorming effect with our task and reporting medium. We expected the pooled results of the Nominal groups (with duplicates removed) to be superior to the results of the Interacting Serial groups. By comparing the Interacting Parallel with the Interacting Serial groups we can see the direct effect of parallel entry of ideas within normal interacting groups. We expected the Interacting Parallel groups to do better than the Interacting Serial groups. Also, by comparing Interacting Parallel with Nominal groups, we can directly asses what is the effect of interaction among group members. We had no basis prior to the study for predicting the relative performance of the Nominal and Interacting Parallel groups.

METHOD

Subjects

There were 116 subjects used in the study. They were recruited from the local community, and ranged in age from 17 to 47. They all had some fluency with the use of Macintosh computers. Subjects were scheduled to show up in groups of four, with all members of the same gender. Group members did not know each other prior to the experiment. Experimental conditions were randomly assigned to time slots, and the groups were balanced by time slot and gender across conditions.

Tasks

Each group of subjects did two brainstorming tasks. For each of the tasks, subjects were given standard brainstorming instructions in which they were asked to generate ideas freely, to avoid commenting on their ideas or those of others, and to avoid deleting ideas that had been generated. Each of the two brainstorming tasks lasted for 15 minutes. The first was a warm-up task whose purpose was to familiarize the subjects with use of their computer setup, and to make them comfortable and proficient in brainstorming itself. For this task they were asked to generate things that they found annoying, irritating, or frustrating in their everyday lives. The second task, whose results are the focus of this study, was designed to be as unaffected as possible by the different backgrounds of the subjects and easy enough so that all subjects could be expected to contribute. The instructions for this task were:

> Imagine you are going to be visited by a person from a low technology environment, say a Siberian Eskimo who has lived as a hunter gatherer all their life. Generate the longest list of as many things around a modern, middle class house that this person would likely find bewildering.

Physical set-up

The study was run in the Collaboration Technology Suite (CTS), a special computerized meeting room that has been designed to be as similar to a regular meeting room as possible [15] The four subjects in each group were seated at a cluster of four computer stations, with computers embedded in the glass topped tables in front of the subjects. Subjects in the Nominal condition sat at the units as well, but partitions were placed between them so they could not see each other while they worked. We considered this to be acceptable even though the subjects were not physically isolated, since Street [16] and Harkins [17] found no difference between individuals working alone and isolated versus those working alone with others working on the same task around them. All typing was saved in time-stamped files for later analysis.

Software

ShrEdit is a multi-user text editor that runs on the Apple Macintosh. It allows all users to type and edit the same document at the same time. There is actually only one document that all users see and work on simultaneously but each user has a channel into it. Each user has their own cursor and pointer in the document, and they can place that wherever they wish. The only form of concurrency control is selection locking, which means that when a person makes a selection no one else is allowed to make the same selection. This could either be a single insertion point or a highlighted region of text. As the individuals edit, the other members of the group see the changes immediately. Users can scroll through the document, or resize their windows without disturbing the view of the others. In essence, ShrEdit provides a shared electronic workspace that all members of the group could access at all times. The Nominal and Interacting Serial groups used UnShrEdit, a single-user version of ShrEdit which had the identical editing functions but had the multi-user aspects removed. For more information about both ShrEdit and UnShrEdit, see [14].

Procedure

The subjects first filled out various permission forms and detailed questionnaires on their years of education, computer experience and attitude toward computers in general. Then they were trained to use the particular computer hardware/software combination that they would be using. Subjects in all conditions performed a few simple editing tasks on a small document. Prior to the brainstorming task all subjects were given scripted instructions explaining the brainstorming rules. The groups in the Parallel Interacting and Serial Interacting conditions were told they could talk or not as they wished, but that their ideas should be entered into the computer. Subjects in the Serial Interacting condition were told they might want to use a conversational protocol to organize their access to the editor. Subjects in the Nominal group silently entered their ideas into the computer. The subjects in all groups were then given the warm up task and brainstormed for 15 minutes. Following a short break to reset the machines they were given the target task, on which they worked for another 15 minutes.

Analysis

Nominal groups were formed by sampling same-sex sets of four people from the total pool of people who had been assigned to this condition. The files of these four people were merged to create a single file for that nominal group.

For all groups lexically identical items were removed automatically. A copy of each remaining list was given to two judges, who separately pruned the lists further by eliminating semantic duplicates. Each judge scored every group, and the final score of a group was computed by averaging the scores of the two judges.

MANOVAs performed on the questionnaire data showed that the groups did not differ in computer experience, computer skills, group activity skills, or education.

RESULTS AND DISCUSSION

Table 1 shows the means and standard deviations for the number of unique ideas produced in each of the three conditions.

Table 1

Number of Unique Ideas Generated

Condition	N	Mean	Standard Deviation
Interacting Serial:	11	91.7	38.2
Interacting Parallel:	10	148.6	30.2
Nominal:	8	172.5	54.6

A one-way ANOVA revealed a significant difference among the three conditions, $F(2, 26)=10.0$, $p < .0006$. Planned comparisons among the pairs of conditions revealed the following: the Nominal groups produced many more ideas than the Serial Interacting groups, $F(1, 26)=17.9$ $p<.0002$; the Parallel Interacting groups produced many more ideas than the Interacting Serial groups, $F(1, 26)=10.1$, $p < .0038$; but the Nominal and Parallel Interacting groups did not differ, $F(1, 26)=1.5$, $p < .23$.

We will discuss each of these contrasts in turn. First, the significant difference between the Nominal groups and the Serial Interacting groups replicates the standard advantage of Nominal groups in brainstorming tasks that has been found so repeatedly [6]. Thus, both our specific brainstorming task and our particular reporting method produced results that are consistent with the 30+ years of prior research. This shows that we are dealing with the same issues and underlying psychological phenomena as previous work even though computers and keyboards were the main method of communication. Had no difference been found between the Interacting Serial group and the Nominal groups, this would have raised serious doubts about the applicability of this work to the previous body of brainstorming work.

The Interacting Serial condition produced the same kind of production blocking that has been identified as the key factor in brainstorming [6] . Loss due to production blocking occurs in the time between the idea being generated internally and when it can be externally reported. One-at-a-time paradigms like conversations and the Interacting Serial condition mean that subjects must hold their ideas until another person stops. The similarity of results between our computer-based situation and the rest of the literature on brainstorming means that our task is comparable to those that have been used before.

The superior performance of the Parallel Interacting groups compared to the Serial Interacting groups showed that giving the members of a group parallel access to the medium used for recording ideas has a major effect on their productivity. This is exactly what one would expect if air time and production blocking were major factors in inhibiting the performance of interacting groups in brainstorming tasks. Giving the groups a software tool that reduced production blocking significantly enhanced productivity. This is true even for our very informal tool and normal group set-up in which conversation and interactions were allowed. The computer was the sole method of recording ideas, and thus in most groups the computer was the primary method of communicating during the tasks. Group members could easily see the output of others on their own screens, and could react by typing in further ideas of their own. But subjects also reacted to the ideas of others with comments, such as surprise or laughter. Interestingly, subjects also used the computer to joke and kid around, to comment about their feelings about the task and ideas, and to respond immediately to others' ideas by typing something in reply. These groups clearly interacted with each other, both by talking and by typing, all in an informal, unstructured environment.

Finally, there was no difference between the Nominal groups and the Parallel Interacting groups. This conflicts with the work of Dennis et al.[10, 11] , who found that Electronic Brainstorming groups did better than nominal groups who also used a computer-based reporting method. What might be going on here? There are a couple of possibilities. First, Dennis et al ran much larger groups than we did. Dennis, Valacich and Nunamaker [7] have reported that larger groups produce more ideas than smaller groups with the Electronic Brainstorming tool. So it is possible that the lack of superior performance by our Parallel Interacting groups is due to the fact that our groups of four are relatively small. We deliberately chose groups of four because this is the most common group size in the brainstorming literature [6].

However, we have identified another source of difference, the task. In our task subjects produced ideas at a very high rate, and were clearly nowhere near exhausting their repertoire of ideas when the 15 minutes were up. Figure 1 shows the rate of output for our Nominal and Parallel Interacting groups across the sessions, and it's clear that both groups were still generating ideas at the end of the session. Averaged across the entire session, our groups reported unique i

Table 2

Rate of Idea Production and Relative Advantage of Electronic Brainstorming

Study	Rate of Idea Production	Relative Advantage	Group Size
Dennis et al [11]	.7	+20.0%	9
Dennis et al [10]	1.1	+19.0%	12
Dennis et al [10]	.9	+14.9%	18
Gallupe et al [13]	3.4	-6.4%	4
Hymes & Olson	10.7	-13.8%	4

deas at the rate of 11.5 ideas/minute for the Nominal groups and 9.9 ideas/minute for the Parallel Interacting group. In contrast, groups performing the Dennis et al. task generated ideas at a drastically different rate. In their studies, business school students were asked to list people who would be affected by the requirement that all students have their own microcomputer. Their groups using computers generated ideas at the rate of less than one idea/minute on average. The rate of idea production might be a factor?

There is one other study that provides a point of observation in this, namely, one of the sets of conditions in the Gallupe et al.[13] paper where both Nominal and Electronic Brainstorming groups used computers. Table 2 summarizes a set of characteristics of the studies that sheds some light on matters. The first column of data shows the average number of ideas generated per minute. The second shows the relative advantage of the Electronic Brainstorming groups to the nominal groups by means of the following figure:

Relative Advantage=
(Electronic Brainstorming - Nominal)/Nominal.

That is, it shows a percentage advantage or disadvantage for the Electronic Brainstorming groups, scaled relative to the Nominal groups. What Table 2 shows quite clearly is that there is a strong negative relationship between the size and direction of the Electronic Brainstorming effect and the rate of idea production. The third column in Table 2 lists group size, which is a confounded factor in these data.

Why might rate of idea generation be an important factor? In order to benefit from the extra stimulation of knowing the ideas of others in the groups, one must have time to both perceive the ideas (e.g., in electronic tasks, reading them) and think about them. We can think of this as a form of input blocking. In other words, there is a cost associated with reading and thinking about the ideas of others. If ideas are appearing quite slowly in a session, then there is plenty of time for the participants to perceive them and think about them. But if the ideas are flowing quickly and continuously, then processing those of others will take time away from generating one's own ideas.

With ShrEdit and with our task that stimulated a high rate of ideas, input blocking occurs in the time lost from producing due to subjects reading the output of others. Although they did not have to (in the instructions, duplication of previous ideas was explicitly allowed), all subjects chose to read their co-workers' ideas in order to stimulate their own generation of ideas. ShrEdit exaggerates input blocking because all the output of the participants is always available for the participants to scroll through, and subjects chose to do this often.

Furthermore, input blocking may be related to group size. As group size increases, in normal groups production blocking gets worse because it is harder to get the floor. However, input blocking could also get worse with larger group sizes if the rate of idea generation is high. As the document gets larger, there is more for the subject to read, and it might become harder for the subject to pick out new and stimulating ideas from the ideas that are common or duplicates of each other. The Electronic Brainstorming tool used by Dennis et al [10,11] has less of an input blocking effect because the tool does not present all the ideas generated by all the participants at one time, and the participants cannot control what they see. There is less to read, and there are no actions to take to access the information. But they also had a task where the flow of new ideas was very slow compared to our task.

We have follow-up research underway whose aim is to sort out the relative contributions of group size and input blocking to Electronic Brainstorming. The simplest way to do this is to present the same task that Dennis et al. [10,11] used to groups of four using our tool and design. We could also run larger groups with our tool. We could also run our task with more time, or with some mechanism for slowing down the rate of idea generation. Our initial impression is that the rate of idea production is the more important effect in explaining the relative ranking of our Nominal and

Figure 1

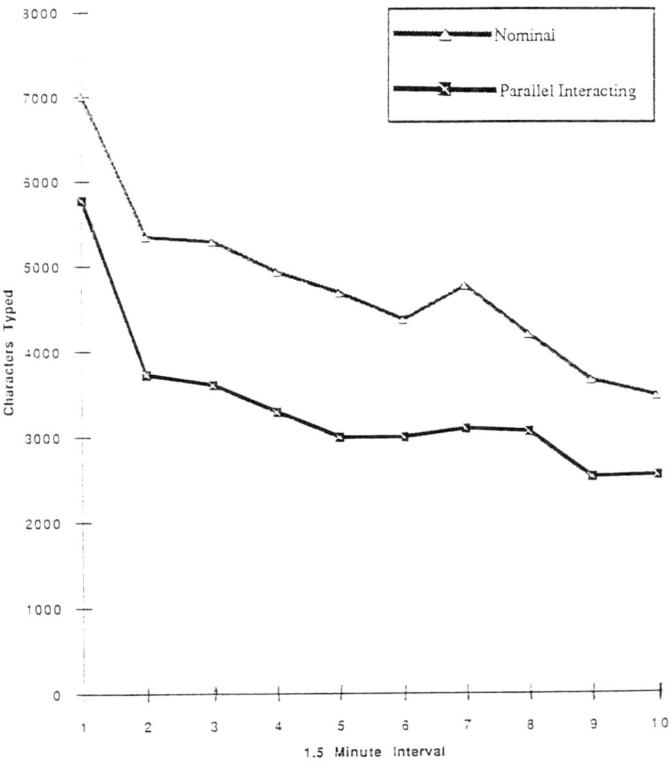

Parallel Interacting groups, but the research will have to sort this out. We have shown that as has been hypothesized in the major reviews, production blocking is a major factor in the poor relative performance of real groups as compared to nominal groups. Production blocking can be substantially reduced through the use of a simple electronic workspace that allows parallel entry of ideas. Whether this simple tool can produce a true brainstorming advantage in which interacting groups would produce more ideas than nominal groups will require further research. This work is solid step along the exploration of how specific features of CSCW systems effect group process.

ACKNOWLEDGEMENTS

This work has been supported by the National Science Foundation (Grant No. IRI-8902930), by the Center for Strategic Technology Research (CSTaR) at Andersen Consulting, by Arthur Andersen & Co., by Apple Computer, and by Steelcase, Inc.. Special thanks to Adrienne Royce and Suzanne Schuon. Judy Olson provided useful feedback on the manuscript.

REFERENCES

1. Hollingshead, A.B. and McGrath, J.E. The Whole is Less than the Sum of its Parts: A Critical Review of Research on Computer Assisted Groups. In *Team Decision Making in Organizations.* Guzzo R. (Ed.), San Francisco: Jossey-Bass, in press.

2. McLeod, P.L. An Assessment of the Experimental Literature on Electronic Support of Group Work: Results of a Meta-analysis. *Human Computer Interaction.*, in press.

3. Nunamaker, J.F. Dennis, A.R Valacich, J.S., Vogel, D.R., & George, J.F. Electronic Meeting Systems to Support Group Work. *Communications of the ACM*, 34,7 (1991) 40-61.

4. Gallupe, R.B., De Sanctus, G., Dickson, G.. Computer-Based Support for Group Problem Solving: An Experimental Investigation. *MISQ*, 12, (1988) 277-296

5. Osborn, A.F. *Applied Imagination* (Rev Ed.) New York: Scribner. 1957

6. Diehl, M., & Stroebe, W. Productivity Loss in Brainstorming Groups: Toward the Solution of a Riddle. *Journal of Personality and Social Psychology*, 53, (1987) 497-509

7. Dennis, A.R., Valacich, J.S., & Nunamaker, J.F. Jr. An Experimental Investigation of the Effects of Group Size in an Electronic Meeting Environment. *IEEE Transactions on Systems, Man and Cybernetics*, 20 (1990) 1049-1057

8. Delbecq, A., Van de Ven, A., & Gustafson, D. *Group Techniques for program planning: A Guide to Nominal Group and Delphi Processes.* Glenview, IL: Scott Foresmann. 1975

9. Madsen, D.B., & Finger J.R Comparison of a Written Feedback Procedure, Group Brainstorming and Individual Brainstorming. *Journal of Applied Psychology*, 63, (1978) 120-123

10 Dennis, A.R., Valachich, J.S., & Nunamaker, J.F., Jr. Productivity Loss and Gain in Brainstorming Groups: More Evidence on an Old Riddle. Manuscript. Dated 1990

11 Dennis, A.R., Valacich, J.S., & Nunamaker, J.F. Jr. Group, Sub-group and Nominal Group Idea Generation in an Electronic Meeting Environment. In J. Nunamaker (Ed.) DSS and Knowledge-Based Systems and Collaboration Technology. Proceedings of the Twenty Fourth Annual Hawaii International Conference on Systems Science.3, (1991) 573-579

12. Gallupe, R., Dennis, A.R., Cooper, W.H Valacich, J. S., Bastianutti, L. M., & Nunamaker, J. F. Jr. Electronic Brainstorming and Group Size. *Academy of Management Journal*, (1992), 35, 350-369.

13. Gallupe, R.B., Bastianutti, L.M., & Cooper, W.H., Unblocking Brainstorms. *Journal of Applied Psychology*, 76, (1991) 137-142

14. McGuffin, L.J. & Olson G.M., ShrEdit: A Shared Electronic Workspace, *CSMIL Technical Report, # 45* The University of Michigan, 1992

15. Olson, G.M., Olson, J.R, Killey, L., Mack, L.A., Cornell, P., & Luchetti, R. Flexible facilities for electronic meetings. In S. Kinney, R. Bostrom, & R. Watson (Eds.), *Computer Augmented Teamwork: A Guided Tour.* (in press). Van Nostrand Reinhold.

16. Street, W.R. Brainstorming by individuals, coacting and interacting groups. *Journal of Applied Psychology* (1974) 59, 433-436

17. Harkins, S.G., Social Loafing and Social Facilitation. *Journal of Experimental Social Psychology*, 23, (1986) 1-18

Awareness and Coordination in Shared Workspaces

Paul Dourish and Victoria Bellotti

Rank Xerox EuroPARC
61 Regent St
Cambridge CB2 1AB UK
dourish@europarc.xerox.com, bellotti@europarc.xerox.com

ABSTRACT

Awareness of individual and group activities is critical to successful collaboration and is commonly supported in CSCW systems by active, information generation mechanisms separate from the shared workspace. These mechanisms penalise information providers, presuppose relevance to the recipient, and make access difficult. We discuss a study of shared editor use which suggests that awareness information provided and exploited passively through the shared workspace, allows users to move smoothly between close and loose collaboration, and to assign and coordinate work dynamically. Passive awareness mechanisms promise effective support for collaboration requiring this sort of behaviour, whilst avoiding problems with active approaches.

KEYWORDS: Awareness, information sharing, coordination, shared workspaces, shared feedback.

INTRODUCTION

Studies of collaborative writing [*e.g.* 2, 7, 16] highlight the extent to which information sharing, knowledge of group and individual activity, and coordination are central to successful collaboration. These factors are clearly critical concerns in the design of computer systems to support collaborative writing, and mechanisms for their support are the subject of this paper.

Information relating to these factors contributes towards what we refer to as *awareness*. In these terms, awareness is an *understanding of the activities of others*, which provides a *context for your own activity*. This context is used to ensure that individual contributions are relevant to the group's activity as a whole, and to evaluate individual actions with respect to group goals and progress. The information, then, allows groups to manage the process of collaborative working.

It is particularly important to recognise that the context within which group members collaborate is comprised of both the object of that collaboration and the way in which the object is produced. We must therefore consider as context not just the *content* of individual contributions, but also their *character*; their significance with respect to the whole group and its goals. It is only by providing awareness of both aspects of group members' work that systems enable each individual to make sense of others' activity and tailor their own work accordingly.

Awareness information is always required to coordinate group activities, whatever the task domain. Although we deal largely here with collaborative text editing, other collaborative activities can benefit equally from the approach we outline.

Systems described in the research literature take various approaches to the provision of awareness information. A primary distinction between these mechanisms is whether the information is *explicitly generated*, directed and separate from the shared work object; or *passively collected and distributed*, and presented in the same shared work space as the object of collaboration. The latter mechanisms are frequently restricted to synchronous systems (*i.e.* those in which all collaborators are virtually co-present and working at the same time); however, there is no need for this restriction and later we will discuss their value in what we term *semi-synchronous* systems, which incorporate synchronous and asynchronous working.

In the following sections, we describe in more detail some approaches to the provision of awareness information in particular systems, and we highlight a number of problems with these approaches. We then discuss a case study of groups performing an open-ended design problem using a particular shared text editor which embodies an alternative approach to the provision of awareness information. We show how the groups used this alternative approach, point to the ways in which it overcomes some of the problems in the more traditional approaches, and the ways in which it supports

Permission to copy without fee all or part of this material is granted provided that the copies are not made or distributed for direct commercial advantage, the ACM copyright notice and the title of the publication and its date appear, and notice is given that copying is by permission of the Association for Computing Machinery. To copy otherwise, or to republish, requires a fee and/or specific permission.

© 1992 ACM 0-89791-543-7/92/0010/0107...$1.50

important aspects of awareness information for collaborative working.

AWARENESS IN COLLABORATIVE WRITING SYSTEMS

We will begin our discussion by looking at three particular collaborative writing systems, and the mechanisms they provide for sharing awareness information between collaborators. The designers of these systems explicitly acknowledge the importance of issues such as information sharing and coordination, and mechanisms for their support, but the approaches they take result in problems for groups, which we shall discuss.

Quilt

Quilt [6, 11] is an asynchronous collaborative authoring system developed at Bellcore. Rather than managing all aspects of document production, Quilt essentially forms a superstructure which manages the specifically collaborative aspects of group authoring; for instance, Quilt makes no assumptions about the underlying editors which might be used to enter and modify text. The Quilt developers identify the primary problems in collaborative authoring as *coordination*, which includes ensuring that work progresses and that redundant work is minimised, and *information sharing*, which includes both information about the substance of the work, the management of the work, and the interpersonal relationships within the group.

Quilt provides a range of explicit facilities to help support these aspects of the collaborative authoring process. The primary mechanisms available to Quilt users are a hypermedia system representing the document along with annotations, audit trail recording, and integrated electronic mail and conferencing systems. Annotation provides a mechanism by which users can comment to each other about the document material. Audit trail recording allows collaborators to review each other's activities. Electronic mail and conferencing provide mechanisms by which users can discuss document-related and activity-related issues, and distribute information about current or planned activities.

Underlying these mechanisms is a system of configurable role-assignment, which controls the degree of access which individuals have to the document. The use of explicit roles provides information about the character of a participant's activity; if you know that a colleague is a "reviewer", then your uncertainty about her potential activities is reduced

Quilt, then, takes a very active approach to the challenges of information sharing and coordination in asynchronous collaborative authoring. The distribution of awareness information is an explicit activity on the part of each member of the group. Any uncertainty about the character of others' work is reduced by imposing roles on all participants. Quilt manages roles through formal mechanisms, which means that explicit actions must be taken to change them.

PREP

PREP [14] is an asynchronous "work in preparation" editor which can be used by groups to collaboratively author documents. It concentrates in particular on the early stages of the writing process; idea generation and collection, initial text production, commenting and revision. The structure of information in PREP is very general. Information "chunks" can be linked together to form "drafts", and to form matrices which relate parallel information streams. The interface simplifies this model by displaying the information in a column structure, presenting the information streams in parallel and using spatial layout to emphasise the linkages between them. A typical view, for instance, might present four such columns; one to hold a plan structure for the document, one to hold draft text, and two for the annotations made by two collaborators.

Like Quilt, PREP uses role assignment to structure and delimit areas of responsibility and to control access to the information streams. The developers, however, acknowledge that, in natural collaboration, roles are typically fluid and continually re-negotiated, and warn of the danger of "premature" definition of roles in collaborative activity. Similarly, they point out that a direct mapping from roles to edit activities may be inappropriate; a reviewer may wish to be able to edit the text being reviewed, rather than merely make annotations, if that suits her particular work style. As a result, PREP tries to support a model of "communication about comments", such that comments, annotation and linkages which collaborators may make are not their only means for expressing ideas relating to the text in preparation. Even so, collaborators are still restricted in their roles, and consequently in the activities which they can undertake at any time.

So, like Quilt, PREP uses roles, explicit annotation and structured or directed messaging to provide means for generating awareness and coordination information. Information about the content of activities in progress is divorced from the activities themselves, but must be provided separately through some other channel.

GROVE

GROVE [4] is a synchronous, multi-user editor for the creation and editing of textual outline documents (tree-structured documents which may be viewed at various levels of specificity). It is designed for use in both face-to-face and remote collaborative situations. While GROVE takes advantage of audio communication to support informal awareness between participants, the system's representations of other users' activities are implicit. A GROVE window will show other users' text entry for any outline nodes which are also opened on the local user's screen, and each node is marked as open, closed or terminal (*i.e.* without any sub-nodes). Parts of the document are presented to each user through a *view*, which may be public, private or shared. In addition, access control mechanisms can be used at each point in the tree to control who can see, edit or create a node.

GROVE differs from Quit and PREP in a number of significant ways. It has no explicit notion of role, although the use of access control does correspond to some of the (non-awareness) aspects of role use in collaborative systems. The notion of "view" serves to differentiate the information presented to each user, which reduces the extent to which the shared document can act as a common resource for reference. Although the dOPT synchronisation algorithm [5] which underlies GROVE can manage simple text streams as well as outline documents, GROVE's structuring of the document also implicitly serves, in some ways, to structure the activities in which the group engages. So, while GROVE is based on a model of synchronous collaboration and external communication channels, it constrains some task elements in an effort to prevent editing conflicts and provide a mutual awareness of activities.

All of these systems clearly embody an assumption that a simple awareness of other's activity needs to be augmented with other explicit, or restrictive mechanisms for ensuring an easy collaboration, such as annotations, role assignment, access rights and so forth. In the next section, we begin to question such assumptions by considering a number of problems implicit in these awareness support mechanisms.

MECHANISMS FOR AWARENESS INFORMATION

The previous section briefly described three collaborative editing systems, with an emphasis on the mechanisms they use to support sharing of awareness information between participants. In this section, we describe two general models which are used, and some of the problems which they generate.

Existing CSCW systems vary in the mechanisms they provide to support awareness. One mechanism, which we refer to as *informational*, is to provide explicit facilities through which collaborators inform each other of their activities. For instance, software control systems such as RCS [18] ask users to provide text for an "edit log" which describes the nature of changes; or electronic mail can be integrated with an authoring system as a channel for sharing this information, as in Quilt. A second mechanism, which we refer to as *role restrictive*, arises from explicit support for roles in collaborative systems. A role describes an individual's relationships to the shared work objects and to other participants, and is typically linked to a set of operations which can be performed. In a shared authoring system, for instance, an "author" role might be associated with the read, write, create, delete and edit operations, while a "reviewer" might be limited to read and annotate. One of the effects of explicit role support, then, is to reduce uncertainty about the actions an individual might take, and hence provide greater awareness amongst participants of each others' likely activities. However, awareness through roles provides information only about the *character* of the activity, not the *content*.

Problems with Informational and Role-Restrictive Approaches to Awareness

While both the informational and role restrictive approaches are useful in conveying to collaborators an awareness of progress and joint activity, they also have some problems. We identify three in particular.

Firstly, the user who provides the information does not directly benefit. In the role restrictive case, we encounter a significant trade-off with respect to benefits. The price of heightened awareness for the group is clearly *restriction in the potential activities* of individuals. However, there is a further problem for role restrictive CSCW systems. This is that, although explicit roles may allow for easier social organisation of collaborative activity in conventional interactions and collaborations, one often observes roles being negotiated and reassigned dynamically. This phenomenon has been identified in other computer supported meeting situations where participants are released from the tyranny of restricted access to shared work spaces [*e.g.* 1, 13]. There seems to be justification for arguing that role-switching in CSCW systems should, therefore, not be a complex, time consuming operation which hampers this negotiated process.

In informational systems supporting awareness, the individual is required to supply the information; again, this cost is repaid to the group rather than the individual, and adds an extra work load in the case of computer support over natural collaborative work. The problem of correctly matching benefits to the individuals who incur costs is one of the problems cited in Grudin's analysis of the failures of some collaborative systems [9].

A second problem with these approaches to awareness can be seen as a proviso to our previous statement that other individuals benefit from the action of one group member in reporting activity. The others *may* benefit, but this is by no means guaranteed. Individuals will receive *what the initiator of the information deems to be appropriate*. However, appropriateness can only be determined in the context of the other individuals' activities. So, information provided in this way may not be at the appropriate level of specificity for the receiving individuals, or it may not be relevant to their particular activities at the time, or it may reflect different assumptions about aspects of the joint work.

The final problem concerns the way in which the information is made available by informational mechanisms such that *delivery is controlled more by the sender* than by the recipient. However, the sender cannot predict what information will be needed and when. The information is not continually available to be browsed and particularly relevant information cannot necessarily be separated from other information which is less relevant to the recipient's particular activity at that moment. Thus, not only is the producer of the information burdened in the act of producing, but the recipient is restricted in ways of using the information.

SHARED FEEDBACK

In contrast to these approaches, we present a case study of a collaborative text preparation tool which embodies some (but not all) aspects of what we call the *shared feedback* approach. Shared feedback makes information about individual activities apparent to other participants by presenting feedback on operations within the shared, rather than the private, workspace. We will describe the particular system under examination, and then proceed to show the way in which users exploited the shared feedback features in the completion of their task.

A Case Study—ShrEdit

We collaborated with Judy and Gary Olson in a study of groups of designers using an application called ShrEdit [12] whilst solving design problems. ShrEdit is a synchronous, multi-user text editor which runs on a network of Apple Macintoshes. It was developed as a tool to explore the support of design meetings. Before discussing observations from the study we will describe some of ShrEdit's features.

ShrEdit allows multiple users to edit a set of documents collaboratively. Each user can have a number of shared and private windows. A shared window presents a view onto a shared document; each user has an edit cursor within each shared window, allowing them to edit text concurrently. Views of documents are unique to each user; each user's window can be differently sized, and aligned on a different part of the document. Private windows contain documents which only one user can see and edit, and can be used for making notes or creating text which may later be pasted into a shared document.

ShrEdit locks shared windows at the level of text selections. No user can edit text which has been selected by another user. Similarly, it is not possible for two users to have their edit cursors at the same point in the document. ShrEdit does not have telepointers which would allow individuals' mouse-cursor movements to be seen by other collaborators, and other users' edit cursors are not displayed to an individual. However, other users' edit actions are displayed in all shared windows with a low latency, and cursor "collisions" are indicated with an audio signal and a pop-up window.

A control window associated with each edit window displays the names of the participants in the session. Through this window, users can "find" other users; ShrEdit scrolls to the current location of their edit cursor in the document in the window. They can also "track" others, which means that they see another user's view (as far as possible given differences in window shape) complete with the edit cursor and text selections; this persists until switched off. Each control window records whether participants have a selection in the associated window, are tracking someone else, or tracking you. Figure 1 shows a typical layout of public, private and control windows.

ShrEdit avoids imposing a structure upon users' activities. There is no strong model of the collaborative editing *process* behind its design. All participants have equal access to the shared document windows and can type at any time. Nor does ShrEdit provide sophisticated functionality to support awareness beyond showing everyone's text as it is input, and giving rudimentary information about whether participants are editing, or are tracking someone. This freedom allows users to adopt very different working styles.

Description of Study

Groups of three designers (all with previous experience of working together) tackled open-ended design problems using ShrEdit. Since one of the aims of the study was to simulate remote collaboration, we placed them in separate locations, linked via video and/or audio. The informal channel of verbal communication, whether across a meeting room table or via audio, is important for supporting a system of this flexibility.

After a training period, each group was given two 20 minute practice problems and finally a 90 minute design problem to be collaboratively solved using ShrEdit. The final problem was to design a 24-hour unstaffed "automatic" post office offering a subset of the usual post office services, such as selling stamps and weighing parcels. The designers were asked to write a plan for the services their design would provide, how it would work, and things they would need to investigate further, as well as to make notes on their reasoning. The design problem was carefully worded so as to avoid the need for drawing, which ShrEdit cannot support. The experiment ended with a debriefing session where the designers were interviewed about their use of ShrEdit, criticising and suggesting improvements to it. All stages of the study were video-recorded for later analysis. For a fuller description of the study see [15].

Designer groups were free to choose the number of shared windows they wanted, how they would use these, and the way they would work together. We were struck by the diversity, not just of the design solutions generated using ShrEdit, but also of the ways in which groups produced them, which they later commented were compatible with the way they would normally work together.

In the next section we highlight some ways in which awareness information was critical to ShrEdit users, and some examples of how its absence was problematic. We base our report on analysis of video-tapes of four groups of users and restrict our examples to the final experimental problem.

Some Observations on Use

The shared workspace provided a focus for the designers' work and discussions. Talk dominated the activity of the designers with many periods when nobody in a group was typing, whilst two or all three talked. Even when everyone was typing, there were frequent sporadic or more sustained bursts of conversation. Subtle inflections of voice, interruptions, humour, or just grunts were also used to convey or cut off information where appropriate. Not only was speech allowing exchange of design ideas, it was also used to maintain awareness of group members' activities with a very low overhead in terms of effort required.

This talk was very much contextualised by, and related to, the shared grounding which the synchronous shared editing allowed. Much of the conversation referred to or implied a shared context provided by the shared documents. We also observed many instances where the information being generated in the shared workspace, and the way it was being organised, acted as a focus that tended to curb digressions and to keep the group working in a coordinated fashion. So awareness of others' work through ShrEdit enabled group members to organise their activities and provided impetus for design contributions.

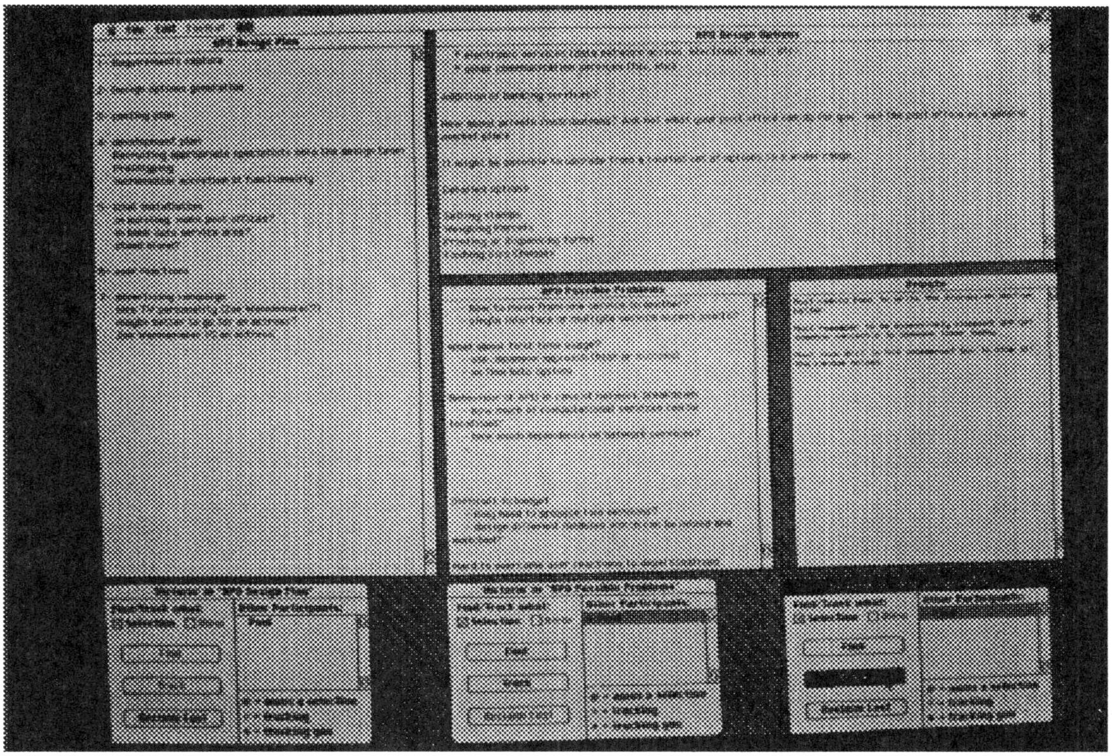

FIGURE 1. A ShrEdit screen, showing three public windows, one private window (middle right) and, at the bottom, three control windows.The control windows show other active users and provide "find" and "track" facilities.

Participants continually moved between concurrent, but more or less independent, work, through discussions and coordination, to very tightly focused group consideration of single items. These movements were opportunistic and unpredictable, relying on awareness of the state of the rest of the group.

The activities of the group also varied continuously, comprising permutations of individuals typing, editing (*i.e.* correcting spelling, indenting and so on), reading, talking, listening or thinking. For example, we frequently observed that one designer would stop typing and watch the contributions of one or both of the others. This might prompt further debate and reorganisation of the document or participants' roles. Sometimes two designers would stop and talk whilst the third might ignore them and continue working independently or suddenly chip in. Occasionally one participant would act as a scribe during discussions, but here, of course, the record could be seen and modified by others.

Designers were clearly aware of the special status of authorship and tended to partition responsibility for and rights over different parts of shared documents. They would ask who had written certain things or warn each other about changes which affected others' work. In the example below, the group has adopted a convention under which each user has their own window, which nobody else should write in but everyone can read.

D3: Um guys, maybe we should copy the stuff from window three, which seems to be the heading, into the main window and then start doing our own thing in our own window.

D2: Into our own, OK.

D1: Do you want to do that [D3] seeing as it's your stuff?

The lack of structure in ShrEdit removed work-process constraints, and continuous awareness allowed users to vary their activities dynamically and opportunistically in response to the changing state of affairs with the group and the growing document.

Some problems with ShrEdit concerned the extent to which users could observe others' activities. There were two facets to this; seeing the *character* of another's activity, and seeing the *content* of another's activity. Often users would watch each other typing, or ask what they were doing. Surprisingly, not much use was made of the "find" and "track" facilities. In debriefing sessions users claimed that this was due to clumsiness in the control window interface. Users preferred to ask where others were, or just scroll to where they knew they would be. One group developed an indexing and indentation scheme so they could give accurate location references. This scheme also gave implicit information about the character of the work being done by participants.

There were also problems with informing others about what you were doing. Users often volunteered such information to the group, as below:

Two designers are working together on part of the document whilst the third is attending to another part. The third designer alerts the other two to a change, as opposed to an addition, he wants to make.

D1: Lets make the first, designer stamps from preset selection.

D2: OK... Now I'll copy this; I'll cut this...

D1: Yeah cut that stuff below and put it in phase three.

D2: ...I can't cut that, I'll just copy that down to...

D3: I don't think there's "no salaries to pay", it's "fewer". You've got to have some kind of fix it.

D1: Huh?

D1: What are you doing [D2]?

D2: What? ... I'm doing... I'm down in the fax stuff.

Having others in the group be aware of what one was doing seemed to be extremely important. Very little use was made of private windows, although this could be due to pressure on group members to produce as much joint work as possible during the experiment. Designers frequently described what they were doing and sometimes would explicitly ask others to look at their work. One group, mentioned earlier, assigned each participant a shared window into which, by consensus alone, only they could type. They also had a window into which all three could type. In this way everyone could see each other's individual work, and, furthermore, the status of that work although public, was clearly an individual's contribution rather than the group's offering.

During debriefing, the users repeatedly emphasised the importance of awareness of work activities, by making design suggestions for easier access to this information. At the same time the designers were very positive about the freedom that ShrEdit gave them to work in a manner which suited them.

Use of Shared Feedback in ShrEdit

ShrEdit provides some of the functionality of the shared feedback approach, in that it automatically represents activity within the shared space. It does so without any explicit informational and role restrictive mechanisms to facilitate collaboration, such as role assignment, setting access rights and so forth. In spite of the lack of such mechanisms, its users are still amply aware of each other's activity, such that they can negotiate and adapt the content and character of their own work with respect to the context of group activity, and can organise the group's activity in a flexible but coordinated manner. In other words, they succeed in organising their collaboration without requiring the effort of explicit, system-structured exchanges of information about their activity, or the restriction of their contribution to some predetermined, inflexible role. They do so in a manner which is subtle and dynamic rather than formal and static. There is clearly much to be learnt about the way people collaborate before we can presume to preordain how that collaboration should be structured.

It should be pointed out that, although ShrEdit embodies aspects of the shared feedback approach, it still lacks certain other features which we would see as important; indeed, in providing some features of shared activity awareness, ShrEdit highlights the lack of some others. For example, whilst users could see other's input, they could not see their edit cursors. It is not surprising, then, that they complained about this during the debriefing.

DISCUSSION

"Awareness", principally of participants' activities with respect to a collaborative context, is a critical issue for collaborative systems and one to which the developers of Quilt, PREP and Grove explicitly address themselves. It is fundamental to coordination of activities and sharing of information, which, in turn, are critical to successful collaboration. Awareness plays a number of key roles. First, high-level awareness of the *character* of other's actions allows participants to structure their activities and avoid duplication of work. Second, lower-level awareness of the *content* of others' actions allows fine-grained shared working and synergistic group behaviour which needs to be supported by collaborative applications.

We have already discussed problems which arise from the approaches to awareness in some existing CSCW systems. We have also shown how a system which embodies aspects of the *shared feedback* approach was used by groups to flexibly coordinate their activities. We now consider some aspects of shared feedback more generally, and show how it relates to the problems with other approaches which we identified earlier.

Shared Feedback: An Alternative Approach

An alternative approach to increasing awareness, which we have successfully used in other collaborative systems is to automate collection and distribution of information, and to present it as background information within a shared space. This is the *shared feedback* approach; presenting feedback on individual users' activities *within the shared workspace.* The emphases of this approach are on low overheads for the providers and recipients of awareness information, availability of information as and when needed as a context for individual activities, and avoidance of restrictive pre-structuring of group activity. This approach is commonly associated with exclusively synchronous applications, although this is not, in fact, a requirement. The notion of semi-synchronous, persistent shared workspaces leads to non-synchronous shared feedback, and we shall return to this presently.

What are the particular benefits of this workspace-based shared feedback approach? The ShrEdit study begins to suggest some of these. We have observed how individuals have the opportunity to peripherally monitor others' activities, and comment on them, so that an individual, even when working independently, is both communicating her activities (allowing others to avoid duplicating her work) and providing others with the opportunity to comment on the activity or observe consequences for their own actions. This is achieved without increasing the workload of the individual "producing" the information. Conversely, users can explicitly tailor their contributions knowing that others can see them, so as to convey information and solicit responses, via the shared workspace or some other communication channel. At the same time, by reducing the need for role restriction, this approach is compatible with a more flexible model of role-assignment which supports the fluid negotiation and reassignment of role we see in a number of collaborative activities. These mechanisms for coordination and information sharing can be made available in a collaborative tool orthogonally to the task itself; they can be applied to a range of tools which embody particular work styles, or to a single tool which can be used in multiple ways. This approach is the one taken by ShrEdit and allows for the adoption of different working styles and self-organisation of the collaborative process which we remarked on in discussing our study.

We should not find it surprising that these features (the ability to passively monitor other's actions, and to tailor indirect productions for other individuals who can see/receive them) are useful ways of coordinating shared activities like collaborative writing, drawing or programming—they are mechanisms which we see groups use to coordinate natural collaboration in other settings. For instance, Heath and Luff [10] show how precisely these mechanisms are used to coordinate activities between individuals working together in the control rooms of a major urban transportation system. The same mechanisms also underpin the role of shared awareness in other contexts, such as the support for informal interactions within distributed work groups [3]. Tatar *et al* [17] point to a clear need in Cognoter, a group brainstorming support tool, for co-reference; feedback enabling users to see others' work and actions as they occur, which allows them to communicate, interpret and coordinate their activities more efficiently. In addition to verbal and visual information, non-speech audio information can also provide a means for shared feedback in a variety of environments [8].

Semi-Synchronous Systems

In looking at different approaches to providing awareness of individual and group activities in shared workspace systems, a correlation emerges between synchronous collaboration and passive, workspace-based group feedback. It is worth considering whether this distinction in awareness mechanisms is intrinsic in the choice of synchronous versus asynchronous approaches. There are two related questions here: is it possible to imagine workspace-based awareness mechanisms in asynchronous systems, and is the distinction between synchronous and asynchronous approaches necessarily such a strong one?

Tackling the first question, we can certainly imagine asynchronous awareness information presented in the same workspace as the work object. A primitive example of this type of asynchronous awareness information is the use of "change bars"; margin marks indicating text areas which have been changed. Change bars are examples of document-based representations of activity. There is no reason why change bars or similar representations[1] cannot provide further information, such as the nature of changes, the identity of the collaborator making the change, and so forth. Details of past activity can be held within the document, and retain the advantages of passive collection and distribution. What's more, such document-based representations can be presented at various levels of specificity, so that users can access information as it becomes relevant. Such information can also change over time to reflect the progress of activity on the part of individuals; and it can be presented differently to the various collaborators, as is appropriate for their different involvements in the activity and for the way these involvements change over time. The work space, then, holds more than merely the object of group activity, but also becomes a persistent record of that activity.

When we consider presenting past activity information within the shared workspace, the division between synchronous and asynchronous activities becomes less distinct, and we can take this further. A *semi-synchronous* system supports both synchronous and asynchronous work modes. In asynchronous use, the workspace presents past activity information, so as to give an individual awareness of the activities of other participants integrated with the work object itself. In synchronous use, this information is presented as it happens, providing participants with awareness of others' current activities. However, these are not two different modes of the system, but rather are two facets of a single view of awareness information. A semi-synchronous system presents current information on synchronously co-present collaborators, at the same time as representations of past activities by other collaborators who are not synchronously present. The workspace becomes a persistent space in which collaborators can interact, rather like a room in which one can either talk with other people who happen to be there at the time, or leave notes (or other, more passive, representations of one's activity) for those who arrive later.

CONCLUSIONS

We have discussed approaches to the critical issue of group activity awareness in collaborative systems. This awareness provides a context for individual activities and thus facilitates group progress. Two existing approaches have been described. The first is an explicit approach which uses directed messaging and the second uses a "strong" notion of roles and activities to convey information to the group about individuals' actions and plans. A third approach is to present shared feedback and results from individual activities to the group at large through the shared workspace. This conveys a continually-updating sense of the actions of individual collaborators and the overall progress of the group.

We have discussed systems which embody each of these approaches. Shared feedback overcomes problems with informational and role-restrictive approaches. In particular:

1. Shared feedback reduces the costs to individuals of information production by collecting information passively and avoiding restrictions on activities.
2. Shared feedback allows participants to look for and extract the awareness information which is most relevant to them.

1. One interface metaphor which frequently crops up in discussions with colleagues is that of the "slime trails" left by snails.

3. Shared feedback presents awareness information through the shared workspace and linked to it, so that users can (i) find relevant information along with the shared object, and (ii) browse awareness information and the work object concurrently.

Shared feedback can be applied more generally than merely synchronous collaborative systems through the use of persistent, semi-synchronous workspaces and systems.

We are continuing to explore the relationship between explicit and implicit generation of information to support awareness in collaborative systems as part of our research on design principles and generic architectures. It is clear that there is more to learn about each approach and its impact on collaborative work practices.

ACKNOWLEDGMENTS

We would like Judy and Gary Olson for their important role in organising the ShrEdit study, Ian Daniel and Mike Molloy for making it work, and Beth Anderson, Sara Bly, Graham Button, Wendy Mackay, Eliot Miranda and Abi Sellen for comments on earlier drafts of this paper. The development of ShrEdit was supported, in part, by the National Science Foundation under grant IRI-8902930.

REFERENCES

1. Laurel Austin, Jeffrey Liker and Poppy McLeod, *"Determinants and patterns of control over technology in a computerised meeting room"*, Proc. CSCW'90 Computer-Supported Cooperative Work (Los Angeles, CA, October 1990).

2. Eevi Beck, *"A Survey of Experiences of Coauthoring"*, to appear in Sharples (ed.), "Computer-Supported Collaborative Writing", Springer-Verlag (in press).

3. Paul Dourish and Sara Bly, *"Portholes: Supporting Awareness in Distributed Work Groups"*, Proc. CHI'92 Human Factors in Computer Systems (Monterey, Ca., May 1992).

4. Clarence Ellis, Simon Gibbs and Gail Rein, *"Design and Use of a Group Editor"*, in Cockton (ed.), "Engineering for Human-Computer Interaction", North-Holland, 1990.

5. Clarence Ellis and Simon Gibbs, *"Concurrency Control in Groupware Systems"*, Proc. SIGMOD'89 Management of Data (Seattle, Wa., 1989).

6. Robert S. Fish, Robert E. Kraut, Mary D. P. Leland and Michael Cohen, *"Quilt—A Collaborative Tool for Cooperative Writing"*, Proc. COIS'88 Office Information Systems (Palo Alto, Ca, March 1988).

7. Jolene Galegher and Robert Kraut, *"Computer-mediated Communication for Intellectual Teamwork: A Field Experiment in Group Writing"*, Proc. CSCW'90 Computer-Supported Cooperative Work (Los Angeles, October, 1990).

8. William Gaver, *"Sound Support for Collaboration"*, Proc. ECSCW'91 European Conference on Computer-Supported Cooperative Work (Amsterdam, September 1991).

9. Jonathan Grudin, *"Why CSCW Applications Fail: Problems in the Design and Evaluation of Organisational Interfaces"*, Proc. CSCW'88 Computer-Supported Cooperative Work (Portland, Or., September 1988).

10. Christian Heath and Paul Luff, *"Collaborative Activity and Technological Design: Task Coordination in London Underground Control Rooms"*, Proc. ECSCW'91 European Conference on Computer-Supported Cooperative Work (Amsterdam, September 1991).

11. Mary Leland, Robert Fish and Robert Kraut, *"Collaborative Document Production Using Quilt"*, Proc. CSCW'88 Computer-Supported Cooperative Work (Portland, Or., September 1988).

12. Lola McGuffin and Gary Olson, *"ShrEdit: A Shared Electronic Workspace"*, CSMIL Technical Report, Cognitive Science and Machine Intelligence Laboratory, University of Michigan, 1992.

13. Marilyn Mantei, *"Capturing the Capture Lab Concepts: A Case Study in the Design of Computer Supported Meeting Environments"*, Proc. CSCW'88 Computer-Supported Cooperative Work (Portland, Or., September 1988).

14. Christine M. Neuwirth, David S. Kaufer, Ravinder Chandhok and James H. Morris, *"Issues in the Design of Computer Support for Co-authoring and Commenting"*, Proc. CSCW'90 Computer-Supported Cooperative Work (Los Angeles, Ca., October 1990).

15. Judy Olson, Gary Olson, Marianne Storrøsten and Mark Carter, *"How a Group-Editor Changes the Character of a Design Meeting as well as its Outcome"*, Proc. CSCW'92 Computer-Supported Cooperative Work (Toronto, Canada, November 1992).

16. Ilona Posner, *"A Study of Collaborative Writing"*, Unpublished Master's thesis, University of Toronto, 1991.

17. Deborah Tatar, Gregg Foster and Daniel Bobrow, *"Designing for Conversation: Lessons from Cognoter"*, Intl. Journal of Man-Machine Studies, 34, pp 185–209, 1991.

18. Walter Tichy, *"RCS—A System for Version Control"*, Software—Practice and Experience, 15(7), pp. 637–654, July 1985.

Faltering from Ethnography to Design

John A. Hughes, David Randall and Dan Shapiro

CSCW Research Centre
Sociology Department
Lancaster University
Lancaster LA1 4YL, UK
Email: shapiro@lancaster.ac.uk
Phone: +44 524 65201
Fax: +44 524 844788

ABSTRACT

The aim of this paper is to explore some ways of linking ethnographic studies of work in context with the design of CSCW systems. It uses examples from an interdisciplinary collaborative project on air traffic control. Ethnographic methods are introduced, and applied to identifying the social organization of this cooperative work, and the use of instruments within it. On this basis some metaphors for the electronic representation of current manual practices are presented, and their possibilities and limitations are discussed.

KEYWORDS

Ethnography, CSCW design, Qualitative methods, Air traffic control, Database visualisation.

INTRODUCTION

There is an almost universal agreement in CSCW on the desirability of interdisciplinary design. While the integration of cognitive psychology in HCI already has a substantial body of achievements on record, the objective now is to incorporate perspectives on the social organization of work – at a theoretical but, more importantly, at a practical level – into the canon. With some exceptions, however, these remain pious hopes, or else independent analyses of work at some remove from the context of real system design. This paper makes a modest contribution to realising the goal of integration. It does so by taking a particular design project: a prototype system for air traffic control; and by carrying an ethnographic analysis of the social organization of the work involved through to specific implications for the design of a computer-based system to support that work.

Permission to copy without fee all or part of this material is granted provided that the copies are not made or distributed for direct commercial advantage, the ACM copyright notice and the title of the publication and its date appear, and notice is given that copying is by permission of the Association for Computing Machinery. To copy otherwise, or to republish, requires a fee and/or specific permission.

© 1992 ACM 0-89791-543-7/92/0010/0115...$1.50

UK AIR TRAFFIC CONTROL

The whole of the airspace of England and Wales is controlled from a centre near London. The airspace is divided into 16 sectors, each of which is controlled from a suite (see Figure 1).[1] Typically, a suite is staffed by two air traffic controllers, two assistants, and one sector chief.

The purpose of air traffic control (ATC) is to direct flights safely and efficiently to their destinations. Safety is attained by keeping aircraft separated from each other, and the standard distances for this are five miles laterally and 1000 feet vertically.[2]

Controllers have three main instruments to aid them. First, secondary *radar* displays which show a trail of 'blips' representing a particular flight, with a data block alongside showing the flight number and flight level (height). Second, *telephone and radiotelephone* communications enabling controllers to talk to pilots, to controllers on other suites, and to neighbouring airspaces. Third, flight progress *strips*, which are strips of card approximately 8 inches by 1 inch, and which are divided into fields containing information for a particular flight (see Figure 2). This information comes from a database holding the flight plan filed by the pilot, modified by radar data and sometimes by inputs keyed in by controllers or assistants. It includes the aircraft's callsign, its flight level, its heading, its airspeed, its planned flight path, the navigation points on its route and its estimated time of arrival at them, the departure and destination airports, and the aircraft type.[3] Strips are arranged in racks, and within the racks in bays, above and below a fixed marker representing a particular navigation point inside the sector.

The strip turns out to be a vital instrument for ATC. It is possible, and on occasion necessary, to perform ATC with the strips but without radar. To do so with radar but no strips, however, would pose extreme difficulties. When a controller gives an instruction to a pilot, for example to ascend to flight level 220, s/he marks this on the strip: in this case, with an upwards arrow and the number 220. When the pilot acknowledges the instruction, the controller

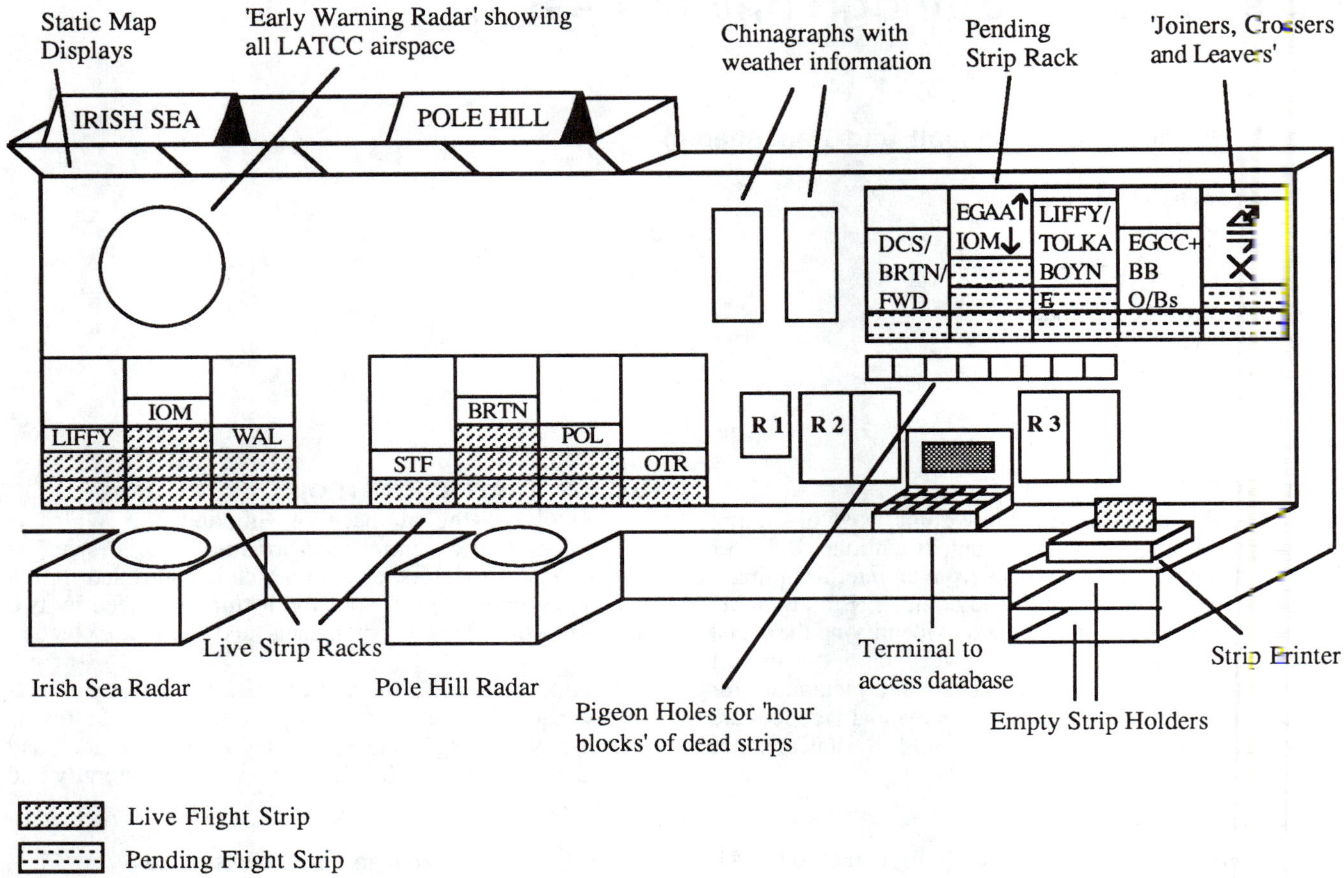

Figure 1. Layout of an en-route suite: Pole Hill and Irish Sea sectors

crosses through the old flight level on the strip. When the new height is attained, the controller marks a check beside it.

The aim of the joint research project[4] reported here is to consider issues involved in command and control systems in which a shared information space comprises a mixture of computer-mediated and manual elements. Specifically, we are concerned with designing a prototype display generator which will provide an electronic replacement for the paper flight progress strip. The reason for this is that as aircraft change position in response to controllers' instructions, the underlying database which generated the flight strip becomes progressively incongruent with the true 'state of the skies', which is accurately represented on the manually amended strips. This limits the flexbility with which the database information can be used and makes it harder, for instance, to design a confliction warning system which would not generate a high proportion of misleading false alarms. This in turn is needed because of the increasing pressure on UK airspace (halted, probably temporarily, by the Gulf War and the current economic recession). Between 1980 and 1989 UK scheduled passengers increased from 22m to 35m, while charter passengers more than doubled from 9.5m to 20.5m (source: UK Civil Aviation Authority). And it is compounded by the complexity of movements in UK airspace, which one sector chief described as, "like a giant terminal manoeuvring area – you hardly ever see planes entering and leaving sectors at the same height."

ETHNOGRAPHIC ANALYSIS

There is no one method of ethnographic analysis (see, for example, 7, 6, 9, 10, 16]. The approach we have adopted involves various practices, alerting concepts, and semi-technical terms, which we can indicate but have no space to defend in detail. The field workers immersed themselves in the work by spending several months observing activities on and around the suites, talking to staff, and discussing with them the researchers' developing understanding of what controllers do.[5]

While attempting to avoid prejudices and to allow the work situation to 'speak for itself' as much as possible, researchers cannot claim to address it innocent of any theoretical orientation; and their results would be much impoverished if they did. The purpose of an ethnographic approach is not so much to show *that* work is socially organized (which is rather easy) but to show *how* it is socially organized. This does not necessarily contradict claims and observations made from an individual or cognitive perspective, but it is likely to cast them in a different light.

The *sociality* of work is not a matter of discovering the linkages which connect individual work together, but is rather what permits that 'individuation' in the first place. People are able to work 'individually' because they know, flexibly and in the particular *context*, what is collectively understood and accepted as *their* task, and how that stands *interdependently* with the tasks of others. While often routine and repetitive, work can hardly ever be completely standardised. The particular circumstances and *contingencies* within which procedures and rules have to be applied are constantly changing, so that work is always *situated* [17], and is to varying degrees *discretionary*. It is oriented to in terms of *structures of relevance* [13] through which *practitioners* exercise *judgement* as to appropriate courses of action given the prevailing aims, circumstances and relations to other practitioners.

In making this match, *members* call on reserves of *tacit knowledge, skills and experience*, which go well beyond any formal procedures.[6] Work is not encountered as a set of discrete tasks involving chunks of data and distinct procedures, but rather as a *free flowing gestalt contexture*, with activities overlapping, and moving through foreground and background in response to (and constituting) the situation as it develops. 'Gearing into' the work [5] is about having the resources of knowledge and practice with which to understand these elements and relations, and inserting oneself into the flow.

The result is a *working division of labour* [1: 160] in which the separation, individuation and combination of activities is *accomplished* in an *accountable* way [3] through a collectively developed, negotiated and evolving knowledge and practice – though one which is not, of course, perfectly matched over all members, or able to cope effortlessly with every mix of circumstances. Where such *problems* arise, *running repairs* will be required, and become the subject of specific discussion and negotiation.

The orientation of the individual within the social organization of the work is not primarily to the work as a whole, but rather to the tissue of connections and separations as they fan out from the particular position which s/he occupies. The orientation to the working division of labour is an *egological* one [11, 1: 60], concerned with engaging one's own activities, the boundaries with the activities of others, and the technology and other resources at hand, in terms of 'decisions-that-I-can-make' and 'actions-that-I-can-take', as against those that others deal with. Working through the stream of tasks means 'doing-what-I-can-do', and passing tasks on to others so that they can do what they do. Though often involving extremes of skill, judgement and coordination, and thus intensive 'work', its smooth accomplishment can render the working division of labour silent and virtually invisible.

Technological artefacts encountered in the course of work are treated by members in a similar way. To be usable, they have to be turned from a machine into an *instrument*, by being incorporated into the flow of the work and finding a place within the practices and contingencies of the working division of labour. A computer-based system or any other tool can, on the basis of its material properties, be known about, geared into, made to work, tinkered with, taken advantage of, used in unanticipated ways, modified, circumvented, or plain rejected by those who work with it, implement it, invest in it, or manage it. That is, it is densely woven into the activities of doing the job, and in highly particular ways.

These precepts cannot be simply 'applied to' or 'mapped onto' a domain in such a way as to yield, in mechanical fashion, a set of results. Rather – and in a manner which mirrors the overall relationship between ethnographic studies and systems design – they act as a resource, as a set of alerting mechanisms, and as a means of orientation. As a hermeneutic, interpretive or phenomenological approach, the aim is to produce a 'thick description' [4] as a means to

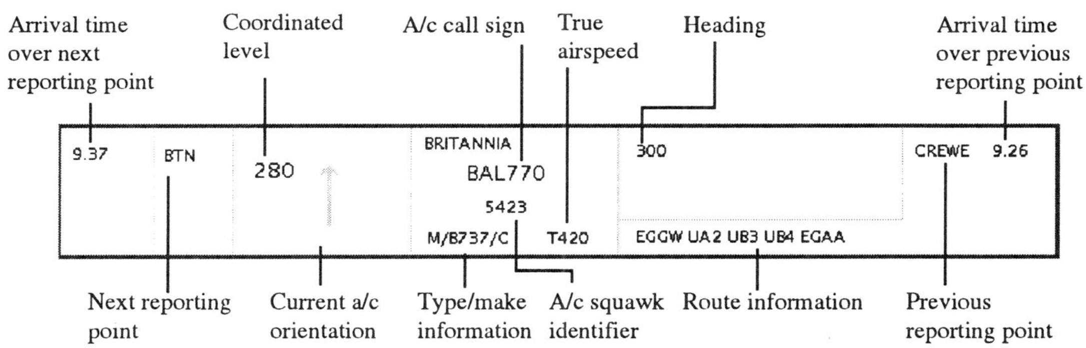

Figure 2. An en-route flight progress strip

discovering the sociality of these activities in context, or situated actions. In the end – and somewhat elusively – the aim is to grasp 'what is really going on' in the course of a piece of work, 'what is really the problem' about doing it, and what instruments might be devised to help resolve these problems.

USING FLIGHT STRIPS IN AIR TRAFFIC CONTROL

The strip as work site

In introducing the flight strip we claimed that it is more than just a repository of information. One aspect of this is the use of the strip as the site where much of the work of ATC takes place. As an example we described the way that a change of flight level would be 'actioned' on and through the strip. Coordination between sectors, changes in heading, eta, route, call sign, and much more are all actioned in similar ways. Most of the activities discussed below are carried and performed on the strip, and do not merely take its contents as 'input'.

The strip as history, memory, trajectory and record

It can be seen from the description of how strips are annotated that previous states and conditions do not disappear, but are available as a series of instructions and crossings-through alongside the current values. They embody a history of the controlling of that flight since entering the sector and, taken together with other strips, a recent history of the state of the sector overall. Controllers can therefore use them to recover the 'trajectory': a sense of 'what they have done' with a flight, and how (and why) they reached the current situation. As one controller told us, "Strips are like your memory – everything you need is there." But they are also *publicly* available to all the members of the suite as a resource with which to make sense of what is going on. They have a *documentary* character as a record or witness of what has been done, and so help to constitute the *accountability* of controlling as a collective process.[7]

'Getting the picture' and 'creating order'

The strip and the radar are used in conjunction, though in different proportion for different purposes (and with different personal styles[8]). In general, radar predominates in the immediate business of coping with a very heavy load, while the strips predominate in planning. Beyond this, however, they are mutually informing for the controller in gaining and holding an understanding of individual flights and of the traffic flow. Controllers will 'build a picture' of the state of the sector by relating traffic within it to a 'schematic' of that sector's characteristics. For example, in a sector where two airways cross each other, building up the picture means looking for the alignment of traffic in a 'single file' relation relative to the main axes, though not simply so, since planes have different performances and some may be 'catching up' while others 'fall behind' (we return to this example in Section 4.2 below). This feature is both a *characteristic* of the sector, and a condition which the controller needs actively to *create*. It is only a schematic in that many flights will not conform straightforwardly to this pattern. Some will turn from one airway onto another, which may involve them crossing through flights coming in the opposite direction. Others may be completely non-standard, such as military flights crossing through the airlanes from air bases (mostly on the flat east coast of the country) to training areas (mostly on the hilly west coast).

Getting the picture therefore means working out what proportion of flights fit the scheme, and with what variation within it, and what proportion are exceptions; it means assessing these for the kinds of control actions that will be required, and planning for those actions; and it means issuing the instructions to create an appropriate current order, and make the traffic flow. One main way in which flights are assessed is therefore their degree of deviation from the scheme, and the kind of problem which that poses. The information for making that assessment is predominantly to be found on the strip. The ordering and marking of the strips reflects the ordering and assessment of the scheme and its problems. The orderliness of the strips stands proxy for the orderliness of the skies; and ordering the strips is a means to creating order in the sky.

Teamwork and the sociality of strip use

Working the strips is team work. When a strip is first printed, the assistant places it in a holder of the colour appropriate to the direction in which it is flying, and in the course of this scans the strip for 'sense'. There are often errors – for example, an indicated route inconsistent with the flight number. In this event the assistant will sort out the error, in discussion if necessary, and may generate a new strip by inputting corrected information from the terminal. The strip acts as a notepad and worksite for all the team members, any of whom may write on it, and each of whom uses a pen of a different colour so the source of the anntoations is immediately apparent. Anyone who notices a problem with a strip or pair of strips – perhaps two flights due at the same navigation point at a similar time and at the same height – can 'cock out' the strips – move them noticeably out of alignment in the racks. This makes it immediately obvious that, when it becomes time to deal with those flights, a problem will need to be considered, and to the practiced eye it will be obvious from a glance at the strips what that problem is. The vocabulary and syntax of annotation and ordering are a language through which the members of the team communicate with each other, and create a 'common statement' about the state of the flight and of the sector.

Nevertheless, it is clear that the activities of the team are 'focussed in' on the support of the active controller, and our account of ATC has reflected this. There is a sense in which a 'protective cocoon' is built around the controller, such that all the resources required for the job are at hand, and s/he can concentrate on doing the job. It is important to recognise, however, that this is not a condition which just arises by accident, or as the result of a simple division of labour and allocation of tasks and responsibilities.

Rather, it is something which needs to be actively and variably created, on a moment-to-moment basis, in response to the constantly changing circumstances, by the other members of the team. Thus it is a crucial aspect of the controller's ability to focus 'single-mindedly' on the job that s/he knows that the strip delivered by the assistant has already been scrutinised by someone with immediate knowledge and experience of what is going on; that particular coordination problems and non-standard flights can be passed to the chief to handle; that the active management of the strips is available for all to see so that they can work up 'the picture' for themselves without having to ask for explanations, and so can be expected to handle tasks delegated to them competently; that puzzling situations or apparent errors can be discussed with other members of the team; and that they are independently and competently on the 'qui vive' for problems and looming catastrophe. Hence it is a working division of labour which is social through-and-through, if in rather distinctive ways. It constitutes a special case of what we might term an *'alterological'* working division of labour.

FROM ETHNOGRAPHY TOWARDS DESIGN

Having touched on several aspects of the sociality of the strip as an artefact in use, we will here take up just two of very many possible consequences for design.

Trusting the system

Taken as a whole, the system is trustable and reliable. There has never been a civil collision in UK airspace which was attributed to air traffic control. It would seem that in this the UK has the best record in the world. Yet if one looks to see what constitutes this reliability, it cannot be found in any single element of the system. It is certainly not to be found in the equipment. The 'Mediator System' technology dates back to the 1960s, it has no backup, and for a period of several months during our fieldwork it was failing regularly[9] (it still fails occasionally). Nor is it to be found in the rules and procedures, which are a resource for safe operation but which can never cover every circumstance and condition. Nor is it to be found in the personnel who, though very highly skilled, motivated and dedicated, as are as prone as people everywhere to human error. Rather, we believe it is to be found in the cooperative activities of controllers across the 'totality' of the system, and in particular in the way that it enforces the active engagement of controllers, chiefs and assistants with the material which they are using and with each other. This constitutes a continuing check on their own work and a cross-check on that of others.

This cross-checking arises in part as an explicit aim of all team members to 'keep an eye' on the state of the sector with a view to safety, since everyone is all too aware that mistakes can be made. But it arises much more reliably in the attention members are forced to give to "each others' business" (and to their own) as a routine part of doing their job. The guarantee resides in the team character of work on the suite and in the coordinating activities which go on between sectors, and the trustability of the strips does not lie in any technical failsafe but in their accessibility by various members of the team. It comes from the very actions of moving the strips, organizing them, writing on them, and discussing them: the checking of information through talk begins as soon as the strip is printed. It occurs not only 'on the job' but during informal conversations, such as in meal breaks, where stories are recounted, or explanations, complaints or apologies are tendered. It can easily appear as an overhead or burden or inefficiency resulting from inadequate equipment or procedures, and so, in a sense, it is. But it is also, we suggest, largely responsible for the trustworthiness of the system as a whole. An obvious path in redesigning the technical support for the job is to seek to do away with these 'redundant' activities and exchanges. Indeed, one of the standard ways in which the division of labour has always been achieved is by devising socio-technical mixes which transform complex cooperation into simple coordination.[10] Yet this may well have the effect of undermining the present trustability.

It cannot follow that the system must be left alone: circumstances and possibilities are constantly changing, and all systems evolve. But it does mean that each of the manual procedures involved in using the strip must be reviewed in a new light, with a view not only to the overt function that it performs, but also to its contribution to the 'knowability', 'checkability' and 'cross-checkability' of the system – with a view, that is, to its part in 'active controlling'. This may mean retaining 'unnecessary' manipulations for some procedures in an electronic equivalent. For example, if a controller has chosen to order strips in a display by estimated time of arrival at a navigation point, then it would seem obvious that any new strips should be automatically inserted in their appropriate place. But it may be better to deliver each new strip to a neutral location, so that the controller is forced actively to review its contents in deciding where to place it [2]. Alternatively, it may mean devising entirely new equivalents for the trustability of some of the old procedures, such as automatic checks on the consistency of the various field values.

Anticipating the load

Our second instance is almost the contrary of the first, since having previously been concerned with the properties of the system as a whole, we are here concerned with the multiple properties of single elements. The ATC system can usefully be conceived in terms of the historical evolution of methods to deal with problems of the *trustability* and *significance* of information. There are two questions controllers must constantly ask themselves. First, "What information do I need to deal with the situation I am now confronted with and the situations that will arise shortly?" (the significance problem). Second, "How do I know that the information which I have is accurate?" (the trustability problem). We argue that it is the cooperative activity that has developed which provides for much of the trustability and significance. At the same time, of course, those historical methods involve considerable overheads, including labour cost, duplication, and time. The capacity constraints of the ATC system are a feature of the means adopted to meet the crucial goals of expedition and safety.

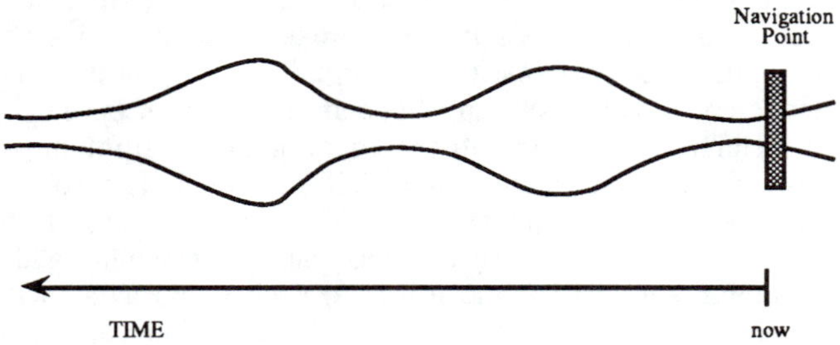

Figure 3. Traffic density indicator

The problem in system redesign is to provide a means to support or enhance those goals, without compromising the very methods that act as their guarantors. Historically, the information resides above all in the strip, and it is through its team-working that trustability and significance are accomplished. At the same time, the strip is the embodiment of the constraints that are inevitably associated with a highly patterned working method. Change in ATC can only be incremental so as to provide continued guarantees of safety. Yet a transformation of working methods is needed if sector capacity is to be increased. Hence the design of the user interface, and the metaphors appropriate to its represesentation of the skies, become critically important. While the strips provide immensely flexible resources, they also impose constraints. There is therefore some purpose in exploring alternative metaphors to see what resources they provide and what constraints they engender. The metaphor we introduce below is just one such possibility.

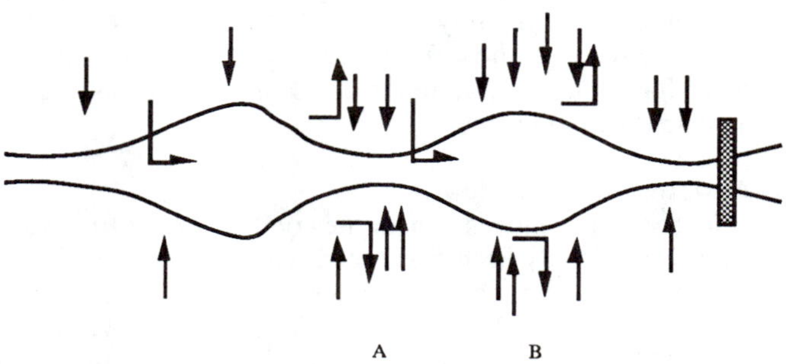

Figure 4. Crossing airways

We have discussed how controllers construct the 'picture' of the state of the skies through the 'schematics' of the sector, as a means to anticipating problems and creating an order and flow, for which the order of the strips is both a proxy and a resource. The varying conditions affect not only the amount of attention which a controller will give, but also the kind of attention which is appropriate. It is important for the controller to anticipate, amongst other things, the 'busyness' of the sector which s/he will have to cope with in, say, the next 10 to 30 minutes. 'Busyness' results not only from the volume of traffic but also from the complexity of the configuration and the proportion of 'standard' to 'non-standard' manoeuvres. The controller will use this anticipation both to clear some space for a busy patch by getting as much as possible of the current controlling requirements out of the way, and also in order to 'gear into' the amount and kind of concentration and planning that will be required.

Currently, the sheer number of strips in the racks (and in the racks of neighbouring sectors) provides a simple 'at-a-glance' indication of how busy things are likely to be. Their distribution over different routes, represented in different bays of the rack, gives a rough indication of the complexity. The estimated times of arrival at a navigation point give, with a rather higher cognitive load, an indication of potential problems in the interrelation of the flights. And the particular flight and destination indicate what kind of manoeuvres can be anticipated. This combination of strip features is therefore used, under these particular circumstances, to address this particular problem. In some sectors, for example, the characteristic problems arise from a 'crossroads' of two airways, with some flights crossing each others' paths, and others turning to leave one airway and join another. In other sectors (or indeed as additional elements within the same ones), flights will be dropping down from or rising up into the airways from an airfield, 'passing through' flights at other levels.

Radical alternatives to the flight strip

An appropriate way of devising an electronic equivalent for the flight strip may, therefore, for these particular purposes, be nothing like a strip at all. An alternative would be to present the controller with a display showing the volume of traffic approaching a particular navigation point as a band of varying width, by time relative to the present, calculated as a moving average. This is illustrated in Figure 3.

Considering next a problem such as the crossing of airways described above, this might be addressed by showing the main stream as a band as in Figure 3, with the incidence by time of crossing, joining and leaving flights shown as arrows at right angles to the band. This is illustrated in Figure 4. It shows, for instance, that there is a high density of crossers at point A, but this coincides with a low main stream density and so indicates a limited scale of problem. At point B, however, there is a high density both of crossers and of the main stream.

Actually coping with the likely difficulties thus revealed could be tackled by, for example, enabling controllers to 'mouse around' the problem area, as illustrated in Figure 5. In response, the corresponding 'captured' electronic strips and radar blips could all be highlighted.

As described so far the 'replacement' of the strip, although radical, has not automated or 'proceduralised' the system, or constrained the field of action and decision open to the controller. It has in a proper sense 'computer supported' the work, by offering an additional resource to the controller in the exercise of judgement and discretion. It has not replaced the ordering eta and route values of the strips 'in general', since under other circumstances these will be used for other purposes. 'Phenomenally', one could say that the same value of the same field of the same strip is a 'different thing' when it is used in a different relation to other elements in a different context.

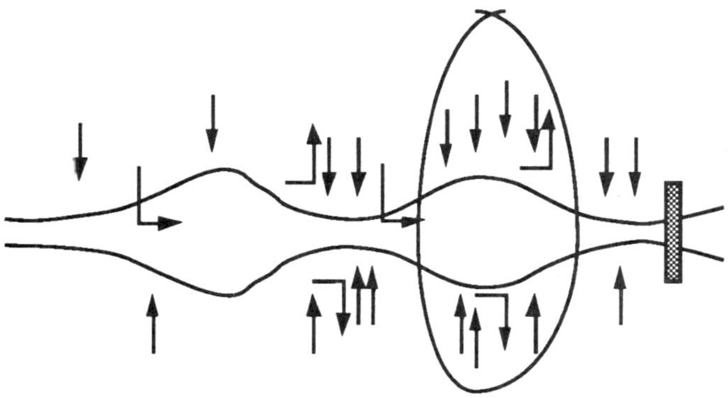

Figure 5. 'Capturing' the problem

But it would not be difficult to go further. For example, if the flights within the main stream were represented by bullets then it would be possible for the controller to try out control solutions by directly manipulating the bullets and arrows – separating them by pulling them forward or backwards, or side to side. The system could then offer the corresponding changes of speed and of heading on the respective strips, for the controller to issue as instructions to pilots if s/he chose. As a next step, the computer could offer its own manipulations to optimise separations. And, with the long-planned Mode S radar transponder which would establish a data link between ATC and aircraft, controllers could authorise the system itself to issue these automatically generated instructions.

Yet somewhere along this path – and we suspect rather soon – the point would have been crossed where, for these sequences of activity, active controlling is turned into human monitoring of controlling performed by the system. And it is crystal clear that humans perform very badly as mere monitors of automated systems. That point therefore cannot safely be crossed until there is a sufficient level of confidence in the automated system that it does not require to be monitored; and that is not in prospect at the moment.

The design platform being developed by our colleagues in computer science allows for a full range of such metaphors to be developed and explored. The purpose of the metaphor discussed here is to illustrate some aspects of the relationship between ethnographic studies of work in context and the generation of ideas for redesign. It is not proposed as a solution, since it will only be possible to tell if these and similar design ideas will work by going on to discuss and test them intensively with working controllers, to evaluate them against alternatives, and to consider systematically a full range of human factors and workload issues in their implementation. While we suggest that the ethnographic approach offers an important additional resource in the artful and creative work of designing systems, the setting is far too complex for its findings to be simply predictive. It would, amongst other things, remain to be seen how many separate 'instruments' would result when the uses of the strip were fully decomposed, and how this would compare to the efficiency and flexibility of this one small piece of paper.

In the space available it has only been possible to skim the surface of the issues, and of the empirical material.[11] The work we have discussed goes to the heart of safety-criticality in complex cooperative systems; but it does so in a way that may be strange and troublesome from a software engineering (or indeed from an HCI) perspective. There is no formal modelling of functions or requirements, no analysis of data flow, no tabulation of viewpoints, no separation between function, implementation and interface [15]. There are only descriptive, interpretive, incomplete and seemingly quite subjective accounts of the accomplishments and the troubles involved in socially organized action. Formal methods are – and for very good reason – most heavily stressed where safety-critical systems are involved. Yet a crucial aspect of safety-critical performance is that a system be built on a proper understanding of the qualitative character of the work involved. Many errors and 'violations' arise precisely out of the necessity to tinker with a troublesome system to make it capable of serving its purposes at all. Hence the characteristics of systems do not exist in the abstract, as absolute features of their design, but are emergent properties of systems in use.[12] These boundaries and paradoxes form the context of our current collaborative work. They are, we believe, key questions for the CSCW research community.

ACKNOWLEDGEMENTS

We would like to acknowledge the very great and of course indispensable contribution of air traffic controllers and others in the UK Civil Aviation Authority; the earlier contributions of Richard Harper, now at Xerox EuroPARC; and Dick Bentley for drawing Figures 1 and 2.

REFERENCES

1. Anderson, R.J., Hughes, J.A. and Sharrock, W.W. *Working For Profit: The Social Organization of Calculation in an Entrepreneurial Firm.* Avebury, Aldershot, UK, 1989.

2. Bentley, R., Rodden, T., Sawyer, P., Sommerville, I., 'A prototyping environment for Dynamic Data Visualisation', in *Proceedings of the 5th IFIP TC2\WG2.7 Working Conference on Engineering for Human-Computer Interaction*, Ellivuori, Finland, 10-14 August, C. Unger and J. A. Larson (eds), Elsevier Science, 1992.

3. Garfinkel, H. *Studies in Ethnomethodology*. Prentice Hall, Englewood Cliffs, 1967.

4. Geertz, C. *The Interpretation of Cultures.* Basic Books, New York, 1973.

5. Gurwitsch, A. *Human Encounters in the Social World.* Duquesne University Press, Pittsburgh, 1979.

6. Hammersley, M. What's Wrong with Ethnography? The Myth of Theoretical Description. *Sociology,* 24, 4 (Nov. 1990), 597-615.

7. Hammersley, M. and Atkinson, P. *Ethnography: Principles in Practice.* Routledge, London, UK, 1983.

8. Hughes, J.A., Shapiro, D., Sharrock, W., Harper, R., and Randall, D. *Ordering the Skies: the sociology of coordinated work.* Routledge, London, UK (in press).

9. Lofland, J. *Analyzing Social Settings: a guide to qualitative observation and analysis.* Wadsworth, Belmont CA, 1971.

10. Lofland, J. *Doing Social Life: the qualitative study of human interaction in natural settings*, Wiley, New York, 1976.

11. Natanson, M. *Anonymity.* Indiana University Press, Bloomington, 1986.

12. Schäl, T. and Zeller, B. A Methodological Approach to Computer Supported Cooperative Work, in *Proc. Fifth European Conference on Cognitive Ergonomics* (Urbino, Italy, 3-6 September 1990), 291-304.

13. Schutz, A. *Reflections on the Problem of Relevance.* Nijhoff, The Hague, (ed. M. Zaner), 1970.

14. Shapiro, D., Hughes, J.A. and Randall, D. Qualitative approaches to the verification and validation of systems for air traffic control, in *Proc. NATO ASI on Verificaton and Validation of Complex and Integrated Human-Machine Systems* (Vimeiro, Portugal, 6-17 July 1992), forthcoming.

15. Sommerville, Ian (1989) *Software Engineering.* Addison-Wesley, Reading, UK, 1989.

16. Stanley, L. Doing Ethnography, Writing Ethnography: A Comment on Hammersley. *Sociology,* 24, 4 (Nov. 1990), 617-627.

17. Suchman, L. *Plans and Situated Actions: The Problem of Human-Machine Communication.* Cambridge University Press, Cambridge, UK, 1987.

NOTES

1 This is necessarily a simplification. Sometimes, as circumstances dictate, the airspace is divided into more or fewer sectors. In this paper we only discuss one of the three kinds of UK air traffic control, that for 'en-route' sectors. The others are terminal manouevring areas, and airfield control.

2 Again, this is a simplification since under certain circumstances other separation standards are applied

3 Other information available to controllers on the suite can include weather displays and forecasts, notes of temporary restrictions or changes in procedures, etc.

4 The project is entitled *Social Analysis of Control Systems for HCI Design.* It is funded by the Joint Cognitive Science/HCI Initiative of the UK Medical, Science & Engineering, and Economic & Social Research Councils, under grant number SPG 8931598. Our colleagues on the project in the Department of Computing at Lancaster are Ian Sommerville, Tom Rodden, Peter Sawyer and Richard Bentley.

5 The precise time devoted is difficult to gauge because three research projects were involved, with the flight strip accounting for a different proportion of effort and attention in each.

6 The use of the term 'tacit knowledge' is different in sociology than in cognitive psychology, in that sociologists are not very careful to distinguish between knowledge which is unarticulated, and that which is *unarticulable*; while in cognitive psychology the term is usually reserved for the latter sense. Sociological 'tacit knowledge' is therefore closer to cognitive psychology's 'scheme' (the authors are grateful to Gerrit van der Veer for pointing out this distinction).

7 This is, of course, not the only form of record. A voice log of telephone and R/T communications among controllers and between controllers and pilots is kept, as is a recording of the computer-generated radar display. However, these are not available to controllers as part of the routine of doing the job but are only used for investigation and monitoring.

8 Some older controllers were trained in a period when radar was not available or was much less reliable. Some tend still to focus more on the strips.

9 Due, it eventualy emerged, to power-supply problems.

10 The sense of these terms which we use here is that of Schäl and Zeller [12], where 'cooperation' entails interdependency in the actual performance of the work, while 'coordination' entails the combination and sequencing of work which can otherwise be independently performed.

11 It will be presented in greater detail in [8].

12 These matters are considered further in [14].

Ethnographically-informed systems design for air traffic control

R. Bentley*, J. A. Hughes†, D. Randall†, T. Rodden*, P. Sawyer*, D. Shapiro†, I. Sommerville*

CSCW Research Centre
Computing* and Sociology† Departments,
Lancaster University,
Lancaster, LA1 4YR
UK.
E-mail: is@comp.lancs.ac.uk
Phone: +44-524-65201
Fax: +44 524 381707

ABSTRACT

This paper relates experiences of a project where an ethnographic study of air traffic controllers is being used to inform the design of the controllers' interface to the flight data base. We outline the current UK air traffic control system, discuss the ethnographic work we have undertaken studying air traffic control as a cooperative activity, describe some of the difficulties in collaboration between software developers and sociologists and show how the ethnographic studies have influenced the systems design process. Our conclusions are that ethnographic studies are helpful in informing the systems design process and may produce insights which contradict conventional thinking in systems design.

KEYWORDS

Air Traffic Control, Systems Design, Ethnography

INTRODUCTION

One of the most significant influences of CSCW has been to lend a respectability amongst software developers to sociological methods of empirical research. The contribution of sociology, and anthropology, is through the description and analysis of the 'real world' settings in which systems will have to find their place. The social world of work is so rich and varied as to defy adequate representation by individualised, cognitive models of users. The notion of the user as a stable generic entity with fixed cognitive capacities is a chimera, and a model which cannot survive the move toward larger scale, distributed systems. Also important is the growing realisation that one of the major causes of system 'failure' is the mismatch between the functionalities of the system as conceived by designers and its contexts of use [5].

Seminal work in this area has been carried out by Suchman [12] and by other investigators such as Hughes *et al.* [9], Harper *et al.* [6] and Heath and Luff [7]. These ethnographic studies have involved a sociologist observing workers in their environment over a period of several months and hence gaining a deep understanding of the actual rather than the formal working practices. For example, Suchman has studied office systems, Heath and Luff have studied a control room for the London Underground railway and Hughes *et al.* studied air traffic control.

The work reported in this paper is a continuation of this last study. It is distinct from previous ethnographic studies of controllers in that the explicit objective of the ethnography is to inform the design of a user interface to a reactive data base system which provides the essential information for air traffic controllers to carry out their work. A reactive data base is a data base where the information is continually updated either from external sensors (radars and aircraft data links in this case) or from concurrent inputs from different users.

There have been several previous experiments with automating the user interface to the flight data base system so that instructions issued by a controller are captured in the data base. Apart from speeding up the communication between controllers, computer-processable information about controllers' intentions could be used to support an effective conflict alert facility. However, given the incremental style of innovation which dominates in air traffic control, any technical change must require minimal changes to working practices not only to avoid the huge cost of retraining but also because the data base interface is only a part of the complex of systems that is air traffic control.

Permission to copy without use all or part of this material is granted provided that the copies are not made or distributed for commercial advantage, the ACM copyright notice and the title of the publication and its date appear, and notice is given that copying is by permission of the Association for Computing Machinery. To copy otherwise, or to republish, requires a fee and/or specific permission.

© 1992 ACM 0-89791-543-7/92/0010/0123...$1.50

Previous experiments in automating the UK system have been undertaken primarily from a technical viewpoint. They have not been acceptable to air traffic controllers and we believe that this is because these systems have not effectively supported the 'working division of labour' [1] as adopted by controllers. Hopkin [8] identifies the problem:

> "One striking aspect of automation applied to air traffic control systems is that most of the forms of automation for the controller to use, as distinct from those which sense or process or compile data automatically, are for one controller at a human-machine interface. They are aids to an individual controller's decisions, problem solving or predictions, yet they are being introduced into contexts where many of these functions have previously been performed by teams"

Our work is different. We are starting from the position that air traffic control is a subtle cooperative activity and we believe we must understand the nature of that cooperation in order to build effective computer support.

This paper is not concerned with the details of the automated system which is under development and which is described elsewhere [2, 3]. Rather, we discuss how the ethnographic studies have helped us gain an understanding of the cooperative processes of air traffic control and how this understanding has influenced the design of our prototype software system. In the remainder of this paper we briefly describe the current system for UK air traffic control and the cooperation in the air traffic control process. We describe some problems of cross-disciplinary working and discuss how the ethnographic studies have led us to question some widely-held assumptions about systems design.

THE UK AIR TRAFFIC CONTROL SYSTEM

Air traffic control in the UK is managed through two sites which control all domestic and international air traffic. Our studies were concerned with the larger of these sites, the London Air Traffic Control Centre (LATCC). Within LATCC, there are 8 radar suites each of which is responsible for controlling 1 or more sectors of the airspace. Each suite provides a working area for two teams of controllers (one team per sector), radar screens and facilities for communications between aircraft and other suites. The radar is a 2-dimensional, 'real time' representation of the sector's airspace and the positions of aircraft within it. It can display other information about a controlled sector including sector boundaries, coast lines, major and minor airports, etc. However, the radar only shows what is 'happening now' but not what 'might be happening' in a few minutes time. Controllers need to anticipate potential problems so, to supplement the radar, they use paper *flight progress strips* which carry information about expected and current flights being controlled, together with controllers' instructions to the controlled aircraft. The ATC system is described in more detail by Hughes *et al.* [10] who discuss the ethnographic studies of controllers and who describe flight strip layout more fully.

An example of a flight strip (as replicated in our automated system prototype) is illustrated in Figure 1. The strip contains static information such as the flight number, aircraft identifier, beacon identifier, source and destination, and dynamic information such as time over beacon, heading, current height and airspeed.

Strips are produced from a data base consisting of flight plans filed prior to the aircraft's departure. The data base is updated through Radar Data Processing (RDP) and by controllers and their assistants directly inputting flight data.

Flight strips are organised on a *flight progress board* where strips are aligned and organised in a rack according to the reporting points over which a flight will pass (Figure 2). To the accomplished controller this display is an 'at a glance' means of showing the flow of traffic through the sector and its characteristics. To the experienced and knowledgeable eye, different indicated ETA times and different heights may represent problems, for example, 'climbing through' or 'catching up' given the relative performances of aircraft. The way in which the controller organises the strips, for instance, according to arrival time over a reporting point, or according to flight level, or to possible confliction points, provides information about the state of the sector.

The controller issues instructions to aircraft and verifies, using the radar, that the instructions have been carried out. Controllers coordinate the air traffic safely by maintaining separation levels, directing course changes, airspeed, ascents and descents. They have to take the traffic as it comes and blend incoming aircraft into a steady flow. To this end, they spend time organising strips into a sequence of aircraft, using the radar to check and assess the current 'state of play' and, using the strips, anticipate likely problems. They also spend time coordinating activities with other members of the team, arranging flight levels, discussing 'best' procedures to expedite the flow of traffic, sometimes passing flight level changes to assistants to coordinate with adjacent sectors, and so on.

The active organising of the strips themselves on the flight progress board by the controller is an essential feature of the work. At its simplest and most general, the controller's problem is a scheduling one. For any segment of airspace the traffic has to be taken as and when it arrives and threaded into an orderly pattern before each individual plane is handed on to the next sector. This scheduling has to be achieved in and through making the traffic flow. Aircraft cannot be parked and even when they are 'on hold' they are still on the move and part of the traffic flow. Organising the strips is a way of achieving a solution to the scheduling problem by organising the strips as a scheduling of work tasks.

Figure 1 A flight strip

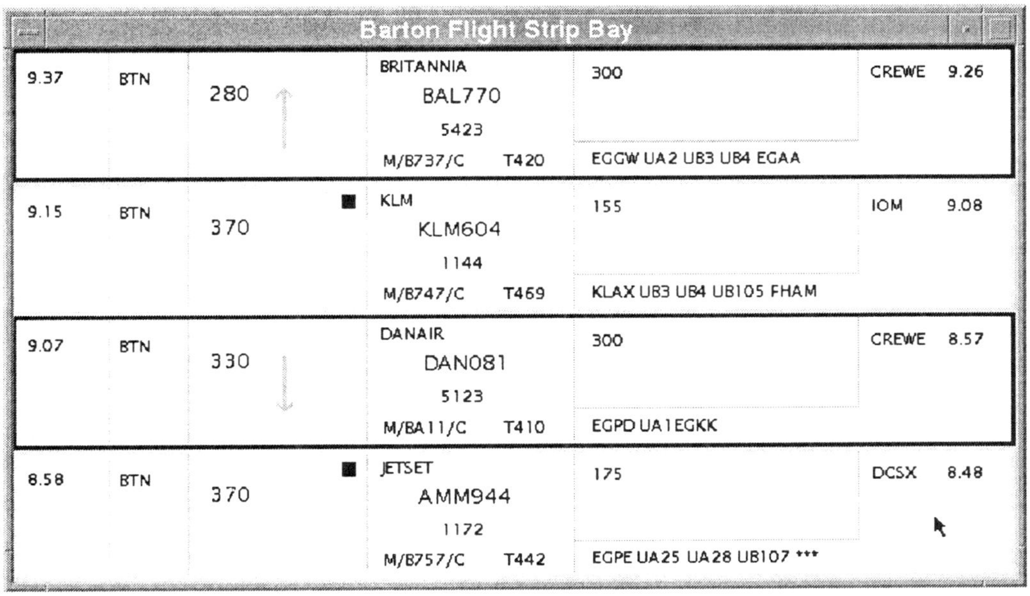

Figure 2 Flight strips representing aircraft due to arrive at the Barton beacon organised by arrival time

COOPERATION IN THE ATC PROCESS

The air traffic control system is deliberately organised to minimise explicit coordination and cooperation between controllers. For example, so long as flights are as planned, the handover of a plane from a controller in one sector to a controller in an adjacent sector does not require any communication between them. A task-based systems analysis would therefore fail to reveal the subtle and complex cooperation which is actually going on. This cooperation only became apparent through the ethnographic studies.

A typical radar suite is manned by a chief controller, two radar controllers, and two assistants with military liaison officers in close attendance. Each of these is responsible for particular tasks, though there is a very important informal sharing of some of them. Assistants perform apparently routine servicing tasks, such as tearing off the printed strips from the printer, placing them into their correct coloured holders, ensuring that each strip is placed in the correct rack. However, during this action, they informally check the information on the strip. Errors are not uncommon and this initial checking is an important first level check. For example, in our observations, we noticed an assistant controller recognise that a flight destination was obviously wrong. As he glanced at the strip, he saw that the destination airport specified was a private manufacturer's airfield yet the flight was a normal scheduled flight. From his knowledge of that specific flight, he corrected the strip before passing it to the controller. Assistants may also update flight plans by editing route and ETA changes.

The radar controllers are responsible for the actual control instructions issued to the aircraft and the chief's responsibilities normally include coordinating traffic between sectors by telephone calls or by visits to the relevant sector suite. His or her main task, however, is monitoring the flow of traffic at a strategic level, making judgements about the allocation of flight levels, and so on, to facilitate the traffic flow. Chiefs may also act as a

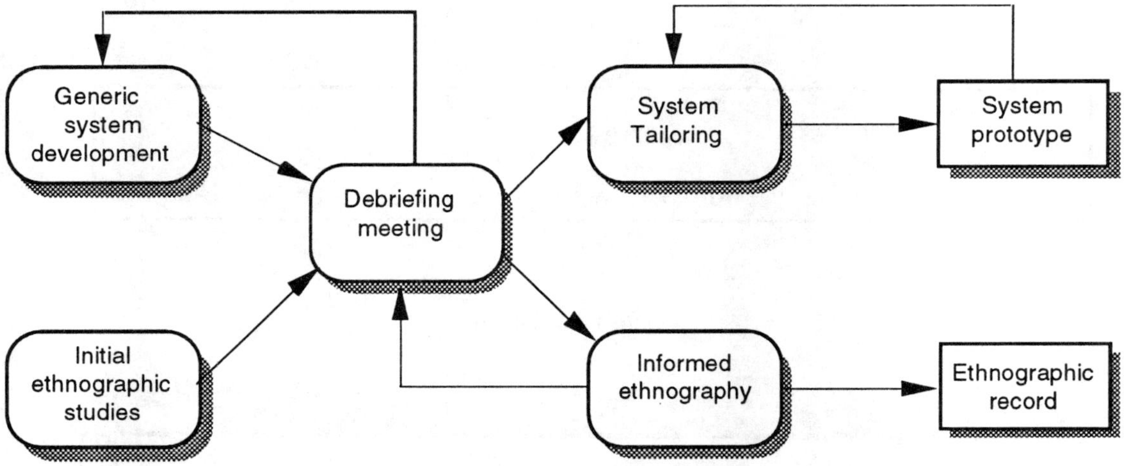

Figure 3 Ethnographically-informed systems development

backup to the radar controller by dealing with unscheduled traffic, drawing attention to potential problems by 'cocking out' strips (setting them at an angle in the rack), or by writing on them. The chief also coordinates military aircraft with the military liaison officers.

What is important about the teamwork is not so much that the respective team members have individual tasks to perform, which they do, but that they are woven into a 'working division of labour'. This means the division of labour is organised dynamically according to need and does not necessarily follow a prescribed form. The individuals are individuals-in-a-team, and much of their work consists in the ability to organise the distribution of individual tasks into an ongoing assemblage of activities *within* the 'working division of labour'.

Our ethnographic studies revealed that the teamwork character of the work was manifested in myriad ways in the ongoing work itself. Not as an adjunct to the work but integral to it. There was no one thing, or set of things, that manifested teamwork since it saturated the work itself - in the talk around the suite, in the activities performed, in the stories and anecdotes told, and more. Indeed, this was much the way in which the ethnography recorded the work, by stories, descriptions of activities, anecdotes, vignettes of events, and so on. But teamwork is very much an aspect of its members' tacit knowledge which is not normally explicitly expressed except on the occasions when 'normal and routine' working breaks down.

Effective use of flight strips is the key to 'good controlling'. As one controller put it, 'You have got to have a complete picture of what should be in your sector and what should be in your sector is on those strips'. Strips become a documentary record of an aircraft's passage through the sector. The initial information on the strip is amended as instructions are given to and confirmed by the pilot. The strip accumulates information about actions which have been recorded on the strip. Essentially, the strip is a shared note pad conveying to members of the team what actions have been taken with respect to particular aircraft, who authorised these actions and how these might affect other aircraft in the traffic configuration.

Amendments may be done by the controller, by the chief or, less often, by an assistant. Attention-getting information may also be written on the strips, such as arrows indicating unusual routes, symbols designating 'crossers, joiners and leavers', circles around unusual destinations, and so on. Information indicating that coordination between sectors has taken place, changes in ETA or to route, changes in call sign, etc., can be indicated using standard notations, each member of the team using a different coloured pen to annotate the strips, thus adding responsibility and accountability to the record. The strip, in other words, is a public document for the members of the team; a working representation of an aircraft's control history and a work site of controlling.

WORKING TOGETHER: ETHNOGRAPHERS AND SOFTWARE ENGINEERS

The challenge which we faced was how to utilise the insights of the ethnographic study of air traffic controllers in the design of user interfaces to a flight data base which would provide comparable functionality to that provided by the flight strip system. Furthermore, because of the time constraints on our project, we could not carry out an ethnographic study then develop the software system rather the ethnography and the systems development had to be concurrent activities. The approach we have adopted is illustrated in Figure 3.

The debriefing meetings are a particularly important part of the process. During these meetings, the ethnographer discussed his findings and was questioned by other team members. The software developers' questions focussed on systems requirements and, while it was rare to identify an explicit software requirement during the debriefing meeting, the developers gained an intuitive impression of the facilities required by controllers.

During the debriefing meetings, the system developers identified particular areas of interest and particular problems which should be investigated in the next phase of the ethnography. Thus, the ethnographer was informed of the system requirements and focussed his observations to answer the questions posed by the system developers.

In the first phase of our work, we have developed a prototyping system [2] which has been designed so that we can rapidly generate user interfaces to a reactive data base. In the second phase, which is now underway, we are experimenting with different approaches to user interface design. The ethnographer plays a key role in this activity as he acts as a substitute for the air traffic controller, and represents his or her view of the system. This allows us to have some of the advantages of participative design but without the requirements that an end-user should be regularly available for system evaluation. In the final phase, we will expose the system to real controllers and evaluate the interfaces which we have designed.

In our work, we have had the advantage that the people involved from both sociology and software engineering were willing to be flexible and willing to recognise that the other discipline's viewpoint may be valid irrespective of how alien it might be. In this respect, we believe our collaboration has been successful but there have been difficulties which we believe are likely to arise in other collaborative projects of this nature.

1. The fundamental approach of each discipline is totally different. Sociology is analytic. It is concerned with gathering and interpreting data about some social situation or process and drawing some conclusions from that interpretation. By contrast, software engineering is concerned with synthesis - designing and building new abstract models of the real-world. Thus, sociology focuses on and pays great attention to detail; software engineering strives to hide detail through abstractions.

2. Social analysis is a fairly prolonged activity. Typically, ethnography will take place over a period of several months with at least the same amount of time spent in analysis and interpretation of the observations. To inform the systems development process, however, software engineers need quick results and make demands on the sociologists to provide rapid assessments of their work.

3. The roots of ethnography are in anthropology so ethnographers are trained to avoid making judgements about a social situation or process and, as far as possible, to avoid letting their own prejudices interfere with their observations. By contrast, engineers *must* make judgements, often with inadequate information, as to what is and is not significant. Engineers therefore may find the more remote attitude of sociologists difficult to understand.

These differences in working styles were highlighted by four questions which systems designers posed to the ethnographer studying air traffic control. These questions were motivated by the need to make design decisions about the system which was being built to support prototype generation and the data base interfaces themselves:

- what characteristics of the existing manual system are unimportant and need not be supported in an automated system?
- what are important manual activities which need not be supported in an automated system because the activities are a consequence of the fact that no automated support is available?
- what characteristics of the manual system must be replicated without change in an automated system?
- what activities from the manual system may be supported in a way which is different from that used in the manual system?

From the point of view of the sociologists, what was interesting about such questions was their directedness in the sense that almost for the first time the service role of the sociological analysis was explicitly formulated. The questions were not easily answerable, not least with reference to a way of working as subtle and as complex as controlling. Moreover, the sociologists' own methodological point of view which treated the system as a fusion of working practices and technology made it difficult to draw the distinctions necessary to answer such questions. For example, deciding what were the 'important manual activities', irrespective of the availability of automated support, was not straightforward. Was 'idle chat' among the team 'unimportant', and in what sense? Even though such talk might not be directly related to the specific tasks of controlling, a case could be made that it was important for morale, the sharing of experiences, providing support, and so on. Similarly, although a number of manual activities of the 'manual system' may be supported in different ways, it is difficult to anticipate the likely consequences of such a shift.

Moreover, the actual performance of some manual activities, such as writing on the strips, manipulating them in the racks, coordinating by telephone with adjacent suites, and more, serve to keep the controller, and other members of the team, 'geared into' the work. Though some of these could be automated, the important question of whether this would reduce the controller to a more passive role of system monitor rather than an active participant in a system-in-use is hard to determine in advance.

The sociologists have recognised the reason why these questions need to be answered; the software engineers have recognised the difficulties in providing such answers. We believe that finding a means to answer questions such as these is the key to the systematic use of ethnography in the systems design process.

ETHNOGRAPHY AND SYSTEMS DESIGN

Our work has now reached a stage where we are generating system interfaces whose design has been informed by the ethnographic observations. We have found that the information provided by ethnography is essentially background information which has provided a deeper understanding of the application domain. The ethnography did not result in specific, detailed systems requirements; rather it provided pointers to appropriate design decisions.

From our observations we have become convinced that some 'conventional' assumptions made by systems designers may be invalid when cooperative systems are being developed. Examples of these assumptions are:

1. Computer systems should always automate tedious manual tasks which involve comparisons of similar information and ordering of records in a data store. Therefore, the computer system not the human operator should be responsible for sorting and maintaining the sort order when new information is added to the system.

2. User interface designers should always provide facilities for end-users to tailor interfaces to suit their own personal ways of working and personal preferences.

Our ethnographic observations revealed that the manual manipulation of flight strips and the manual re-ordering of the flight strip racks were significant activities. To provide an analogue of this manual manipulation, our prototype system incorporates the following design decisions:

1. Strips are not positioned according to some default order when they are added to a display.

2. Some activities have been deliberately retained as requiring manual intervention because the manual activity allows a feasibility check of the strip information to be made.

3. There is no standard, enforced model of flight progress board organisation. Support is provided for many different possible orderings or ordering as specified by the controller.

When a controller is using strips ordered by time of arrival to a beacon and new strips have to be added to the display, it would seem natural for these strips to be positioned automatically in the right place on the user's display. However, the ethnographic work suggested that the controller's action of manually placing a strip in the appropriate position in a bay focussed attention on that strip and to related strips. This was an important safety device as it allowed the early identification of potential problems. Automated positioning is undesirable because these problems may not become apparent until there is an explicit need to use the new strip.

A further example of manual intervention forcing data checking occurs when strips are first printed in the current system. They are then placed into different coloured holders by assistant controllers to distinguish between flights on different headings. In this action, the assistants read the strip information and detect irregularities such as known flight numbers flying to the wrong airport, an arrival time which is inconsistent with the aircraft type, etc. They either correct these errors themselves or draw the controller's attention to them.

The colour of a strip holder is determined by the aircraft's heading and it would be a simple matter to automate the assignment of coloured borders to electronic strips. However, because of the important checking function, we do not propose any default border colour but require the controller to make a manual choice of possible display formats for a strip.

The manual of air traffic control specifies that strip bays should normally be ordered according to the time of arrival of an aircraft over a beacon. This model is followed by the majority of controllers but our ethnographic observations revealed that some controllers have evolved an alternative way of working which uses a different strip ordering. Therefore, while we provide explicit facilities which allow a controller to order his or her display according to the manual, we also immediately switch off this automatic ordering as soon as strips are manually re-ordered

It is a common belief amongst developers of user interfaces that end-user tailorability is essential. Indeed, Fischer and Girgensohn [4] state:

> "End-user modifiability is not a luxury, but a necessity in cases where systems do not fit a particular task, a particular style of working or a personal sense of aesthetics".

While this may be true for applications designed for single-user use, we do not think it valid for cooperative systems where the representation is shared with a common understanding of the syntax and semantics of that representation. Our work has shown the importance of such a common representation for communication amongst controllers. Much of their work requires 'at a glance' observations of strips and flight progress boards. This can only be effective if all controllers can rapidly assimilate flight strip information and this rapid assimilation is hindered if even slight differences in strip representations are supported. We have therefore limited tailorability to surface features such as highlighting and have curtailed the controller's ability to tailor the strips in such a way that extensive explanation to other controllers would be required.

As well as influencing the systems design process, we believe that the ethnographer has a further role as substitute user during initial system validation. User-centred design where users participate in the interface design process from an early stage in that process is likely to lead to more effectively usable user interfaces. However, a serious constraint to the practice of user-centred design is the availability of users, particularly where these users are an expensive and scarce resource. This is a particular problem during early stages of the design process where the design is unlikely to satisfy the user's requirements so the user gets little reward from participation in the design process.

Because of the understanding of the user's work which is gained by the ethnographer in the course of his or her studies, our experience has shown that ethnographers can act as 'user's champions' in the early stages of the design process. Thus, initial inappropriate designs can be detected with very limited end-user involvement so that expensive user time is only used at later stages of the process where design details have to be resolved. This issue is discussed in more detail by Sommerville *et al.* [11]

CONCLUSIONS

Our general conclusions about our collaboration and our studies of air traffic controllers are as follows:

1. Observational methods such as ethnography can play an important role in informing the process of automated systems design. However, there is not an obvious mapping from an observational record and a systems requirements document. The extent of the contribution which observational methods can make to the system specification process has still to be demonstrated.

2. Software engineers and sociologists can work together effectively. However, there is a wide gulf between these disciplines and entrenched philosophical positions will probably ensure that that gulf cannot be bridged. Effective inter-disciplinary cooperation requires much flexibility on both sides and requires both sides to question their own assumptions and working methods.

3. Some conventional principles which are normally thought of as 'good design' may be inappropriate for cooperative systems. Manual intervention and manipulation of information may be essential implicit methods of communication and cooperation.

4. An important role for ethnographers is to act as substitute users in a 'user-centred' systems design process. Because of their close involvement with end-users, ethnographers are well equipped to understand their problems and can be effective in discovering gross errors in the systems design.

The collaboration on studies of air traffic control is continuing with evaluation studies planned for 1993. A further project is also underway where a much less structured cooperative activity (systems design) is being studied and we anticipate that it will be possible to draw interesting comparisons between these projects.

REFERENCES

[1] Anderson, R. J., Hughes, J. A. and Sharrock, W. W. 1989, Working for Profit: The Social Organisation of Calculability in an Entrepreneurial Firm, Aldershot: Avebury.

[2] Bentley, R., Rodden, T., Sawyer, P. and Sommerville, I., 1992, 'A Prototyping Environment for Dynamic Data Visualisation', To appear in the Proceedings of the 5th IFIP Working Conference on User Interfaces, (Ellivuori, Finland), Elsevier Science, 10-14 August, 1992.

[3] Bentley, R., Rodden, T., Sawyer, P. and Sommerville, I., 1992, 'An architecture for tailoring cooperative multi-user displays', To appear in the Proceedings of CSCW'92.

[4] Fischer, G. and Girgensohn, A., 1990, 'End-User Modifiability in Design Environments', Proceedings of CHI '90, (Seattle, Washington), ACM Press, 183-191.

[5] Grudin, J., 1991, 'CSCW: The Convergence of Two Development Contexts', Proceedings CHI'91, 91-98, Reading, Mass.: Addison Wesley.

[6] Harper, R., Hughes, J. and Shapiro, D., 1991, 'Harmonious Working and CSCW: Computer Technology and Air Traffic Control', in J. M. Bowers and S. D. Benford (eds): Studies in Computer Supported Cooperative Work. Theory, Practice and Design, North-Holland, Amsterdam.

[7] Heath, C. and Luff, P., 1991, 'Collaborative Activity and Technological Design: Task coordination in the London Underground Control Rooms', in Proceedings of ECSCW'91, Kluwer.

[8] Hopkin, V. D., 1991, 'The Impact of automation on Air Traffic Control Systems', in. J. A. Wise, V. D. Hopkin and M. L. Smith (eds.), Automation and Systems Issues in Air Traffic Control, Berlin: Springer-Verlag.

[9] Hughes, J. A., Shapiro, D. Z., Sharrock, W. W., Anderson, R. J., Harper, R. R. and Gibbons, S. C., 1988, 'The Automation of Air Traffic Control', Final Report SERC/ESRC Grant no. GR/D/86257, Department of Sociology, Lancaster University.

[10] Hughes, J. A., Randall, D. W. and Shapiro, D. Z., 1992, 'Faltering from Ethnography to Design', To appear in Proceedings of CSCW'92.

[11] Sommerville, I., Rodden, T., Sawyer, P. and Bentley, R., 1992, 'Sociologists can be Surprisingly Useful in Interactive Systems Design', To appear in Proceedings of HCI'92, York, UK, September 1992.

[12] Suchman, L., 1987, Plans and Situated Actions, Cambridge: Cambridge University Press.

Consultants and Apprentices:
Observations about Learning and Collaborative Problem Solving

Lucy M. Berlin
Robin Jeffries

Hewlett-Packard Labs
1501 Page Mill Rd., Palo Alto, CA 94303
(415) 857-7049
berlin@hplabs.hpl.hp.com

ABSTRACT

Informal consulting interactions between apprentices and experts represent a little-studied but common collaborative work practice in many domains. In the computer industry, programmers become apprentices as they retool themselves to new computer languages, programming environments, software frameworks and systems. Our empirical study of consulting interactions has provided insights into the nature of this informal collaborative work practice.

We describe the variety of "hard-to-find" information provided by the expert, the incidental learning observed, and the pair's strategies for managing joint and individual productivity. Given these observations, we discuss how computer-based tools could help apprentices encapsulate task context, switch among subtasks, facilitate collaborative interaction, and supplement consultants.

KEYWORDS

Apprentice, consultant, programmer, incidental learning, shared artifacts.

INTRODUCTION

In the computer industry, professional programmers must often retool themselves. A project change may require working with a new software system, in a new programming language, and using a new toolset. Modern object-oriented frameworks of reusable software components have increased the amount to be learned, since frameworks commonly have hundreds of interdependent classes to be learned about.

In a decade of work as computer scientists in an industrial research setting, we've informally noted the frequency and value of consulting interactions. This is supported by studies of software customization behavior and spreadsheet use. Mackay [8] found that preferred strategies for getting information about software customizations were, in order: asking a person, copying and experimenting, and reading documentation. Nardi and Miller [9] uncovered extensive sharing and collaborative development of spreadsheets within organizations. And, in a rare study of experts on huge software projects, Riedl, Weitzenfeld, Freeman, Klein and Musa [11] showed that debugging expertise largely involves social and psychological expertise — their experts "preferred not to read code at all, if they could help it; certainly not to read unfamiliar code without assistance."

Knowing that people are seen as prime sources of task-relevant information, we undertook an empirical study of the interactions between programmers learning a new system and the system's designers. Our original goal was to study the effect of the object-oriented methodology on programmers' problems in understanding and modifying large systems. By audiotaping interactions with the systems' designers, we expected to focus on the apprentices' most severe understanding problems.

However, even in the first few weeks of the study, we realized that the study provides a window on an important collaborative work practice — one which we broadly describe as an *apprenticeship interaction.*

Apprenticeships are common in intellectually complex domains. For example, multi-year internships are standard in medicine and clinical psychology. Teacher internship programs [4] increase the effectiveness, retention and satisfaction of the mentored. Informal on-the-job training is also a form of apprenticeship. This is used in teaching secretaries, or librarians new to a job. In such on-the-job training, veterans help the new hires become effective by teaching a combination of facts, procedures, decision-making strategies, and the local culture. Understanding on-the-job computer training is becoming more important in society, as even blue-collar jobs become computerized [14]. Apprenticeships and consulting interactions are also common, although less formally recognized, in the computer industry. Besides

Permission to copy without fee all or part of this material is granted provided that the copies are not made or distributed for direct commercial advantage, the ACM copyright notice and the title of the publication and its date appear, and notice is given that copying is by permission of the Association for Computing Machinery. To copy otherwise, or to republish, requires a fee and/or specific permission.

© 1992 ACM 0-89791-543-7/92/0010/0130...$1.50

the implicit references in Mackay, Nardi and Miller, and Riedl et al, a study of design meetings by Olson, Olson, Storrosten, Carter, Herbsleb and Rueter [10] describes the practice of including "greenbeans" in design meetings at one company, so they could observe experienced designers working on a real project.

Our study has provided insights into the collaborative process by which apprentices become proficient in their task and tools, the value of the artifact-centered sessions with a mentor, and both participants' productivity management strategies for accomplishing their individual and joint goals. We've begun to characterize this collaborative work practice and to identify the constraints and work styles that would need to be addressed by technological support for such interactions. Besides guiding tool development for local and remote collaboration, an understanding of the processes in effective apprenticeship interactions may eventually improve this cooperative work practice by teaching people how to be better consultants and better apprentices.

In the remainder of the paper, we first briefly describe the methodology, the complexity of the apprentices' task, and their main strategies for making progress. Then, we introduce the range of help that mentors give, and the valuable incidental learning that occurs within the consulting sessions. With this as a background, we describe the apprentices' strategies for minimizing their impact on the experts' time, and the joint negotiation of the content of the sessions. We finish by discussing some implications for cooperative work technology. We suggest that technology can help facilitate cooperative apprenticeship learning by helping apprentices switch among subproblems while they wait for the consultant, by facilitating communication about the expert's interruptibility, by making consultations more productive, and by complementing the human consultants with other computer-based aids.

THE STUDY OF CONSULTING INTERACTIONS

We conducted an exploratory observational study that focuses on consulting sessions between programmers who are learning one of two complex software systems (whom we call apprentices) and experts in the systems, who serve as consultant/mentors.[1]

The three apprentices were either graduate students in computer science, working at HP Labs over the summer, or researchers within the laboratory. Each apprentice was new to the object-oriented language, C^{++}, and to the software system. All were proficient in other high-level languages, and had been application-level programmers for over four years.

The experts were researchers at HP Labs, with around ten years programming experience. C1 was the architect/engineer of an application-builder. C2 and C3 were the architect/engineers of a hypertext toolkit. These toolkits not simple systems, but application frameworks — architectures of reusable software components, designed to fit together to facilitate building applications. Such design for reusability requires flexibility, and this contributes to complexity. Each consisted of some 200–300 C^{++} interrelated classes. In addition, both systems' user interfaces were built using another C^{++} toolkit of more than 100 C^{++} classes.

Data gathering started in the first three weeks that the apprentice worked on the project and continued for 2–4 months, resulting in around eight hours of interactions on questions that nominally dealt with program understanding or object-oriented programming. To allow recording of unscheduled interactions, informants kept tape recorders in their offices and turned them on at the start of a consultation. Taped sessions ranged from 30 seconds to over an hour long.

The audiotape transcripts provided valuable data. One can read the apprentice's initial questions, the joint discussion and troubleshooting, and incidental learning. However, to give context to the consulting sessions, we also periodically interviewed each of the apprentices, giving about six hours of interview data.[2] In the interviews, apprentices described their current tasks and problems, their strategies for resolving problems before going to a consultant, their use of information sources such as source files or documentation, and the program analysis tools they wish they had. We also opportunistically collected a few data points on four other apprentices who consulted with C1 or C2, and interviewed one of those.

All methodologies have their limitations. This study did not include fleeting hallway conversations, project meetings, design discussions, or e-mail; however our audiotape-based method has the advantage of unintrusively capturing what collaborators *actually do* on real projects in event-driven interactions in one another's offices. Interviews showed that we obtained good coverage of system-understanding and debugging interactions. The study focuses attention on the apprenticeship interaction as an important context for complex collaborative work — the observed patterns characterize features and roles to be supported by CSCW technology.

THE APPRENTICE'S TASK

The complexity of 'getting simple tasks done'

The transcripts expose the range of domains that the apprentice had to learn simultaneously and the result-

[1] We will often refer to these experts as consultants or mentors, since our focus is on their educational role.

[2] The interviews and consulting interactions were collected by the first author. We use the plural "we" here for expository ease.

ing complexity of the start-up process. To make changes to the software framework, apprentices had to learn everything from the details of C^{++} syntax, object-oriented concepts and their use, the framework's information layout, and then of course the data structures and the dynamic information flow within the system.

In addition to this core learning, to accomplish their tasks the apprentices had to learn a host of auxiliary tools and programs. These included the compiler and linker, the file dependency maintenance program, *make*, various C^{++} program analysis and development tools, and the *Emacs* text editor.

The apprentices, who are competent programmers in other languages and environments, usually have the right generic strategies for accomplishing their goals. However, given this set of domains to learn simultaneously, they get tripped up by the details of programs and domains they must use.

Since they're still learning C^{++} and the software framework, apprentices make many mistakes in implementing their ideas; thus, they spend most of their time tracking down framework behavior, experimenting semi-blindly, and troubleshooting problems. This experimentation leads them to encounter many vague or misleading error messages from debuggers, compilers, linkers, and makefiles. As the following two examples show, the tools themselves can wind up compounding the apprentices' problems.

Example 1: Apprentices have to figure out the environment's tools. A2 got sidetracked while debugging a problem, when his debugging output was unexpectedly getting buffered (got printed late). He understood the concept of buffering, figured out that that's what was going on, but didn't know whether C^{++} or the HP-UX operating system was responsible. The concept of *buffering* isn't covered in basic books on C^{++} or UNIX. So, instead of working on his original problem, A2 got stuck trying to figure out different C^{++} printing functions, hoping that one of them wouldn't buffer.

Example 2: Uncertainty about tools' behavior slows them down. Apprentices stay with sub-optimal strategies since they aren't sure of what's possible in this toolse. Here, A1 described the tediousness of trying different solutions to one compiler error (caused by an interaction between her program and the software framework).

> **A1:** It is especially annoying in C^{++} because the compiler is so slow ... it doesn't just say, okay, she's just changed that one little thing, I don't have to worry about the rest of the world. ... I am using a makefile and it seems to take just as long when I do the compile, every single time, even when I have only changed one little teeny thing. So I don't have a good feel for how incremental it is. ... [perhaps] it just feels very slow to a person who is used to LISP.

A1 correctly thought the makefile *should* prevent the recompilation of the whole framework. However, to be sure there even *was* a problem, she'd have had to know how fast the C^{++} compiler is, how *make* really works, and the framework's compilation dependencies. So, she was uncomfortable, but rather than setting her original problem aside and investigating all those factors, she put up with the slow compilation and the resulting slow experimentation. A1 described her progress this way:

> **A1:** basically what it feels like to me is I am kind of solving one little teeny problem after another. ... It is like one pile of dirt after another. ...
>
> When you are working with these big systems, often it is some little piecemeal thing that you have to kind of solve before you can get beyond it and go on to the bigger problems. ... it is often these little teeny things that can hold you up and you have to go to your information sources to solve.

The examples show that, at least for a while, the apprentices are bombarded by 'learning opportunities' in the guise of obstacles due to a variety of domains. However, the apprentices primarily want to make progress on their original tasks.

How do they do this? One strategy is to ask a consultant, but these are scarce resources. As we'll show later, apprentices try to reduce their use of consultants and their impact on the consultants' time. They can do this by by being goal directed, reducing what they try to master, and getting by with limited knowledge. This leads to the expedient *copy and experiment* programming strategy.

Copy and experiment strategy

Both observations and interviews showed that apprentices recognize the overwhelming number of things to learn and consciously put off learning some of them. They minimized their learning of auxiliary tools and even in the core system, they ignored concepts and details they didn't feel they had to immediately understand.

As a result, a primary programming strategy became *copy and experiment.* The apprentices search their own and the system's files for code that looks like it does something similar to what they want, copy it, and then try to figure out what to delete and what to change to make the code meet their goal.

All apprentices said that they do this to get past obstacles, to make progress without having to understand all the details. However, they were somewhat embarrassed about relying on magic. They said that such a strategy backfires; they feel they "should" understand the system and the tools better, but they believe they don't have a choice – to progress on their primary task, they have to minimize the side trips of learning. In an interview, A1 described how (with the mentor's help) she has a makefile that mostly works, although she doesn't understand it; and how ambivalent she feels about putting off learning it.

> **A1:** I think I can patch in little things as needed, but I do find *that* a really confusing feature and that is an area where I probably will do programming by example and I don't know that I will take the time, at least in the near term, to really understand [makefiles]... It's against my religion to do that [modifying code without understanding it]. This is a violation...
>
> I think it is justified not to delve into that kind of thing if you can just get something that will allow you to work on the stuff that you really want to work on. Even though I am sure this policy will come back to bite me at some point ... but at least I think that I can delay that moment right now.

The strategy of limiting their learning continues throughout the learning process; apprentices developed expertise in framework components central to their goal, but continue to rely on consultants for help with unfamiliar sections or interactions.

THE MENTORS' ROLE: NOT 'JUST THE FACTS'

The previous section hints at two of the consultants' roles: helping the apprentices over incidental obstacles (such as C^{++} syntax or makefile problems), and helping the apprentices with their core framework-specific problems.

However, an interesting finding is that joint problem-solving about the apprentice's question triggers exploration of many other topics, topics tangential to the initial question, but crucial to the apprentice's growth into an expert. Within minutes, conversations jump around multiple domains and levels as questions are triggered by the code itself, the mentor's explanations, and the physical actions of either participant. Discussions range from strategic, conceptual and procedural information (e.g. what is broadcasting and how does it work), to historical notes, pointers to information sources, down to syntactic details, and side-trips to discuss commands or tools that would increase the apprentice's productivity.

The information in these discussions (a) generally is triggered by the computer-based files the pair view in order to problem solve, (b) is important to the apprentice's growth in proficiency, and (c) focuses on information that would be hard for an apprentice to find.

Artifacts are crucial. Very quickly, the apprentice and consultant bring up files related to the problem — framework source files, the apprentice's code, error output, etc. As the mentors (re)familiarize themselves with the framework code's intent, they remember or reconstruct the design decisions, control flow, historical twists and turns, the code's assumptions, and quirks in the implementation.[3] If they are viewing the apprentice's code, they may give a running commentary, pointing out errors, asking questions, and using the code to trigger discussions about algorithms, concepts, style, or auxiliary tools that would help the apprentice.

When the pair bring up a new file, the apprentice may ask about a feature brought into view — a syntactic expression, a function — or may just make an implicit request such as "this piece is confusing". Apprentices use this as an opportunity to ask incidental questions. As mentors talk through the behavior and concepts embodied in code, apprentices' reactions guide the conversation. They serve to confirm understanding, request clarification, or steer the conversation back to the apprentice's immediate question.

One question leads to another. Not only do the artifacts serve as the source of information needed to answer the apprentice's question, but they also serve as a starting-off point for additional learning.

Both the apprentice and the consultant take initiative in this, and negotiate about what's worth learning, and what the apprentice wants to learn. Sometimes this is explicit, such as the following, in which A2 requests an explanation of event-handling.

> **A2:** You say "it figures out". Who figures out, what figures out, where?
>
> **C2:**. ... you don't really have to know that.
>
> **A2:** Is it the X system at some level? ... I haven't worked with this kind of stuff before, ... in some sense I don't really need to know a lot of detail but I just would like to have a little understanding of it.
>
> **C2:** [askes A2 to bring up another file, and, pointing at the code, describes the next layer of behavior]

Frequently, the consultant uses the task or the code to bring up relevant, interesting, or otherwise valuable information. For example, here C2 not only explained

[3] Note that frequently it is their own code whose intentions and flow they are reconstructing.

what the intent of a function is and how it interacts with other code, but also volunteered how it should have been written:

> **C2:** ... So the whole purpose of it is.... Actually, you know what should happen — I didn't think of this at the time, but now looking back, that should probably be defined to be a pure virtual function... [and goes on to explain how that would be structured]

Given the apprentices' dominant strategy of copying and modifying code fragments, such meta-information about existing code is especially valuable.

Emphasis on "hard to find" information. We were struck by how much of the information in the sessions would have been difficult for apprentices to find written down. First, in answer to a question, mentors' explanations tend to be much more general than what the apprentices need to fix the specific problem. Mentors focus on describing complex behavior, the rationale for a strategy, and elements of good style. This type of information is rarely documented, yet apprentices must learn this to become proficient.

An important factor of expertise is knowing about and understanding the characteristics of information sources. Not surprisingly, the mentors point these out. Again, they focus on attributes unlikely to be written down. When describing other experts, mentors and apprentices discuss how approachable other experts are and their areas of expertise. For tools, they discuss the tool's purpose, speed, robustness, etc. For written information sources, they describe whether the source is accurate, readable, up-to-date, and where it is located. For example:

> **C1:** [that's a] Question that [the local C^{++} expert] could answer ... Or, you could go and read the 'Annotated Reference Manual'.
>
> **A1:** What's that?
>
> **C1:** The Annotated Reference Manual is ... [it focuses on] explaining why things are done the way they are. In fact, it is the only positively authoritative definition. The 2.0 notes that came with C^{++} are inaccurate.

Interactions provide crucial "incidental learning"

The transcripts vividly show that interactions with the expert are much richer than a simple answer to the apprentice's question. A major aspect is the *incidental learning* we see above — triggered by the the question or the problem-solving, but about facts, domains, history, assumptions, strategies beyond the apprentice's original question.

Apprentices learn incidental information from what the consultant volunteers, from questions they ask opportunistically, and from observing the consultant's troubleshooting strategies and tool use. As the above examples show, incidental doesn't mean unimportant. We believe this represents a valuable mechanism by which the programmers become proficient in a new environment, and that this incidental learning in fact represents a major benefit of the interaction.

BALANCING APPRENTICE AND MENTOR PRODUCTIVITY

To simultaneously learn a language, software system, and toolset is a prolonged task. As we've seen, experts significantly reduce the apprentice's learning difficulties. They help apprentices localize and solve problems, understand and apply concepts, and they critique programmers' partial solutions, thus helping avoid time-consuming detours.

However, mentors are a scarce resource; they aren't always available. Also, both parties are aware that mentors have multiple apprentices asking them for help, and that they have their own work to do. The mentors may even be working on a module which the apprentice needs for another subproblem.

Since our study focused on apprentices' questions and use of information, our primary data is on the apprentices' strategies. We have shown how apprentices use the *copy and modify* coding strategy to get answers without going to the expert. Here we discuss apprentices strategies for reducing their impact on the mentors, and for making effective use of the interaction time.

Minimizing the impact on the expert's time

The apprentices emphasized that the consultants were easy to approach, interruptible, and friendly. However, it was clear that apprentices explicitly work to minimize their impact on the expert's time.

First, they spend up front time to try to understand or narrow the problem before going to the consultant. This is visible in the sessions, where the apprentices guide the consultant to look at specific files, describe their hypotheses, or summarize what they've already tried to do. Also, as consultants scan a source file and comment on the code, the apprentices interject to show they understand a segment, that they have figured out a connection, or that that's where they're confused.

How long they wait before approaching the expert depends on many factors. These include the urgency of the problem (whether there's something else they can be productive on), the perceived length of the interruption, the apprentice's personal style, their view of the consultant's style, the consultant's proximity, and as one apprentice said, "how lazy I'm feeling".

Apprentices seem to have one of two preferred communication styles — either quickly walking over, or spending more time trying to puzzle the problem out, and then send e-mail. Generally all agreed that for non-trivial problems, interactivity and being able to see context on the screens is crucial. Apprentices who send e-mail do it to be less intrusive. The ones who walk over emphasize the benefit of maintaining momentum and being able to discuss the problem interactively, in the context of the relevant artifacts. Both types recognized the value of the other style, but found it difficult to adopt.

Second, they multi-task. They switch from one subproblem to another as they reach obstacles. This context switching has multiple causes. Sometimes, the apprentice and consultant work different hours — A1 was on an early schedule, while C1 tended to work late; another consultant sometimes worked from home, and two apprentices with looming deadlines worked late into the night. Thus, apprentices sent e-mail to the consultants and went on to another subtask.

An effect of task switching is that one can easily build a stack of subproblems. Thus, when the two meet, the apprentice may have a set of questions about a variety of artifacts and domains. A1, who accumulates questions, has developed strategies to reduce forgetting. She keeps a list of questions in a file and keeps a project notebook in which she writes notes during her meetings with the consultant. After each meeting, she marks the action items. Thus, even though programming is only one of about three major tasks for her, the notebook helps in "swapping everything back in and starting up and just going through and doing the action items".

Negotiating the conversation's content

The conversation's content is implicitly negotiated between the apprentice and the consultant. Sometimes, as we've seen, the apprentice asks for clarification about a term or why something happens. Often the consultant volunteers information about a concept, or some historical information on code they're skimming (e.g. how it should have been written, or that the code will go away in the future). Or, a discussion about an error leads to a discussion about C^{++} style or the system's design.

The breadth and depth of the discussion is negotiated between the two. Each person frequently restates what they're hearing or clarifies a question. This often serves as a trigger to raise or lower the level of abstraction. If the apprentices don't understand a concept and care about it, they request clarification. On the other hand, mentors frequently volunteer information they believe the apprentices *should* know. The apprentices don't always want to learn the theory, or can't yet follow the detailed rationale and control flow. Thus, they bring the conversation back to the problem at hand, with statements such as "pop up a couple of levels, please". Experts sometimes explicitly reduce the scope by saying things like "we don't have to worry about that. I don't even know what code decides that..".

In general, the apprentices know better what they want out of the interaction, but the experts introduce what they believe should be relevant to the apprentice. Apprentices guide the flow of the conversation — switching to a new question once they're satisfied, interjecting with a side question on a function on the screen, asking for additional explanations, or asking for more details of how to proceed next. So, the overall pattern seems to be that the apprentice starts the conversation, the consultant brings up relevant (or incidental) information, and the apprentice then guides the conversation to get more breadth, depth, or to follow a random useful side track.

HOW CAN CSCW TOOLS HELP?

Computer support for the cooperative learning can take a number of forms. Here we focus on three: support for encapsulating the information related to a problem, support for remote consultations and the negotiation of availability, and support for getting answers from a distribution list or an archive of previously asked questions.

Encapsulating Context and Task-Switching

Problems whose source isn't obvious, and more general questions, like 'how should I write this?', or 'how does this work?' require examining examples and data from many sources. Thus, when the apprentice and consultant meet after the apprentice has gone on to another problem, it would be useful to be able to bring up the problem, its *working set* of files, plus notes of the apprentice's specific questions and hypotheses raised by the files.

Support for task-switching could also help in the high-pressure situations near a deadline. At those times, everyone tries to make progress on multiple threads. Programmers switch among multiple separate subproblems on an interrupt-driven basis in order to make progress while waiting for a response from someone else, to respond to another's pressing problem, or to figure out the source of an error.

Encapsulating a set of files and the apprentice's local questions is quite doable. It requires separating files and programs spatially into workspaces, allowing elements to reside in multiple workspaces. These workspaces then form task-based contexts that the user may switch between [6]. Since different solutions often require incompatible changes to multiple files, pathnames, etc. a more interesting extension of current workspaces is one that would support cloning a context and simultaneously trying out divergent solution paths – with separate file versions, environment variables, etc. in each context.

Facilitating remote consultations

All subjects said they'd still walk over to talk to someone physically separated by most of a building or a floor, because there is such great utility in seeing the same screens, drawing on a whiteboard, or together moving around files, directories, or modifying and testing code.

In situations where walking over is impractical, props for high-context collaboration have to be provided [3]. Some aids already exist for sharing windows and pointers across a network, including HP's X Window System extension, HP SharedX, prototype shared editing tools such as GROVE [5] and ShrEdit [13], and shared drawing tools such as TeamWorkStation [7], or VideoDraw [15]. If the shared work-surfaces' performance and the audio and video quality are good, such tools may allow high-quality collaborative work.

A major problem of remote collaborations is deciding whether and when to interrupt. From a group productivity perspective, if the apprentice simply needs an answer to a quick question or a confirmation that they're on the right path, it often makes sense to interrupt. When the pair are nearby or in the same room, there's low-cost or implicit signaling of needs and availability, allowing for more frequent but less-intrusive interruptions. As Root [12] points out in discussing Cruiser, people use a host of audio-visual clues to determine another's availability.

In distributed teams, or in organizations in which many tools and systems are used simultaneously, experts are often distant from other users. Thus we need aids that provide similar mutual awareness, access to one another's computers, and low cost interruptions as are available in a shared office, but that make possible the privacy and concentration time of individual offices.

Other collaborative learning aids

Besides facilitating task-switching and communication with a consultant, computers can help the apprentice get information from a broader community of programmers, or tap into knowledge from others' previous questions.

On the Unix system, there are electronic news groups organized around a software system (e.g. Andrew, the X Window System). There, experts and novices discuss bugs, features, and give examples of how to do things. Thus, in a larger community, apprentices can learn from each other as well as from experts. Late-comers to the notes can either ask questions, or they can browse the already collected information. Apprentices may browse the archive of the discussions to pick up terminology, concepts, techniques, and query it to get an answer to a previously asked question. In some news groups, a few experts collect and periodically post "Frequently Asked Questions" (FAQ). These experts donate their time to the maintenance and periodic posting of the FAQ. This heads off many novice questions, and the experts avoid repeated collection and (re)validation of information.

A variant on this informal mechanism is Answer Garden [1], an e-mail based system with a growing tree structure of diagnostic questions and answers. If the learner's question isn't answered within the system, the diagnostic questions are used to identify the appropriate expert to whom the question should be directed.

Since, consultants often use interactive discussion or other context on the apprentices' screens to clarify the problem or its cause, an e-mail forum is not as effective at troubleshooting as a face to face session. Even more serious is the fact that these mechanisms do not provide the high-bandwidth communication and the opportunities for incidental learning that our apprentices had. Thus, even in the e-mail interaction, apprentices are more likely to get just the answer they asked for, without the richness and breadth seen in our consulting interactions. However, the archive of previously asked questions, backed by access to users makes such captured expertise very important, especially in contexts where local experts are unavailable or where there is a large stream of mostly repetitive questions.

CONCLUSIONS

Apprenticeship learning is a collaborative work practice of theoretical and practical significance. It is a common context by which real problems get solved and learners pick up the range of knowledge needed to become experts. Apprenticeship should be especially interesting to the CSCW community because of its characteristics: a focus on intellectually complex activities, cooperative problem-solving with shared computer artifacts, a very fluid negotiation of content, and a rich shared context that enables both task-oriented and incidental teaching. Also, the apprentices' desire to reduce their impact on the consultants' time impacts their work pattern and interaction style in ways relevant for technology design.

This study characterizes the consulting interaction in complex, computer-supported domains, and exposes issues to be addressed by technologies for supporting collaborative work. The interaction pattern we've seen may generalize far beyond computer programmers to other workers in many complex computer-based domains — from reference librarians to engineer CAD users to spreadsheet users — in which employees must accomplish complex tasks with little training. Apprenticeships are costly in terms of the expert's time. However, we believe that the rich transmission of expertise which this study has shown makes them appropriate in many domains — domains where there is an immense amount to learn, where there isn't formal support, where people have good working relationships with colleagues [2], and where the goal is for *everyone* to become proficient in the toolset.

We have confirmed that computer-based tasks require knowing details about many tools and concepts, often details conceptually peripheral to the goals of the apprentices. We found consulting interactions to involve a complex negotiation of the content, with the apprentice in charge of the overall direction. The shared artifacts and cooperative problem-solving trigger much incidental learning, learning necessary for the apprentices to grow into experts. Thus, we believe that consulting interactions are crucial, not only in helping the learners past immediate obstacles, but in transmitting a variety of useful, hard-to-find information essential to proficiency.

Because technology users are often not co-located with experts, CSCW tools are needed to make remote interactions effective. We've suggested that tools for consulting must address multiple aspects of the work situation: enabling apprentices to encapsulate information as they prepare for a meeting, enabling apprentices to switch tasks, facilitating negotiation about the consultant's availability, facilitating the interaction itself, and extending the apprentice's community of consultants via electronic bulletin boards and other information sharing tools. Given the richness and task-appropriateness of the learning in the consulting interactions, this is an unparalleled educational mechanism, one that should be explicitly supported by both organizational structures and by cooperative work technology.

ACKNOWLEDGEMENTS

Many thanks to Mike Creech, Allan Kuchinsky, Bonnie Nardi, Andreas Paepcke, and Craig Zarmer for their helpful comments on drafts of this paper. We are grateful to the informants who gave their time to this study, who took care to turn on the tape recorders, and who shared their travails and their insights with us.

References

[1] Mark S. Ackerman and Thomas W. Malone. Answer Garden: A tool for growing organizational memory. In *Proceedings of the Conference on Office Information Systems*, 1990.

[2] Gary Blau. An investigation of the apprenticeship organizational socialization strategy. *Journal of Vocational Behavior*, 32(2), Apr 1988.

[3] Sara A. Bly. A use of drawing surfaces in different collaborative settings. In *Proceedings of CSCW'88*, 1988.

[4] Linda H. Chiang and James McElhinney. Principals' judgments of experiences with beginning teacher internship program. In *Mid-Western Educational Research Conference*, 1990.

[5] Clarence A. Ellis, Simon J. Gibbs, and Gail L. Rein. Design and use of a group editor. Technical Report STP-263-88, MCC, 1988.

[6] D. Austin Henderson, Jr. and Stuard K. Card. Rooms: The use of multiple virtual workspaces to reduce space contention in a window-based graphical user interface. *IEEE Transactions on Graphics*, 5(3), 1986.

[7] Hiroshi Ishii. TeamWorkStation: Towards a seamless shared workspace. In *Proceedings of CSCW'90*, 1990.

[8] Wendy E. Mackay. Patterns of sharing customizable software. In *Proceedings of CSCW'90*, 1990.

[9] Bonnie A. Nardi and James R. Miller. Twinkling lights and nested loops: distributed problem solving and spreadsheet development. *International Journal of Man-Machine Studies*, 34(2), 1991.

[10] Gary M. Olson, Judith S. Olson, Marianne Storrosten, Mark Carter, James Herbsleb, and Henry Rueter. The structure of activity during design meetings. In *HCIC 92 workshop*. (Similar to a chapter in *Design Rationale* by T. Moran and J. Carroll, in preparation), 1992.

[11] Thomas R. Riedl, Julian S. Weitzenfeld, Jared T. Freeman, Gary A. Klein, and John Musa. What we have learned about software engineering expertise. In J.E.Tomayko, editor, *Software Engineering Education*. Springer-Verlag, 1991.

[12] Robert W Root. Design of a multi-media vehicle for social browsing. In *Proceedings of CSCW'88*, 1988.

[13] Cognitive Science and Machine Intelligence Laboratory. Shredit, a multi-user shared text editor: Users manual. Technical report, The University of Michigan, 1989.

[14] Sylvia Scribner and Patricia Sachs. On the job training: A case study. *National Center on Education and Employment Brief*, (9), August 1990.

[15] John C. Tang and S. L. Minneman. VideoDraw: A video interface for collaborative drawing. In *Proceedings of the Conference on Human Factors in Computing Systems, CHI'90*, 1990.

Supporting Collaborative Writing of Hyperdocuments in SEPIA

Jörg M. Haake & Brian Wilson[1]

GMD-IPSI
P.O. Box 104326
D-6100 Darmstadt
Federal Republic of Germany
haake@darmstadt.gmd.de

ABSTRACT

Today, most cooperative systems support primarily either asynchronous or synchronous (real time) cooperative work. We feel that both synchronous and asynchronous cooperation are extremely important aspects of working in groups, and to ignore one or the other is to supply only half a solution to users. In this paper, we describe the extension of the hypertext authoring system SEPIA developed at GMD-IPSI to support cooperative work among hypertext authors. Cooperative SEPIA is unique not only in its ability to support cooperative work in both of these categories, but also in how smoothly and naturally it supports the transition between these two categories.

KEYWORDS

CSCW, Hypertext, Hypertext authoring, Collaborative Writing, modes of collaboration

INTRODUCTION

It is a well known fact that documents are often created by a group of authors. This is especially true for large hyperdocuments. Adding further to this complexity, authors are commonly distributed over different locations. Current computer systems do not adequately support the distributed creation of multi-author hyperdocuments.

There are several requirements a system must satisfy when attempting to solve this problem. Grudin points out that supplying aids to cooperative work a system must not hinder or interfere with the productivity of individual work as compared to the past [6]. In other words, adding cooperation support to a writing tool should not affect an author's ability to write an individual document. This implies that the cooperation support should not be intrusive when it is not used, and furthermore that the transition from individual authoring to cooperative authoring should be supported in a comfortable and natural way. Finally, systems that attempt to support cooperative authoring must recognize and support geographically distributed authors.

CSCW systems can benefit from three current streams of technological development: hypertext, computer networks, and database management. First, **hypertext systems** [7] allow for concurrent and incremental modification of documents as well as organizing and clustering documents as contexts of work. Second, **computer networks** and advanced communication facilities provide means for communication between distributed user sites and synchronization of concurrent work. Third, **database management systems** allow for shared data, multi-user access, and transaction management.

The system presented in this paper makes use of all three of the above mentioned technologies. It is based on the hypertext authoring system SEPIA [17] which supports the creation and browsing of hyperdocuments and the hypermedia engine HyperBase [15] which provides database support. In this paper, we describe an extension to the single authoring system providing authors with support for cooperative writing in a distributed computing environment in a very natural and elegant way.

In the next section we give a brief overview of related work. Following this section, we describe the hypertext authoring system SEPIA, and introduce a sample work situation to illustrate how SEPIA can provide support for collaborating authors. Next, the design and implementation of cooperative SEPIA is described. We conclude with a discussion of our system and plans for future work.

Permission to copy without fee all or part of this material is granted provided that the copies are not made or distributed for direct commercial advantage, the ACM copyright notice and the title of the publication and its date appear, and notice is given that copying is by permission of the Association for Computing Machinery. To copy otherwise, or to republish, requires a fee and/or specific permission.

© 1992 ACM 0-89791-543-7/92/0010/0138...$1.50

1. Brian Wilson can now be reached at Apple Computer, Mail Stop 35-RJ, Cupertino, CA, brianw@apple.com

RELATED WORK

Computer systems that recognize and deal with collaborating users are labelled "group aware" systems [9]. There have been many research projects and articles in the past few years on how to support cooperative work. Due to the limitation of space in this paper we limit the review of related work on cooperative authoring applications. Most of these applications belong to one of two categories. In the first category are applications that support only asynchronous cooperative work. In this context, "asynchronous" means that although a document may have two or more authors, only one author may actually work on the document at any given point in time. The second category contains applications that support only synchronous (or real time) cooperative work. This is where two or more authors work on a document at the same time. We assume a (relaxed) WYSIWIS (What you see is what I see) view sharing as a general property of this kind of system. Another criterion is the geographical location of the users (distributed vs. co-located) [13] [4]. In this paper, we are concerned with distributed collaboration.

By their very nature, many hypertext systems support asynchronous cooperation between multiple authors working on the same document. In the NoteCards system of Xerox PARC [8], multiple users may open and read the same node, but only one user has the ability to modify the node's content at one time. This limitation leads to draft passing back and forth between authors working on the same document.

The Aquanet system [11] currently developed at Xerox PARC is a hypertext tool supporting the task of collaborative knowledge structuring. It provides a "What you see is what I did" (WYSIWID) view on a shared knowledge structure. Based on a central database and a data/view architecture it allows for semi-synchronous collaboration. Synchronous shared views and communication facilities are not provided.

In the NLS project users could link two terminal screens together for real time conferencing [5]. Since then, several synchronous groupware applications have been developed.

The rIBIS hypertext editor at MCC [12] supports the concepts of Loosely-Coupled (LC) and Tightly-Coupled (TC) modes of synchronous cooperation. In LC mode, a user sees the actions of other users and is allowed to independently scroll, edit nodes, and operate the private mouse. In TC mode, users' interfaces are all tightly locked together so that if one user scrolls or edits a node the other users' rIBIS browsers also scroll or show the editing of that node.

The rIBIS hypertext system is a step in the direction of supporting both synchronous and asynchronous cooperation. Being a hypertext system rIBIS supports asynchronous cooperation. Per folio (hypertext document) there is only one TC session supported and inside this TC session users take turns using the one "Group Mouse" for all mouse based-activities. Since rIBIS does not support composite nodes it requires that all authors working on the same hypertext document (folio) must be in the same browser. Composite nodes (cf. [7]) contain a set of nodes and links. Finally, the system architecture of rIBIS is not very scaleable in that it uses a central server which handles all requests and then broadcasts the new system state to all members.

Dewan and Choudhary [2] argue for supporting flexible coupling among various windows displaying a shared workspace. In their collaboration support environment users can control various aspects of coupling in order to tailor their user-interface to the specific requirements induced by their role, or by the cooperation state.

Systems such as GROVE [3] and WSCRAWL [22] are systems geared entirely towards shared editing sessions among two or more users. The CaveDraw system [10] provides shared transparent layers to extend the shared workspace. These layers have to be explicitly synchronized to set up a shared view. The transition from single person editing to multiple person editing is very abrupt, and shows one of the major shortcomings of these systems.

One concept bridging the gap between synchronous and asynchronous cooperation was described as "Cruiser" [14]. Root identified that chance and informal meetings in the office are an integral part of the workplace. In the Cruiser multimedia concept, users work on their normal office tasks, but the system supports synchronous meetings with other users of the office environment. Furthermore, the system can be asked to set up such meetings at random times simulating the informal office environment. While this is an interesting idea it strikes us as too contrived, and in fact, we would expect users to turn off these random meetings so as not to be bothered.

Grudin [6] points out that if CSCW tools require more effort to use than single user systems, or if the tools ignore existing social protocols, then users will reject the system and it will likely fail. The rest of this paper describes extensions to the hypertext authoring system SEPIA which, while not disrupting the single author in any way, allows asynchronous **and** synchronous collaboration to take place between users in an elegant and natural way.

THE SEPIA HYPERTEXT AUTHORING SYSTEM

SEPIA [17] [18] is a hypertext authoring system developed in the division Cooperative Hypermedia Systems of the GMD Institute for Integrated Publication and Information Systems (IPSI). It supports the creation of hyperdocuments by providing several different *activity spaces*. Each activity space can be viewed as a task-specific browser which supports a part of the creation process of hyperdocuments.

SEPIA's basic hypertext objects are atomic nodes, composite nodes, and labelled links [19]. Furthermore, annotation nodes and links are provided as specializations of atomic nodes and labelled links. Therefore, collaboration based on draft passing which uses annotated hyperdocuments is already supported in SEPIA. Composite nodes are heavily used as organizational means (e.g., clustering and nesting of related document parts).

Users create a hyperdocument by interacting with four activity space browsers dedicated to the tasks of content generation

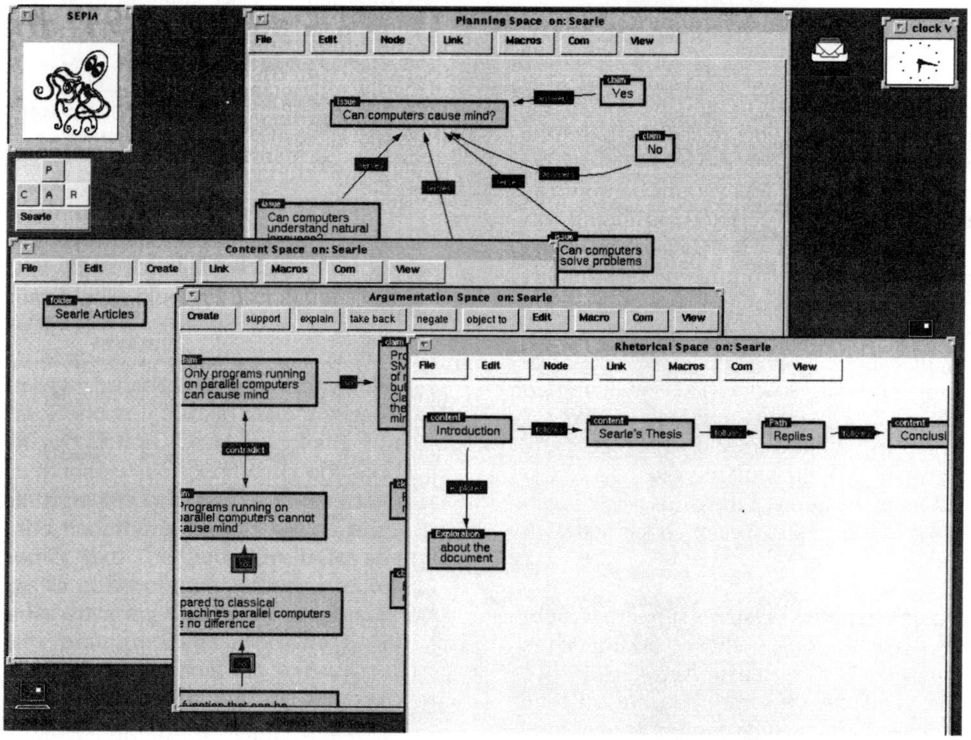

Figure 1: SEPIA's user-interface

and structuring, planning, arguing, and writing the final hyperdocuments under a rhetorical perspective (Content Space, Planning Space, Argumentation Space, and Rhetorical Space respectively). Each space browser provides task-specific hypertext objects and operations. It serves as the top-level of the corresponding task-specific hypertext structure. Users may open composite nodes at the top-level to navigate through the next level of the hypertext structure. Opening a composite node leads to the creation of a new activity space browser which displays the contents of the composite node. Figure 1 shows an example SEPIA authoring session.

SEPIA's user-interface is based on two design decisions: First, one scrollable browser window per space and per composite node is used to display and manipulate the composites' content. Multiple browsers on the screen displaying different composite nodes are supported. Second, the state of an object is signalled by using colors. E.g., selected objects are drawn in yellow. Nodes and links of the same type may be drawn differently according to their internal state.

SEPIA is implemented in Smalltalk-80 Release 4 using X-Windows on Sun Sparc-2 workstations running Unix. The implementation (see Figure 2) is based on the hypermedia engine HyperBase [15] which provides a persistent storage and retrieval mechanism for hyperdocuments. Every hypertext object has an unique object identifier (OID) used to refer to or retrieve it. HyperBase is built on top of the relational DBMS Sybase.

SEPIA is a general hypertext authoring tool that can be used for the production of a variety of documents such as manuals, scientific articles, project proposals etc. The base system allows already asynchronous collaboration among authors. In the next section we will examine an example of cooperative authoring and present an approach to support this task.

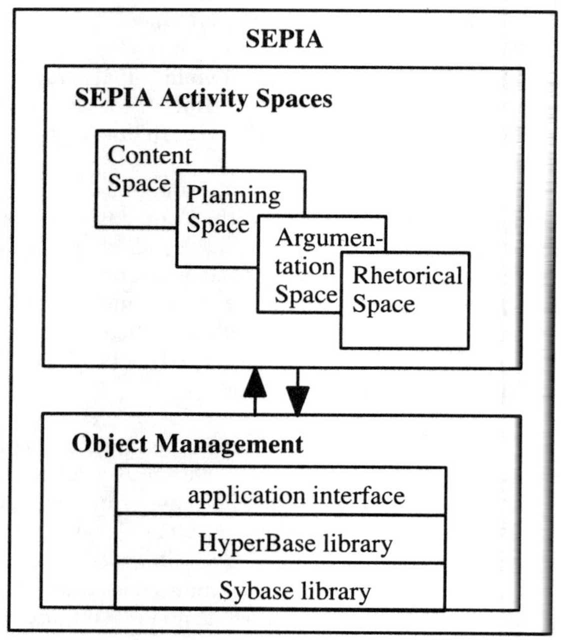

Figure 2: System architecture of SEPIA

THE COOPERATIVE SEPIA SYSTEM

We will now examine a scenario of cooperative work. Three issues arise from this scenario which have to be answered in order to design a system supporting the collaboration process. We then discuss the user-interface of cooperative SEPIA.

A sample scenario of cooperative work

Imagine a software company which is about to deliver a new software product to the market. To do so, three different manuals are needed: a beginners' introduction manual, a users' manual, and a system administrators' manual. Our innovative company decides to produce these manuals as hyperdocuments partially sharing the same data. A group of five people from different disciplines (e.g. technical writers, marketing people, and programmers) which are located at different sites of the company are given the task of producing the manuals. The manager responsible for the manuals divides the work into several subtasks and outlines a time schedule. She then distributes the work among herself and the four others who must create the manuals. All three of the manuals will share parts with the others, and each of the five authors will contribute to several of the joint subtasks. Therefore, there is a need to coordinate the author's efforts and also to access shared states of the document in order to preserve consistency. At specific dates, the authors must integrate their different drafts to produce a consistent version of the hyperdocument manuals.

What are the basic characteristics of the above scenario?

First and most fundamental, the manuals themselves are based on the sharing of hyperdocument data and the views on that data. Second, the authors have to organize their individual and their group work. Third, the authors are working on individual parts of the document while simultaneously working on shared parts of the document with other authors. Notice that cooperation and conflict will occur not only at preplanned locations and times, but also unpredictably as two or more authors begin working on shared parts of the document. Finally, the authors need to discuss parts of the shared document in order to resolve conflicts as they arise and to coordinate the merging of individual contributions.

Design of cooperative SEPIA

Writing a hyperdocument requires support for the creation of nodes and links, the navigation through the document, and the modification of the document structure and content. In order to support the above scenario of writing, we have to address three issues:

How should SEPIA support shared hyperdocuments and shared views on such documents?

We decided to use a shared, multi-user database for holding and accessing hyperdocument data and view information. All document data and view objects are uniquely identifiable by their OID. Every coauthor works on the same document database containing private and shared information thus providing the basis for cooperation.

How should SEPIA support the organization of the collaboration process?

Today the collaboration process between people is organized outside and not reflected in the document under preparation. But hypertext provides an opportunity to reflect some organizational decisions in the structure of the hyperdocument. One example is to assign parts of a document to a given task associated with selected authors. In a hyperdocument, the affected document parts can be clustered accordingly.

In SEPIA, composite nodes are used to cluster related information and to maintain hierarchical, nested structures. In order to organize the work to be done by different authors while writing a hyperdocument, composite nodes are used to cluster information needed to perform a task or work on a specific topic. Each of these composite nodes can then be associated with one or more authors. This way, one composite may be associated with several people who need to work on the same shared data. Access rights may further restrict possible modifications. Several composite nodes can contain the same hypertext object thus enabling multiple organizational structures.

In this paper we do not consider project management issues (like time schedules, activity charts etc.). This is a research topic of its own which can be dealt with once a sound basic cooperative system has been developed.

What are our different modes of collaboration?

In order to cooperate several authors (at least two) have to visit the same composite node. From our scenario we can derive three situations of collaborative writing of a shared hyperdocument:

1. We call working on any node currently not visited by other authors **individual work** as part of a larger collaborative effort.
2. We call working on a composite node that is currently shared by other authors **loosely coupled mode.**
3. We call group work situations where coauthors share the same view on the same composite node's content **tightly coupled mode**. (Obviously, an additional communication channel, e.g. audio/video link, is almost necessary in order to make effective use of this mode.)

To support these three modes, we decided to use:

- color to signal the status of hypertext objects,
- a status line indicating the status of each participant in this collaborative effort with respect to her/his collaborative mode,
- locking of objects when parameters for a subsequent operation are selected,
- the shared database for synchronization purposes between different SEPIA installations.

Individual work on a shared hyperdocument is already supported by SEPIA's shared hyperdocument database.

Loosely coupled work puts two more requirements on the design of the activity space browser: First, authors must be able to recognize presence and actions of concurrent users of the same composite node (group awareness). This is extremely important to detect possible conflicts and possibilities for closer cooperation. Second, avoiding counter-productive behavior (such as concurrently moving the same node to two different positions) is useful. Therefore, in loosely coupled mode, each author may see the actions of other authors but is free to navigate through the document. In SEPIA, one has to select the object(s) before one can execute an operation on them. If an author selects a node or link this object is locked and is displayed in yellow on the author's display. Simultaneously, the collaborating activity space browsers are notified and display the selected object in red. Thus, locking atomic objects is used to avoid counter-productive actions. Color coding provides a simple way to recognize the activities of other coauthors. Note, only selections visible in the currently displayed part of a composite node must lead to an update of the browser display. On request, locked objects display the lock owner's name to indicate where co-authors work.

Tightly coupled work adds another three requirements to those of individual and loosely coupled cases. In order to perform synchronous cooperative work on a shared composite node our requirements are:

- shared views (i.e., each coauthor sees the same browser in terms of size and content),
- a telepointer device used for pointing to items visible in the shared view,
- an audio connection supporting verbal exchange among coauthors.

Therefore, all browser windows in tightly coupled mode have to display the same part of the composites' content and must be of the same size. Scrolling in one of the browsers must lead to corresponding scrolling events in every coauthor's browser. Each coauthor must be able to do any action which is eventually visible to his colleagues. A telepointer device for each participant is necessary to support communication among the coauthors. A shared telepointer [16] is a cursor controlled by one user that appears on all of the collaborating users' screens. This allows the controlling user to point at objects on the screen, usually by providing a verbal explanation. In the first implementation, we decided to establish an audio connection between tightly coupled coauthors supporting verbal communication (e.g., a phone conference, or a Netfone installation [20]).

Note that our usage of the terms "loosely coupled" and "tightly coupled" differs from the usage in [12]. SEPIA's loosely coupled mode broadcasts renaming of objects and visualizes the locking of objects. SEPIA's tightly coupled mode implements a shared view (WYSIWIS), provides multiple concurrent telepointers, supports multiple tightly coupled sessions, and allows for parallel activities and audio communication instead of rIBIS' restricted shared views, and floor-controlled group mouse.

Supporting the smooth transition between modes of collaboration

If several authors concurrently work on a shared hyperdocument some of them may work on the same composite node. In this case, SEPIA automatically sets up a loosely coupled session among the concurrent users of the composite node. Here, a session is constituted of at least two coauthors, and it can be dynamically extended and reduced over time. Once a session consists of only one coauthor it is finished. All (or some) coauthors in a loosely coupled session may decide to start a tightly coupled session supporting synchronous cooperation to facilitate focused discussion of the document under preparation. Two modes of initiating a cooperative session can be distinguished: either several coauthors independently decide to work on the same composite node, or they may plan their cooperative session in advance. Inviting people to participate in a future cooperative session can be done by using conventional means (e.g., e-mail, bulletin board, (ether)phone).

When an author enters a composite node already shared by other people all activity space browsers opened on the node notice the new coauthor and update their status information (thus resulting in a loosely coupled mode). The status information reflects the set of currently collaborating authors (see next section). When an author closes a specific browser (i.e., leaves this specific composite node) all collaborating activity space browsers change their status information correspondingly.

In loosely coupled mode, any author can request that SEPIA establishes a tightly coupled session among a selected set of coauthors. They may confirm or reject the request, but once they agree, all coauthors in a tightly coupled session share the same view (i.e., window content) on the composite node's content. Every coauthor can leave the composite node (i.e., close the corresponding browser) thus leaving the tightly coupled session.

Currently we do not apply premature restrictions on the tightly coupled mode. Therefore, it is also possible to have multiple tightly coupled sessions on the same composite node by different groups of authors. We are aware of the fact that this might cause some confusion for the actual cooperation (see discussion section). Each coauthor can participate in at most one tightly coupled session per composite node. It is also possible that several tightly coupled sessions together with some people in loosely coupled mode are simultaneously working on the same composite node. Because tightly coupled cooperation is a restriction of the loosely coupled behavior they all see their actions, but scrolling, resizing, and telepointing is only synchronized (and visible) within a tightly coupled session.

In the way described above, the transition between all three modes is very simple and easily controllable by the user. There is no need for a user to learn complex commands to start and stop cooperation! Simply navigating through the hyperdocument will start and stop cooperation where necessary.

The handling of tightly coupled sessions requires no knowledge about the physical distribution of partners across a network, their network addresses etc. So far, this design provides enough freedom for users to use social protocols among coauthors rather than enforcing some predefined collaboration style or behavior.

Interaction with cooperative SEPIA

There is no difference between single authoring SEPIA and cooperative SEPIA in the way users manipulate and navigate hyperdocuments. SEPIA users can have as many browsers open as they like. Each browser displays the content of a composite node. There is only one browser per composite node.

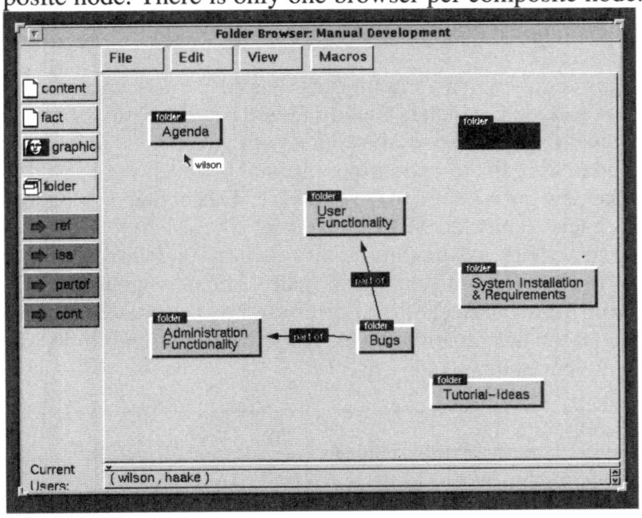

Figure 3a: The browser of Wilson tightly coupled with Haake

After issuing the operation "start TC session" the system displays a menu of the names of the current loosely coupled coauthors. The author requests SEPIA to connect to a set of coauthors by selecting their names from the menu. The selected users get a dialog box displayed on their screen which asks for accepting or rejecting of the tightly coupled session. Every user has to answer (or the system rejects automatically after a time out). Once SEPIA received all replies, a tightly coupled session is set up between all coauthors who confirmed. In addition, SEPIA establishes an audio conference between all members of the tightly coupled session. An example derived from the scenario of developing software manuals is shown in the screendumps of figure 3a and 3b. Two authors (Haake and Wilson) opened the composite node called "Manual Development". Then they decided to start a tightly coupled session. This is reflected in the "current user" line at the bottom of the browser window by placing brackets around the tightly coupled users. Loosely coupled users are shown by listing their names separated by commas. Note that every browser displays the name of its user at the beginning of the "current user" line. In figure 3a author Wilson selected the node "Examples" which is displayed in yellow and uses his telepointer to point to this node while talking to his coauthor using the audio connection. Figure 3b shows the browser of author Haake at the same time. He sees the telepointer of

The support for the loosely coupled mode is provided automatically by the system at all times. In an author's browser, the nodes and links currently selected by other authors are displayed in red and show the lock owner's name. These objects are not available for update operations by other coauthors (i.e. they are write locked). Remote actions such as move, create, and delete eventually lead to changes of the displayed hypertext graph. The only extension of the activity space browser is the list of concurrent users connected to this browser and the color coding of locked objects. This requires no additional effort from the user. Of course, to work in tightly coupled mode the users must specify their interests. Thus, the system offers three items in the new Collaboration Operations menu: start TC session, TelePointer on, and Video Conference.

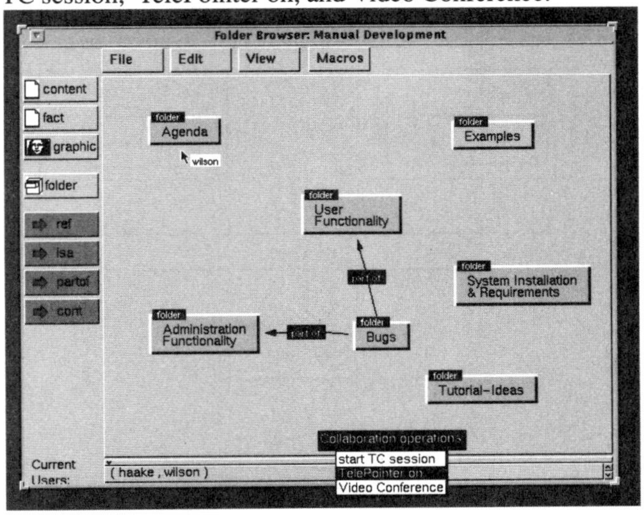

Figure 3b: The browser of Haake showing the collaboration operations menu

Wilson and is about to select an operation from the Collaboration Operations menu (note that each user can operate her/his menus independently).

The operation "TelePointer on" switches the telepointer on. If the author activates her/his telepointer the current position of the cursor is shown on each tightly coupled coauthor's screen (as an arrow with the owner's name). The telepointer remains visible to everybody in this session as long as the left mouse button is pressed.

Note that except for the two tightly coupled operations, none of the collaboration functionality requires explicit commands from the user. An advantage of this design is that the user does not feel restricted by the cooperative work situation. This is in accordance with the overall design requirement of not interfering with the way authoring has been done previously (i.e., without computer supported cooperation).

Our prototype system also includes a video conference device which will not be described further in this paper. This is the reason for the third operation in the collaboration operations menu called 'Video Conference'.

THE TECHNICAL SOLUTION

This section deals with the implementation of the loosely and tightly coupled mode. In extending the SEPIA architecture to support cooperation explicitly, we used the following strategy:

1. use the shared database to synchronize concurrent work and to resolve race conditions via a locking mechanism. Figure 4 shows two workstations, each running an instance of cooperative SEPIA. Each client accesses the shared hyperdocument database across the Ethernet in order to store and retrieve both private and shared data.

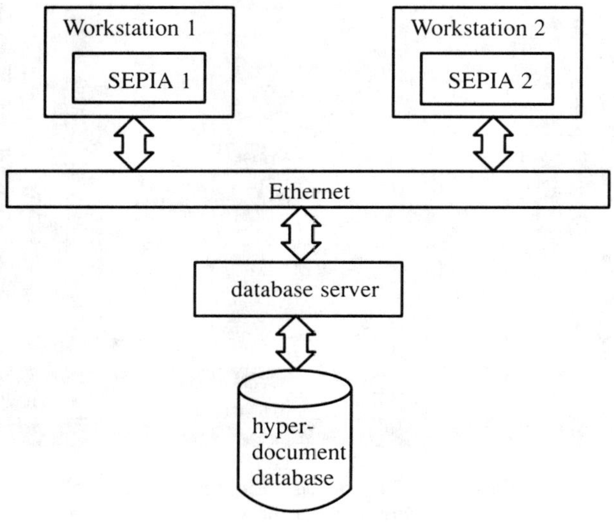

Figure 4: Overview of distributed computing environment

In order to provide access to the shared hyperdocument data, the hypermedia engine HyperBase [15] is used to implement a persistent, multi-user storage for all SEPIA data. Furthermore, we extended the single-user hyperdocument objects with additional attributes to support cooperation. First, each object carries a lock attribute. In addition, each composite node carries a list of all users who have opened this node. Every list entry consists of the necessary data to install a communication channel between a SEPIA program and the potential concurrent user's SEPIA. The general lock attribute of each object is used to synchronize access to objects in the loosely and tightly coupled mode. Changes of hypertext objects are broadcast to every connected SEPIA using a broadcast server.

2. extend the authoring tools (activity space browsers) to communicate with other authors' browsers viewing the same composite node in a way that is transparent to all authors involved, thus implementing loosely and tightly coupled mode. The relevant communication structure between two SEPIA systems is shown in figure 5. Note, there may be several communicating browsers between two SEPIA installations at the same time.

The implementation of loosely coupled mode

To support the loosely coupled mode, we use the update mechanism provided by the broadcast server. Every database server has an associated Broadcast Server which receives change notifications from any SEPIA instance modifying a database object. It broadcasts this notifications to every other SEPIA program. This messages are received and processed by each Broadcast Listener Process ensuring data consistency among cooperating SEPIA's. Three groups of activities are supported:

Setting up or joining a loosely coupled session

This occurs when an author opens a new browser on a composite node C which is already shared by other coauthors. The new browser retrieves the content of C from the database and updates the list of concurrent users of C by adding itself to it. The new list is stored in the database. This update is broadcast to each connected SEPIA instance. There is one Broadcast Listener Process dealing with incoming update requests. In case of an attribute change of node C the new value is loaded from the database, and the corresponding browser is informed about the new coauthor. This causes a transition into loosely coupled mode.

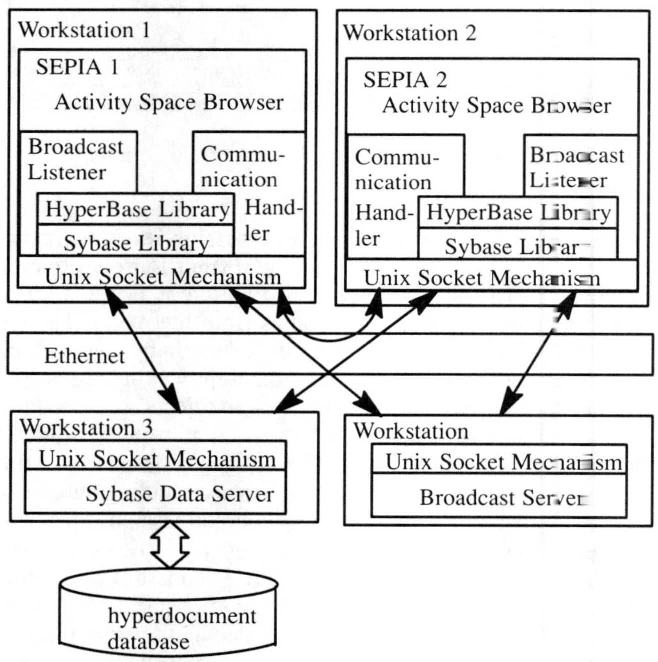

Figure 5: Communication Structure

Working in loosely coupled mode

When an author executes an action that must be reflected on a remote author's browser, the action modifies the state of some hypertext objects. These changes are automatically broadcast, thus leading to updates of browser's remote siblings.

Leaving the loosely coupled mode

If an author closes a browser belonging to a loosely coupled session this browser deletes itself from the concurrent user list. The remote browsers receiving the update request recompute their status line showing the remaining concurrent users.

The above design enables us to deal with dynamically adding and removing concurrent users to activity space browsers. The system supports both individual work as well as collaborative work. All race conditions and synchronization problems are solved using transactions of the underlying hypermedia engine HyperBase.

The implementation of tightly coupled mode

To support the tightly coupled mode, we introduced a tightly coupled session protocol with messages for synchronizing tightly coupled activity space browsers. They deal with

- the initialization of a tightly coupled session,
- simultaneous scrolling of all browsers controlled by one coauthor,
- simultaneous resizing of all collaborating browser windows,
- displaying a telepointer (arrow with coauthor name at a certain position) or removing it from the browser window.

These messages are sent from browsers to the Communication Handler processes of their remote siblings (see Figure 5). Activities supported in tightly coupled mode include:

Initiating a tightly coupled session

A user can initiate a tightly coupled session by executing the operation "start TC session" at her/his browser (called TCInitiator browser). This leads to sending participation requests from the TCInitiator browser to the remote browsers (or to subsets of these). Those who like to join the tightly coupled mode answer with an accept message and their view (i.e., window size, visible area, and scrolling ability) is coupled to that of the TCInitiator browser. In addition, the audio channel will be established. Anyone can leave a tightly coupled session but joining (again) after a session has been set up already is currently not supported.

Working in tightly coupled mode

In tightly coupled mode specific operations are scrolling, resizing and telepointing. To avoid scroll wars atomic scrolling and resizing events are provided for each tightly coupled session. Note, every activity space browser can participate in only one tightly coupled session at a time.

During the tightly coupled session we support a telepointer which is simultaneously visible on all screens together with the name of its owner. To avoid an abundance of cursors and names, the telepointer of a user is only visible as long as the corresponding mouse button is pressed. Concurrent telepointing is supported. This facilitates discussions about a document when concurrently using a video and/or audio conference connected to SEPIA.

In addition to the shared screen functionality of the tightly coupled session, SEPIA provides automatically an audio connection between different coauthors. It is used for multilateral exchange of verbal explanations supported by telepointing in the shared browser window. Note, each coauthor shares the same view but is able to perform his own operations independently from other coauthors (except for scrolling, resizing the window, and selecting objects which are already locked).

Leaving a tightly coupled session

Leaving a tightly coupled session is done by simply closing the browser (see loosely coupled sessions) thus decreasing the number of collaborators in the session by one.

SUMMARY AND DISCUSSION

Referring to the scenario introduced, we can state that cooperative SEPIA supports individual as well as cooperative work (collaboration in loosely coupled mode, synchronous cooperation in tightly coupled mode). Collaboration can be organized using composite nodes. The system provides access to shared hyperdocument data and supports the smooth transition between different modes of collaboration.

Comparing cooperative SEPIA with some of the systems introduced in the related work section yields the following observations.

The Grove group text editor [3] uses local editors and replicated documents together with a central coordinator serializing all editing operations. SEPIA is geared towards hyperdocument authoring and synchronization is done using transactions and locking of objects in the database.

The rIBIS system [12] is based on a central server architecture providing one TC session per hyperdocument and supporting only one mouse, a group mouse, within a TC session. SEPIA is implemented following the replicated architecture approach providing multiple TC sessions per composite node and supporting a private mouse for each coauthor. Switching between cooperative modes is very smooth in SEPIA.

While Dewan and Choudhary's [2] collaboration support environment requires users to tailor the coupling behavior to their needs (and, of course, provides a lot of freedom to do so) cooperative SEPIA implements a specific kind of coupling dedicated to each mode of collaboration. This relieves users from constructing a specific coupling behavior. Furthermore, SEPIA provides concurrency control and maintains dynamic sessions.

The CaveDraw system [10] is a drawing tool providing shared layers whereas SEPIA is a hypertext authoring system. CaveDraw requires explicit synchronization between layers, whereas cooperative SEPIA does not require explicit set up of connections to other coauthors. CaveDraw does not support an audio communication channel.

Aquanet [11] follows also the replicated architecture approach and makes use of a database, but does not support synchronous cooperation in terms of shared views, telepointers, and audio communication.

Our first use of the prototype system is concerned with project plan maintenance and proposal writing. Early experience shows that the system is easy to use. The response time within our in-house Ethernet is sufficiently good. As mentioned earlier, the current design does not support the dynamic expansion of a tightly coupled session to include more authors. To support the dynamic expansion of tightly coupled sessions several issues have to be answered, e.g., how should the current coauthors decide that someone new is allowed to join? We feel, that after some experience with the current system (which supports expansion by closing a tightly coupled session and reinstalling it with an increased set of coauthors) we are able to extend cooperative SEPIA adequately.

In the future we will extend cooperative SEPIA to explicitly support persistent activity tracking (e.g., who made which changes during a given time period?). The history cards in NoteCards [8] addressed this issue by listing a log of updates. But in addition, one is interested in the content of previous versions. For this purpose we will use a version server for structured electronic documents which is under development at our institute [21].

Finally, we discuss how the system will scale up when more users use it on large hyperdocument bases. Because of the replicated architecture approach communication is only necessary between those people who work on the same objects (composite nodes). Thus, partitioning the document base according to the nature of work and collaboration is important to reduce communication overhead. In addition, response time depends on network speed. Note that synchronization without video/audio communication requires only small packets to be exchanged. Distributed databases can further reduce communication costs (i.e., accessing distant databases may be more expensive). Instead of the currently used TCP/IP stream connections multicast protocols could increase performance. Furthermore, we are interested in using SEPIA across wide area network connections.

ACKNOWLEDGEMENTS

This work was supported by a special grant from GMD-IPSI to Brian Wilson as a visiting scientist from Stanford University. We thank Norbert Streitz for initiating our collaboration leading to the work on cooperative SEPIA and for his detailed comments and suggestions on draft versions of this paper. We thank Andreas Lemke and Helge Schütt for the fruitful discussions and comments on all phases of this work. Special thanks to Anja Weber and Jörg Hannemann are due to their detailed remarks on earlier drafts. All contributions lead to significant improvements of this paper.

REFERENCES

[1] J. Conklin. Hypertext: An Introduction and Survey. *Computer Magazine*, 20(9): 17-41, September 1987.

[2] P. Dewan & R. Choudhary. Flexible user interface coupling in a collaborative system. In *Proceedings of the CHI'91*, pages 41-48. New Orleans Louisiana, April 27- May 2, 1991.

[3] C. A. Ellis & S. J. Gibbs. Concurrency Control in Groupware Systems. In *Proceedings of the ACM SIGMOD'89 Conference on the Management of Data*, pages 399-407, Seattle Wash., May 2-4, 1989.

[4] C. A. Ellis, S. J. Gibbs, G. L. Rein. Groupware: Some issues and experiences. In *Communications of the ACM*, 34 (1), pages 38-5[illegible], January 1991.

[5] D. Engelbart & H. Lehtman. Working Together. In *BYTE*, pages 245-252, December, 1988.

[6] J. Grudin. Why CSCW Applications Fail: Problems in the Design and Evaluation of Organizational Interfaces. In *Proceedings of the Conference on Computer-Supported Cooperative Work (CSCW '88)*, pages 85-93, Portland, OR, September 26-29 1988.

[7] F. G. Halasz. Reflections on Notecards: Seven Issues for the Next Generation of Hypertext Systems. *Communications of the ACM* 31(7):836 - 852, July 1988.

[8] P. M. Irish & R. H. Trigg. Supporting Collaboration in Hypermedia: Issues and Experiences. In *Journal of the American Society for Information Science*, 40(3), pages 192-199, May, 1989.

[9] J. C. Lauwers. *Collaboration Transparency in Desktop Teleconferencing Environments*. PhD Thesis, 121 pages, Stanford, CA, July 1990.

[10] I. M. Lu, M. M. Mantei. Idea management in a shared drawing tool. In L. Bannon, M. Robinson, K. Schmidt (eds), *Proceedings of the 2nd European Conference on Computer-Supported Cooperative Work (E-CSCW '91)*, pages 97-112, Amsterdam, Netherlands, September 25-27 1991.

[11] C. Marshall, F. G. Halasz, R. A. Rogers, W. C. Janssen Jr.: Aquanet: A hypertext tool to hold your knowledge in place. In *Proceedings of the 3nd ACM Conference on Hypertext (Hypertext '91)*, page 261-275, San Antonio, Tx, December 15-18, 1991.

[12] G. L. Rein & C. A. Ellis. rIBIS: a real-time group hypertext system. In *International Journal of Man-Machine Studies*, 34, pages 339-367, August 1991.

[13] T. Rodden. A survey of CSCW systems. *Interacting with Computers*, 3 (3), p. 319-353, December 1991.

[14] R. W. Root. Design of a Multi-Media Vehicle for Social Browsing. In *Proceedings of the Conference on Computer-Supported Cooperative Work (CSCW '88)*, pages 25-38, Portland, OR, September 26-29 1988.

[15] H. Schütt & N. A. Streitz.: *HyperBase*: A Hypermedia Engine Based on a Relational Database Management System. In A. Rizk, N. Streitz, and J. Andrè (Eds.), *Hypertext: Concepts, Systems, and Applications.* Proceedings of the European Conference on Hypertext 90 (November 27 - 30, 1990). pages 95-108. Cambridge: Cambridge University Press, Electronic Publishing Series.

[16] M. Stefik, G. Foster, D. G. Bobrow, K. Kahn, S. Lanning, L. Suchman. Beyond The Chalkboard: Computer Support for Collaboration and Problem Solving in Meetings. In *Communications of the ACM*, (30)1, pages 32-47, January 1987.

[17] N. A. Streitz, J. Hannemann & M. Thüring. From Ideas and Arguments to Hyperdocuments: Travelling through Activity Spaces. In *Proceedings of the 2nd ACM Conference on Hypertext (Hypertext '89)*, pages 343-364, Pittsburgh, PA, November 5-8, 1989.

[18] N. A. Streitz, J. M. Haake, J. Hannemann, A. Lemke, W. Schuler, H. Schütt, M. Thüring. SEPIA: A Cooperative Hypermedia Authoring Environment. To appear as Technical Report: Arbeitspapiere der GMD. August 1991.

[19] M. Thüring, J. M. Haake, J. Hannemann: What's ELIZA doing in the Chinese Room? Incoherent hyperdocuments - and how to avoid them. In *Proceedings of the 3nd ACM Conference on Hypertext (Hypertext '91)*, pages 161-177, San Antonio, Tx, December 15-18, 1991.

[20] J. Walker. Netfone Release 1. Posted in news group *comp.sources.sun*. 12 Sep. 1991.

[21] A. Weber. Versioning Isues in Hypermedia Publishing Environments. Technical Report: Arbeitspapiere der GMD No. 542. June 1991.

[22] B. Wilson. WSCRAWL 2.0: A Shared Whiteboard Based on X-Windows. To appear as Technical Report. August 1992.

Flexible Diff-ing In A Collaborative Writing System

Christine M. Neuwirth
Ravinder Chandhok
David S. Kaufer
Paul Erion
James Morris
Dale Miller

Carnegie Mellon University
Pittsburgh, PA 15213
prep-project+@andrew.cmu.edu

ABSTRACT

An important activity in collaborative writing is communicating about changes to texts. This paper reports on a software system, *flexible diff*, that finds and reports differences ("diffs") between versions of texts. The system is flexible, allowing users to control several aspects of its operation including what changes are reported and how they are shown when they are reported. We argue that such flexibility is necessary to support users' different social and cognitive needs.

KEYWORDS

Text comparison, collaborative writing, flexible differencing

INTRODUCTION

In the course of a collaboration, co-authors often make changes to each other's documents. A principal difficulty co-authors face is coping with those changes, especially understanding why the other person made them. For example, in a study of eight writers' production of an insurance company's two-page annual report, Cross [3] observed that each writer "omitted, added, highlighted or modified" the text to agree with his or her preconceptions, with unexplained changes causing "considerable frustration" for other writers (p. 193).

This paper describes an approach to communicating about changes to documents. At the heart of the approach is a flexible text differencing system, *"flexible diff,"* that allows collaborative writers to tailor difference reports to their various social and cognitive needs. The program is imbedded in the PREP Editor [13; 14; 2], a writing environment being developed to study and support collaborative writing processes. The PREP Editor allows difference reports to be annotated with such things as explanations of changes.

Permission to copy without fee all or part of this material is granted provided that the copies are not made or distributed for direct commercial advantage, the ACM copyright notice and the title of the publication and its date appear, and notice is given that copying is by permission of the Association for Computing Machinery. To copy otherwise, or to republish, requires a fee and/or specific permission.

© 1992 ACM 0-89791-543-7/92/0010/0147...$1.50

ISSUES IN THE DESIGN OF A FLEXIBLE DIFF-ING SYSTEM

The technical question in the design of a difference finding program is how to take an original text and a revision, and to produce--in a time and space efficient way--an edit script (or difference report) that describes changes between the two versions. From a time/space efficiency standpoint, the "optimal" difference report is in the form of a list that describes the minimal number of editing changes required to transform the original text into the revision. This technical question has received considerable research attention [7; 10; 11] and is not the focus here. The focus in this paper is on the following human interface design questions and our approach to answering them:

- What changes should be reported?
- How should changes that are reported be pinpointed?
- What should the user interface to the change report be like?

In the course of answering these questions, we argue that, from a human factors standpoint, an optimal time/space difference report is not necessarily optimal.

What Changes Should Be Reported?

The most fundamental design question we addressed was "What changes should be reported?" One might think that the answer is obvious: "All of them." This answer, however, is not unconditionally correct. Nachbar [12] argues compellingly that reporting all changes is inappropriate for some tasks, such as comparing the output of floating point calculations (where roundoff errors result in spurious differences) and comparing program source code (where differences in white space and comments have no effect on the operation of compiled code). In response to these task demands, Nachbar's *spiff* (spiffy diff) provides a flexible diff-ing interface; for example, a user can instruct *spiff* to ignore differences between floating point numbers that are below a user-settable threshold, a feature that allows users to compare the outputs of a statistical package running on two different machines approximately 200 times faster than when using *diff* [7] to generate the report.

We identified three aspects of collaborative writing tasks that require developing a flexible difference finding algorithm:

- Different roles within a writing group;
- Changes in the needs of collaborative writing groups over time;
- Different types of collaborative writing groups.

Different roles within a writing group

A writing group is usually composed of different people fulfilling several different social roles. While a co-author may not be interested in seeing every change that a trusted co-author made, he or she may want to check every change from a less trustworthy editor. For example, Cross [3] observed that a secretary acting as editor changed "crises that could not be overcome" to "crises," because of a belief that crises, by definition, could not be overcome.

Changes in the needs of collaborative writing groups over time

A writing group's needs for detecting changes may be different at different times during the lifetime of a project. At the beginning of a project, co-authors may be changing a draft so radically that it would not be useful to see changes at a detailed level. In those cases, it is less likely that a co-author would want to detect what was inserted, but he or she may want to answer the question, "Where did my 'good bit' go?" At later stages of the project, for example, when responding to reviewer's comments, it may be useful to look at each change a co-author made.

Different types of collaborative writing groups

Different groups often need very different ways to detect changes. For some tasks, writers want to see every last change that was made from the previous version--for example, lawyers doing contract work. If, for example, the reader is a lawyer whose task it is to find all the changes that may have legal implications, then it certainly makes sense to report all of them. To illustrate, Figure 1.a. depicts the original of a legal document; Figure 1.b., a revised version, and Figure 1.c, a change report with all changes shown.[1]

[1] Strike-through corresponds to deleted material; underline corresponds to inserted material. Example based on material from [15].

But in another type of writing group, writers might actually be distracted by seeing every last change because the task might be quite different. If the reader is a co-author, for example, the tasks might be to read the new draft for meaning and, at the same time, to build a representation of the problems that remain in the paper. Such a reader may not be interested in all the changes, many of which draw attention to problems in the previous draft that are no longer of interest because they have been solved.

a. Original	The Pennsylvania law also establishes a time limit within which injuries or occupational diseases must be reported to an employer. Under this provision, compensation will be paid based on the date of the injury only if the injury is reported to your employer within 21 days of its occurrence. After 21 days, compensation will begin based on when the report is made. The law bars compensation for any injury or disease reported more than 120 days after the occurrence.
b. Revised	The Pennsylvania law establishes a time limit within which injuries or work-related illnesses must be reported to an employer. In order to receive full compensation, that is, compensation based on the date of the injury or the onset of illness, you must report it to your employer within 21 days of its occurrence. If you report it between the 22nd and 120th day, you will receive partial compensation, that is, compensation based on the date you file the claim. If you report it more than 120 days after the injury or onset of illness, you will receive no compensation.
c. All changes reported	The Pennsylvania law ~~also~~ establishes a time limit within which injuries or ~~occupational diseases~~ work-related illnesses must be reported to an employer. ~~Under this provision,~~ In order to receive full compensation, that is, compensation ~~will be paid~~ based on the date of the injury ~~only if the injury is reported to~~ or the onset of illness, you must report it to your employer within 21 days of its occurrence. ~~After 21 days, compensation will begin based on when the report is made. The law bars compensation for any injury or disease reported~~ If you report it between the 22nd and 120th day, you will receive partial compensation, that is, compensation based on the date you file the claim. If you report it more than 120 days after the ~~occurrence.~~ injury or onset of illness, you will receive no compensation.

Figure 1. An example revision and difference report.

Instead, the reader may prefer to see only some changes--for example, sentences or paragraphs that have been deleted, on the grounds that destruction of "hard won" sentences or paragraphs is an interesting event (see Figure 2.c). Indeed, a difference report of all the changes to the document might induce such a reader to focus on task-irrelevant information at the expense of building meaning and a representation of problems remaining (Figure 2.b.).

To understand how a change report might interfere with the tasks of building meaning and a representation of remaining problems, it is useful to look at what role attention plays in the process of reading. Most reading models assume that attention is required in order to derive meaning from texts and that the amount of attention available is limited, so attention must be allocated [15]. When two or more tasks exceed attentional capacity, the tasks cannot be performed simultaneously and readers engage in "attention switching," first allocating attention to one task, then the other. For example, beginning readers have difficulty decoding words and building meaning simultaneously, and must often switch attention from one task to the other; however, attention switching comes at a cost: It is time consuming, puts a heavy demand on short-term memory and tends to interfere with recall [8].

a. Original	Finally, and somewhat speculatively, we wondered if more experienced teachers would use electronic communication modes differently than less experienced teachers. New computer technologies do not, in and of themselves, create educational improvements; instead, they create opportunities for improvements.
b. All changes reported	Finally, and somewhat speculatively, we ~~wondered if more~~ hypothesized the following about individual teachers: More experienced teachers ~~would~~ and their students will use electronic communication modes ~~differently~~ more than less experienced teachers. ~~New computer technologies do not, in and of themselves, create educational improvements; instead, they create opportunities for improvements.~~
c. Sentence level changes reported	Finally, and somewhat speculatively, we hypothesized the following about individual teachers: More experienced teachers and their students will use electronic communication modes more than less experienced teachers. ~~New computer technologies do not, in and of themselves, create educational improvements; instead, they create opportunities for improvements.~~

Figure 2. All changes reported vs. sentence level changes.

Based on our initial experience with difference reports,[2] it is our hypothesis that reading for meaning, building a representation of remaining problems and detecting differences are tasks that require attention-switching for many readers. Indeed, the report of a change seems to invite the reader to focus on the change.[3] But an "invitation" can distract the reader from more appropriate tasks. Lesser and Erman [9] define "distraction" as the degree to which an agent's focus can be shifted. Positive distraction shifts an agent to tasks that are more useful; negative distraction shifts the agent to tasks that are redundant or diversionary. The distraction in a difference report might be negative, leading the reader to switch tasks and focus on the changes to the detriment of constructing the gist of the new material. Moreover, a reader with limited metacognitive capacity may fail to detect distraction or may recover from the problem only after considerable misspent time.[4]

This framework allows us to give a general answer to the question, "What changes should be reported?" In general, only those changes should be reported that will reduce negative distraction and increase positive distraction. Since this depends, as we have argued, on the reader and the task, a differencing program for collaborative writing needs to be flexible, to allow readers to specify what changes to ignore.

Like *spiff* [12], *flexible diff* achieves flexibility by allowing users to specify whether to ignore changes in whitespace (spaces, tabs, and newlines) or to treat it as any other non-alphanumeric character (i.e., to parse each whitespace character into its own token). In both systems the goal is to avoid the introduction of spurious and semantically meaningless entries in the difference report. For numerical values, *spiff* goes one step further and allows numerical differences within a threshold "epsilon" to be ignored. For text values, however, there is a question of how to measure differences. To address this issue, we have extended the *spiff* paradigm to text by introducing a heuristic for measuring differences. The user can instruct the program to ignore differences that are smaller than a specified grain size, with the choices for grain size being word, phrase, sentence, or paragraph.

---

[2] Users have been members of the PREP Editor project group, their collaborators, and first-year students in a selected section of a college writing course.

[3] This observation is consistent with the work of Gibson who observes that events--such as the notification of a change--have "affordances," that is, they demand or invite certain behaviors.

[4] With time and practice, frequent readers of change reports may become skilled at "decoding" them and be able to process them at the same time as reading for meaning and representing remaining problems; however, such a development is not inevitable. For example, it is generally **not** possible for proofreaders to become so skilled at finding errors that they are able to build meaning at the same time as they proofread (cf. [6]).

Differences are measured by the following heuristic: differences between two units are ignored if some percentage of their parts are equal. Setting the value to anything except 100% places the burden of difference detection on the reader.[5] For example, a co-author interested in not losing any "hard won" sentences might specify a grain size of a sentence, and a 70% change threshold (Figure 2.c). While we have not had any experience with lawyers using *flexible diff*, the appropriate setting for examining revisions of contracts might be 100% (Figure 1.c.). To complement our notion of "change threshold," we are experimenting with notations for showing relative amounts of differences in the interface. In other words, if some of the actual differences are suppressed from the report via the change threshold, the interface might still (through change bars, color or shading) indicate that there are changes to be explored. Paramount to the effectiveness of such a visual notation is its unobtrusiveness--it must *not* draw undue attention to the suppressed changes, or it will subvert the purpose of the change threshold completely.

Another aspect of the question "*What changes should be reported?*" concerns the type of events that should be reported. In particular, a "move" can be defined as a deletion followed by an insertion of the same material elsewhere. Our initial experience with difference reports, however, suggests that readers appreciate a move being signalled explicitly, because it reduces their search task. We developed a simple technique that searches for insertions and deletions of identical text and remaps them to a move operation. The user can control a parameter, "minimum length for a move," in units of the current grain size, that controls the minimum length of an insertion/deletion before it is interpreted as a move, on the grounds that multiple occurrences of short strings such as "the" and so forth should not be interpreted as moves. Based on our initial experience, it appears to be useful to allow larger units of text, such as sentences and phrases, to be treated as moves even though they have some changes within them, but this is not yet implemented.

How Should Changes That Are Reported Be Pinpointed?

Our experience with differencing tools for texts suggests that several factors--the number, density, and complexity of changes--should condition how changes in a text are pinpointed. Above a certain threshold of change intensity, writers seem to prefer a report that shows the entire region of text as changed rather than one that pinpoints each change piecemeal. To illustrate, Figure 3.a. depicts an original text and Figure 3.b., a revision. Figure 3.c. is a change report with the changes pinpointed at the word level; Figure 3.d. pinpoints the changes by concatenating replacements that are closer together than a user-controlled number of words away. Notice that the change report in Figure 3.d. is no longer strictly accurate: The word "brown" is reported as having been deleted and inserted, even though it was constant across the two versions. Yet many readers prefer the second version, reporting that it increases the readability.

In response to this observation, *flexible diff* defines several parameters that allow users to control how changes are pinpointed. The first parameter is "coarseness" of pinpointing: character, word, phrase, sentence, or paragraph. For example, if the user sets the coarseness parameter for how the change should be pinpointed to the sentence level (and the grain size parameter for what changes are to be reported to the word level), then an insertion of a word in a sentence will be reported, but it will be reported as the whole sentence having been deleted and inserted.

a. Original text	It was cold. The quick brown fox jumps over the lazy dog. Her bowl is over there, by the car.
b. Revised text	It was morning. It was cold. The slow brown dog jumps over the lazy cat. Her bowl is over there, by the truck.
c. Fine pinpointing	It was morning. It was cold. The ~~quick~~ slow brown ~~fox~~ dog jumps over the lazy ~~dog~~ cat. Her bowl is over there, by the ~~car~~ truck.
d. Medium pinpointing	It was morning. It was cold. The ~~quick brown fox~~ slow brown dog jumps over the lazy ~~dog~~ cat. Her bowl is over there, by the ~~car~~ truck.
e. Coarse pinpointing	It was morning. It was cold. ~~The quick brown fox jumps over the lazy dog~~ The slow brown dog jumps over the lazy cat. Her bowl is over there, by the ~~car~~ truck.

Figure 3. Pinpointing changes.

In addition to grain size, the user can control how precisely replacements (insertion/deletion pairs) are pinpointed. Three parameters are defined: "maximum distance to look for commonalities," "maximum percent of differences," and "maximum distance to concatenate." The first two parameters control the recursive top-down application of the differencing process which is applied, for example, at the phrase level before it is applied at the word level: If two phrases are very different in length ("maximum distance to look for commonalities") and have a great many differences ("maximum percent of differences"),[6] a replacement is reported at the phrase

[5]It is important to note that this is not to say that a co-author might not notice a change below the sentence level; simply that the change report would not point it out.

[6]The number of differences is computed by the first phase of the differencing algorithm. Our experiences are that the first phase of the algorithm (which yields the number of changes but not their exact values) generally executes in less than one-half the time required for a complete comparison.

level on the grounds that it is less worthwhile to examine them for commonalities, many of which may be cryptic and fortuitous (e.g., they may contain function words in common such as "the," "of," etc.); otherwise the differencing algorithm is continued and the replacements are pinpointed more exactly. Figure 3.e. depicts a change report that results when the parameters are set so that the algorithm does not recurse to the word level for the phrases "The quick brown fox jumps over the lazy dog" and "The slow brown dog jumps over the lazy cat."

The third parameter, "maximum distance to concatenate," controls a bottom-up concatenation process. As the list of differences (or edit script) is being built by the differencing process, it is examined for replacements that occur within the range of "maximum distance to concatenate" on the grounds that concatenating replacements that are adjacent or relatively close together increases the readability of the report. Figure 3.d. depicts a change report that results when the "maximum distance to concatenate" parameter is set so that "~~quick~~ slow brown ~~fox~~ dog" (cf. Figure 3.c.) is concatenated to "~~quick brown fox~~ slow brown dog." Depending on how the user sets the parameters controlling the top-down and bottom-up processes, they will produce identical or different results for any given example.

Incidentally, the parameters described in this section allow users to trade-off accuracy of pinpointing changes and execution speed because the speed of the differencing algorithm is proportional to the number of input tokens and to the number of differences between the two versions. Thus, users have an additional motivation to select parameters that are appropriate to their cognitive and social needs. In particular, users are motivated to initially generate an initial coarse description of changes (which is faster) and then to look selectively at the details of particular changes (which is more accurate). Our implementation actually uses heuristics like this to improve overall performance.

What Should The User Interface To The Change Report Be Like?

We have implemented an interface for *flexible diff* in the PREP Editor, a writing environment that supports side-by-side columns of text, with horizontal alignment that enables "at-a-glance" viewing of large numbers of annotations and related texts. The comparison interface produces its report in a new column, with the differences linked to the original column for easy, side-by-side evaluation. To illustrate, Figure 4 depicts four columns: an original draft, its revision, the comparison report and an evaluation column. The evaluation column in Figure 4 consists of annotations to the comparison report that a co-author produced in order to explain some of the changes or to solicit advice about them.

This interface has two important features. The first is horizontal alignment of the changes to the point of difference in the text. There is evidence that readers accustomed to horizontal writing read faster in the horizontal direction than in the vertical (*cf.* [17], p. 137). Thus, side-by-side, horizontal alignment of the changes to original and revised documents is consonant with what we know about the cognitive processing demands of the task of seeing what changed. The following excerpt from a "think-aloud" protocol of a reviewer looking at an author's original text, the reviewer's comments on that text, the author's revised text, and a change report is typical of those we have observed when changes are aligned horizontally and illustrates that users are able to understand changes quickly:

> ...*the object-oriented developers encountered fewer of the classic and costly surprises.* So he didn't actually change anything really here. Well all right--he changed a little, but it wasn't exactly what I wanted him to do.[7]

Because the comparison exactly links the changes to the source text, it is possible to provide a mechanism to accept or reject each change easily (as in InterNote [1]), though we have not yet implemented this.

The second important feature of the interface is the ability of users to annotate changes with explanations of the change or questions to co-authors. Our group's experience with this feature suggests that reviewers will annotate changes selectively in order to draw their co-authors' attention to changes they want to discuss or explain. Likewise, a co-author can ask a reviewer to explain a change. Our hypothesis is that the ability to annotate changes will greatly alleviate writers' frustrations with unexplained changes that Cross [3] observed.

The column layout just described requires a significant amount of screen real estate. In order to be usable with smaller screens, PREP provides flexibility in the comparison interface by allowing the user to display the text with the changes interspersed between the unchanged text (a common format used in commercial differencing tools). In this format, users can also annotate the changes.

Besides the interface to the change report, there is an interface to the parameters (described above) that control how the differencing process operates. While the parameters we have described allow enormous flexibility in our comparison tool, we also recognize that most users will not care to change the defaults. We chose the default values after testing the algorithm against widely varying input texts, including texts jointly written among ourselves in PREP (this paper was co-authored in PREP).

---

[7] In a "think-aloud" protocol, subjects are asked to think-aloud--to say whatever it is they are thinking--and are video-taped or audio-taped. In the transcription italics indicate that the subject is reading, and each "-" indicates a pause of 1 second duration. The author and reviewer, who were subjects in an experiment evaluating aspects of the PREP Editor, were working on an actual paper intended for publication.

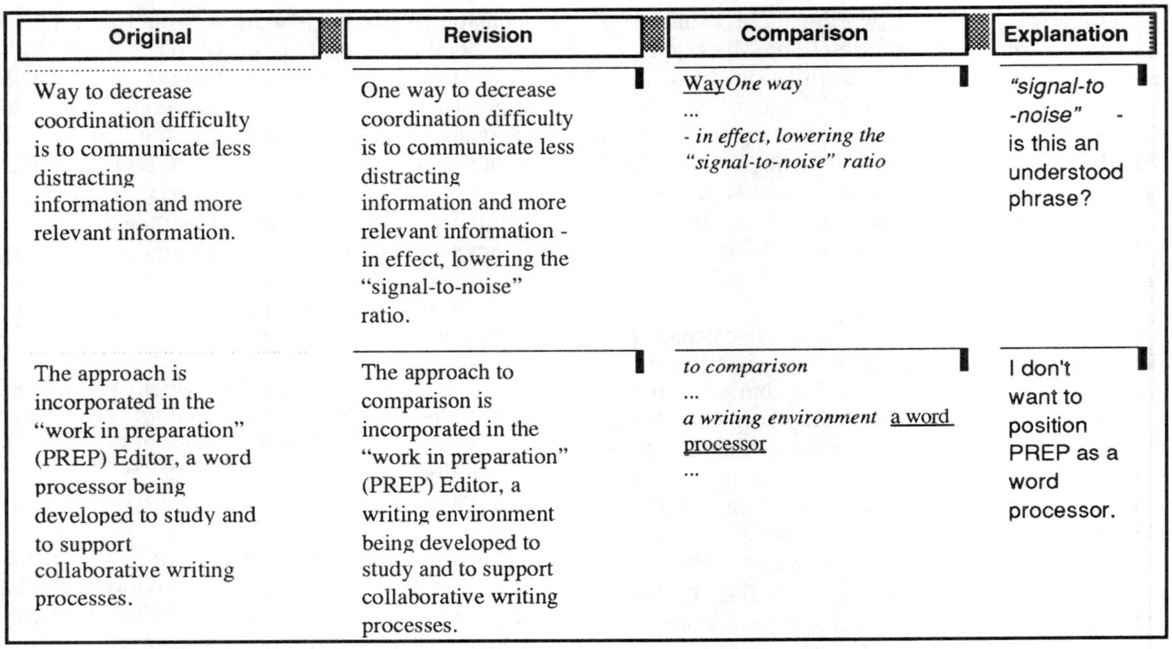

Figure 4. Actual PREP Editor column interface showing *flexible diff*. Note that the current implementation of PREP shows insertions as *italic* text, and deletions as underlined text.

It is essential to note that we do not claim to have discovered the mappings between our heuristics, the parameter settings and output that is optimal for a reader trying to make sense of a report of differences across versions of text. We only claim to have created a tool where these settings and their effect on interpretability can be systematically explored. How the heuristics should be applied (and perhaps the proper defaults based on different task scenarios) is something we regard as important future research.

Currently, comparisons are generated only upon request from the user. We plan to experiment with heuristics for automatically generating comparison reports, depending on role relationships among writers. For example, if the annotated draft is from a co-author, then display changes upon request; if from a reviewer, then display all changes automatically. Apart from generating the comparison before returning the revision (which we, as co-authors, currently sometimes do), the revision's author has little control over how the comparison might be done. As this information might lead to a more productive exchange, we plan to experiment with adding "comparison settings" information to revisions that would serve as hints from the co-author to anyone who would generate a difference report. For example, as a teacher, I might wish to hide/suppress character level changes (e.g., spelling corrections) so that my student's attention would be directed towards the more meaningful, higher-level changes.

OPERATION

Initially, *flexible diff* does a lexical analysis of the input streams based on the settings the user has specified. During this tokenizing process, any white space is distinguished and usually ignored. The resultant streams are then fed into the differencing process for generation of the edit script. Note that even this simple abstraction of separating the actual characters of the input stream from the sequence comparison gives the engine considerable flexibility in terms of generating reports based on different grain sizes[8].

The Differencing Process

The differencing algorithm is modelled after the Myers [11] O(ND) longest common subsequence/shortest edit script algorithm.

In *flexible diff*, the basic Myers algorithm is applied with a hierarchical decomposition strategy that exploits the grain size (character, word, phrase, sentence, paragraph) of comparison reports. For the sake of illustration, assume that the user has set the grain size to the word level (the default setting). The hierarchical application of the Myers algorithm can be described by the following psuedo-code:

1. Compare text-A and text-B at the phrase level.
2. **For** all string replacements in the edit script **Do**
If the original has little in common with its replacement
Then report the whole string as changed
Else compute & report diffs for the two strings at the word level.

After building a list of differences at a higher level (Step 1), several factors are examined to determine whether to

[8] In our implementation, a tokenizer is a subclass of a generic "tokenizer" C++ class, so adding different tokenizers is an easy task--ones for sound and graphics would be possible.

diff recursively the corresponding strings at the next level (Step 2). The decision as to whether strings have "a lot" or "a little" in common are controlled by the parameters "maximum distance to look for commonalities" and "maximum percent of differences" described above.

Finally, concatenations of the edit script, controlled by the parameter "maximum distance to concatenate," are done as the edit script is produced. This concatenation reduces co-located edit operations to one larger operation.

Performance

The Myers algorithm performs especially well when differences are small (i.e., sequences are similar) and is consequently fast in an application in which users adjust grain size to fit the stage in the writing process.

RELATED RESEARCH

Several researchers have argued recently that computer-support for cooperative work requires flexibility, that is, the ability to tailor the behavior of collaborative systems both to differences between groups and to differences among group members [4; 5]. We are especially indebted to Dewan and Choudhary's [4] work on flexible coupling. Their thoughts about the collaborative negotiation that might occur and parameters for such negotiation have influenced our entire approach.

The technical problem of efficient and optimal change detection has been explored in detail by other researchers, most notably UNIX™ *diff* [7] and Miller and Myers [10; 11]. We have not tried to improve on the efficiency and compactness of differencing algorithms themselves, but instead on the readability of the report. Our implementation based on their techniques is able to process realistically sized texts, from 10 to 40 pages and up to 15,000 words, in a user-perceived "reasonable" amount of time.

The notion of flexible diff-ing in *spiff* [12] is closest to our research in its application of domain knowledge to reduce spurious difference reporting. Our work extends this idea by defining parameters we argue are appropriate to the domain of collaborative writing. Some of the settings for the parameters allow users to trade accuracy for efficiency. Others allow for tradeoffs between correctness of the difference report versus cognitive distraction due to unimportant information.

Surprisingly, little work has been done on how best to display difference reports to user. Existing tools pay little attention to the presentation of the comparison information. In the case of *diff*, the output is simply a list of the changed lines with an indication of whether the particular line was replaced, inserted, or deleted (Figure 5.b). Likewise, editors that include "change bars" indicate which lines have changed and do not report the actual site of the revisions (Figure 5.a). Note that while "diff" gives information such as which lines were inserted, deleted, or changed, the change bar interface does not show that detail. With change bars, the location of the change is less precisely pinpointed and the type of change is not specified. Commercial word processors and comparison tools produce output based on word-level differences, such as shown in Figure 3.c. None of these interfaces support commenting on change reports in order to explain changes.

FUTURE WORK AND CONCLUSIONS

The notion of flexible differencing is clearly related to versioning and concurrency control. As techniques for dealing with inconsistencies improve, there may be less need for strict concurrency control, since users could resolve conflicts that have arisen more easily. We have plans to explore the application of *flexible diff* in this context.

▌It was morning.	*** 1,6 ****
It was cold.	It was cold.
▌The slow brown dog	!The quick brown
▌jumps over the lazy	!fox jumps over the
▌cat, her bowl is	!lazy dog, her bowl
over there, by the	is over there, by
▌truck.	!the car.
	--- 1,7 ----
	+It was morning.
	It was cold.
	!The slow brown dog
	!jumps over the
	!lazy cat, her bowl
	is over there, by
	!the truck.
a. Change bars	**b. "diff" output**
	!" Indicates a changed line
	"+" Indicates an inserted line

Figure 5. Typical difference reports in existing systems.

Our approach can be improved in many ways. It will probably be useful to exploit semantic information such as a knowledge of function words (e.g., "and," "the" "of" etc.). Likewise, it might be useful to exploit the semantic and pragmatic knowledge of users themselves. For example, a facility might be useful that would allow a co-author to select a region of text to draw to his or her co-author's attention in a change report, regardless of grain size or change threshold. Also, full support of collaborative writing groups may require supporting difference finding and reporting for objects other than text. Our observations of a group of physicists working collaboratively on a paper suggest that we may need to explore diff-ing pictures.

While we have designed *flexible diff* specifically for PREP and the context of collaborative writing, many aspects of it apply to any collaboration system.

In collaborative writing systems of the future, users will want to automatically recover changes that they made themselves at an earlier time or that are the result of work by another writer. In such a world, good comparison reports of versions will be essential. We have argued a good comparison report depends not only on a tool's efficiency in detecting change but also on the tool's ability to be tailored to different contextual assumptions of change and to a user's cognitive capacity to process information about change in various social contexts. In this paper, we have reported some progress toward the development of such a tool that, we have argued, will support a wide variety of tasks and texts. It remains to be seen which parameters make the biggest difference to which editing contexts. That determination awaits future empirical work. Such a tool, however, allows for a systematic study that varies number, density and complexity of change and could help us discover more about how each factor affects the task definition processes and goals of collaborative writers.

ACKNOWLEDGEMENTS

The work reported here have been supported by the National Science Foundation (grant number IRI-8902891) and by a grant from External Research at Apple Computer, Inc. Special acknowledgement is due to Paul Erion who was chiefly responsible for our implementation of the diff-ing. Thanks to David Banks for consultation on parameters for string similarity measures and to Davida Charney for comments on an earlier draft of this paper.

REFERENCES

1. Catlin, T., Bush, P., and Yankelovich, N. InterNote: Extending a hypermedia framework to support annotative collaboration. In *Hypertext'89 Proceedings* (Pittsburgh, PA, Nov. 5-9). ACM, N.Y., 1989, pp. 365-378.

2. Cavalier, T., Chandhok, R., Morris, J., Kaufer, D., and Neuwirth, C.M. A visual design for collaborative work: Columns for commenting and annotation. In *Proceedings of the Twenty-fourth Hawaii International Conference on System Sciences (HICSS-24)* (Kalua Kona, Hawaii, Jan. 8-11), J.F. Nunamaker, Jr., Ed. IEEE Press, Washington, D.C., 1991, pp. 729-738.

3. Cross, G. A. A Bakhtinian exploration of factors affecting the collaborative writing of an executive letter of an annual report. *Research in the Teaching of English 24*, 2 (May, 1990), 173-203.

4. Dewan, P., and Choudhary, R. Flexible user interface coupling in a collaborative system. In *Proceedings of the CHI'91 Conference* (New Orleans, April 27-May 2). ACM, N.Y., 1991, pp. 41-49.

5. Greenberg, S. Personalizable groupware: Accommodating individual roles and group differences. In *Proceedings of the Second European Conference on Computer-Supported Cooperative Work* (Amsterdam, The Netherlands, Sep. 25-27), L. Bannon, M. Robinson, and K. Schmidt, Eds. Computer Sciences Company, Slough, UK, 1991, pp. 17-31.

6. Haber, R.N., and Schindler, R.M. Error in proofreading: Evidence of syntactic control of letter processing? *Journal of Experimental Psychology: Human Perception and Performance 7*, (1981), 573-579.

7. Hunt, J.W., and McIlroy, M.D. *An Algorithm for Differential File Comparison*, Bell Laboratories, N.J., Computing Science Technical Report No. 41, 1975.

8. Kahneman, D. *Attention and Effort.* Prentice-Hall, Englewood Cliffs, N.J., 1973.

9. Lesser, V.R., and Erman, L.D. Distributed interpretation: A model and experiment. *IEEE Transactions on Computers C-29 12* (Dec. 1980), 1144-1163.

10. Miller, W., and Myers, E.W. A file comparison program. *Software-Practice and Experience 15*, 11 (1985), 1025-1040.

11. Myers, E.W. An O(ND) difference algorithm and its variations. *Algorithmica 1* (1986), 251-266.

12. Nachbar, D. Spiff--A Program for Making Controlled Approximate Comparisons of Files. In *Proceedings of the Summer 1988 USENIX Conference* (San Francisco, CA, June 21-24). USENIX Association, Berkeley, CA, 1988, pp. 73-84.

13. Neuwirth, C.M., and Kaufer, D.S. The role of external representations in the writing process: Implications for the design of hypertext-based writing tools. In *Hypertext '89 Proceedings* (Pittsburgh, PA, Nov. 5-8). ACM, N.Y. 1989, pp. 319-342.

14. Neuwirth, C.M., Kaufer, D.S., Chandhok, R., Morris, J.H. Issues in the design of computer support for co-authoring and commenting. In *Proceedings of CSCW'90 Conference on Collaborative Work* (Los Angeles, CA, Oct. 7-10). ACM, N.Y.,1990, pp. 183-195.

15. Samuels, S.J., and Kamil, M.L. Models of the reading process. In *Handbook of Reading Research*, D. P. Pearson, Ed. Longman Inc., N.Y., 1984, pp. 185-224.

17. Taylor, I., and Taylor, M. M.*The Psychology of Reading*. Academic Press, N.Y., 1983.

Computer-Mediated Communication and Collaborative Writing: Media Influence and Adaptation to Communication Constraints

Jolene Galegher

Department of English
Carnegie Mellon University
Pittsburgh, PA 15213
(412) 268-6448 galegher@andrew.cmu.edu

Robert E. Kraut

Bellcore
Room 2E-232
Morristown, NJ 07960
(201) 829-4513
kraut@thumper.bellcore.com

ABSTRACT

According to contingency theory, tasks involving high levels of uncertainty and equivocality require a communication medium that permits interactive, expressive communication. The theory of adaptive structuration, however, takes a more dynamic view of the relationship between communication technology and communication behavior, recognizing the malleability of human behavior as well as the adaptability of technology. According to the structuration perspective, individuals can adapt their behavior to achieve their goals despite obstacles in the technological environment. To assess the relative validity of these formulations, we examined media choices and responses to communication constraints in a collaborative writing task. The results of this experiment indicate that contingency theory has some general validity in that the task/technology matches it defines do, indeed, occur spontaneously and do contribute to ease and efficiency in task performance. However, the results also draw attention to the human potential for behavioral adaptation, and imply a need for further research designed to identify likely patterns of adaptation in particular technological environments.

KEYWORDS

Adaptive structuration, Computer-mediated communication, Collaborative writing, Contingency theory

Permission to copy without fee all or part of this material is granted provided that the copies are not made or distributed for direct commercial advantage, the ACM copyright notice and the title of the publication and its date appear, and notice is given that copying is by permission of the Association for Computing Machinery. To copy otherwise, or to republish, requires a fee and/or specific permission.

© 1992 ACM 0-89791-543-7/92/0010/0155...$1.50

INTRODUCTION

The advent of computer-mediated communication prompted both intellectual curiosity and practical concerns about how it would affect communication and task performance within and between small groups and organizations. A stream of investigations designed to assess reactions to this new medium and examine its effects on a wide variety of communication behaviors and task outcomes quickly followed [14,15]. To a large extent, these studies have been guided by variants of contingency theory, a rather loose formulation embodying the idea that communication will be more efficient and effective when the communication modality matches the requirements of the message to be communicated or the task to be accomplished [6]. The theory proposes that, when faced with some communicative task and a choice about how to carry it out, individuals will seek the communication modality that best matches the demands of the task. Further, it predicts that communication effectiveness and task performance will be positively related to the degree of fit between communicative requirements and the carrying capacity of the modality. Although the variants of contingency theory differ in emphasis and in the terminology they employ [2,13,18] they have in common the idea that work on ill-structured problems requires interactive, expressive communication.

These are disconcerting ideas for advocates of computer-mediated communication, because technologies such as electronic mail and computer conferencing are generally rated as "lean" media, lacking the potential to support intricate communication about complex topics. If contingency theory is valid, communicators should be reluctant to rely on computer-mediated communication for many important aspects of their work, substantially limiting its utility. The data that have been collected to date, however, are not entirely supportive of the contingency hypothesis. Some studies tend to support the theory's core propositions [1,3,16], but other investigators have questioned the reasoning behind these propositions and have collected contradictory data [15].

Among the theoretical critiques of contingency theory is the observation that it is based on an unjustified assumption of technological determinism. That is, it assumes that the characteristics of technologies are fixed and objectively knowable, and that those characteristics govern the behavior of users in predictable ways. An alternative perspective, developed in detail by Orlikowski & Robey [9] and Poole and Desanctis [10], holds that information technologies are "social object[s], with fixed material features, but indeterminate social implications" [9, p. 151]. According to this formulation, the relationship between technology and human behavior should be seen as constantly evolving; humans create technologies with particular physical features, and, in their encounters with those technologies, behave in ways that are partly a function of pre-existing patterns and partly a function of the opportunities and constraints made manifest in the technology. As a result of these encounters, new patterns of human action may emerge, but technologies might also be modified to better serve human goals. Unlike contingency theory, this perspective, called adaptive structuration, acknowledges both the malleability and the agentic potential of human behavior.

The structuration approach does not, however, directly contradict contingency theory. Because it acknowledges the physical reality of information systems and the potential of that reality to influence human action, it might be more appropriate to say that the structuration approach subsumes contingency theory, directing attention to the causal influence of information technology, but arguing that its influence is mediated by human agency and adaptability. In our own research [5], we have obtained results that are consistent with this analysis. A previous investigation comparing the experiences and performance of groups who used either computer-mediated or traditional face-to-face communication to complete a collaborative writing project revealed that the groups who communicated by computer had substantially more difficulty doing their work, but were nonetheless able to perform as well as those who met face-to-face. In that experiment, the negative effects of computer-mediated communication on the processes by which groups produced their reports could be interpreted as a direct confirmation of contingency theory, but contingency theory does not provide an explanation for the absence of differences in group performance. The structuration perspective, however, allows us to understand both of these outcomes. It suggests that groups adjusted their work processes to create documents that met their standards, but that doing so involved considerable cost.

These outcomes and the interpretation offered here raise obvious questions about which aspects of the work were viewed as most problematic and what social and technological mechanisms were used to overcome the obstacles associated with computer-mediated communication. As Poole & DeSanctis [10] point out, understanding structuration involves understanding technology-in-use. Unfortunately, the data from that experiment do not allow us to speak to these questions because we did not include direct measures of the way groups did their work. Furthermore, because the design of the experiment restricted students to particular communication modalities, we were unable to observe students' media choices. This is a serious shortcoming, both from the viewpoint of contingency theory and from the structuration perspective. According to contingency theory, individuals should prefer media that fit the communication requirements of their tasks over those that are less suitable. For instance, to carry out the intricate communication required to plan a complex project, they should, when possible, choose a rich medium such as face-to-face communication. According to the theory of adaptive structuration, choosing an appropriate communication medium is an instance of structuration, that is, an instance of individuals shaping the world in which they work [9]. Thus, although the theory makes no specific predictions with regard to the medium students will choose, it does suggest that, given the physical realities of the available media and the objectively specifiable demands of the task, their choices should be non-random.

In the experiment to be described below, we attempt to answer some of the questions raised by our previous study. In particular, we have again assigned students to work in groups to produce a complex document, and we have assigned these groups to communication conditions that create a particular combination of opportunities and constraints. This experiment differs from the previous one, however, in that it includes a communication condition in which students could choose at will from among the set of communication modalities (face-to-face interaction, telephones, exchange of documents and computer conferencing) typically available in a contemporary office. Further, we have created projects that differ in the extent to which they appear to require intricate communication and coordination among group members. The combination of these variables makes it possible to determine whether students' media choices reflect the task/technology fit predicted by contingency theory. Moreover, each project involves multiple tasks which differ in their demands for intensive communication; this within-project variation provides us with a second opportunity to assess the validity of the contingency hypothesis regarding the effects of task characteristics on media choice. Finally, we have included measures that allow us to determine how students cope with the constraints imposed by computer-mediated communication when no choice is available.

Based on contingency theory, we hypothesize that students will choose face-to-face communication for the most communicatively intense aspects of their work. This means that, to the extent that projects and tasks within projects differ in the extent to which they appear to demand intricate coordination, students should be more likely to choose to communicate face-to-face. For the between-project comparison in this experiment, we expect that students will be more likely to choose to communicate face-to-face when they are working on the Integrative project; within projects, they will be more likely to choose to communicate face-to-face when they are planning, rather than executing (i.e., drafting and revising their work). Also based on contingency theory, we expect that when students are restricted to communicating by computer, they will experience substantial coordination problems. Last, drawing on the insights offered by the adaptive structuration approach, we expect that when students are restricted to communicating by computer, they will adapt to this constraint by working more independently. The first two of these three hypotheses could be derived from either contingency theory or the structuration perspective, but only the structuration perspective prompts us to consider how individuals adapt their behavior to make it possible to achieve their goals when the material features of the available technologies are at odds with the tasks to be accomplished.

METHOD

Design

The subjects in this experiment were 114 first-year MBA students enrolled in a managerial communication course conducted by the first author. The students were randomly assigned to three-person groups, which were, in turn, randomly assigned to experimental conditions. Each student participated in two groups, one for each of two projects.

This distinction between the two projects represents the first independent variable, Project Type. The first project, hereafter called the Divisible project, was designed to make it possible for group members to decompose the project into tasks that could be carried out with relatively little coordination and communication among individuals. The second project, hereafter called the Integrative project, was designed to make it necessary for group members to coordinate their work more closely in order to produce a coherent product.

For each project, there were three communication conditions (Computer/Phone, Face-to-Face, and Free Choice). For the first project, half of the groups were assigned to the Computer/Phone condition and the rest were evenly divided between the Face-to-Face and the Free Choice conditions. For the second project, new groups were formed with the restriction that workgroups were made up of different individuals than in the first project. Students who had previously been in Computer/Phone groups were assigned to either the Face-to-Face group or the Free Choice group.[1]

[1]Because this project was carried out within a university class, it was necessary to assign groups to conditions in a way that appeared fair to the participants. Thus, for each project, half of the groups were assigned to a communication condition that permitted face-to-face communication (either the Face-to-Face or the Free Choice condition), and half were assigned to the Computer/Phone condition, in which face-to-face communication was not permitted. This arrangement, of course, produced unequal numbers of groups in the three communication conditions. Conducting the experiment in a class setting also precluded counterbalancing the order of cases; that is, it was impossible to have half of the class working on one case and the other half working on the other case at the same time.

Procedure

Students were required to complete two projects, each of which involved responding to the dilemmas presented in a business case. Following class discussion of the case, students were given a set of guidelines that defined the substantive goals they were to try to achieve and a two-week deadline for completing the project. In that interval, they were free to work on the project in any way that did not violate the terms of their experimental conditions. Packets containing blank copies of daily work reports were handed out, and students were instructed to complete one form on each day of the project. Post-project questionnaires were completed during class sessions.

Students assigned to the Computer/Phone condition conducted their computer-mediated communication via a system called ICoSy, a program that supports both electronic mail and computer conferences. Using the e-mail function, individuals could send private messages to other individuals or to several people at a time. Using the conference function, an individual could post entries, much as one would post notices on a bulletin board. These entries could be of any length or type (e.g., personal messages, outlines, draft versions of documents, or comments on entries submitted by other group members). The system also contains a reference function which enables users to follow a sequence of entries (i.e., comments on a draft document and revised versions can be linked to the entry containing the draft). In addition, mail messages could become conference entries and vice versa by copying the relevant message to a "scratchpad," and forwarding it to the appropriate destination. Finally, the system supports uploading and downloading, making it possible for individuals to create and manipulate documents in their own word processors and transmit ASCII versions of those documents to the conference space.

To complete their work, students in the Computer-Mediated conditions could use either their own computers or computers in a university lab open only to MBA students. Modems and communications software (either KERMIT or ProComm) were provided for any student who needed them. The students were reasonably experienced computer users; on a 3-point scale of previous experience with word processing (where 3 = experienced, and 1 = no experience) the class mean was 2.4[2], and 39% reported some previous experience with electronic mail. The rest, however, were new to computer-mediated communication, and almost all were new users of ICoSy. Thus, several weeks prior to the beginning of the experiment, a training session was held to demonstrate the use of the computer conference. At the demonstration, participants were given specially created documentation to guide them as they acquired the necessary computer skills, and were encouraged to begin learning the system immediately. A teaching assistant

[2]Note that these data were collected on the first day of the semester, but the project described here began about four weeks after the beginning of the class. By that time, all subjects had had to complete several assignments using word processors; thus, this value would likely have been somewhat higher when the experiment began.

was appointed to provide technical assistance in using the computer conference, and participants were invited to call him at any time. In addition, students could obtain follow-up advice about the use of the computer conference on-line in the open conference or through mail messages, by telephone, or in person, from the experimenter, from university computer consultants or from their classmates.

For practice using the conferencing system prior to beginning work on their projects, all students joined an open conference. For project work, however, each group had its own computer conference. Thus, each individual was a member of two conferences---an open conference that remained accessible throughout the course as a vehicle for communication among students and between students and the professor, and a closed conference accessible only to the student and the other members of his or her workgroup.

Participation in this research was voluntary; students were asked to sign consent forms indicating their willingness to participate and, except for two individuals, all of them did so. Those two individuals indicated that they were willing to participate in the experiment, but were unwilling to complete questionnaires. Executing the experiment within a regular class meant that students were aware of the variations in communication conditions. To minimize students' concerns about the potential effect of these variations on their performance (and the biases that such concerns might introduce into the research findings), the instructions pointed out that any advantages or disadvantages associated with communication condition would be evenly distributed because each individual would participate in one group that permitted face-to-face communication and one that did not. In addition, students were told that the instructor would eliminate any effects of the experimental manipulations in determining grades. To preserve the students' privacy, they were also told that none of their responses would be examined until after the end of the course.

Independent Variables

To operationalize the Project Type variable, we selected cases that varied in the level of interdependent activity required to complete the project. For the Divisible case, the students were to write a multi-part report for the CEO of a medium-size firm concerning the issue of employer-sponsored childcare. The assignment required that the report contain a section summarizing employees' concerns, a section reviewing possible approaches for responding to those concerns, a section reviewing state regulations for childcare facilities, and an executive summary encompassing the contents of these sections and recommending a course of action to the CEO. Each of the substantive parts of the report was to be a distinct unit, and the executive summary was to briefly restate the contents of those sections. Thus, we believed that the likely approach to this assignment would be to assign responsibility for each section to a single group member, and to work together only enough to generate the recommendations to be presented in the executive summary.

The Integrative case, drawn from Schuler & Youngblood [12] described an organization facing a number of complex personnel problems. The students were to analyze these problems and recommend solutions in a report to management. The problems in the organization were inter-related, and the most probable solutions involved broad-scale organizational change reflected in a large variety of specific measures. Thus, we believed that the likely approach to this assignment would be to work together to come to a decision about a general approach to these problems, as well as to design a coherent set of recommendations.

To operationalize the Communication Modality variable, students were assigned to one of three communication conditions. In the Free Choice condition, the participants could choose whatever means of communication they preferred, including both familiar modalities such as face-to-face meetings and telephone conversations, as well as computer-mediated communication. As noted above, each workgroup had its own conference, and any member of the group could read any message posted in its conference. The other two communication conditions restricted students' communication alternatives, either by disallowing face-to-face communication or by restricting access to the computer conference. In the Computer/Phone condition, students were required to conduct all project-related interactions, including both substantive and procedural discussions of their work and the exchange and review of interim documents, using either the ICoSy system or the telephone. In the Face-to-Face condition, the participants could meet, conduct telephone conversations, and exchange documents, but were not allowed to use ICoSy.

Dependent Variables

Daily Work Reports

Measures of students' behavior and of their subjective assessments of their experience were obtained from their daily work reports. On these reports, they used a checklist to record the type of work they had done each day. They also reported how many "communication occasions" they had had with other group members that day, and provided detailed information (time of day, type of contact, duration, identity of individuals involved, topics discussed, and assessments of enjoyableness and productivity) about a selected communication occasion. In addition, the students provided daily evaluations of several aspects of their experience including the difficulty of coordinating work, the fairness of the division of labor, the quality of their communication procedures, and their attachment to other group members. These evaluations, as well as the evaluations of the enjoyableness and productivity of the focal communication occasion, were reported on 7-point Likert scales.

Retrospective Data

After each of the two projects, students completed questionnaires designed to assess several aspects of their experience in their groups. Here, we concentrate on the extent to which they carried out their work together vs. independently. To determine how the students carried out their work, we asked them two sets of questions. First, they were asked to assess the level of interdependence in their work on the project as a whole. The two 7-point scale items that made up this measure (i.e., the extent to which the people in their groups had "one-person jobs" at which they worked independently, and the extent to which the people in their groups had to work together to make their ideas and individual contributions mesh) were drawn from Van de Ven *et al.* [18]. This measure serves as both a manipulation check for the Project Type variable, and a dependent variable in the analysis of whether the Communication Modality variable affects project execution. Second, we asked them to indicate (again, on 7-point scales) the extent to which they completed a set of specific tasks independently. Some of these tasks were common to both projects (e.g., developing a sense of direction for the project) and some were unique to each project (e.g., creating specific portions of the document).

Performance Data

Each group's project was scored by three people, the first author and two individuals who were employed as graders for the course. These individuals were blind to experimental condition. Their evaluation of the completed projects followed the usual practices in the course. That is, after the projects had been turned in, the first author scanned the submitted papers and selected a small number of examples (without regard to experimental condition) to illustrate successful and unsuccessful responses to the assignment; these were then discussed in a meeting with the graders. Subsequently, each rater worked independently, assigning holistic scores to each paper. At .83, the effective reliability [11] of these ratings was satisfactory, and the mean of the scores assigned by the three raters was used as the measure of performance.

Analysis

In this experiment, we are interested in group-level phenomena such as coordination difficulties and performance on a jointly created product. Some dependent variables, such as group performance, are naturally group-level outcomes. Others, such as time spent on various tasks, were measured on a daily basis at the level of the individual. Still others, such as the extent to which specific project tasks were completed independently, were measured in relation to each project at the level of the individual. For these two kinds of measures, we calculated group means to create the group-level measures needed. In addition, in the analyses reported here, we are primarily interested in the effects of the independent variables, and the effects of within-project task type, rather than in temporal variations in behavior and subjective experience. Thus, for those items measured on a daily basis, we also averaged across days. Our dependent measures, then, are, in most cases, individual scores, averaged across group members, and, in some cases, averaged across project days.

Finally, we are most interested in contrasting outcomes in conditions where the participants could choose whatever means of communication they preferred with outcomes in conditions in which their communications were restricted in some way. Thus, in analyzing the effects of variations in Communication Modality, we focus on the Free Choice vs. Computer/Phone (i.e., no face-to-face communication) contrast and the Free Choice vs. Face-to-Face (i.e., no computer-mediated communication) contrast.

RESULTS

Manipulation Check

An analysis comparing subjects perceptions of the two projects indicates that the Project Type manipulation was, indeed, effective. The integrative project was seen as involving a significantly higher level of interdependence than the divisible project ($F = 27.96$, df = 1, 68, $p < .0001$).

Patterns of Media Choice

Based on contingency theory, we hypothesized that students would choose communication media that permit richer communication for work on projects that required a high level of integration. (Recall that all students were allowed some choice of communication modality. Those in the Computer/Phone condition could use either of those two media; those in the Face-to-Face condition could meet or talk on the phone and those in the Free Choice condition could, of course, communicate in any way they chose.) To assess the validity of this hypothesis, we examined the proportion of focal communication occasions conducted via each communication modality, for each of the two projects. A chi-square analysis of the Project Type x Communication Modality contingency table showed that the distribution of communication occasions across the three communication modalities was significantly different for the two projects, $x^2 = 10.214$, df = 2, $p < .01$. Table 1 shows that for the Integrative project, the percentage of focal communication occasions conducted face-to-face was about 1.5 times as great as the percentage of focal communication occasions conducted either by telephone or by computer. No such difference occurs when students were working on the Divisible project; for that project the distribution of communication occasions across communication modalities was approximately equal.

Table 1. Proportion of Communication Occasions in Each Communication Modality.

Communication Modality	Project Type	
	Divisible	Integrative
Computer	30.70	26.09
Telephone	32.67	29.94
Face-to-Face	36.63	43.98

The data in Table 1 are drawn from reports of students in all communication conditions. When we look only at students in the Free Choice condition, we see that the pattern holds. Using a scale of communication richness in which 1 = computer-mediated, 2 = telephone and 3 = face-to-face, we observed that, on average, students chose richer communications media (Mean = 2.71) for work on the more Integrative project than for work on the Divisible project (Mean = 2.41, $t = -2.02$, df = 17, $p < .06$). Most of this difference is attributable to lower levels of computer use when working on the Integrative project (4% of focal communication occasions) than on the Divisible project (17% of focal communication occasions, $t = 2.47$, df = 17, $p < .05$). There were no significant differences in the proportion of focal communication occasions conducted via the telephone or in face-to-face meetings across the two projects.

Thus, at the project level, we find some support for the contingency hypothesis regarding media choice. In addition, when we look within projects to see how individuals communicated during specific phases of their work, we find further evidence in support of the contingency hypothesis. When groups report that they are planning their work, they are, indeed, also more likely to report that they are using a rich communication modality than a lean one (F = 3.88, df = 1, 68, $p < .05$ for the regression of media richness on planning). However, counter to the contingency hypothesis, the effect of planning on media choice is not project-specific. Groups are as likely to choose a rich modality to plan the Divisible project as they are to plan the Integrative project. Furthermore, there is no comparable effect of task on media choice for execution. The regression of media richness on execution (drafting and revising documents) is non-significant.

Media Effects on Work Outcomes

In addition to its predictions regarding media choice, the contingency perspective suggests that work can be accomplished more successfully---more efficiently and with better results---when there is an appropriate match between task and technology. Once again, our data regarding the validity of this hypothesis are mixed. We do find a strong main effect of communication modality on coordination success. Students who were allowed to communicate face-to-face report fewer coordination problems than those who were not permitted to do so (F = 33.9, df = 1, 68, $p < .0001$ for the Free Choice vs. Computer/Phone contrast). But this effect did not depend on project type or on within-project task type. Furthermore, the other work outcomes we examined---perceived product quality, perceived quality of the focal communication occasion, and group performance---revealed no effect of Communication Modality. Thus, our data do not support the idea that the deleterious effect of computer-mediated communication is task-specific, nor do they support the idea that restrictions in communication will necessarily undermine group performance. They are, however, consistent with the idea that it is difficult to do complex intellectual work without the intricate communication that such work requires.

Patterns of Adaptation to Media Characteristics

Given an inappropriate task/technology match, contingency theory predicts failure, inferior outcomes, or at best, difficulties in achieving a given level of performance. As we have observed, students who used computer-mediated communication conditions did experience coordination problems, but they were nonetheless able to achieve a performance level equal to that of the students who could communicate face-to-face. The adaptive structuration perspective suggests that this performance must have been achieved by adapting their behavior to suit---or, given their reports of coordination problems, to cope with---the constraints on their communication.

Based on this analysis, we hypothesized that when students are restricted to communicating by computer, they will adapt to this constraint by working more independently. In general, our data are consistent with this hypothesis. For instance, on the project-level measures of interdependence drawn from Van de Ven et al., students in the Computer/Phone groups, who were unable to communicate face-to-face, reported lower levels of interdependent work than students in the Free Choice groups (F = 4.79, df = 1, 68, $p < .01$), despite the fact that groups in both conditions were working on the "same" project. On measures of the extent to which they performed particular tasks (e.g., creating materials, refining interim versions of the text) individually vs. jointly, students in the Free Choice condition were more likely to report that they did their work together than students in the Computer/Phone condition. This is true for both project-specific tasks, such as creating a specific portion of the report, (F = 9.99, df = 1, 68 , $p < .001$), and for tasks that were common to the two projects, such as developing a sense of direction for the project (F = 10.56, df = 1, 68, $p < .005$). This pattern of results in shown in Figure 1; the data in the figure are for tasks common to both projects, but the pattern is the same for both common and unique tasks.

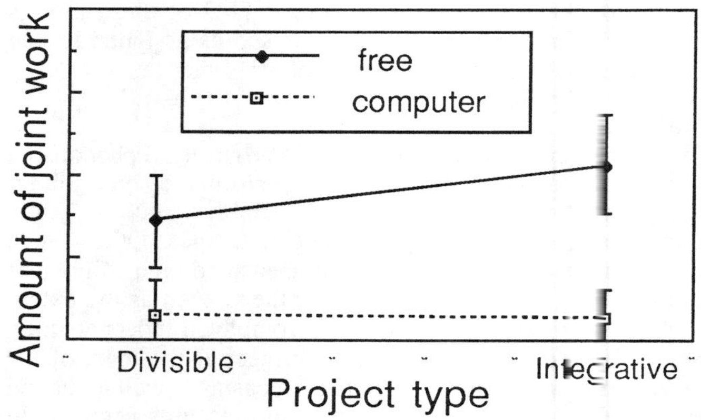

Figure 1. Influence of project type and communication modality on joint task performance.

Students in the Free Choice condition were not only more likely to report having done their work jointly than students in the Computer/Phone condition; not too surprisingly, they also report having invested more time in communicating about it (F = 5.9, df = 1, 68, $p < .05$). More interestingly, however, the experimental manipulations of communication modality produce differential effects on group members' efforts to respond to the demands of the two projects. In particular, groups in the Free Choice condition spent more time communicating when they were working on the Integrative project than when they were working on the Divisible project. This outcome is consistent with our expectations about the sort of interactions required to carry out a complex project involving a high level of interdependence. But the difference in time spent communicating about the two projects disappears for groups in the Computer/Phone condition (F = 3.3, df = 1, 68, $p < .10$ for the Project Type x Free Choice vs. Computer/Phone interaction). In effect, not having the means to work integratively seems to prompt the Computer/Phone groups to convert the Integrative project into a Divisible project, a pattern of behavior that is consistent with the difference in perceived project requirements noted above. A similar effect occurs for the duration of the focal communication occasion. When face-to-face communication is available, the focal communication is longer when groups are communicating about the Integrative project than when they are communicating about the Divisible project, but when they are constrained to communicating by computer or telephone there is no project-related difference in the duration of this interaction (F = 6.51, df = 1, 68, $p < .05$ for the Project Type x Free Choice vs. Computer/Phone interaction).

In sum, with regard to the idea of adaptation, we find that when groups have a project that seems to call for a joint effort, and when they have the means to work together easily, they carry out a substantial portion of their work jointly, investing time in the communication required to coordinate their ideas and actions. Groups faced with the same project, but lacking the means to work integratively, do their work more independently, and invest less time in communicating about it.

DISCUSSION

The data reported here are partially consistent with contingency theory. In particular, group members preferred to work face-to-face, especially for the integrative project, and especially when planning their work. Moreover, those who could not communicate face-to-face experienced a substantially increased level of difficulty in coordinating their work. But two aspects of our results are inconsistent with the contingency perspective. First, group members were not more likely to prefer a lean communication medium during the less communicatively intense aspects of their work. Although inconsistent with the theory, this result is not hard to understand. The issue is apparently one of distinguishing between tasks that require a particular communication medium and those that can be performed equally well regardless of the characteristics of the medium. Tasks that involve intricate communication (e.g., planning) appear to require a richer medium, but tasks that do not involve such elaborate interaction can be carried via whatever medium is most available, familiar or inexpensive. The "excess capacity" provided by a rich medium may not be required for these tasks, but neither is it detrimental. Although we were unacquainted with these investigations when we planned our research, similar results have been obtained in recent studies by Trevino, Lengel, Bodensteiner & Gerloff [17] and by Alexander *et al.* [1].

The second inconsistency with contingency theory in our results is our observation that group performance was unaffected by constraints on interactive communication. This result presents a more serious challenge to the contingency perspective, because it implies a need to consider variables other than the fixed characteristics of tasks and technologies in making decisions about information technology. In particular, this result suggests that it is important to consider the potential for adaptation in human behavior and, although not represented in our study, the malleability of information systems. Our study provides clear evidence that such adaptations do occur, permitting people to accomplish difficult tasks under demanding conditions. Thus, although we do not claim to have invalidated the contingency perspective, we join other researchers [4,8,19] in calling into question its dominance as a framework for shaping research about human uses of information technology, and for making practical decisions about technologies to build or purchase.

Although the technology-induced shifts in patterns of work we observed can be neither predicted nor explained by contingency theory, they can be readily understood within the framework provided by the adaptive structuration analysis. This perspective acknowledges the human capability for adaptation that permits groups to spontaneously adjust to extreme limitations on interactivity and expressiveness in communication, without reducing the quality of their work. Nevertheless, despite its more comprehensive scope, the structuration approach remains somewhat unsatisfactory as a guide for research or design. Orlkowski & Robey [9] point out that the theory of adaptive structuration is "non-propositional"; that is, it does not give rise to specific predictions about patterns of adaptation in human behavior, nor does it suggest ways in which humans are likely to appropriate and modify extant technologies. Rather, it simply suggests classes of variables that might be examined to develop a fuller understanding of technology-in-use. To overcome this liability, Poole & DeSanctis [10] have begun to hypothesize about factors that are likely to promote "stable" appropriations of technology, by which they mean patterns of appropriation and adaptation that are consistent with the intended use of a particular technology. More generally, their approach is an effort to specify when particular adjustments, whether adaptations in human behavior or modifications of information systems, are likely to occur or to be needed. The observations reported here suggest that this approach is needed and is likely to be fruitful.

REFERENCES

1. Alexander, E.R., Penley, L.E. & Jernigan, I.E. The effect of individual differences on managerial media choice. *Management Communication Quarterly*, 1991, *5*, 155-173.

2. Daft, R.L. & Lengel, R. Organizational information requirements, media richness and structural design. *Management Science*, 1986,*32*, 554-571.

3. Daft, R.L., Lengel, R. & Trevino, L. Message equivocality, media selection and manager performance: Implications for information systems. *MIS Quarterly*, 1987, *11*, 355-366.

4. Fulk, J., Schmitz, J. & Steinfield, C.W. A social influence model of technology use. In J. Fulk & C.W. Steinfield (Eds.), *Organizations and communication technology. Sage*, Newbury Park, CA, 1990, pp. 117-140.

5. Galegher, J. & Kraut, R.E. (in press). Computer-mediated communication for intellectual teamwork: An experiment in group writing.

6. Gutek, B.A. Workgroup structure and information technology: A structural contingency approach. In J. Galegher, R.E. Kraut & C. Egido (Eds.), *Intellectual teamwork: The social and technological bases of cooperative work. Lawrence Erlbaum, Inc.*, Hillsdale, NJ, 1990, pp. 63-78.

7. Kraut, R.E., Galegher, J. & Egido, C. Informal communication and scientific work. Unpublished manuscript, 1991.

8. Markus, M.L. Toward a "critical mass" theory of interactive media. In J. Fulk & C.W. Steinfield (Eds.), *Organizations and communication technology. Sage,* Newbury Park, CA, 1990, pp. 194-218.

9. Orlikowski, W.J. & Robey, D. Information technology and the structuring of organizations. *Information Systems Research*, 1990, *2*, 143-169.

10. Poole, M.S. & DeSanctis, G. Understanding the use of group decision support systems: The theory of adaptive structuration. In J. Fulk & C.W. Steinfield (Eds.), *Organizations and communication technology. Sage*, Newbury Park, CA, 1990, 173-193.

11. Rosenthal, R. Estimating effective reliabilities in studies that employ judges' ratings. *Journal of Clinical Psychology*, 1973,.*29*, 342-345.

12. Schuler, R.S. & Youngblood, S.A. *Case problems in personnel and human resource management. West Publishing Company*, St. Paul, MN, 1986.

13. Short, J., Williams, E., & Christie, B. *The social psychology of telecommunications. Wiley*, New York, 1976.

14. Sproull, L.& Kiesler, S. *Connections: New ways of working in the networked organization. MIT Press*, Cambridge, MA, 1991.

15. Steinfield, C. Computer-mediated communications in organizational settings: Emerging conceptual foundations and directions for research. *Management Communication Quarterly*, 1992,*5*, 348-365.

16. Trevino, L.K., Lengel, R.H., & Daft, R.L. Media symbolism, media richness, and media choice in organizations. *Communication Research*, *14*, 1987, 553-574.

17. Trevino, L.K., Lengel, R.H., Bodensteiner, W. & Gerloff, E. The richness imperative and cognitive style: The role of individual differences in media choice. *Management Communication Quarterly*, 1990, *4*, 176-197.

18. Van de Ven, A., Delbecq, A. & Koenig, R. Determinants of coordination modes within organizations. *American Sociological Review*, 1976, *41*, 322-338.

19. Yates, J. & Orlikowski, W.J. Genres of organizational communication: A structurational approach to studying communication and media. *Academy of Management Review*, 1992, *17*, 299-326.

Tasks-in-interaction: paper and screen based documentation in collaborative activity

Paul Luff, Christian Heath and David Greatbatch

Cambridge EuroPARC
61, Regent Street
Cambridge CB2 1AB
United Kingdom
(44) 223 341528
luff.europarc@rx.xerox.com

Department of Sociology
University of Surrey
Guildford GU2 5XH
United Kingdom
(44) 483 300800
scs1ch@soc.surrey.ac.uk

School of Social Sciences
University of Nottingham
Nottingham
United Kingdom

ABSTRACT
Drawing on field studies of three, real world, organisational environments, namely an architectural practice, a medical centre and the Control Rooms on London Underground, this paper explores the ways in which personnel use paper and screen based documentation to support synchronous and asynchronous collaborative activity. It discusses how collaboration involves a complex configuration of co-participation by personnel in a range of activities, ranging from seemingly individual tasks to mutually focussed, real time cooperation. By addressing the ways in which personnel manage collaboration and interactionally organise a range of activities, we discuss the ways in which paper and screen based media provide rather distinctive support for cooperation. These observations form the basis for some suggestions concerning requirements for CSCW systems.

INTRODUCTION
In relation to the concern for uncovering the details of collaborative work there has recently been a growing interest in undertaking naturalistic studies of technologically mediated collaborative activity in 'real world' organisational environments. These studies have focussed on a variety of activities including ship navigation, piloting helicopters, airport ground control air traffic control, and traffic management in an urban railway network (i.e. Hutchins [14], Linde [16], Suchman [19], Goodwin and Goodwin [7], Harper et al. [10], Heath and Luff [12]). and they have begun to delineate a range of practices and reasoning utilised by organisational personnel in using a variety of tools and systems to coordinate real-time tasks and activities. As yet however, these studies have not been primarily concerned with the ways in which their observations and findings might inform the design of tools and technologies to support co-present or physically distributed collaborative activity in the settings in question or the development of more generic requirements for cooperative work.[1]

In this paper we wish to consider how findings generated through the naturalistic analysis of work, interaction and technology in a variety of 'real world' environments might provide some generic issues for the design of systems to support collaborative activities. We will draw on material gathered in three settings, namely, general medical practice, architecture and the Line Control Rooms on London Underground.[2] The analysis of work and interaction within these very different settings has begun to reveal how participants have developed a body of indigenous practices and procedures for utilising paper and screen-based documentation to support various forms of collaboration. These local, 'practical' solutions to the 'intrinsic' properties of particular media provide some interesting implications for the design of systems to support both co-present and physically distributed cooperative work.

THE USE OF PAPER DOCUMENTS
A variety of paper documents are used in each of the settings. For example, in the architectural practice, architects use large paper plans; in the medical practice,

1 But see Bentley et al. [1] for a recent discussion of issues concerning the relationship of ethnographic studies to system design.

2 Details of preliminary analyses of these materials can be found in Heath and Luff [12], Luff and Heath [17] and Greatbatch et al. [8].

Permission to copy without fee all or part of this material is granted provided that the copies are not made or distributed for direct commercial advantage, the ACM copyright notice and the title of the publication and its date appear, and notice is given that copying is by permission of the Association for Computing Machinery. To copy otherwise, or to republish, requires a fee and/or specific permission.

© 1992 ACM 0-89791-543-7/92/0010/0163...$1.50

doctors consult handwritten cards containing their patients' medical histories; and in the London Underground Control Rooms, personnel use paper timetables to manage traffic and passenger movement. Practices have been developed for using these documents to support both synchronous and asynchronous collaboration in these settings which appear to be informed by three factors: (1) the documents' tailorability, (2) their ecological flexibility, and (3) restrictions on the movement of personnel.

In each of the settings the participants customise or tailor their documents in order to differentiate and highlight particular items. For example, staff in the line control rooms cover their timetables with cellophane sheets and mark temporary changes with a felt pen - the various arrows, figures and notes being wiped away when the events to which they refer are no longer relevant.[3] Similarly, doctors use a range of markings to annotate their patients' medical record cards; and architects sketch in and ring changes to their plans.

Although the customisation of documents often seems to involve a distinct task undertaken by a particular individual for their own benefit, it may support various forms of collaborative work. For instance, in looking through plans produced by their colleagues, architects can quickly locate any changes by looking for areas that have been circled; at the start of their shifts, controllers can quickly get a sense of the current state of the service by using their predecessors' markings to locate any changes that have been made to the running times and order of the trains; and in general practice, doctors may pay special attention to items in a record that have been underlined, capitalised or placed in inverted commas by their colleagues. Participants may also make use of textual features which are not necessarily the result of customisation, such as handwriting, ink colour, spacing between entries etc. If, for example, a doctor wishes to determine when a patient last saw either themselves or a particular colleague they can quickly scan a record for the last entry involving the relevant persons handwriting. Similarly architects can recognize who 'marked up' particular plans from the handwriting of the annotations. Both the customisation and the unavoidable differentiation of contributions to the document provide personnel with a rich body of resources with which to draw various inferences concerning some matters at hand and the specific contributions of their colleagues.

The ecological flexibility of paper may also be relevant to the character of the practices that have evolved to facilitate the use of documentation for collaboration in the three settings. The medical records are small enough to be held in the hand and can readily be moved about. As such, their use can be adapted to a range of situations and contingencies. For example, a doctor may prop a medical record card on the corner of the desk so as to be able to glance at it while conducting an examination of a patient seated before him; or the doctor may read a record while facing the patient rather than turning away to read it on the desk. The ecological flexibility of the records contributes to their collaborative use within both the consultation and the practice more generally. Occasionally, doctors may want a patient to look at an item in their paper-based records. In such instances they can place the document between themselves and the patient or hold it up in front of the latter, so as to make it visible to them. They can also carry a document from one room to another in order to discuss aspects of it with colleagues. Similarly, in London Underground Control Rooms, pairs of controllers can jointly read a timetable by moving it between them.

In the architectural practice, the plans are too large to be easily transported around the office. However, the architects are able to move around the office in order to look at the plans of their colleagues. As such, the documents can become the focus of discussion between groups of architects, who relocate themselves to facilitate shared reading and drawing. Here practices that have evolved for using documents to support collaboration have been shaped by the need for personnel to relocate themselves.[4]

Consequently, in all three settings the collaborative use of paper documentation is facilitated by the ecological flexibility of the document and the participants' ability to move around the environment. Even without making use of these features of paper documents it may be possible to distribute information around the environment. For example, in the medical consultations doctors may point to items on the record or explicitly quote from it in order to refer to information on the document, thereby rendering that information public without having to move the card.

Within the London Underground Control rooms there are severe limitations on the participants' abilities to pass paper documents to each other or change their physical position to enable them to read the documents of colleagues. For instance, the London Underground runs according to a conventional timetable which specifies the order, destination and crewing of trains. When problems emerge such as a suicide or the discovery of a suspect package, the Line Controller rewrites or 'reforms' his timetable to reschedule the traffic covering the gaps within the service. As noted earlier, these changes are marked on the relevant pages of the paper timetable and then rubbed off when the event has passed. It is critical that changes to the timetable and the reasoning which lies behind them are communicated to the Controller's colleagues within the Line Control room, since those colleagues are responsible for adjusting the signalling and providing information to passengers. Yet during a crisis the Controller rarely has the time nor the opportunity to break from dealing with the emergency to tell colleagues or inform them of the reasons behind a particular action. In consequence, the Controllers have developed a simple, yet effective way of rendering their

3 Moreover, the customisation of the documents is tailored to the demands of particular occupational groups within the control rooms; while some changes are relevant to all the staff, others are of concern to some but not to others.

4 An alternative means of collaboration, which trades on the flexibility of small paper documents, involves provisional changes to plans being relayed around the office through the use of Post-it stickers.

potentially private paper-based activities publicly visible, at least within the immediate environment of the Control Room. As Controllers reform the service and rewrite the paper timetable they talk outloud to themselves, speaking about the changes they are making. On occasions these apparent mumblings simply consist of, for example, numbers, the replacement of one sequence of numbers with another: '213 216, 240 243, 257 267'. More often than not these numbers are interdispersed with a self discussion explaining why one change is being made rather than another. Through this talk, the Controller not only communicates decisions whilst remaining primarily focussed on the tasks at hand, but reveals 'potentially' private features of the paper-based activity to colleagues within the Control Room. As the Controller talks, the Information Assistant and the Signalmen often mark the changes on their own copies of the paper timetable; without necessarily abandoning other activities in which they are simultaneously engaged.

There are therefore very different ways in which individuals can share, or collaborate through, a paper document. Clearly documents may be tailored and exchanged and thereby support the exchange of information, but they also support synchronous real time collaboration. The ecological flexibility of paper can allow participants to view collaboratively a document and discuss the various details it contains, whether it is the specifics of a particular treatment, the detailed design of a staircase or the running schedule of trains. The document facilitates a variety of cooperative orientations and lookings, which both support, and are engendered through, the particular actions and activities at hand. But as the materials from the Underground and the medical consultations powerfully demonstrate, individuals have ways of making aspects of a document public to support collaboration, even when it is physically unavailable to a co-participant. Nor is the collaborative use of a paper document limited to reading and looking. In the various settings we can witness the ways in which the activity of writing and rewriting can be made public to enable colleagues, who are co-present and yet engaged in potentially unrelated activities, aware of the real time reasoning in making changes to a paper document. Within the settings, personnel have developed a body of conventional and routine practices for dealing with the potential constraints of a particular media, so as to provide a necessary foundation for document-based collaboration.

The ways in which participants use paper-based documentation within these various settings, also begins to reveal how difficult it is to differentiate whether an activity or task is individual or collaborative. So, for example, reforming the train service or writing a medical record card would initially appear to constitute a distinct task undertaken by a particular individual. But as we hope to have shown even such apparently individual and localised tasks are frequently produced with respect to the ongoing interactional demands within the immediate environment. The organisation of the task is shaped in the light of the conduct and sensibilities of co-present participants, and the contingencies which arise within its production. Collaborative activity is simply a gloss for a myriad of ways in which co-present and physically distributed individuals can shape actions and activities in the light of the synchronous and asynchronous contributions of others. Moreover, in the settings discussed here we find the various individuals simultaneously participating in multiple activities, so that even the most mundane and apparently individual task is interactionally organised. The task is constituted in and through the interaction and is perhaps inseparable from it.

SCREEN-BASED DOCUMENTATION

In each of the settings, paper documents are being used alongside recently introduced computer systems. These provide facilities for the performing tasks similar to those for which paper documents are being used; the doctors have access to a computerized medical record system which is accessed through a screen and keyboard placed on their desks; the architects each have an Apple Macintosh on which they are able to draw their plans, sections and elevations; and, in one of the control rooms the staff have access to a screen-based timetable which is embedded in the semi-circular console at which they sit.

Computer systems provide unprecedented support for collaborative work in organisational domains. The ability of the technology to store and coordinate substantial bodies of information gathered by multiple personnel, to facilitate the quick and easy transfer of data between physically distributed individuals, and to provide immediate access to documentation, has had an extraordinary impact on work and communication. In general medical practice, doctors now have immediate and legible access to each others' notes, and can even elicit details of the relevant treatment for particular complaints. Moreover, systematic and accessible information concerning diagnostic decisions and treatment details can not only provide a useful data base to coordinate the various facilities that a particular practice might offer, but also allow the practice as a whole to monitor more closely the activities of its individual practitioners. In architecture, we can discern the ways in which new technology allows both for the re-use of particular components in and across designs and also for different architects and other related personnel to access and utilise the drawings of others. Within the Line Control Room, screen-based technologies can provide precise real time information concerning the movement of trains (perhaps even passengers), and also allow signalmen and others to communicate and coordinate changes to the service with colleagues working within other locales within the organisation.

These facilities, however, seem to encompass a rather restricted view of collaboration in their design; a perspective that focuses on the asynchronous and distinct use of computer systems by individuals. Nevertheless, users of such systems do develop ways of supporting synchronous, real-time, co-present collaboration. For example, one of the doctors places the screen between himself and his patient so that it can be jointly used as a resource during the consultation. In our data, shared readings of the screen are normally initiated or invited by the doctors who, for example, may ask patients to identify which drug(s) they want prescribing from a screen-based list.[5] Computer hardware may be similarly deployed and used to support shared readings in other settings; travel agents, for example, use computer screens that swivel so that they can turn the screen towards customers while discussing various options.

Screen-based systems, even those primarily designed to support tasks by single users, can also be used for less focussed collaboration. In both the Bakerloo Line and Docklands Light Railway Control Rooms, each individual is provided with a configuration of monitors which displays interrelated information concerning the movement of traffic and passengers. For each member of the Control Room however, it is only possible to display a certain configuration of information on their own monitors, which at times can handicap their management of particular problems. These difficulties however, are in part dealt with by using monitors 'belonging' to a colleague which may be configured to provide alternative information. Indeed, it is not unusual for Control Room personnel to be sensitive to concurrent information demands of the activities of their colleagues and maintain particular displays on their monitors in order to allow others peripherally to monitor, for example, changes in traffic movements in a different locations.

In both the Bakerloo Line and the Docklands Light Railway Control Room a number of monitors and information displays are designed to be used by various personnel. For example, in the Docklands Control Room there are a bank of CCTV monitors which provide successive views of the various platforms utilised by all staff within the Control Room, and are regularly used to point out, discuss and manage a particular problem (such as a passenger attempting to avoid payment). The use of these publicly available displays to support various forms of collaboration is far more subtle and complex than merely providing a common information source for focussed discussion. For the Bakerloo Line a large fixed line diagram runs the whole length of the room, say thirty feet or so, and displays in real time through illuminated sections of the track where trains are located on the North and Southbound service. The diagram provides for focussed discussion concerning problems such as gaps in the service, but more importantly perhaps, allows personnel within the Control Room to be able peripherally to monitor their colleagues' orientation to the diagram. So for example, a Signal Assistant may notice a colleague 'looking at' the diagram, and thereby scan the display to discern what may be demanding his or her attention. The very size and position of the diagram, provides personnel with the ability not only to monitor each others' lookings, but to use those 'lookings' as a way of gaining access to the actions and activities in which they may be engaged.

5 However, on occasion patients may unilaterally point to items on the screen, using their presence to warrant the introduction of a topic into the talk. In one instance a patient enquires about the results of a test displayed on the screen.

Utilising a person's orientation towards a screen or diagram to draw certain inferences and coordinate actions and activities, may also facilitate collaboration even when the contents of the display are not accessible to the co-participant. In the medical consultation we find patients systematically coordinating their talk with the doctors' use of the computer, even though the patient may not be able to see the contents of the screen and may well be ignorant of the sorts of information that the doctor is entering or retrieving from the system. For example, patients attempt to coordinate the initiation and delivery of utterances with the keystrokes of the doctor, orienting to potential boundaries within the production of the activity with the computer. Moreover, the ways in which the doctor glances and looks at the screen and its contents, coupled with the movement of the hands and fingers across the keyboard, provide the patient with resources with which to draw various inferences concerning the organisation of the activity and thereby to attempt to coordinate their own contribution. Despite the relative inaccessibility of the activity, the patient makes sense of visible aspects of the doctor's use of the computer, and coordinates his or her contributions with the co-participant. *Mutatis mutandis*, it is often found that the doctor, in entering or retrieving information from the system, produces the activity with respect to the concurrent contribution and participation of the patient, shaping the use of the system with the ongoing conduct of the patient. In consequence, the doctor's use of the system, whilst not collaborative in the conventional sense of the term, is systematically and interactionally coordinated with the concurrent actions of the patient; the systems use *in situ* is unavoidably embedded in the interaction between the participants.

To a large extent the systems found within the various settings discussed here, have been primarily designed to support individual tasks and to provide ways in which distinct asynchronous contributions may be interrelated. It is clear however, that in each of the settings the various tasks and activities which the systems are designed to support are undertaken within a 'public' and cooperative domain; a domain in which each individual whilst responsible for a distinct realm of activity, undertakes tasks which are thoroughly dependent upon and interrelated to real time contributions of colleagues or clients. Not surprisingly, despite the shape of the systems, participants within each of the settings have developed various practices and procedures in and through which they can use these rather crude technologies to support various forms of real time, synchronous, collaboration and cooperation. Even the most apparently individual tasks, such as entering specialised and 'private' information into the medical computer system, is found to be systematically coordinated with the concurrent contributions of the patient. Actual focussed collaboration, however on a single task or activity, the form of collaboration most favoured by CSCW systems, is just one amongst a myriad of ways in which individuals, in real time, coordinate their actions and participate in the various tasks at hand. Indeed, it may the case that in attempting to support collaborative activity we consider mutually focussed collaborative activity on a single task, as perhaps one of the rarer forms of real world cooperation, and that by beginning to delineate the wide range of ways that individuals participate in each others actions and activities in the work place, we can begin to build more sensitive and relevant technologies.

THE RESILIENCE OF PAPER

Despite computer systems being introduced to perform similar tasks, paper documents are still being used in all the settings we have been considering. The doctors continue to rely largely on their medical record cards during diagnosis; architects, despite having more up-to-date versions of the drawings on their own machines, discuss changes to their plans on versions printed out on paper; and the use of the paper timetable is still critical to work in the Bakerloo Line Control Room. There appear to be several reasons for the resilience of paper in the face of computerized alternatives. While some of these are due to the ecological flexibility of paper and the 'reactivity' of the screen, perhaps the most significant issues relate to the differing properties of the two media for documenting and retrieving information.

Although screen based text is often more legible than handwriting, it can be easier to write with pen or pencil on paper than type using a keyboard, particularly when interacting with colleagues or clients, or engaged in concurrent activities. Whereas, writing on a medical record card, marking a paper plan and altering a train timetable can be interleaved into the interaction, users of a computer system tend to have to 'break off' from the interaction in order to type into the machine. Therefore, in medical consultations doctors usually make additions to their paper records during the diagnostic phase and only later will they type the information into the system.

As the range of marks that can be entered into them is often restricted, systems offer less possibilities for tailoring documents. This may mean that they do not support critical work practices. Architects cannot 'mark up' screen-based plans, both because on an individual screen the plans are not publicly visible and because the range of marks and jottings which they make on the paper cannot be easily achieved on the CAD system. Doctors cannot flexibly annotate a screen-based medical history nor can their colleagues scan these histories by identifying the handwriting of the originators of particular entries.[6] Moreover, screen-based timetables do not support the practices that control room staff use in making temporary changes to their paper timetables. As mentioned above, marking up changes to a design, keeping a record of the medical consultation and noting changes to the running order of trains are all crucial to the tasks in which participants in the relevant domains are engaged. However, by not providing a range of the resources upon which the doctors, architects and control room staff have come to rely, the computer systems do not support the differing degrees of collaboration associated with these domains.[7]

A related problem with documenting information on computer systems is that they can structure the ordering in which various activities are performed. Thus, the VAMP system used in the general practice requires doctors to enter data in a particular sequence and places constraints on the ways in which they can move around the screen-based medical record. There are similar difficulties in retrieving information from documents. For example, the CAD system used by the architects inevitably has to restrict the ways in which they can move around and between plans on the screens. Therefore locating, changes to a design may well be easier on the large, paper plans. Furthermore, information may not be available in the electronic form. In the Control Rooms relevant and up-to-date information may be distributed between several documents and artifacts, and in the medical consultation historical records written before computerisation results of tests are only kept on paper.

Screen-based systems also offer fewer ways of differentiating a document than paper. Thus, it is easy for architects to locate annotations on a plan consisting of circles, their colleagues' handwriting and other marks. Similarly, doctors can utilise those features of a medical record card that are due to the paper document's tailorability (e.g. handwriting, spacing) to find !relevant entries. However, when operating the computer system they are confronted with large blocks of undifferentiated text on the screen.

As mentioned above, computer systems can localise particular activities, their immobility restricting the degree of ecological flexibility they have within the work environment. Whereas medical record cards can be moved around the environment in ways which are sensitive to a range of situations and contingencies, the screen-based medical record is in a fixed position. The immobility of the screen-based record means that it is incompatible with a range of work practices that have been based around the ecological flexibility of the paper document, for example, those related to conducting examinations and carrying out tests. The architects are faced with paper as well as screen-based plans being in fixed positions. However, they rarely discuss plans on the screen, either talking over the paper plans or utilising the mobility of smaller pieces of paper, such as Post-it stickers, to inform colleagues of changes to the design. One additional problem faced by architects using CAD systems is pacing their talk with the operation of the computer. As the drawings tend to be complex, the time it takes to move around the building while the image is being displayed and redisplayed on the screen may be substantial and irregular. Thus, coordinating their talk with a changing and reactive display can be problematic, and

6 In fact, on the VAMP system doctors are only given a space of 19 characters for comments. However, a more substantial free-text editor has just been introduced into the system.

7 See also Harper et al's [10] discussion of the uses of paper flight strips for air traffic control.

instances where architects refer to the screen can be fragmented by perturbations, restarts, pauses and the like.[8]

In sum, each of the settings is in a state of transition and it maybe that work practices may develop around the computer systems. However, as yet in our studies, we have not witnessed screen-based systems being utilised with the flexibility of paper documents. Paper is customisable for documenting and retrieving information, ecologically mobile and can be deployed around the work environment, tailorable for individual and shared tasks and it provides a range of ways for individuals to orient to their collaborative activities, supporting this work without having to become a focus for it. Despite computer systems being designed to support various forms of collaboration and users developing ways of utilising them for co-present work, screen-based systems localise the user's activities to the screen, constrain the user's ability to differentiate the documents at hand and are interactionally inflexible. Moreover, unlike paper documentation, they are active in the local environment and place demands upon users. Faced with these constraints, it is not surprising that paper is used alongside the screen-based technology, resilient in the work environment.

RECONSIDERING TASK

It is increasingly recognised in CSCW that the term "cooperation" serves as a gloss for a disparate collection of working practices and communicative arrangements, ranging from asynchronous interaction with a distant colleague, through to real time, mutually focussed activities within the same physical location. Despite the recognition that many real world tasks necessitate cooperation, it is possible that the emergence of CSCW allows more traditional work in human-computer interaction and even cognitive science to preserve a clear demarcation between individual and collaborative activities. As Grudin [9] suggests, whilst we might welcome a growing concern in designing for the 'user', research and design continues to be primarily focussed on supporting a single individual entering or retrieving information from a workstation. And yet, even by briefly examining the use of computing technology in settings ranging from medical consultations through to Line Control Rooms, we can see the ways in which a system can appear to undermine the performance of indigenous tasks that it was designed to support.

The resilience of paper in these various environments does not simply derive from problems with the design of the systems which have been introduced into these settings. Rather, one suspects that the problems result from a more general orientation which informs the design of computing systems. Whilst perhaps recognising the importance of cooperation and asynchronous interaction, the systems are primarily designed with respect to facilitating tasks performed by a single user. The individual, plan based conception of task which one suspects informs the design of the various systems, is insensitive to the ways in which the tasks are accomplished *in situ* and in concert with others in the practical circumstances of the day to day work. In each of the settings we can see the ways in which personnel rely upon their abilities to manoeuvre and improvise with paper and screen based documentation to support a rich and diverse body of practices for accomplishing certain tasks in interaction with others. So for example, in producing an apparently individual task such as entering information into the medical record, the task will be produced with respect to the concurrent participation of the patient in that self-same activity. It is not simply that specific individual tasks and technologies are adapted to the practical circumstances, but that the very tasks themselves are of a different character; they are thoroughly embedded in and dependant upon the indigenous constraints and local interactional organisations. The very nature of the task is embedded within the situation of its accomplishment.

The resilience of paper within these various settings emerges from the ways in which the medium can be flexibly used to support the wide diversity of ways in which apparently individual tasks are accomplished *in situ*. In each of the settings, we can observe how the production of tasks demands that personnel are able to move freely between the individual and collaborative accomplishment of activities, ranging from entering information without apparent regard to the presence of another, through to a mutually focussed discussion of the contents of a file or the arrangement of a document. In general, however the production of paper or technological supported activities within these settings, demands a complex array of techniques and interactional arrangements somewhere between these polar extremes, and necessitates fluid and flexible participation within the activities at hand. The production format of the task and the ways in which it requires, or engenders, co-participation is continually accomplished, in and through the interaction between those within 'perceptual range of the event' (cf Goffman [6]). The 'interaction' may be no more than simply remaining sensitive to a colleague's physical orientation towards a screen, or keeping an ear to the chit-chat in the office, it may involve quietly listing items as they are entered into the patient's record, or it may include pointing to and explaining some change in a document. In each case however, the production of specialised and technologically supported tasks is embedded in the individual's orientation and sensitivity to actions and activities of others within the local milieu; the accomplishment of a task is inseparable from interaction with others.

Whilst CSCW in part derives from a commitment to distributed systems and groups, it is important that it does not disregard more conventional domains of human-computer interaction. By reconsidering the individualistic and largely cognitive notion of task which has infused

8 In a related examination of the issuing of prescriptions using the VAMP system Greatbatch et al. [8] reveal some of the difficulties in attending to the operation of the system while interacting with patients. For example, doctors whilst typing often confine themselves to minimal responses to patients' utterances; delay responses until they have completed a sequence of keystrokes; produce talk with extended perturbations as they await screen changes; glance at patients while a screen-change takes affect and then immediately return their gaze to the monitor as screen-change is completed; or abruptly shift topic in order to elicit information required by the system.

research and development in computing technology, we can begin to see ways in which issues within CSCW are highly relevant to more conventional applications, and perhaps avoid oversimplifying the concepts of cooperation and collaboration. By recognising that almost every task in whatever setting is dependent upon an indigenous body of work and communicative practices, it becomes increasingly relevant to consider the ways in which new technologies need to support both the individual and the collaborative, the private and the public, and the multifarious ways in which personnel coordinate their activities with colleagues and clients.

CONCLUSION AND DESIGN IMPLICATIONS

With these issues in mind, it may be worth considering possibilities for novel developments in CSCW system design. One path may be to explore supplements and alternatives to screen-based systems and to design systems for supporting co-present, rather than distributed, work. New technologies and methods being developed by colleagues at EuroPARC, PARC and elsewhere can be viewed as steps in this direction.

For example, it may be possible to enhance certain aspects of the private work on a conventional computer system to provide public resources for other individuals in the environment. In systems to support service enquiries, sounds could be implemented that reflect patterns in the human-computer interaction. As the user types on the keyboard, sounds could make boundaries in the interaction between user and machine available to a co-participant.[9] Obviously, such sounds would require subtle design to avoid further intrusiveness of the computer system into the interaction.

To address the issue of tailorability, recent developments in computer technology could be utilised. For example, gestural interfaces could enable individuals to write on the screen. The studies outlined above reveal that in some domains and on some occasions it may be preferable not for the computer to 'recognise' and transform the writing of participants into type. Furthermore, as such facilities are being offered on small notepad computers, these systems have the capability of providing a similar ecological flexibility to paper.

Alternative systems could dispense with the screen-based documents entirely. Utilising scanners and facsimile technologies, systems could be devised that store and retrieve paper documents (cf. the PaperWorks™ system developed at PARC). In addition, where possible and useful, some processing of documents could be performed. Obviously, such systems would support both the customisable and ecologically flexible aspects of paper documents.

It may be that larger screens laid flat may provide for objects on the screen to be more publicly accessible. However, such screens would still not provide for the mobility and tailorability of paper mentioned above. A more radical development may be possible. Rather than trying to replace the use of paper, systems could allow users to manipulate both screen objects and paper documents on their work surfaces. Already prototype systems like VideoDesk (Tang and Minneman [20]), TeamWorkStation (Ishii [15]) and DigitalDesk (Wellner [23]) are attempting to achieve this by utilising video projections of screen displays, camera views of desks and locational information generated by digital tablets. DigitalDesk, for example, enables users to place paper documents on a desk from which a camera can 'read' items. Meanwhile a projector displays a screen image back onto the table. On such a system it is possible to engage in work on documents and screen objects, preserving the advantages of each. It may also be possible to support the way individuals orient to activities on paper and to offer a smooth and versatile means of moving between these orientations.

These technological developments can be seen as a move away from a dependency on screen-based systems to support computational activities, towards a state where systems are less visible and intrusive, a state that has been characterised as 'ubiquitous computing' (Weiser [22]). Many of the issues that developers of such systems are addressing will have to be explored by designers of distributed technologies. The relationships between shared and individual screen objects and workspaces have been a longstanding concern of CSCW system designers; recurrent problems with groupware are how users can determine common references to screen objects, how they can establish ownership over screen objects and how these references and ownerships can be displayed to others. The examination of work in real-world environments suggests that the nature of communication and collaboration may be more complex than these current technologies imply. The simple distinction between shared and individual tasks may not be sufficient to capture aspects of the nature of collaborative work, designers of CSCW systems may have to take into account the ways individuals participate in the workplace. Recent developments in audio-visual environments may be beginning to adopt such an orientation. Rather than attempting to simulate face-to-face collaboration and adding facilities for distributed representations of their shared work (e.g. Gale [3], Olson et al. [18]), it may be possible to provide participants with a sense of the orientation of their co-participants to the artifacts they are using (Tang and Minneman [21], Condon [2]). These developments may overcome some of the apparent deficiencies of video-mediated communication (Heath and Luff [13]), as well as beginning to tackle fundamental concerns for supporting collaborative work.

In studying three workplaces we made the recurrent observation that paper documents were being used to

9 Suggestions for the uses of sounds in single-user and CSCW systems have been made by Gaver [4, 5]. It appears to be already the case that in medical interaction certain sounds of the computer are oriented to by participants. For example, Heath [11] gives an instance of an interaction where the talk appears to be tied to the sound of the computer accessing a disk.

perform certain tasks even though a computer system had just been introduced to carry out those tasks. By focussing on the activities that surround both paper and screen-based documents we have suggested why the use of paper persists. This is not only due to the intrinsic properties of paper or the intrinsic constraints of screens, it is also because paper affords an interactional flexibility that allows individuals a range of ways of participating in tasks-in-interaction. Such a reconception of task may be essential for developing systems that provide the sensitivity to the activities of others inherent in collaborative work.

ACKNOWLEDGEMENTS

The issues discussed in the paper have benefited considerably from discussions with colleagues at EuroPARC, the Universities of Oxford, Lancaster and Paris who participated in several meetings concerning work, interaction and technology and systems design.

REFERENCES

1. Bentley, R., Rodden, T., Sawyer, P., Sommerville, I., Hughes, J. A. Randall, D. and Shapiro, D. Ethnographically-informed systems design for air traffic control. *Proc. of CSCW '92* (Toronto. Oct. 31 - Nov. 4, 1992), ACM Press.
2. Condon, C.C. The Computer won't let me - cooperation and the ownership of information. Paper presented at the *Workshop on CSCW: Cooperation of Conflict?* (London, Oct. 23, 1991).
3. Gale, S. Adding audio and video to an office environment. In *Studies in CSCW: Theory, Practice and Design,* J.M. Bowers and S.D. Benford, Eds., North Holland, Amsterdam. pp. 49-62. 1991.
4. Gaver, W.W. Auditory icons: using sound in computer interfaces. *Human-Computer Interaction,* 2 (1986), 167-177.
5. Gaver, W.W. Sound Support for Collaboration. In *Proc. of ECSCW 1991,* (Amsterdam, Sept. 24-27, 1991) pp. 293-324.
6. Goffman, E. *Forms of Talk.* Blackwell, Oxford. 1981.
7. Goodwin, C. and Goodwin, M.H. Formulating Planes: Seeing as a Situated Activity. In *Cognition and Communication at Work,* Y. Engestrom, and D. Middleton, Eds., Sage, London. Forthcoming.
8. Greatbatch, D, Heath, C.C., Luff, P. and Campion, P. *Interpersonal Communication and Human-Computer Interaction.* EuroPARC Working Paper. 1992.
9. Grudin, J. 'interface', In *Proc. of CSCW '90,* (Los Angeles, Oct 7-10, 1990), pp. 269-278.
10. Harper, R., Hughes, J. and Shapiro, D. Harmonious Working and CSCW: Computer Technology and Air Traffic Control. In *Studies in CSCW: Theory, Practice and Design,* J.M. Bowers and S.D. Benford, Eds., North Holland, Amsterdam. pp. 225-234. 1991.
11. Heath, C.C. *Body movement and speech in medical interaction.* Cambridge University Press, Cambridge. 1986.
12. Heath, C.C. and Luff, P. Collaborative Activity and Technological Design: Task Coordination in London Underground Control Rooms. In *Proc. of E-CSCW 1991* (Amsterdam, Sept. 24-27 1991), pp. 65-80.
13. Heath, C.C. and Luff, P. Disembodied Conduct: Video Communication and Collaborative Work. In *Proc. of CHI' 91,* (New Orleans, April 27 - May 2 1991), pp. 99-103.
14. Hutchins, E.L. The Technology of Team Navigation. In *Intellectual Teamwork: The Social and Technological Foundations of Cooperative Work* J. Galegher, R.E. Kraut, and C. Egido, Eds., LEA, Hillsdale, NJ, 1990, pp. 191-221.
15. Ishii, H. TeamWorkStation: Towards a Seamless Shared Workspace, in *Proc. of CSCW '90,* (Los Angeles, Oct 7-10, 1990), pp. 13-26.
16. Linde, C. Who's in charge here? Cooperative work and authority negotiation in police helicopter missions. In *Proc. of CSCW '88,* (Portland, Sept. 26-28, 1986), pp. 52-64.
17. Luff, P. and Heath, C.C. System use and social organisation: observations on human computer interaction in an architectural practice. In *Technology in Working Order,* G. Button, Ed., Routledge, London. In press.
18. Olson, J.S., Olson, G.M., Mack, L.A. and Wellner, P. Concurrent editing: the group interface. In *Proc. of Interact '90 - Third IFIP Conference on Human-Computer Interaction,* (Cambridge, Aug. 27-30, 1990). pp. 835-840.
19. Suchman, L. Constituting Shared Workspaces. In *Cognition and Communication at Work,* Y. Engestrom and D. Middleton, Eds., Sage, London. Forthcoming.
20. Tang, J.C. and Minneman, S.L. VideoDraw: A Video Interface for Collaborative Drawing, *ACM Transactions on Information Systems,* 9, 2 (1991), pp. 170-184.
21. Tang, J.C. and Minneman, S.L. VideoWhiteboard: Video Shadows to Support Remote Collaboration. In *Proc. of CHI' 91,* (New Orleans, April 27 - May 2 1991), pp.315-322.
22. Weiser, M. The Computer for the 21st Century, *Scientific American,* (September 1991).
23. Wellner, P. The DigitalDesk Calculator: Tactile Manipulation on a Desk Top Display. In *Proc. of the ACM Symposium on User Interface Software and Technology,* (November 1991).

A Collaborative Medium for the Support of Conversational Props

Tom Brinck and Louis M. Gomez

Bellcore
445 South St.
Morristown, NJ 07962
hammer@bellcore.com, (201) 829-5238
gomez@bellcore.com, (201) 829-4451

ABSTRACT
Our work focuses on providing computational support for informal communication among people who are geographically separated. To better understand the use of artifacts in communication, we looked at the contents of office whiteboards after they had been used in conversations. Our analysis revealed that whiteboards are used to present and discuss various classes of objects with specific semantic properties. We call these objects "conversational props," and we have come to think of a whiteboard as a conversational medium in which props are introduced and manipulated. This study motivated our design of the Conversation Board, an experimental prototype of a multi-user drawing tool which allows remote use of conversational props. We compare the Conversation Board to various other multi-user drawing tools along a number of dimensions.

KEYWORDS: design methodology, collaborative systems, group work, informal communication

INTRODUCTION
We have been exploring the design of multi-user applications to be used along with video communications systems, such as the CRUISER™[1] system [9][14]. The Cruiser system attempts to recreate a sense of informality common to workplace interactions among people. The intuition that video can add a new sense of presence to telecommunications stems from its ability to add facial expressions and gestures to standard audio-only conversations.

Recent observations of use of the CRUISER system [5] indicate that people find it to be a valuable communications tool which enhances standard telephone communications. They also indicate that the CRUISER system is not currently a viable competitor to face-to-face conversation. One of the reasons for this is that the CRUISER system does not allow people to easily share artifacts like drawings, graphs, or photographs, which are often part of face-to-face meetings. We have come to refer to these media as "conversational props". In the same sense as theatrical stage props, they add communicative realism to situations. In face-to-face conversation, almost anything can serve as a prop, from a napkin to a snapshot of the kids.

In the work reported here we explored the design and implementation of a shared "whiteboard", called the Conversation Board, that could make electronic props available for informal office communication when the participants are geographically separated. There are a number of domains in which this kind of capability for shared props is useful. For example, doctors could share x-rays and medical illustratrions that are used during medical consulting. Electronic conversational props and desktop video could also enable new forms of classroom education over a distance where students not only see and hear their peers but have access to shared educational material.

To understand how geographically-separate office workers might use conversational props, we started by examining the use of office whiteboards as a medium for conversational props in face-to-face communication. We chose office whiteboards because they seemed to be commonly used in the support of conversation in the workplace. Our goal was not to build an electronic duplicate of a physical whiteboard, but instead to discover the communication intent that is supported by the office whiteboard and to use that information to inform the design of an electronic medium which supports the use of conversational props.

THE STUDY OF OFFICE WHITEBOARDS
Procedure
Our approach was to conduct spontaneous interviews of people in their offices about the current state of their whiteboards. Participants were asked to describe the sketches, writing, and diagrams that were currently on their boards and the conversations that led to them. This was entirely retrospective. We observed the whiteboard artifacts left behind after conversations had been completed.

The participants were 18 Bellcore employees. Ten were technical employees with backgrounds in mathematics,

1. CRUISER is a trademark and service mark of Bellcore.

Permission to copy without fee all or part of this material is granted provided that the copies are not made or distributed for direct commercial advantage, the ACM copyright notice and the title of the publication and its date appear, and notice is given that copying is by permission of the Association for Computing Machinery. To copy otherwise, or to republish, requires a fee and/or specific permission.

© 1992 ACM 0-89791-543-7/92/0010/0171...$1.50

computer science, and electrical engineering. Eight were administrative employees who had financial and budgetary assignments. The interviews were conducted in their offices, and lasted 10 to 15 minutes. Photographs were taken of the whiteboards which were later analyzed. The interviewer also made sketches of the whiteboard contents, annotating a sketch with information the participant supplied during the course of the interview.

General Whiteboard Observations

The 18 whiteboards we studied contained remnants of about 76 conversations. Of those, 17 conversations were on whiteboards of administrative participants, and the remaining 59 conversations were on whiteboards of technical participants.

Most whiteboard conversations involved two people, although four of the whiteboards contained entries which were generated only by a solitary user. Several people used their boards both alone and with others. Some reported that when they used the whiteboard alone it was to create objects which would later play a role in a meeting. Very few whiteboard conversations involved three or more people.

Color

All the whiteboards we observed contained multiple colors, as few as two and as many as five. This is perhaps not surprising, since whiteboard markers are sold in small sets of multiple colors. Some people used color to distinguish between different conversations whose scribblings were on the board at the same time. In this way, even if a board was crowded with a previous conversation which had used a *black* marker, people could avoid erasing the previous conversation and avoid confusing the two conversations by using a *red* marker for the new one. Others used color to distinguish between categories of information (e.g. home phone numbers versus work numbers) and to distinguish levels of detail.

Persistence

Seven of the people interviewed said that they would not want all or part of their whiteboards to be erased on the day of the interview. This is because people anticipated that they would find the props currently on the boards useful for subsequent conversations or for future reference. In addition, 17 of the 18 people reported that some aspect of the whiteboard had been or would be copied into some other more permanent medium, such as a computer file or viewgraph.

Classes of Objects

Our characterization of whiteboard objects had the explicit goal of determining how we might create software that supports the objects observed and maintains those semantic properties that an object has in conversational use. Each class of objects in Figure 1 has certain properties that people said they use when they introduced them into a conversation as props. For example, tables were sometimes used in the same way as spreadsheets. People reported that row/column sums in tables were modified dynamically throughout the course of meetings. From the perspective of our analysis, therefore, it was not sufficient to determine that a drawing tool could, with enough effort on the part of users, recreate the *appearance* of every object we observed. It was much more important to motivate the design and structure of an electronic whiteboard with features that captured the *semantics* of the objects that people used in whiteboard conversations.

With this purpose in mind, we totaled the number of objects occurring on the whiteboards within various categories. These totals are imperfect due to the uncertain recall of the interviewees as well as the occasional difficulty in clearly categorizing objects, but they capture the general trends. Figure 1 shows eight different kinds of objects that we were able to classify and their relative frequency of use by technical and administrative people. Since technical and administrative participants had different numbers of conversations represented on their boards, we chose not to present total counts of objects, but instead to present the average number of objects per conversation. Some of these objects and their use bear further explanation.

Text and lists. Figure 1 shows that an average conversation had about one text object (an average of .83 text objects per conversation for technical participants and .88 for non-technical participants). Text refers to objects that people appeared to treat as blocks of connected text, that is, short phrases, sentences, or paragraphs. Other instances of text, used simply to label things, were much too numerous to count. Since these were so numerous, it is clear that text was by far the most common kind of object found on a whiteboard. Many instances of text were serving the more specific conversational function of lists (based on, for instance, their linear and unconnected character), and so these were counted in a separate category.

Geometric objects. Objects such as circles, lines, and rectangles are categorized as geometric pictures. Figure 1 shows that during a conversation involving administrative participants, an average of 1.4 geometric objects were drawn. Administrative participants used lines and boxes much more frequently than technical participants to separate and organize information. This accounts for much of the disparity between administrative and technical groups in this category.

Graphs. The objects labeled as graphs were, by and large, stylized representations of data. They were usually squiggles on unlabeled axes, which we presume were generated quickly to make a point and not to provide numerical accuracy. Graphs, block diagrams, and equations were used almost entirely by the study's technical participants.

Sketches. Objects were classified as sketches when it appeared that they could not easily be interpreted as belonging to a general category of structured object. For the most part, sketch objects appeared to be used for emphasis or highlighting or as gestures in the conversation.

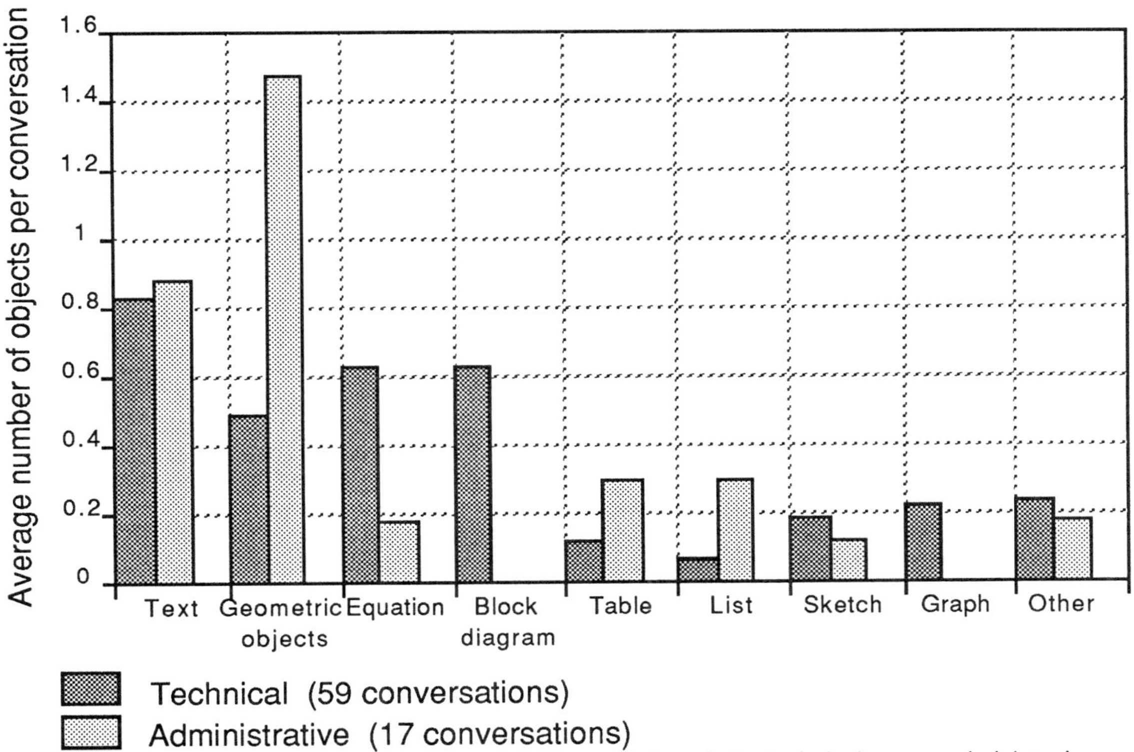

Figure 1. A categorization of the contents of office whiteboards for technical versus administrative users.

Other objects. The "Other" category in the figure was a collection of various other structured objects that people drew or imported to their boards. For example, two people had maps placed on their board, one of which was a floor plan. Other people used graphical trees to outline various relationships among objects. Two people also constructed layouts of computer screens.

Our analysis strongly suggests that whiteboards are not simply "drawing spaces" where people sketch forms devoid of intrinsic semantic content. Since intuitively we had viewed whiteboards primarily as a sketching medium, the most compelling aspect of the objects we observed was their rich semantic content. For instance, text was used more often than any other category. This is true despite the fact that whiteboards do not provide any specific facilitation for the use of text. The whiteboard marker merely facilitates sketching, but the way people use whiteboards suggests to us that they would prefer a medium that preserves the semantic structure of objects placed on the board. Physical whiteboards are sketch mediums because of the constraints provided by the physical environment, but electronic whiteboards need not simply provide sketch functionality as some previous ones have done. They should give people an easily-accessible and rich palette of objects that retain their structure once displayed and can be manipulated in terms of that structure.

Our observation indicates that text and geometric objects are props with wide applicability to both technical and administrative people. However, other props seem to have less generality. It is no surprise that different domains of work will require different kinds of conversational props. For instance, in the medical domain we expect that high-resolution images will be used quite frequently. In the design domain, we might expect the need for more sophisticated sketching capabilities. In the interface design domain, we would expect the use of menus, icons, and buttons.

THE DESIGN OF THE CONVERSATION BOARD

From this study and the experience of other investigators (e.g. [3]) we formulated requirements for the Conversation Board. In this section, we describe our current prototype. Then we discuss how we approached our three central design goals: supporting structured props, supporting persistence, and providing fast high-bandwidth communication, both between the users and between the users and the whiteboard.

Our Prototype

The Conversation Board is a structured graphics editor with a palette of tools and a canvas which serves as the shared conversation space. The structured graphics are similar in style to MacDraw™[2]. However, unlike MacDraw, the Conversation Board is not intended to support the creation of high-quality drawings, but to facilitate the conversational use of objects.

The Conversation Board is being developed in the RENDEZVOUS™[3] system, an experimental toolkit designed at Bellcore to support multi-user interfaces [7]. The RENDEZVOUS language is built on top of

2. MacDraw is a trademark of Apple Computer, Inc.
3. RENDEZVOUS is a trademark of Bellcore.

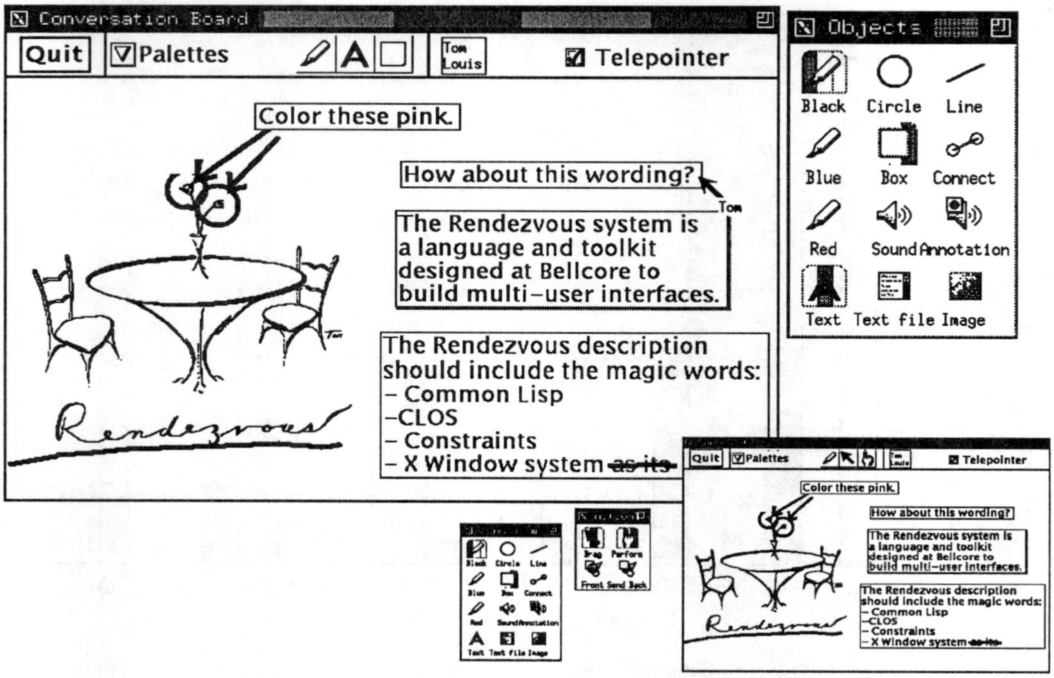

Figure 2. This shows a view of the Conversation Board for one user and a miniature of the view of a second user. It is being used to brainstorm a description of the *Rendezvous* system. The main window consists of a control region at the top and a canvas where all the drawing occurs. There are several tool palettes available. The main one is shown at the top right.

Common Lisp and uses the X Window™[4] system as its terminal model. The Conversation Board prototype has been used informally within our lab. New users have adapted very quickly to its interface. The current version of the Conversation Board has tools for multi-user sketching with various colored markers, editable multi-line text, circles, rectangles, lines, connectors, and the ability to import images and sound clips. It includes features such as telepointers, saving and loading, undo, and cut & paste.

Structured Props

The fundamental lesson we obtained from our study is that there are common categories of objects on office whiteboards with a structure that reflects how they can be manipulated in conversational use. We provide a tool palette of basic "drawing" tools for access to the most common kinds of objects which we observed on office whiteboards. Since users can edit these structured objects, they can manipulate the props with the semantic operations that are conceptually appropriate. These props can be created on the canvas as complete units and then moved, edited, and deleted independently. Figure 2 shows the Conversation Board's palette and canvas.

Sketches. For sketches that couldn't be classified as other structures, we chose to provide markers of 3 different colors. This allows color to be used much as it was on physical whiteboards. The markers will also be appropriate for creating graphs that show general shapes of curves but not numerical data.

Geometric objects. Oval, line, arrow, and rectangle tools should be sufficient to support most cases of geometric pictures we observed.

Text, lists, and equations. A tool for editable text supports these three categories. Because text was quite frequently used for simple labeling, the text tool should facilitate short, one-line pieces of text. This clearly won't be appropriate for all types of equations — in the general case the sketch tool may be necessary for supporting equations. Providing any tool to support a broad range of math notation poses a considerable design challenge if it must also support rapid communication.

Tables. A simple table tool would be sufficient for duplicating the use of a table on a whiteboard, although we suspect that office users would ask for more and more spreadsheet functionality in this tool, since the ones who use tables on their whiteboards are often the same people who use spreadsheets in their work and would want to transfer data between the two forms.

Connectors. To support the use of block diagrams, we provide a connector tool that draws a line or arrow between two other objects and remains connected to them even when the objects are moved. The block diagrams we observed contained a wide variety of different nodes, drawn as circles, rectangles, text, or

4. X Window is a trademark of MIT.

more complicated objects. They were also labeled in a wide variety of ways with text. The one structural aspect they had in common was the use of connecting lines and arrows that stay attached to the objects they link, even if those objects are moved. This behavior is reasonably well captured with a connector tool.

Images. Hand-drawn pictures of real-world objects were rarely observed on whiteboards, though we saw cases in which photographs and maps were placed on whiteboards. We believe one reason for this is that people can't draw pictures in a sufficiently timely fashion to support a rapidly evolving conversation. For this reason, we provide an on-line library of pictures that can be brought into the whiteboard. Our current library contains, for example, maps and personal photographs. We would also like to have a scanner readily available for adding images, although it would have to work quickly in order to mesh with the flow of the conversation.

Object Persistence

Many users leave the contents of their whiteboards unerased for long periods of time just in case they feel a need to reuse their previous sketches. These results imply a need for users of the Conversation Board to be able to save and retrieve the contents of their whiteboards. Many users need to copy their tables into spreadsheet files or their text to text files. It may also be useful to save the entire conversational context — the date and time of the conversation and any associated audio or video communication.

Fast, High-Bandwidth Communication

Here we describe a few approaches to improving the speed and the bandwidth of communication.

Optimized tool access. As we noted, central to our design philosophy has been the support of spontaneous, informal conversation. But there exists a tension between improving the rapidity of whiteboard interaction by providing specialized structured tools and the need to provide a minimal toolset for simplicity of interaction. A design providing only a simple sketch tool might, for example, improve spontaneity by decreasing the range of alternatives the user must consider and removing the time necessary to switch between tools.

Given the advantages of editable structures, we feel it would be a mistake to be too austere in the choice of tools an application supports. Instead, we suggest that there should be user interface accelerations to move between tools. One idea we are trying in our current implementation of the Conversation Board is customizing the use of a three-button mouse. If we had only 3 tools, we could use each mouse button to perform the operations of a single tool. However, there are many more tools available than mouse buttons. With a one-button mouse, a single tool is selected from the numerous possible tools available in a tool palette. Our design extends this notion so that there is a tool selected from the palette for each button of the three-button mouse. Instead of just inverting the chosen tool in the palette, the selected tools have a picture highlighting the left, middle, or right mouse buttons to indicate the mouse buttons with which the tools are associated (see Figure 2, where the black marker is assigned to the left mouse button, the text tool to the middle, and the rectangle tool to the right). Each Conversation Board user can make the tools that are currently most valuable to the conversation the easiest to access.

We believe that this will be no more difficult to use than a one-button mouse, since this tool palette functions the same as a one-button mouse as long as the user only chooses to use one mouse button. However, this gives an advantage over a one-button mouse in that it gives the user the ability to use a larger "working set" of tools, thus reducing the amount of time spent switching tools.

Gesturing. Gesturing is something that is often done in the context of a face-to-face conversation [3], but can be difficult when the prop is no longer something people can physically point to. People often used sketching in order to gesture. We believe that in many cases a telepointer can be used to support the same purpose. A telepointer (used in several other systems, e.g. [11]) displays to users the screen pointers of the other users with whom they are interacting. Telepointers widen the bandwidth of communication between users by conveying information without creating further work for them. However, when telepointers convey irrelevant or distracting information or otherwise just get in the way, the Conversation Board provides a checkbox to turn off a users telepointer. Other systems (e.g. Commune [12]) always provide a telepointer. At least one (WScrawl [19]) provides the telepointer as a tool, thus making it impossible to gesture and draw simultaneously.

Simultaneous Work. The ability to work simultaneously on a shared surface helps people to communicate more quickly since more work can be done in parallel. Bly [3] observed people interacting in design sessions and indicated that most drawing events occurred on regions of the drawing that were shared. We would like to support this, and also allow users to work at the same time on the same region. Therefore, the Conversation Board canvas is shared, but control is not. Different users have the ability to select different tools, select different objects, and perform different commands at the same time. In addition, their views of the whiteboard contents may need to be customized. For instance, when working on a large piece of text, each user may want to scroll to different portions of the text to work on it.

RELATED WORK

Our goal has been the creation of an electronic conversation space, where a conversation space is a space into which props are introduced and manipulated. We use the following set of issues to distinguish between other systems that are similar. Each of these will be discussed in turn.

Drawing characteristics
Structured vs. bitmap graphics
Level of functionality
Speed vs. quality
Degree of specialization

Multi-user characteristics
Number of users
Custom vs. duplicated views
Multi-user awareness
Simultaneous vs. token-passing interaction
Same vs. different place
Same vs. different time

Structured vs. bitmap graphics
The Conversation Board is a structured graphics tool — after objects are placed on the shared canvas they can still be edited and moved. Xsketch [11] is another shared structured drawing tool. It supports polyline, box, and text objects, and allows some limited editing capabilities. The NeXT Greyboard is a mutli-user structured graphics editor built on top of the NeXT Draw program. In addition to supporting standard structured drawing tools, it allows users to drop in arbitrary files which are shipped and opened on each users system. A number of electronic whiteboards use bitmap graphics. These whiteboards more closely emulate the model of a physical whiteboard. They primarily focus on supporting sketching functionality, and often also support erasure, uneditable text, and telepointers. These tools include BoardNoter [16], WScrawl [19], WE-MET [20], Commune [12], and GroupSketch [6].

Level of functionality
An important tradeoff is involved in deciding how many capabilities to provide a user. With fewer capabilities, there is less for a user to learn and fewer decisions to be made. But each new capability can, once learned, make the situations it was designed for easier. This tradeoff is especially important in conversational use. If the tools take too much time to learn, they either won't be used or will disrupt the conversation.

A physical whiteboard has basically two operations available at any time — draw or erase. Though a physical whiteboard has very limited functionality, these tools are nevertheless powerful enough to create complex imagery (with sufficient time) and are very simple to use. Systems such as BoardNoter and GroupSketch, which in many ways try to emulate the functionality of physical whiteboards using bitmap graphics and simple markers (though they also support text entry), seem to be successful at achieving the spontaneity and ease-of-use that physical whiteboards embody.

The Conversation Board provides many more tools than these systems. Another application which provides more functionality is WScrawl, which has tools such as text, line, and box, and the ability to read in a bitmap from a file. There is a careful balance that must be considered when determining level of functionality. For instance, our study indicated that text would be used so often that it seemed worth the time it takes to learn to use it. On the other hand, the connector tool may just be another distraction for administrative users who have no need to draw block diagrams.

Speed vs. Quality
We chose to build a tool that would be used in conversation, therefore the emphasis of the Conversation Board is rapid and unobtrusive construction of a shared drawing, rather than the production of high-quality imagery. Some applications of shared drawing surfaces may require very polished results, such as the cooperative design of a logo or advertisement. One approach to producing high-quality results is to share a high-end single-user graphics editor with a window-sharing system, such as Dialogo [10], Shadows [13], or Rapport [1], or a screen-sharing system such as Timbuktu™[5] [4]. For instance, the Timbuktu software allows an application like MacDraw to be shared among multiple users. However, a high-end single-user graphics editor will not always be appropriate in general communication situations. The use of an office whiteboard is an excellent example where high-quality is not as important as the communicative value of rapidly expressing ideas.

Rulers and the ability to precisely adjust pixel locations and sizes of objects are examples of features the Conversation Board willingly omitted under the assumption that this simplified the interface and that these features which enabled enhanced quality of resulting images were not critical to the ability to communicate effectively. Of course, speed and quality do not always have to be conflicting goals. For instance, by providing an invisible grid, we could make it easy for users to align objects without slowing down the interaction.

Degree of specialization
SharedARK [15] is an example of a system aimed at very specific types of interactions, shared physics problem-solving. Systems such as the Conversation Board or WScrawl are designed with very general-purpose tools, such as markers and text, which have very little behavior associated with them.

Number of users
Our study of whiteboard use indicated that typical office conversations involving a whiteboard had only 2 or 3 participants. It is unclear whether this will remain true for electronic boards since physical interference between people will no longer be a problem in using the board. Though it wasn't a specific design goal, the Conversation Board is built to support any number of users — any limitation on the number of users is due to limited computational power and a need for good response time.

One set of electronic whiteboards incorporate video into the shared design space. These systems have difficulty supporting more than 2 or 3 users simultaneously since

5. Timbuktu is a trademark of Farallon Computing, Inc.

overlaying multiple videos can be confusing and results in image degradation. VideoDraw [17] provides a small workspace onto which users can draw with actual markers, and shows video of the hands of the users as they work on their sketches. TeamWorkStation [8] is similar to VideoDraw but also allows video overlays of computer windows. This enables users to draw by hand or with any computer drawing package. VideoWhiteboard [18] is a wall-mounted whiteboard which portrays a shadow of the other user on the surface of the board. These systems are unique in that they can convey a class of gesture and personal expression that is extremely difficult to capture in a whiteboard surface lacking video. They can also incorporate physical props into the shared workspace. However, these systems require specialized hardware and the interaction on these systems is limited by the fact that it is not possible for users to modify the work of their conversational partners.

Custom vs. duplicated views

Several parts of the Conversation Board interface are customized to each user. Only the canvas is shared identically between all users. Users can have different tools selected at the same time. Thus, one user can be drawing with a red marker, another with a blue marker, and another creating text, all simultaneously. Shared-window systems allow single-user applications to be shared by multiple users with completely duplicated views. Since single-user applications are written without any knowledge of multiple people, they cannot control how much information will be shared between users (all of it will). For instance, using MacDraw with Timbuktu gives users the last tool that *anyone* selected, since the tool selection is duplicated.

Multi-user awareness

Applications that are written specifically for multiple users can be multi-user aware — they can provide customized views and provide information about the conference itself and the roles of the various participants. Single-user applications running under shared windowing systems were not written with the anticipation of multiple users and therefore can't provide these features. For instance, they could not provide users with a list of the current conference participants. Shared windowing systems typically provide conference information and telepointers, but the application cannot use this information.

Simultaneous vs. token-passing interaction

Some multi-user drawing programs, such as the NeXT Greyboard, require users to pass a token (the "marker") between them. The user who currently holds the marker gets to draw. The other users can watch, but cannot interact with the drawing. This method can be easier to implement because user inputs don't need to be synchronized — only one user can draw at a time, and the actions of the one user are broadcast to the other users. The quality of interaction is similar to that of a physical whiteboard, where typically only one person draws at once.

Many multi-user drawing surfaces allow the users to draw simultaneously as the Conversation Board does, including for instance, VideoDraw and WScrawl. Bly [3] and Whittaker et al [19] both give evidence that this may be preferred in conversation.

Same vs. different time

We started our design with the assumption that our tool would support conversation at a distance. Thus, we assumed that these interactions would occur at the same time and in different places. All of the above systems are designed for synchronous interaction. Any system, such as the NeXT Greyboard, which allow the contents of the interaction to be saved and later retrieved, can to some extent be used asynchronously.

Same vs. different place

Most of the systems mentioned have been designed for users who are viewing the interaction on separate monitors — these tools can be colocated but typically are not. Boardnoter [16] was designed for use in a single meeting room. MMM [2] is a collaborative environment for multi-user editors, such as a text editor and a rectangle editor, that is explicitly designed for users sharing a single monitor.

CONCLUSION

The dimensions of comparison between multi-user drawing systems that we've described enables us to distinguish among systems which seem to serve very similar goals. However, the choices made along each of these dimensions depend on the particular way each system is intended to be used. We made our choices based on our goal of supporting informal conversation.

Our study of office whiteboards was motivated by the desire to learn the gross characteristics of the use of props in conversation. This analysis drove our choice of providing structured objects and deciding which types of structured objects to provide and what their behavior should be.

The research reported here has established the value of structured props to conversation. It has also given us initial design guidelines for artifacts that may enhance communication by supporting the straightforward introduction of props into informal conversation.

ACKNOWLEDGEMENTS

We wish to thank the other members of the RENDEZVOUS team — Ralph Hill, John Patterson, Steve Rohall, and Wayne Wilner — for their many contributions to both this paper and the work itself. We also thank Scott Stornetta and Will Hill for valuable comments on an earlier version of this paper.

REFERENCES

1. Ahuja, S.R., Ensor, J.R., & Lucco, S.E. A comparison of application sharing mechanisms in real-time desktop conferencing systems, in *Proc. COIS '90 Conference on Office Information Systems* (Cambridge, MA, Apr. 25-27). ACM, New York, 1990, pp. 238-248.

2. Bier, E.A. & Freeman, S. MMM: A user interface architecture for shared editors on a single screen, in *Proc. UIST '91 Symposium on User Interface Software and Technology* (Hilton Head, SC, Nov. 11-13). ACM, New York, 1991, pp. 79-86.

3. Bly, S.A. A use of drawing surfaces in different collaborative settings, in *Proc. CSCW '88 Conference on Computer-Supported Cooperative Work* (Portland Oregon, Sep. 26-28). ACM, New York, 1988, pp. 250-256.

4. Farallon Timbuktu User's Guide. Farallon Computing, Inc. Berkeley, CA, 1988.

5. Fish, R.S., Kraut, R.E., Root, R.W. & Rice, R.E. Evaluating video as a technology for informal communication, in *Proc. CHI '92.* ACM, New York, 1992.

6. Greenberg, S. & Bohnet, R. GroupSketch: a multi-user sketchpad for geographically-distributed small groups, in *Proc. Graphics Interface '91* (Toronto, June 3-7). Canadian Information Processing Society, Toronto, 1991, pp. 207-215.

7. Hill, R.D. A 2-D graphics system for multi-user interactive graphics based on objects and constraints, in E. H. Blake & P. Wisskirchen (Eds.) *Advances in Object-Oriented Graphics I.* Springer-Verlag, New York, 1991 .

8. Ishii, H. TeamWorkStation: towards a seamless shared workspace, in *Proc. CSCW '90 Conference on Computer-Supported Cooperative Work* (Los Angeles, CA., October 7-10). ACM, New York, 1990, pp. 13-26.

9. Kraut, R.E., Fish, R.S., Root, R.W., & Chalfonte, B.L. Informal communication in organizations: form, function, and technology, in S. Oskamp & S. Spacapan (eds.), *Human reactions to technology: the Claremont symposium on applied social psychology.* Sage Publications, Beverly Hills, 1990.

10. Lantz, K. An experiment in integrating multimedia conferencing, in *Proc. CSCW '86 Conference on Computer-Supported Cooperative Work* (Austin, TX, December). ACM, New York, 1986, pp. 267-275.

11. Lee, J.J. Xsketch: a multi-user sketching tool for X11, in *Proc. COIS '90 Conference on Office Information Systems* (Cambridge, MA., April 25-27). ACM, New York, 1990, pp.169-173.

12. Minneman, S.L. & Bly, S.A. Managing à trois: a study of a multi-user drawing tool in distributed design work, in *Proc. CHI '91 Human Factors in Computing Systems* (New Orleans, LA., April 27 - May 2). ACM, New York, 1991, pp. 217-224.

13. Patterson, J.F. The good, the bad, and the ugly of window sharing in X, in *Proc. the Fourth Annual X Technical Conference* (Boston, MA, January 15-17). 1990.

14. Root, R.W. Design of a multi-media vehicle for social browsing, in *Proc. CSCW '88 Conference on Computer-Supported Cooperative Work* (Portland Oregon, September 26-28). ACM, New York, 1988, pp. 25-38.

15. Smith, R. B., O'Shea, T. , O'Malley, C., Scanlon, E., Taylor, J. Preliminary experiments with a distributed, multi-media, problem solving environment, in *Proc. EC-CSCW '89 1st European Conference on Computer-Supported Cooperative Work* (Gatwick, U.K., September 13-15). Computer Sciences House, Slough, U.K., 1989, pp 19-34.

16. Stefik, M., Foster, G., Bobrow, D.G., Kahn, K., Lanning, S., & Suchman, L. Beyond the chalkboard: computer support for collaboration and problem solving in meetings. *Communications of the ACM* 30,1 (1987), pp. 32-47.

17. Tang, J.C. & Minneman, S.L. VideoDraw: a video interface for collaborative drawing, in *Proc. CHI '90 Human Factors in Computing Systems* (Seattle, WA., April 1-5). ACM, New York, 1990, pp. 313-320.

18. Tang, J.C. & Minneman, S.L. VideoWhiteboard: video shadows to support remote collaboration, in *Proc. CHI '91 Human Factors in Computing Systems* (New Orleans, LA., April 27 - May 2), ACM, New York, 1991, pp. 315-322.

19. Whittaker, S., Brennan, S.E., & Clark, H.H. Co-ordinating activity: an analysis of interaction in computer-supported co-operative work, in *Proc. CHI '91 Human Factors in Computing Systems* (New Orleans, LA., April 27 - May 2). ACM, New York, 1991, pp. 361-367.

20. Wolf, C.G., Rhyne, J.R., Zorman, L.A., & Ossher, H.L. WE-MET (Window Environment-Meeting Enhancement Tools), in *Proc. CHI '91 Human Factors in Computing Systems* (New Orleans, LA., April 27 - May 2). ACM, New York, 1991, pp. 441-442.

Groupware Experiences in Three-Dimensional Computer-Aided Design

Li Shu

MIT, Room 3-443
77 Massachusetts Avenue
Cambridge, MA 02139
(617) 253-2349 lishu@athena.mit.edu

Computer-Aided Design Laboratory
Department of Mechanical Engineering
Massachusetts Institute of Technology

Woodie Flowers

MIT, Room 3-461a
77 Massachusetts Avenue
Cambridge, MA 02139
(617) 253-6234 flowers@athena.mit.edu

ABSTRACT

A system that allows people to simultaneously modify a common design in a graphically rich environment was developed to identify and examine groupware interface issues unique to three-dimensional computer-aided design.

Experiments confirmed that a simultaneous mode of edit access is preferred over a turn-taking mode for two-person interactions. Also, independent points of view (e.g., isometric versus top view) between designers optimized parallel activity. Further experiments that aimed to transfer software-usage knowledge through the groupware system led to the development of the *viewpoint*. The viewpoint is a tool that indicates the points of view of different designers as well as provides a method of pointing effective in an environment where arbitrary, contrasting points of views are allowed.

KEYWORDS

Computer-aided design, graphics, three-dimensional.

INTRODUCTION

Motivation

Many people realize the impact of the human-computer interface on the success of a software product [14][3][4]. The significance of the human-computer interface extends naturally to groupware products where interface-design choices are even more complex. Moreover, [9] asserts that many of the perceptions and perspectives acquired from experience with single-user applications will not be helpful for the groupware domain. Unfortunately, only recently have there been interface research on group systems, which involve not only the human-computer interaction existing in a single-user application, but also the person-to-person interaction through the groupware system [13]. Much of this work has focused on primarily text editors that support group creation and modification of documents and software code [10][12][8][15]. One of the few systems that specifically supports computer-aided design (CAD) for example, is TOPES [18]. Studies that involve the collaborative use of a two-dimensional drawing surface include [2] and [24].

Not surprisingly, the existence of "profound occupational and suboccupational differences in the way in which workgroups share space and structure activities in their work environments" has been documented:

> "...we observe that some occupational groups, such as artists, architects and mechanical engineers (designers of physical objects whose development is shared in posted drawings or sketches), tend to prefer open workspaces through which colleagues are encouraged to browse. Other occupational groups (e.g., software engineers, academics, writers) tend to prefer more enclosed and private workspaces which offer fewer intrusions and interruptions." [19].

This suggests that designers and authors need systems with inherently different orientations to best support their work; an editor which tolerates graphics capabilities may not be sufficient for supporting the graphics activities of collaborative design work. It is then possible that there exist issues unique to a drawing or CAD system that will not be recognized and appreciated in the context of a group editor which primarily supports the manipulation of text. Also, representation of three-dimensional objects may present situations not applicable to systems that only provide a planar sketching surface.

Permission to copy without fee all or part of this material is granted provided that the copies are not made or distributed for direct commercial advantage, the ACM copyright notice and the title of the publication and its date appear, and notice is given that copying is by permission of the Association for Computing Machinery. To copy otherwise, or to republish, requires a fee and/or specific permission.

© 1992 ACM 0-89791-543-7/92/0010/0179...$1.50

System
Clearly, to study interface issues, an appropriate system is needed. A brief description of Teledesign, the system implemented, follows.

Teledesign was built from scratch, specifically designed to support multiple users, although it can also be used by a single designer as needed. An alternative option is to write a shell program to transform existing single-user applications into multi-user applications, examples of which are SharedX from Hewlett-Packard Co., [11], and [17]. Although this alternative method can take advantage of existing software, designing a groupware application from the ground up provides an interface more suited for group use. Teledesign supports *real-time*, physically dispersed as well as face-to-face meetings of several people using a *replicated architecture*. In a replicated architecture, a local copy of the application, the graphics editor in this case, runs at each node of the conference. Inputs from designers at each node are broadcasted to all other nodes where the outputs are determined and executed locally. This option is in contrast to a centralized architecture, where only one application accepts input from the nodes and then determines and broadcasts all resulting output. Benefits of the replicated architecture over the centralized architecture are identified in [6]. Teledesign supports both *sequential access*, where only one designer can input edits at a time, and *simultaneous access*, where all the designers can edit at the same time. In sequential edit-access mode, an *implicit floor change policy* is implemented, where designers do not have to perform explicit actions such as selecting a particular button or key to request and relinquish floor control. During simultaneous access, *reversible execution* [20] was used for concurrency control. Reversible execution involves executing commands locally, before they are broadcasted, in a way such that they can be undone if they lead to inconsistencies between databases. The taxonomy used above is delineated in [21] and [7].

Teledesign has two main parts. A graphics editor runs at each workstation connected to the conference, and a communication system propagates changes between the workstations. The graphics editors are connected to a *hub*, which uses UNIX interprocess communications sockets to receive and distribute updates. The hub follows the client-server model of interaction, and accommodates connections across different remote networks as easily as those on the same network. The three-dimensional graphics editor, implemented on Silicon Graphics Personal Irises, provides a user-friendly and graphically rich environment where designed objects are *built* out of blocks and cylinders of various colors and shapes.

The Teledesign graphics editor is simple. Difficulties with explaining a previous, more complex editor to potential users resulted in streamlining which led to the current editor. In the current Teledesign editor, there is only one window. This avoids a sense of clutter [23] and reduces the computational load of redrawing many complex surfaces in multiple windows. Although some more experienced users have expressed a preference for simultaneous display of multiple views, a single window was chosen both to avoid overwhelming the new user and to provide a larger workspace. In this window, a single view of the color-shaded objects is displayed. A different view is obtained by using special keyboard keys to navigate about in the virtual world of the objects. A set of axes whose origin coincides with the origin of the world may be toggled on and off. It was found that it is easier to manipulate an object in a three-dimensional world using a two-dimensional input device, such as the mouse, by being able to *snap* to and work from views perpendicular to one of the three reference frame axes (see Figure 1). A single pop-up menu is used to create, duplicate, or destroy a cylinder or rectangular block. Setting the material or color for subsequent creations is also accomplished using the menu. Editing functions to translate, rotate, and change the shape of the cylinders or blocks, were made as intuitive as possible by using mouse click-and-drag operations. A detailed description of the system and available functions can be found in [22].

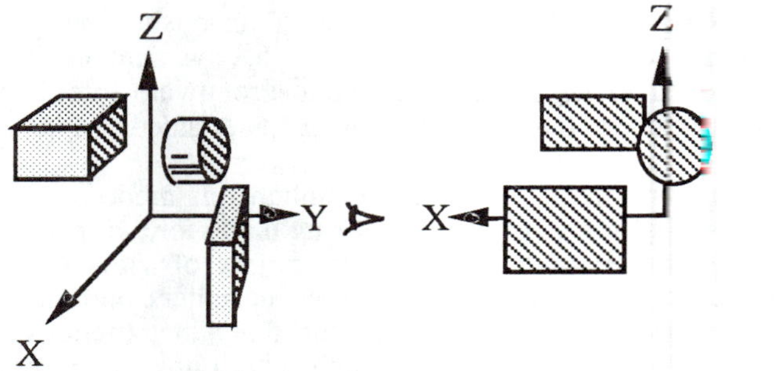

Figure 1. Perspective View vs. Orthogonal "Snap" View.

Experiments in which two-person groups performed design tasks cooperatively were conducted on Teledesign. The first set of experiments examined the issues of floor-control passing and display-consistency enforcement, while the second paired designers of contrasting Teledesign-usage experience in order to transfer software-usage knowledge through the groupware system.

Figure 2. Product of an Experimental Collaboration Session on Teledesign.

EXPERIMENT 1

A useful metaphor for Teledesign is a virtual meeting place for designers collaborating from afar. In this virtual meeting place, the designers are gathered around a set of objects, representing a prototype of a design, and with minimal physical effort, the meeting participants would modify or build upon this prototype.

Questions

Should everyone be able to manipulate the objects simultaneously or should they have to take turns? What would be the appropriate protocol for taking turns? This is a question common of all groupware systems: what, if any, edit-access or floor-passing protocol should be implemented?

Another common interface-design issue in groupware involves the degree of sharing. [23] introduces WYSIWIS (What You See Is What I See), the foundational abstraction for multi-user applications that embodies many of the attributes of a face-to-face meeting. A strict enforcement of WYSIWIS produces an environment where everyone sees the same thing all the time. One dimension along which WYSIWIS can be relaxed is congruence, which results in allowing alternative views, or "visual variations" such that a remote selection can be displayed differently from a local selection. [7] defines a *shared context* as "a set of objects where the objects and the actions performed on the objects are visible to a set of users," and a *view* as a "visual representation of some portion of a shared context." The same information may be presented differently in different views, or different sections of the shared context may be viewed using the same presentation format. For example, an array of numbers can be shown as either a table or a graph, and different people may be looking at different sections of the table [7].

To further illustrate the difference between a shared context and a shared view, particularly in the Teledesign environment, return to the meeting metaphor where designers are manipulating a shared design prototype. When one person modifies the set of objects, her actions are seen by everyone else. This group of people has a shared context since an identical set of objects is discussed at all times. Yet, since each person has a different point of view of the objects depending on where the person is standing or seated, this group does not have a shared view of the context. What degree of sharing, or WYSIWIS, is most appropriate? Should all the computer screens look identical all the time?

Methods

In this experiment, the effects of two edit-access modes, or "meeting styles", a free-for-all, simultaneous mode and a simple turn-taking mode were observed on the performances of two types of collaborative design tasks. The first type of task was a loosely defined, loosely linked task, an example of which is the cooperative design of a room. Much freedom is given to the designers, and what one person does at one end of the room usually does not substantially affect the other. The other type of task was a well-specified interdependent task, such as the collaborative building of a bookcase. This was a more interdependent task because the dimensions of one panel may depend on the dimensions of other panels, which may be designed by different people.

Research Setting

Two SGI Personal Irises located side-by-side were used for the experiments. A partition was placed between them so that the participants could see neither the other person nor the screen of the other person. Although they were visually separated, the participants were allowed to talk freely. All the sessions were videotaped.

Subjects and Group Task

This experiment used five groups of two each. The participants were MIT and Tufts graduate students in engineering who were unfamiliar with the program. They were trained in a structured half-hour session immediately prior to the experiment. In the training session, the participants first familiarized themselves with commands of the editor in a single-user environment by performing simple tasks, such as the creation and subsequent manipulation of blocks and cylinders into specified shapes and orientations. The single-user environments were achieved by executing two hubs, and connecting each graphics editor to a different hub. Next, they performed a similar task cooperatively to become accustomed to the presence of another designer in the same workspace.

The goals of the experimental tasks were to collaboratively design objects and sets of objects using the cylinder and rectangular block as primitives. Each of the two edit-access modes was paired with each of the two types of tasks as described above, so that each group performed a total of four tasks, a well-specified, interdependent task under both the simultaneous and sequential modes, and a loosely linked, loosely specified task under both the simultaneous and the sequential modes. Two different tasks of the same type were performed under each of the floor-passing modes since the subjects would have gained familiarity with an identical task performed twice. All four tasks were completed in approximately one-and-a-half to two hours.

Observations

Independent Environments

It was found that independent environments were necessary to optimally perform independent parallel tasks, especially during the simultaneous edit-access mode. One example involves the status of *edit-mode*. When edit-mode is toggled on, the shape of objects can be changed by selecting the corresponding highlighted outlines, or *edit-lines*. During edit-mode, objects can also be translated using the same mouse button when edit-lines are not selected. Unfortunately, it is difficult to avoid the edit-lines of a very small object. Consequently, users turn edit-mode off to translate a small object without inadvertently changing the size. This results in a conflict when the edit-mode status is common across workstations, and one designer is editing shapes while the other wants to move small objects.

Another example of the need for independent environments involves points of view. When the designers are working on separate tasks, it is intuitive that they prefer to be in the view that best accommodates their task. For example, someone rearranging the floor plan of the room would work best from the top view while the designer modifying the height of a door would work best from a side view. Additionally, it was observed that having different points of view is beneficial even when designers are working cooperatively on a single task. For example, when one designer is maneuvering an object, the other can see the position of the object, which as shown from another view, is not apparent to the first designer from his view (see Figure 3).

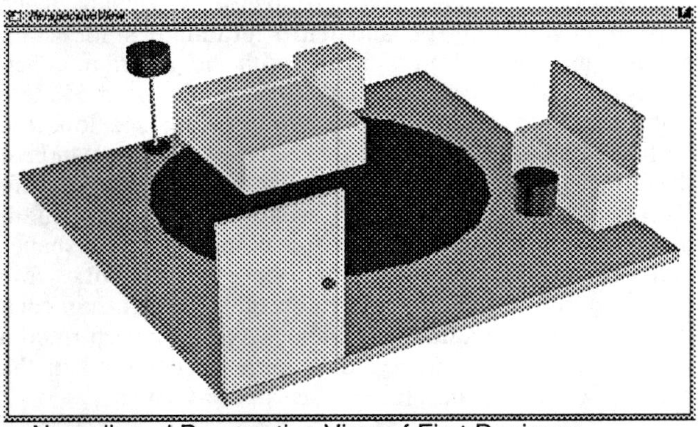

a. Non-aligned Perspective View of First Designer.

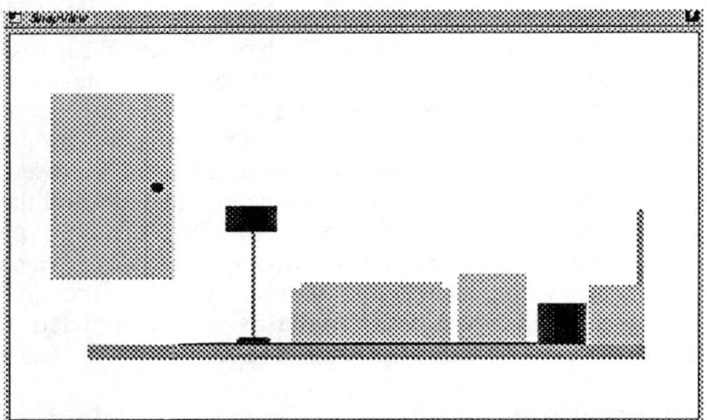

b. Same Geometry, Aligned Snap View of Second Designer.

Figure 3. Misleading Apparent Object Position Due to Point of View. (Note position of door in both views.)

[20] recognized the need for presenting the same data in different ways when participants have varied interests. [23] found that the broadcast of a participant's input command to modify an environment parameter, such as the changing of the position of a public window, would result in obstructing private work on other screens. Such conflicts were resolved by relaxing the congruence constraint of WYSIWIS to allow independent environments.

Yet when people were allowed to have independent views, a need for common reference points ensued. One of the most commonly asked question between designers was, "Where are you?" or "What view are you in?" This suggested a need for a representation of other participants' views in each designer's screen.

Edit-Access Style

It was found that forced turn-taking was not necessary for two-person interactions, regardless of task type. Contrary to intuition, the confusion caused by simultaneous editing was minimal. Occasionally, after some pause in verbal communication, two people would try to grab and move the same object without being aware of the other person's actions. When this happens, the designers need to first recognize that they are trying to move the same object, and then they need to resolve the conflict. During this experiment, the total time spent both on recognizing and resolving such conflicts was on the order of five seconds per fifteen minutes. The appropriate meeting metaphor is that there is no need for a moderator for two-person meetings. When turn-taking is necessary, it will usually occur naturally out of social protocol. [7] also found that simultaneous editing is not chaotic due to intervention of social protocol, and that, "Collisions are surprisingly infrequent." To further prevent accidental collisions, a "busy signal" such as the graying of teleselected objects, or the use of a cloudburst around changing text, has been implemented in text editors to warn other participants not to modify the same data [23] [7]. Likewise, if the virtual positions of other designers in the meeting room were somehow represented in each workstation screen, people would more likely avoid other designers' workspace.

Furthermore, the experiment participants unanimously preferred the simultaneous edit-access mode over the sequential edit-access mode for both types of tasks. The designers found it frustrating to be forced to take turns when parallel work was possible. [7] also recognized that the sequential-access mode is "limited to those situations in which a single active user fits the dynamics of the session, (and that) it is particularly ill-suited for sessions with high parallelism, inhibiting the free and natural flow of information." [25] reports that the type of floor mode selected depends on the type of meeting, noting that when persons of equal rank met, the "baton mode and first-come-first-served mode" were used most frequently, the "designation mode" was used when a clear chairperson was present, and that brainstorming sessions used the "free mode" most often. [1] presents additional factors that affect patterns of control in a computerized meeting room. [20] also favors less structured methods of access control, finding that "participants in a real-time conference change roles quite frequently, and complex access controls may be a hindrance." [20] promotes verbal negotiations as an alternative to a rigid floor-passing scheme, admitting however, that verbal negotiation may break down when the size of the meeting group increases since "the voice channel itself becomes an object of contention." Returning to the meeting metaphor, when the size of the meeting increases, more structure may be needed for the meeting to remain effective.

EXPERIMENT 2

The use of groupware to gain software knowledge has been cited by many. [4] points to the need to support informal collaboration to learn how to use the technology, further suggesting that the system help match learners with experts. [18] categorizes three areas of interaction of TOPES, which is an interactive graphics teleconferencing system used for the planning of building construction. One area was related to the discussion of drawings and the exchange of technical information, while the other two were related to the training of new operators and the deployment of the systems. Novice TOPES users who came upon difficulties would set up conferences with more experienced persons. [18] affirms, "The teleconferencing feature has facilitated user mastering of the command language."

Methods

In this experiment, designers of contrasting levels of Teledesign-usage experience were paired. The goal of the task was to transfer knowledge of software use across the system to a person who has never been exposed to Teledesign. This situation is different from the first set of experiments, which paired designers of comparable expertise, and may reveal implications for transferring more general technical, or other, knowledge across the groupware system. Again the participants were visually separated but allowed to talk freely. First the system expert steps the novice through each of the available functions, demonstrating how to best take advantage of the system features. Next, the team performs a simple collaborative design task suggested by the novice, which lasts approximately half an hour. Examples of designs selected include those of a desk and chair set, a wheelchair, a trailer, and various room layouts.

Observations

Pointing

Pointing was important. The need for a *telepointer*, a pointer that can be seen on multiple displays, was more pronounced in the context of this experiment than in the first. The need to reference objects and parts of objects specifically occurred more frequently than during experiment one. An example of a typical verbal exchange is, "To change the shape of *this* block in *this* dimension, it would easiest to select *this* corner, while editing from *this* view." Designers who were new to the system assumed that their cursor was visible in the other's display. Unfortunately, pointing in three dimensions is more complex than sending the two-dimensional cursor location on the computer screen from one workstation to another. Two cursors in identical positions relative to the workstation screen may be pointing to completely different objects if the two workstations are displaying the objects from different points of views. [23] came across the two-dimensional analogy of this telepointer problem when individualized preferences for window placements were allowed, which was solved by a calibration to make the telepointer window-relative rather than screen-relative. There is no equivalent solution for pointing in three dimensions. The participants of the experiment improvised by actually "picking up" and jiggling an object. This method has the disadvantage of disturbing the position of the referenced object. A less intrusive method involved creating a makeshift pointer out of an appropriately dimensioned block, and then moving the block to the vicinity of the object being discussed. Still, this method is guaranteed to work only if both designers have identical points of view.

Point of View

Knowledge of the other person's point of view was more essential in this situation than it was in experiment one. Since designers were allowed independent points of view, it was difficult to convey the concept that certain things were easier to do from certain points of view. The novice, not being able to see the more experienced user change between views to accomplish particular tasks, tended to try to do everything from an unaligned perspective view, only to become frustrated in the process. It was also difficult for the system expert to recognize that the other person was having difficulties because he was editing in a view which was not best suited for the task.

[16] suggests that in training simulations, instructors and students may want to have identical views to share both context and view. [11] suggests the option of "snapping back" to a common view. [23] "teleports" people to view the appropriate windows. It would seem that enforcing strict WYSIWIS is a simple way of solving both problems: there would be no confusion about point of view, and pointing reduces to the two-dimensional case. In fact, strict WYSIWIS, such that the position of cursors relative to objects and menus are visible across workstations with identical views, may be the most efficient mode for several training tasks, especially when there is a language barrier or other communication hindrance. However, sudden changes in point of view can be disorienting, especially when the change is not self-initiated [7], just as "scrollbar wars" are disruptive [23]. Perhaps voluntary teleporting, where users can choose to align their views, as suggested in [20] would be more acceptable. Alternatively, [7] identifies real-time animation as a technique of smoothly reflecting changes. The example given involves having text materialize gradually or change color as it is entered. Animation use in Teledesign could involve the more continuous panning of views to get from one point of view to another, such that the transition is less abrupt. Nevertheless, animation is computationally expensive and may jeopardize system responsiveness.

Perhaps the idea of displaying representative vectors of all other designers' views in each person's window, as suggested in results of experiment one, would be a more effective way of conveying how and when which views are used by other participants. Still, if designers continue to have independent points of views, an effective method of pointing which would accommodate the different views would have to be developed.

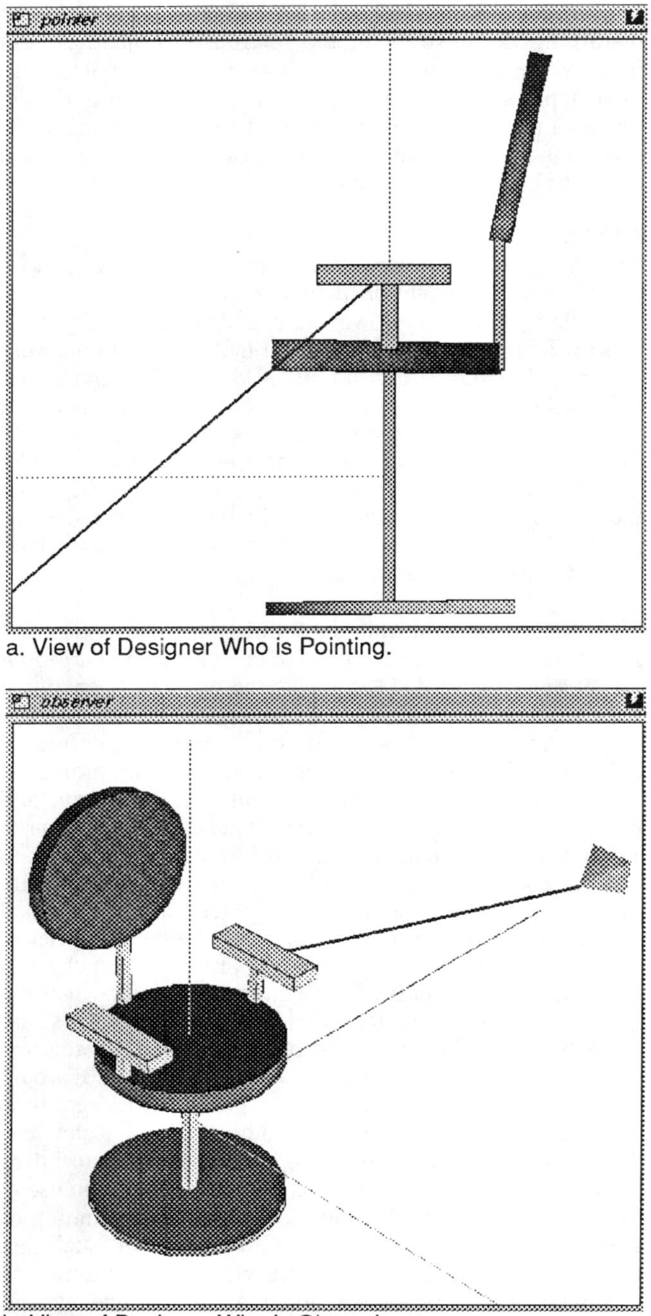

a. View of Designer Who is Pointing.

b. View of Designer Who is Observing.

Figure 4. Implementation of Viewpoint.

Solution

In answer to both the point-of-view and the three-dimensional pointer issues, the *viewpoint* was implemented. A viewpoint is a pyramid that represents the view of a designer and is visible in all other designers' displays. When a designer wants to point, the pointer is turned on using the pop-up menu, after which a gray line, extending from a lower corner to the center of the screen, appears to show that the pointer is available and ready. When an object is selected, the line brightens and terminates on the corresponding object. In the views of observing designers, a ray runs between the tip of the viewpoint representing the designer who is pointing and the selected object (see Figure 4). Local pointers are colored differently from remote pointers.

A possible feature of the viewpoint that had not been implemented, is to be voluntarily teleported to the view of another designer by selecting the corresponding viewpoint. A way of returning quickly to the original position, much like the "backdoor" of [23] should be provided.

One advantage of the viewpoint is that it serves its purpose without being unnecessarily distracting, at least no more distracting than the presence or movement of another designer in a real-world room. [7] supports that "an active user is only marginally interested in others' changes, which should therefore be indicated subtly and not disruptively." Implementation of the viewpoint is not only less disruptive, but also computationally cheaper than opening additional windows to show particular views, since only one additional object is displayed per designer in an existing window. Proper scaling of the viewpoint makes it easy to recognize if someone else has the same point of view without being an obstruction to the view itself. When the pointer is used, it does point to the correct object effectively regardless of the view of any particular designer. Alternatively, a telepointer in the form of a three-dimensional arrow has a higher chance of being obstructed in another designer's display that is in a different point of view.

SUMMARY

Teledesign was built to investigate human-machine interface situations particular to cooperative work in three-dimensional computer-aided design. Experiments confirmed that a two-person collaborative effort called for a simultaneous rather than a forced turn-taking mode of edit access. It was also found that allowing designers to have independent points of view optimized parallel activity when independent tasks were performed, as well as assisted the designer with crucial feedback from another participant in a different perspective. The need for both a three-dimensional pointer and the knowledge of the other designer's point of view was established. Consequently, the viewpoint was developed as a tool that indicates the points of view of different designers and provides a method of pointing which is effective in an environment where arbitrary, contrasting points of views are allowed.

Clearly, much territory remains to be explored. For one, Teledesign has not been tested for groups of more than two persons. An increase in group size may uncover entire realms of new issues. As the group size expands, the degree of active participation of the average meeting member may reduce, thereby intensifying the need to access private work.

A larger group size mandates a system capable of accommodating the various needs of many people. Time is one dimension along which the system can be made more flexible. Since it is difficult to schedule a meeting time for several people, participants may wish to drop in and out during the course of a meeting. [16] recognized the need to update a late-joining user. [19] recommends that a system support both synchronous and asynchronous modes of interaction since this represents the "natural patterns of communication" of workgroup members. [18] supports asynchronous interaction in addition to real-time teleconferencing by allowing collaborators to send messages and transfer drawings. [5] describes the Design Journal, a hypertext system that captures and documents design rationale. A "history file" had been implemented as part of an earlier version of Teledesign. The history file records edits of all designers in chronological order, and identifies which edits were performed by whom. When a late comer, or even someone who has entirely missed the meeting, logs on, he is presented with the current state of objects, and has the option of running through the history file to witness the edits which resulted in the current state. A combination of the history file and the Design Journal may be implemented as a voice-annotated, animated graphical segment, much like a videotape segment, which explains the rationale behind the changes as they are replayed.

ACKNOWLEDGMENTS

Financial support for this research was provided in part by the Office of Naval Research through an academic fellowship.

REFERENCES

1. Austin, L.C., Liker, J.K., and McLeod, P.L. Determinants and Patterns of Control over Technology in a Computerized Meeting Room, in *Proceedings of the Conference on Computer-Supported Cooperative Work* (Los Angeles, CA, October 7-10, 1990), ACM, New York, pp. 39-52.

2. Bly, S.A. A Use of Drawing Surfaces in Different Collaborative Settings, in *Proceedings of the Conference on Computer-Supported Cooperative Work* (Portland, OR, September 26-29, 1988), ACM, New York, pp. 250-256.

3. Bullen, C.V. and Bennett, J.L. Learning from User Experience with Groupware, in *Proceedings of the Conference on Computer-Supported Cooperative Work* (Los Angeles, CA, October 7-10, 1990), ACM, New York, pp. 291-302.

4. Clement, A. Cooperative Support for Computer Work: A Social Perspective on the Empowering of End Users, in *Proceedings of the Conference on Computer-Supported Cooperative Work* (Los Angeles, CA, October 7-10, 1990), ACM, New York, pp. 223-236.

5. Conklin, J. and Begeman, M.L. gIBIS: A Hypertext Tool for Exploratory Policy Discussion, in *Proceedings of the Conference on Computer-Supported Cooperative Work* (Portland, OR, September 26-29, 1988), ACM, New York, pp. 140-152.

6. Crowley, T., Milazzo, P., Baker, E., Forsdick, H., and Tomlinson, R. MMConf: An Infrastructure for Building Shared Multimedia Applications, in *Proceedings of the Conference on Computer-Supported Cooperative Work* (Los Angeles, CA, October 7-10, 1990), ACM, New York, pp. 329-342.

7. Ellis, C.A., Gibbs, S.J., and Rein, G.L. Groupware, Some Issues and Experiences. *Communications of the ACM.* Vol. 34, No.1, (January 1991), pp. 38-58.

8. Galegher, J. and Kraut, R.E. Computer-Mediated Communication for Intellectual Teamwork: A Field Experiment in Group Writing, in *Proceedings of the Conference on Computer-Supported Cooperative Work* (Los Angeles, CA, October 7-10, 1990), ACM, New York, pp. 65-78.

9. Grudin, J. Why CSCW Applications Fail: Problems in the Design and Evaluation of Organizational Interfaces, in *Proceedings of the Conference on Computer-Supported Cooperative Work* (Portland, OR, September 26-29, 1988), ACM, New York, pp. 85-93.

10. Kaiser, G.E., Kaplan, S.M., and Micallef, J. Multiuser, Distributed Language-Based Environments, *IEEE Software*, Vol. 4., No. 6 (November 1987), pp. 58-67.

11. Lantz, K.A. An Experiment in Integrated Multimedia Conferencing, *Proceedings of the Conference on Computer-Supported Cooperative Work* (Austin, TX, Dec. 3-5, 1986), ACM, New York, pp. 267-275.

12. Leland, M.D.P., Fish, R.S., and Kraut, R.E. Collaborative Document Production Using Quilt, in *Proceedings of the Conference on Computer-Supported Cooperative Work* (Portland, OR, September 26-29, 1988), ACM, New York, pp. 206-215.

13. Mantei, M. Capturing the Capture Concepts: A Case Study in the Design of Computer-Supported Meeting Environments, in *Proceedings of the Conference on Computer-Supported Cooperative Work* (Portland, OR, September 26-29, 1988), ACM, New York, pp. 257-270.

14. Martin, J. *Design of Man-Computer Dialogues*, Prentice-Hall, Englewood Cliffs, New Jersey, 1973.

15 Neuwirth, C.M., Kaufer, D.S., Chandhok, R., and Morris, J.H. Issues in the Design of Computer Support for Co-authoring and Commenting, in *Proceedings of the Conference on Computer-Supported Cooperative Work* (Los Angeles, CA, October 7-10, 1990), ACM, New York, pp. 183-196.

16 Patterson, J.F., Hill, R.D., and Rohall, S.L. Rendezvous: An Architecture for Synchronous Multi-User Applications, in *Proceedings of the Conference on Computer-Supported Cooperative Work* (Los Angeles, CA, October 7-10, 1990), ACM, New York, pp. 317-328.

17 Perreault, D.J. *Interactive Computer Support for Remote Design Teams: A New Approach,* MIT S.M. thesis, Cambridge, MA, 1991.

18. Pferd, W., Peralta, L.A. and Prendergast, F.X., Interactive Graphics Teleconferencing, *IEEE Computer*, Vol. 12, No. 11, (November 1979), pp 62-72.

19. Reder, S. and Schwab, R.G. The Temporal Structure of Cooperative Activity, in *Proceedings of the Conference on Computer-Supported Cooperative Work* (Los Angeles, CA, October 7-10, 1990), ACM, New York, pp. 303-316.

20. Sarin, S. and Greif, I. Computer-Based Real-Time Conferencing Systems, *IEEE Computer*, Vol. 18, No. 10, (October 1985), pp. 33-45.

21. Schooler, E.M., Casner, S.L., and Postel, J. Multimedia Conferencing: Has It Come of Age? *Proceedings of the 24th Hawaii International Conference on System Sciences,* Vol. 3, (January 1991), pp. 707-716.

22. Shu, L. *Groupware Experiences in Three-Dimensional Computer-Aided Design,* MIT S.M. thesis, Cambridge, MA, 1992

23. Stefik, M., Bobrow, D.G., Foster, G., Lanning, S., and Tatar, D. WYSIWIS Revised: Early Experiences with Multiuser Interfaces, *ACM Transactions on Office Information Systems,* Vol. 5, No. 2, (April 1987), pp 147-167.

24. Tang, J.C. and Leifer, L.J. A Framework for Understanding the Workspace Activity of Design Teams, in *Proceedings of the Conference on Computer-Supported Cooperative Work* (Portland, OR, September 26-29, 1988), ACM, New York, pp. 244-249.

25. Watabe, K., Sakata, S., Maeno, K., Fukuoka, H., and Ohmori, T. Distributed Multiparty Desktop Conferencing System: MERMAID, in *Proceedings of the Conference on Computer-Supported Cooperative Work* (Los Angeles, CA, October 7-10, 1990), ACM, New York, pp. 27-38.

An architecture for tailoring cooperative multi-user displays

Richard Bentley, Tom Rodden, Peter Sawyer and Ian Sommerville

CSCW Research Centre
Computing Department
Lancaster University
Lancaster LA1 4YR.
U.K.
Email: {dik, tom, sawyer, is}@comp.lancs.ac.uk
Phone: (+44) 524 65201
Fax: (+44) 524 381707

ABSTRACT

A range of architectures have emerged which support real-time cooperative user interfaces. These architectures have tended to centralise the management of the interface and thus provide only limited support for user-centred development and interface tailoring. This paper considers the problems associated with the development of tailorable cooperative interfaces and proposes an architecture which allows such interfaces to be developed using an incremental, user-centred approach.

The architecture presented in this paper has emerged within the context of a project investigating cooperative interface development for UK air traffic control. We conclude that the architecture is equally applicable to other Command and Control domains, where a shared information space forms the focus for the work taking place.

KEYWORDS

Multi-user interfaces, CSCW architectures, Command and Control systems, Database visualisation.

INTRODUCTION

The merging of computer and communications technology and the development of network based windowing systems has seen the development of a range of real-time cooperative systems. These systems often exploit multi-user interfaces which allow application sharing across a number of workstations and many examples have been reported within the CSCW literature [1,2].

The approach taken by the majority of these systems has been to extend existing windowing technology to provide replication of output on a number of displays. This approach has been most successfully applied within shared window or desktop conferencing systems. A number of more recent examples of real-time cooperative systems have considered the development of architectures to support multi-user applications with more control over the user interface [3,4].

Most existing approaches have tended to consider user interface construction as a task for application developers and have provided only limited support for user-centred development and tailoring. In contrast, this paper presents an architecture which supports rapid user-centred development of multi-user displays and its realisation within a prototype system for generating cooperative interfaces.

The development of the architecture and system described in this paper has taken place within the context of an on-going multi-disciplinary project investigating the application of user interface technology to support the work of air traffic controllers. The project involves the extensive use of ethnographic observation with the intent to inform the development of cooperative systems to support the controlling process [5].

SYSTEM RATIONALE AND REQUIREMENTS

Air traffic control (ATC) systems are a type of Command and Control (C^2) system and, like many classes of C^2 system, involve controllers cooperating using a shared information space which reflects the external processes being controlled. This shared space is updated by controllers and by input from external sensors such as radars, transponders, etc. (figure 1). Each controller maintains and interacts with their own view of the shared space, with cooperation between controllers supplemented by direct audio communication facilities.

Currently, most C^2 systems are hybrid systems where a computer-maintained database is supplemented by paper

Permission to copy without use all or part of this material is granted provided that the copies are not made or distributed for commercial advantage, the ACM copyright notice and the title of the publication and its date appear, and notice is given that copying is by permission of the Association for Computing Machinery. To copy otherwise, or to republish, requires a fee and/or specific permission.
© 1992 ACM 0-89791-543-7/92/0010/0187...$1.50

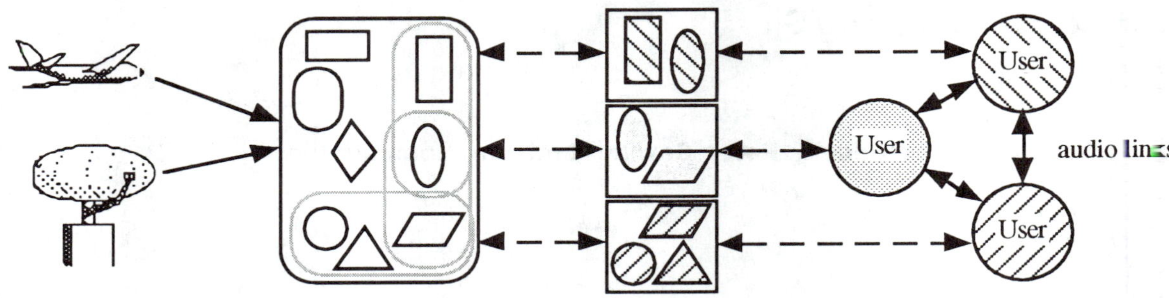

Figure 1 Cooperation via a shared space

work and a variety of manual procedures to form the shared information space shown in figure 1. Controllers evolve a complex and subtle way of working which often involves coordinating their decisions with other controllers. In making decisions, they must often anticipate how other controllers will react to particular configurations of the system being controlled. In order to reflect this complexity we are attempting to use an on-going ethnographic study [6] to inform the derivation of user requirements.

The ethnographic observation of controllers and control rooms has been a central theme within CSCW and has been reported elsewhere by [7,8,9]. Our work aims to extend this previous history by using the ethnographic study to inform the construction of a computer system. In many ways this is a new field for both computer scientists and sociologists with methods of working and respective roles in the requirements capture process still being established.

Given the lack of any established working method we use a prototyping approach to system development. The focus of our work has been the development of a prototyping system which allows specific instances of cooperative interfaces to be rapidly constructed in conjunction with the results of on-going studies [10].

Architecture Requirements

The overall objective of the architecture, therefore, is to support an environment for the prototyping of interfaces for users cooperating via a shared information space. The architecture should be flexible enough to allow the interactive development of these interfaces by informal consultation between user, interface developer and ethnographer. The role of the prototype generator and initial observations highlight a number of requirements for the underlying architecture.

1) Support for multi-user displays

Cooperating users access the shared information store through individual workstations. This form of access will often be supplemented by the informal cooperation gained from screens being located within a common control room. Given the reliance on controllers' awareness of the activities of others, the supporting architecture should :-

- Allow the construction of different user display formats.
- Allow displays to be shared across different workstations.
- Support the visualisation of shared entities within user displays.
- Allow the manipulation of shared entities on different workstations.
- Allow the set of cooperative displays to be dynamically changed with workstations being easily added and removed.

2) Support for different views

Cooperating users may wish information to be presented in different ways. For example, in ATC a particular controller's view of an aircraft could be different to that of an officer concerned with controlling the flow of traffic. The architecture should support different views of entities within the shared information space so must :-

- Allow the definition of different interactive representations of shared entities.
- Maintain these different representations as underlying entities change.
- Allow the updating of entities through interaction with these representations.

To promote rapid interface construction the architecture should allow these facilities to be provided in a highly visible and accessible manner.

3) Support for tailorability

Our focus is on the construction of cooperative interfaces in conjunction with the observation of users and it is difficult to predict the exact nature of these interfaces in advance. It is important that the architecture allows interfaces to be easily constructed and tailored by domain experts and developers in line with the results of observational studies. In particular the architecture should :-

- Allow system features to be presented in such a way that details are readily understood.
- Allow displays to be easily tailored to support different working practices.
- Support the personalised presentation of shared information to different users.

An end-user could be given complete freedom to tailor the appearance of his or her display by the architecture. However, results of initial observations have suggested that end-user tailorability needs to be bounded within a cooperative setting. For example, in ATC it is important that controllers understand each others displays at a glance. In fact when controllers change at the end of shifts the in-coming controller monitors the work of the out-going controller he or she is replacing for some minutes prior to switching position. The limits and bounds of the tailorability eventually provided to end-users will be a matter of consultation between developer, controller, observer and management.

SHARED INTERFACE ARCHITECTURES

The merging of workstation technology and real-time computer conferencing has played an important role in CSCW. This merging has been termed *desktop conferencing* and an integral part of desktop conferencing is the use of *multi-user interfaces*. Lauwers [11] outlines two approaches for the development of multi-user interfaces. The development of special purpose applications which are *collaboration aware*, and the adapting of existing single user applications to provide *collaboration transparent* shared applications. Examples of work which exploit collaboration transparency include Vconf [12], Rapport [13], SharedX [14], and MMConf [15].

Most of the collaboration transparent synchronous interfaces exploit network based window systems such as X or NeWS. These systems assume a client-server or virtual terminal model of interaction where the application and the display are separate and connected by an interaction protocol. This approach allows local graphical events to be handled by each display with interaction details being passed to the application using this protocol.

The majority of shared window systems use a centralised agent to multiplex output from applications onto a number of display screens and to route input from each display to the appropriate applications. In this approach an application does not know that it is being shared between users. Consequentially it is impossible to support different views of the shared information within these systems.

An additional problem with this approach is that an assumed model of cooperation based on many readers but only one writer is embedded within the system. As a result it is difficult to customise these systems and any tailorability which exists has concentrated on the development of techniques to support different forms of turn taking protocols [16].

In contrast to the transparent approach outlined above, collaboration aware solutions provide facilities to explicitly manage the sharing of displays between different users. This approach has been adopted by a range of applications including Cognoter [1], Grove [17] and rIBIS [2].

As a result of the centralisation of user interface management, multi-user cooperative applications can support different user interfaces and many of them provide facilities which allow individual views to be supported. Recently researchers have started to examine how this arrangement can be generalised to provide supporting architectures for a variety of applications. Systems adopting this approach include the Rendezvous system [4] which has the ability to support different user views on application objects and interactions with these views. This is provided by maintaining a separation between *underlying objects*, which contain the application semantics and *interaction objects*, which maintain details of users' views on these objects.

Collaboration aware applications require a significant degree of logical centralisation. Systems which are physically centralised and directly support a number of displays have been criticised for their inability to provide the responsive interfaces required by cooperative systems [11]. Replicated architectures exist for collaboration aware applications [16] which significantly improve this performance. However, many of these systems involve an additional overhead in maintaining consistency between application processes and often require significant re-configuration when adding or removing displays. As a direct result of our need to provide responsive user interfaces whilst also supporting the addition and removal of displays we have adopted a hybrid approach in our architecture.

Existing architectures for collaboration aware systems do not concentrate on tailoring. They embed user interface management facilities within the cooperative application. For example, in Rendezvous each user's interaction is managed by lightweight processes embedded within the application process. Facilities tend to be application specific and provide only limited tailorability. In contrast, our architecture attempts to localise and make visible many features of user displays in order to support and encourage tailorability by exploiting independent, active display agents.

USER DISPLAY AGENTS

Traditional models of interaction consider the user interface as a presentation of an application with users interacting through some form of dialogue. User interface systems have reinforced this model by supporting the development of user displays as fixed system entities. User interface details are often closely coupled with application semantics with the result that tailorability is inhibited.

In contrast to previous dialogue models our approach is based upon the application of shared interaction objects. The state of these objects characterise the information presented to the user by the application. Users interact directly with these objects with state changes directly affecting the state of the application. The interaction semantics of the application are thus captured by the set of objects presented to the user and how the system reacts to changes in these objects.

Our architecture considers user displays as active entities with individual properties which can be tailored by systems designers in conjunction with users. We refer to these active

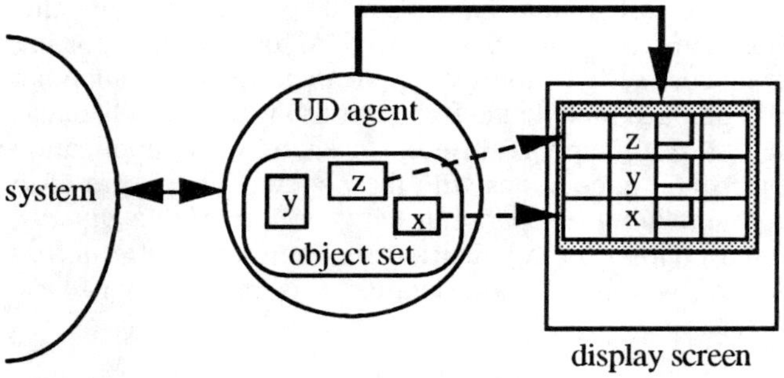

Figure 2 Detaching interaction semantics with a User Display agent

entities as *User Display Agents* (UD agents) and the parts of the user's screen managed by an agent is called a *User Display* (UD). These agents maintain state and use this state to determine details of interaction with the user. This state information includes the interaction and presentation details of the shared interaction objects relevant to a User Display. Each User Display agent allows this information to be directly manipulated with changes occurring dynamically. This arrangement represents an extension of the separation between interaction and underlying objects supported by systems such as Rendezvous.

Under this arrangement, details of the user interface can be held within the User Display agent rather than the system (figure 2). This allows users to access the details of the user interface semantics through mechanisms provided by the User Display agent. This approach is analogous to the difference between deep and surface object interaction highlighted by Took [18].

The User Display Agent Model
Our architecture exploits active User Display agents as the primary mechanism of interaction with a shared information store. The following properties are central to this interaction:

FOCUS: Cooperating users are only interested in a subset of entities within the information store. As the state of an entity changes, its relevance to each user may change. Consequently a representation of that entity may have to be added to or removed from existing User Displays.

VISUALISATION: Whilst cooperating users may require representations of the same information, the form of these representations may vary depending upon the user and task the representation is supporting. Representations should therefore reflect the user-task context, and changes in the state of represented entities may require changes in the form of representation used.

POSITION: The spatial arrangement of entity representations on the user's screen may provide information concerning relationships between those entities. As the state of represented entities change, it may be necessary to adjust the spatial arrangement to reflect changes in these relationships.

Our model of a User Display separates the notions of the entities to be displayed, their representations and their spatial arrangement. A User Display has three separate components: a *Selection* representing focus, a *Presentation* representing visualisation and a *Composition* representing position. A User Display agent manages the affects of entity updates on each component of its User Display.

A *Selection* is a set of entities which are dynamically chosen from the information store according to *Selection criteria*. Selection criteria are predicates over entity attributes and are specified by the interface designer The Selection criteria filter entities to select which should be included in the User Display. As entities' states change, the selection changes accordingly.

A *Presentation* is a set of *Views* used to represent entities in the selection. A View is a graphical representation which defines the appearance, attribute positioning and interaction mechanisms for an individual entity. Views are selected for each entity dynamically, according to the *Presentation criteria*. These define a guard for each View which an entity must pass if it is to be represented by that View. As an entity's state changes, it may be necessary to change the View used to represent it in the User Display.

A *Composition* is a set of positions which represent the spatial arrangement of the Views in the User Display. These positions can be absolute or relative to other Views. As an entity's state changes, the positions of the Views also change, to remain consistent with the arrangement defined in the *Composition criteria*.

This abstraction of User Displays as autonomous entities allows cooperative systems to be constructed of a federation of agents interacting and responding to changes in a shared information store. Each User Display agent contains sufficient information to allow the presentation aspects of shared entities central to cooperation to be readily tailored without system re-configuration.

COOPERATIVE USER DISPLAY AGENTS

A characteristic of the kind of cooperative system we are considering is that shared data provides the focus for the cooperation taking place; different users working at separate screens interact with shared information entities. In our cooperative setting, users accessing a shared information store each have a working set of User Display agents which manage different displays of the shared information for them (figure 3). Each agent can present the User Display it manages in one or more screen windows, and agents can be added to and removed from the working set as required.

Changes in the state of entities in the information space potentially affect the selection, presentation and composition components of each User Display. For example, a change in the longitude of an aircraft will require a change in composition in a User Display which presents a radar (ie the radar blip for the aircraft will be seen to move). Thus the architecture must allow relevant User Display

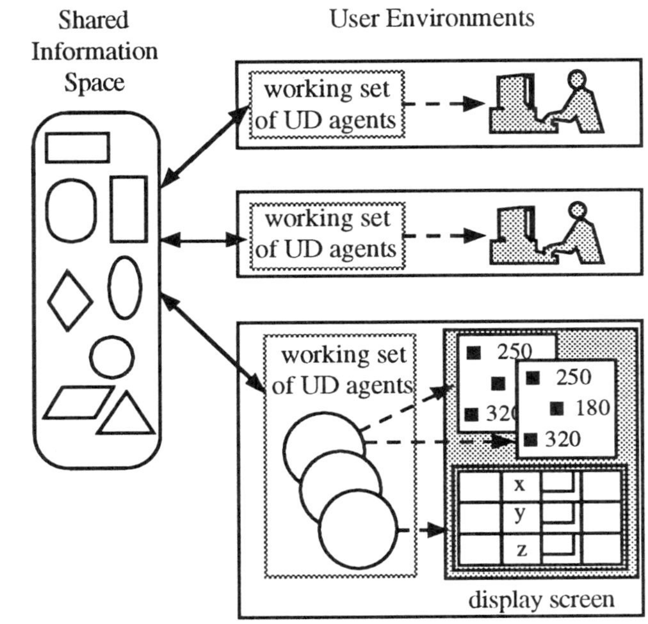

Figure 3 User Display agents cooperating via a shared information space

agents to be informed of such changes, these agents to compute the effects on their User Displays and all windows presenting that User Display to be brought up to date.

Maintaining User Displays

A requirement for our architecture was the need to allow the same User Display to be presented on separate display screens. Referring to figure 3, this means that users may hold copies of the same User Display agent as part of their working set. However, changes in the state of entities in the information space will affect each of these copies in the same way, and thus the effects of such changes on selection, presentation and composition need only be calculated once.

To support this, each user may hold a copy (or *Surrogate*) of each of the User Display agents as part of their working set. These Surrogate agents are minimised, in that each holds only the current state of the User Display; the definition of the User Display is held by the *Master* User Display agent. This receives notification of relevant changes in the state of entities, computes the effects on the User Display (using the selection, presentation and composition criteria), and informs each of its Surrogates of the new state (figure 4).

This factoring out of display semantics supports local tailorability of information displays without requiring system re-configuration. Local tailoring operations performed on a display, such as selection of alternative Views for represented entities, are retained by the Surrogate agent. Machines can be added and removed at any time during system execution; added machines will contact the Master User Display agents and create the Surrogates required, establishing communication links to receive the

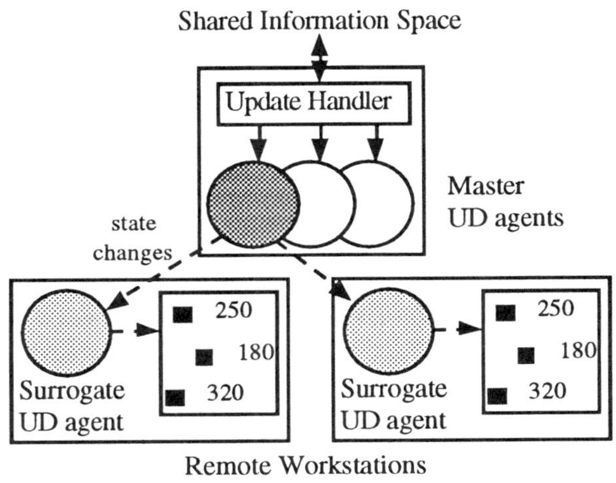

Figure 4 Surrogate User Display arrangement

current state of the User Display and future update information.

All access to the information store is made via a well-defined interface, which informs the Update Handler component (figure 4) of any changes made by external (ie non-user) sensors. In addition, the Update Handler must pass on user-sourced changes to the information store using this interface. Thus, our architecture can support a range of storage technologies and places no requirements on the information store for broadcasting update information.

The Update Handler is responsible for passing update information on to those Master User Display agents potentially affected by an update. For this, the Update Handler uses information regarding each agent's *interest set*, which is registered when the User Display the agent manages is defined. (For example, an agent managing a radar Display will register changes in longitude and latitude as part of its interest set). In the event of a change in definition of a User Display, the User Display agent must register the new interest set with the Update Handler as well as computing the new state.

Figure 5 shows the *dispatching* mechanism of the Update Handler, which minimises the communication (and so the cost) involved in informing User Display agents of updates.

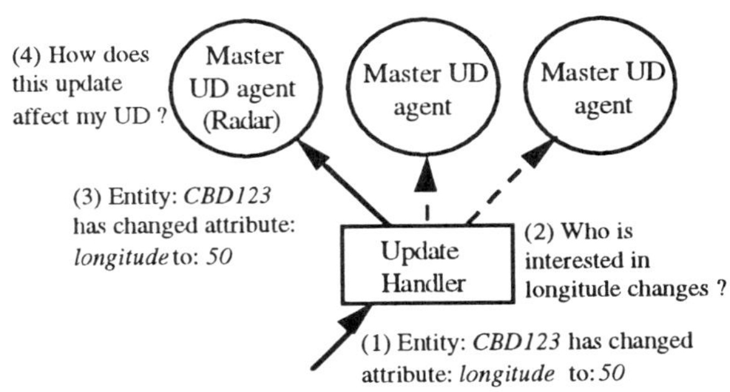

Figure 5 The dispatching role of the Update Handler

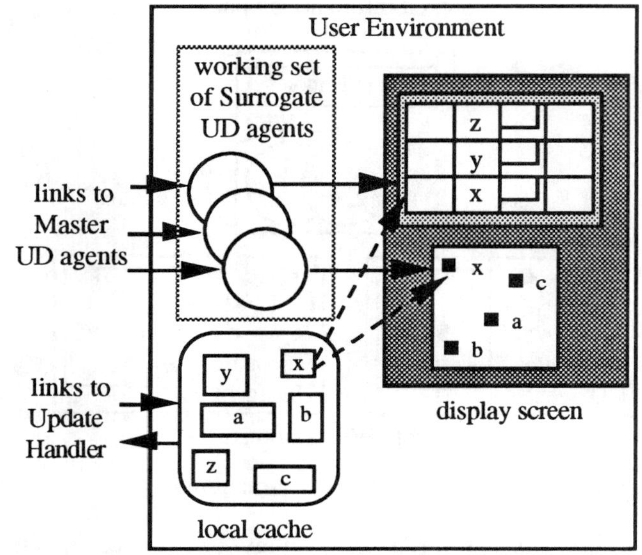

Figure 6 Local caching mechanism

It is possible (and quite likely) that entities in the information store may be represented in different User Displays by different Views. As updates occur, these Views must also be updated to remain consistent with the entities they represent. Routing such updates through the User Display agents would require each agent which maintains such a View to be informed of the update, even though the update may not affect the selection, presentation and composition components of that agent's User Display. These agents would then have to inform their Surrogates of the change, potentially resulting in many communications to the same workstation to update the Views.

To minimise this communication, we have adopted a caching mechanism where replicated subsets of the information store are held locally (figure 6). It is the Update Handler's responsibility to broadcast changes in the state of entities to all caches which maintain replicated copies of these entities. Views are connected directly to these cached entities, removing the need for complex mechanisms to maintain entity-View links across workstations. The links between the Update Handler and caches are bi-directional to allow the Update Handler to receive updates in the state of a cached entity caused by user interaction with one of that entities Views. The Update Handler can then inform the information store of such updates, selectively multicast updates to caches which maintain a copy of the updated entity and inform relevant User Display agents in case the update requires changes in the state of any User Displays.

IMPLEMENTATION

Our implementation of this architecture forms the basis of a prototyping environment which allows the construction and refinement of cooperative displays [10]. We have found that this implementation, developed in Smalltalk-80 for Sun workstations, meets our performance requirements for real-time updating.

The prototyping environment makes visible our model of a User Display, whilst hiding the complexity of the Update

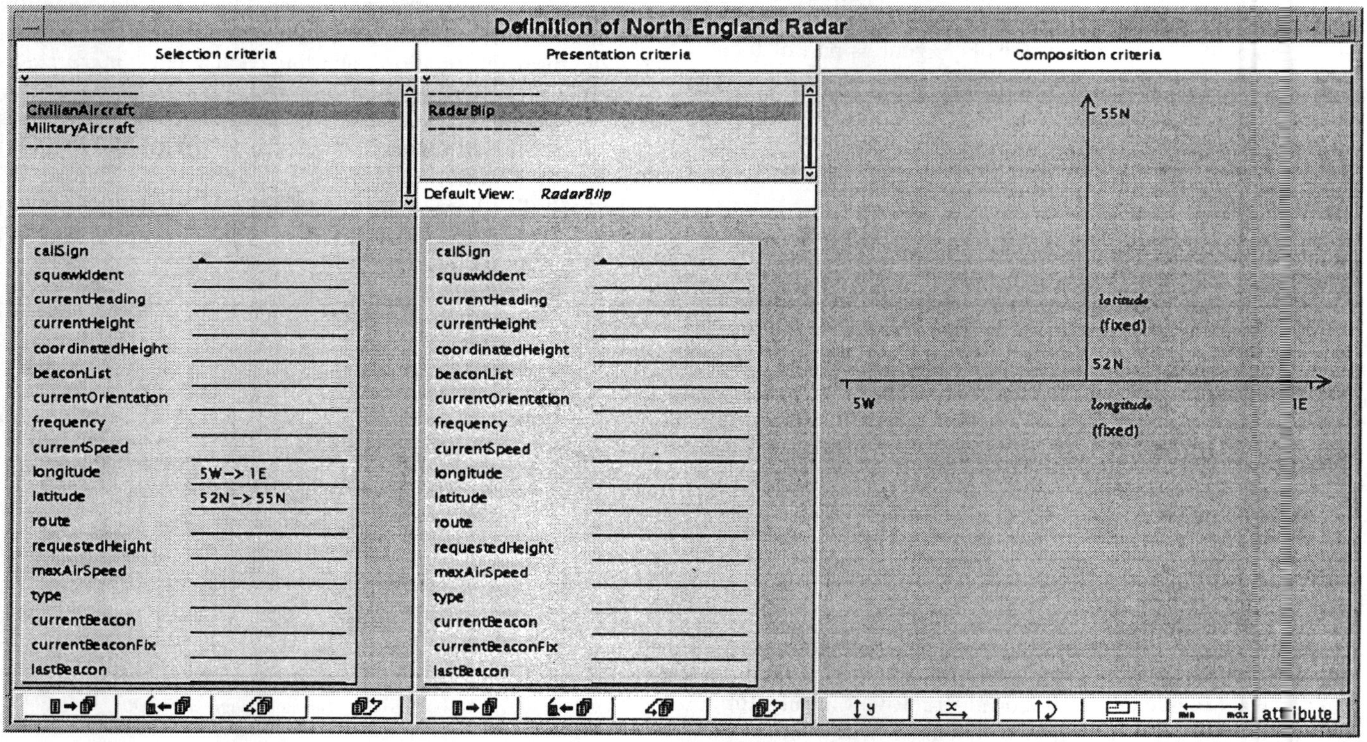

Figure 7 The User Display definition tool

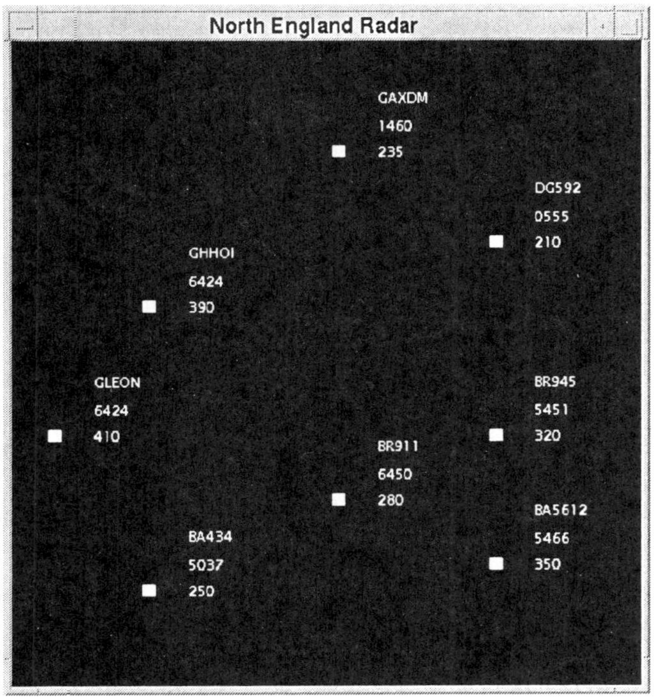

Figure 8 A window presenting the 'North England Radar' User Display

Handler, Surrogate agent and local caching mechanisms. The interface designer, in consultation with a domain expert and/or end-user, defines the selection, presentation and composition criteria of each User Display. Libraries of such criteria can be constructed and re-used, shortening the time required to construct new User Displays. Our tool used to capture these criteria is presented in figure 7, which shows the definition of a radar User Display.

The task of defining a User Display is partitioned, so that the interface designer completes a separate 'form' for each of the selection, presentation and composition criteria. For the selection and presentation criteria, these forms are represented as Pattern templates [19] which can be used to capture the criteria in a by-example manner.

A pattern defines a guard and an entity must meet all conditions specified in the pattern to pass that guard. (A pattern with no conditions implies all entities pass that pattern's guard). To meet the selection criteria of the User Display defined in figure 7 (and thus be represented in that display), the values of longitude and latitude attributes for 'CivilianAircraft' type entities must be between 5°W-1°E and 52°-55° N respectively.

The presentation criteria are defined by specifying the conditions under which different Views will be used to represent entities of each type. View templates are defined using a different tool, which captures each template's appearance, attribute positioning and interaction mechanisms. Templates are associated with one or more entity types and entities of these types can be represented by directly manipulatable instantiations of these templates. Both User Display and View definition tools are integrated, so that the User Display definition tool knows which Views are associated with which entity types. In figure 7, entities of type 'CivilianAircraft' will use a 'Radar Blip' representation.

For each type of entity which can be represented in the User Display, the composition criteria define how entity representations will be arranged. The model of composition is relatively simple, but allows Views to be positioned in two dimensions, absolutely or relative to other Views in the User Display. For example, the composition criteria defined in figure 7 will position Views of 'CivilianAircraft' type entities absolutely, depending on the values of their longitude and latitude attributes.

Figure 8 shows a window presenting the User Display defined in figure 7, as it would appear on the user's display screen. Aircraft represented are taken from a small example information store created from actual flight plan data.

The definitions of the selection, presentation and composition criteria are translated into directly evaluatable expressions by the User Display agent. The agent can use these expressions to determine the effects of updates on the User Display it manages. By using these form-based representations to capture the definition, the underlying complexity of these expressions is hidden from the designer, allowing rapid development and modification of different display formats. Our environment makes no distinction between design and run time, so User Display definitions can be modified and the effect on currently displayed information immediately observed.

CONCLUSIONS AND FUTURE WORK

We have presented an architecture to support the development of cooperative interfaces for C^2 systems which is intended to support the rapid prototyping of different formats of information display. The envisaged development model is that interfaces will be constructed in informal consultative sessions and informed by the results of observational studies. These interfaces can then be evaluated by controllers in actual control environments.

The architecture allows the construction of multi-user interfaces by the definition of User Displays which present information from a shared information space. User Displays can be shared across different workstations and a single workstation can support multiple User Displays. Each type of entity has an associated set of Views which can be used to represent entities of that type. Besides information presentation, these Views also define the interaction mechanisms which allow users to update the entities they represent. These updates are submitted to the shared information store and propagated to all other representations of the shared entity, as well as relevant User Displays.

Our approach to development has been to make as few assumptions as possible regarding the coordination the architecture must support. Rather, we have built general mechanisms which can be tailored to conform with the results of observational studies. The propagation of change is an example of this philosophy; our update mechanism is 'policy free', with changes propagated to other users without interference from the architecture. More specialised update strategies will be tailored from this general mechanism to meet the specific needs of controllers.

Although our architecture has evolved to support the development and management of cooperative interfaces in the domain of ATC, we believe it is equally applicable to a wide range of C^2 systems. Within such systems, shared system entities provide the focus for cooperation, with changes to the state of these entities being the smallest granularity of update requiring propagation.

The domain that we have addressed allows us to consider the shared information store as devoid of embedded procedure, so that information is held as state, without considering methods which operate on that state. This simplifies our model of distribution and our local caching mechanisms. Future investigations will consider the problems of embedded procedure, such as method mutability, information migration and propagation of change within the information store.

REFERENCES

1. Stefik, M., Foster, G., Bobrow, D. G., Kahn, K., Lanning, S., Suchman, L., 'Beyond the chalkboard: computer support for collaboration and problem solving in Meetings', *Communications of the ACM*, 30(1), January 1987, pp 32-47.
2. Rein, G. L., Ellis, C. A., 'rIBIS: A real-time group hypertext system', *International Journal of Man Machine Studies*, 34(3), March 1991, pp 349-368.
3. Greenberg, S., 'Personalisable Groupware: Accommodating Individual Roles and Group Differences', in *Proceedings of ECSCW '91*, Bannon, L., Robinson, M., Schmidt, K. (eds), Sept 25-27, Kluwer, 1991, pp 17-31.
4. Patterson, J. F., Hill, R. D., Rohall, S. L., Meeks, W. S., 'Rendezvous: An architecture for synchronous multi-user applications', in *Proceedings of CSCW '90*, October 7-10, Los Angeles, Ca., ACM, 1990.
5. Bentley, R., Hughes, J.A., Randall, D., Rodden, T., Sawyer, P., Shapiro, D. and Sommerville, I., 'Ethnographically-informed systems design for air traffic control', in *Proceedings of CSCW '92*, November 1-4, Toronto, Canada, ACM, 1992.
6. Harper, R., Hughes, J. A., Shapiro, D. Z., 'Working in harmony: An examination of computer technology in air traffic control', In *Studies in Computer Supported Cooperative Work. Theory, Practice and Design*, eds J. M. Bowers and S. D. Benford, Amsterdam: North-Holland. 1991.
7. Heath, C., Luff, P., 'Collaborative Activity and Technological Design: Task Coordination in London Underground Control Rooms', in *Proceedings of ECSCW'91*, Bannon, L., Robinson, M., Schmidt, K. (eds), Sept 25-27, Kluwer, 1991, pp 65-80.
8. Suchman, L., 'The Situated Structuring of Cooperative Work', *Inaugural Lecture*, CSCW Centre, Lancaster University, October 3, 1991.
9. Hutchins, E., 'The technology of team navigation', in *Intellectual Teamwork: Social Foundations of Cooperative Work*, Galegher, J., Kraut, R. E., Egido, C. (eds), Hillsdale, New Jersey, Erlbaum, 1990, pp 191-220.
10. Bentley, R., Rodden, T., Sawyer, P., Sommerville, I., 'A prototyping environment for Dynamic Data Visualisation', in *Proceedings of the 5th IFIP TC2\WG2.7 Working Conference on Engineering for Human-Computer Interaction*, Ellivuori, Finland, 10-14 August, C. Unger and J. A. Larson (eds), Elsevier Science, 1992.
11. Lauwers, J. C., Lantz, K. A., 'Collaboration awareness in support of collaboration transparency: Requirements for the next generation of shared window systems', in *Proceedings of CHI '90*, April 1-5, Seattle, Washington, ACM, 1990, pp 303-311.
12. Lantz, K. A., 'An experiment in integrated multimedia conferencing', in *Proceedings of CSCW '86*, Austin, Texas, December 1986.
13. Ahuja, S. R., Ensor, J. R., Horn, D. N., 'The Rapport Multimedia Conferencing system', in *Proceedings of the Conference on Office Information Systems* (COIS88), Allen R. B. (ed.), March 23-25, Palo Alto, Ca., 1988.
14. Gust, P., 'Shared X: X in a distributed group work environment', *presented at the 2nd Annual X conference*, MIT, Boston, January 1988.
15. Crowley, T., Milazzo, P., Baker, E., Forsdick H., Tomlinson R., 'MMConf: An infrastructure for building shared multimedia applications', in *Proceedings of CSCW '90*, October 7-10, Los Angeles, Ca., ACM, 1990, pp 329-342.
16. Greenberg, S., Bohnet, R., 'GroupSketch: A multi-user sketchpad for geographically-distributed small groups', in *Proceedings of Graphics Interface*, June 5-7, Calgary, Alberta, 1991.
17. Ellis, C., Gibbs, S. J., Rein, G., 'Design and use of a group editor', Technical report STP-263-88, MCC, September 1988.
18. Took, R., 'Surface Interaction: A paradigm and model for separating application and interface', in *Proceedings of CHI '90*, April 1-5, Seattle, Washington, ACM, 1990, pp 35-42.
19. Larson, J. A., 'A Visual Approach to Browsing in a Database Environment', *IEEE Computer*, 19(6), June 1986, pp 62-70.

Architecture of the Artifact-Based Collaboration System Matrix

K. Jeffay, J.K. Lin, J. Menges, F.D. Smith, J.B. Smith

University of North Carolina at Chapel Hill
Department of Computer Science
Chapel Hill, NC, USA 27599-3175
(919) 962-1700 {*jeffay,linjk,menges,smithfd,jbs*}*@cs.unc.edu*

ABSTRACT The UNC Collaboratory project is concerned with both the process of collaboration and with computer systems to support that process. Here, we describe a component of the Artifact-Based Collaboration (*ABC*) system, called the *Matrix*, that provides an infrastructure in which existing single-user applications can be incorporated with few, if any, changes and used collaboratively. We take the position that what is needed is not new tools but better infrastructure for using familiar single-user tools collectively. The paper discusses the Matrix architecture, a Virtual Screen component, and generic functions that provide conferencing, hyperlinking, and recording of users' actions for all applications.

INTRODUCTION AND MOTIVATION

Our research is concerned with both the process of collaboration and with computer systems to support that process. We focus on shared intellectual activity as required, for example, in system design and other similar tasks, in which groups of scientific and technical professionals work together to build a large, complex structures of ideas. Further, we assume that these groups are geographically distributed, interact with one-another using communications networks, and that they normally produce some form of tangible *artifact* as the goal of their work.

Our project is attempting to address the fundamental issues of collaboration in a comprehensive way. First, we are a multidisciplinary group including cognitive psychologists, anthropologists, and computer scientists that is conducting studies of collaborating groups and developing theories of the collaborative process. A study of four software development groups is described in [6]; a discussion of Collective Intelligence as the basis for a process model of collaboration is presented in [12]. Second, we are building a collaboration-support system called the Artifact-Based Collaboration (*ABC*) system that supports both *asynchronous* work — individuals working alone on different parts of a project — and *synchronous* work — people, perhaps geographically distributed, working together on the same part of the artifact at the same time through high-speed communications networks. An overview of the *ABC* system appears in [13].

This work supported in parts by the National Science Foundation (Grant # IRI-9015443), the IBM Corporation, and the Digital Equipment Corporation.

Permission to copy without fee all or part of this material is granted provided that the copies are not made or distributed for direct commercial advantage, the ACM copyright notice and the title of the publication and its date appear, and notice is given that copying is by permission of the Association for Computing Machinery. To copy otherwise, or to republish, requires a fee and/or specific permission.

© 1992 ACM 0-89791-543-7/92/0010/0195...$1.50

We have taken as our driving problem the design of software systems. Brooks has described the essence of software design as follows:

> The essence of a software entity is a construct of interlocking concepts: data sets, relationships among data items, algorithms, and invocations of functions. The essence is abstract in that such a conceptual construct is the same under many different representations. It is nonetheless highly precise and richly detailed. I believe the hard part of building software to be the specification, design, and testing of this conceptual construct, not the labor of representing it and testing the fidelity of the representation. [2]

We agree with Brooks but go further to suggest that the problem of building large "conceptual constructs" is *fundamental* not just for software design, but for all large collaborative projects. For software systems, this construct typically consists of concept papers, architecture documents, requirements, specifications, programs, diagrams, user documentation, and maintenance manuals, as well as various administrative documents. Similar sets of materials are produced by other types of collaboration, such as designing aircraft, planning projects, or defining military doctrine. Some materials represent the final goal of the project; others assist the development process. However, if the work of the group is to have integrity, then this entire conceptual construct — including instrumental as well as target products — must be consistent, coherent, and correct. To emphasize this requirement, we consider the entire construct to be a single artifact that is developed and maintained as a whole.

For organizing the group's shared artifact, we have adopted a hypermedia data model; its hyperlinking capabilities allow users to explicitly denote dependencies within the artifact so that when changes are made in one place, users (or automated processes) can follow these links to other places to verify or modify those parts of the artifact, accordingly. We have also developed a small group of browsers that allow users to navigate through the artifact, to visualize its structure, and to reorganize it; these tools help users comprehend the artifact and provide a sense of context.

Our system design is based on our hypothesis that what is most needed is not new tools for collaboration, but better infrastructure to support collaborative use of existing tools. We believe our system must allow users to incorporate, with minimal effort, familiar single-user applications of their choice, such as editors, drawing tools, spreadsheets, CAD/CAM programs, *etc.* Users should be able to use for group-related work — in both asynchronous and synchronous modes — the same computer tools they are accustomed to using as individuals. Consequently, the emphasis in the rest of this discussion is devoted to describing an architecture in which much of the large base of existing software can be incorporated for collaborative use.

This approach is practical only if existing single-user applications can be incorporated with few, if any, modifications to those programs. To meet this requirement, we are developing a set of generic functions that can be attached to existing applications. These functions include *hyperlinking* between *anchored* points within different applications; a shared-workspace *conferencing* function that can be invoked from any application or group of applications; and tools for *recording* and *recreating* the behaviors of group members for studying the collaboration process from a human point of view.

The architecture of the *ABC* system can be divided into three large components, as shown in Figure 1. A Distributed Graph Storage System (DGS) [11], provides the hypermedia data model implemented in a distributed architecture. A set of browsers and an extensible set of existing application programs provide tools for the user. A third component, shown in the middle of the figure, launches browsers and applications, joins them to the storage system and to one-another, and provides a set of generic collaboration functions that apply to all tools. We call this component the *ABC* System *Matrix* — in the geological sense of a surrounding context in which objects are embedded; in this case, the objects are browsers and applications.

In following discussion, we will focus on the architecture of this encompassing matrix. Section 2 describes the user's mental model of the system. Section 3 provides an overview of the architecture. After that, individual components are described that support generic collaboration functions. Section 4 describes the Generic Function Manager. Section 5 describes a conferencing facility available to all applications within the system. Section 6 describes a general hyperlinking and anchoring component. Section 7 relates this work to other systems and other research. Section 8 provides a summary and discusses our future plans.

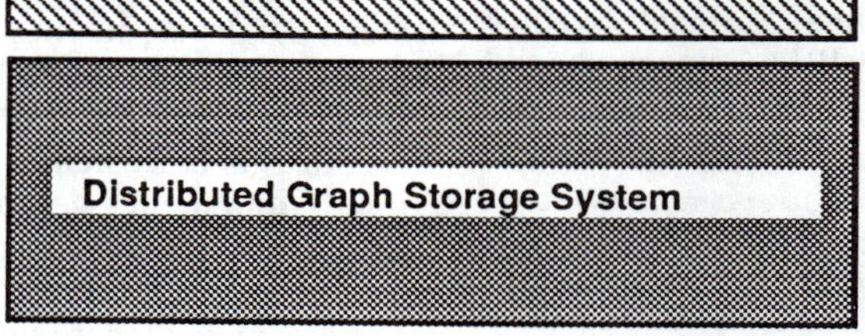

Figure 1. ABC system components.

USER'S MENTAL MODEL

Here we describe the visual appearance of the *ABC* system and the user's mental model of it. Much of what gives *ABC* its particular character as a system derives from its hypermedia data model, supported by the underlying DGS and presented to the user through a set of browsers. Consequently, we begin the discussion with the data model and then discuss other components the user sees and works with.

Data Model. The basic model for the artifact is a collection of separate *graphs*, each consisting of a set of nodes and a set of links that denote structural relationships between nodes. A node's content can consist of a block of data — such as a conventional file — or it may be another graph. By storing individual graphs as the content of nodes, graphs can be composed to form a structure that can be viewed both as a single large, integrated artifact but also as separate objects that permit multiple users to work concurrently. *ABC* supports several different graph types, including trees, lists, general directed graphs, etc. Finally, a special type of link, called a hyperlink, is provided to define semantic relationships that would violate the integrity of a graph type if they were denoted by structural links (*e.g.*, a relationship between siblings in a tree) and to join separate graph structures.

Virtual Screen Environment. The *ABC* system runs within the X Window System environment under the UNIX operating system. Because the underlying *ABC* storage system is based on a hypermedia model instead of a conventional file system model, it is important to signal the user that a given window or application is referencing the *ABC* storage system versus the UNIX file system. We elected to do this by providing a separate contiguous area within the overall X display for the *ABC* system and its associated browsers and applications rather than marking individual *ABC* windows and permitting them to be intermingled with conventional X windows. Thus, users have a sense of "entering" and "leaving" the *ABC* environment, which they do simply by moving the mouse from one area of the screen to another. We call this environment a Virtual

Screen because it resembles the entire screen in appearance; it can contain multiple windows within its borders, as shown in Figure 2; and users may use within it any X window manager they choose, including one that is different from that for the rest of the screen [9].

Browsers and Applications. Within the *ABC* virtual screen, individual tools display output as X windows. A collection of some half-dozen browsers written by our project are provided for developing, navigating, and accessing individual graph structures within the artifact. A set of familiar applications, not written by our project, are provided for creating and editing conventional forms of data, such as text, diagrams, spreadsheets, etc., stored as node content in the DGS. This set of applications is open-ended. Thus, users may bring into the *ABC* environment familiar tools of their choice that can run without modification so long as hyperlink anchoring capabilities (explained in a later section) are not required. If anchoring is needed, the application program must be modified; however, we have tried to minimize these changes by providing a generic anchor-support toolkit. Both browsers and applications are opened on the content of nodes, and the graph or data object they produce is viewed by the user as being stored "inside" the node.

Generic Function Management. Across each *ABC* window is a menu bar that provides access to an additional set of functions common to all *ABC* browsers and applications. The functions accessed through this bar, which we call a Generic Function Manager, include starting, stopping, and anchoring hyperlinks, and sharing an application or browser in a conference with other users. The same underlying architecture that supports generic functions also supports the tracking and replay functions mentioned above.

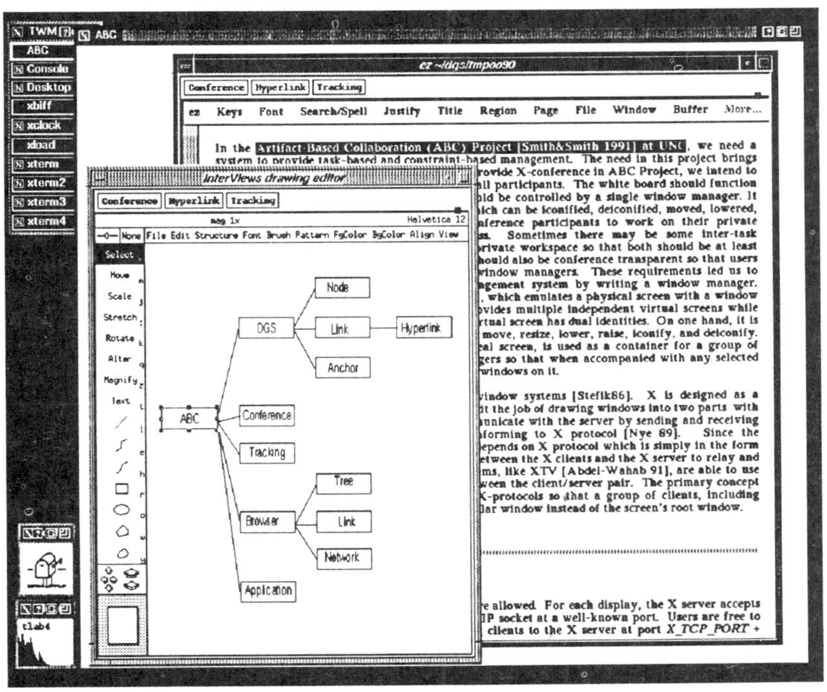

Figure 2. An ABC Virtual Screen and Generic Function Manager.

ARCHITECTURAL OVERVIEW

The design of the *ABC* system has been driven by two general principles. The first is our desire to support synchronous collaboration over networked computer systems. This lead to our adoption of the X Window System as the software platform for the *ABC* system. Standardizing on X also allows us to maximize the number of hardware and software platforms that can support the *ABC* environment (given the constraints of a moderate sized university research project). Although all of our development efforts to date have taken place on UNIX workstations, the *ABC* system could, in principle, run on any computer that supports X. For example, we have demonstrated the conferencing portion of the *ABC* system (the shared windows) between an Apple Macintosh and a UNIX workstation.

The second principle is the desire to integrate as many existing applications (*e.g.*, editors, drawing programs, text processing utilities) as possible into the *ABC* system. This allows users to retain significant portions of their traditional working environment while using the *ABC* system. There are two levels of integration within the *ABC* system. At a minimum, any X application can be launched and used within the *ABC* system. By virtue of executing within the *ABC* system, such an application is automatically capable of being conferenced and having user interactions recorded for later study. Moreover, one can create and follow node-level hyperlinks from or to unmodified applications. In this manner, the *ABC* system adds powerful collaboration functions to existing single-user applications. Existing applications that operate on byte streams (*e.g.*, UNIX files) can also be used to create and modify the contents of nodes in the DGS. (Any temporary or auxiliary files needed by an application reside outside the DGS.) A second data integration function, allowing the contents of UNIX files to be imported into a DGS object, is also provided. X cut/copy/paste functions can also be used to move data into and out of applications.

The second level of integration is the integration of anchoring functions (*e.g.*, *create anchor, delete anchor*, *etc.*) into existing applications. This requires modification and recompilation of the application. The extent of the modifications is a function of the complexity of the application. Hyperlinking and anchoring are discussed in more detail below.

Figure 3 shows the basic structure of the *ABC* System Matrix. It can be thought of as a pipeline of processes that filter streams of X Window System protocol data. At the highest level, the Matrix itself exports an X server interface to applications (*e.g.*, browsers, editors, *etc.*) and an X client interface to an X server. Therefore the Matrix can be viewed as an X "pseudo-server." All applications manipulate their visual interface indirectly through the Matrix. Similarly, the X server interacts with user applications indirectly through the Matrix. If applications are "*ABC* system aware," such as the browsers we have constructed, they also interact with the graph server. For example, screen management for the *ABC* system, that is, the placement of windows within the larger, encompassing, *ABC* system window is the responsibility of the Virtual Screen component of the Matrix described in Section 2. The Virtual Screen is an X protocol filter, *i.e.*, it intercepts and modifies X protocol data sent between an X client used in the *ABC* system and an X server. The modifications re-parent clients to the virtual screen instead of the root window of the workstation console. (The Virtual Screen is simply a window as far as the X server is concerned.) As is the case with all our protocol filters, the Virtual Screen filter modifies very few of the messages (typically less than 10%) that are sent between an application and an X server.

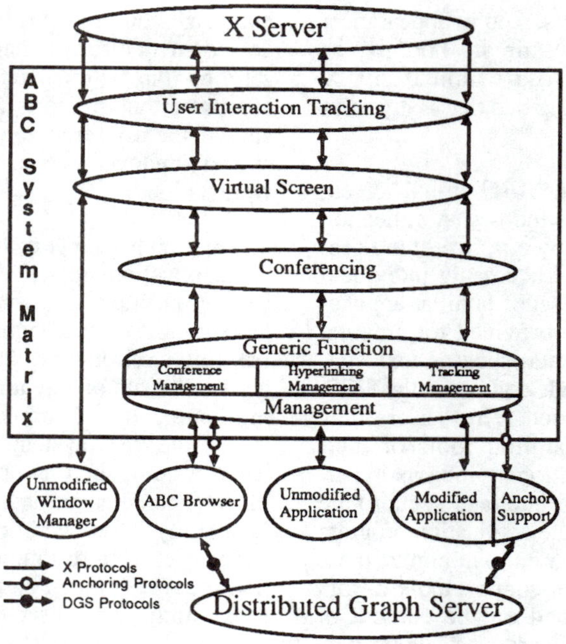

Figure 3. Architecture of the *ABC* System Matrix.

Starting at a user application and working towards an X server, an application's X protocol data stream is first processed by the *ABC Generic Function Manager* (GFM). This is a program that the user interacts with to create conferences, or to create or manipulate hyperlinks. The output from the GFM (a valid X client protocol stream) is processed by a second protocol filter that implements conferencing. A third filter implements the user interaction protocol recording. A final filter is the Virtual Screen. The filters that implement the conferencing and screen management are described in greater detail in separate sections below. The filter that implements user interaction protocol recording is similar to the conferencing filter. The implementation of anchored hyperlinks is distributed between individual user level applications and the GFM. This is also discussed below.

GENERIC COLLABORATION FUNCTION MANAGEMENT

Any application that is used within the *ABC* environment (*i.e.*, within a Virtual Screen) is transparently endowed with conferencing, hyperlinking, and user interaction recording functions. By modifying applications, anchoring function can also be added. These functions are referred to as *generic collaboration functions*. These functions are invoked and controlled via an entity called the *Generic Function Manager* (GFM). To the user, the GFM appears as a title bar that resides between each top level window of an application and the associated window manager's title bar as shown in Figure 2. Our title bar is created and managed by the GFM, in the same way that the window manager's title bar is created and managed by the window manager. The GFM "re-parents" the application's window so that the application window and the generic function buttons appear to the user as a single coherent window. The GFM maintains one connection (*e.g.*, one socket) for each application displayed within the virtual screen. Indeed, for each application, the X server displaying the Virtual Screen windows considers the GFM/application pair as a single X client with multiple subwindows (the GFM title bar and the application window(s)). The appearance and interaction of the GFM title bar is customizable on a per-user basis. That is, how the user invokes various operations and how feedback is displayed are not prescribed, but can be defined in a GFM initialization file. We do, however, provide reasonable defaults. The GFM is capable of managing buttons, pop-up and pull-down menus, dialogue boxes, miniature icons, *etc.* The GFM provides a framework for extending the an application's capabilities without disturbing its user interface.

CONFERENCING

Conferencing refers to the use of an application by multiple users simultaneously. In the Matrix, conferencing is implemented by (1) distributing the visual interface of an application to one or more remote workstations thereby allowing remote users to view the interactions of other users with the applications, and (2) providing input paths from each conferee back to the application so that any participant in the conference may interact with the application. Since all applications we currently use within the *ABC* system are single user applications, it is not possible in general to allow more than one user to interact with a conferenced application at any one time. The Matrix supports a simple protocol for negotiating access to a conferenced application. The basic paradigm of group input to a conferenced application is that of "passing the keyboard." The model is one of cooperative collaboration wherein users might gather in an office and take turns interacting with an application by passing the keyboard among themselves. While this paradigm is certainly not a panacea for group conferencing, it is necessitated by our desire to work with existing single user applications. The conferencing subsystem requires no modifications to applications. The conferencing subsystem is based on our earlier work on a stand-alone conferencing system [1, 3].

One X protocol filter in the Matrix is dedicated to implementing conferencing. The filter records every message an application sends to an X server that effects the state of the

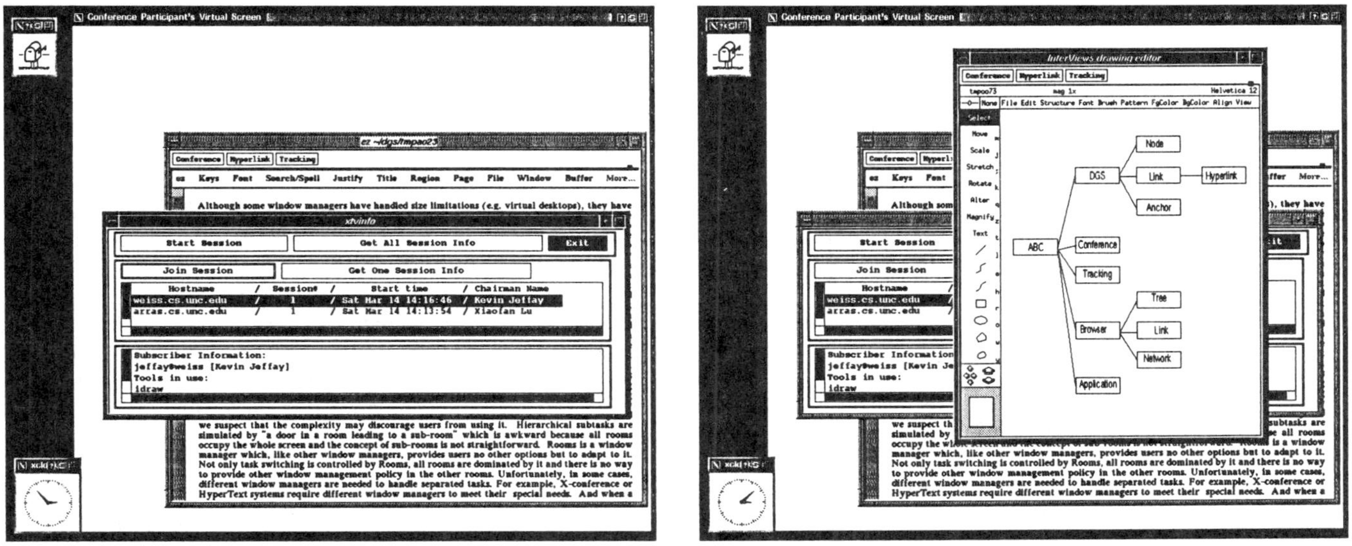

The idraw window in Figure 2 has been placed into a conference. A remote user (left) joins the conference by contacting an *ABC* conference server via a Matrix-provided conference management application and selecting a conference from a menu of on-going conferences. An exact copy of each window of each application in the conference then appears on the remote user's virtual screen (right).

Figure 4. An example of joining a conference.

internal data structures the server maintains for the application's visual interface. (In more technical X terms, the filter records all X resources created by the application.) When an application is used in non-conferenced mode (the common case), the conferencing protocol filter passively records salient X information that is later used to create a copy of the application's visual interface on a remote machine.

A conference is initiated when a user presses the conference button on the GFM menu bar for an application. The GFM then contacts a global conference server and registers the user's name, unique machine identifier (*e.g.*, its internet address), and the name of the application in the conference. The user can then invite other users to act as participants in the conference by notifying them of the existence of this conference. Participants join the conference as shown in Figure 4. In the present system there are no access control mechanisms for joining conferences. The initiator of a conference may, however, eject a participant from a conference at any time.

When a remote participant joins a conference, the remote participant's conference management application creates a process on the participant's workstation that acts as a surrogate for the conferenced application as shown in Figure 5. The surrogate application is responsible for maintaining a visual image of the conferenced application on the participant's display that is consistent with the view on the conference originator's workstation. When an application is placed in a conference, it is actually conferenced as an GFM/application pair. This is in keeping with our "passing the keyboard" paradigm of interaction. By including the GFM in the conference, remote participants can create, for example, hyperlinks to and from data object viewed in conferenced applications. A network connection is established between the remote surrogate process and the conference originator's protocol filter and all X messages sent by the application are distributed to all surrogate processes. In addition, the original X filter and the surrogate process speak a Matrix conference control protocol that negotiates access to the input path back to the application from remote users.

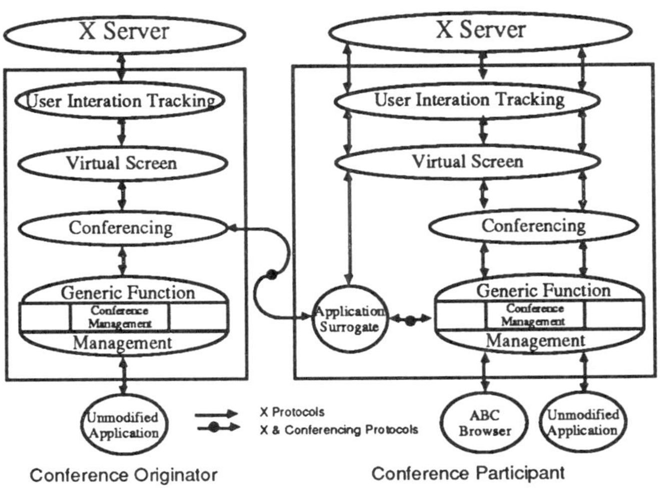

Figure 5. Conference architecture.

Two paradigms of conferences are supported in the *ABC* system. The first is conferencing of individual applications (described above). The second is conferencing of Virtual Screens. The latter is useful for providing a coherent visual context for conferences that involve multiple applications. Conferences in the *ABC* system are "lightweight" in the sense that they can be started at any time. For example, if a user is editing a document and would like to review a section with a colleague, she could initiate a conference around her current editing session, independent of how long she had been using the application in non-conference mode. When the colleague joins the conference, a window will appear on their workstation that is identical to that of the initial user's.

In order for conferences to be effective, higher bandwidth communication media than simple "talk" windows are required. We are interested in providing integrated digital voice and video communication links to the workstation and are pursuing this in a parallel research effort [7]. For high-bandwidth communication in the present system we use an in-house broadband CATV system.

HYPERLINKING AND ANCHORING

One of our major goals is to provide a mechanism for adding anchored hyperlink capabilities to existing X applications. A hyperlink in the *ABC* system is a directed reference from a node in one graph to a node in the same or another graph. Either the source or the destination endpoint (or both) of a hyperlink may be unanchored (in which case the endpoint refers to a node as a whole) or anchored (in which case it refers to some portion of the content of a node). For example, suppose $node_1$ is a text document and $node_2$ is a drawing. If a hyperlink relates a paragraph in $node_1$ to the entire drawing represented by $node_2$, the source of that hyperlink is anchored to the paragraph, and the destination is unanchored [11]. Examples of hyperlinks and anchors are presented in Figure 6.

The implementation of anchors for hyperlinks requires application source code modifications. We wish to minimize this effort by keeping per-application code changes small and reducing the need to understand the implementation of each application in detail. We also want to make it possible to invoke hyperlink operations without changing the user interfaces of existing applications and window managers (*e.g.*, key and mouse bindings). This minimizes interference with the user's established work habits. Moreover it enables hyperlink functions to be invoked similarly for all applications. In order to make anchors fit the semantics of each application, we do not prescribe how any particular application should define or display anchors, or how the user should specify them.

Hyperlinking operations are invoked via buttons on the GFM titlebar. Unlike conferencing, hyperlinking functions require interactions between the user application (the GFM client) and the GFM. For example, for the *Create Hyperlink* function the GFM should just notify the client that the *Create Hyperlink* operation was invoked and wait for feedback on the success or failure of the operation; it then displays the feedback as the user-defined means of invoking the function and user-defined feedback specifications dictate. Other operations, *e.g.*, *Follow Hyperlink*, might require the GFM to ask the client for information to display in a menu or dialogue box; in this case a list of hyperlinks associated with the currently selected anchor. The user would then select one of the links and the GFM would tell the client which was selected and wait for feedback as before. A hyperlinking example is illustrated in Figure 7.

Most X-based applications already have some means of selecting and highlighting items to be operated upon; most likely these same items are appropriate anchors for the data manipulated by the application. In this case we do not need a new mechanism for specifying anchors; we only need to add new operations on selected data (*e.g.*, *Create Anchor*, *Follow Hyperlink*, *Modify Hyperlink*). These operations are invoked via the GFM as described above. It is the application's responsibility to maintain the values of anchors created by the user. Unfortunately, existing mechanisms for selecting items typically assume that such selections are not persistent; that is, there is only one selection and it can be discarded when the data is edited or the application exited. Anchors, however, must be persistent. Their values must remain constant (or be modified in intuitively appropriate ways) when the data is edited, and they must be maintained between application invocations. This is the area in which the application implementation must be understood in the

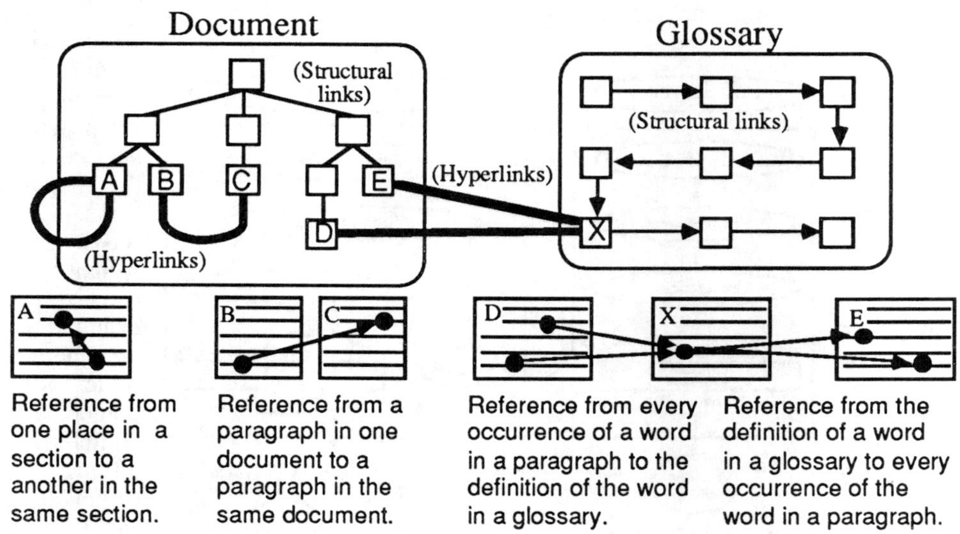

Figure 6. Examples of anchored hyperlinks in and between graphs.

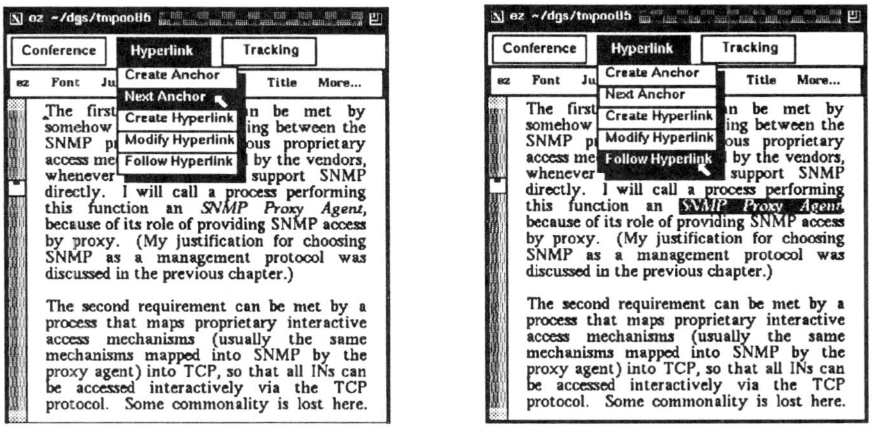

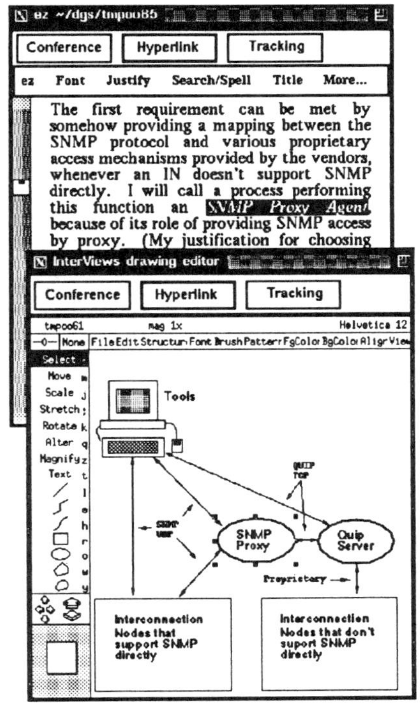

In step one (left), the user is requesting via the GFM title bar that the next anchor in the document be highlighted. The GFM forwards the request to the (modified) *ez* editor, which inverts the text of the next anchor ("SNMP Proxy Agent"). In step two (center) the user requests that the hyperlink associated with the selected anchor be followed. The GFM forwards this request to the *ez* editor which queries the graph server to determine the node and anchor value at the other end of the hyperlink. The GFM then launches the *idraw* editor on the content of this node and asks the modified *idraw* application to highlight the relevant anchor (right). Note that *idraw* uses its own highlighting mechanism; the *idraw* anchor (the "SNMP Proxy" oval) is surrounded by small square "handles."

Figure 7. An example of following a hyperlink.

most detail and where the most code changes must be made. One must either modify the application's internal data structures to store anchor values, or maintain an anchor table separate from the application's internal data structures and modify all editing operations so that they update this table appropriately.

Creating and modifying hyperlinks requires communication between multiple applications. The entity performing the hyperlink operation must gather information as to which nodes and anchors are to be the endpoints of the hyperlink. We use the X selection mechanism to effect this communication. We define five selections: *SourceAnchor*, *SourceNode*, *HyperlinkID*, *DestNode*, and *DestAnchor* for hyperlink operations. Ownership of these selections is obtained by applications when the user performs the appropriate actions. For example, to create a hyperlink, the user would put application *A* in source mode, create or select an anchor (which grabs the *SourceAnchor* and *SourceNode* selections), put application *B* in destination mode, create or select an anchor (which grabs the *DestNode* and *DestAnchor* selections), and invoke *CreateHyperlink*. The entity creating the hyperlink would request these four selections and send the *CreateHyperlink* request to the graph server. The *HyperlinkID* selection is then grabbed by the entity creating the hyperlink for use in subsequent *ModifyHyperlink* operations. Splitting Anchor selections from Node selections simplifies the creation of unanchored hyperlinks and adding or deleting anchors to or from existing hyperlinks.

In summary, existing applications must be modified to maintain anchors, communicate with the GFM to provide a user interface to new operations, communicate with the graph server to effect hyperlink operations, and communicate with other X clients via hyperlink X selections. With the exception of anchor maintenance, these code modifications can be made by simply inserting calls to library routines at the appropriate places. We also expect to be able to facilitate anchor maintenance by providing a set of library routines to perform common functions.

RELATED WORK

The collaboration-support environment based on Suite [5] focuses on flexible methods for coupling users' views of shared objects. Where most shared-workspace systems strictly replicate an application's windows for all users, the Suite architecture allows each view to be tailored in several dimensions. Views may be customized to specify which values in shared windows are coupled (change when the underlying object changes), how "committed" a value must be before it is used to update a view, when and in which views changes are reflected, how formatting may differ among views, and which window elements (*e.g.*, scrollbars, menus) are coupled. Applications (*e.g.* text or line drawing editors) must be written as multi-user programs using the Suite environment.

Rendezvous [10] is another framework specifically designed for creating multi-user programs. A rule and constraint system provided in an underlying UIMS is used to control three major aspects of sharing: how underlying objects are shared, how views of objects are shared, and how input (update) access to objects is shared. These appear to be similar in spirit to Suite facilities (but perhaps less flexible). Rendezvous also provides a session (conference) manager for dynamic creation, joining, and leaving a multi-user application. Another framework for creating shared multi-user applications is MMConf [4]. MMConf focuses on conferencing issues such as conference management, input access (floor control), and distribution of shared data files. No functions for tailoring views are provided. "Conference-aware" applications are created using the MMConf toolkit for these functions.

On the surface, ConversationBuilder [8] has greater similarity to *ABC* — it supports artifacts with hypertext storage and browsers, can accommodate conventional editors such as Epoch and idraw, and does tracking of user interactions. It represents, however, a fundamentally different approach to collaboration support. ConversationBuilder is best understood as a framework for creating a coordination system using protocols based on speech/act theories. Protocols are templates that define roadmaps for various interactions among group members. For example, process protocols coordinate activities and checkpoints in a goal-oriented process such as joint paper writing; discussion protocols can be invoked to resolve questions or issues; and transient protocols can be used for simple ad hoc coordination.

Suite, Rendezvous, and ConversationBuilder all take a strong role in structuring the user's working environment, either by view tailoring and control over sharing, or by activity coordination. In contrast, *ABC* takes a "hands off" approach; it provides a suite of tools useful in both synchronous and asynchronous activities by group members but takes no direct role in tailoring or coordinating user interactions. Unlike MMConf, Suite, and Rendezvous, the only toolkit needed in *ABC* is for extending conventional applications to maintain anchors for hyperlinks.

SUMMARY

The UNC Collaboratory Project is concerned with both the process of collaboration and with computer systems to support that process. Because so many of the problems associated with collaboration derive from the fundamental problem of constructing a coherent, integrated whole from a collection of individual contributions, we have attempted to build a comprehensive system that supports equally collective, synchronous work and individual, asynchronous work. In this discussion, we emphasized the second issue by focusing on the *ABC* System Matrix that provides an infrastructure in which an extensible set of browsers and existing single-user applications can be incorporated. We have purposely and with considerable effort taken a minimalist approach to make the system approachable. We were able to do this by capitalizing on the generality of the X Windows System architecture and by developing a set of generic functions for conferencing, hyperlinking, and tracking, that gracefully extend familiar application programs.

Our future agenda includes incorporating voice and, perhaps, video into the workstation, extensions to the set of generic functions, and increasing performance and robustness to support actual use studies.

REFERENCES

1. Abdel-Wahab, H. M. and Feit, M. A. XTV: A framework for sharing X Window clients in remote synchronous collaboration. In *Proceedings, IEEE Conference on Communications Software: Communications for Distributed Applications & Systems*, Chapel Hill, NC, April, 1991, pp. 159-167.
2. Brooks, F. P., Jr. No silver bullet: Essence and accidents of software engineering. *IEEE Computer*, 20, 4 (April 1991), 10-19.
3. Chung, G., Jeffay, K., and Abdel-Wahab, H. Dynamic Participation in a Computer-based Conferencing System. *Computer Communications* (to appear).
4. Crowley, T., P. Milazzo, E. Baker, H. Forsdick, and R. Tomlinson. MMConf: An Infrastructure for Building Shared Multimedia Applications. In *Proceedings ACM CSCW'90 Conference*, October 1990, pp. 329-342.
5. Dewan, P. and R. Choudhary. Flexible Interface Coupling in a Collaborative System. In *Proceedings ACM CHI'91*, New Orleans, LA, April 1991, pp. 41-48.
6. Holland, D., Reeves, J. R., and Larme, A The construction of intellectual work by programmers. Dept. of Computer Science Tech. Report 92-013 (March 1992), Univ. of North Carolina, Chapel Hill, NC, 27599.
7. Jeffay, K., Stone, D.L., and Smith, F.D. Kernel Support for Live Digital Audio and Video. *Computer Communications*, 16, 6 (July 1992), pp. 388-395.
8. Kaplan, S.M., A.M. Carroll, and K.J. MacGregor. Supporting Collaborative Processes with ConversationBuilder, *Proceedings ACM Conference on Organizational Computing Systems*, Atlanta GA, November 1991, pp. 69-79.
9. Lin, J.K. Virtual Screen: A Framework for Task Management, *The X Resource*, 1, 1 (Winter 1992), pp. 191-198.
10. Patterson, J.F., R.D. Hill, S.L. Rohall, and W.S. Meeks. Rendezvous: An Architecture for Synchronous Multi-User Applications, *Proceedings ACM CSCW'90 Conference*, October 1990, pp. 317-328.
11. Shackelford, D. E., Smith, J. B., and Smith, F. D. *A Distributed Graph Storage System for Artifacts in Collaboration.* Department of Computer Science Tech. Report 92-012 (March 1992), Univ. of North Carolina, Chapel Hill, NC, 27599.
12. Smith, J. B. *Collective Intelligence in Computer-Based Collaboration: An Introduction.* Dept. of Computer Science Tech. Report 92-011 (March 1992), Univ. of North Carolina, Chapel Hill, NC, 27599.
13. Smith, J.B., and Smith, F. D. ABC: A Hypermedia System for Artifact-Based Collaboration. *Proceedings Hypertext '91*, San Antonio, TX, December 1991, pp. 179-192.

System Support for Computer Mediated Multimedia Collaborations

Harrick M. Vin
P. Venkat Rangan

Multimedia Laboratory
Department of Computer Science and Engineering
University of California at San Diego
La Jolla, CA 92093-0114
E-mails: vin@cs.ucsd.edu, venkat@cs.ucsd.edu; Phone: (619) 534-5419

Mon-Song Chen

IBM T. J. Watson Research Center
P. O. Box 704
Yorktown Heights, NY 10598, USA
E-mail: monsong@watson.ibm.com, Phone: (914) 784-7209

ABSTRACT

Future advances in networking and storage will enable a wide spectrum of computer mediated structured collaborations among individuals. In this paper, we present a model that can capture diverse types of structured collaborations. The model combines both efficiency and power via a hierarchy of three abstractions, at the lowest level of which are *streams* for media communication modulated by access rights of participants within collaborations. The higher two levels of abstractions are *sessions*, which represent collections of semantically related media streams, and *conferences*, which represent temporally related sequences of sessions. Using these abstractions, the model supports unification of both synchronous and asynchronous collaborations, sophisticated access control, and intra-group and inter-group collaborations, yielding a powerful set of building blocks for constructing multimedia applications and a rich environment for carrying out structured multimedia collaborations.

KEYWORDS

Multimedia collaboration management, synchronous and asynchronous collaborations

Permission to copy without fee all or part of this material is granted provided that the copies are not made or distributed for direct commercial advantage, the ACM copyright notice and the title of the publication and its date appear, and notice is given that copying is by permission of the Association for Computing Machinery. To copy otherwise, or to republish, requires a fee and/or specific permission.

© 1992 ACM 0-89791-543-7/92/0010/0203...$1.50

MOTIVATION

Future advances in networking and storage will enable a wide spectrum of computer mediated structured collaborations among individuals, ranging from simple meetings and conferences to classrooms and examinations, and from corporate negotiations, work flow tasks, and team design endeavors to courtroom hearings, each with its own unique set of requirements for media communication. The system support necessary for supporting the establishment of such a wide range of collaborative activities, and subsequently managing and controlling their progress, is the subject matter of this paper.

Collaborations involve exchange of media information among all their participants, with media exchange being either synchronous (as in a telephone conversation), or asynchronous (as in electronic mail). Structured collaborations, whether synchronous or asynchronous, usually involve diverse modes of participation by their various participants. For instance, a session at a convention usually involves a sequence of presentations by its speakers and questions posed by its attendees, each of which must be permitted by its chairperson. A classroom is similar to a conference session except that it has only one speaker, who also serves as the chairperson. An examination, on the other hand, involves a proctor and examinees, with communication restricted to that between the proctor and examinees, but absolutely no communication among examinees themselves. Negotiations among corporate groups may involve both intra-group and inter-group communication, which may need to be separated for purposes of confidentiality. If such a wide range of collaborative activities are to be supported using computer systems, a common software framework with a sufficiently rich semantic expressibility is essential.

In this paper, we present a model that can capture diverse types of structured collaborative activities and develop software paradigms for carrying out such activities in distributed multimedia systems. The model combines both efficiency and power via a hierarchy of three abstractions, at the lowest level of which are *streams* for media communication modulated by access rights of participants within collaborations. The higher two levels of abstractions are *sessions*, which represent collections of semantically related media streams, and *conferences*, which represent temporally related sequences of sessions. Using these abstractions, the model supports unification of both synchronous and asynchronous collaborations, sophisticated access control, and intra-group and inter-group collaborations, yielding a powerful set of building blocks for constructing multimedia applications and a rich environment for carrying out structured multimedia interactions. A prototype collaboration management system based on this model is being implemented at the UCSD Multimedia Laboratory.

REQUIREMENTS FOR MANAGING MULTIMEDIA COLLABORATIONS

The simplest of collaborations involve exchange of media information among all their participants, with media exchange being either synchronous or asynchronous. Whereas synchronous collaborations involve contemporaneous exchange of media information, asynchronous collaborations are characterized by recipients' discretionary delays after transmission by senders. During such intervening delays, the media information in transit may have to be managed by servers (such as storage and mail servers). Traditionally, collaborations have been classified into these two categories, and different paradigms have been used by the system to manage them, thereby necessitating separate programming as well as user interfaces for their management. Unification of both synchronous and asynchronous collaborations into a single paradigm permits co-existence of both types of collaborations within a single multimedia application, and even the same collaboration may sometimes be synchronous and at other times asynchronous, shuttling from one to another depending on users' participation schedules.

Collaborations, whether synchronous or asynchronous, can be established by setting up media communication channels among its participants. Establishing a structured collaboration requires mechanisms for the initiator to specify the permitted modes of participation for each of the invitees, as well as for each of the invitees to express their desired mode of participation.

Controlling the progress of a collaboration requires mechanisms for changing the set of participants and their modes of participation dynamically, (either by the initiator or by a participant himself), a special case of which is floor control. Alterations of modes of participations may also need to be constrained depending on the collaboration semantics (e.g., in a courtroom hearing, witnesses cannot change their desired mode of participation after its initiation). A participant may be permitted to simultaneously participate in multiple collaborations (using same or different media). Furthermore, a collaboration may itself be an aggregation of other collaborations, since such a multi-level collaboration is a natural paradigm for expressing meetings between two or more sub-groups of users (e.g., corporate meetings in which managers together with their multi-level groups participate).

Thus, a system for managing structured multimedia collaborations should provide: (1) a model for unifying the representation of synchronous and asynchronous collaborations, (2) a high-level framework for specifying access rights that can characterize the semantics of structured collaborative environments, and (3) techniques for instantiating and managing the progress of collaborations.

MODELING MULTIMEDIA COLLABORATIONS

At the most basic level of multimedia collaborations is the need for transport of media information between participants. Media transport can be built upon either 1-to-1, or 1-to-n, or m-to-1, or m-to-n communication paradigms. However, the chosen paradigm will have to be implemented on the underlying network, and must, hence, be designed so as to make use of network services efficiently. Since most networks currently provide multicast services, the paradigm at this lowest level of our model is a communication channel from a sender to a set of receivers, which we will call as a *stream*. Each stream encapsulates the permitted access rights of both the sender and the receiver with respect to the media exchanged on the stream. In order to capture both synchronous and asynchronous collaborations, it is necessary to associate temporal attributes with each media stream. If the earliest and the latest times defining the transmission interval of a stream are denoted by: [ETT, LTT], and those of reception by: [ERT, LRT], a completely synchronous collaboration requires that ERT not exceed ETT. On the other hand, in a wholly asynchronous collaboration, ERT exceeds LTT. In fact, in all, there can be 13 possible temporal relationships [3, 6] (namely, *before*, *meets*, *during*, *overlaps*, *starts*, *ends*, and *equal* plus the inverse relations - except *equal*) between two intervals, and each of them results in a different kind of stream. Furthermore, since each stream may have multiple receivers, the same stream can be characterized differently relative to different receivers.

A stream, however, is a very rudimentary form of communication. A collaborative activity consists of a collection of media streams carrying media information from various senders to various receivers, who are all taking part in a collective endeavor during a common activity period. Such a collection of streams is referred to as a *session*, and is the paradigm at the next higher level above streams in our model.

Each session is characterized by a start time and an end time. We have chosen to regard the ERT of the streams constituting a session as the start of the active period of the session, and the LTT of those streams as the end of that period. In order to have a well-defined period of activity of a session, the ERTs of all its streams are constrained to be identical, and so should their LTTs. Thus, the ERT and LTT of a stream become attributes of the session containing the stream, and are presented as part of the specification of the session but not the stream.

Whereas the session provides a convenient abstraction for a collective activity in a common time span, a complete collaborative endeavor may, in general, involve several periods of collective activity, possibly with dependencies between the outcomes of some periods and causations of others. All such sessions, whose activity periods are temporally related, go to constitute a *conference*, which is the term denoting a complete collaborative endeavor. In our model, a conference is also the unit of resource allocation for information archival, and hence, the latest time, until which the information transmitted on any of the streams during any of the sessions constituting a conference is available for retrieval, is considered to be common to all the streams. Hence, LRT is identical for all streams of all sessions of a conference, and is, therefore, stored as part of specification of conferences, rather than as part of either streams or sessions. Based on these intuitive ideas, we present precise definitions of the stream, session, and conference abstractions in the following subsections:

Stream

A stream S is defined as a 4-tuple:

$$S = [\text{media, sender, receiverList, ETT}]$$

where media represents the communication media (such as, audio and video); sender denotes the permitted sender of media information; receiverList represents list of permitted receivers; and ETT defines the earliest time at which the transmission of media can be initiated. A user is a member of the receiverList if and only if he possesses access rights to receive media transmitted by sender. Media transmission from sender cannot be initiated before ETT. The association of ETT with streams provides an important feature: participants can pre-record the media information that they intend to be made available during a collaboration. An excellent illustration of the use of this feature is in the case of an examination, in which the instructor can pre-record the questions, but students can begin to access the questions only during examination. In cases where the transmission of media on a stream is initiated in advance of reception by its receivers, the media information in transit is stored by storage servers for subsequent retrieval by receivers.

Session

A session ψ is formally defined as a triple:

$$\psi = [\mathcal{S}, \text{ERT}, \text{LTT}]$$

where $\mathcal{S} = \{S_1, S_2, ..., S_n\}$ represent a set of media streams; and ERT and LTT denote the earliest receive time and the latest transmission time, respectively. Media streams can have existence only insofar as they are associated with a session, but never independently. The interval [ERT, LTT] defines the activation period of a session.

Since a stream encapsulates the permitted access rights of both sender and the receiver with respect to the media exchanged on the stream, a session denotes collective access rights of all participants with respect to all of its constituent streams. Furthermore, the inheritance of activation period by the streams constituting a session enables each participant to transmit and receive media information simultaneously, thereby yielding a well-defined period of activity. Thus, a session represents a semantic context, and aggregates all the media streams associated with the context.

Nested sessions can be captured by permitting the sender or any member of receiverList in a stream to be either an individual user or a session. If the sender is a session (rather than an individual participant), then the stream carries a mix of the media information transmitted by the session's participants intending to communicate with the stream's receivers. On the contrary, if a member of the receiverList is a session, then, effectively, each participant of the session has the rights to receive the media information transmitted by the stream's sender. Even though such streams containing sessions as participants can always be flattened into streams containing purely individual participants, the former approach provides a mechanism for separating intra-group and inter-group communication, and serves as a better (more natural and efficient) abstraction to model inter-group and inter-organization collaborations.

As an illustration, consider a meeting between two groups of managers belonging to two different organizations, for deciding upon policies for technical cooperation between their organizations. The nature of the meeting requires that members of each group discuss a policy among themselves before communicating it to the other group. Such a meeting can be modeled so as to consist of two sessions ψ_1 and ψ_2, each handling intra-group discussions within an organization. Each session serves as a sender of a stream for which the other session serves as a receiver, yielding two such streams, both of which constitute a nested session ψ, with participation in either ψ_1 or ψ_2 automatically implying participation in ψ.

In general, a session can be represented by a directed graph $G = (\mathcal{P}, \mathcal{E})$, where $\mathcal{P}$ represents the union of the sets of sender and receiverList for each of its constituent streams, and for each $P_i, P_j \in \mathcal{P}$, a directed edge $(P_i, P_j) \in \mathcal{E}$ if and only if user P_j has the access right to receive media information transmitted by P_i. Each node which has at least one outgoing edge is a *transmitter* in the session, and that which has at least one incoming edge is a *receiver*.

A special kind of a session, in which all the participants receive exactly the same set of media streams is referred to as a *confluence*. In a confluence, all the participants can be regarded as transmitting media information to the confluence as a whole, and all the receivers can be regarded as receiving mixed media stream from the confluence as a whole. Most commonly held sessions fall under this category. Confluences provide an excellent opportunity for optimizing network bandwidth usage. This is because, in a confluence, rather than transmitting individual media streams from senders to receivers, media streams transmitted by all the senders can be mixed together and broadcast to all the receivers on the network [7]. Given a graph representing a session, a sub-graph within the graph can be identified as representing a confluence if and only if the degree of incoming edges at each receiver is exactly equal to the number of transmitters in the sub-graph. This principle can be used to automatically detect confluences within a session, and optimize network bandwidth usage. This is illustrated in Figure 1, which represents an inter-organizational meeting session through mediators (namely, M_1 and M_2). Members of each organization (namely, $\{P_1, P_2, P_3\}$ and $\{P_4, P_5, P_6\}$) have closed-door discussions amongst themselves, and then communicate the consolidated views of their organization to the other through the mediators. Such a session is amenable to decomposition into three confluences c_1, c_2, and c_3, consisting of the set of participants $\{P_1, P_2, P_3, M_1\}$, $\{P_4, P_5, P_6, M_2\}$, and $\{M_1, M_2\}$, respectively.

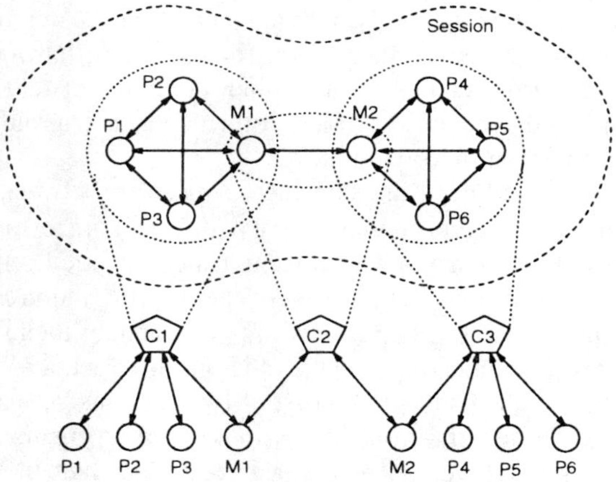

Figure 1: Decomposition of a session into confluences

Conference

A conference C can be formally defined as a pair:

$$C = [\mathcal{T}, \mathsf{LRT}]$$

where $\mathcal{T} = \{T_1, T_2, ..., T_k\}$ denotes the set of temporal ordering relations between sessions constituting the conference; and LRT represents the latest time until which media information transmitted on any of the streams during any of the sessions constituting the conference is available for retrieval. In general, ordering of the activity periods of sessions ψ_i and ψ_j can be represented by any of the 13 temporal relations possible (mentioned at the beginning of this section).

Since a session encapsulates the collective access rights of all its participants with respect to all its constituent streams, temporal ordering of sessions denote dynamic changes in the access rights of its participants. Furthermore, recursive temporal relations among sessions constituting a conference makes the conference persistent (as opposed to transient). Mutual recursion yields periods of activity separated by periods of inactivity, and can be used to realize periodic meetings. For example, a temporal relation $\psi_i \overset{\tau}{\rightsquigarrow} \psi_i$ indicates that session ψ_i is to be re-activated τ units of time after the termination of its previous activation. Even a meeting room may be regarded as a conference that becomes active when it is being used, but reverts to being inactive when not in use. For such conferences, the needed system resources (such as network bandwidth) can be reserved in advance, and their periodic invocations can be made automatic. Conferences such as telephone conversations, on the other hand, are transient ones.

Discussion

Whereas a stream encapsulates the permitted access rights of both the sender and the receiver with respect to media exchange, a session represents a collaborative activity consisting of a collection of media streams, and a conference denotes temporally ordered sequence of sessions that together constitute a complete collaborative endeavor. These abstractions together provide a framework for capturing the semantics of various structured collaborative environments.

The inclusion of temporal attributes in the model unifies the interfaces and management of both synchronous and asynchronous collaborations, thereby permitting participants to inter-operate between synchronous and asynchronous collaborations. Specifically, based on the values of ETT, ERT, LTT, and LRT associated with a media stream, it can be characterized as synchronous or asynchronous as follows: If ETT = ERT = LRT, then the stream denotes synchronous exchange of media information. On the other hand, if ETT < LRT, then media information transmitted by the sender may be requested by a recipient after its discretionary delays, thereby capturing the asynchronous nature of media exchange. For such asynchronous media exchange, a storage server records the media being transmitted, and retrieves it upon request. However, the involvement of servers (such as, storage or mail servers) in the media exchange is completely transparent to the users, yielding complete unification of synchronous and asynchronous collaborations.

INTERFACES FOR MANAGING CONFERENCES

Basic Operations

- INSTANTIATE[conferenceSpec, participantList, timingInfo] → [conferenceDesc, confController]

  Instantiating a conference requires the specification of the type of the conference, a set of invitees, and a set of timing values that define the activity periods of session. Invocation of this operation by the instantiator (who becomes the confController) results in invitations being sent to all the invitees.

- JOIN[objectDesc] → objectInfo

  Each invitee, on receiving an invitation, can independently accept or decline the invitation. An invitee can accept the invitation by JOINing, and thereby becoming a *participant* of the conference. JOINing a conference returns information regarding its constituent sessions (through objectInfo). A participant can then JOIN any of the sessions, which in turn provides information regarding its constituent streams. Transmission or reception of media information to or from the streams can be initiated by the invocation of SEND and RECEIVE operations, respectively.

  A participant can terminate his or her participation within a session or a conference by invoking the LEAVE operation. Similarly, a conference controller can terminate a conference by invoking the TERMINATE operation.

- SEND[sessionDesc, streamList, duration]

  A participant can initiate transmission of media information to streams constituting a session by invoking the SEND operation. Whereas invoking SEND on a synchronous media stream initiates the transmission to only the participants who have desired to receive media information from that stream, invoking SEND on an asynchronous stream initiates an additional transmission to a storage server.

- RECEIVE[sessionDesc, streamList]

  A participant can initiate reception of media information from streams constituting a session by invoking the RECEIVE operation. If a RECEIVE is invoked on a synchronous media stream, reception directly from the media stream is initiated. On the contrary, invocation of a RECEIVE by a participant with respect to an asynchronous stream initiates reception of media information either from a storage server or from the sender of the stream.

  The transmission or the reception of media information on a stream can be terminated by either a STOP or a PAUSE operation. A PAUSE operation may either have a *destructive* semantics, which causes resources (such as, bandwidth and processing time) to be deallocated during the PAUSE, or a *non-destructive* semantics, in which resources remain allocated. If a destructive PAUSE is specified, a subsequent RESUME has to acquire the necessary resources before resuming the operation.

- CHANGEACCESSLIST[sessionDesc, newStreamList]

  The permitted access rights of participants associated with a session can be altered, or new participants can be invited to join a session already in progress using the CHANGEACCESSLIST operation.

- CHANGETEMPORALRELATION[conferenceDesc, newTemporalRelations]

  The sessions constituting a conference can be altered by the conference controller dynamically by invoking the CHANGETEMPORALRELATION operation.

- CHANGECONTROLLER[conferenceDesc, newController]

  The controller of conferenceDesc can be changed by the invocation of this operation. This operation can be invoked only by the conference controller.

Editing Operations

Streams can also be manipulated in a manner similar to string manipulation using INSERT, DELETE, and REPLACE operations. Precise semantics of these operations depend on synchronous or asynchronous nature of the streams being manipulated. Interesting effects can be obtained by inserting asynchronous streams into synchronous streams, and vice versa. For instance, while receiving media information transmitted on a synchronous stream (say S_1), insertion of an interval from another stream (say S_2) terminates the reception of media from S_1, and initiates the reception from S_2. On completion of the inserted interval from S_2, the reception from S_1 is resumed. However, since S_1 is a synchronous stream, media information transmitted on S_1 during the interval cannot be retrieved. On the contrary, if S_1 represents an asynchronous media stream, then reception from S_1 can be resumed from the point at which it was terminated.

Multiple sessions can be coalesced into a single session using the MERGE operation. There are several alternatives by which temporal attributes and streams of component sessions can be combined to obtained a merged session. Whereas temporal attributes can be derived by taking the minimum or the maximum of those of the component sessions, component streams can be combined by taking the intersection or union of their respective attributes (such as media, sender, and receiverList). For instance, two streams with identical media and sender can be combined to yield a single stream with the receiverList computed as either the union or intersection of receiverLists of the component streams. Similarly, taking the merge via union of two streams with different senders and **media** yields four separate streams, each with a different combination of **sender** and **media**, but all of them with the same **receiverList** (obtained by taking the union of the **receiverLists** of the two streams being merged). The dual of MERGE is SPLIT, which partitions a session to create two or more new sessions. MERGE and SPLIT operations can be optionally *destructive* to the sessions on which they operate. The interfaces provided for the MERGE and the SPLIT operations are as follows:

MERGE[listOfSessionDesc]
SPLIT[sessionDesc, listOf [listOfStreams]]

Query Operations

A set of query operations are necessary to determine properties of sessions, and conferences, such as the name of its creator, current set of participants, controller of a conference, etc. A common interface for all such operations is given by:

QUERY[opcode, objectDesc, listOfParameters]

where opcode identifies the operation, objectDesc identifies the session or the conference being queried, and the listOfParameters represent operation-specific parameters.

ILLUSTRATION

In order to illustrate the use of the collaboration model presented in the abover sections, let us consider a collaboration that involves both multiple media exchanges (some of which maybe serial and some of which overlapped), and dynamic changes in access rights. An example is a panel discussion (usually held at professional conferences, conventions, etc.), that involves prepared presentations by a set of panelists followed by on-the-fly questions and answers between panelists and attendees. Whereas the prepared presentations by panelists' can be pre-recorded (and hence may need to be handled as asynchronous collaborations), the question-answer period requires contemporaneous participation of panelists and the attendees. During his or her presentation, a panelist alone has the right to transmit media information, whereas during the question-answer period, any participant may transmit. Furthermore, it is desirable to permit any of the panelists to join the panel at any time after its instantiation, and pre-record their presentations.

The sequence of presentations of panelists during the progress of the panel can be handled through a simple floor control mechanism. However, this would require physical presence of panelists during the panel, and does not afford the flexibility to permit an arbitrary subset of panelists' presentations to be asynchronous (i.e., pre-recorded), while retaining the question-answer session as synchronous. A realization of the panel based on our model, on the other hand is independent of whether or not some of the panelists pre-record their presentations.

In our model, each of the presentations as well as the question-answer period can be realized as separate sessions, each with its own set of access rights for all the panelists and attendees. The entire panel discussion can be represented as a temporally ordered sequence of these sessions. Figure 2 shows such a representation for a panel discussion consisting of three panelists (namely, P_1, P_2, and P_3) and n attendees (namely, $A_1, A_2, ..., A_n$), where sessions ψ_1, ψ_2, and ψ_3 represent the prepared presentations of the panelists P_1, P_2, and P_3, respectively; and ψ_4 represents the question-answer session. Whereas, during session ψ_1, ψ_2, and ψ_3, only panelist P_1, P_2, and P_3, respectively, have the right to transmit media information and all the other participants can only receive information, during session ψ_4, any of the panelists or attendees can transmit and receive media information (as shown by the directed arcs in Figure 2).

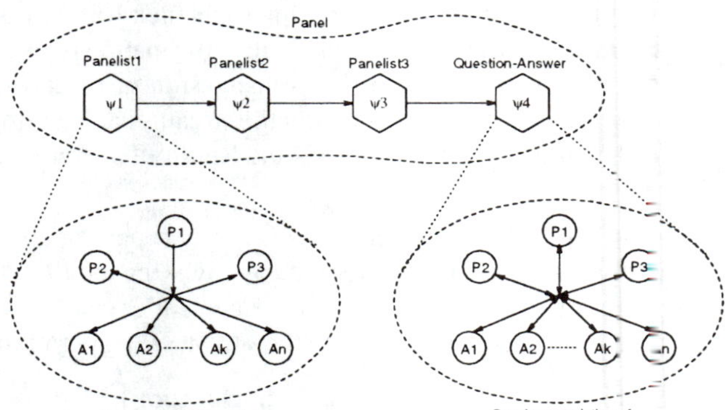

Figure 2: Semantic representation of a panel

Notice that the specification of a panel discussion as described in Figure 2 is independent of the origin of media information and the type of media exchange (namely, synchronous or asynchronous). Consequently, several different instantiations of panel discussions with various combinations of pre-recorded and contemporaneous presentations by panelists' can be derived from such a unified specification.

In order to instantiate a panel discussion, the initiator (whose role is possibly taken up by the panel chair) has to specify the list of panelists and attendees, the time of initiation of the panel, the order of presentations, the duration of each presentation, and the duration for which the proceedings of the panel may be retrieved. The temporal constraints resulting from such an instantiation are depicted in Figure 3.

Sessions ψ_1, ψ_2, and ψ_3 permit their panelists to pre-record their presentations prior to ERT1, ERT2, and ERT3, but after ETT1, ETT2, and ETT3, respectively, permitting the panelists to participate in an asynchronous manner. However, ψ_4, which represents the question-answer session, requires synchronous participation of both panelists and atten-

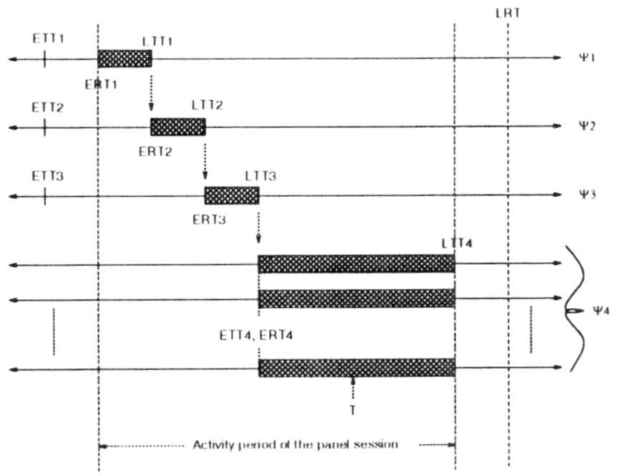

Figure 3: Instantiation of a panel

dees. An attendee joining the panel, say at time T (ETT4 < T < LTT4), can retrieve panel proceedings upto time T in an asynchronous manner, after which the attendee is automatically switched into a synchronous mode of participation.

CONCLUDING REMARKS

In recent years, several conferencing systems have been proposed and prototyped to improve the effectiveness of person-to-person collaborations. Lantz [5] have studied conferencing architectures for text and graphics. Dewan [4] has addressed the issue of sharing and coupling among windows displaying shared workspace. Ahuja et al at AT&T Bell Laboratories [2] and Aguilar et al at SRI [1] propose architectures for person-to-person audio and/or video conferencing. Connection management architectures for providing flexible control of media connections among users and/or servers were addressed in [8, 10], and a preliminary framework for modeling collaborations was proposed in [9]. However, most of these systems have separately considered synchronous and asynchronous collaborations, and unification of the two into a single paradigm have not received much attention. Additionally, system support abstractions based on formal specification of access rights and temporal relations have not been explored.

Our model presented in this paper employs temporal relations and a general access control mechanism (in place of simple floor control) to support a wide spectrum synchronous and asynchronous multimedia collaborations. The model combines both efficiency and flexibility via a hierarchy of abstractions, the lowest level of which are streams for efficient media communication on networks, and the higher two levels of which are sessions and conferences that capture synchronous and asynchronous collaborations. These abstractions provide a powerful set of collaboration building blocks and yield a rich environment for constructing multimedia applications. A prototype collaboration management system based on this model is being implemented at the UCSD Multimedia Laboratory.

REFERENCES

[1] L. Aguilar, J.J. Garcia-Luna-Aceves, D. Moran, E.J. Craighill, and R. Brungardt. Architecture for A Multi-Media Tele-Conferencing System. *Proceedings of the SIGCOMM'86 Symposium on Communications Architectures and Protocols, Stowe, VT*, pages 126–136, August 5-7, 1986.

[2] S. R. Ahuja, J. Ensor, and D. Horn. The Rapport Multimedia Conferencing System. In *Proceedings of COIS'88 Conference on Office Information Systems, Palo Alto, CA*, pages 1–8, March 23-25, 1988.

[3] J. F. Allen. Maintaining Knowledge about Temporal Intervals. *Communications of the ACM*, 26(11):832–843, November 1983.

[4] P. Dewan. A Tour of the Suite User Interface Software. *In Proceedings of the 3rd ACM SIG-GRAPH Symposium on User Interface Software and Technology*, pages 57–65, October 1990.

[5] K.A. Lantz. An Experiment in Integrated Multimedia Conferencing. In *Proceedings of CSCW'86*, pages 267–275, December 1986.

[6] T.D.C. Little and A. Ghafoor. Synchronization and Storage Models for Multimedia Objects. *IEEE Journal on Selected Areas in Communications*, 8(3):413–427, April 1990.

[7] Srinivas Ramanathan, P. Venkat Rangan, Harrick M. Vin, and Thomas Kaeppner. Optimal Communication Architectures for Multimedia Conferencing in Distributed Systems. *In Proceedings of the 12th International Conference on Distributed Computing Systems, Yokohama, Japan*, June 1992.

[8] P. Venkat Rangan and D. C. Swinehart. Software Architecture for Integration of Video Services in the Etherphone Environment. *IEEE Journal on Selected Areas in Communication*, 9(9):1395–1404, December 1991.

[9] P. Venkat Rangan and Harrick M. Vin. Multimedia Conferencing as A Universal Paradigm for Collaboration. In *Multimedia Systems, Applications, and Interaction, Chapter 14, Lars Kjelldahl (editor), Springer-Verlag, Germany*, April 1991.

[10] Harrick M. Vin, P. T. Zellweger, D. C. Swinehart, and P. Venkat Rangan. Multimedia Conferencing in the Etherphone Environment. *IEEE Computer - Special Issue on Multimedia Information Systems*, 24(11):69–79, October 1991.

Ubiquitous Audio: Capturing Spontaneous Collaboration

Debby Hindus
Chris Schmandt

MIT Media Lab
20 Ames Street
Cambridge, MA, USA 02139
Email: hindus@media.mit.edu or geek@media.mit.edu

ABSTRACT

Although talking is an integral part of collaborative activity, there has been little computer support for acquiring and accessing the contents of conversations. Our approach has focused on *ubiquitous audio*, or the unobtrusive capture of voice interactions in everyday work environments. Because the words themselves are not available for organizing the captured interactions, structure is derived from acoustical information inherent in the stored voice and augmented by user interaction during or after capture. This paper describes applications for capturing and structuring audio from office discussions and telephone calls, and mechanisms for later retrieval of these stored interactions.

KEYWORDS

Stored voice, semi-structured data, ubiquitous computing, collaborative work, software telephony, multimedia workstation software.

INTRODUCTION

People spend much of their workday talking. In Reder and Schwab's recent study of professionals, phone calls comprised about 20% of the workday, and face-to-face meetings accounted for an additional 25-50% [23]. Yet this time spent talking has been to a great extent out of reach of computer technology. This loss of speech information is all the more striking, given the dominance of the audio medium in influencing communication outcomes regardless of the presence of visual and other media [22]. Furthermore, speech communication fulfills different communicative purposes than text communication and "is especially valuable for the more complex, controversial, and social aspects of a collaborative task" [4].

Nevertheless, audio is, in a sense, a forgotten technology for CSCW. Multimedia has received considerable attention as a CSCW technology area in recent years, and many applications have focused on synchronous video communication. Because the social and technological issues involved in supporting video calls are so demanding, synchronous video conferencing remains a research topic [7, 12, 20], whereas audio communication is already part of daily life—telephones sit on every desk. Eventually, however, simply supporting synchronous conversations will be insufficient and the research emphasis then will shift to storage and retrieval of the *contents* of interactions.

Permission to copy without fee all or part of this material is granted provided that the copies are not made or distributed for direct commercial advantage, the ACM copyright notice and the title of the publication and its date appear, and notice is given that copying is by permission of the Association for Computing Machinery. To copy otherwise, or to republish, requires a fee and/or specific permission.

© 1992 ACM 0-89791-543-7/92/0010/0210...$1.50

In many ways, storing and retrieving communication for later review is much more demanding than merely establishing the synchronous channel. Both audio and video are time-dependent media with few sharp boundaries for indexing or classification. If it were practicable, speech recognition and natural language processing techniques could convert speech to text. Such processing will not be reliable and as fast as human speech for perhaps decades [35], and in any case would cause the loss of nuances carried by the audio signal but not in the words themselves. In the meantime, extending audio technology to spontaneous conversation will require automatic derivation of structure without understanding the spoken words. This *semi-structured audio* will assist in later retrieval as well.

This paper is about various means of capturing voice interactions in everyday work environments; we call this *ubiquitous audio*. We discuss applications for capturing audio in work situations and deriving structure during or after capture, leading to semi-structured audio. We describe user interfaces for later retrieval of these stored voice interactions. Finally, we briefly mention how voice records of meetings and conversations fit into the broader context of utilizing voice as a datatype.

BACKGROUND

To motivate ubiquitous audio, we will first review the current role audio plays in CSCW. Audio as a communication medium has received attention in computer conferencing applications, although the related technological problems have obscured its potential as a source of data. Recorded speech has been used in a limited role, in applications that require little structuring of the audio data. Structure is what is needed to make audio more useful in CSCW, and we describe semi-structured audio and its antecedents. Looking ahead to ubiquitous computing, stored voice will be more readily available, and access and retrieval will be significant issues. A glimpse of this future is available by examining current projects.

Audio in CSCW Applications

Audio in most CSCW applications is only a medium for synchronous communication and not yet a source of data. Audio conferencing over telephone lines has proven to be of limited utility. In teleconferencing applications, echo cancellation and feedback are common problems, particularly with speakerphones that are half-duplex (i.e., only one party can speak at a time) [8]. This has led to computer conferencing systems that support voice through a custom network, such as MMConf [11]. A recent desktop conferencing system, MERMAID [30], uses ISDN and so can support full-duplex conversations; that is, all parties can talk simultaneously.

Short pieces of recorded speech—voice snippets—are the main use of speech as data in current CSCW applications. These snippets are used in message systems, e.g., voice mail, and in multiuser editing systems. (The categories follow Ellis, et al.'s taxonomy [8].) Voice can also be used to annotate text, as was done in Quilt [9]. Voice snippets can be stored in a personal calendar or within spreadsheet cells. The stored voice is not itself structured in these applications; the recorded speech is treated as a single unbroken entity and the application maintains an external reference to the sound, such as a message number, calendar date, or position within the text or spreadsheet.

Semi-structured audio

Semi-structured media have not, to date, been extensively explored. In the text domain, Information Lens is an example of the power of a semi-structured approach [18]. Information Lens users add extra fields to electronic mail messages; this extra information provides attributes to messages but is not part of the message body itself. Users can then write rules to route and sort received mail, based on these additional attributes [17].

Similarly, semi-structured audio provides a framework for organizing and manipulating audio data. Information inherent in the speech signal and in the audio interaction can be combined with situational constraints and user annotations to create semi-structured audio data. An early example of semi-structured audio was Phone Slave [27]; it used conversational techniques to take a telephone message, asking callers a series of questions and recording the answers. These sound segments could be highly correlated with structured information about the call. For example, the response to "At what number can you be reached" contained the phone number. Recently, structured data capture has been applied by Resnick [24] to a voice-driven application that uses the form-entry metaphor for a telephone-based voice bulletin board. After recording their messages, contributors to the bulletin board are asked to fill in additional fields, using appropriate mechanisms. For instance, the headline field is filled in with a brief recording and expiration dates are given by touch tones.

Ubiquitous computing

Technological advances are leading to small, portable computers that will communicate through wireless networks; current examples are laptops, palmtops, alphanumeric pagers, and smart cellular phones. Xerox PARC is exploring technologies ranging from electronic whiteboards to wearable computers in the context of *ubiquitous computing*: the concept that explicit computer interactions will be replaced by specialized smart devices that are unobtrusively present in all aspects of day-to-day pursuits [31].

The advent of ubiquitous computing will permit the acquisition of previously inaccessible data about daily activities. The Activity Information Retrieval (AIR) project at Rank Xerox EuroPARC has been exploring how ubiquitous computing can provide people with access to their own previous activities. In one effort, laboratory members wear "active badges" (originally developed by Olivetti) that can be tracked [29], and personalized diaries are created that summarize each badge wearer's whereabouts and meetings. Another component of AIR is a system that continually videotapes lab members. The stored video can be retrieved by using situational information such as where the person was at a particular time, and by using timestamped notations made on pen-based devices during meetings [16].

A portable prototype for capturing user-structured audio has been developed at Apple. A handheld tape recorder was modified so that users could mark interesting portions of recordings of meetings or demarcate items in personal memos. A key point is that these annotations could be made in real time, as the sound was being recorded [5].

THE HOLY GRAIL: AUTOMATIC TRANSCRIPTION OF FORMAL MEETINGS

Conspicuously absent from our discussion so far is the notion of capturing the spoken contents of formal group meetings without human transcription. Given the importance of meetings, this is an obvious CSCW application, as indicated by the body of work on electronic meeting systems [19, 6]. Due to technological issues, however, it is very difficult to automatically structure recordings of meetings.

The first issue is obtaining high-quality recording of the participants' speech. Individual microphone placement is critical and may encumber the participants. Using a single wide-area microphone is simpler, but will compromise the audio quality.

The next issue is associating each utterance with a participant. Ideally, each person's speech would be recorded on a separate audio channel. But room acoustics make it quite difficult to get each attendee's speech to be transmitted by only one microphone, and using highly directional table microphones greatly constrains participants' movements. For large groups, an auto-directional microphone can orient itself towards the podium or towards the audience [10], although its discrimination when talkers are sitting side-by-side is unproven. Signal processing techniques based on spectral analysis might be capable of determining who is talking from among multiple talkers on one recording; these techniques are being researched.

Transcription of the spoken words is the third issue. Speech recognition of fluent, unconstrained natural language is nowhere near reality yet. Even keyword spotting, to produce partial transcripts, is very difficult when applied to spontaneous speech, especially from multiple talkers [28]. However, wordspotting techniques have recently been incorporated into an audio indexing and editing system [32], and keyword spotting need not be perfect; the Intelligent Ear [26] was an early system that made use of a graphical color display and indicated the confidence of the word recognition through luminance levels.

THE CAPTURE AND STRUCTURING OF SPONTANEOUS AUDIO

Common workaday activities other than formal meetings provide a starting point for exploring ubiquitous audio, both in terms of user interfaces and audio processing. Ubiquitous audio can come from a number of sources and through a variety of physical input devices. The ubiquitous computing approach will eventually lead to large quantities of stored information; for example, all the conversations that occur in an office in a year could be saved on a single disk drive *.

The semi-structured approach defines a framework for making these quantities of audio usable by incorporating acoustical cues, situational and contextual data, and user-supplied structure. Acoustical structure includes speech and silence detection, and associating portions of the audio signal with the correct talker. Semi-structure provides enough structure for flexible access to the data later, without relying on the explicit creation of structure by the source or recipient of the audio. Users *can* create structure as they see fit, but they do not *have* to create structure in order for the audio data to be manageable and accessible.

We have explored ubiquitous, semi-structured audio in varied tools that support informal meetings, personal notes, and telephone conversations. This section describes two such tools and issues in structuring the audio they capture. The first of these applications is a digital "tape loop" that provides short-term auditory memory in the office, with no inherent structure to the recording. The second application allows users to selectively mark and save portions of telephone conversations, and utilizes the conversants' turn-taking for structure. For each application, we consider both the capture phase, during which the spoken collaboration is recorded and accessed immediately thereafter, and the retrieval phase, wherein the stored voice can be used at a later time.

Capturing office discussions

When multiple authors are working on a collaborative writing project, one may suggest a new wording to a paragraph, which the other strives to write down but cannot. By the time the second author says, "That was perfect, say it again," the

*Assuming eight-hour days, wherein conversing takes four hours (of which 30% is silence), and 10:1 compression of telephone-quality speech, a year's worth of office speech would require approximately 2 gigabytes of storage.

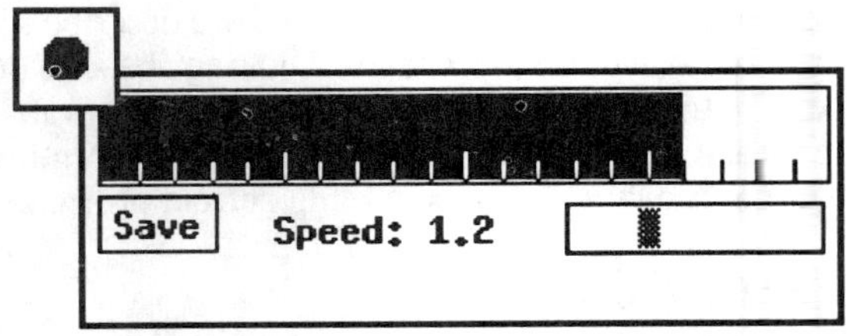

Figure 1: Xcapture after an office discussion.

words have already been forgotten. Xcapture is meant to supply exactly this short-term memory; the user remembers the flow of the recent conversation, so xcapture makes no direct use of any structure in the recorded audio.

Many workstations are now equipped with a speaker and microphone, but in practice the microphone is rarely used. Xcapture provides short-term audio memory in the office by making use of workstation resources in a background task. Whenever the microphone is not in use by another application, xcapture records ambient sound into a circular buffer; five to fifteen minutes is a typical length.

Retrieving office discussions

Xcapture records until the user clicks on its animated icon, causing a new window to appear. This window displays the entire audio buffer using a SoundViewer widget (see Fig. 1). The SoundViewer, used extensively in our work, provides a direct manipulation user interface to sound files. Time is displayed horizontally as tick marks. When the user clicks on the SoundViewer, the sound plays and a cursor bar flows into the window from left to right. The mouse can be used to move this cursor and cause the replay to jump to the new location; that is, the mouse provides a time-based offset into the sound, allowing random access.

During retrieval, the xcapture user is faced with the task of finding the interesting speech segment from within multiple minutes of recorded audio. The SoundViewer indicates time, but gives no clue to the contents of the sound it represents. A longer recording buffer makes xcapture more useful, but retrieval is onerous for a lengthy recording, even with the random access mechanism described above. Therefore, xcapture and the SoundViewer support scanning through the recorded audio by replaying the speech back in less time than was required to record it. A slider under the sound viewer allows the xcapture user to increase playback to up to three times normal speed; although intelligibility is significantly reduced beyond twice normal speed, the upper limit allows faster scanning through familiar material.

Time-compressing speech so that it remains intelligible is not straightforward. Simply increasing the rate at which samples are played is inadequate; this raises the pitch, as with the cartoon chipmunks. Discarding chunks of sound during playback is a better approach; quality is improved by finding and discarding complete pitch periods, and smoothing the boundaries. For a survey of time compression techniques, see Arons [2].

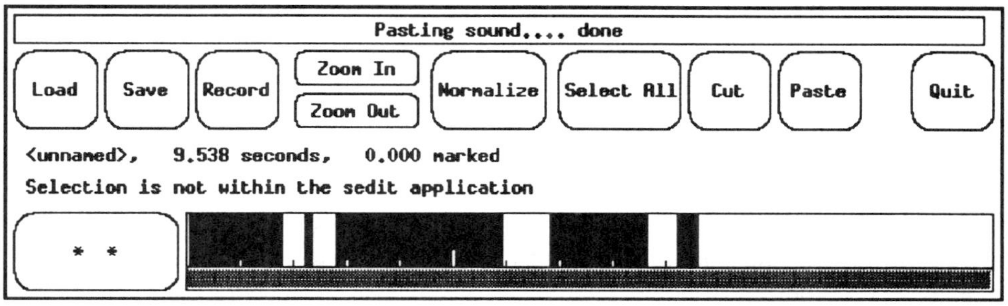

Figure 2: A sound editor showing speech and silence intervals

Xcapture allows the entire buffer to be saved to a file, but this does not turn out to be very useful. Instead, using the mouse, the xcapture buffer can be cut and pasted into an audio editor that displays speech and silence intervals (see Fig. 2), and from there a snippet of a few seconds can be pasted into other audio-capable applications such as a calendar (see Fig. 3) or things-to-do list.

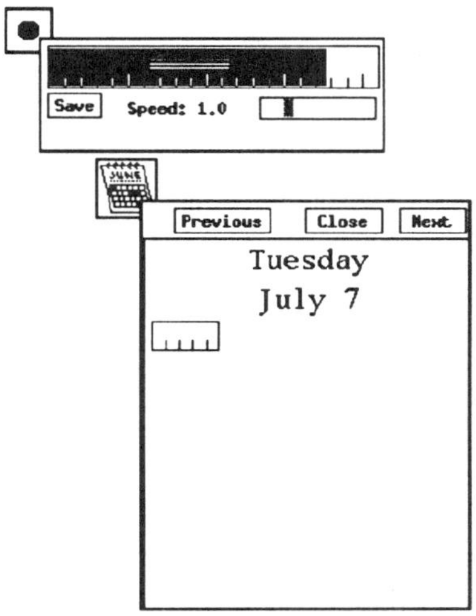

Figure 3: Sound fragment being pasted into a calendar entry

Xcapture provides a means of transforming ubiquitous speech into manageable chunks that can be incorporated into databases that supply structure, e.g., the short list of things to do on a particular day. But the lack of structure limits the utility of xcapture; even for short-term memory, audio structure is required for direct manipulation interfaces. We provide an improved interface incorporating structure in an application to record telephone calls.

DYNAMIC CAPTURE AND DISPLAY OF TELEPHONE CONVERSATIONS

Xcapture supported structuring during retrieval; this portion of our work addresses creation of structure at the time of capture and allows interaction during capture. In addition to structuring during capture, this project addresses the visual representation of free-form conversations and dynamic displays for real-time capture. It features the Listener, a telephone listening tool that allows users to identify and save the relevant portions of telephone calls as the phone conversation progresses. Telephone conversations are a practical choice for demonstrating semi-structured audio; very little equipment is required beyond audio-capable workstations, and who is speaking can be detected because the two audio channels can be separated. In this sense, phone calls can be thought of as two-person meetings. Also, telephone conversations will be increasingly mediated by workstations, so situational information can be associated with a digitized telephone conversation [34, 15].

The Listener captures structure from telephone calls, as described in the following scenario: You receive a telephone call. The Listener pops up a notification window on your screen. You choose to record the call. While you are talking, a graphical representation of the conversation is constructed on your screen, showing the shifts in who is speaking and the relative length of each turn. You can click on a segment to indicate that it should be saved. At the end of the phone call, you can listen to segments and decide which ones to save, or just save all the marked segments.

Capturing and Displaying Conversational Structure

Studies of audio communication provide parameters for automatically structuring conversations. Business telephone calls are brief and therefore tractable; the expected duration of business telephone calls is 3–6 minutes [23]. Speakers alternate turns frequently, and utterances are typically either very short, or 5–10 seconds long [25, 33]. Furthermore, turn-taking pauses are not distinguishable from other pauses by their length, and many turns happen with minimal pausing [3]. The inherent structure of a conversation therefore consists of the naturally-occurring pauses at the end of phrases and sentences and the alternation of utterances between talkers. Audio data can be automatically segmented into understandable pieces on the boundaries between talkers and between phrases.

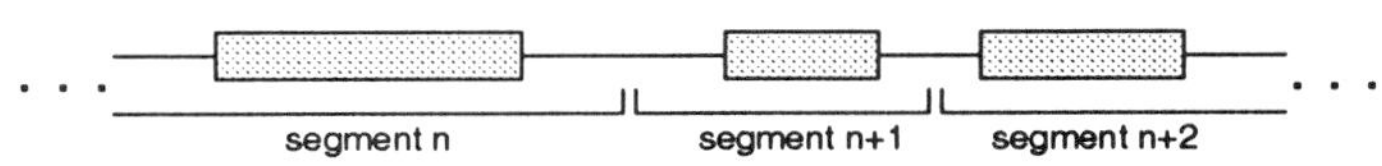

Figure 4: Silences are divided between segments

Two microphones collect audio signals for the Listener. One

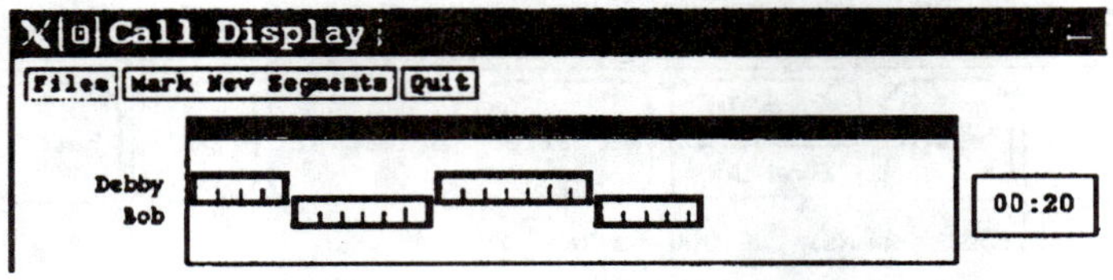

D: Hello, this is Debby Hindus speaking.
B: Hi Deb, it's Bob. I'm just getting out of work, I figured I'd call and see how late you're going to stay tonight.
D: Well, I think it'll take me about another hour, hour and a half, to finish up the things I'm doing now.
B: OK, I'm just going to head on home, I'll probably do a little shopping on the way.

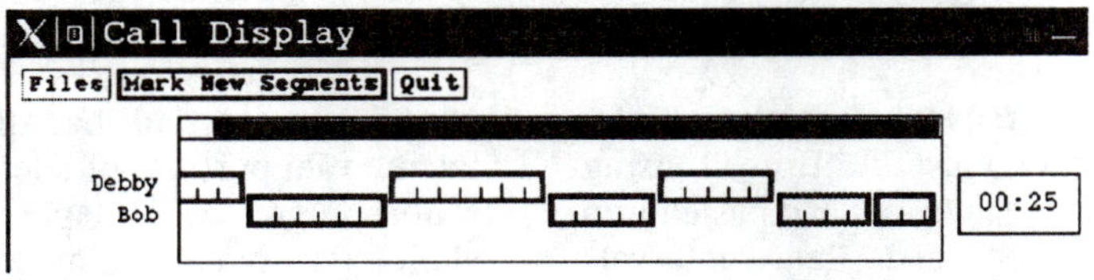

D: Well, if you think of it, maybe you could get some of that good ice cream that you got last week.
B: OK. By the way, somebody, uh...
B: mentioned an article you might be able to use

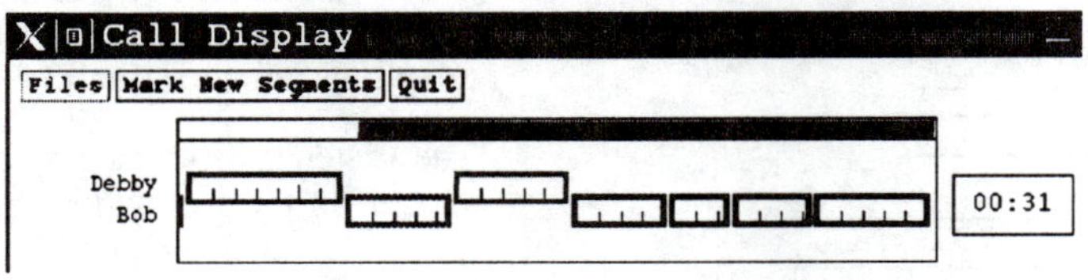

B: in your tutorial. Debby: Oh really? [Debby's very short turn is ignored.]
B: Yeah, it's by Graeme Hirst, in the June '91 Computational Linguistics.

Figure 5: Sequence of segments during a phone call, with transcriptions

is connected to the telephone handset and carries speech from both talkers. The other microphone sits in the user's office near the telephone and carries just that person's speech (assuming that the handset is used rather than a speakerphone). This second, single-talker audio stream enables the Listener to distinguish between the two talkers. The Listener receives audio data from both mikes, performs pause detection on each source, synchronizes the sources, and then locates changes of talker between pauses. This last step is needed because turn-taking pauses can be undetectable with just pause detection. To determine the segment boundaries, the Listener incorporates a state machine that takes into account who is talking, the previous state, and the segment duration. As shown in Fig. 4, segment boundaries are calculated so that they fall in the pauses between utterances; this makes segments sound complete when played individually. The new segment is then added to the call display. (Other visual representations have shown speech as periods of sound and silence [1]. Both forms highlight the temporal aspect of sound and provide structure for display and graphical interaction.)

The call display that appears during the conversation must be unobtrusive, so as not to interfere with the conversation. Also, short-term memory constraints imply that only the recent portions of the conversation are salient, and interesting segments can be identified only shortly after the segment takes place.

Figure 5 shows the call display during part of the conversation. As the conversation proceeds, a visual representation of approximately the previous 30 seconds is displayed retrospectively. Each conversational turn is shown, reflecting the phrase-level utterances of the talkers. Each segment, or portion of the audio signal, is displayed within a SoundViewer, the same audio representation that is used throughout our applications. Each tick mark within each SoundViewer represents one second of audio. New segments appear at the right-hand side, and older segments scroll out of view to the left. Segments from each talker can be visually distinguished by their relative positioning and by different border colors when unmarked.

The Listener is an X Window System client application that communicates with several server processes, and it is built on top of a generic sound-and-text handling mechanism called the ChatViewer [13]. The ChatViewer is a widget designed to manage and display *chats*: collections of recorded speech segments and short text strings.

Adding User-Supplied Structure

The derived conversational structure makes it possible to identify the segments worth saving for later reference. The Listener provides mechanisms for marking, or indicating to the Listener, these interesting segments. When the conversation turns to substantial matters, the user can toggle automatic marking so that all new segments are marked. Furthermore, a user can mark individual segments at any time by clicking on them, and marking is reversible. Marking a segment also highlights it visually.

During the phone call, the user's attention is focused on the conversation and not on interacting with the Listener program. Therefore, the only feasible user actions are clicking the pointer on segments of interest or just toggling the Mark New Segments button. The nature of the user interaction changes from capture to review, however, once the conversation is completed. The entire conversation is available for review at this point through a browsing application. The post-call browser displays the conversation and provides additional editing functions. A user can replay all or part of the conversation, revise the choice of segments to store, annotate with text, and save the chat for later retrieval. Once these post-call revisions are made, only the marked segments are saved.

Browsing Stored Telephone Conversations

Chats may be retrieved long after the phone call took place. There are two levels of retrieval. The first is finding the specific audio segments within a chat that contain the desired conversation extract. The second is locating a particular chat from among numerous stored chats. Our focus has been narrowly focused on capturing and retrieving single conversations. Future efforts will need to address mechanisms for navigating among many chats, making use of the situational data to locate one chat among many in a fashion akin to locating a specific electronic mail message.

Audio cannot be searched in the fashion that text can, and so situational and supplemental structure will be needed to provide memory cues as to the content of the stored audio. The user's choice of which segments to save is one form of supplemental structure; textual tags are another.

The Listener collects and stores contextual, or situational, structure, along with the stored audio. For telephone calls, contextual data includes the other party's name and phone number, if known; the time and date of the call; and the extension of the user. Marked segments will typically occur in consecutive groups, or paragraphs. When the chat is retrieved in the future, these paragraphs are reflected in the chat's layout, as shown in Fig. 6. Users can provide an optional descriptive tag for each conversation and one for each paragraph. Tags are not required; the timestamp is sufficient identification for retrieving a conversation.

DISCUSSION

The goal of this paper has been to introduce the concept of ubiquitous computer gathering of audio and to present applications and user interfaces to manage ubiquitous audio. We do not claim that the applications presented herein have solved the problems associated with managing large amount of semi-structured stored voice. We have presented preliminary work, and we expect to continue this research and extend it into new domains over the next several years.

We have used the applications ourselves enough to be confident that they have value. We have, for example, used the Listener while collaborating long-distance on this paper and mailed impromptu office discussions to group members not present at the time. Our research group has gained significant experience with audio snippets in a number of applications described in this paper, and one of the lessons learned has been the utility of audio cut and paste between applications. The SoundViewer supports a built-in X Windows-based selection mechanism, and so a portion of any sound in any application, including the telephone conversation browser, can be selected and moved to another application.

Obtaining high-quality audio from microphones in offices is still problematic, and acoustic structuring is limited to speech and silence detection. The audio quality from telephones is good, but using two microphones to segment based on talker is awkward and imperfect. When workstations are equipped with ISDN telephone lines, talker-based segmentation will be more realistic because the audio signal from each talker will be carried separately.

We have only begun to explore capturing and structuring large amounts of audio. One future direction, of course, is to start to extend our applications to meetings of more than two persons. Another direction is in new approaches to deriving structure. For example, although real-time speech understanding systems are a number of years away, non-real-time partial transcriptions could be made available as an overnight service by a specialized server in a network. Another approach to structuring is to classify (and perhaps delineate) segments by correlating the prosody of the segments with templates of classes of utterances. For instance, questions can be identified by the ending rising pitch [14].

A final point concerns privacy issues. Office discussions and telephone calls are already vulnerable to inappropriate or surreptitious recording, and conventions and laws govern what is considered appropriate with respect to current recording technology. As the technologies described in this paper become more widespread, users will continue to invent or adapt social protocols for negotiating levels of privacy that suit their needs.

CONCLUSION

The work presented in this paper demonstrates that every-

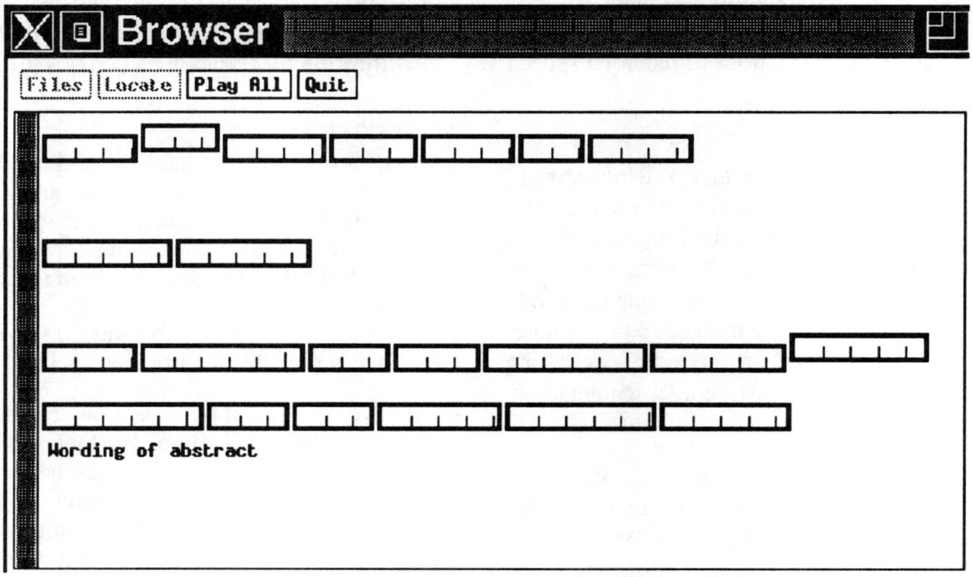

Figure 6: Browsing a stored conversation with three groups of saved segments

day audio interactions can be captured in various ways, and semi-structuring the audio data aids in storage and retrieval. Real-time structuring and display is feasible by making use of situational constraints and by adopting simple segmentation strategies. It is exactly the mundane nature of audio that makes it a worthwhile focus for CSCW. As Moran and Anderson [21] point out, technologies should be mundane in the workaday world and are successful when ordinary activities interact seamlessly with technology. Conversations and telephone calls are examples of such ordinary activities, and they provide a good starting point for exploiting the potential of ubiquitous audio.

ACKNOWLEDGMENTS

The work presented in this paper relies upon software developed by members of the Media Lab Speech Research Group. Barry Arons wrote the audio server used by both `xcapture` and the Listener. The SoundViewer widget was written by Mark Ackerman and Chris Horner, and the mechanics for audio cut and paste were implemented by Sheldon Pacotti. `Xcapture` was written by Lorin Jurow, and `sedit` was enhanced by Jordan Slott. Finally, Lisa Stifelman and Eric Ly worked on related audio applications.

We would like to thank Mark Ackerman for his thoughtful review of an early draft of this paper and Wendy Mackay for her incisive comments on a later draft. She and Kate Ehrlich also contributed to the research on semi-structured telephone conversations. The major portion of this work was funded by Sun Microsystems, Inc.

REFERENCES

1. S. Ades and D. C. Swinehart. Voice annotation and editing in a workstation environment. Technical Report CSL-86-3, Xerox Palo Alto Research Center, Sept 1986.

2. B. Arons. Techniques and applications of time-compressed speech. To appear in Proceedings of 1992 American Voice I/O Society Conference.

3. G. W. Beattie and P. J. Barnard. The temporal structure of natural telephone conversations (directory enquiry calls). *Linguistics*, 17:213–229, 1979.

4. B. L. Chalfonte, R. S. Fish, and R. E. Kraut. Expressive richness: A comparison of speech and text as media for revision. In *Proceedings of the Conference on Computer Human Interaction*, pages 21–26. ACM, Apr 1991.

5. L. Degen, R. Mander, and G. Salomon. Working with audio: Integrating personal tape recorders and desktop computers. In *Human Factors in Computer Systems – CHI'92 Conference Proceedings*, pages 413–418, May 1992.

6. A. R. Dennis, J. F. George, L. M. Jessup, J. F. Nunamaker, Jr., and D. R. Vogel. Information technology to support electronic meetings. *MIS Quarterly*, 12(4):591–624, 1988.

7. C. Egido. Teleconferencing as a technology to support cooperative work: its possibilities and limitations. In J. Galegher, R. E. Kraut, and C. Egido, editors, *Intellectual Teamwork: Social and Technological Foundations of Cooperative Work*, chapter 13. Lawrence Erlbaum, 1990.

8. C. A. Ellis, S. J. Gibbs, and G. L. Rein. Groupware: Some issues and experiences. *Communications of the ACM*, 34:38–58, January 1991.

9. R. S. Fish, R. E. Kraut, and M. D. Leland. Quilt: a collaborative tool for cooperative writing. In *Conference*

on office information systems, pages 30–37, Palo Alto, CA, 1988. ACM.

10. J. L. Flanagan, D. A. Berkeley, G. W. Elko, J. E. West, and M. M. Sondhi. Autodirective microphone systems. *Acustica*, 73(2):58–71, February 1991.

11. H. C. Forsdick. Explorations into real-time multimedia conferencing. In *Proceedings Second International Symposium on Computer Message Systems, IFIP Technical Committee on Data Communications*, Washington, D.C., September 1985.

12. C. Heath and P. Luff. Disembodied conduct: communication through video in a multi-media office environment. In *Human Factors in Computer Systems – CHI'91 Conference Proceedings*, pages 99–103, 1991.

13. D. Hindus. Semi-structured capture and display of telephone conversations. Master's thesis, MIT, Feb 1992.

14. J. Hirschberg and J. Pierrehumbert. The intonational structuring of discourse. In *Proceedings of the Association for Computational Linguistics*, pages 136–144, July 1986.

15. R. Kamel, K. Emami, and R. Eckert. PX: supporting voice in workstations. *IEEE Computer*, 23(8):73–80, Aug 1990.

16. M. Lamming and W. Newman. Activity-based information retrieval: Technology in support of human memory. Technical Report 92-002, Rank Xerox EuroPARC, Jan 1992.

17. W. E. Mackay, T. W. Malone, K. Crowston, R. Rao, D. Rosenblitt, and S. K. Card. How do experienced information lens users use rules? In *Human Factors in Computing Systems, CHI 89 Proceedings*, pages 211–216. ACM, 1989.

18. T. W. Malone, K. R. Grant, K.-Y. Lai, R. Rao, and D. Rosenblitt. Semi-structured messages are surprisingly useful for computer-supported coordination. *ACM Transactions on Office Information Systems*, 5(2):115–131, 1987.

19. M. Mantei. Capturing the capture lab concepts: A case study in the design of computer supported meeting environments. In *Computer Supported Cooperative Work – CSCW'88 Conference Proceedings*, pages 257–270, 1988.

20. S. Minneman and S. Bly. Managing a trois: a study of a multi-user drawing tool in distributed design work. In *Human Factors in Computer Systems – CHI'91 Conference Proceedings*, pages 217–223, 1991.

21. T. P. Moran and R. J. Anderson. The workaday world as a paradigm for CSCW design. In *Computer Supported Cooperative Work – CSCW'90 Conference Proceedings*, pages 381–393, 1990.

22. R. B. Oschman and A. Chapanis. The effects of ten communication modes on the behavior of teams during co-operative problem solving. *International Journal of Man/Machine Systems*, 6:579–619, 1974.

23. S. Reder and R. G. Schwab. The temporal structure of cooperative activity. In *Computer Supported Cooperative Work – CSCW'90 Conference Proceedings*, pages 303–316, 1990.

24. P. Resnick. HyperVoice: A phone-based CSCW platform. To appear in CSCW'92 Conference Proceedings.

25. D. R. Rutter. *Communicating by Telephone*. Pergamon Press, 1987.

26. C. Schmandt. The Intelligent Ear: A graphical interface to digital audio. In *Proceedings IEEE Conference on Cybernetics and Society*, pages 393–397, October 1981.

27. C. Schmandt and B. Arons. Phone Slave: A graphical telecommunications interface. *Proceedings of the Society for Information Display*, 26(1):79–82, 1985.

28. M. Soclof and V. Zue. Collection and analysis of spontaneous and read corpora for spoken language system development. In *Proceedings of ICSLP*, pages 1105–1108, Nov 1990.

29. R. Want and A. Hopper. Active badges and personal interactive computing objects. *IEEE Transactions on Consumer Electronics*, 38(1):10–20, Feb 1992.

30. K. Watabe, S. Sakata, K. Maeno, H. Fukuoka, and T. Ohmori. Distributed desktop conferencing system with multiuser multimedia interface. *IEEE Journal on Selected Areas in Communications*, 9(4):531–539, 1991.

31. M. Weiser. The computer for the 21st century. *Scientific American*, 265:66–75, September 1991.

32. L. Wilcox and M. Bush. HMM-based wordspotting for voice editing and indexing. In *Proceedings of Eurospeech 91*, pages 25–28, Sep 1991.

33. C. Wilson and E. Williams. Watergate words: A naturalistic study of media and communications. *Communications Research*, 4(2):169–178, 1977.

34. P. Zellweger, D. Terry, and D. Swinehart. An overview of the etherphone system and its applications. In *Proceedings of the 2nd IEEE Conference on Computer Workstations*, pages 160–168, Santa Clara, CA, March 1988.

35. V. W. Zue. From signals to symbols to meaning: On machine understanding of spoken language. In *Proceedings of the 12th International Congress of Phonetic Sciences*, August 1991.

HyperVoice
A Phone-Based CSCW Platform

Paul Resnick

MIT Center for Coordination Science
1 Amherst Street, Room E40-181
Cambridge, MA 02139
(617) 253-8694 presnick@mit.edu

ABSTRACT

A major shift is underway in how we think about telephones. For decades, they were used solely for one-to-one, synchronous communication. The increasing use of answering machines and voice messaging, however, is shifting the public perception of telephones, thus opening a space for more innovative applications. Five years from now, some of the most interesting and popular cooperative work applications will probably use telephones as the primary means of access. This paper presents evidence that there are practical phone-based cooperative work applications and describes a set of software tools that facilitate the development of such applications.

INTRODUCTION

Telephones are the most ubiquitous, best-networked, and simplest computer terminals available today. This makes telephones an attractive platform for cooperative work applications such as event calendars, issue discussions, task tracking, and question and answer gathering applications, especially those in which local-area network connection of all users cannot be assumed. The limitation of telephones is that they provide only sound for output and only sound and twelve buttons for input. Many skeptics who are familiar with existing telephone interfaces believe that this limitation is so strong as to eliminate the possibility of creating practical phone-based cooperative work applications. A new telephone interface style called Skip and Scan [15], however, opens up the possibility of more complex telephone-based applications, including cooperative work applications.

Permission to copy without fee all or part of this material is granted provided that the copies are not made or distributed for direct commercial advantage, the ACM copyright notice and the title of the publication and its date appear, and notice is given that copying is by permission of the Association for Computing Machinery. To copy otherwise, or to republish, requires a fee and/or specific permission.

© 1992 ACM 0-89791-543-7/92/0010/0218...$1.50

Field trials of several applications, totaling more than 7000 calls, demonstrate that it is possible to build usable and useful phone-based cooperative work applications. The field trials also highlight some of the factors that will influence the success or failure of applications. These factors include the value of the expressiveness of voice, the need for anonymity, the need to remember large chunks of information, and the distribution of costs and benefits among users.

HyperVoice is an application generator for phone-based cooperative work applications. Several features distinguish HyperVoice from other software tools for building telephone applications:

1) The specification language primitives are at a high level of abstraction. An interpreter automatically determines the details of dialogue sequencing and the text of prompts.

2) Messages have internal structure. Using telephone forms, callers can add new information objects (messages) that consist of several fields. The fields can contain recorded voice, typed-in dates, phone numbers, and quantities, or even links to other information objects. Sorting and filtering operations can act on the non-voice fields.

3) Presentation formats are separate from information objects. Multiple presentation formats can present the same information objects in different ways, depending on the context. In addition, callers can add new information objects without specifying details of how to present the information, since existing presentation formats can be reused.

SAMPLE APPLICATION: EVENT CALENDAR

Consider the following scenario for a phone call to an event calendar application. The computer answers the phone and prompts the caller to select one of six event categories. The caller selects the lectures and seminars category. The system tells the caller that there are twelve announcements in this category. The announcements are arranged in the order of the event dates and the caller then uses two buttons, **9** and **7**, to move forward and back through the announcements. Each announcement begins with a headline, so that the caller can quickly decide whether to listen to the rest of the announcement. If the caller chooses to keep listening beyond the headline, several other "fields" are played back, including the date, the time, the location, a contact phone number, and details. The caller can also press #, the "smart" fast-forward button. Unlike an ordinary fast-forward button, which advances a fixed amount of time, the "smart" fast-forward skips to the next logical segment in the recording, in this case the next field of the announcement.

After listening to some of the announcements, the caller presses **3**, which initiates the entry of a new announcement. The caller then fills out a "telephone form." Each field of the event announcement becomes one entry blank in the form. The caller can press **9** and **7** to skip back and forth between the entry blanks. In some entry blanks, the caller speaks information. In other entry blanks, such as the one for the date field, the caller presses buttons to enter data, such as **082192** for August 21, 1992. For typed in data, the system runs validity checks, ensuring, for example, that the caller enters a date in the next 90 days. The caller can review and replace the contents of any of the entry blanks before deciding to save the form. Once saved, the new announcement is added to the lectures and seminars category.

Now consider the scenario of a moderator calling up to make sure that no one has added an inappropriate announcement. Instead of selecting a category, the moderator enters a special code and the system goes to a list of all the event announcements. In this case, however, the announcements are sorted in descending order by the date on which they were entered, so that the newest announcements are at the beginning of the list. When listening to an announcement, the moderator hears all the same fields that regular callers do, plus the 'date added' and 'category' fields. The system automatically had added those fields to each announcement that was posted to the system. If the moderator finds an inappropriate announcement, entry of a special code removes that announcement from the system.

This scenario illustrates a number of important features of applications developed using HyperVoice. 1) The information in the system can come from many sources, since anyone with a touch-tone phone can add a new announcement. 2) The event announcements consist of several pieces. While recording, that allows the system to remind the callers of important information to record, and allows callers to re-record smaller pieces when they make mistakes in recording. During playback, it permits callers to use a smart fast-forward button to skip between fields. 3) Some of the fields of event announcements are symbolic rather than recorded, including the date, date added, and category fields. This allows the system to provide validity checks during data entry and to sort announcements during playback. 4) There are multiple presentation formats for the same information objects. For example, a moderator hears the announcements sorted in a different order, and with additional fields played back.

HYPERVOICE

HyperVoice is an application generator for telephone bulletin-board applications. To create an application, a programmer specifies a login procedure, a collection of linked information objects, how to filter and sort the information, and how callers can add new information objects. A pre-processor automatically generates the text of prompts that need to be recorded. At run-time, an interpreter generates state-machines that determine the details of dialogue sequencing.

Existing telephone application toolkits require programmers to specify state-machine representations directly [5, 13]. These tools provide programming environments analogous to HyperCard. By contrast, HyperVoice provides a specification language that abstracts away from many of the details of dialogue sequencing and navigation prompts. It is analogous to recent research on generating screen-based interfaces from higher-level abstractions [6, 17, 18].

This section briefly describes the HyperVoice application generator and presents part of the specification of the event calendar application. For more details, see [14].

The Language

A programmer begins by specifying object types. In the event calendar application, for example, there is an event announcement object type that has eight fields: headline, date, time, location, contact number, details, date added, and category.

Lists are ordered sequences of objects. The same object can appear in more than one list. In the event calendar, for example, there is one list of events for each category, plus a master list that contains all the announcements.

Login

Some applications require login procedures to restrict access and to determine the initial list of information objects to present to different callers. The HyperVoice Login primitive includes two parameters for whether callers need to enter ids and passwords to access the system. If no registration is required, two other parameters specify the initial privileges callers should get and the initial list to present. If registration is required, a parameter specifies a list of User objects. The id and password that a caller enters pick out a User object, which contains fields that specify the initial privileges and list to present.

Presenting a List

A List Format specifies how to present a list of objects. The List Format has a number of parameters, as summarized in Table 1. The filter selects a subset of the list to present. The Sort Formats determine the order in which to present the selected objects. The Item Formats specify which fields of the objects to play back, in what order, and whether to play the field names before the contents of the fields. One Item Format specifier is included for each of the object types that can appear in the list.

A menu is a special case of presenting a list of objects, as determined by the two parameters, 'how to advance' and 'how to select'. Callers can advance to the next item either by waiting until the end of the current item (WAIT) or by pressing a button (SKIP), or both. With numeric selection, callers press **1** to select the first object, **2** to select the second and so on. With positional selection, a single button selects the current object. For a discussion of the relative merits of the menu styles that these two parameters can generate, see [14].

The 'Name for Objects' parameter is used in generating the text of prompts that will tell the caller how to navigate through the list. For example, if the parameter has the word "announcement" as its value, a number of prompts will be generated, including, "For the next announcement, press 9," and, "For the previous announcement, press 7."

The 'Response List?' parameter determines what recordings will be played back to introduce the list. Each list that is not a response list has its own recording to introduce the contents of the list. Response lists, however, are generated automatically when information objects are added, so that the description of those lists needs to be generated automatically as well. HyperVoice plays the phrase "Responses to:" and then the contents of the specified field of the object that the list contains responses to.

Adding New Information by Phone

A List Action specifies how a caller can add new objects. It determines the privileges required to add a new object and the locations in the list from which the addition can be initiated.

The List Action also includes an Extension Format specification (Table 2). The Extension Format determines what kind of object to add, which lists to add it to, and where in those lists to add it. Finally, an Extension Format determines initial values for the fields, which fields will appear in the form, maximum recording lengths, and validity checks on typed in data, such as accepting dates only in the next 30 days.

Parameter Name	Alternative Values	Description
Filter		Selects a subset of the list to present.
Sort Formats		The order in which to present the items.
Item Formats		How to play back each item in the list.
How to Advance	SKIP, WAIT, BOTH	Whether the caller presses a button to advance to the next item, or just waits.
How to Select	NONE, NUMERIC, POSITIONAL	The selection mechanism for menus.
List Action		Action that callers can take to add a new information object.
Name For Objects		Used in generating prompts.
Response List?	NO, Field Name	Is this a list of responses to some other object? If so, the field of the other object to play in the list header.

Table 1: The parameters of a List Format specification.

Parameter Name	Alternative Values	Description
Add to Current List?	YES, NO	Whether the new object will be added to the list currently being presented to the caller.
Other Lists to Add To		
Location to Add	END, BEGINNING	Add the new object at the end or the beginning of the list(s).
Type of Object to Add		
Edit Format		A collection of Field Edit Formats that specify which fields will appear in form, initial values, validity checks, etc.

Table 2: The parameters of an Extension Format specification.

Example: The Event List Format

Now consider how to specify the presentation of a category of even announcements, as shown in Table 3. It specifies that the announcements be sorted in ascending order by the date of the announcement. The first six fields of each event announcement will be played back, and all except the headline will have the field name played back before the contents.

There is a List Action (details not shown) that specifies how a caller can add a new announcement. It specifies that the new announcement will be added both to the current list and to the master list that the moderator uses, as described in the scenario above.

A different List Format (not shown) specifies the presentation of the master list of announcements to the moderator. It specifies that the announcements be sorted in descending order by the 'date added' field, so that the moderator can hear the most recent announcements first. The Item Format in the List Format includes two additional fields, 'category' and 'date added'. Finally, the List Format does not include a List Action, since the moderator will not be adding announcements directly to the master list.

Implementation

Programmers specify the primitives described above by filling in screen-based forms in the OVAL system [8], which runs on a Macintosh. These primitives are then written to a database file and transferred to an IBM-compatible PC. A C language program on the PC reads the application specification from the database file and updates the database file whenever callers add new information objects. A commercial add-in card, Watson, handles speech digitization and touch-tone detection.

List Format: Event List Format	
Field Name	Value
Filter	[0 - 90 days]
Sort Order	['Date' ASCENDING]
Item Formats	['Headline' NO 'Date' YES 'Time' YES 'Location' YES 'Contact Number YES 'Details' YES]
How to Advance	SKIP
How to Select	NONE
List Actions	[New Event Announcement]
Name for Objects	Announcement
Response List?	NO

Table 3: The specification of how to present a list of announcements.

SUCCESS FACTORS FOR APPLICATIONS

Previous research on CSCW applications and analysis of the differences between text and voice suggest a number of context variables that will influence the value of HyperVoice applications. Below I discuss both positive and negative factors.

Green Flags

Time-critical information Once entered over the phone, information is immediately available to other callers. For applications with time-critical information, HyperVoice will be more useful than communication systems such as mass mailings that have longer delays to publication.

Need for access from home or while traveling One of the great advantages of the telephone is its widespread accessibility. Applications that benefit from entry or retrieval of information from remote sites will be more likely to succeed, since competing technologies cannot match its accessibility.

Need for expressiveness of voice Voice is more expressive than text; through tone, pitch, and speed, a speaker can convey much information not conveyed by a text transcription. Studies of teleconferencing indicate that voice is the single most important channel to include for collaborative tasks [12] and that voice is a better annotation medium for the more complex, controversial, and social aspects of collaborative tasks [4].

Users have weak composition, keyboarding, or reading skills Unlike text-based systems, phone-based systems do not require these skills.

Opportunity to create a 'honeymoon period' Most communication systems have increasing returns to adoption: the utility of the system to each user increases as the number of other users increases [2, 10]. To achieve critical mass, these systems need an initial honeymoon period in which users adopt based on expectations of future value, when others have adopted, rather than on the current utility of the system. Any opportunity to create a honeymoon period, through sponsorship by a powerful person or through a big splash introduction of the system, will improve its chances of success.

Red Flags

Well-entrenched communication patterns Changes from existing patterns are disruptive and people may not perceive the opportunity for better communication patterns.

Poor distribution of costs and benefits The distribution of incentives is a well-known problem for CSCW systems [7]. While the benefits to the group as a whole may outweigh the costs, the benefits may accrue to some individuals and the costs to others, who may then refuse to participate.

Need for anonymity A person's voice is more easily identified than a person's writing style. Research indicates that the anonymity of bulletin boards can improve participation from shy people [3] and that anonymous suggestions can enhance brainstorming sessions [11]. Using digital signal processing algorithms, it is possible to disguise voices, but only at the cost of losing the expressiveness and some of the intelligibility.

Need to scan large information chunks If there is no way to break information chunks into small pieces, then it will take longer to listen to a message than for a good reader to read or scan a written version of it. If, on the other hand, the information divides naturally into small, meaningful segments, then a consistent set of telephone buttons may allow callers to accomplish the fast changes of attention that eye gaze shifts accomplish in visual scanning. This is the idea behind the Skip and Scan interface style [15].

Need to remember large information chunks The presentation of information by phone is ephemeral. If callers need to take information with them, they will have to engage in the tedious process of transcription.

FIELD TRIALS

HyperVoice has generated working prototypes of many different applications, including a joke collector, several versions of an issue discussion application, event calendars, a question and answer line for teachers, and a task tracking application. These prototype applications demonstrate the utility of the HyperVoice primitives as a specification language for a diverse set of applications. The design process for several of the prototypes also demonstrated the utility of HyperVoice's high-level primitives for discussion of alternative designs with non-programmers.

Table 4 summarizes field trials of several of the prototypes. The field trials demonstrate the possibility of usable and useful telephone-based cooperative work applications. Observations from both the successful and unsuccessful field trials are consistent with the success factors described above.

Issue Discussions

In an issue discussion application, callers can not only listen to what others have recorded, but also record responses. Similar to selecting a category of events, a caller to an opinion forum navigates through one or more menus to select a topic. A topic is a list of comments, each having headline and contents fields. Each time a caller adds a comment, an empty list of responses is automatically created. Then, a future caller who listens to a recorded comment presses a button to go to the responses to that comment.

The first issue discussion was used as an adjunct to a class discussion. Despite some technical and user interface difficulties, a majority of the class called and a number of them recorded comments, including responses to others' comments. The second issue discussion, on the topic of intellectual property rights on software user interfaces, was demonstrated at the Interactive Experience at CHI '90. Experts on the topic recorded comments in advance. Most conference-goers, however, were unwilling to publicly record an opinion on such a controversial topic since their voices might be recognized.

Application Name	Message Types	Participatory Design?	# of calls	# of messages added	duration of trial
Issue Discussion 1: class discussion	Comment	No	~20	~10	4 days
Issue Discussion 2: Intellectual Property	Comment	No	~150	3	3 days
Issue Discussion 3: U-TALK	Comment	No	1030+	152+	2 months +
Mandela Task Tracking	Status Report	Yes	1	0	7 days
Mandela Event calendar and Volunteer signup	Message (unstructured)	Yes	1378	more than 200	10 days
Peace and Justice Events Hotline	Event Announcement	No	4578 +	more than 300	1 year +
Curriculum Questions and Answers	Lesson Plan, Question, Response, Success Story, Meeting Announcement, Comment	Yes	72 by head teacher; 66 by others	57 by head teacher; 10 by others	6 weeks

Table 4: Summary of field trials. Those marked + are ongoing.

The final issue discussion, U-TALK, (pronounced "You talk") was open to the entire MIT community. The letters spell out the internal MIT phone number for the system. I initially hoped for serious discussion of issues such as academic honesty. While some people recorded serious comments, and even one poem, others took advantage of the expressiveness of voice to record music and other entertaining sounds. For example, in response to a question about their worst experience at MIT, two people shouted in unison, "Everything!" To preserve anonymity, some people tried to disguise their voices.

Task Tracking

The people coordinating Nelson Mandela's visit to Boston in June 1990 had the opportunity to use a HyperVoice application to help track the status of plans for events. One or two people recruited from local corporations and non-profit organizations were responsible for each of the approximately ten events. In addition, there were several overall coordinators, including a publicity person and an overall operations coordinator. Because they were an ad hoc group, the only technologies that they all had in common were telephones and fax machines.

Interestingly, the HyperVoice specification language provided a convenient language for discussing alternative designs with the head of the operations committee. We considered several designs, varying the fields of a status report, who would be allowed to add new status reports, and who would be allowed to listen to them. We decided on one list of status reports for each event, with open access, both reading and writing, to all members of the operations committee.

The committee members, however, did not use the phone application. Follow-up telephone calls to them indicate several reasons. First, the system was ready too late in the process. Communication and coordination structures, however inadequate, had already been established. Second, the operations coordinator introduced the system briefly in the middle of a lengthy meeting. Several people could not remember the system being introduced at all. Thus, the introduction process did not create enough excitement to spawn a honeymoon period. Third, there was an incentive distribution problem. The work required to post status reports would have fallen on the event coordinators, while most of them perceived that the benefits would all accrue to the overall operations coordinator. Finally, some of the event coordinators wanted to retain as much control as possible over their events. As a result, they did not want to open their plans to others' scrutiny.

Event Calendars

A more successful HyperVoice application publicized the schedule of events for Nelson Mandela's visit to Boston. In this case, the general public was not permitted to add new event announcements. The event organizers, however, added and removed announcements by phone, and this proved to be quite useful for handling last minute changes to the schedule. Printed flyers and newspaper and radio spots advertised the phone number. Besides listening to the schedule of events, callers could also listen to recorded requests for volunteers and leave (unstructured) messages to sign up.

A second event calendar, called the peace and justice event hotline, allowed the general public to post announcements using telephone forms. While a few people had trouble with the structured input (they recorded their entire announcements in each entry blank of the telephone form), most had no trouble.

Leaflets and announcements at political events around Boston publicized the phone number. During the Gulf War, the emcee at a city-wide rally described it as the best source of up-to-date information about events. While transmission of information about event announcements does not require the expressiveness of voice, a number of people remarked that they liked hearing many different voices on the system. More than a year later, the system is still in active use.

Curriculum Questions and Answers

A group of 38 elementary school math teachers used a HyperVoice application to communicate about a new math curriculum that they were using. The HyperVoice specification language again turned out to be useful in discussing alternative designs with a non-programmer, the head teacher who developed the curriculum. The key decisions again were the structure of information objects and who would be able to listen to and add them. We decided to have publicly accessible lists of success stories, meeting announcements, and general comments, and a list of lesson plans that only the head teacher could add to.

Each lesson plan had an attached list of questions that any teacher could add to, and each question had an attached list of responses that they could add to. The motivation for this was that the head teacher routinely handled the same question from more than one teacher, causing her to be on the phone for several hours each night. By making the questions and answers public, she hoped not to handle the same question repeatedly. Thus, this application embodies some of the ideas in the Answer Garden system [1].

The question and answer system made use of the ability to provide multiple presentation formats for information objects. The head teacher promised to call in each night and respond to any questions that other teachers had recorded. There were as many as forty different lesson plans on the system at any one time. Without a special method of access, she would have had to check all forty question lists for new questions.

Instead, each new question was also added to a master list that she checked. In addition, each new question had a field that contained a pointer to its associated lesson plan. That way, the head teacher could listen to the new question and hear what the associated lesson plan was.

The actual usage differed quite a bit from the planned usage. Almost half the teachers never called. Those who did call listened to the lesson plans that the head teacher posted and listened to the meeting announcements. A few of them recorded success stories or congratulations to other teachers on wedding plans, but only two recorded questions. This application, then, gave the head teacher the additional task of recording lesson plans, without reducing the number of repeat questions that she handled. After six weeks, she stopped recording new lesson plans.

A number of plausible explanations can be made of the usage patterns. First, the system was introduced six weeks into the school year, after communication patterns were already set. Second, while the 38 teachers were distributed among many schools, there were usually two or three in each school, and the whole group met for one day a month, so that many teachers may not have felt the need for greater communication. Third, teachers generally do not get much feedback from peers, so that asking publicly about teaching puts them in an unfamiliar and vulnerable position. Thus, the lack of anonymity of recorded voice appeared to be an important factor. Fourth, at approximately ten minutes each, the recorded lesson plans were too long. To absorb all the detail in a recorded lesson plan, teachers would have had to take extensive written notes. Despite that, some teachers did use lesson plans from the phone system in their classrooms.

RELATED WORK

HyperVoice builds on previous research in two areas, telephone-based interfaces and screen-based information-sharing tools. Overall, this project generalizes the notion of semi-structured information objects and presentation formats from text-based systems to a new medium, and develops a telephone interface style that is suited to the entry and presentation of semi-structured objects.

One previous project investigated the collection of semi-structured information objects over the telephone [16]. The PhoneSlave conducted conversations with callers to elicit structured answering machine messages. The system asked each caller a series of questions ("Who's calling please?"; "What is this in reference to?"; "At what number can he reach you?"; etc.) After playing a question, it recorded whatever the caller said, until it detected a long pause, then went on to the next question. The system automatically filled in the date and time of the call. The structured messages were retrieved using graphical tools on a computer screen. HyperVoice generalizes this dialogue to include entry of non-voice data such as dates and even links to other objects. HyperVoice also generates interfaces that take advantage of message structure in presenting information objects for playback by telephone.

A number of asynchronous text-based systems help coordinate the activities of a set of people. Applications have included conversation management [19], task tracking and scheduling.

Malone et al [9] showed that most such applications can be constructed from the following features: 1) sharing of semi-structured information objects 2) filters and, more generally, agents, that automatically select some objects for presentation to particular users at particular times; 3) views that specify how to present visually single objects or collections of objects in ways that are helpful to particular users at particular times.

HyperVoice generalizes the notion of semi-structured objects in these systems to include voice as a data type. It also generalizes the concept of views, a visual notion, to that of presentation formats, and provides presentation formats that are particularly suited to telephones.

FUTURE RESEARCH

Future plans call for the development and evaluation of additional applications and the integration of two other widely accessible technologies, fax and email. The planned applications include an aid to scheduling meetings and task allocation applications (e.g. a distributed sign-up sheet). Some of these will require extensions to the HyperVoice specification language.

To integrate fax and email with the telephone, I am developing an architecture for sharing semi-structured information objects that will allow users to participate with any combination of these technologies, without requiring any individual user to have all three. For example, a user could enter a semi-structured object using a telephone form, but could send in a fax to be the contents of one of the fields, and an email message to be the contents of another. An extension of this idea would be to make the telephone an alternative mode of access to Lotus Notes or Oval [8] databases, for both entry and retrieval.

CONCLUSION

The main message of this paper is that it is possible and worthwhile to use the telephone as a platform for input and retrieval of semi-structured information objects. HyperVoice provides a language that is useful both in considering alternative designs and in specifying applications. The field trials of applications demonstrate that even some prototype-quality systems were usable and useful. The telephone is a worthy platform for further research on CSCW applications and for the development of commercial products.

ACKNOWLEDGMENTS
Tom Malone provided invaluable guidance and assistance throughout this project. Charlie Welch maintains the Peace and Justice event hotline. Wendy Lee did the fundraising and publicity for U-TALK. Victoria Bill, Leslie Clark, Mary Leer, and Lauren Resnick made the teachers' question and answer application possible and Jolene Galegher and Mark Ackerman helped analyze it. Kevin Crowston, Rob Fichman, Chris Kemerer, Jintae Lee, Wanda Orlikowski, Mike Plusch, Chris Schmandt, Bob Virzi, and Joanne Yates also contributed the content of this paper.

REFERENCES

1. Ackerman, M. S. and Malone, T. W. Answer Garden: A Tool for Growing Organizational Memory. In *Conference on Office Information Systems.* (Cambridge, MA, 1990). ACM, pp. 31-39.

2. Arthur, W. B. Competing Technologies: An Overview. In *Technical Change and Economic Theory,* Volume . G. Dosi, Ed. Columbia University Press, New York, NY, 1987.

3. Chaiklin, S. and Schrum, L. Community-Based Telecommunications. In *Third Guelph Symposium on Computer Mediated Communication.* (Guelph, Ontario, Candada, 1990).

4. Chalfonte, B. L., Fish, R. S. and Kraut, R. E. Expressive Richness: A Comparison of Speech and Text as Media for Revision. In *CHI '91: Conference on Human Factors in Computing Systems.* (Seattle, WA, 1991). ACM Press, pp. 21-26.

5. Magnum Software Corporation. TFLX Quick Manual: A Simple Overview of Magnum TFLX and its Picture Programming System. 21115 Devonshire Street, Suite 337, Chatsworth, CA 91311, 1990.

6. de Baar, D. J. M. J., Foley, J. D. and Mullet, K. E. Coupling Application Design and User Interface Design. In *CHI '92 Conference on Human Factors in Computing Systems.* (Monterey, CA, 1992). ACM, pp. 259-266.

7. Grudin, J. Why Groupware Applications Fail: Problems in Design and Evaluation. *Office: Technology and People.* 4, 3 (1989), pp. 245-264.

8. Lai, K.-Y., Malone, T. and Yu, K.-C. Object Lens: A "Spreadsheet" for Cooperative Work. *ACM Transactions on Office Information Systems.* 6, 4 (1988), pp. 332-353.

9. Malone, T. W., Grant, K. R., Lai, K.-Y., Rao, R. and Rosenblitt, D. Semi-structured Messages are Surprisingly Useful for Computer-Supported Coordination. In *Computer-Supported Cooperative Work: A Book of Readings.* I. Greif, Ed. Morgan Kaufmann, San Mateo, CA, 1988, pp. 311-331.

10. Markus, M. L. Towards a 'Critical Mass' Theory of Interactive Media: Universal Access, Interdependence and Diffusion. In *Perspectives on Organizations and New Information Technology,.* J. Fulk and C. W. Steinfeld, Ed. Sage Publications, Newbury Park, CA, 1990, pp. 194-218.

11. Nunamaker, J. F., Dennis, A. R., Valacich, J. S., Vogel, D. R. and George, J. F. Electronic Meeting Systems to Support Group Work. *Communications of the ACM.* 34, 7 (1991), pp. 40-61.

12. Ochsman, R. B. and Chapanis, A. The Effects of 10 Communication Modes on the Behavior of Teams During Co-operative Problem-solving. *International Journal of Man-Machine Studies.* 6, (1974), pp. 579-619.

13. Repenning, A. and Sumner, T. Using Agentsheets to Create a Voice Dialog Design Environment. In *Symposium on Applied Computing.* (Kansas City, MO, 1992). ACM Press, pp. 1199-1207.

14. Resnick, P. HyperVoice: Groupware by Telephone. Ph.D. thesis, Department of Electrical Engineering and Computer Science MIT, 1992.

15. Resnick, P. and Virzi, R. A. Skip and Scan: Cleaning Up Telephone Interfaces. In *CHI '92: Conference on Human Factors in Computing Systems.* (Monterey, CA, 1992). ACM, pp. 419-426.

16. Schmandt, C. and Arons, B. A Conversational Telephone Messaging System. *IEEE Transactions on Consumer Electronics.* CE-30, (1984).

17. Szekely, P. Template-based Mapping of Application Data to Interactive Displays. In *ACM Symposium on User Interface Software and Technology.* (Snowbird, Utah, 1990). ACM, pp. 1-9.

18. Wiecha, C., Bennett, W., Boies, S. and Gould, J. Tools for Generating Consistent User Interfaces. In *Coordinating User Interfaces for Consistency.* J. Nielsen, Ed. Academic Press, San Diego, CA, 1989, pp. 107-130.

19. Winograd, T. A Language/Action Perspective on the Design of Cooperative Work. In *Computer Supported Cooperative Work: A Book of Readings.* I. Greif, Ed. Morgan Kaufmann, San Mateo, CA, 1988, pp. 623-653.

Cooperative Work Environment Using Virtual Workspace

Haruo Takemura and Fumio Kishino

ATR Communication Systems Reserch Labolarories
2-2 Hikari-dai, Seika-cho, Soraku, Kyoto 619-02 JAPAN
+81-7749-5-1211 takemura@atr-sw.atr.co.jp

ABSTRACT
A virtual environment, which is created by computer graphics and an appropriate user interface, can be used in many application fields, such as teleoperation, telecommunication and real time simulation. Furthermore, if this environment could be shared by multiple users, there would be more potential applications.

Discussed in this paper is a case study of building a prototype of a cooperative work environment using a virtual environment, where more than two people can solve problems cooperatively, including design strategies and implementing issues. An environment where two operators can directly grasp, move or release stereoscopic computer graphics images by hand is implemented. The system is built by combining head position tracking stereoscopic displays, hand gesture input devices and graphics workstations.

Our design goal is to utilize this type of interface for a future teleconferencing system. In order to provide good interactivity for users, we discuss potential bottlenecks and their solutions. The system allows two users to share a virtual environment and to organize 3-D objects cooperatively.

KEYWORDS
Virtual reality, virtual environment, cooperative workspace, shared workspace.

INTRODUCTION
"Teleconferencing with realistic sensation" aims at allowing smooth and intricate communications among users by reproducing various aspects of face to face conferencing. One method for achieving this is a virtual conferencing room created by virtual reality technology. Moreover, if we regard this virtual conferencing room as a shared workspace among users, an environment can be formed where users can cooperatively solve various problems.

There are many studies related to virtual reality technology. Beaton et al. evaluated several input devices for a 3-D workstation[1]. They also made a comparison of graphical tasks on stereoscopic and non-stereoscopic displays. Takemura et al. evaluated a 3-D cursor locating task using several types of input devices[13,14]. It is also reported that a 3-D cursor locating task follows Fitts' Law[2,3] when a 3-D digitizer is used for cursor control. Milgram et al. compared effectiveness of depth perception on a stereoscopic display and on a display with motion parallax[10]. Hirose et al. evaluated remote operation of a hand manipulator with remote stereoscopic camera visual feedback[5]. Tachi et al. proposed design strategies for a stereoscopic TV system for teleoperation and evaluated their system[12]. Fisher et al. built a prototype system of virtual reality for telerobotics application[4]. Sturman et al. studied the possibilities of using a hand gesture in an interactive environment[11]. Codella et al. implemented a demonstration system of multi-person virtual world[18].

However, there are not many reports on cooperative environments created by virtual reality. This paper describes the concept of "telecommunications with realistic sensations", the implementation of a cooperative work environment using this concept and an empirical study of the prototype system.

VIRTUAL SPACE TELECONFERENCING AND VIRTUAL WORKSPACE

Virtual Space Teleconferencing
In order to achieve "Teleconferencing with realistic sensations," the concept of virtual teleconferencing is proposed. As shown in Figure 1, a "virtual teleconferencing" system creates an image of a conference room (virtual conference room) using computer graphics in real time. It also constructs images of the remotely located conference participants. Users of the system can talk to each other or proceed with the conference with the sensation of sharing the same space. There are many problems to be solved

Permission to copy without fee all or part of this material is granted provided that the copies are not made or distributed for direct commercial advantage, the ACM copyright notice and the title of the publication and its date appear, and notice is given that copying is by permission of the Association for Computing Machinery. To copy otherwise, or to republish, requires a fee and/or specific permission.

© 1992 ACM 0-89791-543-7/92/0010/0226...$1.50

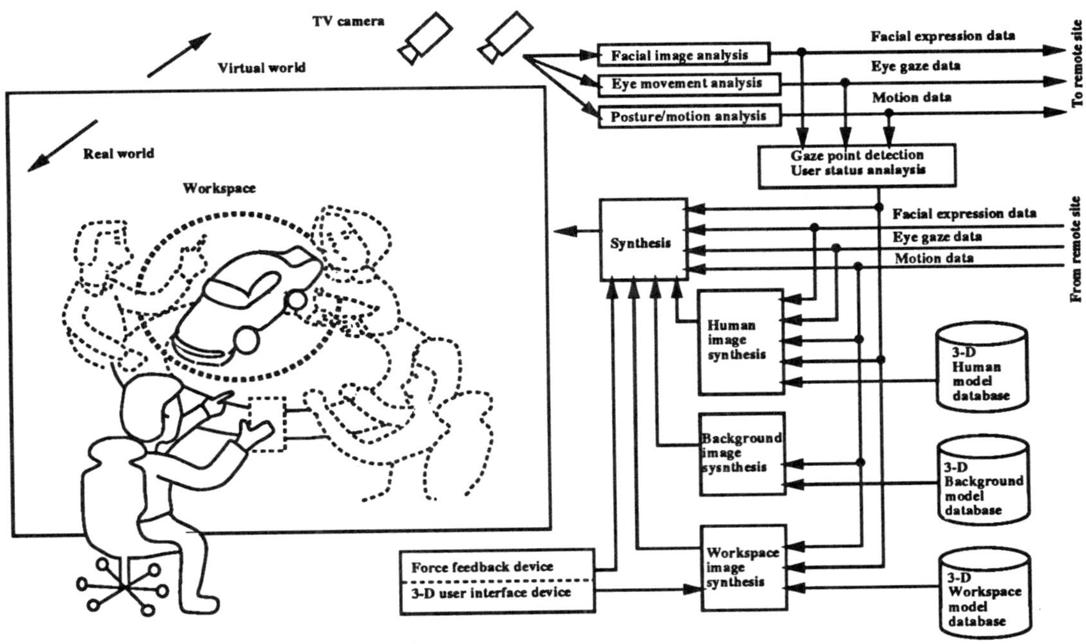

Figure 1. Virtual Space Teleconferencing

however, before this system can be realized. Some of them are now being studied at our labolatories.

A virtual workspace for virtual teleconferencing is to be generated by computer graphics. "Virtual manipulation" is a facility enabling users to interact with the virtual environment. Users can cooperatively work on tasks such as city planning or modeling a new car. In such a case, it is desired that users be able to handle objects in a virtual environment just as they do in a real environment without a sense of incompatibility. If this can be achieved, users can collaborate in various ways without any prior training of teleconferencing operations.

Figure 2(a) shows an overview of "Virtual Manipulation." First, the user's viewing position, hand position and hand

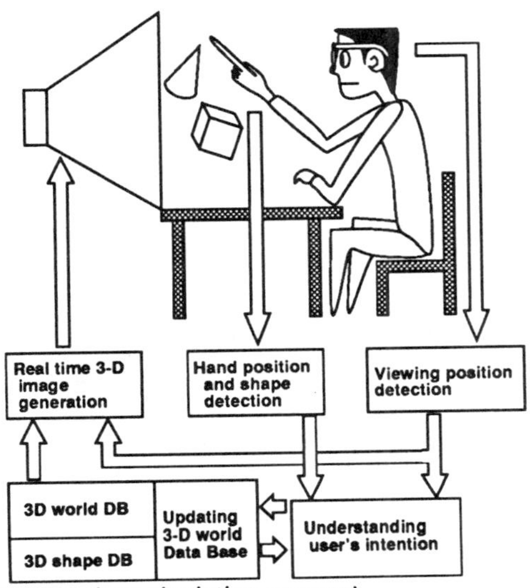

Figure 2. Virtual manipulation concept

shape are measured. The user's intentions are then analyzed to allow grasping, translating or releasing of an object in the virtual environment. The system will be able to select the object of the user's interest with higher order analysis of the user's intention. A prototype system was built for studying feasibility and usability[15].

Virtual Manipulation

Figure 2(b) shows the prototype systems's configuration. A 70-inch CRT projector is used as an image output device for "viewing position tracking stereoscopic display", which is a system for measuring user eye position and generating perspective projection images based on real time measurement.

User eye position is derived from the position of a 6-D magnetic sensor[9] attached to LCD shutter glasses for stereo viewing. Accordingly, the system can present non-distorted images with depth sensations and motion parallax. The screen works as a window into the virtual environment. The

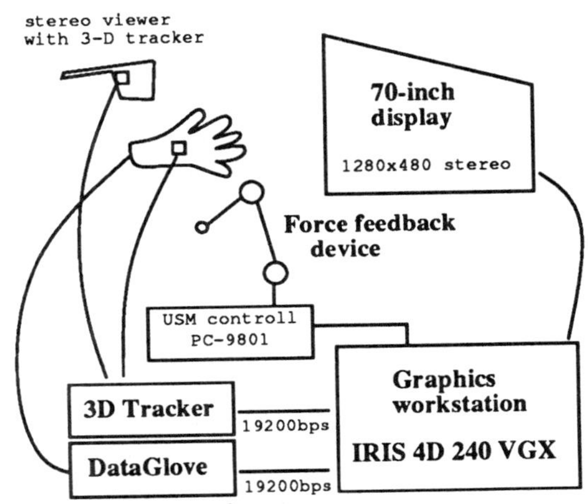

Figure 3. System overview

inside of a quadrangular pyramid determined by the screen corners and the user's eye is the space where virtual objects can be displayed stereoscopically. Viewing a 70-inch diagonal screen at a distance of 1 meter, one can have a viewing angle of 70 degrees and observe objects in an 80 cm × 60 cm rectangular area at a distance of 60 cm. This observation area is sufficiently wide in comparison with a CRT display for direct viewing. Furthermore, the image quality can easily be improved, because the size of the display system is not limited as that of HMD (head mounted display).
Currently implemented features of the system are:

1)Stereoscopic image generation based on the viewing position of the user;
2)Hierarchical object representation;
3)Simple gesture recognition for object handling (Table 1)
4)Simple simulation of physical phenomena.

A user who wears a stereo viewer and a DataGlove[17] can directly grasp the virtual object and perform such manipulation as translation and rotation. Some of the objects in the scene are fixed and some can be moved based on the constraints given to the object.

Neither the 3-D cursor nor computer graphics hand is displayed. The operation, locating one's hand where the object is perceived and grasping it, determines the target of the operation. In comparison with the method which uses an indirect pointer such as a cursor, this method is superior because it does not require users to learn how to operate cursor control devices and allows intuitive operation. By using this system, it is observed that one can manipulate a virtual object with only a slight sense of visual incompatibility.

A force feedback device using a 3-joint master manipulator with a"Torque Controllable Ultrasonic Motor (TOCUS)" has been developed and evaluated to improve system usability[16]. The end of the manipulator and the DataGlove are linked. When the operator grasps an object, the device is so controlled that he feels the weight of the object. This is an implementation of passive feedback. Besides an expression of weight, several types of force feedback are also being studied, as shown in Table 2.

Table 1. Gesture definition

Gesture	Meaning
Grasp	Grasp nearby
Release	Release object
Cancel	Return held object to its initial position
Gravity	Turn on/off gravity simulation
Nextview	Read new view definition file

Table 2. Force feedback type

Name	Control Strategy
Lock	Move the end of the arm to a certain 3-D location
Boundary display 1	Generate force towards surface normal direction
Boundary display 2	Force break on a surface
Area display	Vibrate the arm when the end is in the area
Weight display	Generate force corresponding to the object weight

Auditory or visual feedback, such as operation-related sounds or changing the objects' color, are also effective in improving the way a user interfaces with the system. Such non-contact feedback is compatible with hand shape recognition using image processing. A real time finger tip tracking system based on stereo measurement using two TV cameras is also being studied[6].

COOPERATIVE WORK ENVIRONMENT

"Virtual manipulation" has many applications such as teleoperation, city planning, product design and man-machine interface where a small number of operators must monitor huge amounts of information, e.g., monitoring and operation of electric power plants. Providing a ''virtual manipulation'' environment for collaboration, the system can be used more effectively. The concept of a cooperative work environment in computer networks is known as "computer-supported cooperative work"(CSCW) or groupware. Groupware is also intended to create a shared workspace that supports dynamic collaboration in a work group over space and time constraints[7]. However, a cooperative work environment using virtual workspace is more flexible than the traditional CSCW environment which is based on conventional user interface devices, such as mice, keyboards or CRT displays.

Prototype System

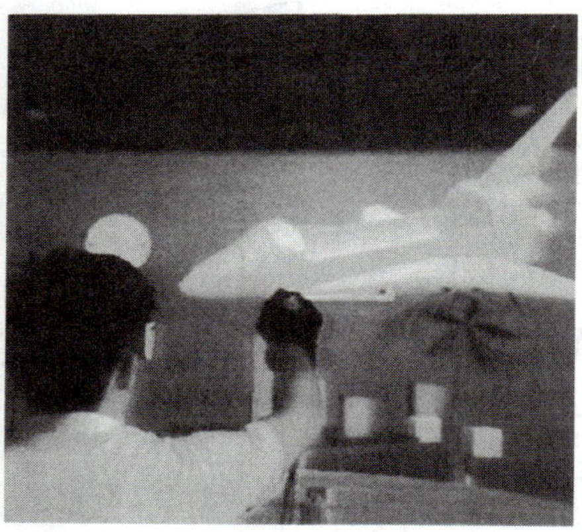

Figure 4. Virtual manipulation system

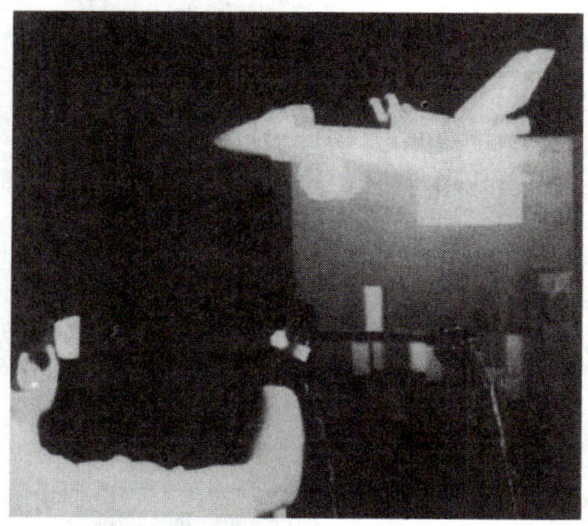

Figure 5. Force feedback user interface

Two of the systems in Figure 2 were used to implement a cooperative work environment. Object layout tasks, such as toy block layout, office furniture layout, and city building layout, were chosen as a model task to be performed in this environment. It is known that understanding the final image of a layout from a 2-D plan requires plan reading skill. From this point of view, such tasks are better suited for a 3-D virtual workspace.
Figure 6 shows the system configuration. Data communication was carried out using a local area network and auditory communication by means of an in-house telephone network.
Figure 7 shows the system processing diagram. A "3D Shape Data Base" is installed at each site for faster computer graphics(CG) image generation, as is a copy of the " Virtual World Data Base." Only retrieval is allowed with the "3D Shape Data Base." CG images are locally generated based on the user's head position data (HPD), "3D Shape Data Base" and "Virtual World Data Base." HPD and " hand shape data"(HSD) are also transmitted to the other site and the "Virtual World Data Base Manager" (VWDBM). VWDBM updates the "Virtual World Data Base" according to incoming data and predefined hand gestures. The updated portion of the data base is then distributed to each site. The sites communicate with each other via a TCP/IP socket connection.

This implementation structure has the following characteristics:
1)Each site can rapidly generate a CG image, because a copy of the data for the image generation is distributed to each site.
2)Gesture understanding and data base updating are performed only by VWDBM. Therefore, it is relatively easy to implement a mutual exclusion facility, such as prohibiting two users from simultaneously grasping the same object.
3)Once the ''3D Shape Data Base'' and ''Virtual World Data Base'' are distributed to each site, there is relatively little data traffic.

Figure 6. Shared workspace configuration

However, the communication link between the two sites is subject to a transmission delay and results in a delay in the user's getting results of their operation.

Implementation Issues
In this section, system implementation issues are described, as follows.

Consistency Each site must share the status of a virtual world, which changes according to operations performed at multiple sites. Therefore, there must be a mechanism to maintain consistency.
The simplest way to maintain consistency of a distributed virtual world database is to restrict manipulation, such that only one site can perform operations to alter the status of the virtual world at one time, such as grasping, rotating or translating an object. This mechanism can be easily implemented by token passing. A site which has a token is allowed to manipulate objects in the virtual world. When there is no need for manipulation, the token is passed to the next site However, this mechanism obviously narrows the possibility of cooperative work. When N sites are used, a single site is the source of actual operation and the other N-1 sites present the results of operation.

Another way to solve this problem is assuming that an operation on one object does not interfere with an operation on another object. By making this assumption, it is possible to allow N different sites to simultaneously manipulate N different objects. The results of an operations at each site are collected at the master site and then redistributed to all sites. In our prototype system, this method is used.

Mutual exclusion If users simultaneously try to alter the status of a virtual world, the status may end up contradictory. For example, two users may simultaneously try to grasp the same object and translate it in different directions. These operations must be prohibited to avoid inconsistency in virtual world status.
Mutual exclusion to avoid simultaneous manipulation of the

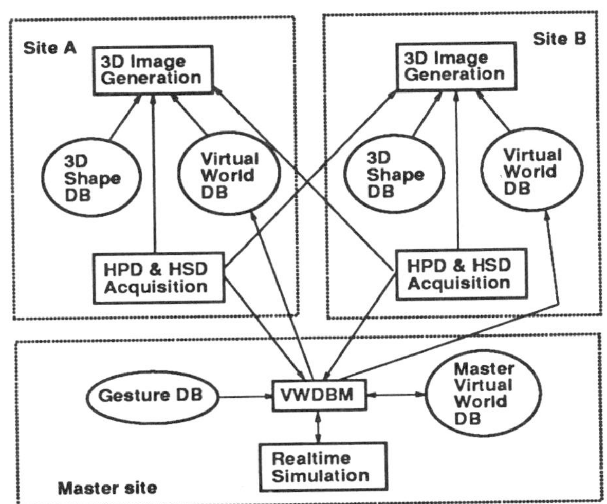

Figure 7 Processing architecture

same object must also be incorporated. If the system has a master site in which all requests for an operation are concentrated, this can be accomplished by simply giving a priority to each request. When two sites request an operation at the same time, the master site allows an operation by the site with higher priority. Objects being manipulated are marked in order to prohibit manipulation by the other site.

Interactivity In order to provide good interaction, the system must respond to users' reactions as quickly as possible. Unlike a single user system, interactivity in a cooperative work environment is affected by the time required for data transmission. Therefore, processing which can be performed locally must be selected and should be implemented at each local site. Distributing redundant data to each site may significantly reduce communication between two sites and improve system response. In particular, the following strategies are actually used:

1)3-D shape data of objects in the virtual environment are distributed to each local sight. A user's head position is also measured locally. Using this head position data and 3-D data, a 3-D scene can be rendered locally. Thus, a user at a local site has a minimum delay in image generation based on one's head position.

2)When a user grasps an object in the virtual environment, a lag between one's hand motion and object motion is minimized by locally binding one's hand position data and object position (Figure 8). At the same time, hand position data is transmitted to the master site to update the master virtual world database, the updated database of which is then distributed to other local sites. This local binding does not cause any inconsistency in the virtual world database provided that each object in the virtual world is manipulated by a single hand at any one time.

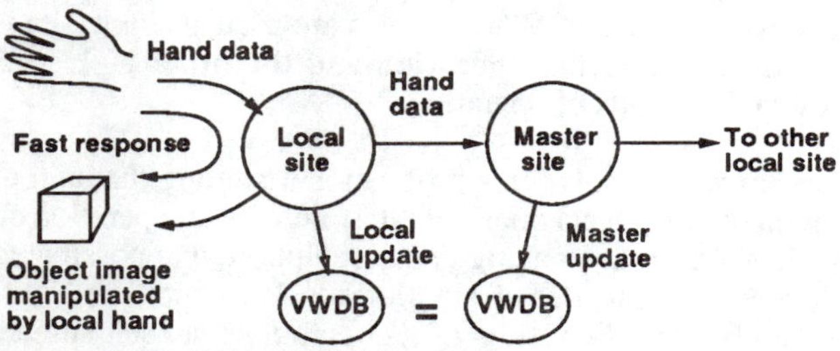

Figure 8. Local loop for fast response

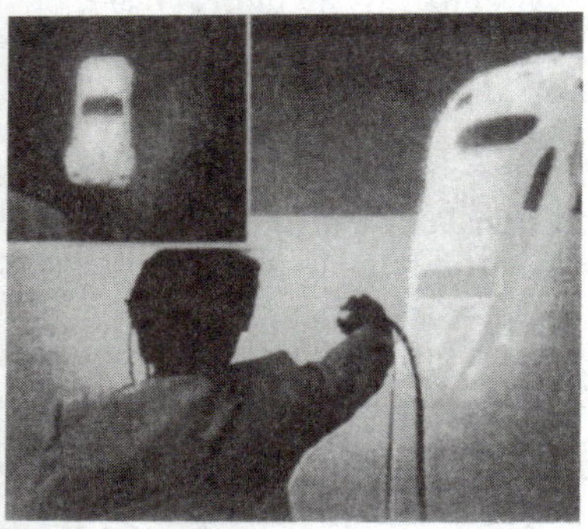
Figure 9. Opposite view orientation

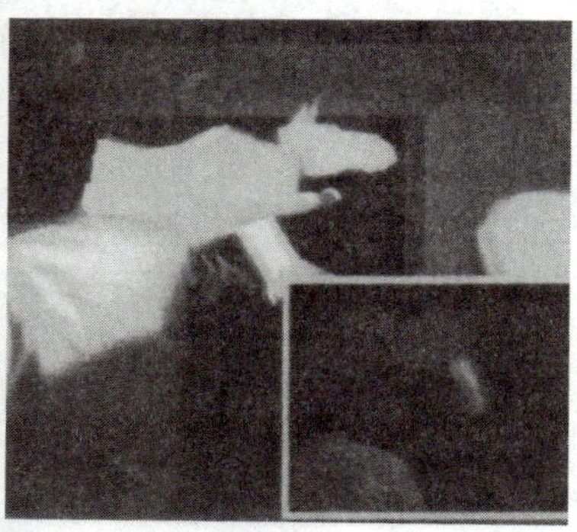
Figure 10. Common view orientation

Using The System

Figure 9 shows two users facing each other and manipulating the CG image of an automobile, located between the two users. Figure 10 shows two users looking in the same direction and sharing the same view. The users are cooperatively assembling a horse-shape 3-D puzzle. In this case, the configuration of looking in the same direction enables the users to share more visual information.

When the opposite view configuration is used, work space which can be shared, is limited as shown in Figure 11(a). The area marked S can be accessed by both users. The area marked E can be viewed by only either of them. Neither of them can perform operations in area E because it is behind the screen. This configuration is useful provided that the task performed requires observation of objects from different points of view. For example, office furniture layout requires an evaluation of the layout from various points of view and is very suitable for this configuration.
On the other hand, when two users are facing in the same direction, the background, which is marked B in Figure 11(b) is also shared by the two users. This configuration also enables them to share a view. Such view sharing is difficult in a real environment because of physical constraints. This configuration is useful for explaining, training or teaching an operation on objects, for example, teaching engine maintenance.

Experiment

Anoperator performance during a simple object moving task was measured using the prototype system. Twenty-seven cubes were placed in a virtual workspace with cubic configuration (3 x 3 x 3) as shown in Figure 12. One surface of a cube was colored with either red or blue. The other 5

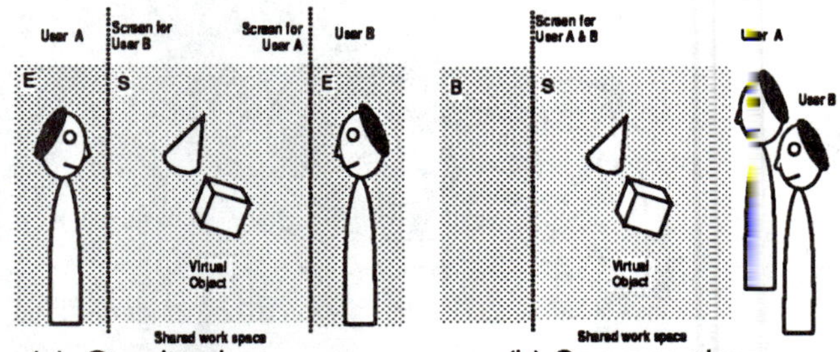

(a) Oppsite view (b) Common view
Figure 11. Shared workspace comparison

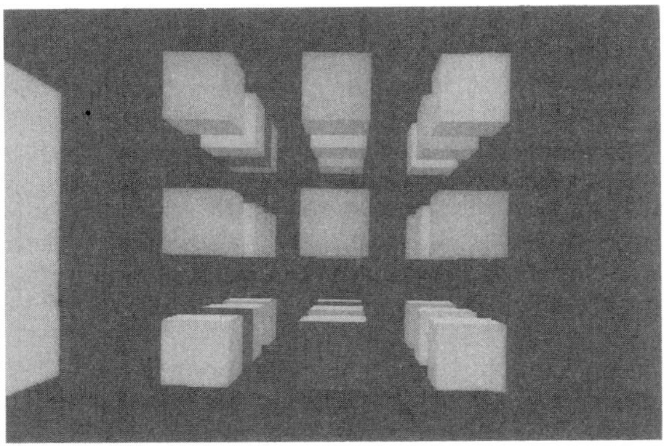

Figure 12. An example of cube layout

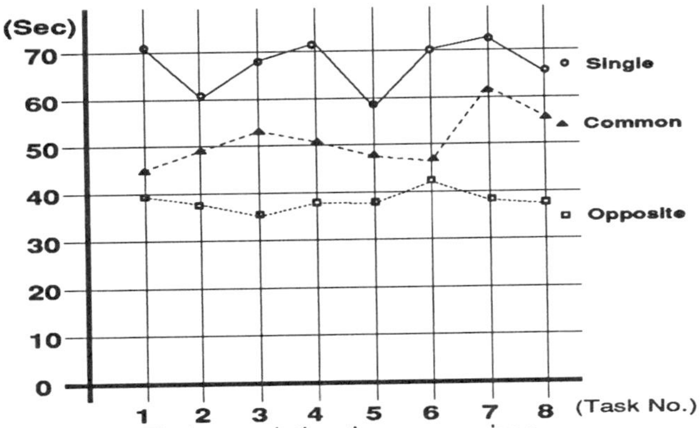

Figure 13. Task completion time comparison

surfaces of a cube were not colored. The orientation of each cube was randomly chosen between two possible orientations. One is an orientation where a colored surface faces towards a user. The other is an orientation which is opposite to the former one. The colored surface is located behind the surface which faces to a user. Therefore, the subject cannot determine color of the cube without rotating it. A subject was asked to move cubes to two specific target areas according to their color as quickly as possible. The time required for placing all (twenty-seven) cubes to the target area was measured. The system also recorded the time required for a single cube placement, which consists of grasping a cube, translating it to its target area and releasing it.

The task was performed eight times in three different situation, respectively. these are,
1)A single subject operator performed the task;
2)Two subject operators performed the task with common view;
3)Two subject operators performed the task with opposite view.

The task completion time is shown in Figure 13. Apparently, cooperative work environments have much better performance compared to a single operation. Among cooperative environments, an opposite view configuration shows significantly better performance to a common view configuration.

Figures 14 and 15 show the distribution of single cube placement performance by one operator with common view and with opposite view configuration, respectively. In case of common view, there are two peaks in the distribution. This is because cube placement tasks are divided into two different types. When colored face is visible to the operator, the cube can be directly placed to the target area. When invisible, the cube must be rotated by the operator to determine its color. The peak at 2.6 second is the latter case. In case of opposite view, each operator choose cubes for which colored the face was visible to them. Therefore, there is an single peak in Figure 15. These results show that this experimental task are suitable for opposite view configuration. Further study of simple, but component, operations are planned for usability analysis of the environment.

SUMMARY

The concept of "Virtual Manipulation" in "Teleconferencing with Realistic Sensations" has been described. A cooperative work environment using "Virtual Manipulation" has been proposed and its implementation issues discussed. A prototype system, where two people can solve problems cooperatively, has been implemented, tested and found to be satisfactory in object arranging tasks. Specific design criteria of the system, such as concurrency and interactivity control have also been described.
A subjective evaluation of the environment is in progress

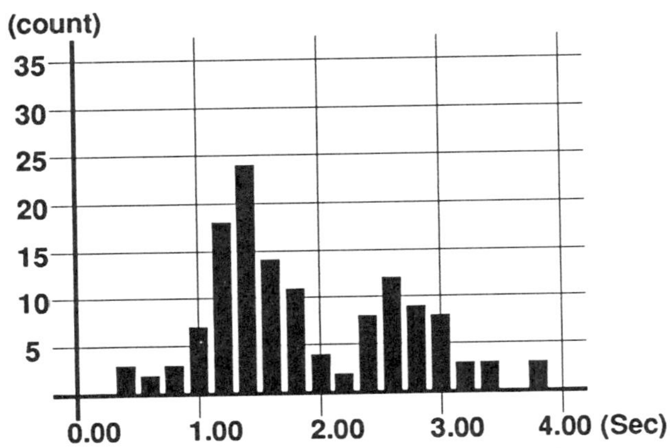

Figure 14 single cube operation with common view

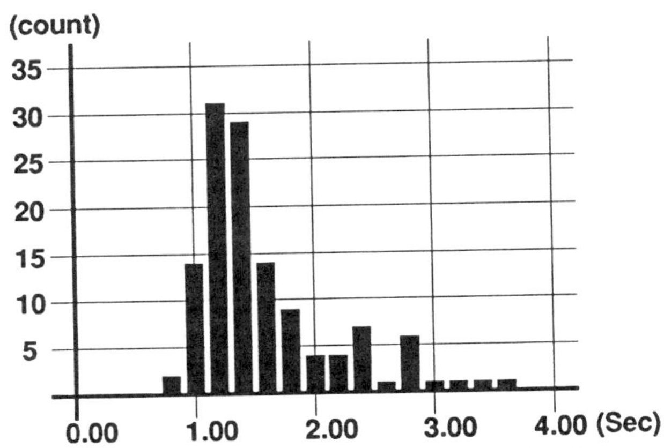

Figure 15. Single cube operation with opposite view

and will help us to understand the feasibility and ramifications of this new communication media.

ACKNOWLEDGMENTS

The authors wish to thank Dr. N. Terashima - President of ATR Communication Systems Research Laboratories, and Dr. K. Habara - Executive Vice President of ATR International (Chairman of the Board of ATR Communication Systems Research Laboratories), for their thoughtful advice and encouragement on this research. The authors also wish to thank their colleagues who voluntarily took part in discussing this study.

REFERENCES

1. Beaten R.J., DeHoff R.J., Weiman, N and Hildebrandt, W . An Evaluation of Input Devices for 3-D Computer Display Workstations, in *Proceedings of SPIE*,vol. 761(1987) The International Society for Optical Engineering, pp. 94-101.

2. Card, S.K., English, W.K. and Burr, B.J. Evaluation of mouse, rate-controlled isometric joy-stick, step keys and text keys for text selection on a CRT, *Ergonomics*, 21, 8(1978), pp. 601- 613.

3. Card, S.K., Moran T.P. and Newell, A. Models of Devices for Text Selection. in *The Psychology of Human-Computer Interaction*, Lawrence Erlbaum Associates Publishers, New Jersey, 1983, pp.229-256.

4. Fisher, S.S., McGreevy, M., Humphries J, Robinett, W. Virtual Environment Display System, in *Proceedings of 1986 ACM Workshop on Interactive Graphics* (1986), ACM Press, pp. 77-87 .

5. Hirose, M., Sudo, J. and Ishii, T. Human Interface of Remote Operation in Three-Dimensional Space(in Japanese), in *Proceedings of the 2nd Symposium on Human Interface*(1986), Society of Instrument and Control Engineers, pp. 237-244.

6. Ishibuchi, K., Takemura, H. and Kishino, F. Real time hand shape recognition and its application for man-machine interface (in Japanese), in *Proceedings of IEICE conference 1991 Autumn* (1991), IEICE.

7. Ishii, H. and Miyake, N. Toward an Open Shared Workspace, *Communications of the ACM*, 34, 12(Dec. 1991).

8. Kishino, F. Communication with Realistic Sensation(in Japanese), *3-D image*, 4, 2(1990).

9. Raab, F.H., Blood, E.B., Steiner, T.O. and Jones H.R Magnetic Position and Orientation Tracking System, *IEEE Trans. on Aerospace and Electronics system*, AES-15,5(1979). pp.709-718.

10. Sollenberger, R.L. and Milgram, P. Stereoscopic Computer Graphics for Neurosurgery, in Proceedings of HCI '89(1989), Elsevier Science Publisher.

11. Sturman, D.J., Zeltzer, D. and Pieper, S. Hands-on Interaction with Virtual Environments, in *Proc. of UIST '89*(1989), ACM Press.

12. Tachi, S., Tanie, K., Komoriya, K. and Kaneko, M. Tele-existence(I): Design and Evaluation of A Visual Display with Sensation of Presence, in *Proceedings of the 5th International Symposium on Theory and Practice of Robots and Manipulators*(1984).

13. Takemura, H., Tomono, A. and Kobayashi Y. An Evaluation of 3-D Object Pointing Using A Field Sequential Stereoscopic Display, in *Proceedings of Graphics Interface '88*(Edomonton, 1988).

14. Takemura, H., Tomono, A. and Kobayashi, Y., A Study of Human Computer Interaction via Stereoscopic Display, in *Proceedings of HCI '89*(Boston, 1989), Elsevier Science Publishers, pp. 496-503.

15. Takemura, H., Tomono, A. and Kishino, F. A Usability Study of Virtual Environment, in *Proceedings of the 6th Human Interface Symposium*(Tokyo, 1990), The Society of Instrument and Control Engineers, pp. 577-582.

16. Takemura, H., Tomono, A. and Kishino, F. A Study of Force Feedback in Virtual Workspace(in Japanese), in *Proceedings of IEICE Conference 1991 Spring*(1991), IEICE.

17. Zimmerman, T.G. and Lanier, J. A Hand Gesture Interface Device , in *CHI+GI '87 Proceedings(1987), ACM Press*, pp.189-192.

18. Codella, C. et al. Interactive Simulation in a Multi-Person Virtual World, in CHI '92 Proceedings (Monterlay, 1992), ACM Press, pp. 329-224.

Identifying Potential CSCW Applications by Means of Activity Theory Concepts: A Case Example

Kari Kuutti

University of Oulu, Department of Information Processing Science
Linnanmaa, SF-90570 Oulu, Finland
+358 (81) 352602 kuutti@rieska.oulu.fi

Tuula Arvonen

City of Espoo Council, Department of Health Care, SOPU-project
Kamreerintie 5, Rahatoimisto 5 krs., SF-02770 Espoo, Finland

ABSTRACT

The paper presents some novel concepts and models derived from Activity Theory for to identify a potential CSCW application. It is suggested that the six elements of the structure of the activity concept might be useful for differentiating between areas of support, and that three levels of support are needed in order to cope with both routine and emergent features of cooperative work situations. Thus a 3x6 support type classification is formed and its usefulness studied by means of a real-world example. A work situation is analyzed, problems identified and possible areas of support defined. A temporary solution is produced and, by evaluating it, possible directions for the development of a "real" new CSCW application and the usefulness of the classification are discussed.

KEYWORDS

CSCW applications, work support types, requirements analysis, emergent features, activity theory.

INTRODUCTION: THE DIFFICULTY OF DESIGNING CSCW APPLICATIONS

Given that the Computer-Supported Cooperative Work (CSCW) research community has not yet been able to reach a generally accepted formulation of what is a CSCW application, it is no wonder that the methods for designing such applications have been slow to emerge. In fact, CSCW design is still practically a non-existent discipline. One reason for this is the lack of appropriate conceptualizations of cooperative work on which design could be based.

Permission to copy without fee all or part of this material is granted provided that the copies are not made or distributed for direct commercial advantage, the ACM copyright notice and the title of the publication and its date appear, and notice is given that copying is by permission of the Association for Computing Machinery. To copy otherwise, or to republish, requires a fee and/or specific permission.

© 1992 ACM 0-89791-543-7/92/0010/0233...$1.50

This paper suggests that by using suitable core concepts and by layering the support types it might be possible to take some initial steps towards practical design. Two areas in particular are addressed in this paper: dealing with the emergent features of the work and finding suitable metaphors to guide the design.

How does one design for emergent features?

One problem has been the situational and elusive character of cooperative work: if it is something which just "emerges" in situations (e. g. [12], [13]), how can one design support for it at all, because that would require fixing many aspects of the work beforehand and thus the emergence would be restricted – and so on. There have been many attempts to base CSCW design on models of the allocation of tasks or prescribed patterns of communication, but they lead to a rigidity which is incapable of coping with the open nature and emergent features of cooperative work (for an accurate criticism, see [12]).

So how should emergent and unanticipated features be supported in a meaningful way?

Where do the design metaphors come from?

The study of computer support types for CSCW has been quite limited, with the most common approach being the use of popular metaphors, like "tool", "medium" or "shared material". Even a "panopticon" – an instrument for increased social control [2] and "shared knowledge or memory" [3] have been mentioned. It is clearly difficult to locate the support and to produce good analytical descriptions of the relationship between work and information technology – although CSCW research is not alone in suffering from this inability. I have suggested elsewhere [9], [10] that one reason for this may be that information technology penetrates the structure of a work activity and changes it so deeply that "the support" is in fact inseparable from the structure of the work itself.

Some of the suggested metaphors can obviously be of considerable value for design, at least heuristically. If the models of organizational structures do lead to rigidity, perhaps CSCW design could proceed by relying only on heuristic metaphors. But where do the design metaphors come from? Do we already have a complete reservoir of them – and if not, where should we begin the search for new ones?

Approach taken in this paper

The initial assumption of this paper is that the conceptualization of work given by Activity Theory could form a fruitful starting point for tackling the problems presented above. They are addressed here as follows:

Emergent features.

Although 'tailorability' or 'constructability' is obviously one of the features CSCW applications should possess (see [4] and [12]), it is clear that 'tailorability' alone cannot form a CSCW application – otherwise programming languages would be the best possible applications. There must be something to be tailored, something so much work context dependent that it can support the work. That part has to be pre-specified, and the larger it is the more support an application can deliver – at least quantitatively. Thus there should be a balance between the 'closedness' and 'openness' of the application: if it is totally closed, it will not support the necessary adaptation to changes, and if it is totally open, it may not help sufficiently in dealing with those aspects which do not change so rapidly.

In real life both features can and do naturally coexist in same systems. As a first step for helping to deal with these differences, the paper suggests a three-level layering schema based on the different (theoretical) roles a person can have in an activity:

- user of a ready-made artifact in a pre-specified way

- user of a ready-made artifact in a self-specified way

- creator of a new artifact.

This gives us some kind of elementary scale for discussing the level of support a system is aiming to offer.

Design metaphors.

It is plausible that a good theory of cooperative work could help us in finding new design metaphors. This paper attempts to use one Activity Theory conceptualization, the structure of (work) activity, for that purpose. As mentioned before as an initial assumption, information technology penetrates the whole work structure. Since the structure of the activity has six major elements, it is simply assumed that information technology can help in dealing with each of them, and new metaphors are formed accordingly.

Definition of a CSCW application

Following Bannon & Schmidt [3] and Kuutti [10], CSCW is defined in this paper as *work by multiple active subjects sharing a common object, supported by information technology*. The definition can cover a great part of the recent research and still be able to draw acceptable clear boundaries around the object of it. The existence of active subjects gives us a means to delineate CSCW from "traditional information systems", where predetermination of work sequences by the system has been the normal case. On the other hand, a common object of work is clearly different from a shared goal (criticized as too restrictive) or shared material (criticized as too loose). Negotiators may have opposite goals, but they have a common object, a problem space. Database users may share material, but the objects of their work need not have anything in common. Similarly a community which shares a common object of work can usually be fairly easily delineated in practice, whatever the contributions of the different participants in that community may be.

THE CONCEPT OF ACTIVITY IN THE DESIGN OF CSCW APPLICATIONS

This section gives a short glimpse of Activity Theory and introduces the concept of activity and a work support typology based on it.

Activity Theory

There have been several attempts recently to search for a suitable theoretical background for CSCW in different social theories, like those proposed by Heidegger, Habermas and Giddens, for example. Activity Theory is one more, albeit less well known possibility among these social theories. It may be the only school of social thinking which has originated in Soviet Union and has been able to gain a foothold in western world, too. Although the concept of activity as a scientific tool was first formulated within Soviet cultural-historical psychology, it has gained users around the world. It has also been found to be useful and flexible for the analysis of other disciplines, such as education, the social sciences, cultural research, anthropology, work science etc.

Broadly defined, Activity Theory is a philosophical framework for studying different forms of human praxis as developmental processes, both individual and social levels interlinked at the same time. Although the framework is still more an agenda for a research programme than a 'complete' theory, the conceptual tools developed thus far have had promising qualities. For those with a deeper interest, reference [9] contains a more comprehensive introduction to Activity Theory (AT) and also relevant bibliographical references. Reference [5], in the same volume, considers AT from a more practical (Information Systems) viewpoint, and reference [7] studies the use of AT in different empirical research settings.

The behavioural and social sciences have always suffered from a dichotomy between the individual and the social. If one uses a social system as a unit of analysis, there are problems in maintaining human agency. If one studies individual actions, there are problems in maintaining contextuality. Social systems in general are too big and messy to be used as contexts, but actions without context are often meaningless. On the other hand, arbitrarily selected contexts (like those in many lab studies) do not help much in theory-building.

The solution offered by Activity Theory is that there is a need for an intermediate concept – a minimal meaningful context for individual actions – which must form the basic unit of analysis. This unit – better defined and more stable than just an arbitrarily selected context, but also more manageable than a 'whole' social system – is called an activity. Because the context is included in the unit of analysis, the object of our research is always essentially collective, even if our main interest lies in individual actions. The concept of activity is elaborated further in the next section.

The concept of activity

The following contains a short description over some properties of the concept of activity. Because of the scope of the theory and the space limitations of this paper, the description is quite superficial and several topics are just mentioned.

As stated earlier, the basic idea is that there exists a "fundamental type" of context, which is called an activity. It is meaningless to study essentially human qualities using a smaller object of research, because without that basic context one cannot grasp the essence of the phenomenon.

Activities in which humans participate are the basic units of development and human life and thus form the basis of the study of all contextuality. Activities – an individual can participate in several at the same time – have the following properties:

- an activity has *an object* and activities can be distinguished according to their objects. The transformation of the object towards some desired state or direction motivates the existence of the activity.

- an activity is a *collective phenomenon.*

- an activity has an active *subject (actor)*, who understands the motive of the activity. This subject can be individual or collective. Not all participants involved in an activity necessarily understand the motive of the activity in which they are participating or even recognize the existence of one. In this case they are not active subjects of the activity.

- an activity exists in *a material environment* and *transforms it.*

- an activity is a *historically developing* phenomenon.

- *contradictions* are the force behind the development of an activity.

- an activity is realized through conscious and purposeful *actions* by participants.

- the relationships within an activity are *culturally mediated.*

Y. Engeström [6] has made an attempt to establish a simple structural model of the concept of activity and culturally meditated relationships within it.

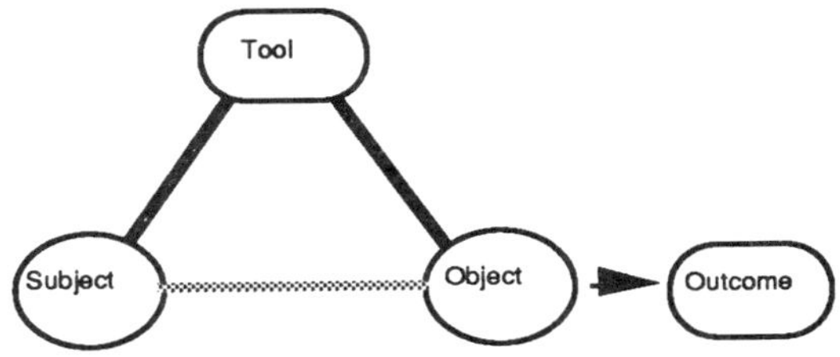

Figure 1: Structure of an individual, mediated action

Cultural mediation is dealt with in Engeström's model by replacing binary relationships with mediated relationships. This is carried out by introducing a third, intermediate term which carries with it the cultural heritage of the situation. Thus the central relationship – that between the *subject* and the *object* of activity – is mediated by a *tool (instrument)* into which the historical development of the relationship between subject and object thus far is condensed. This simple structure is not adequate to fulfil the needs of a consideration of the systemic relations between an individual and his environment, however, and thus Engeström adds a third main component, namely *community* (those who share the same object of activity). Thus two new relationships are formed: subject-community and community-object. Both of them are also mediated and thus we have the structure described in Figure 2.

This systemic model – which according to Engeström is the simplest possible in terms of a unit of analysis– contains three mutual relationships between subject, object and community.

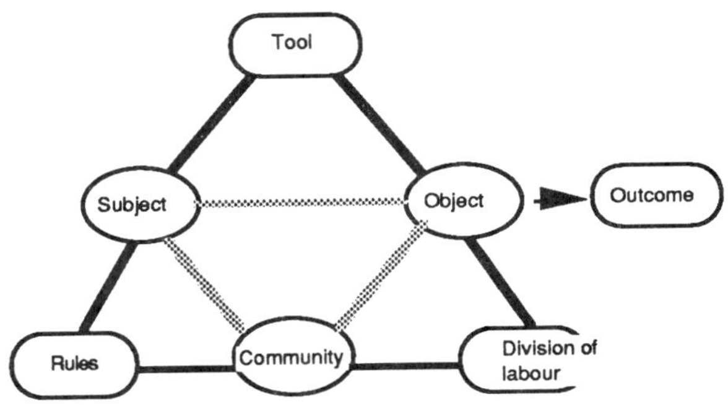

Figure 2: Basic structure of an activity

The relationship between subject and object is mediated by tools, that between subject and community is mediated by *rules* and that between object and community is mediated by the *division of labour*. Each of the mediating terms is historically formed and open to further development. In fact, during the existence of an activity the corresponding mediating members are continuously reconstructed. This development is not a smooth linear one however, but uneven and discontinuous, driven by different contradictions.

Persons generally participate in several parallel activities in work, home and social life. For example, an IS development project for, say, a departmental application can apparently be described as an activity. It has a collective subject – the development group – which uses a development methodology as a tool in order to transform an object – the work practice to be improved. There is a community which shares the object: at least the manager of the department and those workers whose work will be affected. There is a set of explicit and implicit rules controlling the relationship between the subject and the community: administrative procedures, accepted work practices, union rules etc. There is also a certain division of labour in transforming the object: what the development group is expected to do, what belongs to the role of the departmental manager, the role of workers etc.

At the same time there is another activity in which the subject is the leader of the development project, his or her tools are project management tools and the object is the development project itself and its successful completion. The community consists of the members of the project group. Again, there is a certain – but different – set of rules and division of labour.

We can imagine a third connected activity in which the subject is the departmental manager, who is using the whole project as a tool to change the power structure of the organization for his or her own benefit. The community consists of his or her peer managers and the upper administration, and again a set of rules and a division of labour can be found.

So, in real life situations there always exists an interconnected web of activities, which can be distinguished according to their objects. Participation in interconnected activities having very different motives can cause tensions and distortions (e.g. the position of the departmental manager in the example).

Work activity as a basic element in analyzing organizations

It is obvious that the concept of work activity is in a good harmony with the tentative definition of the basic unit of work to be supported. The concept allows the analysis to span from the individual to an organization-wide level and even broader, but it is far more flexible than the concept of formal organization. On the one hand, it is possible to study formal organizational units as activities – to the extent that a community of active subjects sharing the same object can be found. In most traditional, hierarchical organizations the formal borders of an organization do not necessarily fit together nicely with the activities, because often only the managers of organizational units are 'active subjects', who use their units as tools to strive after their goals. Thus the activities found at the traditional organization level are mostly only managerial ones, and other people are treated as wheels in the organizational machinery, invisible in activity analysis. On the other hand, the concept of activity makes it easy to cross any departmental, organizational or geographical borders – only belonging to the group of active subjects sharing an object is significant.

How can a work activity come to be supported by information technology?

The structure of the activity concept is used to generate a classification of basic types of work support (Figure 3). In practice applications usually cover several support types.

Role of a person towards the support system in an activity

Area of support	Pre-determined	Active	Expansive
Instrument	Routine automation	Tool	Automation or tool construction
Rules	Control	Shared meanings	Rule cor-struction, negotiation
Division of labour	Fixed, "forced coordination"	Mutual coordi-nation	Organizing work
Subject, 'thinking'	Triggering of a predetermined action	Searching information	Learning, under-standing
Object	Data	Shared material	Object construction
Community	Fixed hierarchy/ network (invisible)	Malleable, visible network	Community construction

Figure 3: The range of relationships between an actor and a support system in an activity.

The classification of rows is based on the main structural parts of an activity, the internal activity of a subject being (somewhat crudely) condensed here under the title 'thinking'. The classification of columns is based on the different roles a person can have towards artifacts in an activity: a predetermined role, using given artifacts in a pre-specified way; an active role, using given artifacts but deciding actively how, where and when, to use them; and finally, as an active developer of artifacts in an activity.

This classification contains many familiar elements. For instance, the first column corresponds to a "traditional" data processing system: routine automation, potential control of users, fixed division of labour, triggering of actions ("alarms"), no personal relationship with the object of the work ("just data"), a fixed organizational hierarchy or network which many times is invisible to the individual users. The second column contains most – if not all – of the metaphors used in CSCW discussions. The separation between "shared material" and "shared meanings" may not be used commonly. Usually the term "shared material" is used without any differentation. This classification suggests that it might be useful to separate different types of shared material. We will return later to this topic.

The third column describes different areas where information technology may help one to deal with emergent features in a situation. This dimension of "metaphors" has not been widely discussed within CSCW. Here it has been assumed that information technology can somehow support the formation and change of any of the structural elements of an activity. The formation and change of an active subject is a complex issue and only one of its facets – learning – is mentioned here.

A CASE EXAMPLE

An attempt is made in this section to use the concepts introduced above to analyse a real-life case example.

The SOPU project

The background to the case to be elaborated lies in the SOPU project which is currently going on as a joint effort between the social services and health care departments of the City of Espoo Council, Finland. The project began in 1989 and it will continue until 1994, and its goal is to move the organization in a more service-oriented direction and reduce the bureaucracy and the traditionally strong sectoral division between the units involved (for a more accurate description of the project, see [11]).

A new information system with a corresponding infrastructure should play a major role in the organizational change. On the one hand, the highly participative process of developing the system will also be used instrumentally to create and disseminate the necessary new, more holistic work orientation. On the other hand, the new system to be built will hopefully - to some extent - institutionalize the resulting work orientation and enable the realization of corresponding new, cooperative forms of work which have been impossible so far.

The core idea on which the integration of the efforts of the different organizational units is based is that they actually share a common object of work. This common object has been obscured, however, by tightly sectorized practices, and the new information system should thus be designed around it. This approach corresponds closely to the recent theoretical attempts to define CSCW applications by means of a common object, content, issue etc. (e.g. [1], [3], [8], [10]). The project has been able to delineate and conceptualize the common general object as the basis of information system development. It has been defined as the 'life processes' of the citizens, so that the service orientation of all organizational units involved should be to help the citizens to master their 'life processes' themselves. 'Life processes' have different attributes and dimensions. They are partially separate but partially overlapping, and problems within these overlapping areas have been especially difficult solve cured by sectorized practices. The orientation of the approach is quite different from existing systems, where the starting point has been existing organizational practices. Correspondingly, the conceptualization of 'life processes' has not been an easy task, but has called for a demanding, research-like effort.

Information systems can support the service task in a number of ways. Thus the new information system will consist of a common data base, basic administrative routine applications (13 recognized and outlined so far), personal and management tools and CSCW-like applications. The preliminary design of the data base has been completed and construction of the first applications has begun. The number of personal computing, management-oriented and CSCW applications has not been fixed beforehand, because it is believed that they must be identified by the users themselves, and this is impossible before the learning process inherent in the participative design of the basic applications has taken place.

This paper presents an example of how initiatives for CSCW applications may proceed in the future, and also elaborates some initial concepts which may be useful for conceptualizing and defining the boundaries of those applications. It must be noted, however, that while the SOPU project is seriously attempting to help citizens to master their life processes themselves, that dimension is consciously left out of this paper. Issues concerning the agency of clients have been dealt with in the project using the concepts introduced here, but giving them a fair treatment would lead to discussions beyond the scope and space of this paper. Therefore only a partial perspective – that of traditional professionally-oriented care-keeping – is adopted here simply to illustrate the potential of our conceptual framework. Thus the treatment and suggestions in the paper do not necessarily cover those actually made in the project.

A problematic situation

The work situation analyzed here involves a strict sectoral division of labour between different units responsible for health care and social services in a city. A client has multiple problems – a couple of different biomedical diseases, mental problems (depression) and social problems (mistrust, loneliness, inadequate housing). Attempts to help him have been made by different professionals belonging to different organizational units. Little progress is made because each of the helpers can see only a partial view of the situation, and so the advice or help can be insufficient or even conflicting. Over ten people have been involved in different aspects of the case history.

The situation is first analyzed as an activity from the viewpoint of a physician at a health care center (Figure 4).

Several contradictions can be defined in the situation. The tools and instruments available to the physician - aimed

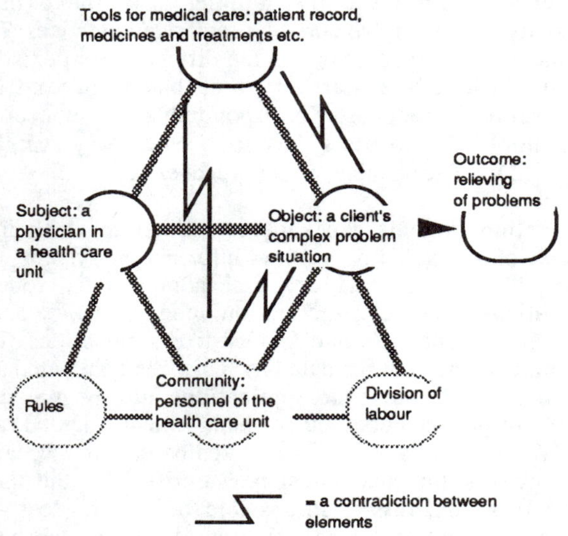

Figure 4. The problem situation described as an activity, from the viewpoint of a physician in a health care unit.

mainly at medical problems - are inadequate to tackle the multidimensionally problematic life situation of the client. There is no actual community sharing the same object and thus there cannot be any real activity - it is nobody's true concern to adopt a 'holistic' view and initiate corresponding treatment. And even if a true community did exist, there is no instrument to tackle the problem. The situation can be described as in Figure 5.

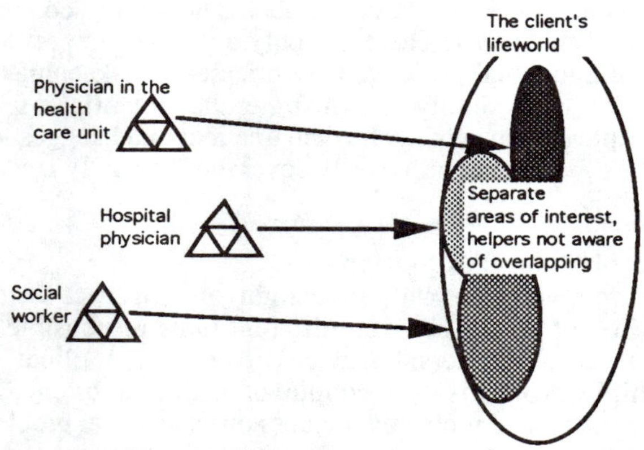

Figure 5. Separate, but overlapping and potentially conflicting areas of interest of different helpers.

The situation should be transformed so that the problem as a whole becomes the common object of all efforts, which are at present separated and unsynchronized. For this it is necessary that the separate helpers should actually be united into a new community.

This alone does not help, however, for there is also a need for new, common instruments, but there are considerable problems in producing this kind of new common effort, because there are no organizational rules or procedures to define how people belonging to different organizations should handle this kind of situation together. Neither there are any convenient means to carry out the necessary negotiation between the people involved.

Analysis of the situation

How could information technology help in resolving this problematic situation? The situation has been analyzed using a work support typology and the potential areas in which information technology could potentially be most useful are shown in Figure 6.

In terms of the typology, it is possible to support the formation of a new community, new instruments and a new work object. Thus there is some potential for alleviating the major problems.

	Pre-determined	Active	Expansive	
Instrument	Routine automation	Tool	Automation or tool construction	IT can be used to create new instruments or enhance old ones
Rules	Control	Shared meanings	Rule con-struction, negotiation	
Division of labour	Fixed, "forced coordination"	Mutual coordi-nation	Organizing work	
Subject, 'thinking'	Trigge-ring	Searching	Learning, under-standing	
Object	Data	Shared material	Object construction	IT can enable that something can be made into an object of an activity
Community	Fixed hierarchy/ network (invisible)	Malleable, visible network	Community construction	IT can be used to create and maintain a new community

Figure 6. (Based on figure 3.) Areas of potential support by information technology (IT) in the activity studied.

Practical attempt to solve the problem using the means available

In this particular case a temporary solution was worked out by a physician. A new community consisting of members of some of the authorities already involved in the case was formed by networking them via e-mail (and telephone + ordinary mail where e-mail was not available).

A number of private individuals involved in the same work were also connected to the network. The resulting network is described in Figure 7.

This means that a new activity had begun to emerge. In order to establish it, several issues had to be negotiated via e-mail (and telephone), e.g. the division of labour (who will

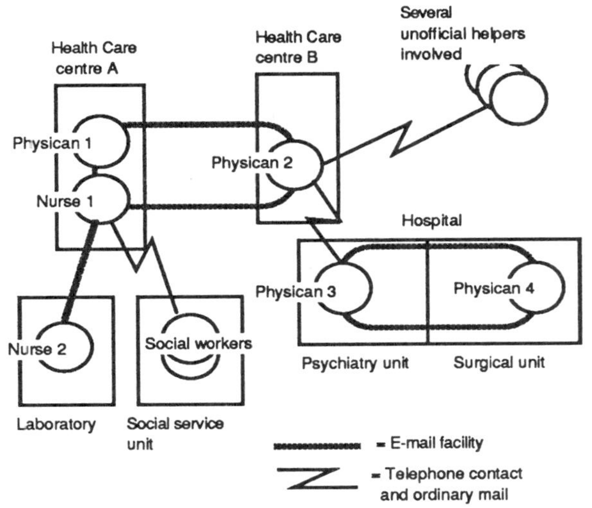

Figure 7. The network built up by a physician (P2) to establish a new community of helpers.

contact whom) and rules (what should be done and in what order when there is a change in situation or plans) etc. New artifacts have been created within the newly forming activity. On the one hand the formerly separate case histories have been collected together, which enables the whole problem situation to become an object for all the members of the community, and on the other hand, a kind of a "master help plan" has started to take shape as an adequate tool for tackling the whole problem. It is based on a collection of the formerly separate "help plans" which are now beginning to be synchronized. It is worth noting that although both the representation of the object and the emerging new tool are both "shared material" and, in fact, consist of very similar data items differing only by their timing (history vs. future), the actual use of them is different. Figure 8 describes the emergent new situation.

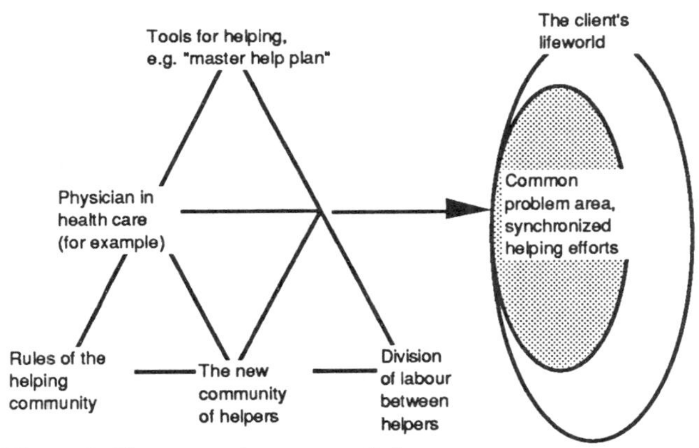

Figure 8. The emerging new activity.

The new 'master help plan' circulating within the community provides a more holistic view, and it will be updated if the situation changes. The new activity with its new instruments has been capable of solving the citizen's problems more successfully than earlier.

Evaluation of the solution and speculation upon a potential CSCW application

What can we learn from the example? Even in this simple case information technology has been used in many different ways to support the activity at both its formulation and operation stages. It is easy to see, however, that the process and the solution reached are not by any means optimal. Perhaps the most obvious obstacle was the lack of e-mail connections between the organizational units which caused a lot of unnecessary work. But even if that had not been the case, some problems would have remained due to the rudimentary nature of e-mail as the only means for technological support. Only within the 'community' area was it possible to achieve an adequate solution - to establish a semipermanent, visible community by means of a distribution list, but although both 'instrument' and 'object' areas were supported in the case, the support offered by e-mail was the minimal one to enable some solution at all.

With an expansive level of support one can cope with the emergent features of a situation, but if the system does not support other levels, one has to build everything from scratch every time, and run the resulting system manually, without much support. The situation is described in Figure 9.

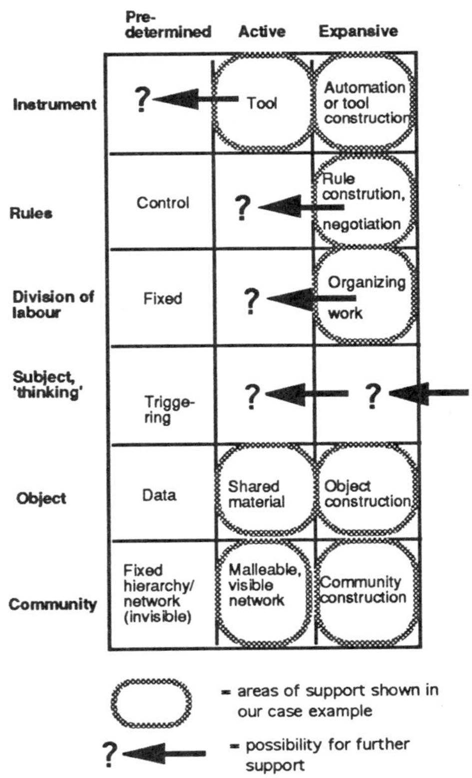

Figure 9. (Based on figure 3) The support given by IT in the example and potential directions for the development of a 'real' CSCW application.

Since clients with multiple problems are not by any means uncommon, it would perhaps be possible to pre-specify certain support types which would be useful in similar situations.

According to Figure 9 there are many potential directions in which a more 'mature', sophisticated CSCW application could be developed. For example, although e-mail in this case has served as a platform for constructing the rules or shared meanings, as a platform for forming an object (represented by the combined case histories) and as a platform for creating a tool to deal with the object (the master help plan), there is very little additional support for using and maintaining them. Is there a need for an "etiquette book" for this type of cases? Should the case history have some predetermined semistructural form - a topic widely discussed in medical information science? Or is there a need for an accessible, complete, annotated history of the corrections made to the master help plan? Is there anything which could be automated? One can invent similar questions for each support area.

By evoking questions of this kind, the classification can be made to direct the design towards finding effective areas of support.

CONCLUSION

The aim of this paper has been to show that the concept of activity is useful for analyzing organizational situations in order to locate places where new CSCW applications could be used, and also for studying different avenues along which more mature and efficient support for work might proceed. In particular, it was found that the "shared material" metaphor may be too broad to be constructive because "shared material" can actually be used for several distinct purposes: in this case, "tool", "object" and "shared meaning" types were recognized, all of which may need different treatment.

ACKNOWLEDGMENTS

The comments of anonymous referees greatly helped us in clarifying the paper.

REFERENCES

1. Applegate, L., Ellis, C., Holsapple, C. W., Radermacher, F. J. and Whinston, A. J. Organizational Computing: Definitions and Issues. *Journal of Organizational Computing*, vol. 1 no. 1, 1991, pp. 1-10.

2. Bannon, L., Bjørn-Andersen, N. & Due-Thomsen, B. Computer support for cooperative work: an apparaisal and critique. In Bullinger, H. J. (ed.) *EURINFO 88*, Nort-Holland, Amsterdam,1988, pp. 297-303.

3. Bannon, L. J. & Schmidt, K. CSCW: Four Characters in Search of a Context? In Bowers, J. M. & Benford, S. D (eds.) *Studies in Computer Supported Cooperative Work.* Theory, Practice and Design. North-Holland, Amsterdam, 1991, pp.3-17.

4. Bowers, J. M. The Janus Faces of Design: Some Critical Questions for CSCW. In Bowers, J. M. & Benford, S. D (eds.) *Studies in Computer Supported Cooperative Work.* Theory, Practice and Design. North-Holland, Amsterdam, 1991, pp. 333-350.

5. Bødker, S. Activity Theory as Challenge to Systems Design. In Nissen, H.-E., Klein, H.K. and Hirschheim, R. (eds.) *Information Systems Research Arena of the 90's.* North-Holland, Amsterdam, 1991, pp. 551-564.

6. Engeström, Y., *Learning by expanding.* Orienta-konsultit, Helsinki, 1987.

7. Engeström, Y *Learning, Working and Imagining. Twelve Studies in Activity Theory.* Orienta-konsultit, Helsinki, 1990.

8. Hartfield, B. & Graves, M. Issue-Centered Design for Collaborative Work. In Stamper, R. K., P. Kerola, R. Lee & K. Lyytinen (eds.) *Collaborative Work, Social Communication and Information Systems.*, North-Holland, Amsterdam, 1991, pp. 295-310.

9. Kuutti, K. Activity Theory and its applications in information systems research and design. In Nissen, H.-E., Klein, H.K. and Hirschheim, R. (eds.) *Information Systems Research Arena of the 90's.* Norh-Holland, Amsterdam, 1991, pp. 529-550.

10. Kuutti, K. The Concept of Activity as a Basic Unit for CSCW Research. In Bannon, L. J., M. Robinson & K. Schmidt (eds.) *Proceedings of the 2nd ECSCW.* Kluwer Academical, Amsterdam, 1991, pp. 249-264.

11. Kuutti, K. & Lönnfors, T. *Using information technology for to integrate separate organizational units around a common object of work.* Manuscript, Univ. Oulu, Dept. Information Processing Science, 1992.

12. Schmidt, K. Riding a Tiger, or Computer Supported Cooperative Work. In Bannon, L. J., M. Robinson & K. Schmidt (eds.) *Proceedings of the 2nd ECSCW.* Kluwer Academical, Amsterdam, 1991, pp. 1-16.

13. Truex, D.P. & Klein, H. K. A Rejection of Structure as a Basis for Information Systems Development. In Stamper, R. K., P. Kerola, R. Lee & K. Lyytinen (eds.) *Collaborative Work, Social Communication and Information Systems.* North-Holland, Amsterdam,1991, pp. 213-236.

Collaboration and Constraint: Middle School Teaching Teams

R. G. (Jerry) Schwab[1]
Sylvia Hart-Landsberg
Stephen Reder
Mark Abel[2]

Northwest Regional Educational Laboratory
101 Southwest Main Street, Suite 500
Portland, Oregon 97204
(503) 275-9592

ABSTRACT

This paper explores the meanings and dynamics of interaction and cooperation in professional activities in the context of middle school teaching. What makes schools particularly interesting and challenging contexts for both the conduct and study of cooperative work is the high degree of temporal constraint and spatial isolation in which teachers must perform their work. The reported research is based on a comparative study of teacher collaboration in two schools, each of which utilized a different strategy for supporting collaborative work amidst these striking constraints. By focusing on the interplay of constructed meanings, history, and temporal and spatial structures which enable and constrain collaboration, we gain a new view of the CSCW enterprise.

KEYWORDS

Collaboration, teachers, teamwork, meaning, constraint

INTRODUCTION

Advances in research and development on computer support for cooperative work depend on a proper understanding of the nature and social organization of work in given settings. Previous research on workgroup collaboration, for example, has reported highly specific spatial and temporal patterns of work activities in studied occupations, e.g., Reder & Schwab [4, 5], Linde [3], Suchman [6], Hutchins and Klausen, [2]. Detailed studies of cooperative behavior in workgroups have ranged across a variety of occupations and settings--from high tech product engineering teams to corporate management teams to helicopter crews to air traffic control teams.

1992 ACM 0-89791-543-7/92/0010/0241

There is a strong suggestion in this research that work activities in many occupations have characteristic temporal and spatial shapes that are highly responsive to the imperatives of the physical and social environments in which they take place. Suchman's [6] elegant description of the collaboration among pilots and traffic controllers to move aircraft safely on the airport ground reveals precise patterns of observation and communication which both create and constrain safe and efficient traffic flows. Linde's [3] study of flight deck collaboration between police and pilot in helicopter pursuit highlights ongoing negotiation of their respective roles and responsibilities within the joint accomplishment of their task. Reder and Schwab [5] report sharply varying temporal patterns of activity among executive management teams that reflect different tradeoffs between solitary and interactive components of team activities across task environments.

As a body of empirical studies accumulates across occupations, it is important to assume a comparative stance in analyzing what is distinctive about the organization of cooperative activity in particular occupations and work settings. In work reported previously to the Computer Supported Collaborative Work (CSCW) conferences, we have emphasized the ways in which individuals and work teams are able to accomplish multiple tasks within the jigsaw like constraints of space and time characteristic of a workplace environment [4, 5]. The work environments reported in this paper--public schools--are particularly challenging ones for collaboration in this regard.[3] The spatial and temporal organization of the schools highly constrain opportunities for collaboration: Teachers spend a preponderance of their workdays in their classrooms, isolated from professional colleagues and others with whom they need to collaborate.

Although previous studies of cooperative activity have tended to focus on the temporal dynamics of cooperation, there is good reason to focus as well on the *meanings* which collaboration carries for participants. Contemporary accounts of the strong meanings individuals take from team experiences in mountain-climbing, combat and athletic competition, to name but a few examples, point to this critical dimension of cooperative work that needs to be better understood. We will see that much of the meaning that collaboration carries for teachers is closely related to the rising external pressures schools and teachers are under to "restructure" their operations in more collaborative ways. Other sources of the meanings collaboration carries for teachers come from the strong tensions between their desires and needs for collaboration on one hand and the strong temporal and spatial constraints on how their work can be accomplished.

Like many occupations and occupational settings, the social organization of public schools has deep historical roots. The subject matter specialization of teachers in these institutions was modeled after the assembly line, with children being the raw materials that pass from station to station. The isolation of classroom teachers from peers has a close analogy with the isolation of factory workers on the line. The conflicts between these structural forms and the humanistic ideals of education and human development--ideals to which teachers have traditionally adhered--have correspondingly deep historical roots as well.

Two middle schools were selected for a careful study of teacher collaboration. The schools were chosen for two reasons: (1) teacher teams had formed for specific collaborative purposes, and (2) the schools had developed a particular strategy for facilitating collaborative activities amidst all the constraints. One school used a CSCW strategy, placing networked computers (with electronic mail, bulletin board and file-sharing software) on each teacher's classroom desk, whereas the other school deployed a spatial and organizational strategy to facilitate collaboration. We will see that each strategy was successful in facilitating collaboration. The resulting patterns of similarities and differences between the schools offers some fresh perspective on CSCW in such contexts and highlight a range of important issues in CSCW and workplace design in relation to the occupationally-specific dynamics and meanings of collaboration.

THE SCHOOL AS WORKPLACE

Susan Petrie's morning at Oak Bluff begins with a 7:15 am committee meeting in the school library. Thirty minutes later she returns to her class room to begin preparing for her teaching day. By 8:00 she has read five email messages, written three replies, and found eight uninterrupted minutes to prepare the day's activities for her students. By the time the bell rings at 8:00, a dozen students have arrived for AM, a fifteen minute "homeroom class" in which attendance is taken, announcements are read and students prepare for the day. Susan's role as a resource room teacher allows her the luxury of assistance from two classroom aides who attend to the students while she scrambles to complete several tasks before her first class begins at 8:19. During the few minutes, Susan greets students, sends one and receives and reads three incoming email messages, two of which she responds to with replies. She makes three phone calls and has four separate interactions with five people in four different parts of the school building.

The next hour, spanning second and part of third period, is relatively quiet, and Susan is able to turn much of her attention to the job most of us imagine teaching to be: instruction. She spends roughly fifty-six minutes instructing students; the remaining four minutes are taken up attending to five incoming email messages, two brief interactions with other teachers, and the creation of two outgoing email messages. One of these is to Peter Dumond, the school counselor, about Gennifer Hayes, a sixth grader with learning difficulties. In her message--marked "urgent"--Susan reports that Gennifer "smells like marijuana" but that she doesn't appear to have been using the drug. Twenty minutes later, Susan's suspicions have grown and she uses the telephone to call Peter and ask if he received her message. "I think I was too kind," she says, " I think there is something else going on." About ten minutes later Peter arrives in the classroom, observes the child's behavior and then takes her to the counseling office.

As this brief glimpse shows, Susan's job involves a combination of instructional and social work, a mix of collaborative and solitary tasks, and requires a special ability to take advantage of every opportunity and resource available to complete tasks at hand; this pattern is common among teachers everywhere. However, because of her special status as a resource room teacher, Susan has several advantages over other classroom teachers. She has a phone in her office, electronic mail to connect her with her colleagues throughout the building, and aides to cover for her if she needs to leave her classroom. Few classroom teachers experience the flexibility Susan enjoys. Indeed, school can be characterized as a workplace where collaboration is required and valued but the workers are isolated from one another for the majority of the workday (behind the doors of their classrooms) and constrained by the largely arbitrary and inflexible school bell. Yet increasingly, Susan's and her colleagues' success as teachers depends on their abilities to collaborate in the face of these and other obstacles which, as we shall see, are deeply embedded in the history, tradition, and patterns of practice of the school as workplace. In the sections which follow we will examine more closely the structures of time and space which pervade the school as a workplace and consider their impact on teachers' abilities to work in collaborative teams.

Time

A bell rings, doors suddenly burst open and a flood of students drains into the empty hall. Amid the slamming of locker doors, books are tossed and retrieved and commotion reigns. Minutes later the tide of young people reverses and bodies flow out of the hallway and back into classrooms. As the bell rings, teachers pull doors shut and the halls are once again silent and empty.

For those of us educated in North American schools, this image is still fresh and sharp; the rhythmic punctuation of the school bell is a defining feature of our school experience. But this image is one-sided, based on our perceptions as students. Teachers' experiences of this periodicity is more complex, and in the schools we studied, the traditional constructions of "school time" have a strong impact on staff members' control over their own activities, including their communication and collaboration.

The delineation of time is relatively constant in schools across the nation--class, passing, prep, lunch, and before and after school periods. Each day has the same general outline of seven or eight classes daily: 50-minute class periods, five-minute passing periods between classes, one 50-minute prep period for each teacher, and lunch (typically two half-hour periods with half the faculty assigned to one and half to the other). At every turning point the tyranny of the school bell determines the time period and thereby influences the type of work teachers take up; the schedule, designed to support instructional work, arbitrarily limits the teachers' options for attending to social and organizational work. Bells curtail conversations and direct people to locations where certain tasks cannot be accomplished. From the teachers' point of view, school time is a given, and teachers develop diverse strategies for handling their time: they come early, stay late, close their doors during prep period, eat in the faculty lunchroom to catch up on business, or employ other techniques to accomplish their long list of daily tasks.

At first glance this temporal predictability would seem to make all the adults accessible to each other during breaks, but distance among rooms, quantity of work, and urgent business reduce the accessibility so much that during most breaks, a teacher sees only those in nearby classrooms unless he or she rushes to other parts of the building. Thus, school days for teachers are characterized by long periods of isolation from adults punctuated by short break periods of intense communication. Since most of the allocated class time is taken up by direct instruction of students, break time is pressured by the demands of curriculum work, student support services, and organizational maintenance. During the short "free" periods, a teacher often takes care of personal needs or faces regular duties or pressing situations (e.g., hall duty; a student needing help on a math concept for a test next period; or parents in the office who want to talk). Longer "free" periods (before and after school, prep, and lunch) are often filled with scheduled meetings, handling unforeseen social crises, and grading and class preparation. In practice, few teachers accomplish all the necessary tasks of a single work day while in the school building; weekends and evenings are filled with phone calls to parents, grading and preparation for upcoming instruction.

Space

Imagine yourself a worker responsible for the various needs of 30 clients, clients so highly valued as to often be described as "our most valuable resource," and "our country's future." A major requirement of your job is effective communication with co-workers, supervisors, and the parents of your clients. Yet your work area is separated from those of your colleagues, so you spend the majority of your day in isolation from your workmates. In addition, you have no tools in your work area (other than pen and paper) to facilitate communication. A telephone on your desk, a tool taken for granted by workers in other "industries," is viewed in your field as an expensive extravagance (in the best case) or a distraction you cannot be trusted with (in the worst case). Welcome to the school as collaborative workplace.

Though as former students we may recall the buzz of crowded hallways and commotion of the playground, few teachers view the school in the same way. More than anything, teachers experience a sense of isolation from colleagues. Indeed, attempts to bridge this traditional gulf are behind many of the current efforts to promote collaboration among educators. History and tradition, however, provide powerful constraints to new forms of cooperative work.

Most North American schools are housed in tall or sprawling buildings with long hallways and self-contained classrooms. Once ideal for the self-contained teachers of 50 years ago, these physical structures provide obstacles to the collaborative needs of today's teacher. Typically, teachers' work is conducted in classrooms, hallways, the main office/mail room complex, and the faculty lunchroom. There are no private places for teachers in the schools; the classroom is considered the teacher's own personal sphere for instruction and paper work but, ironically, teachers have little control over their privacy for those tasks they need to complete alone. Students and/or teachers enter without knocking, regardless of the time period.

Because of the sheer sizes of the buildings, coworkers are often widely dispersed. Long halls mean long walks, and that uses up precious time. When it takes a teacher a minute to go from his or her classroom to the mailroom (at a fast clip) and a minute to open the door, grab the mail and get out, only three minutes of a five-minute passing period remain. If the same teacher needs to use the restroom, some other goal of the journey has to be cut. Still, the hallways are in some ways the school building equivalent of milling around the office water cooler, since they serve as "conduits" in which people converse and hail each other along their way; unlike office workers, however, teachers have little control over their time and they are forced to "mill" on the run.

Faculty lunchrooms are one of the few places students cannot go. Although many teachers take lunch and other breaks there for informality, fun, and food, a substantial portion of the conversation there concerns school politics, curriculum, and individual students' welfare. A central area of communication in any school is "the office." Teachers come to the office to send and pick up mail, use the telephone, make photocopies, and do business with administrators, secretaries, parents and other outsiders. Teachers often conduct more business in the office than planned, because of interactions with others coming in and out on similar errands, but there is rarely time for leisurely conversation--ringing bells soon drive the workers back to their rooms.

THE STRUCTURE OF TEACHERS' WORK

In order to understand teachers' collaboration it is essential to examine the diverse tasks they face on a daily basis. The public mandate for schools to handle social and emotional dimensions of students' lives, and the necessity of doing so in order to have students who are receptive to learning, have dramatically altered the nature of teachers' work. The teachers we studied, like teachers throughout the United States today, are engaged in two interrelated sets of responsibilities which we call Job 1 and Job 2. Job 1 is the instructional work which traditionally has been the main duty of the profession. Job 2 is a modern overlay of guidance and social support activities teachers perform for individual students facing social and academic difficulties which seriously impair their ability to adjust to school and learn the material.

Job 1 has many components. As their foremost activity, teachers lead classes. For seven or eight class periods a day, teachers devote about 50 minutes to instructing their classes--explaining ideas and assignments, leading small study groups, supervising experiments, holding writing conferences, and applying other instructional methods. Behind each instructional scene lie hours of planning--studying the topic; selecting texts; writing lesson plans; and creating materials. Additional hours of deskwork are spent on grading. "Duties" such as monitoring student behavior in halls and at the bus stop are necessary for ensuring smooth movement of students to and from classes.

Job 2 also is multifaceted. Each teacher, in effect, carries a caseload of students who need special attention and support due to their difficulties learning class material or adjusting to school life. To fulfill this responsibility teachers confer with parents, faculty, psychologists and other professionals (inside and outside the school system).

Teachers experiences in two social spheres--the world of children in their classrooms and the world of professional networks outside their classrooms--are leading them to look to collaboration as the means for fulfilling both sets of duties. Within their classrooms, they see that many children do not receive basic support and guidance either from their families or social service agencies, and they feel that *they* must provide it. Caring teachers traditionally have supported students in many ways, but due to the increasing severity of social problems children bring to school, the energy, time and attention teachers put into the "social work" components of their jobs increased manyfold. Teachers do not see Job 2 as a luxury, something to be performed only after Job 1 is done, but as an urgent responsibility, linked to many students' ability to succeed in school and develop fully.

There is increasing pressure from outside teachers' classrooms--administration, colleagues--to adopt high standards of excellence in both jobs but also to *collaborate* in meeting the standards. The widespread efforts to restructure schools also advance this new meaning of professionalism, i.e., as entailing collaborative work. These efforts are based on the view that the success of instructional innovation depends on collegial relationships among teachers. Accordingly, many schools are providing resources for sustained staff interaction focused on school improvement. For teachers this movement is at once appealing and unsettling. While they welcome the increased recognition that professional contacts beyond classroom walls are essential to education reform, they often are shackled in making and maintaining such contacts by traditional structures of time, space and expectation.

Thus internal classroom pressures from the students and external pressures from colleagues and administrators are changing both jobs for teachers. This development is radically transforming teachers' perceptions of the very meanings of teaching as profession.

INNOVATIONS TO SUPPORT COLLABORATION

Ironically, many teachers feel that the growing emphasis on "social work" (Job 2) decreases their ability to provide excellent instruction (Job 1). Both their students and professional colleagues press them to coordinate their efforts with other adults who care for children. This pressure, along with dissatisfaction with their isolation in their classrooms, pushes teachers to innovations which promise to increase their capacity through collaboration. The schools we studied were developing such new strategies and forms for collaboration. At both schools, the innovations represented a complex set of opportunities and obligations for the teachers . On the negative side, collaboration, i.e., the obligation to spend time and energy developing a new style of professional relationships, was one more demand in a seemingly endless stream of innovations. On the positive side, collaboration was distinct from most other innovations in that it provided an overarching avenue for working on both Jobs 1 and 2.

Mountain View Middle School

At the beginning of the school year in which the fieldwork was carried out, Mountain View Middle School implemented a new social and spatial organization intended to increase collaboration among faculty as well as provide more continuity for students. These changes were designed, in part, to address the needs of a diverse and rapidly changing community. At the time of our study, the school's 482 seventh and eighth graders represented a wide range of social and economic backgrounds; a recent influx of highly mobile workers from other regions appeared to correlate with an increasing number of students with special needs for counseling, academic support and disciplinary action. The principal and many teachers hoped to deal with these challenges by creating time, space and social groups to: 1) increase the integration of the curriculum across disciplines, and 2) manage the cases of students at risk of school failure.

In this new structure all teachers and students were grouped into one of four "neighborhoods." Two neighborhoods were comprised of seventh graders and their teachers and two others of eighth graders and their teachers. A neighborhood's students were subdivided into classes of individuals who for the most part remained together as they traveled from one teacher's classroom to another's. From the teachers' vantage point, this structure increased both the opportunities and the reasons for collaboration: Neighborhood faculty members were familiar with the same individual children as well as the same group dynamics (e.g., individuals who "acted out" when paired with certain others).

The Mountain View neighborhood architecture and schedule both supported team communication. Each neighborhood's core classes and meeting room were located along the same hall. Neighborhood teachers met regularly during a daily common "prep" period and a weekly Late Start Day (when students arrived an hour late).

Our research focused on one seventh grade neighborhood team (called the "A Neighborhood Team"). Five core subject teachers (one science, one math, one social studies and two language arts teachers) and one resource room teacher were shadowed.[4] The resource room teacher's room was not in the same hall with the others. Students who required special instruction due to learning disabilities or low achievement came to her remedial classes from all the neighborhoods. However, she frequently met and exchanged messages with A Neighborhood Team teachers concerning their students in her classes, and her role was considered integral to the team's mission of meeting the needs of its students.

As is typical in schools today, several innovations requiring teamwork compete with each other for attention, creating a context in which it was difficult to use the neighborhood team structure for both curriculum and individual student case management. Innovations included (1) a discipline policy with a clear sequence of disciplinary actions requiring communication among faculty and parents; (2) the Outcome-Based Education instructional approach in which teachers took training workshops; and (3) curriculum revisions to prepare for the state review process for accreditation. Due to the small size of the district, administrators (trying to keep up on all education trends) assigned multiple committee responsibilities to the few staff. (To make the point that committee duties were heavy, the principal compiled a list of all building and district committees to which any Mountain View personnel belonged: the list was two pages long.)

Despite these difficulties, the Neighborhood system did provide opportunities for collaboration. With core team members' rooms located on the same hall, a team member could, for example, dash to a colleague's room to get help on a crisis which had just arisen in class, knowing that the teacher visited would be familiar with the background of the student involved and that the school supported the teachers' teamwork on the issue.

Oak Bluff Middle School

Although less radical in its reorganization than Mountain View, Oak Bluff also was trying to restructure teachers' work to create opportunities for collaboration. The social problems which sometimes surfaced during the teachers' work with the 370 sixth, seventh, and eighth grade students from a middle to upper-middle class suburb included drug abuse, delinquency and family tension. In order to better meet the needs of individual students with problems, establish and coordinate school policy, and create cross-disciplinary projects for students, each teacher was assigned to three committees on a subject area, a grade-level, and a school issue. Our research on collaboration targeted five key members of the "seventh grade team": two English teachers, one math and computer science teacher, one science teacher, and one resource room teacher. As at Mountain View, the resource room teacher at Oak Bluff was not formally a member of the team studied but she interacted with team members frequently regarding students she shared with them.

This social organization based on committees was coupled with a technological innovation designed to support collaboration. A year and a half before our study began, networked personal computers (Macintosh) providing electronic mail, bulletin-board and file sharing capabilities had been installed on each teacher's and administrator's desk. Personal messages, information about committee tasks and administrative information filled the network. Daily attendance data were sent to the office staff on the computer. Teachers recorded and computed grades electronically; at the end of grading periods, they were required to communicate them electronically to the office.

While the new team structure at Oak Bluff--as at Mountain View--can be credited in part with increasing opportunities for collaboration, the network supported collaboration by adding a new channel for communication. Without leaving the room or waiting for a "free" period, a teacher could send and receive messages. Electronic mail often expedited business which would have taken more time, some of it class time, to accomplish through other channels. For example, the seventh grade team arranged a meeting to plan a "Fun Day" by first proposing options (e.g., which videos to show) via email and then met in person to finalize plans.

STRUCTURE AND COLLABORATION

In all occupations, available space, time periods, communication channels and personnel interact to form the opportunities and constraints to get the work done. In this section we will draw on observations of teachers' work to show some of the ways these factors combine to shape collaboration.

Regarding the people who were available for collaboration, daily life in the schools provided opportunities for interaction with nearly every individual on the faculty and staff, but individual teachers interacted most frequently with a particular constellation of individuals. On the other hand, teachers did not transact much business with individuals from the world outside the school. Teachers at Mountain View interacted with an average of about 25 individuals a day, teachers at Oak Bluff with about 29. This is an *unduplicated* count of the individuals with whom group members met face-to-face, talked on the telephone, received a letter from or sent a letter to, and so forth. The volume of interaction--when considered in light of the fact that these data do not include interactions with students--is impressive. In fact, in terms of the sheer numbers of individuals they interact with and the number of tasks they face on a daily basis, teachers are as "busy" as senior business executives (and this is *not* counting their instructional and other interactions with students).[5]

Figure 1 portrays communication among adults during class time. Obviously, most of the teachers' attention and energy are consumed by instruction and class management activities during these periods but, given the enormous number of collaborative tasks teachers faced every day some communication with other adults did occur during these periods.

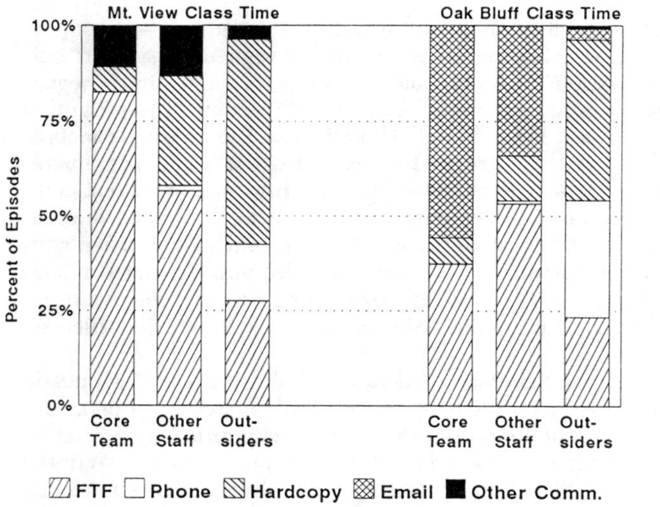

Figure 1. Social Categories - Class Time

When we look at the types of individuals and the channels which comprise this communication during classes, several interesting patterns emerge. When a teacher at Mountain View communicates with another core team teacher, that interaction tends to occur through the face-to-face channel (83%); Oak Bluff teachers tend to communicate with core team members through electronic mail (56%) or to a lesser extent face-to-face (37%). The proportion of face-to-face communication with other staff during class periods is similar for both schools (57% for Mountain View and 53% for Oak Bluff), but electronic mail is again prominent at Oak Bluff (34%), apparently replacing hardcopy and other channels of communication.

At Mountain View, most interactions during class time were face-to-face because the common location of team members' rooms on the same hall made it relatively easy for teachers to contact other team members through this channel. During class time at Oak Bluff, most teachers' rooms were not close to other members' rooms, so they tended to contact them through email rather than face-to-face. In contrast, they were apt to "drop in" on other staff (not members of their own teams) whose classrooms were near. The overall greater proportion of telephone interactions with outsiders (i.e., individuals such as parents or district administrators who do not work in the building) at Oak Bluff as compared with Mountain View appears to be a result of the availability of the telephone and use by the teacher with the responsibility for computer support.

Channel availability in the schools was closely related to location. For example, telephones were available only in the main office, faculty lounge, and a few other rooms. Since teachers spent most hours in their classrooms, their access to phones was limited. Consequently, as we would expect and as our data show, most of the communication with outsiders took place in the office area where telephones were centrally located.

In Figure 2, we see that Mountain View teachers communicated with members of their core team in and from a variety of locations; nearly equal proportions were initiated or received from individuals' own classrooms (28%), classrooms of team members (25%) and from the hallway (24%). Oak Bluff teachers accomplished slightly more than half (51%) of their communication with core team members within their own classrooms. The balance of communication with other core members took place predominantly in the classrooms of other team members (12%), in the office area (14%), hallways (7%) and other areas. Once again, differences between the two schools seem at least partly shaped by the availability of electronic mail to Oak Bluff teachers.

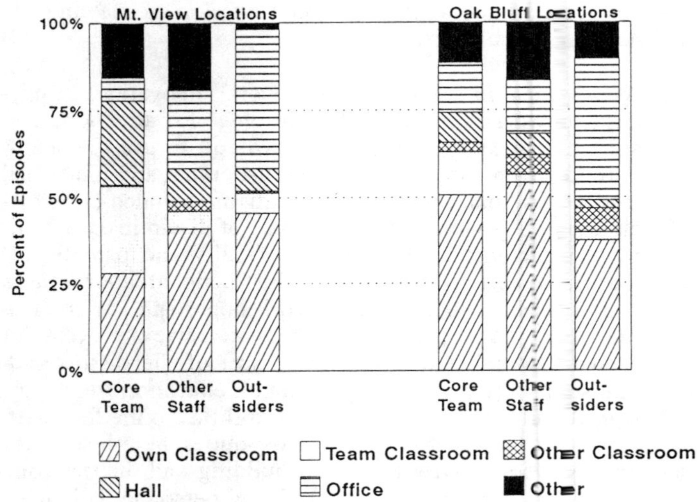

Figure 2. Social Categories - Locations.

Using electronic mail, Oak Bluff teachers were able to conduct much of the communicative work required to complete team tasks from within their own classrooms; the other locations were thus less important as venues for interaction. Similarly, the neighborhood organization at Mountain View increased the likelihood that interactions with core team members would occur in the hallways since their classrooms tended to be located in the same area of the building; core team classrooms at Oak Bluff, it will be remembered, were distributed throughout the building. Both of these attempts to overcome the isolation resulting from spatial and temporal constraints appear to be at least partially effective.

Outcomes of Innovations at Both Schools

Although the two staffs eagerly exploited the innovations, Job 1 was affected less than Job 2; academic matters (including cross-disciplinary planning) were much less often the subject of collaboration than was the business of handling difficult student cases. Occasionally collaboration was directed to the challenge of integrating the curriculum across subjects, one of its original purposes. For example, Oak Bluff faculty organized several special events--an All Species Dance, a milk jug recycling competition, and a field trip to plant trees--intended to enhance the study of ecology across disciplines. And there were more routine jobs associated with the content of education--choosing English books, for instance. But such collaborative work took a back seat to the intense, daily need to monitor the progress of students at risk of school failure. Many days were powerfully shaped by individuals' problems, as faculty held meetings and "caught" each other in the halls to discuss ways to respond to their needs. Teachers' classes and breaks were punctuated by the pressing needs of these students e.g., the need to send assignments to the resource room (for students who could get help on them there), arrange staffings for parents and teachers to determine "treatment," and circulate letters from psychiatrists.

Why did collaboration tend to focus on at-risk students at the cost of cross-disciplinary academic work? One reason lies in the sheer magnitude and urgency of the task of preparing students to learn which left little time for teamwork on curriculum. Teachers throughout the country find themselves facing fundamental challenges to long held understandings of their jobs. What it means to be a "good teacher" is shifting dramatically. Teachers are trying to keep their footing while they construct new understandings and meanings and deploy new models of collaboration. In this sense teachers from Mountain View and Oak Bluff are no different from their colleagues across the nation. But another reason teachers rarely "got to" new cross-disciplinary planning lies in the ways the interlaced structures of time, space, and channel availability powerfully constrained teachers' activities. Our observational data on the fine structure of occupational activities reveal some of the obstacles to collaboration teachers experienced in spite of the positive effects of the innovations. These obstacles are an aggregate of history and tradition and are most visible in the temporal and spatial structures of schools and schooling. These persistent structures are a fundamental reason that the relatively new overlay of social work (Job 2) cannot easily be accommodated in schools as they exist today.

IMPLICATIONS FOR DESIGN

Schools are particularly challenging environments for the accomplishment of cooperative work. A high degree of commitment is necessary to squeeze the extra margins of space and time needed to construct an environment sufficient to support collaborative approaches to the many critical activities teachers face. In addition, ingenuity is required to navigate the complex course of daily interactions and tasks. Teachers, like other workers, both want and need innovations that will help them collaborate better within the powerful constraints of their workplace. While external social pressures contribute to the meaning of collaboration for teachers, the temporal and spatial constraints of the school as workplace inhibit teachers' abilities to achieve the collaboration they envision.

Consider the Context

Any innovation meant to improve collaboration among teachers must consider this complex context of the workplace. For example, an innovation should compensate for the spatial isolation which teachers experience during the many hours they need to stay in their classrooms. For this, innovations like "neighborhoods" (with geographical and social features) and distance-spanning communication channels are indicated.

Teaching in middle schools, while an interesting context for study, is not the only occupation having a rich interlocking web of contextual variables which must be considered in designing collaborative innovation. Reder and Schwab's [5] earlier research showed that senior marketing executives, for example, were dispersed most of the time due to travel. Any office-based collaborative innovation which ignores the contextual framework is likely to fail.

Support Control and Efficient Use of Time

The school bell, not the teacher, dominates a teacher's use of time. Teachers and their students, like assembly-line workers in a factory, have little control over this schedule. The bell tells teachers when (and where) they can teach, communicate with other teachers, approach the counselor or principal with a problem and use the rest room. When a teacher does have discretionary time it is very brief. Often, teachers must use the short breaks between teaching periods to run to the office for information, grab a colleague in the hallway for advice, photocopy an assignment or call a parent. This results in a marked compression of time and opportunity for collaboration.

Due to its asynchronous quality, email gave teachers at Oak Bluff the opportunity to communicate at times when they would otherwise have been "stuck in their classrooms." It thus provided leverage for more control and more time in a situation in which a small amount of gain was a large percentage of increase in the time which could be used for collaboration. As changes in the wider social environment lead schools to emphasize teacher collaboration, other technologies, e.g., voice mail, might provide similar leverage for collaboration between teachers and professionals outside school who focus on children's welfare. These time constraints, so pronounced in the primary and secondary education world, make schools an interesting test bed for learning how to develop collaborative innovations to fit other occupational settings in which time and control are at a premium.

Support Multiple and Emerging Jobs

The social work (Job 2) of teaching entails a set of activities which are emerging dramatically as part of the occupation. Historically, the temporal, spatial and social structure of schools were developed to support the instructional work, Job 1. The structures established for the traditional set of activities are inadequate for supporting the new set. Innovations which enable teachers to operate beyond their traditional classroom milieu are in order.

The teaching profession is not unique in encompassing multiple "jobs". In many occupational settings, existing structures support a traditional set of activities yet they fail to support emerging sets of critical activities. One implication is that system designers must try to develop collaborative innovations which are elastic enough to support shifting and newly emerging multiple "jobs." A broader implication is that designs must be as flexible as possible, so that they can be adapted to the needs of an evolving occupational setting.

CONCLUSIONS

The two schools we studied utilized different strategies for supporting collaborative work among their faculties. Mountain View teachers perceived, acted and interacted as team members on many issues every day in their "neighborhoods." Oak Bluff seventh grade team teachers used the email system to transact team and other school business. Although teachers and other staff in both schools eagerly used the innovations to increase their collaboration, they did not focus their collaboration equally on the two sets of activities they had originally envisioned. Academic work, i.e., the preparation and delivery of new curricula, (Job 1 in our terminology), took a back seat to social work (Job 2).

Though the two schools implemented very different innovations for collaboration, they were remarkably similar in the ways teachers used available personnel, locations, time and communication channels to perform their work. The traditions of U.S. schooling, teachers beliefs and understandings about what constitutes "teaching", the social structure of the two schools, and the demanding nature of the tasks at which teachers labored determined to a large extent how teachers operated. In spite of significant site differences, the same overwhelming reality for teachers at both schools was that they could fulfill only a part of the instructional and social work their communities and their own professional aspirations mandated. Constraints on their time and attention meant that the innovations could increase their effectiveness only to a certain extent. Thus it appears that while schools have evolved particular spatial, temporal and social organizations for conducting their traditional academic work (Job 1), cultural and environmental structures are not in place for the support of the overlaid Job 2. Consequently, innovations supporting collaboration appear to have a greater functional value with respect to Job 2.

The occupation of teaching is complex along lines not normally perceived by the public. While the academic and communication skills teachers exercise in interacting with students are well-known, the extent of their responsibilities and variety of their activities are less well-known. The collaborative aspect of all their tasks is generally hidden from public view. Our research shows that as the tasks which constitute teaching dramatically shift and change, teachers' perceptions, understandings and experiences--*the core meaning of teaching as a profession*--is being reconstructed. As the profession changes, so does the content and meaning of collaboration. This is no doubt true for other occupational groups as well.

ACKNOWLEDGEMENTS

The authors wish to acknowledge the generous support of U. S. West Advanced Technologies.

NOTES

1. Jerry Schwab is now with the Centre for Educational Development and Academic Methods, The Australian National University, GPO Box 4, Canberra, ACT, Australia, (61) (6) 249-5111.

2. Mark Abel is now with Intel Corporation, 5200 Northeast Elam Young Parkway, Hillsboro, Oregon 97124, (503) 696-2862.

3. The research upon which this paper is based is reported in Hart-Landsberg, et al [1].

4. The shadowing methodology is described fully in Hart-Landsberg, et al [1].

5. Compare Hart-Landsberg, et al [1] with parallel studies reported by Reder and Schwab [4, 5].

REFERENCES

1. Hart-Landsberg, S., Schwab, R. G., Reder, S., and Abel, M. J. *Teacher collaboration and constraint: Quantitative ethnographies of two middle schools.* Portland, Oregon: Northwest Regional Educational Laboratory, 1991.

2. Hutchins, E. and Klausen, T. Distributed cognition in an airline cockpit. In Y. Engestrom and D. Middleton (eds.), *Communities of practice: Cognition and communication at work.* New York: Cambridge University Press (In Press).

3. Linde, C. Who's in charge here?: Cooperative work and authority negotiation in police helicopter missions. In *CSCW '88: Proceedings of the Conference on Computer-Supported Cooperative Work (Portland, September 26-28, 1988)*, New York, New York: Association for Computing Machinery, Inc.

4. Reder, S. and Schwab, R. G. *Selection and effects of channels in distributed communication and decision-making tasks.* Portland, Oregon: Northwest Regional Educational Laboratory, 1990.

5. Reder, S. and Schwab, R. G. The temporal structure of cooperative activity. In *CSCW '90: Proceedings of the Conference on Computer-Supported Cooperative Work (Los Angeles, October 7-10, 1990)*, New York, New York: The Association for Computing Machinery.

6. Suchman, L. Constituting shared workspace. In Y. Engestrom and D. Middleton (eds.), *Communities of practice: Cognition and communication at work.* New York: Cambridge University Press (In Press).

TIME-MANAGEMENT
A case for CSCW

Edeltraud Egger
Ina Wagner

Technical University of Vienna
Argentinierstr. 8/187
A-1040 Vienna
(+43) 222 58801/4418

ABSTRACT

This paper focuses on time-management as a cooperative task. Based on an analysis of the cultural complexity of the timing of surgery in a large clinic, possibilities of using computer-support for strengthening the sharing of information and resources as well as participation in decision-making are discussed.

KEYWORDS

Time-management, automatic scheduling, cooperative decision-making

TIME IN ORGANIZATIONS

From a systems theory point of view the introduction of time structures within organizations can be understood as an instrument of activating a larger number of internal relations. Luhmann [1] speaks of a temporalization of complexity. Timing through diachronous sequencing and synchronous differentiation offers organizations an extension of choice. To achieve this, however, an organization has to solve a series of problems. McGrath [2] identifies three such problems inherent in any collective action: temporal ambiguity, conflicting temporal interests and requirements, and scarcity of temporal resources. Organizational responses to these problems can be characterized as scheduling, synchronization, and allocation.

While a conceptualization of temporal orders from a system´s theory point of view seems a useful starting point for identifying and classifying the problems complex organizations encounter when establishing workable temporal structures, a fuller understanding of observable timing practices, including inconsistencies and ambiguities, can only be achieved by examining the social and cultural character of time. A study of time in organizations has to document "how actors experience time as qualitative and heterogeneous; that is, how they obtain meaning through the recurrence of temporally-ordered events, and how they construct their own time reckoning systems" [3]. Industrial sociologists with their interest in the "commodification" of time and in its use as an instrument of control [4] have focussed on the linear-quantitative notion of time. According to this tradition, time is homogeneous, objective, measurable and infinitely divisible. Durkheim [5] has stressed that time is essentially a social category of thought which is derived from social life and subject to collective representations. Analysis of competing concepts of social time helps to understand how organizations solve the tensions between social spontaneity and structure.

Given the social character of time and the plurality of time-reckoning systems in organizations, time management becomes a focus of organizational conflict and a mirror of organizational power. Actors have to engage in ongoing negotiation on how to allocate scarce temporal resources, often without being able to resolve the underlying conflicts. This makes time management a challenge for "technology for collaborative work" [6].

Based on a case-study on the scheduling of surgery in a large clinic, the following paragraphs explore the possibilities of computer-support for collaborative time management.

* Firstly, the social and cultural complexity of timing is analyzed and the main organizational time management tasks are defined.
* Secondly, an understanding of collaborative time management in complex organizations is developed.
* In a third step, a prototype is presented and its collaborative elements are examined.

TIME MANAGEMENT IN A SURGICAL CLINIC

The clinic, part of a large university hospital, consists of six departments, representing different specialties. A main organizational problem this clinic faces is the scheduling of surgery. Prior to prototype development the project team carried out an in-depth study of the clinic´s social practices of managing time. Standard qualitative research methods such as semi-structured interviews and participant observation were used to explore

Permission to copy without fee all or part of this material is granted provided that the copies are not made or distributed for direct commercial advantage, the ACM copyright notice and the title of the publication and its date appear, and notice is given that copying is by permission of the Association for Computing Machinery. To copy otherwise, or to republish, requires a fee and/or specific permission.

© 1992 ACM 0-89791-543-7/92/0010/0249...$1.50

* the staff's planning practices,
* explicit and implicit priorities and values,
* individual and occupational differences in experiencing time, evaluating time loss, coping with temporal constraints,
* individual time calendars including occupational differences with respect to time autonomy,
* perceived organizational and individual failure as sources of temporal problems.

Planning practices

The clinic disposes of six operation theaters and one small room for minor surgery. The planning of surgery is done in a several phase scheduling process. Each department has been alloted a certain number of operation days per week. Pre-planning is done by entering an operation (including name of patient and responsible surgeon) into a book which is located in the clinic's main secretariat. The pre-program for the following day is discussed in an afternoon session in which one representative from each department (normally a doctor), the head surgery nurse and one representative from anesthesiology are present. In this session the schedule for the next day is set up. It contains names of team members and the estimated beginning time of each surgery. The result of these consultations is a time table which shows the distribution of surgery over the available theaters. Nurses decide among themselves who is going to join which surgical team. No pre-planning for the following days is done, although surgeons may enter operations ahead.

Normally, a day's program cannot be realized as it was planned. Due to unrealistic time estimates, unforeseen complications, emergencies and organizational delays, ad-hoc-adjustments have to be made which might result in the cancelling of operations (even though the patient may already be waiting outside the operation theater). Like in many complex organizations the conditions for coordination and planning are poorly developed. Particularly in a hospital people are busy and constantly on the move. Spatial arrangements are not conducive to frequent meetings. Although portable telephones ensure the availability of surgeons, the maintenance of regular communication and feedback patterns is discouraged. Currently, a senior surgeon is responsible for most readjustments of a day's schedule. He bases his decisions on an internalized "map" of individuals' or teams' specific competencies and deficiencies and their capability to mobilize resources under time constraints. These planning practices combine stability-creating elements (e.g. the allotment of fixed operation days) which also create a certain amount of inflexibility with cooperative elements (e.g. the joint afternoon session) and a series of non-collaborative, ad-hoc adjustments to unplanned events.

Various discussions in occupationally mixed and homogeneous groups were held in which the results of this research were presented, feedback elicited and possible changes debated. A simple prototype has been developed which will be used for cooperative prototyping in two different clinics.

MULTIPLE REALITIES: THE CULTURAL COMPLEXITY OF TIMING

Hospitals host such diverse occupational groups as physicians, nurses, technicians, and administrators. Although these groups have many aspects of organizational life in common, they also form distinct "occupational milieus". The thought worlds and social practices which are shared by members of these different occupations profoundly affect the temporal order of an organization. Individual time discipline, for example, reflects the occupational groups's time autonomy. Surgeon's liberty to ignore the beginning time of an operation whenever they are engaged in an important meeting may lead to the anesthesiologist's refusal to introduce the anesthesia until the physician is actually getting dressed. The temporal commitment which a member of a specific occupational group is expected to show bears directly upon the temporal structuring of an operation.

The value of one's time varies dramatically with one's position within the hospital. Patients' time does not count at all. Once they have been admitted they are expected to wait. This waiting time is often totally unstructured since information on how long to wait for what kind of interventions in which sequence is rarely given. Nurses have to be available within their working hours independent of individual time preferences and instantaneous commitments. Physicians' time is valued so highly that they are not expected to join the surgical team for the full duration of an operation. On the other hand surgeons are often prepared to work longer hours. In emergency situations they are more willing to stretch their time than anesthesiologists.

These occupational differences are clearly related to differences in power and opportunity. At the same time, however, they reflect what McGrath calls social entrainment. Time related perceptions and practices are shaped by actors' experiences in different social settings - e.g. working with different surgical teams, handling of emergency cases. Research shows that under time pressure "groups will eliminate much of the communication activity by which they evaluate one another's task ideas, and virtually all of the interpersonal or nontask aspects of their interaction" [2, p. 42].

Subjective time, so it seems, contains elements of diversity and conflict as well as mutual entrainment. With this notion in mind, organizational responses to problems of temporal ordering can be examined.

Temporal ambiguity:

Ambiguity can be interpreted as a result of three factors: the cultural and social nature of time, loose coupling and problematic trajectories. Temporal ambiguity is inherent in patients' trajectories. Work with patients is always of an evolving character, requiring continual readjustment and coordination [7]. The temporal uncertainties created by unexpected complications are aggravated by the organization's loose coupling.

Complex organizations (like a surgery clinic) are usually segmented, the stable units being small units: "Organizations built of small stable segments make sense over shorter spans of time, involving fewer people than we thought. Once these temporal and spatial boundaries are exceeded, orderliness, predictability, and sensibleness decline" [8, p. 118].

One organizational answer to temporal ambiguity is scheduling. The tasks that make up an operation have to be organized in terms of time - namely sequence and duration. Implicit in these task sequences is a specific division of labour which in turn is based upon more or less well defined professional boundaries. So does the main surgeon´s expectation that all preparations be finished before he starts his/her work reflect a hierarchy of knowledge. This hierarchy also affects actors´ temporal images. These, although based on shared experiences, reflect the peculiarities of actors´ perceptive field. Usually it is the surgeon who estimates an operation´s duration. He may be aware of all possible complications and the tempo of this day´s surgery team. But he may not be aware of many of the small tasks that need being done and the uncertainties involved (e.g. the hospital´s elevator being in repair with its consequences for patient transport; a new cleaning lady who needs supervision). In so far the surgeon´s time estimates also reflect a specific set of values.

Temporal dependences:
Moore [9] in his classification of time problems refers to synchronization as the adjustment of various social units with each other. Synchronization becomes necessary when there are temporal interdependences and individual or intermittent activity is inadequate to coordinate tasks. The temporal patterning of an operation team´s action reflects sequential interdependence (the outputs of one unit or actor form the input to another; [10]). Synchronization of the surgical team is largely based on members´ time discipline and their willingness to give their time for collaborative effort. The sequential ordering of operations also involves reciprocal interdependence insofar as the performance of one operation team affects the time schedule of all other units and delays require ongoing mutual adjustment. The ways in which these temporal dependences are handled clearly show the social and cultural character of time. The sequential ordering of operations reflects the status of individual surgeons as well as established priorities of different specialties.

Scarcity :
Given the long waiting line of patients in this clinic this third problem is particularly severe. Different types of constraints work together, on top of them the limited number of operation theaters (which need regular maintenance and occasional repair) and the scarcity of intense care beds. Secondly, actors´ working time schedules restrict time resources. One bottleneck is the time inflexibility of anesthesiologists who are not willing to perform overtime. This conflict is aggravated by anesthesiologists´ treatment as ´service people´ with no right to voice their time priorities (e.g. time for research, time for seeing the patient before the operation).
Time constraints are also created by the clinic´s notorious lack of qualified surgical nurses. This problem points to stressful working conditions as well as to a lack of job satisfaction. Part of nurses´ disenchantment with their work is related to the fact that, although it is technically demanding, there is no time for patient contact. In this way the temporal patterning of operations negatively affects the availability of personnel. A third problem derives from surgeons´ ambition to perform as many complicated operations as possible. This ambition varies with surgeon´s professional biography. As operations offer unique chances for learning (and for producing research papers), allocation of scarce temporal resources within the clinic is a major problem, loaden with a lot of in-fighting.

NEGOTIATING TIME-SCHEDULES

Technology for group work has largely been tailored to examples of "intellectual teamwork" [6]. Underlying this work is the concept of a small, semi-autonomous functional group which can be regarded as a social system in itself, being only loosely coupled to the surrounding organizational environment. This group is usually task centered, goes through a series of stages and exists over a well-defined time span.

Surgical teams as a special form of work groups:
Our example of collaborative time management is different; for two reasons. Firstly, it touches upon the organization as a whole, making differential use of the connections among segments or units. Although there are a shared task - to sequence operations in a meaningful and efficient way - and some stability-creating elements, the planning process is rather open. In Weick´s [8] terminology, the scheduling of operations is only partially bounded by explicit rules, agreement on these rules is minimal and feedback mechanisms poorly developed. On one hand there are a strong hierarchy and well-specified arcs of work. At the same time the hospital is underorganized. There is a lack of explicit organizational responsibilities and rules. Given this weak frame, informal relationships and with them status and power gain influence and an immediacy unmodified by rules and procedures develops. Secondly, although operations are a product of group work, the performing team does not constitute itself as a group nor does it act as one (although individual team members share joint work experiences). Rather people who are based within different substantive and social domains meet at certain physical spaces at particular times to engage in particular tasks [11]. This peculiarity is partly due to the fact that the tasks which have to be performed during an operation are sequentially organized with team members being present at different times and - with the exception of the surgical nurse - only partially overlapping and directly collaborating. After the patient has been brought into the operation theatre, first enters the anesthesiologist, second the assistant surgeon, third the main surgeon (who finds the patient as an "open field" on whom to perform his specialized task) and these persons leave the theater in reverse order.

Cooperation or negotiation?
Contrary to Habermas´ concept of the ideal speech situation "the peculiarly uncompelling force of the better argument which allows for a systematic evaluation of propositions and a rational motivation of decisions on practical questions" [12, p. 137] often cannot unfold under the conditions that have been described as typical of surgical teams. The relevance of focussing system development on organizational conflict and group process has already been extensively discussed (e.g. [13]). Most analyses done from this perspective identify structural antecedents of conflict potential, such as in our case temporal ambiguity, scarce resources, a plurality of time-reckoning systems, power-related differences in time autonomy. They focus on managing conflict and communication in order to obtain "constructive outcomes". Underlying this perspective is the assumption "that the preferences of multiple parties can be satisfied with the same solution ... That is conflict can have constructive outcomes that conflicting parties experience as mutually beneficial" [13]. While Smith and Berg [14] suggest that for groups to work productively conflicts have to be understood, accepted and even tackled, Murnighan and Conlon found: "Successful groups handled conflict with a variety of strategies that allowed the conflict to continue without being disruptive. ... Less successful groups compromised, talked more, and evidenced all the characteristics of groups that were ´stuck´" [15, p. 182].

The strong emphasis on conflict resolution might be due to the fact that much of the research on conflict has been centered on typical examples of group problem solving. Our case challenges this perspective. In an organization characterized by strong authority relations and interpersonal networks many problems are handled locally [11] without resolving the underlying conflicts. Negotiated order theory seems to conceptualize particularly well the organizational procedures for getting things done in such types of organizations. In a series of case-studies Strauss has developed a "paradigm" which helps to analyze negotiative processes and their embeddedness in social settings. Its "key terms include subprocesses of negotiation, of which examples were making trade-offs, obtaining kickbacks, compromising toward the middle, paying off debts, and reaching negotiated agreements" [7, p. 237]. The concept of negotiation implies that, although overt or endemic conflict may exist, actors within an organization are able to develop modes of interacting which help them to reach an agreement. Power forms an important part of negotiation. However, it is not seen as absolute and unchallengeable but in relation to other factors which help actors create coalitions and partnership.

Its applicability to many different types of collaborative effort in complex organizations makes negotiated order theory attractive for CSCW. It encompasses a variety of interactions such as informing, coordinating, collaborating and cooperating [16], without building upon an ex-ante notion of successful group work. Through investigating many different kinds of negotiative contexts Strauss [7] developed an inventory of properties according to which a specific negotiation process can be analyzed. Translated into the organizational context studied, these are:

* *The number of negotiators, their relative experience in negotiating, and whom they represent:* Operation planning involves a limited number of negotiators, representing the clinic´s departments as well as the different occupational groups.
* *The relative balance of power exhibited by the respective parties in the negotiation itself:* Physicians bring a considerable amount of time autonomy and authority into the negotiation process. Anesthesiologists are treated as "service people" with no right to voice their time priorities Nurses have to be available within their working hours independent of individual time preferences and instantaneous commitments.
* *The clarity of legitimacy boundaries of the issues negotiated:* There are multiple and competing sets of priorities derived from patients´ conditions (as evaluated from a medical or a care perspective which need not be identical), the internal ranking of disciplines within the clinic, and surgeons´ seniority and ambition to perform as many complicated operations as possible.
* *The nature of their respective stakes in the negotiation:* Actors´ stakes in the negotiation are high and at the same time representative of different value systems (e.g. patient versus career related).
* *The visibility of the transactions to others; that is, their overt or covert character:* Information sharing is highly selective and temporal commitments not made transparent (e.g. surgeons have an interest in keeping parts of their individual time calendars private; priorities are only partially made explicit).
* *The options to avoiding or discontinuing negotiation; that is, the alternative modes of action perceived as available:* Current practices are characterized by a leadership versus democracy paradox [15] with e.g. nurses being reluctant to participate in decision-making (which they fear might only add to the complexity of their tasks and consume more time than can be spent).

COMPUTER-SUPPORTED TIME-MANAGEMENT: THE PROTOTYPE

The centerpiece of the prototype is an "operation book" which resembles the document used in the clinic´s daily planning sessions. Four basic functions have been developed (see Table 1).

* a planning function which supports face-to-face decision making;
* an additional option for deciding upon and administering ad-hoc-changes of a given operation plan;
* a communication function which has been restricted to the sending and receiving of messages;
* an information function which forms the basis for individual and team planning.

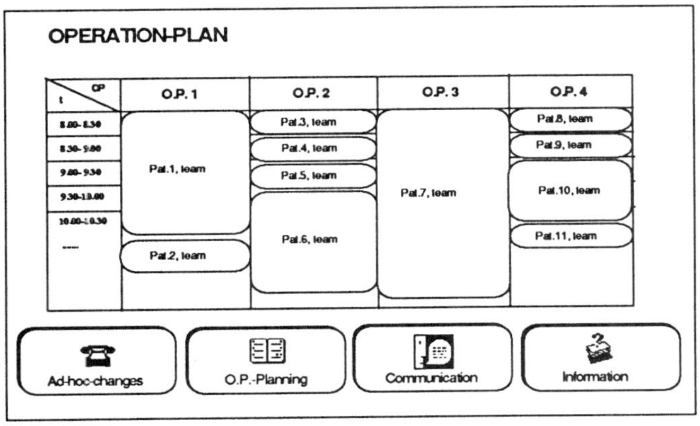

Table 1. The "operation-book"

Three central concerns guided the translation of our observations on the social and cultural complexity of time management into the design of a prototype:

Limits of automatic scheduling

Building an understanding of the social reality of time-planning has made aware of the limits of automation. Given the high degree of temporal ambiguity and the existence of competing priorities, time management cannot be conceptualized as a pure scheduling problem, although there are some clearly defined rules which can be administered by the system. Estimating the time needed for a particular type of surgery provides a good example of temporal ambiguity. Research within both cooperating clinics has shown that neither the head surgeon´s estimate nor statistical averages are reliable indicators of the duration of a surgery. The system has to provide for "buffer" time which needs to be assessed on a day-to-day basis by those persons who have an intimate knowledge of the clinic´s organizational problems and resources.

As a consequence, the prototype´s "planning function" combines an automatic scheduler - a module which "knows" a series of restrictions and tests the compatibility of data - with elements that support face-to-face decision-making (such restrictions are e.g. the availability of operation theaters and personnel, medical-technical conditions which influence the timing of surgery, the compatibility of scheduled operations with personnel´s working hours). Based on this knowledge and on organizational instruments such as local waiting lists, personal calendars and a resource plan, the system identifies collisions- e.g. operations overlapping, a team member´s absence, the non-availability of an OP theatre or IC bed, slots of "unused" OP time.

Strengthening cooperative decision-making

A second central focus is the idea of cooperativity. It is strengthened in four ways:

a) by expanding upon the number of persons who are consulted or informed;
b) by facilitating communication;
c) by providing "coded" information on stated rules, priorities, individual availability and preferences;
d) by systematically introducing information on past decisions into the planning process.

ad a) *Inviting participation:* This can be illustrated using the example of ad-hoc-changes. In order to be able to update the operation plan whenever changes are required, a special function has been added. Options are: to insert emergency cases, to delete a patient (e.g. whose condition has deteriorated), to extend the estimated operation time, and to change the operation team.

In most surgery clinics an operation manager (in our case a low-status secretary) acts as an intermediary in the planning process. He/she takes on some basic critical social functions (even though his/her competencies and responsibilities may vary widely); in particular: taking in messages, initiating communication and moderating decisions. Feenberg argues that such functions, including the "verification of the accuracy of each participant's judgement about the nature of that context.... and relieving some of the anxiety participants experience in a communication setting that is undefined by tacit contexts"[17, pp. 266] cannot be taken over by an "impersonal" coordinator but need competent human intervention.

The system offers support for this role, based on the idea of shared responsibility and decision-making. This is especially important for all types of decisions for which no explicit rules exist or rules should be handled more flexibly. In cases of changes of the surgery team the Operation Manager should e.g. have easy access to staff´s personal calendars and be able to contact the persons involved. Incoming emergencies, unexpected extensions of operation time or the postponement of a scheduled operation require decisions that might affect several other teams and their patients. To administer these the Operation Manager needs to be able to look into local patient queues and to contact persons who can give information on whether another surgery can be performed within the pre-scheduled time (availability of patient, team etc).

ad b) *Facilitating communication:* The communication function is used for several purposes. It serves as a substitute for the traditional "operation book" in which surgeons register operations. Surgeons are required not only to enter their patient´s name and the members of the surgery team. The electronic operation book contains the diagnosis as well as the expected beginning time and end of the operation (including a time buffer as judged by the Operation Manager or a Head Nurse). It offers anesthesiologist and nurses the chance to enter their names in a surgery team (this can be done individually or by a representative).

Secondly, changes which concern a large number of staff such as the closure of an OP theatre can be communicated. The Operation Manager uses this function to contact persons involved in ad-hoc-decisions (e.g. by monitoring portable telephones through the system) and for releasing messages. Lastly, this function may be used as an Electronic Board for individual arrangements (e.g. swapping operation time). There is also the possibility of long term registration (e.g. a surgeon indicating that he/she will need extra operation time at a certain date). The advantage of such a semi-structured communication function is the overall visibility of needs and events in a loosely coupled organization where opportunities for regular meetings and exchange are rare. It is seen as an instrument for increasing the degree of inclusivness and participation throughout the organization.

ad c) *Increasing transparency:* Among the highly controversial planning instruments are staff´s personal calendars (see Table 2). Such calendars seem useful in complex organizations where the availability of persons at certain times is not always known to those who have to make the planning decisions. The applicability of personal calendars depends on two conditions: everyone involved must keep a personal calendar and be willing to let the computer dispose of free time slots. Ehrlich [18] points out that neither of these requirements is generally satisfied. "Free time is never really free" - people usually have strong notions on how to handle unscheduled slots of time and do not want to lose control over how and for what purpose to use this time. This points to a more general problem. Constructing a shared representation of time presupposes that priorities be made more explicit. Explicitness, however, makes individual and group practices and decisions more accessible to discussion and reflection within an organization. It turns hitherto private regions into public ones [19]. The organization faces the problem of negotiating "publicly" the legitimacy of priorities and practices.
A tool has been designed that gives individuals (assistant surgeons, anesthesiologists and OP nurses) the opportunity to delete time thereby indicating non-availability for surgery. Questions that need discussion among users are:

* Who is going to keep such calendars and who should have access?
* Are individuals required to indicate the reasons for not being available?
* Would the possibility of stating individual temporal preferences help planners and increase users´ acceptance of an electronic calendar?

At present nurses and anesthesiologists have to be available within their working hours independent of individual time preferences and instantaneous commitments. To them the option to indicate temporal preferences could be attractive. Surgeons on the other hand have an interest in keeping parts of their individual time calendars private. This is in conflict with the interest of patients and planners in temporal transparency.

ad d) *Learning from the past:* Records of the organization´s "past" (e.g. containing information on average operation times or on past decisions) are likely to influence the management of operation time. So may for instance knowledge on which department or individual surgeon was most affected by past

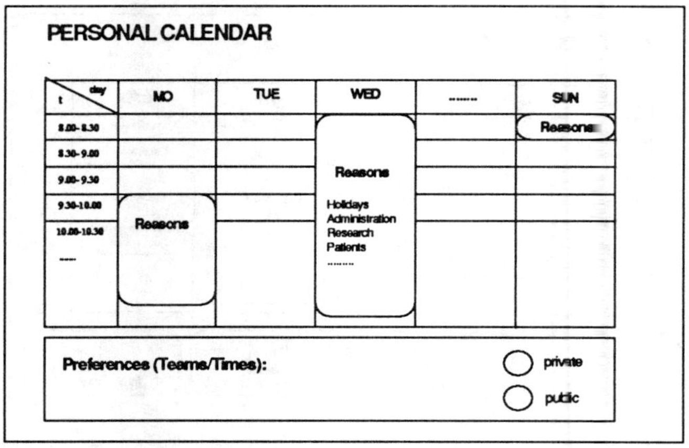

Table 2. Personal calendars

ad-hoc changes (e.g. the head of the clinic frequently disposing of time openings for heart surgery on "his" patients) influence future decisions. A concrete example of computer-assisted learning from past practices is provided by a system in use in a Dutch hospital. During the operation the assisting nurse registers time indicators which the OP managing staff later enters into the computer system. These include starting time of anesthesia, patient´s arrival on OP location, start of operation, end of operation and end of anesthesia. A data analyst has started to develop tools for a statistical evaluation of these data. The aim of such an analysis is to optimize the distribution of OP resources and finetune the schedules. Graphics show e.g. the distribution of OP time over the clinic´s specialties, the number of operations performed within this time and differences between "brutto" time and actual operation time.
The explicit aim underlying this approach is to bridge organizational segmentation. At present each individual surgeon (as a representative of a specialty) plans with the waiting lists of his/her own patients in mind, thereby largely disregarding the development of the clinic as a whole. Research has pointed out the potential for self-management and self-rationalization connected with the mirror function of information technology [20]. Computer-supported mirroring makes it increasingly difficult for actors within an organization to stick to their individual, "egocentric", occupation-specific perspective. They find themselves confronted with a larger segment of the organization. This segment includes the contribution of other actors and groups and puts the individual's performance in relation to those of others.

Changing the organization

A third "lesson" to be learned from the in-depth analysis of time planning practices is their dependence on basic organizational decisions. So can e.g. many problems of synchronizing the activities of a surgical team be traced back to differences in member´s time autonomy and discipline. Often the roots of "bad timing practices" are not primarily technical but organizational. This points to the importance of organizational learning processes.

Organizational decisions	Ethical problems
Synchronization	
Team versus pool Group versus sequential task performance	Value of time of individuals/ occupational groups
Prioritizing and sequencing of operations * cooperatively or hierarchically * synchronous versus asynchronous	Right to dispose of the time of others, to voice temporal preferences
Using temporal 'reserves'	Competing notions of efficiency, differential value of knowledge and activities
Allocation of temporal resources	
Flexible versus stable patterns of allocation	Benefits and burdens of flexibility of operation-time unequally distributed
Flexible versus standardized working time arrangements	
Coping with ambiguity	
Explicitness of priorities	Private versus public regions
Making the use of time transparent	Comparability of individual/ team performance and time discipline

Table 3. Organizational decisions and ethical problems

Whether a cooperativity-enhancing system can be successfully developed and implemented seems to depend on two conditions: Firstly, it presupposes that members of the organization be aware of acute and continuing problems in managing scarce temporal resources and the associated conflicts. Secondly, there has to be a commitment to cooperativity within the organization and proponents of participation be willing to act as coalition partners for the developing team.
In our project designer's commitment to the idea of cooperative planning has proven to be a main source of conflict in an organizational environment in which surgeons claim absolute authority and often argue for "chaos" as the most productive way of coping with contingency. A cooperativity-enhancing system only makes sense if actors are willing to share information and resources. The local autonomy of medical departments (and within those individual senior surgeons) works against developing a culture of transparency and sharing. This requires that organizational decisions be reflected on prior to system development and be questioned at each stage.

The organizational issues and the ethical problems involved (see Table 3) can be translated into a set of questions which serve as guidelines for an intercultural dialogue between systems developers and users [21].

CONCLUSIONS

A central conclusion from first discussions of the prototype is that cooperativity can be supported by a system but not be enforced. Although the prototype has been designed to broaden access to information and to facilitate joint decision-making, there is no way of preventing the organization from using it for making current autocratic planning more efficient. This dilemma seems to be an intricate part of CSCW applications, in particular when they reach beyond the small task-centered group into the organization as a whole.
One salient problem in our project e.g. is that both the complexity of the organization and the urgency with which decisions have to be taken makes the implementation of a "master-level" from which different tasks are coordinated indispensable. This is in conflict with the aim to distribute information as widely as possible and to intensify participation in decision-making. This dilemma in our judgement cannot be solved on the system level. It rather points to the need of a widespread commitment to cooperativity within the organization.

REFERENCES

1. Luhmann, N. Temporalisierung von Komplexität. Zur Semantik neuzeitlicher Zeitbegriffe. *Gesellschaftsstruktur und Semantik Bd I.* Frankfurt, 1980, pp. 235-300.

2. McGrath, J.E. Time Matters in Groups. Galegher J., Kraut R.E. , Egido C. (eds). *Intellectual Teamwork. Social and Technological Foundations of Cooperative Work.* Hillsdale N.J., Lawrence Erlbaum Ass., 1990, pp. 23-61.

3. Hassard, J. Time and Industrial Sociology. Blyton P. et al (eds). *Time, Work and Organization.* London and New York, Routledge, 1990, pp. 13-31.

4. Thompson, E.P. *Organizations in Action.* New York, McGraw-Hill, 1967.

5. Durkheim, E. *The Elementary Forms of Religious Life.* London, George Allen&Unwin, 1976.

6. Galegher, J., Kraut, R.E. Technology for Intellectual Teamwork: Perspectives on Research and Design.

Galegher J., Kraut R.E. , Egido C. (eds): *Intellectual Teamwork. Social and Technological Foundations of Cooperative Work.* Hillsdale N.J., Lawrence Erlbaum Ass., 1990, pp. 1-20.

7. Strauss, A. *Negotiations*. San Francisco, Jossey-Bass, 1979.

8. Weick, K.E. Sources of Order in Underorganized Systems: Themes in Recent Organizational Theory. Lincoln Y.S. (ed). *Organizational Theory and Inquiry.* Beverly Hills, Sage, 1985, pp. 106-136.

9. Moore, W.E. The Temporal Structure of Organization. Tiryakian, E.A. *Sociological Theory, Values and Sociocultural Change*. Free Press, London, 1963.

10. Hassard, J. Time and Organization. Blyton P. et al (eds). *Time, Work and Organization*. London and New York, Routledge, 1990, pp. 79-101.

11. Cicourel, A.V. The Integration of Distributed Knowledge in Collaborative Medical Diagnosis. Galegher J., Kraut R.E. , Egido C. (eds). *Intellectual Teamwork. Social and Technological Foundations of Cooperative Work.* Hillsdale N.J., Lawrence Erlbaum Ass., 1990, pp. 221-242.

12. Habermas, J. *Vorbereitende Bemerkungen zu einer Theorie der kommunikativen Kompetenz*. Frankfurt, Suhrkamp, 1971.

13. Robey, D., Farrow, D.L., Franz, C.R. Group Process and Conflict in System Development. *Management Science 35/10* (1989), pp. 1172-1191.

14. Smith, K., Berg, D. *Paradoxes of Group Life*. San Francisco, Jossey-Bass, 1987.

15. Murnighan, J.K., Conlon, D.E. The Dynamics of Intense Work Groups: A Study of British String Quartets. *Administrative Science Quarterly 36* (1991), pp. 165-186.

16. Blair, J.H. Supporting Cooperative Work With Computers: Adressing Meeting Mania. in *Proceedings COMPCON.* (Spring 1989), Washington DC, IEEE Computer Society Press, pp. 208-217.

17. Feenberg, A. A User's Guide to the Pragmatics of Computer Mediated Communication. *Semiotica 75/3-4* (1989), pp. 257-287.

18. Ehrlich, S.F.: Social and Psychological Factors Influencing the Design of Office Communication Systems. in *Proc. CHI+GI '87 Human Factors in Computing Systems* (Toronto, April 5-9, 1987).

19. Hägerstrand, T. Space, Time and Human Condition. Karlqvist A. (ed). *Dynamic Allocation of Urban Space,* Farnborough, Saxon House, 1975

20. Hirschhorn, L., Farquhar, K. Productivitiy, Technology and the Decline of the Autonomous Professional. *Office Technology and People 2* (1985), pp. 245-26[illegible].

21. Wagner, I. Caught in a Web of Fuzzy Problems. Confronting the Ethical Issues in Systems Design. in *Proc. PDC'92 Participatory Design Conference* (Cambridge Mass., November 6-7, 1992).

* This paper is based on a research project on Computer Supported Time-Management which is funded by the Austrian "Fonds zur Förderung der wissenschaftlichen Forschung" Research Grant No P7743-PHY, and carried out in collaboration with Christian Stary and Alexander Bek, Technische Universität Wien.

“Lazy” Consistency: A Basis for Cooperative Software Development

K. Narayanaswamy
Neil Goldman

USC/Information Sciences Institute
4676 Admiralty Way
Marina del Rey, CA 90292
email: swamy@isi.edu

Abstract

One of the major problems in cooperative software development is that of maintaining certain global consistency properties. Broadcasting changes that have already occured, as many programming environments do, will not resolve this problem. We argue in favor of an architecture where the announcements deal with *impending or proposed* changes as well as changes that have already occurred. One can then formulate consistency requirements on the system that are maintained “lazily” as it evolves. Such an architecture can support a wider range of cooperative processes than traditional software development environments. This paper describes the design and implementation of this architecture.

1 Introduction

In this paper, we are concerned with the problem of providing principled support for the cooperative development of software by programmers distributed over a network of workstations. The main difficulty stems from the distributed nature of the development process, changes made by one programmer can conflict or collide with the changes made by another in various ways. The problem must be solved through negotiations and organizational protocols. The aim of this paper is to identify the technical basis to support such resolutions of cooperative software development(CSD) problems.

Permission to copy without fee all or part of this material is granted provided that the copies are not made or distributed for direct commercial advantage, the ACM copyright notice and the title of the publication and its date appear, and notice is given that copying is by permission of the Association for Computing Machinery. To copy otherwise, or to republish, requires a fee and/or specific permission.

© 1992 ACM 0-89791-543-7/92/0010/0257...$1.50

1.1 CSD Models

A “collision” occurs when two different programmers have changed a system in potentially inconsistent ways while pursuing their disparate goals. One mechanism for coherent CSD is to prevent collisions from ever arising. This entails stringent object locking schemes (such as classical two-phase locking in traditional database systems), which guarantee that access to objects is sequentialized. In effect, no parallel development is actually supported. This is conceptually a simple solution with the advantage that system inconsistencies can never arise. However, its disadvantages are generally deemed unacceptable because programmers would need to wait indefinitely for locks to be released or would risk losing major investment due to rollback [14].

CSD can also be based on more optimistic assumptions about the frequency of collisions in practice. This strategy allows development to proceed in parallel on different work stations, and, when collisions do occur, the programmers are supported in handling collisions. usually by doing a potentially 3-way merge. These ideas are embodied in several systems [1, 8, 12].

There are, of course, ways to combine both of the above schemes to create a hybrid strategy that will allow one to benefit from the advantages of both. The work done by Kaiser et al [14] is a good example of such work. We wish to describe one more such scheme that has features of interest to the larger community of those interested in supporting CSD. In effect, we wish to allow parallel development as much as possible, but without losing all ability to guarantee system consistency.

It has been recognized that one needs to create more flexible notions of consistency when dealing with software evolution. Sutton [16] points out that when it comes to software there are many reasons why one cannot enforce consistency in the same way that one might in a traditional database system:

- It is difficult to discern and/or articulate all the constraints *a-priori* for a software system.
- Automatic detection of constraint violation (let alone automatic repair) is completely unrealistic. Hence, human programmers will need to be part of the process of constraint violation detection and repair for a long time to come.
- It is not always clear *when* one must check for constraint violations or *where*.

The notion of *lazy consistency* and the transaction model that accompanies it provide our answers to the above problems identified by Sutton.

1.2 "Lazy" Consistency

Many researchers note that one must learn to live with inconsistency in complex system data [2, 16]. More accurately, it is important to talk about consistency within the context of a larger evolutionary transaction model, that makes it explicit when the system is expected to be in a consistent state, and when it is tolerable for it to be in an inconsistent state. The problem of consistency gets further exacerbated in a distributed software development context where one cannot assume shared memory.

One common method to address the problems caused by distributed development is to announce or broadcast events of interest across the network. While this might provide the rudimentary basis for coordination of network-wide activities, one cannot guarantee consistency properties of the system if the announcements deal solely with events that have already occurred. This is because the notifications that objects have changed arrive too late for individuals who might have a stake in those changes to object to the changes in the first place. This leads to difficult and unproductive back-tracking and merging when collisions occur. On the other hand, preventing collisions, while it can guarantee system consistency, is too restrictive for parallel development.

An alternative is to base announcements not on changes that have already occurred, but proposed changes (PCs) that are about to occur. Proposed change notifications are broadcast within the context of a larger transactional model which permits the grouping of changes into coherent, logical units called *evolution steps* that together achieve some goal. In informal terms, a step is a collection of PCs to the software system that achieves a software development goal. For instance, the goal could be to fix a bug or to improve the performance of a component. We will present a more formal definition in due course.

PCs to an object could conceivably require changes to one or more of its dependents. Accordingly, PC notifications are broadcast to all impacted programmers (those responsible for maintaining the dependents). These programmers can review the PCs in the step, and have an opportunity to communicate their approval or disapproval of each PC, or modify the contents of the step in specific ways. Through this process, the step gradually becomes a consistent and approved set of alterations. Gradual establishment of intra-step consistency is one aspect of *lazy consistency*.

In addition to intra-step consistency, lazy consistency also incorporates concepts for inter-step consistency. Inter-step consistency is important in large software system because there can be work in progress on several goals at the same time. In this situation, a collision can arise between steps at the level of PCs, e.g., different changes can be proposed for the same object. The notifications of PCs can be used as a basis to support various kinds of policies in response to collisions: collision prevention, automatic collision repair, or manual merging as required by the programmer. Further, if there is a collision between two steps, since both steps are actual transactional units accessible to the programmers, it is possible for the two programmers to negotiate how the impending collision should be handled, and act accordingly. For example, one of them can offer to wait for the other to finish, thereby sequentializing the steps. Alternatively, the steps could be merged. In this manner, the two steps can be modified, and consistency eventually restored. The process of eventually restoring intra-step and inter-step consistency within the step-based transaction model is what we call *lazy consistency*, a compromise between the optimistic and pessimistic extremes discussed earlier.

2 Data Sharing Architecture

The context for this discussion is a distributed network of workstations configured in a Server-Client architecture. In other words, one of the machines on the network is designated to be the Server machine. The programmers are assumed to work at the other machines, which are called Clients. While the Server is assumed to have all the system data, the a Client will often choose to have a local cache of information, called the *local workspace*, for efficiency reasons

Much of the discussion in this paper applies to different data models and information management regimes. We happen to use an "object-oriented" data model to represent system data with the fairly standard notions of class, subclass, attributes, attribute inheritance, etc. Attributes may be single or multi-valued. In the interests of brevity, we will not discuss the details of our schema for system data. Each entity of interest, like a module or a function is simply an object, and all its properties are stored as its attributes.

One attribute of particular importance to defining collisions in a principled manner is the notion of dependency between objects. For example, functions invoke other functions or macros, set or use variables, or employ different data types, causing many kinds of dependency links. We model dependencies with a relation *DependsOn*; with *DependsOn*(S_1, S_2) meaning that when S_2 is changed, S_1 *may* need to be altered as well. While many dependencies can be derived by analyzing the source definitions and/or specifications of objects, it is not, in general, possible to determine automatically when a given change to an object *necessitates* a change to a potential dependent. Therefore, our dependency notion is much weaker, capturing only that the dependent object *might* require change, but defining neither the circumstances under which a change is absolutely required nor the nature of the change.

Another important idea is that of *responsibility* for changing an object. An object can be changed only by someone who has been granted the *responsibility* to change the component. We model this with the relation *responsibility*, with responsibility(s,p) indicating that person p has the responsibility to change object s. A person is allowed to have multiple responsibilities. For simplicity in the following explication, we will assume that each object has precisely one programmer who is responsible for it.

The Server contains all the system data. However, the Clients can cache information in their local workspaces for efficiency reasons. Changes that a Client makes to any object are reflected only in the local workspace, and are invisible to other programmers on the network unless the Client explicitly requests that the changes be committed.

3 CSD Process

The cooperative development process must be flexible without losing coherence and focus, even within a distributed development context. Accordingly, our process starts with the identification of some evolutionary goal. For instance, the goal could be to fix a bug, improve performance, or add a new capability. We do not explicitly model the creative portion of the task where the goal is articulated and a plan to achieve it is created.

To achieve a goal, the programmer(s) start by *proposing* a set of changes to some of the primitives and modules in the system. Each PC by a programmer P could affect other objects. Some of these objects might be the responsibility of P, and others might be the responsibility of other programmers. We require that these programmers (including P if necessary) review all the affected objects, and explicitly approve or reject each of the changes that had an impact on that object. A programmer can approve a change by simply accepting the change without reservation, or by proposing a (presumably compensatory) change to the dependent object.

The programmer can also reject a PC. In this case, the programmer who proposed the original change can retract or alter the PC, reinitiating the approval process, or abandon the goal entirely. When all the changes necessary to achieve the goal have been accumulated, and all the approvals necessary have been obtained, the entire set of changes must be incorporated as a unit, creating a new version of the software system.

We wish to create enough conceptual structure to allow programmers to cooperate, both in achieving the same goal (i.e., a team of programmers trying to cooperate in achieving the same evolutionary goal), and in coordinating multiple active goals at the same time. The basic foundation for coordinating development activities is twofold:

- There is a communication protocol that allows the actions of an individual programmer, where pertinent, to be broadcast to other programmers. The notifications are routed through the Server. Important events for notification in our scheme are, for example, creation of a new goal, proposing changes to objects, etc.

  When notifications are received at each workstation, assertions are made in the local database about the events at other workstations. Rules can now be written to react to these assertions, providing the basic mechanisms for cooperation.

- A transaction model that allows one to group changes into logical units of work is crucial. The notification structure works in conjunction with the transaction model to facilitate cooperation.

4 Transaction Model

Under our scheme, the programmer makes changes to an object by changing its attributes within the database. Typically, many object-level changes are required in order to achieve any particular evolutionary goal. All of these must be grouped together and handled coherently as a single logical unit. We call this unit an *evolution step*.

4.1 Step Status & Operations

When a step is created, it is in the *volatile* state. The term "volatile" reminds us that the set of PCs which comprise it is not fixed. A programmers may, at any time, add more PCs to a volatile step. A programmer may make any volatile step the *focus* of development activity for a given software system. As the programmer uses editing tools to modify his local copies of objects, those modifications are automatically incorporated as prooposed changes in the focussed step.

When all of the PCs necessary to achieve the goal of the step have been made (and other conditions that we will discuss presently) have been met, the step can be *committed.* At this time, the step is made visible to everyone because its PCs are actually incorporated into a new version of the system. Thereafter, the contents of the step (i.e., its PCs) may not be altered. While a step is still in the *volatile* state, it may be *abandoned* if the programmers deem the step superfluous. This puts the step in the *abandoned* state. When a step is abandoned, all its PCs in it and their effects, if any, are retracted from the local workspaces of programmers contributing to the step.

4.2 Structure of a Step

As just described, a step consists of a set of PCs. The PCs are related to the step by the *ProposedChange* attribute. Formally, therefore, a step is a collection of PCs which can be applied to a consistent system state to produce a different, but also consistent system state. A PC is a formal object encoding the following:

Author: `the programmer proposing the change.`
ObjectModified: `Object altered.`
AttributeModified: `Attribute altered.`
DeletedValues: `Set of values to be retracted.`
AddedValues: `Set of values to be asserted.`

Some attributes are restricted to having exactly or at most one value. For these, the DeletedValues and AddedValues are always singleton or empty sets, as required. For every step there can be at most one PC for a given attribute/object pair. The restriction will make the ultimate enactment of the step (section 5.2) deterministic, depending solely on the *set* of PCs that have been attached to the step at the time.

The process by which the contents of a step are elaborated is of importance because this process involves the coordination of programmers at two different levels. First, different programmers can contribute PCs and approvals to a step as required of them. This involves the notion of *intra-step consistency,* the idea that the step is intended to be a completely self-contained and consistent set of changes to a system. The second level of support for CSD is the coordination of *different* steps, involving the interleaving of different evolutionary goals. This involves the notion of *inter-step consistency,* providing the foundation to support parallel development without losing all control over consistency.

PCs to an object, assertions about approval or rejection of any PC with respect to any particular affected object, or actions regarding objects affected by a collision, can only be made a programmer who has been assigned responsibility for that object. This is a constraint that will be strictly enforced by the support system to prevent spurious permissions from being granted.

5 Intra-Step Consistency

Automatic system consistency detection is still unrealistic. Therefore, intra-step consistency conditions ensure that the PCs within a single step have been approved by everyone who has a stake in it. Exactly who has a stake in a change is defined by using the inter-object dependency of *DependsOn*. The idea is that, with help of simple analytical tools (like static analyzers), affected programmers can review PCs in an orderly fashion, and cooperate by taking explicit actions about each PC. For pedagogical reasons, we simplify the discussion of intra-step consistency by ignoring the possibility of having multiple goals.

5.1 Proposed Changes

As said before, evolutionary change within the context of a step is initiated by a programmer who proposes some set of changes to system objects that (partially) accomplish the goal of the step. Anyone contributing PCs to a step is considered an *author* of the step. Programmers affected by PCs are notified (there is a separate notification for each affected object within the purview of the programmer). The programmer then has the following choices of actions:

Approval without Reservation: If the programmer decides there is no need to change the dependent object, he permits the original change without reservations. This is modelled with the relation *ApprovedWithoutReservation*: with *ApprovedWithoutReservation* (pc,O) indicating that object *O* has been reviewed by the programmer responsible for it, who certifies that no changes are necessary to object *O* in response to proposed change *pc*.

Proposing a Compensatory Change: The programmer proposes a compensatory change to the dependent object. This change will become part of the same step as *pc*. This action is accomplished by creating a new PC (or altering an existing one) with the appropriate object, attribute, and add/delete sets. We also allow the programmer to informally characterize the causal relationship between PCs. This is solely for the edification of anyone who later peruses the step. The proposal of a compensatory change is itself modelled with the relation *ImpliesChange*; with ImpliesChange(P_1,P_2) meaning that P_2 was proposed in response to P_1

The relation ImpliesChange also comes into play when a PC, *pc*, is altered or retracted by a programmer. When *pc* is retracted, any PC that is implied by *pc* is deemed no longer valid, and is itself retracted, and the programmers concerned are notified. All its ImpliesChange links are broken. However, if that PC is *also* implied by some active PC other than *pc* (i.e., it was multiply motivated), its author is notified of this event, and is expected to reestablish ImpliesChange links to satisfy the remaining motivations. When a PC is altered (i.e., the programmer chooses to propose a different value for the attribute and object referred to by PC), the effect on PCs implied by it are exactly as though it had been retracted. That is, as might be expected, altering a PC is no different than retracting it and then creating a new one in its place.

Rejection of PCs: The programmer decides that he or she cannot accommodate the original PC. This is modelled with the relation *Rejected*: with *Rejected*(O, *pc*)) meaning that the programmer responsible for O refuses permission for the *pc* because he is unwilling (or unable!) to alter the object O to compensate for *pc*. When a PC is thus rejected, its author is notified. He may alter the PC, propose some alternative change, or reject the change he was attempting to accomodate.

Naturally, if the author of the step proposes more changes to some objects this can initiate the seeking of another round of permissions involving the dependents of *those* objects. PCs to dependent objects behave just like the step author's original changes, leading to notifications reaching further into the influence sets of the originally changed objects. In the typical case, eventually all the necessary permissions will be obtained and required changes supplied. At this point, all the PCs have been reviewed and approved and the *entire set of PCs* in the evolutionary step is incorporated together into the software system by actually creating new versions of the objects in the Server.

We are now in a position to define when permission has been granted for a PC. This notion is modelled in terms of the programmer actions just defined. We define two additional relations:

```
Approved(pc,o) ≡
  ApprovedWithoutReservation(pc,o) ∨
  (∃ pc2 ImpliesChange(pc,pc2) ∧
              ObjectModified(pc2,o))
Permission(pc) ≡
  ∀ c,o (ObjectModified(pc,c) ∧ DependsOn(o,c))
                            → Approved(pc,o)
```

Approved(pc,o) indicates that object o has been reviewed by the programmer responsible for it, and that the programmer grants permission for *pc* either by approving the change without reservation or by defining another PC for o. *Permission*(pc) characterizes the situation in which for every component affected by a PC, the programmer responsible for that component has reviewed the component, and has explicitly permitted the change. Conversely, we can also express when a PC is awaiting permission with respect to one of its affected dependents. This occurs when there has been no action taken with respect to a dependent object. This is modelled with the relation *PermissionNeeded*:

```
PermissionNeeded (pc,o) ≡
  ∃ c ObjectModified(pc,c) ∧ DependsOn(o,c)
      ∧ ¬(Approved(pc,o) ∨ Rejected(pc,o))
```

The above relations allow the progress of the evolution step to be reviewed by either the programmers or by managers who want to visualize the process.

5.2 Final Dispensation of a Step

In order for a particular step to be ready to be committed, all the permissions necessary for its PCs must be explicitly asserted. We define the relation *AllPermissions* to represent this situation.

```
AllPermissions(st) ≡
  ∀ pc ProposedChange(st,pc) → Permission(pc)
```

A necessary condition for a step S to be committed is that AllPermissions(S) holds, given the PCs in S at that time. However, the condition is not sufficient for step commital because it is impossible to say when the author believes the set of PCs is adequate to meet the step's objective. Hence, we rely upon the author to issue the step commital command.

Committing a step has the effect of actually incorporating all the PCs in the step into the definitions at the Server. At this point, the changes become visible to all Clients. All subsequent changes at any client will be with respect to the newly incorporated versions of the different objects. The enactment of a step consists of atomically enacting the following changes:

```
    -- COMMIT procedure for Step S --
  for pc such that ProposedChange(S,pc)
      let A be AttributeModified of pc,
          O be ObjectModified of pc
          for v such that AddedValues(pc,v)
              assert A(O, v)
          for v such that DeletedValues(pc,v)
              retract A (O, v)
```

Conversely, if one of the PCs of the step authors is

rejected, he has only three choices: abandon the step in question; alter or replace the PC and revive the negotiation process; or convince the programmer who rejected his proposal to reconsider. These negotiations are not formally supported, but their ultimate resolution can be reflected by appropriate assertions on steps or PCs.

6 Coordination Between Steps

Step creation and PC notifications are sent to the Server, and distributed to interested Clients. Therefore, all the pertinent Clients have information about PCs asserted into their local databases. An evolution step represents a major transaction unit in software system maintenance. Our model allows a great deal of concurrency within a single step, relying on a supported process of negotiation to arrive at consistent change proposal before changes are actually committed. To provide a coherent semantics for multiple steps taking place concurrently, we must concern ourselves with the serializability of the steps themselves.

6.1 Collisions and their Resolution

The usual database criterion for allowable interleaving of transactions is that the net result be equivalent to some strictly serial execution of those transactions. Although this goal, *serializability*, applies to software development as well, the traditional database mechanism for achieving it are recognized as inappropriate for transactions that take place over an extended time (hours to months) span and involve primarily manual decision making to formulate the content of the transaction.

Our model, via *ImpliesChange* and *ApprovedWithoutReservation*, imposes considerable structure on the content of a transaction, and also, via *DependsOn*, delimits the areas where inter-step conflict might arise. We employ this structure to automatically detect inter-step conflicts as they arise and, using notifications, allow programmers to adapt evolving transactions to eliminate these conflits.

One obvious collision situation between two volatile steps occurs when when each has a PC that involves the same object/attribute pair for a single-valued attribute, such as *source-code*. But in fact *any* outcome of independently considering changes to a dependent object O_d as part of two distinct volatile steps violates serializability. Even if in both cases the result is *ApprovedWithoutReservation*, it may be that consideration of the object in light of the conjunction of *both* motivations would have resulted in some effect upon O_d.[1]

We extend the definition of inter-step conflict to say that potential conflict exists whenever objects being changed in two volatile steps have a common dependent; that is

```
InterStepConflict(pc1,pc2,o) ≡
   ∃ s1,s2 ProposedChange(s1,pc1) ∧
      ProposedChange(s2,pc2) ∧  s1 ≠ s2 ∧
      Volatile(s1) ∧  Volatile(s2)) ∧
      ∃ o1,o2 ObjectModified(pc1,o1) ∧
            ObjectModified(pc2,o2) ∧
            DependsOn(o,o1) ∧  DependsOn(o,o2)
```

When *InterStepConflict* arises, the programmer responsible for the common dependent object "o", is notified of the conflict set, as are the step authors. The approvals and/or implied changes for "o" in the steps, if any, are withdrawn. The team has several alternatives: abandonment or suspension of one of the steps; letting the programmer P responsible for the common dependent object, "o", to consider it in light of *both* steps; or merging the two steps into one. None of these processes is specifically supported formally, but their resolution can be reflected in appropriate database assertions about steps and proposed changes.

6.2 The DependsOn Relation

Because the notion of object dependencies is so crucial in determining the set of affected objects and necessary permissions, an important issue is that of how and when the *DependsOn* relation is updated. As object changes are proposed, the programmer might be changing the dependencies. We model this situation as follows:

- *DependsOn*(s_1,s_2), the Server version of s_1 depends on the Server version of s_2.
- *StepAddsDependency*(step,s_1,s_2), indicates that the step adds a new dependency of s_1 upon s_2.
- *StepRemovesDependency*(step,s_1,s_2), meaning the step removes a previous dependency of s_1 depending upon s_2.

StepAddsDependency and *StepRemovesDependency* may be discovered manually or by appying analysis tools to PCs. When a step is committed, *DependsOn* is updated as indicated by *StepAddsDependency* and *StepRemovesDependency*.

[1]For example, suppose a function F was written using two other functions G and H. Let us say there were two separate PCs, one making G more efficient, and one making H more efficient. Neither of these affects F by itself. However, taken together, it may be advantageous to reconsider the algorithm underlying F and change it as necessary to take advantage of the new G and H.

7 Implementation Experience

We have an implementation testbed that makes it relatively easy to experiment with several of the ideas described in this paper [3, 6]. In particular, relations, constraints, rules, etc, can be directly realized in our environment. We have been using the notion of steps, and PCs for several years. However, all of these were restricted to the address space of a single workstation. A single programmer might be interleaving work on multiple evolution steps, although the great bulk of development consisted of carrying through a single step from creation to commital before beginning another evolution step for the same software system.

Our first effort to promote cooperation was based on optimistic assumptions about the probability of a collision. These assumptions were justified based on the size of our programmer teams. Thus, we provided no locking or coordination in real time for steps across workstations. Collisions would be detected only at commit time, and resolution would involve merging activities by the programmer with some support from the system.

More recently, in order to facilitate cooperation across a distributed network, we have implemented a communication architecture based on the Artifacts system [9]. This system is an example of an event-based architecture featuring the sending of messages about various events to interested nodes on the network. We adapted the Artifacts system to create notifications about different kinds of events such as Step creation; Ultimate Dispensation of steps through *commit* or *abandon*; and Creation, alteration, or retraction of PCs. One effect of these notifications is to change the local workspace to reflect these events across the network. Different rules can be written to react to the events.

We have considerable experience in the area of intra-step consistency, supported by a powerful static analysis tool. Very little experience has been accumulated with inter-step consistency. In particular, we wish to provide the kind of flexibility in collision resolution that is discussed in this paper.

8 Related Work

Any CASE environment targeting production-quality software systems requires mechanisms to support CSD. In most such environments, the chief goal of the cooperation mechanism is to prevent the developers from interfering with each other while changing a system, e.g., [7, 10]. Often, the underlying mechanism is to lock objects (files) conservatively when they are to be modified, but no explicit mechanism for actual cooperation is provided.

Kaiser, et al, [14] have extended the traditional database transaction models to support the notion of *long-term transactions*. They have argued that conservative locking strategies are too restrictive for the distributed software development, and have tried extending database mechanisms to support extended transactions. The work reported here is strongly related in its overall goals to Kaiser's work. We have focused on the logical structure of a step to facilitate negotiations between programmers. Kaiser's work goes well beyond ours in looking at the difficult problem of having different rule sets at different workstations in the network.

SUN Microsystems' Network Software Environment (NSE) [1] follows a philosophy based on optimistic assumptions about collisions. They call their paradigm for evolution *Copy Modify Merge*. One copies any desired objects into one's workspace – regardless of who else might have access to those objects. The modifications are carried out in the local workspace. Before making changes persistent, the system ensures the integrity of the changes – forcing a merge if any problems are discovered. Our communication structure is intended to support a range of policies, including one that is very similar to that of NSE.

Harrison et al, [8] describe a CSD strategy very similar to that in NSE. Their conditions for collisions are somewhat more restrictive than ours, corresponding to those where the changes are to the same object in both transactions. We allow a more open-ended definition of a collision, with analysis tools and people deciding when a collision has arisen.

The Softbench tool [4], now a product of Hewlett Packard Corporation, also features an event notification architecture to support team-oriented development. As we pointed out before, it is difficult to handle consistency problems when one deals with notifications of changes that have already occurred, rather than changes that are yet to occur. This appears to be a major difference from Softbench. Similar remarks apply to another event-based tool called Yeast [15], which provides no mechanism to deal with impending events as one must to prevent inconsistency.

Lee [11] and Potts and Bruns [13] apply models that support general group decision making to the problem of software design. Both advocate, as do we, the use of a network of semi-formal records to represent the deliberation process. Our model does not capture the gradual elaboration of alternative designs as their models do, but provides greater direction of the process through its use of dependencies and responsibilities, as well as a notion of necessary conditions on the closure of the deliberation process.

9 Conclusion

A fundamental impediment to CSD is the resolution of global conflicts introduced by local changes. In this paper, we have discussed a technical basis for CSD which features network-wide notifications of *proposed changes* to objects, rather than actual changes to objects. The proposed change notifications happen within the context of a larger transactional unit called an *evolution step*, which corresponds to a single goal the the programming team. Dependencies between objects are used to define who has a stake in each proposed change. Support is provided for affected programmers to approve or reject each proposed change.

The causal relationships between proposed changes are maintained so that programmer negotiations can be supported. Using these concepts, we are able to support a process of gradually making each step internally consistent and consistent with respect to other volatile steps that might be pursued concurrently.

10 Acknowledgment

The seeds of the concepts described in this paper first appeared in preliminary ideas outlined by Don Cohen and the lead author in a short workshop position paper [5]. The implementation of the ideas described herein was greatly aided by the relational language AP5, whose nucleus was provided by Don Cohen as well. The programming environment for this effort [6] resulted from several years of research and development by various individuals in the Software Sciences Division at ISI.

References

[1] Adams, E., Honda, M., and Miller, T. Object management in a case environment. In *Proc. of 11th ICSE* (1989), IEEE.

[2] Balzer, R. Tolerating inconsistency. In *13th Int'l Conf. on Software Engg* (1991), ACM.

[3] Balzer, R. M. Living in the next generation operating system. In *Proceedings of the 10th World Computer Congress '86* (Dublin, Ireland, September 1986), IFIP.

[4] Cagan, M. The hp softbench environment: An architecture for a new generation of software tools. *Hewlett-Packard Journal* (June 1990).

[5] Cohen, D., and Narayanaswamy, K. A logical framework to support cooperative software development. In *Proceedings of the 6th International Software Process Workshop* (1990), IEEE Computer Society.

[6] Goldman, N., and Narayanaswamy, K. Software evolution through iterative prototyping. In *14th Int'l Conf. on Software Engg.* (May 1992), IEEE.

[7] Habermann, A., and Notkin, D. Gandalf: Software development environments. *IEEE-TSE SE-12*, 12 (Dec 1986), 1117–1128.

[8] Harrison, W., Ossher, H., and Sweeney, P. Coordinating concurrent development. In *Proceedings of CSCW '90* (1990), ACM.

[9] Karr, M. Beyond the read-eval-print loop: Architecture of the artifacts system. Technical Report, Contact Software Options, Inc.,, 199■. 22 Hilliard St., Cambridge, MA 02138.

[10] Leblang, D. B. Configuration management for large-scale software development efforts. In *Proceedings of Workshop on Software Engg Environments for Programming-in-the-Large* (June 1985), pp. 122–127.

[11] Lee, J. Sibyl: A tool for managing group design. In *Proceedings of CSCW '90* (1990), ACM.

[12] Narayanswamy, K., and Goldman, N. A flexible framework for cooperative distributed software development. *Journal of Systems and Software 16*, 2 (October 1991).

[13] Potts, C., and Bruns, G. Recording the reasons for design decisions. In *Proc. of 10th ICSE* (1988), IEEE.

[14] Pu, C., Kaiser, G., and Hutchinson, N. Split transactions for open-ended activities. In *Proc. of 14th VLDB* (1988), ACM.

[15] Rosenblum, D., and Krishnamurthy, B. An event-based model of software configuration management. In *Proceedings of the 3rd International Workshop on Software Configuration Management* (June 1991).

[16] Sutton, S. A flexible consistency model for persistent data in software-process programming languages. In *4th Int'l Workshop on Persistent Object Systems* (1990), ACM.

Implicit Locking in the Ensemble Concurrent Object-Oriented Graphics Editor

R. E. Newman-Wolfe, M. L. Webb and M. Montes

Computer and Information Sciences Department
The University of Florida
Gainesville, FL 32611
(904) 392-1488 nemo@chameleon.cis.ufl.edu

ABSTRACT

Ensemble is an X-Windows based, object-oriented graphics editor based on the *tgif* graphics editor from UCLA. It relies on Unix* 4.3bsd sockets and can be used as a stand-alone program or as an application in the University of Florida's distributed conferencing system (DCS). It uses implicitly placed write locks for concurrency control, with locks placed when an object is selected and removed when it is deselected. Multiple users may read or edit a file concurrently, with all users receiving updates whenever a lock is removed. Pointers are shared by mutual consent, so that users may collaborate to the degree desired. Ensemble is a prototype lock-based approach to object-oriented concurrent graphics editing.

KEYWORDS

Groupware, collaborative editing, graphics editing, distributed conferencing, DCS.

INTRODUCTION - CONCURRENT GRAPHICS EDITING

Traditional graphics editors are not collaboration aware: they cater to a single user editing one file at one time. These editors have no built-in control for voluntary or involuntary multiple invocations attempting to edit the same file. For example, if a file were edited simultaneously, only the changes made through one editor would affect the final version of the file.

Some systems, such as SCCS [3] and RCS [23], support editors externally in preserving the integrity of files. Files need to be checked out through these systems before changes may take place. This method ensures that only one user may edit a file at one time. However, if close collaboration is desired, or if work must proceed in parallel, a collaboration-aware editor is needed.

Collaboration-aware editors provide mechanisms for more fine-grained, real-time sharing. The ability to sketch and gesture are highly desirable for communication of a wide variety of ideas; after all, "a picture is worth a thousand words." More important, recreating a picture from a verbal description is a tedious and error-prone activity. Even when the images can be transmitted the gestures that are used to focus attention are largely lost. Simultaneous access to the same canvas is often desirable, so shared graphics editors are useful for collaboration support.

This paper describes Ensemble, the concurrent, object-oriented graphics editor of the distributed conferencing system (DCS) at the University of Florida. DCS provides broad support for cooperative work, and includes several particular tools, including Ensemble [19]. Ensemble has been in use for the past two years. There are four significant contributions of Ensemble. It uses implicit locking in an object-oriented graphics environment, and gestures may be shared with filtering by both sender and receiver. It has mechanisms to provide concurrency control at the file level in two ways: collaboration groups are formed implicitly simply by accessing a file, and within DCS, access to the file must be made through Ensemble, so that there can be no collisions with edits made outside of Ensemble. Finally, the architecture of Ensemble is simple and efficient, and lends itself well to inclusion of heterogeneous interfaces to the same canvas.

We will first introduce issues in shared graphics editors, then describe some of the existing ones. Ensemble is then described in detail, including its requirements, design, and implementation as well as notes on preliminary experience with Ensemble. We conclude with some observations on what succeeded and what did not with Ensemble, and where future work can take us.

ISSUES IN CONCURRENT GRAPHICS EDITING

There are many philosophical and technical issues in producing a shared graphics editor. One basic question is the degree of collaboration awareness of the application. The reviews by Stefik et al. [22], Ahuja et al. [2], Crowley et al. [6] and Greenberg [12] are excellent, and Greif's book is a good source of seminal papers [13].

This work is partially supported by the University of Florida - Purdue University Software Engineering Research Center.

* Unix is a trademark of AT&T Bell Labs.

Permission to copy without fee all or part of this material is granted provided that the copies are not made or distributed for direct commercial advantage, the ACM copyright notice and the title of the publication and its date appear, and notice is given that copying is by permission of the Association for Computing Machinery. To copy otherwise, or to republish, requires a fee and/or specific permission.

© 1992 ACM 0-89791-543-7/92/0010/0265...$1.50

A good concurrent editing system should support features that provide the user with ease of use, good accessibility to editable objects, hidden seams, and ability to filter remote information. Ease of use is the responsibility of the user interface. Information concerning other collaborators, such as their identification and their roles in participation, should available but unobtrusive. Users should not be hindered by the fact that the file is being shared unless it is necessary: they may be made aware of the collaboration but should not be taxed by its existence. In sum, sharing should be as transparent as possible to the user, yet details of that sharing should be available if desired.

Drawing, gesturing and viewing may be separated from one another in terms of sharing. It is possible that only one user may draw at a time, while any user may gesture (move a cursor around the canvas); likewise, different users may choose to view different parts of the canvas in distinct ways (at different magnifications, for example). On the other hand, even if all users are able to draw on the canvas simultaneously, a user may not see the position of every other user's cursor.

The input sharing paradigm for concurrent graphics editors has usually been all or one: either any user could draw anywhere on the canvas at any time, or input was serialized through some floor passing mechanism. Unconstrained access is usually limited to pixel-oriented drawing editors.

Gesture sharing paradigms range from no sharing of cursors, to having a distinctively shaped cursor for each user visible to all users. Some systems allow serial access to a single "conference pointer," eliminating the distraction found when many cursors are visible at once [22]. This problem can also be addressed by altering the view sharing paradigm, as is done in Ensemble.

The WYSIWIS view sharing paradigm is the earliest and most obvious paradigm for view sharing. WYSIWIS, or What You See Is What I See, supports a chalk-board type of interaction where every one sees the same view of the shared material. A major shortcoming of this method is the lack of privacy to the collaborator as strict WYSIWIS outlaws the presence of a private work space [11, 21-22]. In addition, many problems present themselves in accommodating user control of his view of the shared data [24].

Another abstraction known as WYSIWIMS, or What You See Is What I May See, allows independent viewing perspectives and private work spaces [19]. In Ensemble, just because a user's cursor position is available for another user to see does not mean that the other user must see it unless he requests it. Further, users need not observe the same parts of the canvas, or even view the parts observed in common in the same manner. This paradigm is more general than the relaxed versions of WYSIWIS provided in Mermaid [24]; users need not have the same parts of the shared objects on their screens, and may not even see the same version of a shared object. This WYSIWIMS paradigm is similar to the filtering provided in Suite, which propagates changes depending on syntactic or semantic integrity in a structured editor environment [7]. However, in graphics editors, semantic integrity is somewhat harder to specify than in the more constrained world of structured editors.

Interactions occur between the various sharing paradigms and the implementation approach used. Two main approaches to sharing a drawing/gesturing space electronically are distinguished by the way graphic input is obtained by the system. One approach is to use a video camera to capture a physical drawing or object, which is then transmitted to other users, perhaps merging it with other scenes captured by camera or generated by computer (such as cursor positions). TeamWorkStation is one example of this type of system [15]. This approach makes it difficult to save or modify the shared scenes, but allows very natural input, using familiar drawing tools comfortable to users (such as pencils, brushes, etc.) as well as permitting display of actual objects. However, it depends on costly, specialized equipment at every input site, so that input can only occur at special locations, and only a user physically at the site of a televiewed object will be able to manipulate it.

The other implementation approach for input is to use only canvases produced by graphic editor programs. These come in two flavors: pixel-oriented (or "paint" type programs) and object-oriented editors. Pixel-oriented programs simply change the values associated with pixels of the canvas, and do not associate the value at one pixel with the value at another pixel. For example, once a circle is drawn, it looses its identity as a logical component of the picture: parts of it may be erased and it may not be moved independently of overlapping components. The canvas is stored as a pixel map. Commune, Xsketch, and tools in Augment, Colab and CES are examples of this type of system [5, 18, 8, 20, 22].

Object-oriented graphics editors store the canvas as a collection of parameterized objects, which may be manipulated independently regardless of their relative positions on the canvas: a circle may be resized or moved even though it overlaps a box. Part of a circle may be "erased" only by placing an opaque object over that part of the circle. While in pixel-oriented programs, parts of the canvas are selected for manipulation based on their position (an area is selected), in object-oriented programs, objects are selected for manipulation.

Concurrency control is based on avoidance or resolution of collisions. Within a file, a collision may happen when two or more users edit the same region of the canvas. When a pixel-oriented editor is used, raster operations are performed in the order they arrive and collisions present little problem. In an object-oriented graphics editor, collisions occur only when the same object is selected for manipulation. If modification of graphics objects are allowed, then some form of mutual exclusion must be used to maintain integrity.

After an editing session is completed, the resulting document should be consistent at all sites. During editing, the stable, committed portions of the document should be identical at all sites, within some reasonable update delay. It is incumbent upon the concurrent editor to ensure that all users have access to the same document, at least in the parts that are not under active modification.

Concurrency control is not only important at the level of internal editing within the file, but also at the level of file access. Collisions at the file access level are acceptable only if the application is collaboration-aware and users are only allowed to access the file through coordinated programs. For many editors there is no access control to the file itself forcing use of the groupware system for editing. While some users could edit the file using the groupware system, another could edit it using a single-user application, producing the standard problems of lost updates or inconsistency. Those that do limit users to accessing the file through groupware generally require the group of users editing the canvas to be formed explicitly. In Ensemble, the group is formed implicitly by the act of opening a file to edit.

In addition to the user interface and internal representations, a shared application must have a distributed architecture. A collaboration-aware system may have a centralized or a replicated architecture, or some hybrid schemes combining these.

In centralized architectures, there is only one instance of the application program running (e.g., the graphics editor engine) [2, 12, 16-17]. All input is channeled to that single process, which selects inputs and produces output that is broadcast to display processes at all user sites (see Figure 1).

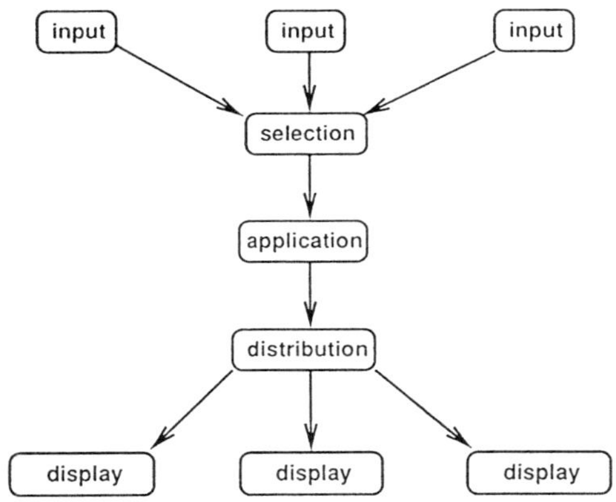

Figure 1. Centralized architecture.

These architectures have the advantage of keeping a consistent state across all views, since the input is serialized and only one copy of the internal structure exists. However, in order for the results of manipulations to be displayed, the input must travel to the central site and back again, potentially allowing some "stickiness" to exist in the system [6]. This is rarely a problem on local area networks [2], but could be significant over slower, longer communication paths.

Replicated architectures have a copy of the application running at each site in addition to an input and a display process (see Figure 2). The input processes broadcast input from each site to all the sites, where each site selects and acts on its application's internal representation. Since input data usually uses far less bandwidth than display information, this reduces load on the network. Further, the response time is excellent since the local display is driven by a local copy of the application reacting to the local input. Another advantage includes

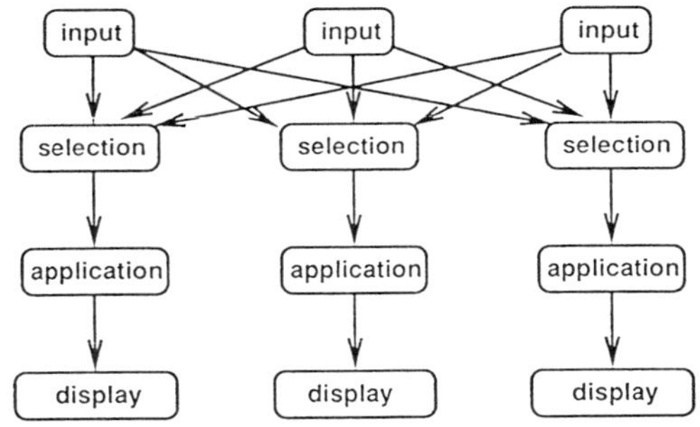

Figure 2. Fully replicated architecture.

the ability to collaborate in spite of some differences in hardware architectures [1]. In principle, if all sites receive the same messages in the same order, the internal representations remain consistent across all copies of the application. However, in practice there can be significant synchronization problems.

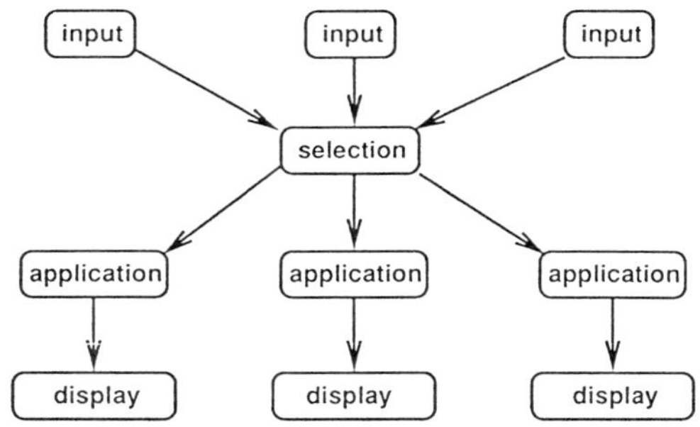

Figure 3. Ensemble's hybrid architecture.

The hybrid architecture used by DCS and most of its applications, including Ensemble, combines these two approaches (see Figure 3). There is a central coordinating process that maintains the master copy of the internal representation, but each site has input, display and application processes as the replicated architecture. The key difference is that input that could cause inconsistency is first sent to the coordinator for approval, while operations guaranteed not to cause inconsistency are handled and displayed locally. This enables the response time to remain good, while input from the central coordinator is broadcast to all copies of the application; thus it also has lower bandwidth requirements than the centralized architecture. In addition, this permits customization of the local copy of the application. Finally, local processes can decide not only when to send input information to the central process, but also to which inputs they will react. This gives a natural mechanism for implementation of the WYSIWIMS view sharing paradigm.

EXISTING CONCURRENT GRAPHICS EDITORS

Collaboration systems may be either open or closed; that is, they may support arbitrary serial applications, or may implement a particular collaboration aware tool. In open systems collaboration, single user programs are shared by input and output multiplexing in a pseudo-serial fashion [16-17]: collaboration awareness is added external to the application program. In this manner, unaltered, serial programs may be shared at the expense of either requiring serial control of the program or risking semantically incorrect concurrent access. In collaboration aware applications, the application itself manages concurrent access to its objects, permitting a much greater degree of control and finer granularity of access. Typically, open systems collaboration restricts not only the types of input sharing possible, but also view sharing, requiring the WYSIWIS paradigm to be used.

Open systems are a very flexible approach to shared graphics editing, using shared terminal emulators and view-sharing facilities for sharing familiar serial applications without modification (NLS [8], Augment [9], Project Nick [4], Dialogo [16], Rapport [1], Timbuktu [10], MMConf [6], Share [12] and Mermaid [24]). However, since the original program is not collaboration aware, it has no provision for concurrency control -- only one user is allowed to edit the canvas at a time. Some floor control mechanism is used to pass control between users to allow access to the editing facility. These systems, while allowing multiple users to observe editing as it occurs, place a substantial collaboration distance between users.

Collaboration-aware graphics applications typically implement a distributed whiteboard, e.g., Commune [5], Colab's Boardnoter [21-22], MBlink [20]. Here it is not necessary to limit editing access since the raster operations may be performed on each pixel as they arrive. Access is generally either serial or totally unconstrained, with real-time broadcast of modifications.

Commune is modeled after a notepad of paper, and is intended to allow geographically separated designers share a drawing surface [5]. Each site has a horizontal monitor and transparent digitizing pad with a stylus that serves as the writing surface. Each user's stylus appears in a different color on the shared screen. Commune supports free-hand drawing, with no notion of lines, boxes, curves, etc. Some problems were found in the interface to the shared canvas due to resolution and sensitivity of the stylus and digitizer used, and to the small size of the shared screen. Also, many pointer movements unrelated to the discussion were distracting, and it was hard to distinguish relevant gestures from random ones.

MBlink allows users within a CES conference to share a bitmap [20]. It runs on a DEC Vax minicomputer, and users view the shared space on Xerox Alto workstations connected by a LAN. The conferencing facility allows workstations to be added and removed from the conference in which a bitmap is shared. All user's cursors are uniquely shaped and visible on all screens. In addition, each user's own cursor is displayed twice: once for local tracking, and once for the position seen by other users after it is echoed by the Vax.

The Boardnoter application in Colab supports the shared whiteboard paradigm. It has an advantage in providing multiple boards through its "stampsheet" mechanism. However, it is designed only to support users in the same room, and its formats are only useful to the other tools in the Colab environment.

All of these shared whiteboards use the pixel-oriented paradigm, which is appropriate for quick sketching and is amenable to uncontrolled access to multiple users. Object-oriented collaboration aware graphics editors are much rarer, and demand more care in coordination of access by multiple users. Ensemble and Xsketch are such tools.

Xsketch supports a cut-and-paste facility for editing, erasing and moving objects on the canvas [18]. Primitive object types include polyline, box, and text, which constitute a subset of types supported by Ensemble. Drawings are saved in Xpic format, and may be imported by other tools. The architecture consists of client, arbiter, and name server agents in addition to the X11 display server, with TCP connections used for communication. Data is replicated over the clients and is managed by the arbiter, which validates and broadcasts edits. Its architecture is similar to that of Ensemble. A significant shortcoming of Xsketch is that it only supports cut-and-paste modification of objects.

The systems above have all dealt exclusively with electronic objects; other systems support access to physical objects as well. TeamWorkStation supports up to six users by integrating desktops with a shared workspace [15]. The shared workspace is captured by a micro-CCD camera focused on a fixed region of the desk at each workstation. The digital video images are then integrated with computer produced objects such as text and lines. Here it is impossible to manipulate the physical objects displayed from other stations, and the collaborative effort put into the session cannot be stored for later use.

Ensemble differs from the editors described above in its implicit locking, WYSIWIMS view-sharing philosophy, implicit formation of editing groups upon concurrent access of an edited file, its architecture, and in belonging to the larger collaboration support environment, DCS.

ENSEMBLE

Ensemble Requirements

Ensemble was built to be used as DCS's graphics editor. The application interface required by DCS suggested an architecture for Ensemble; it also discouraged separate development of meta-communication channels specifically for Ensemble, since they already exist in DCS. Though the main requirement is that Ensemble be the shared graphics editor of DCS, Ensemble is required to exist as a stand-alone system as well.

Other requirements for Ensemble are based mostly on the issues discussed in the preceding sections. Some products, even though powerful, are under-utilized because of their difficulty of use or unfamiliarity [14]. This suggests that editors with heterogeneous command sets and interfaces be able to interact with each other through Ensemble: collaborators may use interfaces familiar to them. Ensemble is intended to be a modular concurrent editor and a basis for development of other concurrent editors.

In Ensemble, the user should not have to know that there is someone else sharing a file unless they are both trying to modify the same part, or unless close collaboration is desired. For example, the user should be able to see the work of a remote site when needed, but remote cursors and multiple edit updates should not clutter the display. Updates from remote sites should be reflected as soon as they are complete, but not while in progress so that distractions are kept to a minimum. Ensemble should also minimize "collaboration distance" by minimizing editable granularity and maximizing the number of users who could access a canvas concurrently. The next subsection describes the capabilities of Ensemble that meet these requirements.

Ensemble Design

Ensemble is invoked through the X Window system. It is based on the tgif graphics editor from UCLA. When it first appears, the user may load a file through the file menu. Each file has a logical edit manager associated with it, so that the concurrency control is automatically started when users start to share a file. When used within DCS, this is the only way in which a user may access the graphics file, so there can be no inconsistent access at the file level by using incompatible or collaboration-unaware editors.

Ensemble appears as another window on the user's screen. It can be iconified and resized without affecting other users. The user is free to move between the Ensemble window and his private work areas. The file to edit is loaded through the window. Multiple Ensemble windows may be invoked by a user to edit the same or different files. Most of the functionality of the tgif serial graphics editor, on which Ensemble is based, is achieved through menu and mouse click operations.

Concurrency control within a file is handled by locks placed implicitly when a user selects an object. If a selected object is already locked by another user, the selection operation fails and the user is informed. Theoretically, any number of writers may edit the file concurrently: locks logically partition the canvas into mutually exclusive sets of objects, so there can be as many active editors as there are objects. Locks are relinquished when the objects are deselected. At this time, and not before, other viewers may see the new version.

Users are informed of locks held by other users by clear boxes, similar to the black boxes a user obtains when he selects an object. Currently, users have no option to observe an edit in progress until the other user releases his locks on the objects. The only continuous, real-time updates received are on pointer positions.

Users may gesture with their pointers. In order to prevent the distraction of many pointers moving around the canvas at once, and to reduce the demands on both the network and the graphics window managers, a user may choose not to export his pointer location, or not to import other users' pointers. So, a remote pointer is displayed on a user's canvas only if he imports pointers and another user exports his pointer.

Ensemble Stand-Alone Architecture

We have chosen the implementational platforms of Ensemble on the criteria of speed, availability, portability, extensibility, and ease of implementation. The first version is implemented on the UNIX operating system, which has a wide usage in academic and scientific circles. The user interface is built on the X Window system for similar reasons. Interprocess communication is done using internet sockets. We preferred socket communication over RPC for reasons of speed, wide compatibility, asynchronous operation, and wide area network (WAN) capabilities.

An important feature of Ensemble's architecture is its process distribution. It uses a hybrid, federated architecture with the processes spread among users' workstations to avoid any overloading (see Figure 4). Ensemble consists of three types of processes. Figure 4 shows process hierarchy and the connection topology of the whole system. Numbers in parentheses in the text below refer to the labels in this figure. The file manager (FM) is first in the hierarchy and handles session control. Each session consists of a graphics manager (GM) and a collection of graphics editor windows (GWs) that make up a partially replicated architecture. The communication and process synchronization of Ensemble depends on broadcasting and multicasting of messages. We have organized the processes in a star topology to minimize discrepancies in message delays, and to provide input synchronization.

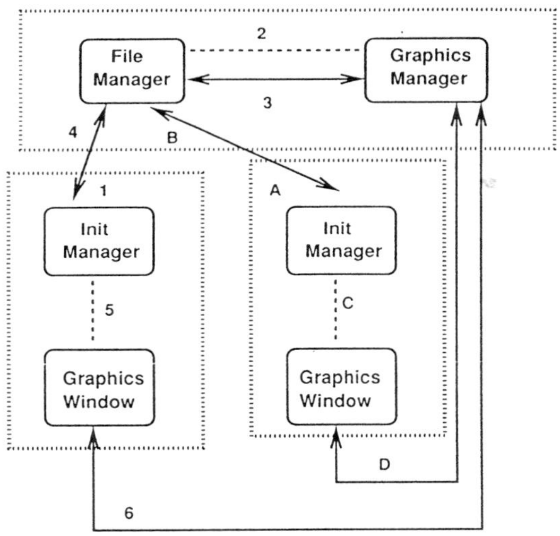

Figure 4. Ensemble's stand-alone federated architecture.

A session starts when a user loads a file in Ensemble. The initial GW contacts the FM to request a file list (1), from which the user chooses the desired file. If there is no GM for the requested file, the FM spawns a new GM (2), which then acts as a coordinator for that file. After the GM informs the FM that it is functional (3), the GM provides the GW with the GM's address (4), and the GW establishes a connection with the new GM (5, 6). As additional users enter the editing session on that file (A), the FM informs them of the existing GM's address (B) and they connect to the GM (C, D) until the session terminates by all users leaving the session. The FM then kills the GM.

The GW is the user's interface to Ensemble. It generally runs on the local machine and is fully replicated at each user location. The GW carries the heavy processing load of editing the canvas, and each GW keeps an internal copy of the representation of the canvas. It may differ from the copy kept at the GM in two ways: the GM may have just received an update from another GW that has not yet propagated to the copy kept at the GW; or the user may be manipulating some selected objects locally that have not yet been committed and sent to the GM. Also, the GM keeps track of all exported pointer positions, which may not be imported by a particular GW.

When a user attempts to select an object for manipulation, a lock request is sent to the GM. If the object is not locked, then a permission is returned to the GW and it is selected, otherwise a denial is returned by a message displayed on the banner line. If the lock was obtained, the user is able to manipulate the selected object using tgif capabilities locally. None of the intermediate forms of the manipulated object(s) are sent to the GM; when the user deselects an object, this is taken as an implicit commit, releasing the lock and sending the update to the GM, which modifies its internal representation and broadcasts the update to other GWs. In this way, the GM is not flooded with input from each editor, and is not required to output large messages describing the entire canvas.

When the local pointer is exported, mouse movements are periodically sent to the GM, which then broadcasts them to all GWs in the session. GWs that are importing remote pointers then display the information received from the GM.

Ensemble Within DCS

In DCS, a set of mechanisms for conference management supports a wide range of control paradigms. The small, flexible message-passing interface to the conferencing management processes permits shared applications to be installed easily in DCS. Currently, in addition to Ensemble, DCS has applications that support concurrent text editing (MACE); single input control, open systems sharing of "glass tty" applications (MATE); a discussion window (multiperson talk); a status window (for conference control and user-defined motions); and automatic creation of transcripts of meetings including motions made and voting results.

Shared applications may be made accessible within DCS by adherence to the DCS message-passing interface within the application code, and by providing a minimal amount of information to DCS regarding the application name and usage. Applications in DCS are required to have a (virtual) application manager (AM) for each instantiation of the application. This AM is created by the conference manager (CM) when needed, and users may be directed to an AM based on parameters of the application requested. These applications then have access to DCS's facilities for registration, communication, and conference control. This distributes the workload within DCS in two ways. First, each process that handles multiplexing within an application can be relatively simple since they handle only a fraction of the communication load. Second, a new AM may be started on a different machine from the CM or existing AMs, so no one machine will become overloaded.

When Ensemble is incorporated in DCS, the conference manager (CM) takes the place of the FM in the stand-alone version. The GW is invoked as a DCS application through the status window. Figure 5 shows the place of Ensemble in the DCS system.

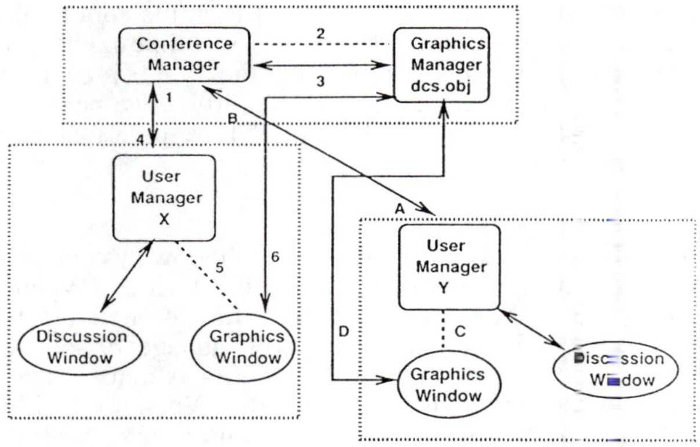

Figure 5. Ensemble in the DCS Architecture.

Incorporation within DCS permits greater control over file access, since users cannot access the files within a conference directly. Rather, files are accessed by launching applications from the status window of DCS once a conference has been joined. This means that file access can be controlled in two ways: first, only users accepted by the conference may gain any sort of access to the conference files; second, DCS can limit access to files by an application it launches. It can force users to edit graphics files using Ensemble only, and no unmanageable collisions at the file level can occur. Further, within DCS users have levels of access rights, including a read-only level as well as a read-write level. In this way, canvases within a conference may be shown to other users without allowing them to modify a canvas.

Ensemble Graphics Manager

Each canvas that is edited is associated with an GM. Together they form a logical object. The GM is the server that controls the edit session. Since the GM is the bottleneck of the topology, we have designed it to carry a minimum process load: the GM is not involved in the actual edit at all. It is responsible for the granting of locks and message multicasting. By using sockets, the lock requests are serialized and the GM may detect colliding locks easily. Since all lock requests for a selection are sent in one message, and failed lock requests are simply returned as failures, there is no possibility of deadlock. If a user has held a lock too long in the opinion of other users, Ensemble has the ability to purge all locks on request.

The internal representation of the canvas is replicated in Ensemble. The GM keeps the primary copy of the object list of the canvas being edited, while each GW holds its version of the canvas, reflecting changes made locally but not yet committed to the GM. Edits are made locally, with changes sent to the GM only when the user saves his edit by deselecting the edited object(s).

Ensemble Graphics Window

What we refer to as Ensemble's graphics window is

really a set of processes, including a local copy of the modified tgif editor and the X11 display process. The GW provides a user interface that is both the editor and drawing surface display and the control panel for communication with the GM or FM. Pulldown menus allow users to import remote pointers and to export their local pointer. A banner line at the top of the screen allows messages from the GM to be displayed to the user. Figure 6 shows two graphics windows in Ensemble, displaying local and remote locks in both windows, and remote pointers in one window.

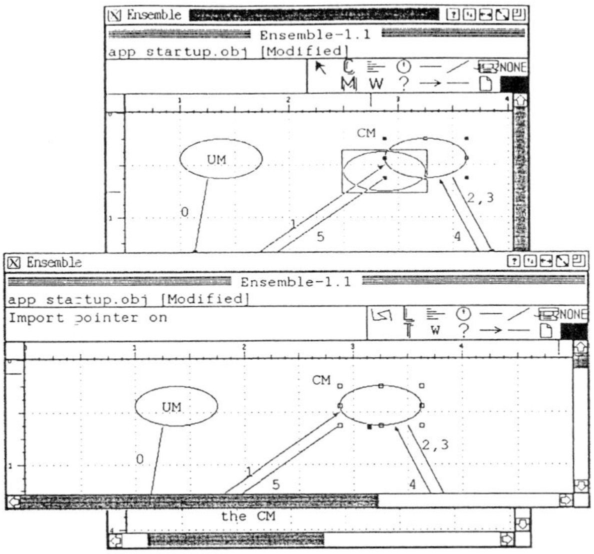

Figure 6. Two graphics windows in Ensemble

The editor supports a superset of the object primitives found in Xsketch, and is able to save its canvas in a superset of the formats used by these other editors. Besides Xpic format, Ensemble can save canvases in postscript format, as was done with the figures in this paper. In addition to the polyline, box, and text primitive types, tgif (and hence, Ensemble) supports ovals, polygons, arcs, and rectangular-circular objects. Objects may not only be moved, but also resized or reshaped. Unlike the whiteboards, it does not support free-hand sketching.

EXPERIENCE WITH ENSEMBLE

We have used Ensemble both within DCS and as a stand-alone tool at the University of Florida for over two years. As a stand-alone tool, we found on occasion that there were collisions at the file level because users applied tgif to a file that was also opened under Ensemble. This was rare, but did happen when other tgif features not supported in Ensemble were desired.

When used under DCS, these collisions never happened. The automatic concurrency management was found to be very smooth, and often users were not aware that others were accessing the same canvas. On several occasions, we deliberately chose to produce a canvas concurrently. We were able to do this without much difficulty once the task was partitioned: in one case one collaborator drew a process box diagram while the other wrote out the steps and labeled the boxes and arrows.

It was convenient not to have to either request the floor, as in serialized access facilities, or to have to place explicit locks, as in MACE and some other lock-based tools. The implicit locking paradigm is very natural to object-oriented editors. It was sometimes a surprise that an object that a user had attempted to select failed; perhaps the clear boxes indicating a remote lock on an object are not obtrusive enough, but this does not seem to be much of a problem.

The ability to import or ignore remote pointers has been found useful. In our experience, the lack of ability to selectively import remotes pointers has not been a problem, since we could limit the pointers that were exported at their source. The shape of the remote pointer was unfortunate, in that it closely resembles one of the selection boxes. It is rare that this causes confusion, and may be fixed easily.

When working in close collaboration, we found that we needed to be able to speak to one another. This was no problem when we were colocated, but when we were in different rooms it became a problem. The discussion window, a text interface, was too slow for much beyond the initial setup of the editing effort. When editing it was cumbersome to move from the graphics window to the discussion window and back again, so we are pursuing an audio channel to augment DCS. Currently we use telephone connections when we need audio augmentation.

CONCLUSIONS

Ensemble is a collaboration-aware, concurrent, object-oriented graphics editor that uses implicit object locking for concurrency control. It makes several types of sharing possible, implementing a WYSIWIMS (What You See Is What I May See) paradigm. The sender (editor) and the receiver (viewer) have joint control over the degree of view sharing. Users see updates from other users as they are committed.

The architecture of Ensemble is federated, a hybrid between replicated and centralized architectures. By using an intermediate editing notation, any number of editing user interfaces may be supported. Because of this modular design, Ensemble may be considered an open system for editing, allowing third party components to be added later.

As a stand-alone tool, Ensemble permits consistent updates to a concurrently edited graphics file. As part of the Distributed Conferencing System (DCS), Ensemble inherits facilities for real time communication with collaborators, mechanisms for controlling the disposition of jointly created objects, and other application windows that may also be useful.

Additional editing interfaces that do not require X Windows, as well as some supporting a command interface more familiar to various users (such as xfig or pubdraw) would permit greater flexibility and more use of Ensemble. Also, the use of a text-based discussion window for communication has been found awkward, particularly when simultaneous gesturing is desired. The incorporation of an audio discussion facility would greatly enhance the usefulness of Ensemble. This is currently under development within DCS, using the audio facilities provided in Sun4 workstations.

REFERENCES

1. Ahuja, S., Ensor R., and Horn D. The Rapport Multimedia Conferencing System, in *Proc. COIS 88 Conf. on Office Information Systems* (Palo Alto, March 1988), ACM Press, pp. 1-8.

2. Ahuja, S., Ensor R., and Lucco, S. E. A Comparison of Sharing Mechanisms in Real-Time Desktop Conferencing Systems, in *Proc. COIS 90 Conf. on Office Information Systems* (Cambridge, MA, 1990), ACM Press, pp. 238-248.

3. Allman, E. An Introduction to the Source Code Control System; Project Ingres, working paper (University of California at Berkeley 1980).

4. Begeman, M., Cook, P., Ellis, C., Graf, M., Rein, G. and Smith, T. Project Nick: Meeting Augmentation and Analysis, in *Proc. CSCW 86 Conf. on Computer Supported Cooperative Work* (Austin, December 1986) ACM Press, pp. 1-6.

5. Bly, S. A. and Minneman, S. L. Commune: A Shared Drawing Surface, in *Proc. COIS 90 Conf. on Office Information Systems* (Cambridge, 1990), ACM Press, pp. 184-192.

6. Crowley, T., Milazzo, P., Baker, E., Forsdick, H., and Tomlinson, R. MMConf: An Infrastructure for Building Shared Multimedia Applications, in *Proc. CSCW 90 Conf. on Computer Supported Cooperative Work* (Los Angeles, Oct. 1990), ACM Press, pp. 329-342.

7. Dewan, P. and Choudhary, R. Flexible User Interface Coupling in Collaborative Systems, Purdue Univ.-Univ. of Florida Software Engineering Research Center, SERC-TR-76-P, June 1990.

8. Engelbart, D. and English, W. A Research Center for Augmenting Human Intellect, in *Proc. of FJCC Fall Joint Computer Conference 33(1)* AFIPS Press, 1968, pp. 395-410.

9. Engelbart, D. Authorship Provisions in Augment, in *IEEE Compcon Conference*, IEEE Press, 1984.

10. Farallon, *Timbuktu User's Guide*, Farallon Computing, Inc., Berkeley, CA, 1988.

11. Foster, G. and Stefik, M. Cognoter, Theory and Practice of a Colab-orative Tool, in *Proc. COIS 86 Conf. on Computer Supported Cooperative Work* (Austin, December 1986), ACM Press, pp.7-15.

12. Greenberg, S. Sharing Views and Interactions with Single-user Applications, in *Proceedings COIS 90 Conf. on Office Information Systems* (Cambridge, MA, 1990), ACM Press, pp. 227-237.

13. Greif, I. (ed.) *Computer-Supported Cooperative Work*, Morgan-Kaufmann Publishers, San Mateo, CA, 1988.

14. Grudin, J. Why CSCW Applications Fail: Problems in the Design and Evaluation of Organizational Interfaces, in *Proc. CSCW 88 Conf. on Computer Supported Cooperative Work* (Portland, OR, 1988), ACM Press, pp. 85-93.

15. Ishii, H. TeamWorkStation: Towards a Seamless Shared Workspace, in *Proc. CSCW 90 Conference on Computer Supported Cooperative Work* (Los Angeles, Oct. 1990), ACM Press, pp. 13-26.

16. Lantz, K. An Experiment in Integrating Multimedia Conferencing, in *Proc. CSCW 86 Conference on Computer-Supported Cooperative Work* (Austin, TX, 1986), ACM Press, pp.

17. Lauwers, J. C., Joseph, T. A., Lantz, K. A. and Romanow, A. L. Replicated Architectures for Shared Window Systems: A Critique, in *Proc. COIS 90 Conf. on Office Information Systems* (Cambridge, MA, 1990), ACM Press, pp. 249-260.

18. Lee, J. J. Xsketch: A Multi-user Sketching Tool for X11, in *Proc. COIS 90 Conf. on Office Information Systems* (Cambridge, MA, 1990) ACM Press, pp. 169-173.

19. Newman-Wolfe, R. E., Ramirez, C. L., Pelimuhandiram, H., Montes, M., Webb M. and Wilson, D. L. A Brief Overview of the DCS Distributed Conferencing System, in Proc. USENIX 91 Summer Usenix Conference (Nashville, TN, June 1991), Usenix Assoc. Press, pp. 437-452.

20. Sarin, S. and Greif, I. Computer-Based Real-Time Conferencing Systems. *Computer* 18, 10 (October 1985), 33-45.

21. Stefik, M., Bobrow, D., Lanning S., and Tatar, D. WYSIWIS Revisited: Early Experiences With Multi-User Interfaces, in *Proc. CSCW 86 Conf. on Computer Supported Cooperative Work* (Austin, December 1986), ACM Press, pp. 276-290.

22. Stefik, M., Foster, G., Bobrow, D., Kahn, K., Lanning, S., and Suchman, L. Beyond the Chalkboard: Computer Support for Collaboration and Problem Solving in Meetings. *Commun. ACM* 30, 1 (January 1987), 32-47.

23. Tichy, F. W. RCS: a Revision Control System, in *Proc. ECICS 82 European Conference on Integrated Computing Systems* (Stresa, Italy, Sep 1982).

24. Watabe, K., Sakata, S., Maeno, K., Fukuoka, H, and Ohmori, T. Distributed Multiparty Desktop Conferencing System: MERMAID, in *Proc. CSCW 90 Conference on Computer Supported Cooperative Work* (Los Angeles, Oct. 1990), ACM Press, pp. 27-38.

Undoing Actions in Collaborative Work

Atul Prakash
Michael J. Knister

Software Systems Research Laboratory
Department of Electrical Engineering and Computer Science
University of Michigan, Ann Arbor, MI 48109-2122
Phone: (313) 763-1585
Email: aprakash@eecs.umich.edu, mknister@eecs.umich.edu

ABSTRACT
The ability to undo operations is a standard feature in most single-user interactive applications. However, most current collaborative applications that allow several users to work simultaneously on a shared document lack undo capabilities; those which provide undo generally provide only a global undo, in which the last change made by anyone to a document is undone, rather than allowing users to individually reverse their own changes. In this paper, we propose a general framework for undoing actions in collaborative systems. The framework takes into account the possibility of conflicts between different users' actions that may prevent a normal undo. The framework also allows selection of actions to undo based on who performed them, where they occurred, or any other appropriate criterion.

KEYWORDS
Undo, collaboration, groupware, conflict analysis.

1 INTRODUCTION

The ability to undo operations is a standard and useful feature in most interactive single-user applications. For instance, the availability of undo facility in editors is invaluable if users are allowed to invoke commands that can modify a document in complex ways (e.g. remove all lines that contain the string "##"). Availability of undo can also encourage users to experiment, acting not only as a safety net, but also allowing users to try out different approaches to solving problems using backtracking [9]. Unfortunately at present, though many collaborative editors and other group applications have been built, such as GROVE [2], ShrEdit [5], and DistEdit [4], almost all lack undo capabilities. Those which provide undo generally provide only a global undo, in which the last change made by anyone to a document is undone, rather than allowing users to individually reverse their own changes.

Compared to single-user applications, performing undo in collaborative applications provides technical challenges in three areas: choosing the action to be undone, determining where the undo should occur, and resolving conflicts between different users. First, choosing the action to undo in a single-user system is usually easy: simply choose the most recent action and use it to revert to the prior state of the document. However, in a group environment, there may be parallel streams of activities from different users, and the undo needs to be more selective. Often, when parallel work on a shared document is going on, users would expect to undo their own last actions rather than globally-last actions, which might belong to other users. Second, once the correct operation is chosen to be undone, the location at which the undo of an action should be performed may be different from the location at which the action was originally performed due to the effects of other users' activity on the document. Finally, if two or more users interleave their work in the same portion of a document, it may not make sense to undo one user's changes without undoing the other users' changes. In this case, there are dependencies between the changes made that need to be taken into account during an undo.

The rest of the paper is organized as follows. Section 2 summarizes basic concepts used in conventional undo algorithms for single-user systems. Section 3 describes related work in the area. Section 4 discusses how our approach extends undo capabilities, particularly for group environments. Section 5 describes the requirements an application must meet to use our undo framework and an example for text editing. Section 6 describes our

Permission to copy without fee all or part of this material is granted provided that the copies are not made or distributed for direct commercial advantage, the ACM copyright notice and the title of the publication and its date appear, and notice is given that copying is by permission of the Association for Computing Machinery. To copy otherwise, or to republish, requires a fee and/or specific permission.

© 1992 ACM 0-89791-543-7/92/0010/0273...$1.50

selective undo algorithm. Section 7 discusses several variations of selective undo that may be useful in collaborative systems. Finally, Section 8 summarizes our conclusions and future work.

2 BASIC CONCEPTS

To provide the raw ingredients for implementing undo, a *history list* needs to be maintained. The history list consists of the sequence of operations that have been carried out so far to modify the state of the document. The operations on the history list are stored in the same order as they were performed. For instance, if the history list is

$$A\ B\ C\ D$$

then, starting from state prior to A, carrying out the operations A, B, C, and D in sequence should lead to the current state.

In this paper, we assume that all operations that modify the state of the document are *reversible*, i.e., for every operation A, we can determine an inverse operation $\overline{A}$ that will undo the effect of A. For instance, in an editor, an *INSERT* operation can be undone by a *DELETE* operation.

Note that, in general, the inverse of an operation A may depend on state of the document prior to A. For instance, on a text document, if a *DelChar(10)* operation is done, which deletes the character at position 10, then in order to determine its inverse, we must know the character that was deleted. We assume that the operations stored in the history list contain sufficient data so that their inverse can be easily determined. For instance, the above operation might be stored as *DelChar(10, c)* on the history list, where *c* is the deleted character.

3 RELATED WORK

There are several basic methods for providing undo capability in single-user systems. We discuss them here. A more detailed discussion of these techniques can be found in [9], and a formalization of undo and redo facilities can be found in [11].

3.1 Single-step Undo

Single-step undo is common in most Macintosh and Windows applications, as well as editors such as *vi*. It allows undo of the last operation. For instance, given the history list

$$A\ B\ C\ D\ E$$

single-step undo allows undoing of operation E, but not a subsequent undo of operation D. Usually redo of the last undo is also allowed (often implemented as an undo of the last undo) so that, in the above example, E can be redone.

3.2 Linear Undo Model and US&R Model

The Interlisp system [8], one of the early systems to provide undo, used the linear undo model. The linear undo model allows undoing of a sequence of operations and keeps a pointer which tracks the last operation undone. Operations can then be redone, after possibly doing some new operations. For instance, given the history list:

$$A\ B\ C\ D\ E,$$

operations E and D can be undone (in sequence), then a new operation F done, and then D redone, giving the following history list:

$$A\ B\ C\ F\ \underset{\uparrow}{D}\ E$$

The pointer indicates that the next operation to be undone is D, and E is the next operation that could be redone. Note that, in this model, undo operations are not explicitly stored in the history list. So, if one wants to back to the original sequence without the F it is not possible. One could undo F, but then D and E must be done manually.

The Undo, Skip, Redo (US&R) model [10] supports redo like the linear undo model, but also allows a more user-friendly skipping of some operations during the redo. Instead of a linear list, US&R model keeps a tree data structure for maintaining history so that it becomes possible to restore state to any point in the history (unlike the linear undo model). In the above example, F would be stored on a different branch of the tree from the sequence $D\ E$ so that F could be undone and then D and E could be redone if the user so desired.

A limitation of both the linear undo model and the US&R model is that in order to undo one operation O several steps back in the history, all subsequent operations must first be undone and then redone (skipping O during the redo). If the implementation is not careful, this can be potentially disruptive in a group environment; other users may see their work undone for at least a short while with no apparent reason. Furthermore, the models do not address the issue that simply redoing operations may not semantically make sense or may lead to unexpected results if an earlier operation is skipped.

3.3 History Undo

The history undo scheme, used in the *Gnu Emacs* editor [7], also allows undoing of a sequence of operations but, unlike the linear undo and US&R schemes, it appends the undo operations to the end of the history list. The undo operations in the history list are treated as any other operations, allowing them to be undone later if desired. For instance, given the history list,

$$A\ B\ C\ D\ E$$

suppose that E is undone. Then in the history undo, the

history list will be as follows, where $\overline{E}$ is the operation that reverses the effects of E:

$$A\ B\ C\ D\ E\ \overline{E}$$
$$\uparrow$$

If one now breaks out of the undo mode by doing some operation other than an undo, say F, the history list will become:

$$A\ B\ C\ D\ E\ \overline{E}\ F$$
$$\uparrow$$

At this point, doing two more undo operations will result in:

$$A\ B\ C\ D\ E\ \overline{E}\ \ F\ \overline{F}\ \overline{\overline{E}}$$
$$\uparrow$$

History undo has the nice property that it is possible to go back to any previous state, and the possibility of conflicts does not arise (in single-user applications) since operations are never skipped.

4 OUR APPROACH

In this paper, we present an approach called *selective undo*. The approach is based on history undo, but we allow operations to be undone selectively and deal explicitly with location shifting and conflicts. In our experience, history undo is simple and intuitive for most users. However, if desired, the techniques given in the paper can also be applied to linear and US&R models.

We use data structures similar to those used in history undo; in particular, upon an undo, the inverse of an operation is appended at the end of the history list. However, in a collaborative application, since the last operation done by a user may not be *globally* last (other users may have done operations subsequently), we need to allow undoing of a particular *user's* last operation from the history list. For example, consider the following history list, where A_i's refer to operations done by user A, and B_i's refer to operations done by other users:

$$A_1\ B_1\ A_2\ B_2\ B_3$$

Now, suppose user A wishes to undo his last action, A_2. Normal history undo mechanisms in single-user systems do not support such a task because they would require undoing B_2 and B_3 as well. In the *US&R* model, it is possible to undo the last three operations and then redo B_2 and B_3, but as pointed out in the previous section, that can be disconcerting to other users of the system and may not even be correct if there are dependencies between A_2 and B_2, B_3. Note that user A may not be aware that operations B_2 and B_3 have been carried out on the document by other users, and the other users may not aware of activities of user A. In the algorithms presented in this paper, it is possible to undo A_2 without undoing/redoing B_2 and B_3.

In the above example, the operation to be undone, A_2, is selected based on the identity of the user. More generally, the operation to undo could be selected based on any other attribute, such as region, time, or anything else. Thus, we term our scheme as *selective undo*, since the operation to be undone is not necessarily the last one, but is selected using some attribute attached to the operation.

To selectively undo an operation, we cannot simply execute the inverse of the operation because later operations could have shifted the location where the undo must be performed. For example, suppose the following two text operations have been applied to the starting state 'abcd': $InsChar(4,'x')$ followed by $InsChar(1,'y')$, resulting in the state 'yabcxd'. The first operation inserted 'x' at position 4, and the second operation inserted 'y' at position 1. Assume that these operations were done by different users. Now the user who did the first operation does an undo. We cannot simply perform the first operation's inverse, $DelChar(4)$, because the second operation has moved the 'x' to location 5. Our scheme takes this possibility of location shifting into account, so that in this example, the first operation will be undone by executing $DelChar(5)$.

We also take into account the possibility of *conflicts*. In the above example, B_2 may have modified the same region of the document as A_2, so that it no longer makes sense semantically to undo A_2 without first undoing B_2. We do not allow an operation to be undone until any prior conflicting operations have been undone.

5 APPLICATION REQUIREMENTS

Our undo framework assumes an application model in which all changes to a document are performed using a set of primitive operations. As operations are performed, they are archived in a history list to provide the basis for undo. The operations must be reversible and capable of being re-ordered when no conflicts between the operations exist.

All applications maintain a current *state* of the document that is being edited. This state can be represented in different data structures, and our framework places no restrictions on the representation.

Primitive operations, or just *operations*, are the only means by which the state of a document can be altered. An operation applied to a state results in a new state. Any given state is simply the result of a sequence of zero or more operations applied to the starting state. Operations can also have parameters which specify exactly what the operation is to accomplish and where it is to be performed. For instance, a DELETE operation would have parameters to indicate what is to be deleted.

We will use the letter S to denote state prior to application of an operation. A $\circ$ indicates that the operation is being applied. For example,

$$S \circ M \circ N$$

denotes the state resulting from application of operation M followed by operation N on a document in state S. Sometimes, we will also use $A \circ B$ to denote the compound operation that first applies A and then applies B.

Two sequences of operations are *equivalent* if they produce the same state. Equivalence is represented by $\equiv$. For example,

$$M \circ N \equiv P \circ Q$$

indicates that the two sequences produce the same state, even though the operations in each sequence are not identical.

5.1 Extensions to the History List

For implementing undo in collaborative systems, some extensions are needed to the basic history list described in Section 2. In order to selectively undo a particular user's operation, we must tag each operation in the history with the identity of the user who performed it. Other tags could be stored as well, such as the time of or the reason for the operation. Our selective undo algorithm allows any such tag to be used to choose operations to undo.

5.2 Conflict, Re-ordering, and Reversibility of Operations

Our model requires that the application supply functions which can detect conflicts between operations, re-order operations, and create inverse operations. In a synchronous group environment, similar functions would usually be needed anyway to ensure predictable results when parallel streams of activities are going on. For instance, if two users are working simultaneously in a document, conflict checking may involve making sure that their changes do not overlap, e.g., through use of locks. Mechanisms for reordering of parallel, independent operations are also needed because the order in which two operations will be done may be unpredictable. The editor must be prepared to accept the two operations in either order with the same resulting effect.

The functions which the application must provide are:

- $Inverse(Operation) \Rightarrow Operation$
- $Conflict(Operation, Operation) \Rightarrow Boolean$
- $Transpose(Operation, Operation)$
  $\Rightarrow (Operation, Operation)$

It is assumed that operations that result from these functions are also primitive operations — or can be expressed in terms of primitive operations (see Section 7.3 for extensions needed for multi-operation undo). This allows the operations that result from applying the above functions to be treated just like other operations in the history list. The *Inverse* function has already been explained in Section 2. The following sections provide descriptions and properties for *Conflict* and *Transpose* functions.

5.2.1 Conflict

A *conflict* between two adjacent operations A and B implies that the second operation, B depends on A and is not meaningful without having performed A.

Suppose, for example, that a graphics document is being edited. Operation A creates a circle in the document, and operation B resizes that circle. In this case, there is a conflict between A and B. If operation A had not been done, operation B would make little sense.

The $Conflict(A, B)$ function supplied by the application must return $True$ if there exists a conflict when the two operations are performed in sequence, and $False$ if no such conflict exists. The importance of the notion of a conflict is that an operation cannot be undone if it conflicts with a later operation, unless the later operation is undone first.

5.2.2 Transpose

If no conflict exists between two operations, we require that it be possible to *transpose* them. That is, by making some adjustments to the operations, it is possible to perform them in a different order and still obtain the same result.

The $Transpose(A, B)$ function, given two non-conflicting operations A and B, will return two new operations B' and A', which satisfy the following two properties:

<u>Transpose Property 1:</u> Performing $S \circ B' \circ A'$ will give the same result as executing $S \circ A \circ B$, irrespective of the initial valid state S.

<u>Transpose Property 2:</u> B' is the operation that would have been done to the document instead of B if operation A had not been done before B.

Property 1 allows us to move operations around in the history list and guarantees that the resulting state will be the same. Property 2 shows that A can meaningfully be undone, leaving only the effects of B. Quite often, but not always, operation A will be identical to A', and B to B', except that the position data may be different.

Our notion of transpose is similar to the one described in [1]. However, we require transpose function to be defined only when the operations do not conflict.

Example 1: Document Model applied to Text Editing

Consider a text editor supporting the following two primitive operations:

- *InsChar(position, char)* to insert a character at the specified position; and
- *DelChar(position)* to delete a character at the specified position.

Note that the model does not dictate the actual data structure which is used to store the document state. The current state could be represented as a linked list of lines, as a single array of characters, or any other way. The application is responsible for correctly applying operations so that its internal data structure represents the correct state.

We will denote operations to be stored in the history list as follows:

- *InsChar(position, char)*
- *DelChar(position, char)*

Note that the character deleted is also stored in the history list as part of the *DelChar* operation so that we can easily derive its inverse. The above two operations happen to be inverses of each other.

Following are the definitions of *Conflict* and *Transpose* for the sequence *InsChar()* followed by *DelChar()*:

$$Conflict(InsChar(p_1, c_1), DelChar(p_2, c_2)) = \begin{cases} true, & \text{if } p_1 = p_2; \\ false, & \text{otherwise.} \end{cases}$$

$$Transpose(InsChar(p_1, c_1), DelChar(p_2, c_2)) = \begin{cases} (DelChar(p_2 - 1, c_2), InsChar(p_1, c_1)) & \text{if } p_1 < p_2; \\ undefined, & \text{if } p_1 = p_2; \\ (DelChar(p_2, c_2), InsChar(p_1 - 1, c_1)) & \text{if } p_1 > p_2 \end{cases}$$

The above definitions say that there is a conflict if the character deleted is the same as the one that was inserted. Otherwise, the two operations are considered to be independent and transposable. Notice the change in position argument in *Transpose()* so that Transpose Properties are satisfied. We leave it to the reader to determine the Conflict and Transpose definitions for the other three combinations of these two operations. A complete definition of these two functions for general string insert and delete operations can be found in [6].

Example 2: Document Model Applied to Graphics Editors

Let's assume that two of the commands that are stored on the history list of a graphical editor are

- *DrawCircle(x,y, radius, CircleID)*: Draw a circle at position (x,y) of the specified radius. *CircleID* is the object identifier returned by the command and stored in the history list to permit easy reversal and transpose.
- *ChangeRadius(CircleID, NewRadius, OldRadius)*: Change the radius of the circle *CircleID* to *NewRadius*. *OldRadius* is stored so that inverse is easy to compute.

In this case, the *Conflict* and *Transpose* functions are straightforward:

- *Conflict:* the two operations will conflict if and only if they refer to the same circle, i.e., their *CircleID*'s match.
- *Transpose:* Transposing the two operations simply requires interchanging the two operations if they refer to different circles; else the *Transpose* is undefined.

Note that the graphical operations, unlike those in text editors, usually will not require parameter changes since graphical operations usually use absolute (x,y) coordinates rather than coordinates that change with the position of other objects; if relative positioning is desired, then different operations should be provided that do use relative coordinates so that they can be correctly transposed.

6 UNDO ALGORITHMS

This section presents two versions of our undo algorithm: a limited selective undo to demonstrate the basic concepts, followed by the full selective undo algorithm. Both algorithms assume that an operation has already been chosen to be undone. Methods of selecting which operation to undo are described in Section 7.

The algorithms are independent of whether a single centralized history list is maintained for all users or every site has its own (possibly different, but equivalent) history list and editor state. For multiple history lists and editor states, the communication protocol between editors should ensure that all editors eventually reach the same state even when operations are being done in parallel at various sites. [6].

6.1 Limited Selective Undo

To demonstrate the principles of our undo technique, we first describe a limited version of the algorithm and present an example.

The algorithm works as follows: the *transpose* function is used to repeatedly shift the operation to be undone until it reaches the end of the history list. If it cannot be shifted to the end due to a conflict along the way, it cannot be undone. If the operation can be shifted to the end, we can simply execute the inverse of the shifted operation to undo it. By shifting the operation, we have effectively determined where the undo must be performed.

An example will help demonstrate the algorithm. Assume that we want to undo A given the history list:

$$A\ B\ C$$

Suppose A conflicts with B. Then $Conflicts(A, B)$ will be true, and the undo will fail, as it should. If A does not conflict with B, the result after one iteration will be:

$$B'\ A'\ C$$

where $(B', A') = Transpose(A, B)$. Note that the the history list need not be actually altered because the only the new A' is used in the next iteration. We show the entire list here for clarity.

Next, if $Conflicts(A', C)$ is true, the undo will fail. Otherwise, another shift will occur, resulting in:

$$B'\ C'\ A''$$

where $(C', A'') = Transpose(A', C)$. Now that A has been shifted to the end of the list, $\overline{A''}$ can be performed giving the history list:

$$A\ B\ C\ \overline{A''}$$

To see that this is correct, note that since $B' \circ C' \circ A''$ is equivalent ($\equiv$) to $A \circ B \circ C$ (by Transpose Property 1), we find:

$$A \circ B \circ C \circ \overline{A''} \equiv B' \circ C' \circ A'' \circ \overline{A''} \equiv B' \circ C'$$

Thus, performing $\overline{A''}$ at the end of the original history gives the same result as if operation A had never been performed (by Transpose Property 2); the undo has succeeded!

This algorithm, while correct, is unable to deal with the results of prior undo operations. For example, suppose that the history contains $A\ B\ C$, where A and B conflict but neither conflicts with C. A user, wanting to undo both A and B, first undoes B, resulting in the history $A\ B\ C\ \overline{B'}$. Then, the user attempts to undo A. The limited undo determines that A conflicts with B, and is unable to shift A to the end of the history. However, since B is undone, we should be able to undo A.

6.2 Selective Undo

We now give a selective undo algorithm which is not limited by prior undo operations (Figure 1). The algorithm is similar to the limited algorithm in Section 6.1, but it uses a more sophisticated conflict-checking technique.

To avoid the prior undo limitation, we must track which operations have already been undone. We do this by placing a pointer into the history list that links an operation to its corresponding undo operation. Thus, upon undoing B from the sequence $A\ B\ C$, the history list would appear as follows; note that the oval line beneath the sequence indicates a *do-undo* pointer:

$$A\ B\ C\ \overline{B'}$$

The undo algorithm works by making a copy of the end of the history list, from the operation to undo onward. The operation to undo is shifted using *transpose* until it reaches the end of the list. Before each shift, we check whether a conflict exists with the following operation. If a conflict is found with an operation which has been later undone (i.e. there is really no conflict), that operation and its undo are removed from the copied history list by procedure *RemoveDoUndoPair*.

The *RemoveDoUndoPair* subroutine, given an operation X which is later undone by $\overline{X}$, shifts X until it is adjacent to $\overline{X}$, and then removes both operations. This is valid because $X \circ \overline{X}$ is an identity operator. X will not conflict with another operation Y in the history between it and $\overline{X}$, unless Y itself has been undone (otherwise, X could not have been undone). In the case of such an intervening Y, *RemoveDoUndoPair* is called recursively to first eliminate Y from the history list.

6.2.1 An Example of Selective Undo

Let us say that the history list at some point is as follows:

$$A\ B\ C\ D$$

Assume that operations B and C conflict, and there are no other conflicts. If the operation C is undone, the history list will be a follows, where C' is the operation that results from shifting C past D:

$$A\ B\ C\ D\ \overline{C'}$$

Now, suppose operation B is to be undone. The algorithm will first copy *HistoryList* from B onwards into *TempHistoryList* so that the original list is not affected by shifting operations. Since there is a conflict between B and C, and C has a *do-undo* pointer, *RemoveDoUndoPair()* will be called to remove the C and $\overline{C'}$ pair. The resulting (temporary) history list from B onwards will be as follows:

$$B\ D'$$

where $(D', C') = Transpose(C, D)$.

Assuming that there is no conflict between B and D', B will be shifted past D' giving the operation B' where $(D'', B') = Transpose(B, D')$. Now that operation B has been shifted to the end of the list, it can be successfully undone using the operation $\overline{B'}$. This operation is carried out and appended to the original history list, with the appropriate *do-undo* pointers added, giving the desired result:

$$A\ B\ C\ D\ \overline{C'}\ \overline{B'}$$

7 VARIATIONS OF SELECTIVE UNDO

Before undo algorithms given above can be used, a means must be provided for a user to select the operation he wishes to undo. There are many variations

```
type HistoryRec = record
   op: Operation;
   next: ^HistoryRec;
   /* Following field is for pairing do/undo */
   undoneBy: ^HistoryRec; end

proc Undo(UndoItem: ^HistoryRec)
   HistTemp: ^HistoryRec;          /* temporary list */
   PrevPtr, HistPtr: ^HistoryRec;/* node pointers */
   ShiftOp: Operation;
   NewItem: ^HistoryRec;

   /* Make a copy of the history list
      from the UndoItem onward */
   HistTemp := CopyTailofList(UndoItem);
   /* Shift UndoItem forward, removing
      all paired do/undo operations */
   ShiftOp := HistTemp^.op;
   PrevPtr := HistTemp; HistPtr := HistTemp^.next;
   while HistPtr <> nil do
      if Conflicts(ShiftOp,HistPtr^.op) then
         if (HistPtr^.undoneBy <> nil)
            RemoveDoUndoPair(HistPtr);
            HistPtr := PrevPtr^.next;
         else return ("Sorry. Conflicts with", HistPtr);
         endif
      else /* Transpose returns two operations;
            store the 2nd in ShiftOp */
         (_,ShiftOp) := Transpose (ShiftOp,HistPtr^.op)
         PrevPtr := HistPtr; HistPtr := HistPtr^.next;
      endif
   endwhile
   /* Perform executes the operation, appends it to
      the end of the history list, and returns a
      pointer to the appended node */
   NewItem := Perform(Inverse(ShiftOp));
   UndoItem^.undoneBy := NewItem;
   return ("Undo successful");
endproc

proc RemoveDoUndoPair(doPtr: ^HistoryRec)
   while doPtr^.next <> doPtr^.undoneBy do
      if Conflicts(doPtr^.op, doPtr^.next^.op) then
         /* if there is a conflict, it must have been
            undone, so can be removed */
         RemoveDoUndoPair(doPtr^.next)
      else /* Transpose the two operations,
            logically and physically */
         (doPtr^.next^.op, doPtr^.op) =
            Transpose(doPtr^.op, doPtr^.next^.op);
         ListSwap(doPtr, doPtr^.next)
      endif
   endwhile
   /* The operation is now adjacent to its undo;
   remove them both from HistTemp list */
   ListDelete(HistTemp, doPtr^.next);
   ListDelete(HistTemp, doPtr)
endproc
```

Figure 1: Selective Undo Algorithm

by which operations to be undone can be selected. Determining the most appropriate variation is a subject of future research and is not the focus of this paper. However, we give some of the interesting variations to illustrate the basic techniques.

7.1 Individual History Undo

The Emacs-style history undo described in Section 3.3 can, with minor modifications, be made to work in our framework, allowing each user to undo his most recent operations one by one.

The first time a user does an undo, the system searches backward from the end of the history list until an operation tagged with that user's identity is located; a pointer to that history record is stored for later use by the user. The selective undo algorithm is then applied to the operation. Should the user immediately do another undo, the history search continues backward from the stored pointer. Thus, the user can proceed back through his most recent changes. When an operation other than another undo is performed, the stored pointer is deleted, making the undo operations appear as normal operations which can be undone.

If the undo algorithm fails due to a conflict, a simple Conflict List Generation [6] algorithm can be used to locate the conflicting operations, which must belong to other users. At this point, the interface can inform the user of the problem and show whose work must be undone. He might then be given a choice of canceling or proceeding to undo the operations of those other users.

7.2 Regional Undo

Another useful criterion for selecting undo operations is a region in the document. For example, a user may want to undo his most recent changes to the abstract of a paper, but not any other changes.

Using a region as a selection criterion is slightly more difficult than using user-id or timestamps, because operations performed historically on a region refer to the location where the region used to be, rather than where it is now.

To locate an operation which affects a region R, we start by defining a special region-identifying operation S which we define to conflict with any operation performed in R. We place S at the end of the history list, and use transpose to shift it backward. If it cannot be transposed due to a conflict, that conflicting operation must be within the region, and can now be undone. Note that for any operation A, *Transpose*(A, S) should give (S', A), where S' is the region that corresponds to S prior to doing A. To implement repeated undo on a region, it is necessary that *Transpose(A,S)* be defined even if A conflicts with S, so that S can be shifted past

A after A is undone for subsequent undos. This apparent anomaly is not a problem since S is not a update operation — it is simply introduced to identify a region and determine which operations were carried out in the associated region.

7.3 Multi-operation actions

Situations often arise in which an application may wish to treat a group of primitive operations as a single, high-level, operation. For instance, consider the following scenarios:

- One user-level action (e.g. *IndentParagraph*) could result in numerous primitive operations (a bunch of *INSERTs*). Users would expect to be able to undo the high-level operation in entirety using one undo operation rather than having to undo the primitive operations one by one.

- Undoing many steps at once could be useful for returning to a known previous state. For example, a user may wish to revert chapter 15 of a paper back to the way it was at 5PM last Tuesday (i.e., undo all operations done on chapter 15's region with timestamps after 5PM last Tuesday), assuming sufficient history with appropriate tags is kept.

Multiple-operation actions and corresponding undo actions are similar to the notion of *transactions* in databases. Either all the primitive operations should be performed collectively, or conflicts should be reported and handled first. For instance, suppose that a paragraph is indented and then modified so that conflicts arise. It would not be desirable to allow a partial undo — its effect is likely to be hard to understand.

Multi-operation undo can be implemented in our framework with the following extensions:

1. The history list needs to be extended to keep sufficient information around so that the set of operations that constitute a high-level operation can be determined.

2. When undoing a high-level operation, all the primitive operations that constitute the high-level operation need to be shifted to the end and then undone as a single transaction. If conflicts arise during shifting, the undo should not be permitted without first undoing the conflicts.

3. Do-undo pointers need to go between corresponding operations, which could be high-level.

8 CONCLUSIONS

We have presented a framework for group undo which is simple and generally applicable to a variety of documents. The techniques proposed in this paper are presently being implemented in the DistEdit toolkit [4]. The techniques are presented in the context of history undo; however, many aspects of the techniques such as the notions of *Transpose* and *Conflict*, are also applicable to implementing undo based on linear and US&R models. The focus of the paper was on developing a general framework for group undo; research is still needed to determine appropriate interfaces for supporting undo in collaborative applications.

REFERENCES

[1] Ellis, C.A. and Gibbs, S.J. Concurrency Control in Groupware Systems, in *Proceedings of the ACM SIGMOD '89 Conference on the Management of Data* (Seattle, Washington, May 1989), ACM Press, pp. 399-407.

[2] Ellis, C.A., Gibbs, S.J., and Rein, G.L. Design and Use of a Group Editor. In *Engineering for Human-Computer Interaction*, G. Cockton, Ed., North-Holland, Amsterdam, 1990, pp. 13-25.

[3] Ellis, C.A., Gibbs, S.J., and Rein, G.L. Groupware: Some Issues and Experiences. *Communications of the ACM*(January 1991), 38-58.

[4] Knister, M. and Prakash, A. DistEdit: A Distributed Toolkit for Supporting Multiple Group Editors, in *Proceedings of the Third Conference on Computer-Supported Cooperative Work*, Los Angeles, California, October 1990, pp. 343-355.

[5] McGuffin, L. and Olson, G.M. ShrEdit: A Shared Electronic Workspace. *CSMIL Technical Report No. 45*, The University of Michigan, Ann Arbor, 1992.

[6] Prakash, A. and Knister, M.. Undoing Actions in Collaborative Work. *Technical Report CSE-TR-125-92*, Computer Science and Engineering Division, The University of Michigan, Ann Arbor, March 1992.

[7] Stallman, R. *GNU Emacs Manual*, 1985.

[8] Teitelman, W. *Interlisp Reference Manual* Xerox Palo Alto Research Center, 1978.

[9] Thimbleby, H. *User Interface Design.* ACM Press, New York, 1990, pp. 261-286.

[10] Vitter, J.S. US&R: A New Framework for Redoing. In *IEEE Software* (October 1984), pp. 39-52.

[11] Yang, Y. A New Conceptual Model for Interactive User Recovery and and Command Reuse Facilities, in *Proc. CHI'88 Conference on Human Factors in Computing Systems* (Washington, D.C., May 15-19, 1988), ACM Press, pp. 165-170.

THE ACTION WORKFLOW APPROACH TO WORKFLOW MANAGEMENT TECHNOLOGY

Raúl Medina-Mora, Terry Winograd, Rodrigo Flores, Fernando Flores

Action Technologies, Inc.
1301 Marina Village Parkway
Alameda, CA 94501
(510)521-6190 rmm@ati.mhs.compuserve.com

ABSTRACT
This paper describes ActionWorkflow™ approach to workflow management technology: a design methodology and associated computer software for the support of work in organizations. The approach is based on theories of communicative activity as language/action and has been developed in a series of systems for coordination among users of networked computers. This paper describes the approach, gives an example of its application, and shows the architecture of a workflow management system based on it.

KEYWORDS
Workflow, ActionWorkflow, Coordination, Coordinator, Business process.

INTRODUCTION
In introducing new technologies into a workplace we are not simply augmenting the work, but are in effect reorganizing it. Technological innovation offers an opportunity for organizational innovation. In providing computer support for cooperative work, we are directly concerned with its potential for business process redesign.

For the past ten years we and our colleagues at Action Technologies have been developing computer software for organizational communication and action, based on a theory of work structure as language action. Previous publications [2][3][10][12] have described the basic elements of the theory and explained its application to computer-supported cooperative work:

- *Language acts*, classified according to a speech-act taxonomy.
- *Conversations*, which are coherent sequences of language acts with a regular structure of expectations and completions.
- *Time tokens* for *completions* in conversations.
- *Explicit mutually-visible* representations of acts, conversations, and times, as a way of facilitating communication in an organization.

This has led us to a new way of characterizing workflow, based on the identification and construction of atomic "loops" of action in which a performer completes an action to the satisfaction of a customer (internal or external). The overall workflow in any organization is an interweaving of these action workflow loops, some of which are highly recurrent (done in a structured way time after time) and others are *ad hoc* (unique to a situation). Our experience with workflow management technology has demonstrated the effectiveness of action workflow analysis in redesigning the action structure in an organization to improve the workflow, along with providing computer support.

BUSINESS PROCESSES
We distinguish three different domains in which to describe activities of an organization:

Materiel processes.
Human activities are rooted in the physical world. Nothing happens without physical things moving and changing state. If we ask "What is happening?" the obvious answer is a description of physical activity.

In the tradition of factory automation this was the relevant domain, in which physical components were transformed and assembled into product unities. Materiel process redesign and technologies have been used to move and process objects more efficiently, from the early analyses of Taylor and the production innovations of Ford, through the sophisticated techniques of modern industrial engineering.

Information processes
With the twentieth-century shift to "information work," the materiel process domain fails to capture what is important about everyday activity. With computer workstations, all of the physical work becomes indistinguishable—talking to people and tapping keys in front of display screens. What is relevant is the nature of what the talk and tapping is about.

Permission to copy without fee all or part of this material is granted provided that the copies are not made or distributed for direct commercial advantage, the ACM copyright notice and the title of the publication and its date appear, and notice is given that copying is by permission of the Association for Computing Machinery. To copy otherwise, or to republish, requires a fee and/or specific permission.

© 1992 ACM 0-89791-543-7/92/0010/0281...$1.50

Theorists and information technology providers have developed sophisticated ways to analyze and facilitate the flow of information. Current techniques of data flow analysis, database storage and retrieval, transaction processing, network communication, and many more have provided a structure of effective information processing. This is the heart of the applications offered by the computer industry today.

Business processes

What is lost in the information perspective is the recognition that information in itself is uninteresting. Information is only useful because someone can do something with it, and we can't define "do something" circularly as just the handling of more information. What do people do that matters?

Here we find the domain of business processes, in which people enter into language actions that have consequences for their future activities. When a customer hands a supplier an order form, there is a physical activity (transferring a piece of paper) and an information dimension (communicating a form with information about a particular set of goods, delivery instructions, etc.). But the true significance is in the business process dimension: It is a request for the supplier to perform some particular actions, in return for which the customer is committed to perform other actions (e.g., payment).

Our theoretical work has been identifying the basic structure of the business process dimension: workflows, roles, acts and the incompletions they lead to, which constitute expectations for further behavior by the participants. It is important to note that business processes are implemented in information processes, just as information processes are implemented in materiel processes. In moving to a focus on the language/action structure of workflow, rather than on the forms or database transactions used when acting, we are revealing a higher existing level of organization.

WORKFLOW

Most current approaches to workflow management are structured around the domain of information processes [9]. They begin with a class of information objects, such as forms or stored images, and define workflow as a sequence of actions to be done on those objects. The primary organizing structure is the "routing" of information objects among users, and the specification of automatic actions to be taken in that routing. In a way, this is very much like the materiel process view, in which parts are passed along from one "station" to another in a factory for processing, and some of the component tasks are taken over by automated machinery.

Traditional work management is well suited to highly structured "heads-down" paper processing, but is not adequate for supporting the realities of work in the 90s, with its emphasis on better educated workers who combine structured work with opportunity-based initiative and individual responsibility for quality and customer satisfaction.

Although our approach also includes capacities for generating and managing forms, these are grounded in the dimension of business process structure, which is constituted of action workflow loops. This provides the basis for allowing individuals to deal directly with the consequences of their work for completion and satisfaction.

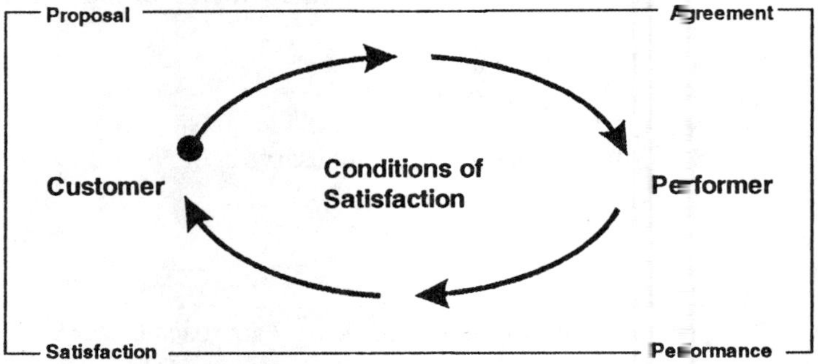

Figure 1. ActionWorkflow Loop

Figure 1 shows the basic sequence of actions in the action workflow loop. There is always an identified customer and a performer, and the loop deals with a particular action that the performer agrees to complete to the satisfaction of the customer.

The loop proceeds in four phases:

1) Proposal

The customer requests (or the performer offers) completion of a particular action according to some stated conditions of satisfaction.

2) Agreement

The two parties come to mutual agreement on the conditions of satisfaction, including the times by which further steps will be taken. This agreement is only partially explicit in the negotiations, resting on a shared background of assumptions and standard practices.

3) Performance

The performer declares to the customer that the action is complete.

4) Satisfaction

The customer declares to the performer that the completion is satisfactory.

At any phase there may be additional actions, such as clarifications, further negotiations about the conditions, and changes of commitments by the participants. (For a more detailed analysis of these possibilities, see [12], p. 65). The structure is defined by the language acts through which people coordinate, not the actions done by individuals to meet the conditions of satisfaction. The key difference in our approach is this shift from the task structure to the coordination structure. In a more traditional workflow approach, actions of coordination are seen as one kind of task or as a flow of information between tasks. In our perspective, tasks are defined by the requests and commitments expressed in the loops. This shift is analogous to moving

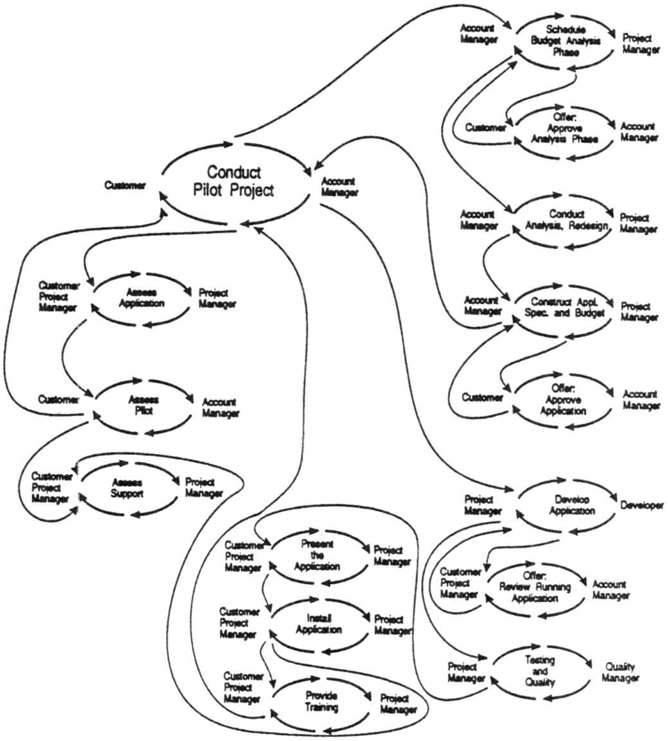

Figure 2. Business process map for pilot projects

from a view of a network as a collection of nodes (with links between them) to seeing it as a collection of links (with shared nodes). Although all the elements are still there, the different starting point leads to different potentials for representing and supporting the activities.

The simple workflow loop structure is both general and universal. It is general in that it occurs whenever there is coordination among people, regardless of what they are doing. The words "customer" and "performer" apply to people within a single organization as well as across boundaries. The loop structure is universal in that it is independent of any culture, language, or communication medium in which it is conducted. There are endless variations in the specifics of how the steps are taken, what other loops are triggered, and how people respond to breakdowns within them, but the basic structure is the same. The action workflow loop is like an atomic element of the chemistry of interactions. By combining these loops, all the complex phenomena of organizations are generated.

Our initial designs, such as The Coordinator™ [1][11][12], based their utility on the universality of this basic structure. They provided tools for creating and managing records of conversations (which correspond to workflow loops) based on the universal vocabulary of speech acts. The research described here follows later developments [2], which expand on this elementary structure as the basis for doing business process design. In place of the sequential tracking of forms found in other approaches to workflow support, we design (and help redesign) a business process as a collection of interrelated loops, each with its own completions and possibilities for breakdown.

Figure 2. shows an example of a business process map that was created to manage the conduct of pilot projects in the Action Technologies development group. The lines connecting loops show dependencies between them, with each connected to the appropriate quadrants of the loop, according to which aspects of the workflow structure they complete. We will examine a smaller example in some detail below.

We approach the task of designing a workflow management system by first analyzing the workflow structure and its possibilities for improvement and new functionality and for new or improved conditions of satisfaction that can be offered to customers. This analysis process, or "work mapping," uses theory-guided observations and interviews to generate explicit representations of the acts, roles, and incompletions that make up the flow of work. We have experimented with more detailed forms of mapping, in which we represent material and information structures in their relationship to the language/action structure [7], but the primary focus in our applied work has been on tools for revealing and highlighting the key elements of workflows and their relationship to completions and incompletions that are vital to the organization.

New opportunities to improve performance come from the ability to identify, observe, and anticipate potential "breakdowns," or failures to reach satisfactory completion. From the maps and associated discussions it is possible to identify places where breakdowns may occur on a recurrent basis and to see what additional steps or workflows can be put into place to anticipate and/or cope with them. The explicit articulation of the structure of customers, performers, and conditions of satisfaction leads to identifying new kinds of offers or requests that can be made. On the basis of these, new workflow structures can be instituted. While "breakdown" (by other names) is a standard concept in other forms of workflow analysis, the loops with their associated completions are unique to our approach.

Finally, we can identify those places where technological support can be valuable:

- Notifying users about actions that need completion.
- Providing users with the specific tools and information to complete a task, in a ready-to-hand way associated with identifying it.
- Managing reminders, alerts, follow-ups, etc. to keep processes moving along.
- Giving users an overview of where their tasks fit into the overall processes, both dynamically and through maintaining records of workflow history and providing structured access to them.

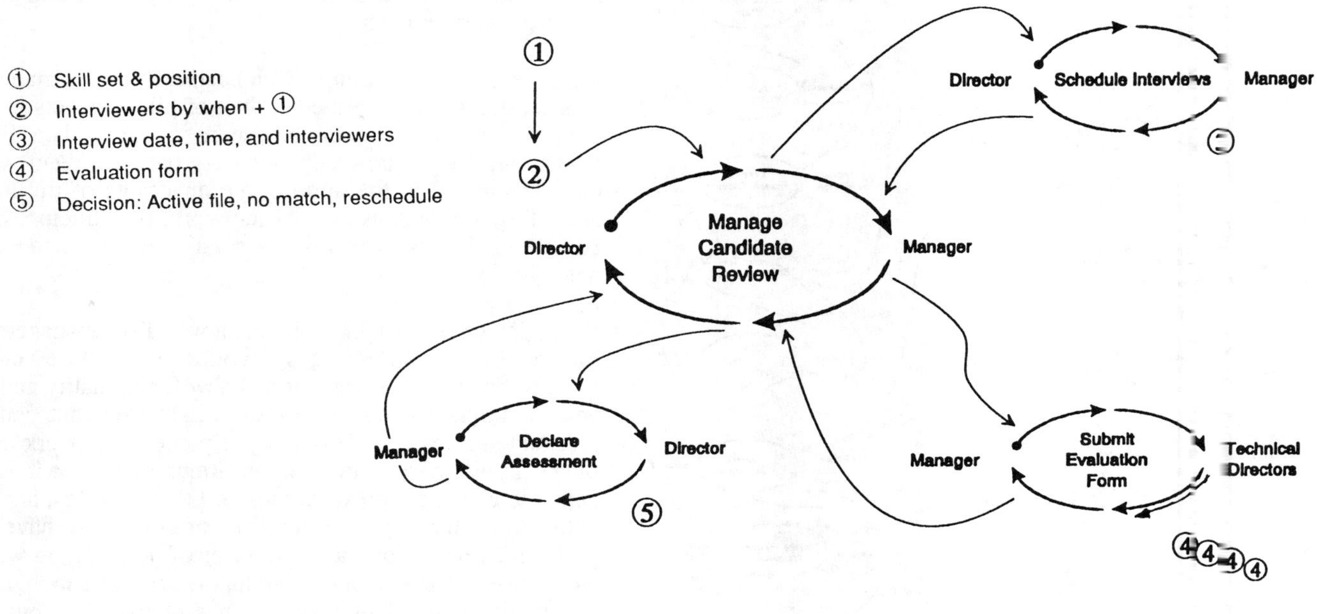

Figure 3. Core structure of the candidate review process

- Giving managers an overview of the status of workflow in the organization, both on demand and through generating regular reports and measures based on workflow structure.
- Automating standard procedures and individualized responses, on the basis of the action workflow structure.

Our methodology for providing workflow support is based on creating a unified conceptual structure and data representation that ties these functions into a coherent whole based on the explicit representation of workflow loops and their interconnections.

AN EXAMPLE

We will illustrate business process analysis and support with an application that was developed for managing the review of job candidates. This process is part of a larger business process for staffing, which is based on several dozen interconnected workflows, including advertising for positions, receiving and evaluating resumes, etc.

The process centers on four central loops, as shown in Figure 3. Each loop stands for a recurrent workflow, with the customer identified on the left and the performer on the right. Lines connecting workflow loops indicate triggering and dependency relationships between them. Numbered circles indicate forms and other external representations that play a role in the process.

The candidate review process starts when the director of personnel makes a request to a personnel manager to manage the review of a particular candidate. The manager starts the process by filling in an on-line form with information such as the interviewers, positions sought for the candidate, required skills, etc., as shown in Figure 4.

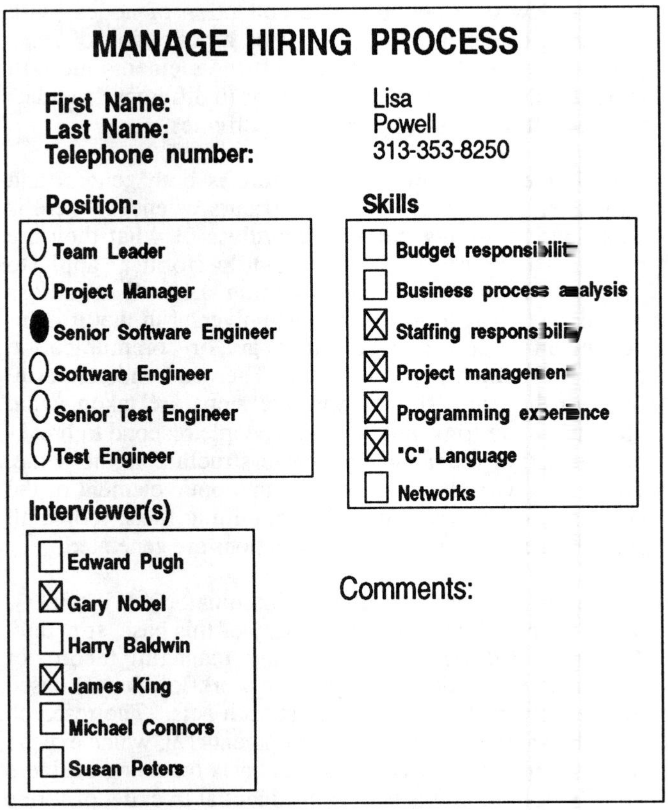

Figure 4. Form for initiating candidate review

This application was developed using the Lotus Notes version of the workflow management system, so the form was defined using the standard facilities for designing Notes forms. Other implementations differ, as described below. The structure of the review process has been defined by the analyst, working with the participants, and is stored in the definitions database maintained by the Workflow Management Server (see below). The server instantiates instances of all the workflows of the process and starts the "Schedule interviews" workflow automatically.

The "Schedule interviews" workflow corresponds to the second phase (agreement) of the main workflow: the manager agrees to do the work as requested by the director once the interviews have been scheduled. By including this scheduling in the agreement phase, a specific completion time can be promised.

Once the review process reaches agreement, the "Performance" phase starts and the "Submit evaluation forms" workflows are automatically started, one for each of the selected interviewers. Again, forms are defined for each of the participants and used in making actions in the workflow.

Once an interview has been scheduled for a particular date, all the workflows for submitting evaluation reports are initiated and directed to the selected interviewers to be completed on the specified date.

Each interviewer can use the workflow database to identify the set of workflows in progress. Figure 5 shows the status of interviews organized by interviewer. The lines showing next actions and times are generated from the action workflow database, using names defined specifically for this workflow.

Candidate	Recommended Action:	By When:
Edward Pugh		
Medina, Raul	Schedule an interview date	03/13/92
Bush, George	Check status of evaluations	0
James, Henry	Check status of evaluations	0
Samson, Dick	Check status of evaluations	0
Frank, Teddy	Thank you for submitting evaluatio	02/29/92
Gary Noble		
[illegible]	Recommit to evaluate	[illegible]
James, Henry	Recommit to evaluate	0
Harry Baldwin		
James, Henry	Recommit to evaluate	0
Wilson, Peter	Recommit to evaluate	02/29/92
James King		
Wilson, Peter	Recommit to evaluate	02/29/92
Bush, George	Recommit to evaluate	0
James, Henry	Recommit to evaluate	0
Michael Connors		
Wilson, Peter	Recommit to evaluate	02/29/92

Figure 5. Status display of interviews

By selecting one item, the interviewer brings up the on-line evaluation form for the candidate, which can be filled in incrementally and submitted when completed (this submission of a completed form constitutes a "declaration of completion" action in the workflow action structure). If the interviewer does not submit the evaluation report by a day after the agreed-upon completion date, the definition has been structured to cause the system to send a "follow-up" reminder to submit the report.

The definition of a workflow structure includes definitions of the forms that are used by customers, performers and observers of each workflow at each phase. When an interviewer accesses the document for the interview, it shows up as an evaluation form to be completed, since the interviewers are the performers of the workflow "Submit evaluation form." Other participants would see the forms relevant to the actions they are able to take, with fields available or protected from editing as suited to their roles.

Once all of the interview workflows have been completed, the system automatically declares the main workflow complete and moves to the fourth phase, where the personnel director declares (or not) satisfaction with the process. The system sends a mail message to the personnel director, as a prompt to act on the workflow for final assessment of the candidate.

At any time the manager can get an overview of the status by examining the workflow database through an appropriate view, as illustrated in Figure 6.

Recommended Action:	By Whom:	By When:
Not in process		
Harris, Mike		
Commence interview process	**Manager**	
Schedule Interviews		
Medina, Raul		
Schedule an interview date	**Manager**	03/13/92
Complete Evaluations		
Bush, George		
Check status of evaluations	**Manager**	0
James, Henry		
Check status of evaluations	**Manager**	0
Samson, Dick		
Check status of evaluations	**Manager**	0
Decision Pending		
Jones, Tom		
Decide on candidate	**Director**	02/29/92

Figure 6. Status overview of workflows

ARCHITECTURE

We have defined a general Workflow Management System architecture for interoperability among different applications and across diverse platforms, integrating the coordination of specific applications along with system enhancements and utilities from users and third-party developers. This architecture has been the basis for several implementations, including a DOS based "Business Process Management" system (BPM1) [2], an extended version of The Coordinator in the Windows environment, and a workflow application development environment in Lotus Notes (from which our example was drawn).

The overall architecture consists of one or more client applications (called *workflow-enabled applications*), and the structures and components that enable them to interact with the workflow management server and receive services from it. Figure 7 shows the major components of a Workflow Management System.

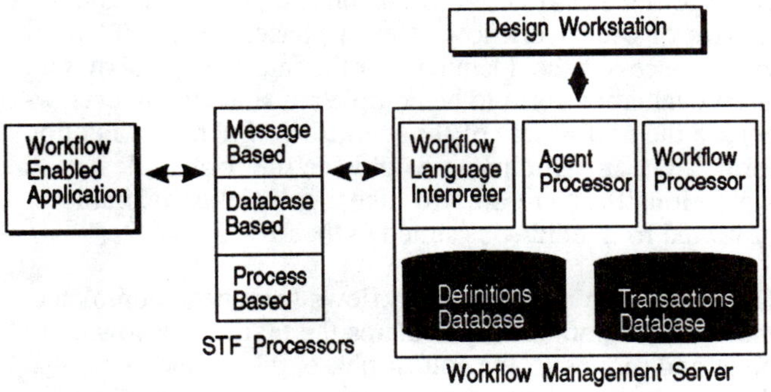

Figure 7. Workflow Management System Architecture

Workflow enabled applications

The goal of the Workflow Management System is to provide workflow capabilities to new and existing computer applications. Adding or integrating an existing or new application is referred to as "workflow-enabling."

Workflow-enabled applications are of three types:

1. Workflow-initiating applications.

An example of a workflow-initiating application would be an existing order-entry application that has been modified to initiate a fulfillment workflow. The task of the order-entry application is complete once the fulfillment workflow takes over and starts a sequence of actions to verify the new order, define customized requirements, alert manufacturing, etc. This level of integration can be done with little or no modification to the existing system.

2. Workflow-participating applications.

In the order-entry example discussed above, the participating applications are those that perform the details of the fulfillment process. The order-entry application first initiates a workflow to verify credit, for example, by sending an e-mail form to a credit manager to which she or he can respond by checking Yes or No. The addition of those buttons to an existing e-mail form, plus the work of defining Yes or No as they are to be understood in this case by the workflow processor are the only steps required to workflow-enable this aspect of the application.

3. Workflow management applications.

Workflow management applications provide managerial views and actions in addition to the operational ones needed to conduct the work. In the above order-entry example, an application that had workflow management built in could be used to keep track of fulfillment cycle times, sources of breakdown, etc. The candidate review example includes workflow management.

STF processors

STF Processors translate between an application's native data format and the Standard Transaction Format of the Workflow Language Interpreter. STF Processors isolate the Workflow Management Server from the interface used by the application and provide a layer for integrating different protocols and technologies. By providing an appropriate STF Processor, any existing database, messaging, or networking system can be incorporated into a workflow management network. If an application communicates by writing to a database, for example, the STF Processor will read the database and look for the records that hold STF transactions.

This architecture makes it possible for existing line-of-business applications, databases, networks, and protocols to be orchestrated by the ActionWorkflow system. Organizations already have tools in place to manage parts of tasks, and parts of workflows. It is an important requirement of a workflow system to integrate with the existing infrastructure, or the benefits will not outweigh the costs of moving to it.

There are three types of STF processors:

1. Message-based.

Message-based applications interact with the Workflow Management System by sending and receiving messages. The STF Processor receives the messages from applications and interacts directly with the Workflow Management Server. Similarly, it constructs messages to be sent back to the application. Message-based STFs are independent of the message transport. Our current implementations use MHS as the messaging system.

2. Database-based .

The client application writes and modifies records in an external database that is concurrently accessed by an STF Processor that has been built for the particular database platform. Applications initiate and participate in workflows by modifying records in this shared database. The STF Processor monitors changes to the database and interacts with the Workflow Management Server for recording and updating transactions. Applications can manage workflows and business processes by querying this shared database to obtain reports about the status of the workflows. We have implemented transaction databases in Lotus Notes and on SQL servers.

3. Process-based.

In the inter-process communication STF interface, a client application receives services from a server by making a process-to-process service request (a remote procedure call, for example). In this case, the STF structures are embedded in the parameter blocks of the service request and service result calls.

Workflow Management Server

The Workflow Management Server uses stored definitions of the workflow structure and of the history of transactions to interpret and initiate acts. It comprises a number of interacting components:

a) Definitions Database

This database describes the workflow of the organization. The definitions include several basic structures. The core is the set of loop types and act names, with associated forms For example, the loop type "Manage candidate review" would have an associated form as shown in Figure 4, and an "accept candidate" act as one of its ways of reaching completion. The definitions database also specifies the linking relationships connecting the different loops, and the actions to be taken automatically by the agent processor.

The linking relationships are used to generate the appropriate sets of "next actions" for each participant as the workflow proceeds, and for automation. They can be of several kinds:

1. Subordinate workflow loops:

In order to complete a part of one workflow it is necessary to initiate and complete a subsidiary one. For example, in order to do the review it is necessary to schedule interviews.

2. Independent triggered workflow loops:

An action in one workflow triggers the initiation of another, which proceeds independently. For example, in a sales workflow the selling of an item from stock may trigger reordering, but the reordering is not a part of completing the sale that triggered it.

3. Resolving workflow loops:

The decision as to which action to take in one workflow requires the initiation and completion of another workflow. For example, a credit approval must be received before accepting or rejecting an order.

In each of these cases, there may be several triggered loops of a given kind instead of just one, with concurrency relationships among them. In the candidate review example all workflow loops for interviews are started in parallel at the moment the agreement is reached in the main loop. The definition of the process indicates that the performance phase of the main loop is completed once all the interview loops are complete.

b) Transactions Database.

This database contains the history of completed workflow loops and workflows-in-progress. It is accessed both for carrying out transactions and for providing status reports and overviews.

c) Workflow Language Interpreter

The Workflow Language Interpreter receives service requests from STF Processors in the form of workflow language constructs: workflow declarations, workflow actions, and requests for workflow management services. It instructs the workflow processor to calculate workflow states and next actions based on specified criteria (such as the current state of the workflow and the role of the person taking an action). It takes actions and makes reports based on the calculations of the workflow processor and the logic of the workflow definitions.

d) Workflow Processor

The workflow processor generates and manages transaction records in the transactions database, which keep track of the current state and history of the workflow, organized according to the component loops and associated completion times.

e) Agent Processor

The agent processor maintains a queue of events and times to trigger workflow actions that have been specified in the definition. We have taken the approach of *incremental automation*, initially assuming human action at each point, and then introducing a program-determined action at any point where rules can be effectively specified. Agent code is written in the workflow definition language and initiated on the basis of the workflow type and act that triggers it. It can take actions both within the workflow structure (making acts and initiating new workflows) and in other functions (printing reports, sending email messages, running other applications, etc.).

There are three ways in which agents are triggered:

1. Triggering act.

For example, a cancellation in a particular workflow initiates a request to a manager to deal with problems caused by cancellation.

2. Status changes in a workflow.

For example, a workflow moving to the state "completed" may trigger actions to cancel all of the subsidiary workflows in progress, whether or not the termination resulted from a cancellation, success, failure, etc.

3. Incompletion times.

For example, a follow-up request to a performer may be initiated when the time for completion of a loop has been reached without a declaration of completion.

Design Workstation

The design workstation is a separate application that is used to generate, modify, and maintain the definitions. We have developed a graphical notation for high-level workflow maps, and have implemented interactive structured drawing tools for creating and manipulating those maps, which can used for business process redesign, both with and without workflow management system development.

CONCLUSIONS

The approach and architecture described here have been developed in a number of prototypes and products. In addition to the development of computer support systems, the theory and analysis methodology has been used as the basis for consulting about redesign of business processes in a number of organizations (For a general discussion of business process redesign, see [5][6]. Kukla [8] describes a case study in a chemical plant, using earlier versions of our approach).

Our experience has demonstrated the effectiveness of business process redesign and computer support based on an ActionWorkflow analysis. The theory provides a starting point that is very different from conventional approaches to workflow. When an analyst first asks people in an organization "What is the work here?," the natural response is to start looking at the forms and procedures. We explicitly reject this, ignoring the forms and asking "What are you actually *doing*?" Without the action workflow structure, this question might seem meaningless, but with it there is a specific direction to move. Who are the customers and performers? What are the conditions of satisfaction in each loop? How is each of the four stages is carried out? How are the loops related to one another?

This questioning leads to identifying those places where gaps and confusions lead to incomplete workflows, misunderstanding of results, and ineffective information flow. This can then lead to new forms and procedures, rather than simply automating the old ones. Traditional methods have been *production-centered*, focusing on efficiency (as measured in standard output for input) and control. Our approach is *satisfaction-centered*, with a central focus on commitments, conditions of satisfaction, and timely completion.

In a significant way, this new methodology corresponds to the shift of concerns in business as we move into the 90s. Guiding concerns of productivity and efficiency have been replaced with others, such as quality (how are conditions of satisfaction set, met, and declared by customers; responsiveness (how are cycle times related to the completion of the structure of loops and how can they be systematically reduced); and customization (how can secondary loops be designed and managed to effectively tailor conditions of satisfaction in the main loops).

Our current efforts are to provide a general platform for action workflow management, which can be incorporated into existing information systems in an incremental way, providing the basis for new understanding of the business processes, and facilitating business process design on a larger enterprise-wide scope. Our goal is to open up the potential to radically improve the functioning of the workflow-enabled organization.

ACKNOWLEDGMENTS

We wish to thank Chauncey Bell, Tom Buchler, Bob Dunham, Pablo Flores, Michael Graves, Manuel Jasso, Juan Ludlow, John McAfee, Russell Redenbaugh, Tom White, and others at Action Technologies who have participated in the development of the concepts and systems described in this paper.

REFERENCES

1. Bullen, Chris, and John Bennett, Groupware in Practice: An Interpretation of Work Experiences, in C. Dunlop and R. Kling (eds.), *Computerization and Controversy*, Academic Press, 1991, 257-287.

2. Dunham, Robert, Business design technology: Software development for customer satisfaction, IEEE Press, *Proceedings of the 24th Annual Hawaii International Conference on Systems Sciences* 1991, 792-798

3. Flores, Fernando, Michael Graves, Bradley Hartfield and Terry Winograd, Computer systems and the design of organizational interaction, *ACM Transactions on Office Information Systems* 6:2 (April, 1988), 153-172.

4. Flores, Fernando, *Management and Communication in the Office of the Future*, Dissertation, University of California, Berkeley, 1982.

5. Hammer, Michael, Reengineering Work: Don't Automate, Obliterate, *Harvard Business Review*, July-August 1990, 104-111

6. Keen, Peter, *Shaping the Future: Business Design through Information Technology*, Boston: Harvard Business School Press, 1991.

7. Kensing, Finn, and Terry Winograd, The language-action approach to design of computer support for cooperative work, *Proceedings of the IFIP TC8 Conference on Collaborative Work, Social Communications and Information Systems*, Helsinki, Finland, 27-29 August, 1991.

8. Kukla, Charles, Anne Clements, Robert Morse and Debra Cash, Designing Effective Systems: A Tool Approach, in P. Adler and T. Winograd (eds.), *Usability: Turning Technology into Tools*, New York: Oxford University Press, 1992, 41-65

9. Moad, Jeff, ViewStar faces many Goliaths, *Datamation* 38:11 (May 15, 1992), 30-31.

10. Winograd, Terry, A language/action perspective on the design of cooperative work *Human-Computer Interaction* 3:1 (1987/88), 3-30.

11. Winograd, Terry, Where the action is, *Byte*, December, 1988, 256-260.

12. Winograd, Terry and Fernando Flores, *Understanding Computers and Cognition: A New Foundation for Design*, Norwood, NJ: Ablex, 1986. Paperback issued by Addison-Wesley, 1987.

Experiments with Oval: A Radically Tailorable Tool for Cooperative Work

Thomas W. Malone, Kum-Yew Lai*, and Christopher Fry

Center for Coordination Science (E53-333)
Massachusetts Institute of Technology
Cambridge, Massachusetts 02139
617-253-6843 malone@mit.edu, cfry@mit.edu

ABSTRACT

This paper describes a series of tests of the generality of a "radically tailorable" tool for cooperative work. Users of this system can create applications by combining and modifying four kinds of building blocks: *objects, views, agents*, and *links*. We found that user-level tailoring of these primitives can provide most of the functionality found in well-known cooperative work systems such as gIBIS, Coordinator, Lotus Notes, and Information Lens. These primitives, therefore, appear to provide an elementary "tailoring language" out of which a wide variety of integrated information management and collaboration applications can be constructed by end users.

INTRODUCTION

For as long as computers have been used for practical tasks, software designers have tried to match their systems to the situations in which they are used. This problem is perhaps nowhere more important than in designing software to support groups of people working together [8]. In some approaches to this problem, software designers study organizations using systems analysis techniques (e.g., [23]) or social science methodologies (e.g., [5], [20], [18]). In participatory design approaches to this problem, the eventual users of a system (who already know about the context of its use) work with software developers in its initial design (e.g., [6], [19]).

An even more extreme version of the participatory design approach is not just to *involve* users in design but to let them *become* designers by giving them end-user programming tools (e.g., [13], [4], [17], [12]). For instance, with products like spreadsheets and Hypercard, end-users, who have no specific training in software development, can create for themselves more and more of the kinds of applications that would previously have required substantial work by professional programmers.

In this paper, we focus on one important class of such end-user programming tools. We call this class of systems *radically tailorable* since they allow end users to create a wide range of different applications by progressively modifying a working system. Radically tailorable systems differ from "ordinary" tailorable systems (such as word processing programs with "Preferences" parameters) in the degree to which users can create a wide range of substantially different applications. For instance, starting with the same blank spreadsheet, users can create applications ranging from personal budgeting to sales forecasting to corporate finance.

Radically tailorable systems also differ from conventional programming languages (including typical fourth generation languages) in that end users progressively modify a working version of an application (such as a blank spreadsheet), instead of specifying instructions in some programming language. In this way, radically tailorable systems reduce the "cognitive distance" between using an application and designing it (c.f., [7]).

Radically tailorable systems are not the only approach to matching cooperative work tools to their contexts of use, but we believe they will be an increasingly important one. One of the key problems in designing radically tailorable tools is picking a set of building blocks at the "right" level of abstraction. That is, the building blocks should not be so low-level that they require significant effort to do anything useful, nor so high-level that they require significant modification whenever the users' needs change (see [3]).

In this paper, we describe a set of experiments with one such set of building blocks. The building blocks are embodied in a radically tailorable system for cooperative work called Oval, the name of which is an acronym for the four key building blocks of the system: *objects, views,*

---

* Current address: McKinsey & Co., 18/F Two Exchange Square, Central, Hong Kong.

Permission to copy without fee all or part of this material is granted provided that the copies are not made or distributed for direct commercial advantage, the ACM copyright notice and the title of the publication and its date appear, and notice is given that copying is by permission of the Association for Computing Machinery. To copy otherwise, or to republish, requires a fee and/or specific permission.

© 1992 ACM 0-89791-543-7/92/0010/0289...$1.50

agents, and *links*.[1] The experiments we describe are tests of the generality of these building blocks: What is the range of different kinds of applications that can be implemented "naturally" with these building blocks and the user level tailoring facilities provided by the Oval system?

To do this, we first constructed a wide range of relatively simple applications for tasks such as project management, software bug tracking, meeting scheduling, and personal information management. These simple applications are not described here. Instead, we focus in this paper on four applications that are already believed by many people to be valuable for supporting cooperative work. Three of these applications were developed elsewhere: gIBIS [2], Coordinator [21], and Notes [11]. One was developed in our laboratory: Information Lens [16].

For each of these systems, we attempted to emulate as much as possible of the functionality of the original system using only the user level facilities provided by Oval. We also identified (and in some cases performed) system level modifications necessary to emulate the functionality of the original systems more closely. With a few exceptions, the basic functionality of the original systems was achieved with only user level modifications.

These tests demonstrate, therefore, that the four key components of Oval (objects, views, agents, and links) provide a *tailoring language* with which a wide variety of cooperative work tools can be constructed. It would, of course, be no surprise to say that we could implement all these applications in a general purpose programming language or that primitives like objects, views, agents, and links were helpful in doing so. The surprising thing, we believe, is that all these applications can be implemented using only the extremely restricted and simplified tailoring language provided by Oval.

OVERVIEW OF OVAL

Oval is based upon four key building blocks (see [9] and [14] for much more detailed descriptions):

(1) Semistructured *objects* represent things in the world such as people, tasks, messages, and meetings. Each object includes a collection of fields and field values and a set of actions that can be performed upon it. The object types are arranged in a hierarchy of increasingly specialized types with each object type inheriting fields, actions, and other properties from its parents in the hierarchy. The objects are semistructured in the sense that users can fill in as much or as little information in different fields as they desire and the information in a field is not necessarily of any specific type (e.g., it may be free text, a link to another object, or a combination of text and links). Users see and manipulate these objects via a particularly natural form of template-based interfaces.

(2) User customizable *views* summarize collections of objects and allow users to edit individual objects. For instance, users can select the fields to be shown in a table display of a collection of objects, or they can select the links to be used to create a network display of the relationships between objects. A calendar display can be used to summarize objects with dates in one of their fields. Any appropriate display format (e.g., table, network, or calendar) can be used to show any collection of objects in any field of any object. Typically, these display formats are used for the "Contents" field of "Folder" objects.

(3) Rule-based *agents* perform active tasks for people without requiring the direct attention of their users. Agents can be triggered by events such as the arrival of new mail, the appearance of a new object in a folder, or the arrival of a pre-specified time. When an agent is triggered it applies a set of rules to a collection of objects. Rules contain descriptions of the objects to which they apply and actions to be performed on those objects. Actions include general actions such as moving, mailing, and deleting objects or object-specific actions such as loading files or responding to messages.

(4) *Links* represent relationships between objects. For example, users can use links to represent relationships between a message and its replies, between people and their supervisors, and between different parts of a complex product. Users can follow these hypertext links by clicking on them, and the knowledge represented by the links can be used by rules or in creating displays.

User tailoring

The primary user level modifications to the system include: (1) defining new object types, (2) adding fields to existing object types, (3) selecting views for objects and collections of objects (from a prespecified set of display formats), (4) specifying parameters for a given view (such as which fields to show), (5) creating new agents and rules, and (6) inserting new links.

Sharing information

There are three primary ways for people to save and share information in Oval: (1) They can save any collection of objects in a file which they (or other people) can load later. For instance, all the objects linked (directly or indirectly) to a given object can be automatically collected and saved in a file. (2) They can mail any collection of objects back and forth to each other in messages. When users load a

---

1 Oval is based upon the Object Lens system ([9], [14]). However, we picked a new name to reduce the widespread confusion between Information Lens and Object Lens. Information Lens [16] was a system for intelligent mail sorting. Oval, as this paper describes, is a much more general system in which Information Lens is only one possible application.

previously saved file or receive a message containing objects, the identity of the objects is preserved (i.e., pre-existing links will point to the newest versions of the objects and the previous versions will be stored as "previous versions"[2]). (3) We have also implemented a rudimentary version of "live" sharing of objects stored on remote databases. Even without this capability, agents can be used to automatically mail and sort "shared" objects thus providing many of the benefits of live sharing.

Implementation status

Oval is implemented in Macintosh Common Lisp on networked Apple Macintoshes. As of this writing, various versions of this system have been used intermittently by up to six people in our research group over a period of approximately 2 years, and by numerous other people for shorter periods. Over 100 copies of the software have been distributed to other researchers and developers for demonstration purposes.[3]

TEST APPLICATIONS

To test our hypothesis that Oval is radically tailorable, we used the system to try to implement the functionality of a variety of cooperative work applications for which descriptions have been previously published. In this section, we will describe briefly how we implemented the major features of each application and what features of the original applications we did not implement. The first application is described in somewhat more detail than the others to illustrate how the system works. More detailed examples of how new applications are created can be found in [9] and [14]. Note that we would not expect beginning users of a system like Oval to be immediately able do all the tailoring needed for some of these applications. Some of the applications require the use of tailoring features (such as defining new object types) that we would expect of experienced users.

For each application, we were primarily concerned with whether the overall user interface paradigm provided by Oval could accommodate in a "natural" way the primary functionality of the application. We did not attempt to mimic exact details of screen layout and command names. Similarly, since our system is only a research prototype, we did not attempt to replicate the level of attention to robustness, speed, access controls, and so forth present in the commercial products we analyzed. In all cases, however, we tried to be faithful to the spirit of the original systems.

---

2 Users are notified of these changes, and if they desire, can undo them in specific cases.

3 For information on how to obtain a copy of the software for research purposes at no charge, contact Peter Richards, MIT Technology Licensing Office, E32-300, 28 Carleton Street, Cambridge, MA 02139 (Telephone: (617) 253-6966. Email: par@eagle.mit.edu.)

gIBIS – Argumentation Support

gIBIS [2] is a tool for helping a group explore and capture the qualitative factors that go into making decisions. Elements of a policy analysis in gIBIS are represented as a network containing three types of nodes: Issues, Positions, and Arguments. Each Issue may have several Positions that "Respond to" it, and each Position, in turn, may have various Arguments that "Support" or "Object to" it.

Defining new object types and creating examples of them

To emulate gIBIS in Oval, we first defined the three types of objects used by gIBIS: Issues, Positions, and Arguments. For instance, to define the new type of object called "Argument", we performed the actions illustrated in Figure 1. First, we selected the basic object type called "Thing" and then chose the "Create Subtype" action (Figure 1(a)). To create individual examples of this type, we selected the new type and chose the "New object" action. The new Arguments have the fields "Name", "Keywords", and "Text" by default, since these fields are present in all Things. To add the fields (like "Supports", "Objects to", and "Entered by") that are present in Argument objects but not in all Things, we used the "Add Field" action on one of the new Argument objects (Figure 1(b)). Finally, we filled in the fields of this (and other objects) by typing and by adding links (Figure 1(c)). The square brackets in Figure 1(c) indicate "live" links to other objects that can be traversed by clicking on them. To add these links in the first place, we simply selected the "Add link" action in a field and then pointed to the object to which the link goes.

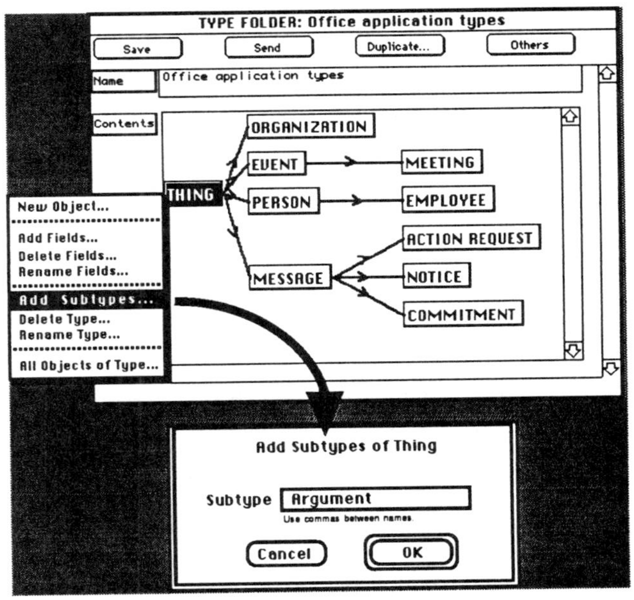

Figure 1(a). To define a new type of object, users create it as a subtype of some existing object type. (Note: In this and subsequent figures, the heavy curved arrow is added for clarity. It is not part of the actual screen display.)

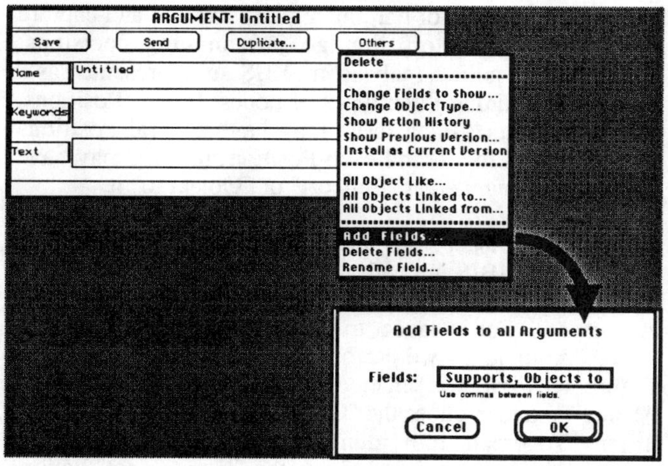

Figure 1(b). Users can add fields to an object type with the "Add Fields" action on any instance of that type. The fields then appear in all objects of that type.

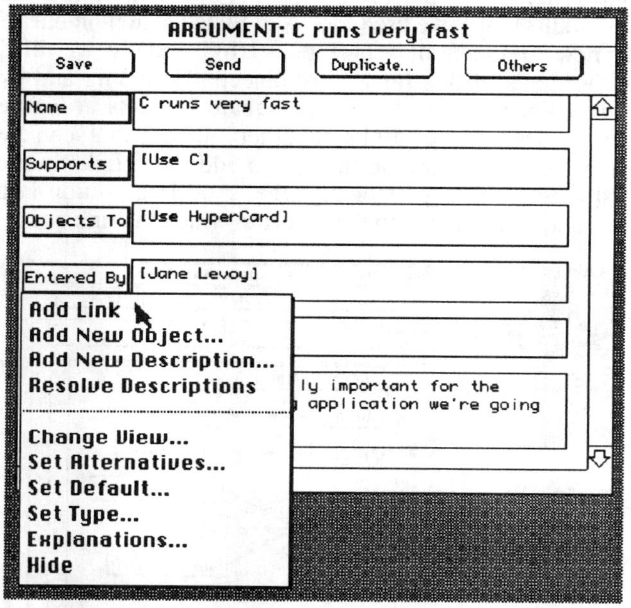

Figure 1(c). Users can fill in the fields of an object by typing or by inserting links to other objects.

Viewing collections of objects

In the original gIBIS system, users can graphically see the relationships between the nodes in an argument network. To do this with Oval, we selected the "Change View" action for a field containing the nodes and then chose the "Network" display format (see Figures 2 and 3). This format allows us to choose the fields from which links will be shown in the network. For instance, in Figure 2, we chose to show links from three fields,"Supports", "Objects to" and "Responds to." We also chose to display in each node the "Name" and "Object Type" fields. The result is shown in Figure 3.

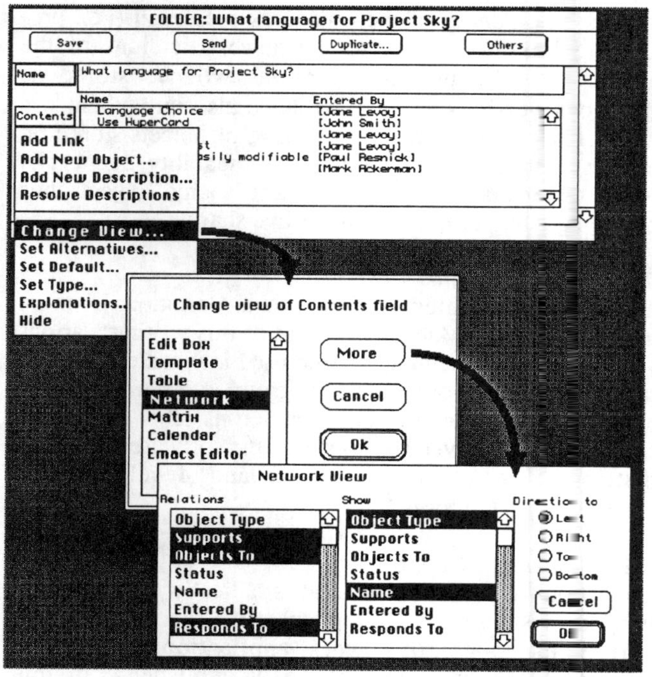

Figure 2. Users can "Change View" on any field. Here, the "Network" view was selected. Then, two other choices were made: (1) the fields from which links will be used to construct the network and (2) the fields to be shown in the nodes of the network

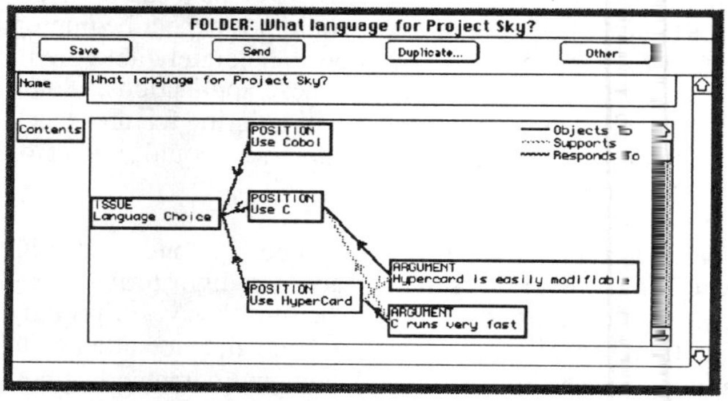

Figure 3. This network view, the result of the choices made in Figure 2, shows the relationships between Issues, Positions, and Arguments as in the gIBIS system.

Note that this simple method of tailoring a network view can be used for any collection of objects whose relationships to each other are represented by links (e.g., organization charts, PERT charts, and software module calling relationships). In one sense, of course, there is nothing new about this notion of using general display formats for many kinds of objects. We have been genuinely suprised, however, at how widely useful and powerful this feature is when users can apply it themselves to create new applications.

Features of the original system not included in our application

We omitted one feature of the original gIBIS system for aesthetic reasons: The original system included a distinction between primary and secondary links of each type. We could have implemented this simply by defining additional fields (e.g., "Supports (primary)" and "Supports (secondary)"), but we chose not to, in order to reduce the complexity of the system.

In addition to a shared "live" database, gIBIS has two other features which would have required new system level programming to implement: (1) aggregate nodes (the ability to automatically collapse a group of nodes into one aggregate node), and (2) a node index that shows nodes in outline format (with indentations indicating their relations). These features did not seem essential to the main point of the application, and we did not include them in our implementation. However, they would both have been quite consistent with the overall Oval paradigm. Aggregate nodes could be implemented with two new actions on folders (one to create aggregates and one to break them apart). An outline display format would be reusable in many other applications as well and would, therefore, be a useful addition to the current display formats for collections of objects (tables, networks, calendars, and matrices).

Coordinator – Conversation structuring and task tracking

The Coordinator is an electronic mail-based system that helps people structure conversations and track tasks ([22], [1]). To emulate the functionality of the Coordinator in Oval, we first made three system level modifications to automatically group a series of messages into "Conversation" folders (see Figure 4): (1) When users create a new message (without it being a reply to an old one), a new conversation folder is automatically created. This folder contains the new message, and the conversation field of the new message is also linked to this folder. (2) When users reply to a message of a given type, they are presented with a choice of message types for their reply. (The choices to be presented are specified in a user-modifiable field called "Reply Types", which is not shown in the view used in Figure 4.) (3) After users select a reply type, the Conversation field in the reply message is automatically linked to the Conversation folder specified in the original message, and the reply is inserted in the Conversation folder.

After these system-level changes to add conversations (which can be useful in any messaging application), the other main functionality of the Coordinator can be added by user-level tailoring. For instance, we added 15 new message types and defined their reply types to provide the same conversational sequences (such as Conversations for Action) used in the Coordinator. The Request message type, for example, has reply types like Counteroffer, Promise, and Decline.

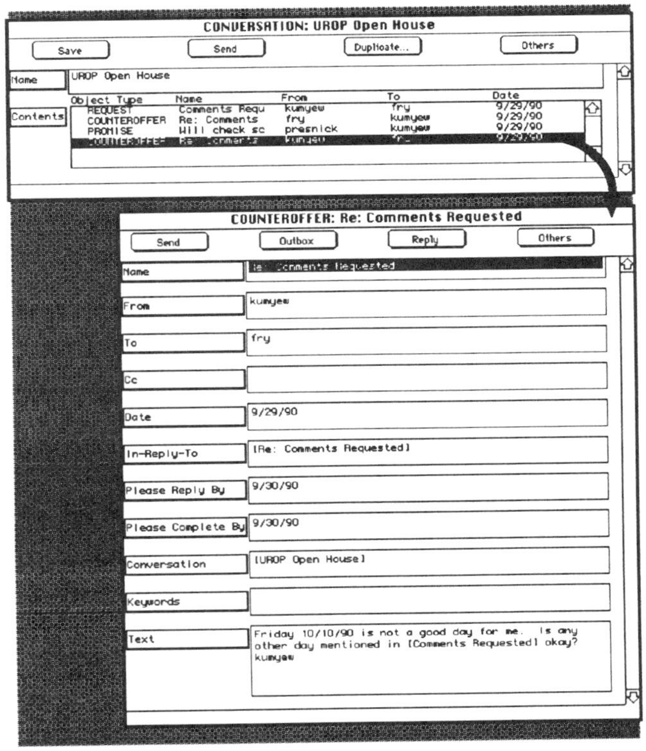

Figure 4: A conversation folder contains messages within a conversation, like those in the Coordinator.

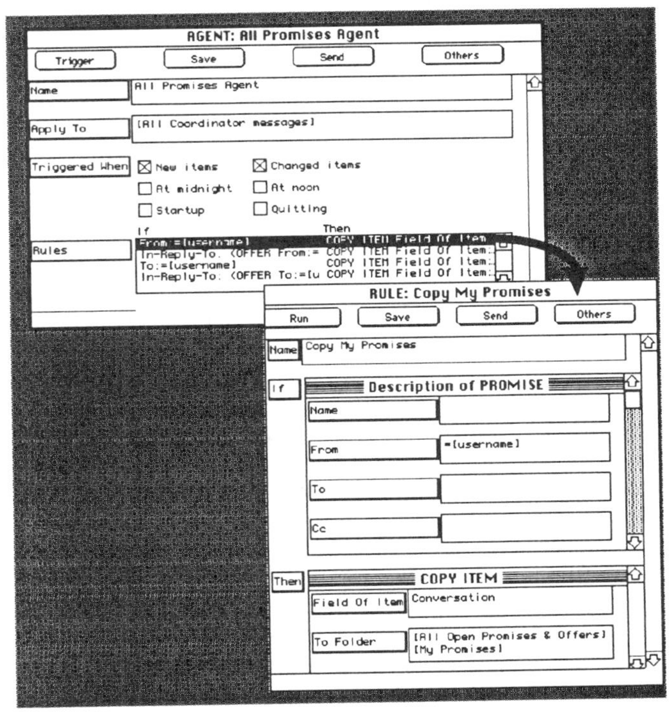

Figure 5: An agent that tracks conversations involving promises. The rule shown puts conversations that include Promise messages from the user into the appropriate folders.

To provide the various kinds of summary displays in the Coordinator we created 23 folders (such as "Open Matters" and "My promises"), and 14 agents with 47 rules that move messages into and out of these folders. For instance, Figure 5 shows an agent that moves conversations into the folders for various kinds of promises. To create an agent like this one, users fill in the fields shown in Figure 5: a folder to which the agent applies, one or more triggering conditions, and a set of rules. Then, when the agent is triggered, it will apply the rules to the objects in the "Apply to" folder. Rules, like agents, are created with a straighforward sequence of menu-picks and form filling. The rule shown in Figure 5, for instance, moves conversations with promises from the user into two folders: "My Promises" and "All Open Promises and Offers".

Some of the agents make use of "all-objects-of-a-type" folders in Oval. An all-objects-of-a-type folder is one which is maintained by the system so that it always contains all objects of a specified type. For example, the "All Coordinator messages" folder is dynamically maintained so that it always contains all the Coordinator messages in Oval.

Features of the original system not included in our application

Unlike the original Coordinator, our application does not provide explicit support for delegation. Instead, someone who has received a request can delegate it to someone else "manually" by sending a new request that contains a link to the original one.

There are also several detailed features of the Coordinator not included in our application. For instance, unlike the Coordinator, our application does not enforce the restriction that people who are only copied (cc:'ed) in a conversation cannot change its state. Furthermore, there are some cases where users of our application would need to do minor things "manually" that are done automatically in the Coordinator. For instance, if someone wants to cancel a request before having received a reply to it, they would have to manually address the cancel message and insert it in the original conversation.

Notes – Semistructured information sharing

Of the other systems analyzed here, Lotus Notes [11] is the most similar to Oval. It is also similar to earlier computer conferencing systems with the important additions that (1) the documents in a database are semistructured templates (with optional "hot links" to other documents) and (2) the documents in a database can be filtered and summarized according to various user-definable views. Like Oval, Notes can be tailored for many different applications. The templates in Notes are equivalent to object types in Oval; the databases in Notes are equivalent to folders in Oval; and the views in Notes are equivalent to views of collections of objects in Oval. Notes views are all variations of a kind of "outline" display format that does not currently exist in Oval, but is similar to the table format display that does

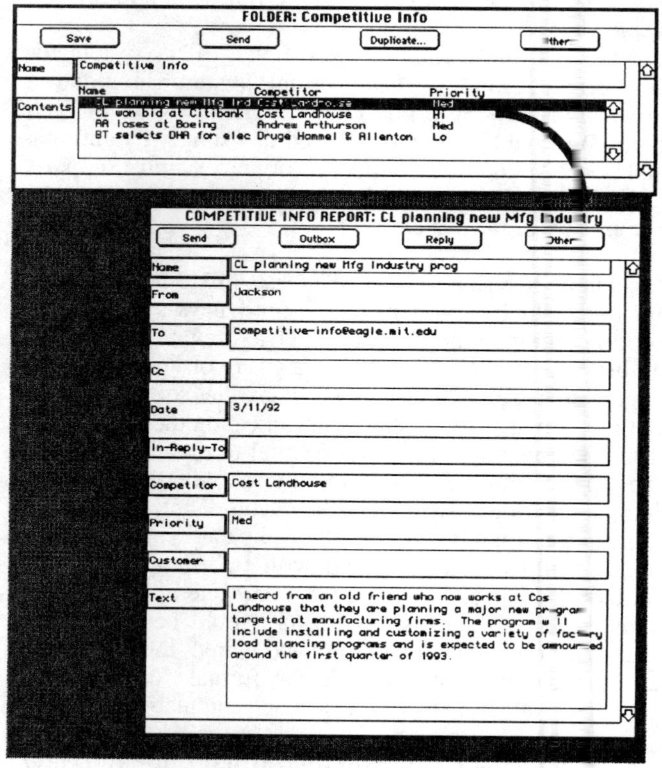

Figure 6. A table format display summarizing documents like those in a Notes database.

exist (see Figure 6). Notes does not include any of the other folder display formats in Oval such as networks and calendars. Similarly, even though Notes allows very knowledgeable users to do certain kinds of sorting and filtering using views, it does not appear to be designed to make this easy for end users, and it does not have active agents like those in Oval.

Unlike Oval, Notes is based on a database replication algorithm which approximates "live sharing" of documents. Also, as a commercial product, Notes includes a number of features such as access controls, "rich text" fields and calculated fields. Even though these features are not currently part of Oval, they would be consistent with its overall user interface paradigm and useful for many other applications.

Information Lens -- Intelligent mail sorting

Information Lens ([16], [15]) helps users by automatically filtering and sorting incoming electronic messages. It also helps users create messages using a set of (optional) semistructured message templates. Implementing Information Lens in Oval is quite straightforward. For instance, users can define new message types as subtypes of Message in the object type hierarchy and create rules to filter and sort messages (see Figure 7).

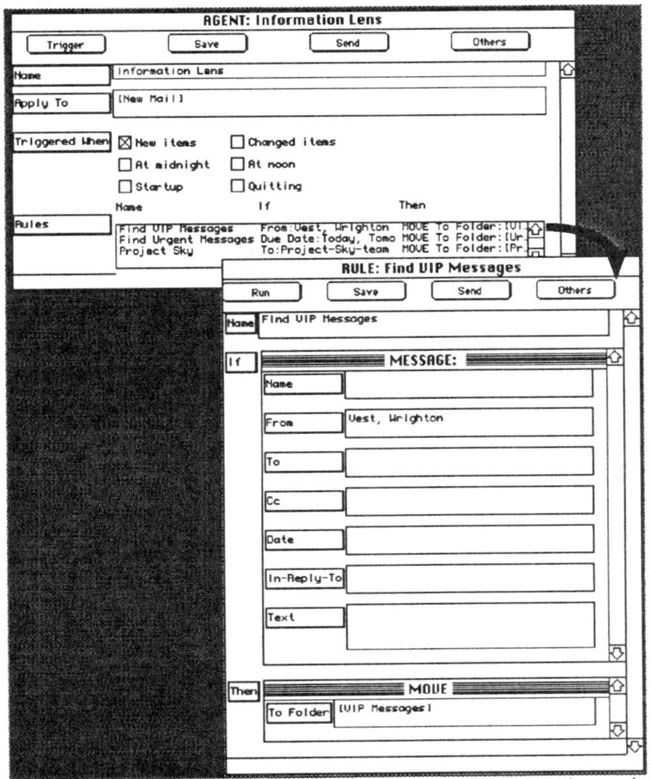

Figure 7. Examples of an agent and a rule like those in Information Lens.

In addition to the local mail sorting agents, the original Information Lens included a second kind of agent that ran on servers and selected potentially interesting messages for a given user from a stream of messages addressed to "Anyone." Implementing remote agents like these would require some additional systems level programming which we have not yet done in Oval but which would be consistent with the overall framework of Oval and useful in other applications.

Summary

Table 1 summarizes the results of the four application experiments described above. In three of the cases (gIBIS, Notes, and Information Lens), some of the features of the previous systems were not included in our emulations. It appears, however, that the functionality omitted in these cases was not essential to the main point of the applications. Also, in all three cases, the functionality omitted would fit naturally within the user interface paradigm provided by Oval and would be reusable in other applications. In the other case (Coordinator), we performed modest amounts of system level programming and believe we emulated all of the major functionality of the original system. The new system level functionality implemented in this case (Conversation folders) should also be generally useful in other Oval applications. Overall, therefore, the primary functionality of the previous systems seems to be captured reasonably well by user-level modifications within the user interface paradigm provided by Oval.

DISCUSSION

Limitations of experiments

Before proceeding, it is important to note several limitations of our experiments. First, even though the experiments establish that the range of applicability of systems like Oval is large, they do not allow us to characterize its limits. In fact, we suspect that it is difficult, in principle, to characterize the limits of radically tailorable tools since ingenious users will always be able to think of unexpected new uses for them.

Second, we have not formally studied the *usefulness* of the applications that could be created with systems like Oval. Instead, since we emulated other systems that are widely believed to be useful, we assume that systems like Oval would be at least as useful as these previous systems are individually. We do not yet know how much additional benefit will come from combining these and other applications that can be created with the system.

Finally, and perhaps most importantly, we have not formally tested the *usability* of this system. That is, we tested whether the system made it *possible* for knowledgeable users to implement the applications using only the user level tailoring facilities. As the descriptions above indicate, the user level tailoring facilities have "face validity" as being simple and easy to use. Another important kind of test, however, would be to examine how

System	**User-level modifications**				**System-level modifications**
	Object Types	*Folders*	*Agents*	*Rules*	
gIBIS	3	1 per discussion	1	1 per query	Aggregate nodes**;"Outline" folder display format**; Live sharing †
Coordinator	19	23	14	47	Conversation folders; Reply types
Notes	*	*	*	*	"Outline" folder display format**; Live sharing †
Information Lens	*	*	1	*	"Anyone" agents**

Table 1. A summary of the modifications required to emulate the systems described in each experiment.
(* = Application specific. ** = "Optional" feature; not implemented. † = Implementation in progress)

well typical users at various levels of sophistication could actually create such applications for themselves.

In practice, we expect that radically tailorable systems like this will be used in very different ways by end users, by power users, and by programmers ([17], [12]). Since the system provides a wide spectrum of tailoring options, we believe that many users would make only minimal changes to applications developed by others, while some power users would develop applications for other people, and programmers would use the system to dramatically reduce the time and effort required to develop completely new applications. In fact, even if the Oval system were not tailorable at all by typical end users, radically tailorable systems like this would still be very useful for programmers as rapid prototyping and iterative development tools.

Lessons from experiments

What can we learn from these experiments? We believe that two of the most important lessons have to do with the power of the four primitives with which we started:

(1) Objects, views, agents, and links provide a kind of elementary "tailoring language" for user interfaces to information management and cooperative work applications. All of the previous systems we analyzed had some form of semistructured objects and some form of summary displays analogous to our views. Most of the systems also had some of the functionality provided by our agents and links. With the exception of Notes, however, the systems were built to handle only specialized kinds of objects (e.g., messages or argumentation nodes) and certain display formats (e.g., tables). By generalizing to the abstract level of semistructured objects, customizable views, rule-based agents, and links, we achieve a great increase in scope of applications with only a relatively modest increase in complexity. For instance, by implementing views (such as tables, networks, matrices, and calendars) once in a way that end users can then apply to any kind of information, a vast amount of programming effort is avoided and the end users' power is significantly increased. We were genuinely surprised at the power of this approach, and we believe that the generality of these basic primitives and their combination methods is not yet widely appreciated.

(2) Radical tailorability facilitates integration. In addition to the versatility that a radically tailorable system provides, there is another important benefit of constructing a variety of different applications within the same system: It is much easier to integrate the different applications. For instance, discussions facilitated by systems like gIBIS often lead to action items, the status of which a group might want to track with systems like Notes or the Coordinator. In an integrated system like Oval, it is a straightforward matter to link these action items to the discussions that generated them and vice versa.

CONCLUSION

Even though the primitives of objects, views, agents, and links provide a powerful basis for constructing information management and cooperative work applications, there are many difficult problems to be solved before the full promise of this approach is realized. For instance, numerous difficult issues arise in trying to manage large numbers of linked objects in a shared, distributed network. One particularly important aspect of this problem involves how to manage the evolution of partially shared object type definitions (e.g., [10]). Finally, even if the approach described here were successful in completely eliminating the programming effort needed to create applications, the task of imagining new and useful things for computers to do is a far from trivial one.

ACKNOWLEDGEMENTS

This research was supported by Digital Equipment Corporation, the National Science Foundation (Grant No. IRI-8903034), Matsushita Electric Industrial Co., Boeing, Information Resources, Inc., Electronic Data Systems, Apple Computer Company, and the corporate members of the MIT International Financial Services Research Center.

We are indebted to Terry Winograd for suggesting the acronym "Oval" after hearing about the four components of our system and to John McDermott for suggesting the term "radically tailorable" as a description of the Oval system. The Oval system has benefitted from the suggestions and work of numerous people over many years, including most recently: Mark Ackerman, Geoffrey Bock, Kevin Crowston, Troy Jordan, Jintae Lee, Charley Osborne, Dave Park, Mike Plusch, and Paul Resnick.

REFERENCES

1. Action Technologies, I. (1988). *The Coordinator, Version II, User's Guide.* Emeryville, CA:

2. Conklin, J. and Begeman, M. L. gIBIS: A hypertext tooling for exploratory policy discussion. In *Proceedings of CSCW '88 Conference on Computer-Supported Cooperative Work* (Portland, OR, Sept. 26-28, 1988), ACM Press, pp. 140–152.

3. diSessa, A. A. A principled design for an integrated computational environment. *Human Computer Interaction.* 1, (1985), 1–47.

4. Fischer, G. and Girgensohn, A. End-user modifiability in design environments. In *Proceedings of CHI '90 Conference on Human Factors in Computer Systems* (1990), ACM Press, pp. 183-191.

5. Galegher, J., Kraut, R. E. and Egido, C. (Eds.). *Intellectual Teamwork: Social and Technological Foundations of Cooperative Work.* Lawrence Erlbaum, Hillsdale, N. J., 1990.

6. Greenbaum, J. and Kyng, M. (Eds.). *Desgin at Work: Cooperative Design of Computer Systems.* Lawerence Erlbaum, Hillsdale, N. J., 1991.

7. Hutchins, E. L., Hollan, J. D. and Norman, D. A. Direct manipulation interfaces. In *User-Centered System Design,* D. Norman and S. Draper (Ed.), Lawrence Erlbaum, Hillsdale, N. J., 1986, pp. 87–124.

8. Kyng, M. Designing for cooperation: Cooperating in design. *Communications of the ACM.* 34, 12 (1991), 65-73.

9. Lai, K. Y., Malone, T. and Yu, K.-C. Object Lens: A spreadsheet for cooperative work. *ACM Transactions on Office Information Systems.* 6, 4 (1988), 332–353.

10. Lee, J. and Malone, T. W. Partially shared views: A scheme for communicating among groups that use different type hierarchies. *ACM Transactions on Information Systems.* 8, 1 (1990), 1–26.

11. Lotus. *Lotus Notes Users Guide.* Lotus Development Corp., Cambridge, MA, 1989.

12. Mackay, W. E. Patterns of sharing customizable software. In *Proceedings of CSCW '90 Conference on Computer-Supported Cooperative Work* (Los Angeles, CA, October 7-10, 1990), , pp. .

13. MacLean, A., Carter, K., Lovstrand, L. and Moran, T. User-tailorable systems: Pressing the issues with buttons. In *CHI '90 Conference on Human Factors in Computer Systems* (Seattle, WA, April 1-5, 1990), ACM Press, pp. 175-182.

14. Malone, T., Yu, K.-C. and Lee, J. (1989). *What good are semistructured objects? Adding semiformal structure to hypertext* (Technical report #102). Cambridge, MA: Center for Coordination Science, Massachusetts Institute of Technology.

15. Malone, T. W., Grant, K. R., Lai, K.-Y., Rao, R. and Rosenblitt, D. Semistructured messages are surprisingly useful for computer-supported coordination. *ACM Transactions on Office Information Systems.* 5, (1987), 115–131.

16. Malone, T. W., Grant, K. R., Turbak, F. A., Brobst, S. A. and Cohen, M. D. Intelligent information-sharing systems. *Communications of the ACM.* 30, (1987), 390–402.

17. Nardi, B. A. and Miller, J. R. An ethnographic study of distributed problem solving in spreadsheet development. In *Proceedings of CSCW '90 Conference on Computer-Supported Cooperative Work* (Los Angeles, CA, October 7-10, 1990), ACM Press, pp. .

18. Olson, G. M. and Olson, J. R. User-centered design of collaboration technology. *Journal of Organizational Computing.* 1, (1991), 61-83.

19. Schuler, D. and Namioka, A. (Eds.). *Participatory Design.* Lawrence Erlbaum, Hillsdale, N. J., 1992.

20. Sproull, L. and Kiesler, S. Computers, Networks, and Work. *Scientific American.* 265, 3 (1991), 84-91.

21. Winograd, T. A language/action perspective on the design of cooperative work. *Human Computer Interaction.* 3, (1987), 3–30.

22. Winograd, T. and Flores, F. *Understanding computers and cognition: A new foundation for design.* Ablex, Norwood, NJ, 1986.

23. Yourdon, E. *Modern Structured Analysis.* Yourdon, Englewood Cliffs, NJ, 1989.

Supporting Exploratory CSCW with the EGRET Framework

Philip Johnson

Department of Information and Computer Sciences
University of Hawaii
Honolulu, HI 96822
(808) 956-3489 • johnson@Hawaii.Edu

ABSTRACT

Exploratory collaboration occurs in domains where the structure and process of group work evolves as an intrinsic part of the collaborative activity. Traditional database and hypertext structural models do not provide explicit support for collaborative exploration. The EGRET framework defines both a data and a process model along with supporting analysis techniques that provide novel support for exploratory collaboration. To do so, the EGRET framework breaks with traditional notions of the relationship between schema and instance structure. In EGRET, schema structure is viewed as a representation of the current state of consensus among collaborators, from which instance structure is allowed to depart in a controlled fashion. This paper discusses the issues of exploratory collaboration, the EGRET approach to its support, and the current status of this research.

KEYWORDS

Collaborative Environments, Exploratory Development, Hypertext, Schema Evolution.

INTRODUCTION

Group work is unpredictable. It is unpredictable for a variety of reasons: the task may be ambiguous, the methods for accomplishing the task may be unclear, the backgrounds and motivations of the group members may lead to unforeseen events, individual group members and their relationships with other members may change, increasing understanding of the task and domain may change the group process, and so forth. As a result, surprisingly little can be determined *a priori* about the way some groups will perform their tasks, or even what tasks these groups will eventually perform.

Permission to copy without fee all or part of this material is granted provided that the copies are not made or distributed for direct commercial advantage, the ACM copyright notice and the title of the publication and its date appear, and notice is given that copying is by permission of the Association for Computing Machinery. To copy otherwise, or to republish, requires a fee and/or specific permission.

© 1992 ACM 0-89791-543-7/92/0010/0298...$1.50

Adapting terminology from software engineering, we call such group work *exploratory* in nature.

This paper concerns computer support for one of the fundamental characteristics of exploratory group work: the dynamic, emergent, and evolving nature of the structure of information and artifacts produced by exploratory collaborative activities. To investigate this phenomena, we have designed a framework for collaborative systems that provides novel mechanisms for evolution of information and its structure as an integral part of the collaborative activities. These mechanisms also provide a historical record of the collaboration, with interesting potential for process improvement and artifact preservation.

This paper describes an implementation of this framework called EGRET[1]. The next section discusses the nature of exploratory group work, illustrating it via an example of collaborative software development. The following section presents the EGRET data and process model for support of collaborative exploration and evolution. The remainder of the paper contrasts EGRET with other research and discusses the status and future directions of the project.

EXPLORATORY COLLABORATION

In [8], exploratory domains are characterized as *experimental* and *embedded*. Experimental means that the appropriate structure and process for problem solving in the domain cannot be well determined except through experimentation with a variety of techniques. Embedded means that the introduction of new support may impact upon the domain in unpredictable ways. Exploration, which often arises in traditional collaborative activities such as software development, document generation, and so forth, implies that the group might not be able to precisely characterize in advance how they will accomplish their task, or even the ultimate result of their efforts.

For these reasons, exploratory collaboration typically results in significant evolution in the structure, content, and process by which information is

[1]Exploratory Group Work Environment

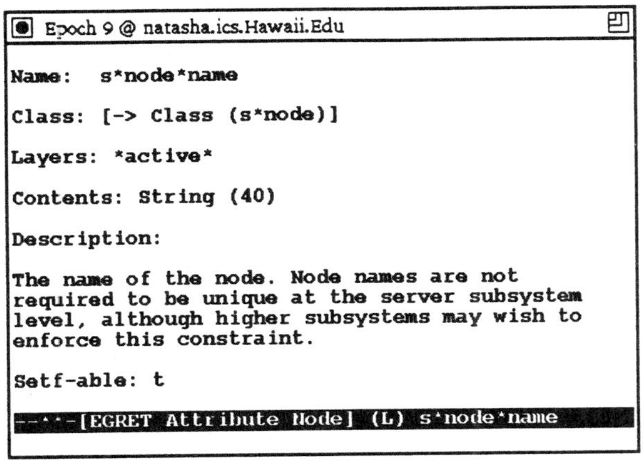

Figure 1. One version of an attribute node used to describe the s*node*name object

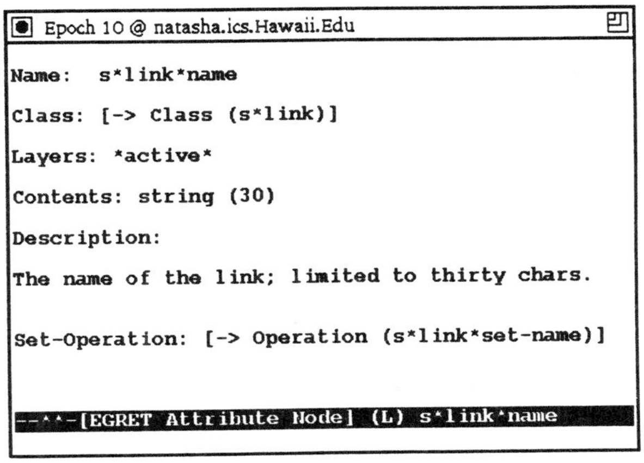

Figure 2. Another version of an attribute node used to describe the s*link*name object

created and manipulated by the group. As the group works, they acquire more knowledge about both the domain and the working styles and skills of the other group members. Indeed, individual working styles and skill levels are typically changed by this collaboration. This circularity further emphasizes the *emergent* nature of exploratory collaboration.

As a concrete scenario, consider a group of software developers collaboratively producing a novel, object oriented application requiring high reliability. Furthermore, assume that these developers have a mixture of backgrounds—some are experienced C programmers, others experienced Lisp programmers, while still others are programming novices. Members also differ in familiarity with object oriented concepts, and of those familiar with object orientation, their understanding of the paradigm differs significantly depending upon whether their background involved C++ (a C-based OO dialect) or CLOS (a Lisp-based OO dialect).

The reliability demands on this application require good software engineering practices: for example, periodic reviews and inspections of the design and implementation during development. As with all review and inspection activities, one major goal is to uncover errors, i.e. points of inconsistency between the specification and implementation of the system. However, this group work scenario also involves significant exploratory activities:

- *Discovery of variations in design/implementation structures and processes among members.* The diversity of member backgrounds will result in a diversity of approaches to design and implementation, regardless of the target language(s) for the application. Most of these prejudices, ranging from the simple (C idioms for iteration) to the complex (CLOS idioms for multiple inheritance) cannot be consciously specified by the developers *a priori*. Instead, most of these techniques and idioms only reveal themselves during actual review of specific design or implementation fragments, usually by members not sharing their mindset.

- *Formation of structure and process-level standards for development activities.* Following discovery of variations, the group must decide upon a consensual course of action. Typical alternatives include: (a) the variation represents one among a number of acceptable alternative possibilities; (b) the variation represents a standard to be mandated for all members; or (c) the variation is unacceptable and requires correction.

- *Adaptation of the review/inspection process to accomodate emergent design/implementation standards.* The standards for design and implementation emerging from the review and inspection process impact upon the process itself. A major purpose of future reviews is to ensure conformance to previously defined standards.

- *Adaptation of review/inspection artifacts to accomodate emergent design/implementation standards.* To support adherence, the structure and content of supporting artifacts used in review/inspection must evolve. Such changes could involve simple additions or deletions to checklists, incremental generation of design guideline documentation complete with hypertext links to examples of correct or incorrect code, integration of automated tools to ensure conformance to a new guideline, and so forth.

Figure 1 illustrates a simple but exemplary situation that arises in this scenario. In the description of the `s*node*name` object, the Lisp orientation of the designer is betrayed by the boolean `setf-able` field implying that updates occur through overloading the `setf` construct. In a different member's design of the `s*link*name` object illustrated in Figure 2, the attribute conforms to a C++—oriented view of updating and encapsulation, using a `set-operation` field that contains a link to the corresponding update operation.

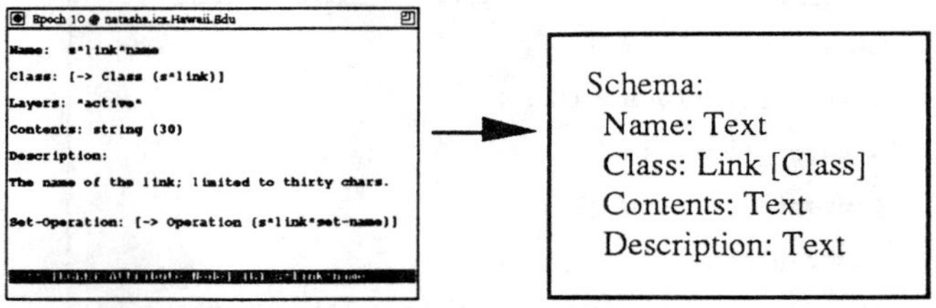

Figure 3. S*link*name and its associated schema.

While the two alternatives are essentially equivalent in semantics, they differ significantly in structure. In one case, a simple boolean value suffices to indicate an updatable attribute, while the other case requires a link rather than a boolean, as well as an additional node documenting the design of the update operation.

While some might believe that such an issue can be easily resolved in advance, there is no obviously preferable alternative. In fact, allowing the group to explore alternative design structures can be useful. For example, if the group becomes polarized over the alternatives, it may be best to simply allow both and let each member use their favored version. If the entire application will be implemented in C++, standardizing on the link version may be preferable. A CLOS implementation may dictate the opposite. If the application is a hybrid of C++ and CLOS, then mandating different structures for different design parts may be best. Some other conclusion might be reached if the boundary between the CLOS and C++ components is not firm.

This scenario of exploratory group work clearly exhibits both experimental and embedded properties. It is experimental because the most appropriate set of guidelines can only emerge through the process of development itself, and the incremental discovery of each member's techniques and preferences and their impact upon other members' work. It is embedded because the incrementally emerging set of guidelines fundamentally affects the future form and course of collaboration.

Computer support for the exploratory definition and evolution of artifacts such as the design template structure above requires addressing several fundamental issues. First, what is an appropriate structure and process model for defining such collaborative artifacts? Second, how can that model support changes in the appropriate structure of artifacts as the collaborative activity proceeds? Finally, and perhaps most importantly, how can the exploratory definition and adaptation of artifacts be accomplished in a truly *collaborative* fashion?

The EGRET framework is our answer to these questions. It defines a data model and a process model that facilitates a collaborative approach to evolution in the structure and content of exploratory artifacts. To accomplish this, EGRET fundamentally redefines the meaning of structural schemas and instances and the relationship between them. These issues are explored in detail in the next section.

THE EGRET DATA AND PROCESS MODELS

At core, EGRET implements a multi-user hypertext model of information, where typed nodes of information are related together via typed links. The key issue explored in EGRET is the relationship between node and link types, their instances, and the changes in these relationships over time. The next section begins this discussion through a conceptual overview of the fundamental entities in EGRET: nodes, schemas, fields, links, and layers. A more formal definition of the EGRET data model is found in [10]

The EGRET Data Model

Nodes.

EGRET *node instances* are the basic repository for information. Each node instance is a composite of an arbitrary number of *fields*. Each node instance has associated with it a *node schema*. A node schema includes a default specification of the internal structure—the set of fields—to be used when creating new node instances conforming to this schema. Figure 3 illustrates this relationship for the node instance `s*link*name` shown previously in Figure 2.

A key difference between the EGRET data model and conventional database models is that node schemas provide only a default, rather than an absolute specification of node instance structure. In fact, the actual structure of an EGRET node instance can depart arbitrarily from the structure specified by its node schema. This capability for (temporary) structural inconsistency forms the core of support for exploratory collaboration in EGRET.

Node instances are created in two ways: by *instantiation*, where a node schema forms a template for the creation of a node instance, or by *cloning*, where another node instance, rather than a node schema, forms the template.

EGRET includes a simple structural inheritance mechanism to create hierarchies of node schemas. One node schema can be defined as the subschema of one or more other node schemas, which means that the structure of those schemas are inherited directly into the new schema.

Fields.

Following a hypertext orientation, fields can potentially contain arbitrary mixtures of text and links to other nodes, although field contents are typically constrained through the use of *field schemas*. Defining a new field schema requires the implementor to supply a *validity function*: a function that is passed the field contents and returns a boolean indicating whether or not the field conforms to the schema. Using this mechanism (and exploiting the power of Emacs), it is relatively straightforward to implement specialized textual fields for structured information such as Bibtex-entry or C-function. It is similarly straightforward to constrain a field to hold only link instances of a single schema or set of schemas.

In the node instance s*link*name illustrated in Figure 2, there are six fields: Name, Class, Layers, Contents, Description, and Set-Operation. Name, Contents, Layers, and Description are simply constrained to hold text. The Set-Operation field is constrained to hold a single link instance with schema Operation. The Class field is similarly constrained to hold a single link with schema Class. The Contents field could easily be constrained to hold "structured text" conforming to a data description language.

Fields can be incrementally added to either node schemas or node instances. When a field is added to a node schema, it changes the default specification for the field-level structure of future node instances of that schema. When a field is added to an existing node instance, its effect is to add that field structure to the single node instance. Fields can also be incrementally deleted from node instances or schemas.

Links.

Links are typed pointers from fields to nodes. As with node instances, link instances are associated with a link schema. Unlike node schemas, however, the purpose of a link schema is to specify the valid domain and range of a link instance. Both the domain and range of a link instance is specified through a link *constraint expression*, which operates over the set of node schemas. (The constraint expressions combine with field validity functions to enforce the field-to-node semantics for links.) The relationship between link instances and link schemas is analogous to that between node instances and node schemas: while the default structure for a link is specified by its associated schema, individual link instances may depart arbitrarily from this structure. EGRET provides functions to modify the constraint expressions associated with both link schemas and link instances.

Referring again to the node instance s*link*name in Figure 2, there are two links displayed, one from its Class field to the node instance s*link, and another from its Set-Operation field to the node s*link*set-name. These links are actually constrained only in their range—in other words, they can link arbitrary node instances to a node with associated schema Class (or Operation).

Layers.

EGRET provides the ability to partition the database into (potentially overlapping) sets of schemas, instances, fields, and links called *layers*. Conceptually, layers can be viewed as a namespace mechanism, or alternatively as a set of tags for EGRET entities that are orthogonal to the type system. For example, both s*node*name and s*link*name are members of the default, active layer.

The fundamental purpose of layers is to support the process of exploratory collaboration. Layers accomplish this by defining both focal points for current collaborative activity, and by delimiting archival instances that may be structurally inconsistent with their schemas but do not require maintenance activities to bring them into conformance.

Structural Inconsistency in EGRET

The single most important (and probably most contentious) result of the EGRET data model is the capability of instance structure to diverge from schema structure. For example, Figures 1 and 2 illustrate two instances of an attribute node with different internal field structure. Figure 3 reveals that neither node is strictly compliant with its schema, since both contain an additional field not present in the schema. This typically occurs when the structure of an object is initially under-specified, and members of a group invent different solutions to filling in the missing structure.

EGRET aids and abets this structural inconsistency through the instance cloning mechanism, which allows new instances to be created from old instances. This allows group members to avoid time-consuming re-derivations of useful divergent structures from their original schema structure.

Left unchecked, instance divergence would inevitably lead to a "spaghetti-bowl" collaborative system lacking any structural uniformity, and of uncertain benefit to the group. To counteract this tendency toward structural entropy, the EGRET framework embeds the structural flexibility of its data model within a process model that helps the group to exploit the utility of this flexibility, while preventing the system from becoming unwieldy.

The EGRET Process Model

Building upon experiences with exploratory software development and other process models, [3,5,15,16], EGRET implements a new process model for collaboration called Ex-Con (for "exploration and consolidation.")

Ex-Con models collaboration as a cyclical process of individual experimentation and divergence from established group norms, followed by a period of consolidation, where the differing experiences of individuals are reviewed and collective, integrative action is taken. The resulting consensual structures and policies form a platform for a new phase of individual experimentation.

In the EGRET data model, schemas represent these consensually agreed upon group norms for the structure of artifacts. In order to support experimentation, the EGRET data model allows individuals to modify the structure of individual instances, and to create whole populations of instances with deviant structures via instance cloning. Fortunately, since the group consensus is explicitly represented by schemas, EGRET can provide analysis mechanisms to help the group (a) determine when consolidation activities should take place; and (b) what form of consolidation might be appropriate.

The Ex-Con model consists of three basic states, or phases of collaborative activity, called the Consensual, Exploration, and Consolidation States.

The Consensual State.
Collaboration begins with some form of consensual (or near consensual) collaborative structure. For the currently active layer, this means that node and link instances are structurally consistent with their schemas.

The Exploration State
Collaboration proceeds, during which time individual members may modify individual instances by addition or subtraction of fields, and replication of these altered instances occurs via cloning rather than via schema instantiation. For example, a C++ programmer may populate the database with dozens of node instances that illustrate her choice of instance-level structure in a variety of contexts. A CLOS programmer might do the same. Metrics are used to monitor the level structural inconsistency in the collaborative database. When indicated by these metrics (perhaps in concert with other domain-specific activities), a period of consolidation begins.

The Consolidation State
Consolidation begins by determining the differences between the consensual schema structures and their associated instances. EGRET provides a summarization function that generates a list of each schema and the number and type of instance deviations in terms of the set of fields. Depending upon the nature of these differences, one or a combination of the following activities may occur:

- Instances are modified into structural conformance with their schemas.
- Schemas are modified into structural conformance with their instances.
- A new active layer is created, and selected EGRET entities are migrated into it.

The first two activities typically occur when differences between the schema and instance structure are relatively minor. For example, in the case of the Attribute schema in Figure 3, consolidation might occur by adding the Set-Operation field to the Attribute schema, implicitly bringing many instances into structural conformance. The remaining instances containing the Setf-able field would be brought into conformance by replacing that field with a Set-Operation field and a link.

Consider, however, a situation in which consolidation activities lead to a major restructuring, in which entire sets of instances and their associated schema will no longer be a part of the new organizational strutcure.

While such entities are inconsistent with the newly defined consensual schema structures, it would be wasted effort to bring them into conformance, since they are no longer relevent to the process. On the other hand, they might be important for design rationale purposes, in that they document an alternative that was explored but not chosen.

EGRET supports this situation by allowing developers to create a new active layer and then "migrate" the appropriate structures and instances to it. Migration occurs in two ways, depending upon whether the schema or instance is migrated with modifications or without modification. When migrated without modification, the schema or instance retains membership in the old layer while acquiring membership in the new layer. When migrated with modification, the prior version of the schema or instance is retained within the old schema, and a new version of the schema or instance is created in the new schema.

The result of consolidation processes is to move the collaborative database back into a consensual state, from which point new exploratory forays can take place.

Support Tools for the Ex-Con Process Model

In order to support effective transition between exploration and consolidation states, EGRET currently provides relatively simple analysis tools for assessment of structural inconsistency in the system. Two of these tools compute metrics called *Schema Divergence* and *Instance Convergence.*

Schema Divergence
Schema Divergence provides a quantitative measure of the degree of structural inconsistency between a schema and its instances. The Schema Divergence metric for a single schema S is a function of the structural difference of S with each of its instances. The structural difference of a schema with an instance is, in the simplest case, simply the sum of number of fields that appear in the schema but not the instance, or vice versa. Aggregating all the individual measures of schema divergence provides a measure for the collaborative database as a whole.

A low Schema Divergence value for S indicates that most of its instances are structurally conforming. In addition, if various group members have created instances of this structure, then S may represent a consensual structure. If most or all of the instances have been created by a single group member, then less can be inferred about the consensuality of S.

A high Schema Divergence value for S indicates structural inconsistency, but this metric alone does not aid in choosing among any of several potential resolutions: (a) Change S to better reflect its instances' structure; (b) Change S's instances into better structural conformance with S; (c) Change both both instance and schema structure toward a common "middle" ground; or (d) migrate the instances, since they have evolved into better conformance with some other schema S'.

Instance Convergence
Instance Convergence provides a quantitative measure of any instance-level structural clustering differing from the clustering that naturally occurs around their schema's structure. The goal of this metric is to identify instances

that should be migrated to another schema, or sets of instances with a common structure that should be elevated to the schema level.

The Instance Convergence metric for an instance **I** is zero if the instance conforms to its schema structure, and is otherwise the number of other instances with an identical field-level structure.

A low Instance Convergence metric indicates that **I** either conforms to its schema, or else **I** is an "oddball" instance with little conformance to other instances (even instances of other schemas).

A high Instance Convergence metric indicates that **I** conforms to a number of other instances structurally, but does not conform to its own schema structure. There are two fundamental ways this can occur. First, the instance might conform to a different schema structure (with a number of conforming instances—this indicates the instance might require retyping. Second, the instance might conform to other instances of its own type that all diverge in the same way. This may indicate the need to modify the schema into greater conformance, or alternatively, to create a new schema with a structure conforming to these instances, and retype the instances appropriately. This second alternative is especially justified when the instances were created by different members of the group, indicating some consensus on their validity and utility.

Parameterizing the Metrics

The Instance Convergence and Schema Divergence can be parameterized in two important ways. The first way is by allowing ``mismatches"—for the Schema Divergence metric, this means allowing a certain amount of divergence between schema and instance before returning a non-zero value. For Instance Convergence, this means reporting a match between two instances even when their field structure differs by a specified amount. Such coarsening of the metrics can help smooth out temporary anomolies in the database structure.

The metrics can also be parameterized to operate only within a certain set of layers. This provides a crucial feature in exploratory databases, where large numbers of inconsistent instances may be temporarily created but not found to be ultimately useful. As noted before, while these instances have value as an audit trail of the design alternatives, they can also artificially inflate the Schema Divergence metrics. By relegating these instances to an inactive layer and parameterizing the metric computations to only currently active layers, this problem can be avoided. Figure 4 illustrates this issue.

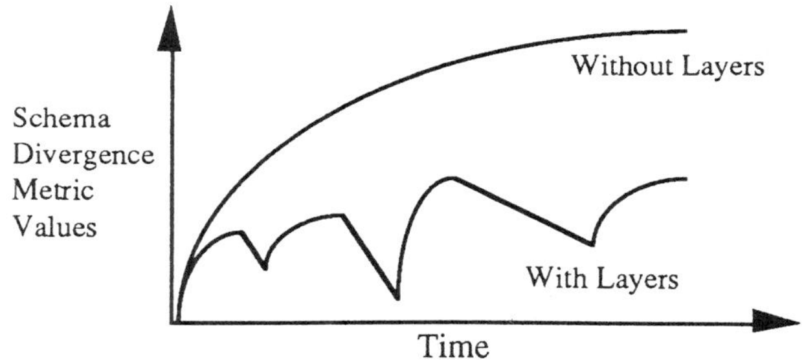

Figure 4. Trends for the aggregate schema divergence metric with and without layer parameterization.

RELATED WORK

While there is a great deal of research on appropriate data models for hypertext and hypermedia systems[2], we know of no other work with EGRET's explicit focus on collaborative structural evolution. For example, other data modelling approaches explore the isomorphism between graphs and hypertext networks [2,20], user interface issues [1], or the application of formalisms such as Petri nets [19].

Support for collaboration in traditional databases and hypertext systems typically involves traditional concurrency control, transaction management, and versioning facilities. EGRET simply "passes on" these facilities from its underlying database server mechanism to the user. The contexts mechanism [7] for providing logical workspaces comes close to our concerns, yet these workspaces do not allow *structural* exploration of the form supported in EGRET.

There has been some work on extensible CSCW systems, for example [14,17]. However, these systems do not attempt explicit data and process model support for representational exploration and change: in an important sense, the extensibility occurs *outside* of the system.

The Object Lens system [11] allows different sites build first class, yet inconsistent schema-level structures. To support communication between sites, mappings must be defined that transform instances of one structure at one site into their analogous form at other sites. Object Lens is the only collaborative system we know of involving research on divergent structural elements.

EGRET, however, takes an architectural and process-level stand against the approach taken in Object Lens. In EGRET, structural diversity (within instances of the same types) is supported, but parallel versions of the same schema-level structure are explicitly disallowed. Stated more prosaicly, EGRET does not allow collaborators to "agree not to agree". Instead, while permitting temporary discord, the data and process model of EGRET tend to coerce progress toward consensual structures.

[2]See [6] for a survey.

Research in database systems is quite active in the area of schema evolution [4,12,18]. However, schema evolution research in database systems is oriented toward definition of truth-preserving schema transformation rules that support automated updating of instances. In other words, the goal of this research is to avoid the inconsistency between schema-level and instance-level structure that EGRET embraces. This paradigmatic disagreement can be resolved by noting the difference between exploratory domains and the domains well supported by traditional databases. In the former, the essential activity is defining what the task is, who the participants are, and how to achieve concensus on the structure and process for accomplishing the activity. In the latter, these activities are assumed to have already been resolved, and the emphasis is on efficiency, reliability, and completeness in large-scale databases. Like exploratory activities in general at this point in time, EGRET will not scale well to hundreds of workers manipulating millions of artifacts.

Finally, support for the philosophy behind EGRET can be inferred from a critical analysis of group support systems [22]. This research argues that a fundamental problem with such systems is their emphasis on the downstream activities of judgement and choice, rather than the upstream activities of sensemaking, which is characterized as:

> *... the effort to construct moderately consensual definitions which cohere long enough that people are able to infer some idea of what they have, what they want, why they can't get it, and why it may not be worth getting in the first place.*

We view sensemaking as fundamentally exploratory, and so hope that EGRET could find application to this problem.

STATUS AND FUTURE DIRECTIONS

An alpha-level prototype of EGRET was implemented in the Fall of 1991 using Unix, X windows, Epoch [13], and the HyperBase database server [23]. Much of the user interface-level features of EGRET, such as multiple fonts, colors, and windows; read-only regions; multi-user support via client-server processing across ethernet; locking; and so forth are provided by this palette of platforms.

While the alpha-level prototype was actively used by the EGRET development team (in fact, the code review scenario used in this paper is directly adapted from actual experiences in our group), it proved too brittle for external release. We have now re-implemented EGRET with improved functionality, reliability, and portability to different database and user interface platforms. On top of this framework, domain-specific collaborative systems for research review [21] and software inspection [9] are under construction.

Our experiences with EGRET suggest several promising future directions. First, EGRET represents the structural history of an entity. This representation could provide useful answers such rationale-related questions as: How did an entity evolve into its current form? What intermediate structures did it go through? How long has it been in its current form? What other evolution co-occurred?

Second, we are interested in combining the EGRET paradigm with more traditional database evolution paradigms. We believe that metrics similar to those for divergence and convergence can serve as a front-end to more formal methods for database re-organization—the EGRET mechanisms identifying what to reorganize, and the database re-structuring methods defining how to carry out this reorganization.

Finally, one result of our twin design goals of extensibility and efficiency has been the design of EGRET *agents*: event-triggered autonomous processes with full access to the contents and structure of the hypertext database that perform simple housekeeping functions. We believe that the EGRET architecture forms an excellent platform for the implementation of more sophisticated agents, and are excited at the prospect of using EGRET to explore coordination among human and non-human agents in semi-structured environments.

ACKNOWLEDGMENTS

The author would like to acknowledge the contributions of Dadong Wan, Danu Tjahjono, Frenky Palit, Kiran Kavoori, and Carol Ezaki to the design and implementation of the EGRET framework. Support for this research was provided in part by the National Science Foundation Research Initiation Award CCR-9110861 and the University of Hawaii Research Council Seed Money Award R-91-867-F-728-B-270.

REFERENCES

1. R. M. Akscyn, D. L. McCracken, and E. A. Yoder. KMS: A distributed hypermedia system. *Communications of the* ACM, 31(7), July 1988.

2. M. Anderegg, B. Elledge, J. Harford, D. Shackeleford, and O. Toki. *User's Manual for Attributed Graph Server*. Department of Computer Science, University of North Calrolina, 1990.

3. R. Balzer. Tolerating inconsistency, in *Proc. of the 13th International Conferenece on Software Engineering,* 1991.

4. Jay Banerjee, Won Kim, Hyoung-Joo Kim, and Henry Korth. Semantics and implementation of schema evolution in object-oriented databases, in *Proc. of the* ACM SIGMOD *1987 Annual Conference,* 1987.

5. B. Boehm. A spiral model of sofware develepement. IEEE *Computer,* 21(5), May 1988.

6. Joan Boon. A survey of data models for hypermedia. Technical Report TR-91-022, The University of

North Carolina, Department of Computer Science, 1991.

7. N. Delisle and M. Schwartz. Contexts---a partioning concept for hypertext. ACM *Transactions on Office Information Systems*, 1987.

8. R. V. Giddings. Accomodating uncertainty in software design. *Communications of the* ACM, 27(5):428--434, 1984.

9. Philip Johnson. Collaborative software review for capturing design rationale. In *Proceedings of the AAAI 1992 Workshop on Design Rationale*, July 1992.

10. Philip Johnson, Dadong Wan, and Danu Tjahjono. EGRET Design Specification: EGRET Version 2.0. CSDL Technical Report 91-02, University of Hawaii Department of Information and Computer Sciences, July 1992.

11. Jintae Lee and Thomas W. Malone. Partially shared views: a scheme for communicating among groups that use different type hierarchies. *ACM Transactions on Information Systems*, 8(1):1-26, 1990.

12. Barbara Staudt Lerner and A. Nico Habermann. Beyond schema evolution to database reorganization. In *Proceedings of the 1990 Conferance on Object-Oriented Prgramming: Systems, Languages, and Applications*, 1990.

13. Chris Love, Alan Carroll, Simon Kaplan, and Dan LaLiberte. Epoch 4.0 manual. Technical report, University of Illinois, 1992.

14. Wendy E. Mackay. Patterns of sharing customizable software. In *Proceedings of ACM CSCW'90 Conference on Computer-Supported Cooperaative Work*, pages 209--221, 1990.

15. D. Partridge. Engineering artificial intelligence software. *Arificial Intelligence Review*, 1(1):27--41, 1986.

16. B. Sheil. Power tools for programers. In D. R. Barstow, H. E. Shrobe, and E. Sandewall, editors, *Interactive Programming Environments*. McGraw Hill, Inc., 1984.

17. Allan Shepherd, Niels Mayer, and Allan Kuchinsky. Strudel - an extensible electronic conversation toolkit. In *Proceedings of ACM CSCW'90 Conference on Computer-Supported Cooperaative Work*, pages 93--104, 1990.

18. Andrea Skarra and Stanley Zdonik. The management of changing types in an object-oriented database. In *Proceedings of the 1986 Conference on Object Oriented Programming: Systems, Lanuages, and Applications*, 1986.

19. P. Stoots and R. Furata. Petri-net-based hypertext: Document structure with browsing semantics. ACM *Transactions on Information Systems*, 1989.

20. F. Tompa. A data model for flexible hypertext database systems. ACM *Transactions on Information Systems*, 1989.

21. Dadong Wan and Philip Johnson. Supporting scientific learning and research review using CORVIEW. In *Proceedings of the 1992 AAAI Workshop on Communicating Scientific and Technical Knowledge*, July 1992.

22. Karl Weick and David Meader. Sensemaking and group support systems. In L. Jessup and J. Valacich, editors, *Group Support Systems*. MacMillan Publishers, 1991.

23. U. Will and K. Osterbye. Experiences with hyperbase--a multi-user back-end for hypertext applications with emphasis on collaboration support. Technical Reprt 90-38, Department of Matematics and Computer Science, University of Aalborg, Denmark., 1990.

Sharing Perspectives in Distributed Decision Making

Richard J. Boland, Jr.
Anil K. Maheshwari
Dov Te'eni

Weatherhead School of Management
Department.of Management Information and Decision Systems
Case Western Reserve University
Cleveland, Ohio 44106-7235
boland@spider.cwru.edu

David G. Schwartz

Department of Computer Engineering & Science and Center for Automation & Intelligent Systems Research
Case Western Reserve University
Cleveland, Ohio 44106-7071

Ramkrishnan V. Tenkasi

Weatherhead School of Management
Department of Organization Behavior
Case Western Reserve University
Cleveland, Ohio 44106-7235

ABSTRACT

Complex organizations are characterized by distributed decision making, and require a sharing of perspectives among distributed decision makers if they are to coordinate activity and adapt to changing circumstances. This paper explains the process of perspective taking and its roles in human communication, mutual trust, and organizational learning. SPIDER is a software environment for enriching communication among managers by improving their ability to represent and exchange understandings of the situations they face. Cognitive maps linked to underlying assumptions are used as a basis for sharing their perspectives and enabling coordination of distributed decision making.

KEYWORDS

Distributed decision making, perspective taking, organizational learning, mutual trust, cognitive maps.

INTRODUCTION

Complex organizations are composed of many diverse, interdependent work groups such as product development teams, manufacturing planning, and marketing which all have unique decision domains. Managers act autonomously within their domains, yet they are affected by each others' actions. We are designing computer support for the coordination of decision making in this type of complex organization, and ultimately, the support of organizational learning. We are not concerned with highly bureaucratic organizations which presume a stable task, technology and environment, and which control themselves through strict adherence to standard operating procedures. Instead, we are concerned with the kind of less hierarchical, more network-like organization that is able to cope with changing tasks, technologies, and environments - what is called a *learning organization* or an *organization of the future* [20, 25, 39].

Permission to copy without fee all or part of this material is granted provided that the copies are not made or distributed for direct commercial advantage, the ACM copyright notice and the title of the publication and its date appear, and notice is given that copying is by permission of the Association for Computing Machinery. To copy otherwise, or to republish, requires a fee and/or specific permission.

© 1992 ACM 0-89791-543-7/92/0010/0306...$1.50

Decentralized organizations with differentiated sub units require mechanisms of integration. Organization sub units develop unique perspectives in response to the different tasks, goals and environments they face, and these different perspectives reveal ambiguity, paradox and conflict [32]. Integration is not achieved by a simple summation of different perspectives, but is instead found through dialogue in which conflicts are recognized and discussed. Lawrence and Lorsch [23] identify many of the ways that integration can be achieved, and they all ideally involve a sharing of perspectives among the differentiated sub units. Organizational arrangements such as liaisons, ad hoc problem solving teams and matrix structures are typical approaches to achieving integration among differentiated units, and each hopes to encourage the diverse perspectives within an organization to be surfaced and discussed more openly.

This paper explores some of the issues involved in sharing perspectives among actors in a complex organization, and describes SPIDER, a software tool we are developing to enable perspective sharing. SPIDER is a software environment for enriching communication by improving each manager's ability to represent an understanding of the situation he or she faces, and exchange it with others. We are working with business unit planners of a large manufacturing company, who will use SPIDER to exchange and critique their perspectives of the market they face in order to better understand both the market place and their interdependencies.

DISTRIBUTED DECISION MAKING

Much effort in computer supported cooperative work is oriented toward the phenomenon of a group decision [14, 24, 13, 31]. A group decision is made by a set of actors who work together to achieve a common purpose in a very immediate and concrete way. There is typically a single, identifiable outcome from the group process: a paper is written, a diagnosis is agreed upon, a budget is allocated, or a policy is set.

In contrast to groups, decentralized organizations are composed of multiple autonomous actors in a distributed decision environment. Brehmer distinguishes distributed decision making from a group decision process in that the former concerns a situation "too complex for one person to understand in its entirety" [4, p. 3]. Agents in a distributed decision making setting "have limited models of the problem as a whole, and...may never achieve a global understanding of the problem" [4, p. 3].

Distributed decision making involves a set of actors who are autonomous within their sphere of concern, and who act independently based upon their own understanding of the situation they confront, but who recognize that they have interdependencies among themselves. Coordination in a distributed decision setting is more likely to emerge when the autonomous agents are able to take their interdependencies into account in deciding on their independent actions. This requires a sharing of their different perspectives among themselves, in a process of *perspective taking.*

PERSPECTIVES

Much of social behavior is predicated upon assumptions an actor makes about the knowledge, beliefs, and motives of others. This process of perspective taking, is fundamental: in any communication, the knowing of what others know is a necessary component [3, 6, 22]. As Brown [5] observed, effective communicating requires that the point of view of the other be realistically imagined. Others such as Rommetveit have affirmed this point; "An essential component of communicative competence in a pluralistic social world...is our capacity to adopt the perspectives of different *others*" [33, p. 126].

The fundamental importance of taking the other's point of view into account is seen in Mead [27] who referred to it as *taking the attitude of the other* and equated our ability to be fully human with our ability to maintain an inner conversation with a *generalized other*. Messages are formulated to be understood by a specific audience, and in order to be comprehensible they must take into account what that audience does and does not know, such as their knowledge, beliefs, preferences, suppositions and the like.

Coordinated behavior of most kinds, including bargaining and similar structured interactions, requires that participants plan their own moves in anticipation of what their partner's motives are likely to be [9]. Festinger's [12] social comparison theory postulates that people evaluate their own abilities and beliefs by comparing them with how they assume abilities and beliefs are distributed in their reference population. Predicting the other's moves requires extensive assumptions about what the other knows, wants, or believes, which is the process of perspective taking.

THE PERSPECTIVE TAKING PROCESS

It has been argued that assumptions about what others know (and hence what is mutually known) are necessarily tentative and probabilistic. Because these assumptions are based on a variety of sources of information that will vary in credibility and relevance, perspective taking at any point in time can be viewed as tentative hypotheses that participants continuously modify and reformulate on the basis of additional evidence [27]. Each communicator acts in response to the hypotheses she has constructed through perspective taking, and revises them based on the outcomes.

Although many conceptualizations of the communication process assert the centrality of perspective taking as the basis for taking each other's knowledge and background into account, there has been surprisingly little discussion of the process by which this might be accomplished [27].

Clark and Marshall [7] describe several heuristics that speakers and listeners might use to establish their *mutual knowledge* or the common ground of knowledge that they share, and know that they share. One such heuristic is the linguistic co-presence heuristic, in which, anything said at time T during the course of a conversation can be mutually assumed to be known at time T+1. However, others have argued that the reasoning communicators employ to assess what they and their co-participants mutually know is much more complex than such simple heuristics suggest [27]. But even with this simple heuristic there is a deep underlying problem, since the thing said at time T is a string of words, and what is assumed to be mutually held at time T+1 is the meaning of that string, which may differ radically between communicators. This is the fundamental distinction between a signal which, by convention, indicates a specified action or object, and a symbol, which always carries a surplus of metaphorical referent and possible meanings [18].

The task of assessing the knowledge held in common by members of a community, such as managers in an organization, is a complex one, and involves a variety of inferential and judgmental processes. Individuals may utilize a variety of knowledge structures, such as schemata, stereotypes, and inference heuristics to estimate what others know. Such structures can facilitate the task of drawing inferences, but they also can induce systematic errors and biases [21, 30]. For example, an actor may use the *availability heuristic* to assess what others know. The ready availability of his own perspective may lead him to overestimate the likelihood that the perspective will be shared by others. This *false consensus* effect, in which subjects assume that others are more similar to themselves than is actually the case [34], is a form of bias particularly relevant to the perspective taking process.

Steedman and Johnson-Laird have proposed that "the speaker assumes that the hearer knows everything that the speaker knows about the world and about the conversation, unless there is some evidence to the contrary" [40 p. 129]. This heuristic should lead to overestimates of the extent to which a speaker's knowledge is shared by others, and studies support the existence of such a bias [10, 27].

SPIDER, the software system we are developing, is designed to facilitate the perspective taking process by enabling actors to depict their understanding of a situation and exchange it with others. SPIDER enables each actor to build a cognitive map of the factors that influence his sphere of concern, and to link each factor to the documents (text, spreadsheets, graphs) that provide its background assumptions. A cognitive map is a directed graph whose nodes represent concepts or factors in the actor's decision domain, and whose arcs represent cause-effect relationships between source and destination nodes. Thus, SPIDER is a tool for portraying an actor's view of the situation with multiple layers of context so that others may better know what that decision maker knows when communication takes place.

Weick and Bougon [43] suggest that building a cognitive map can be evocative for the map creator, as well as informative to its recipient. The effectiveness of the cognitive mapping model is well documented and appears in the literature under a variety of names, including cause maps, influence diagrams, and belief nets. Creating cognitive maps can reveal personal cause and effect logic, which in turn forces the individual to confront the reasonableness and validity of previously tacit cause-effect assumptions. A cognitive map provides an occasion to think carefully, deeply and deliberately about a situation. Knowledge of a cause map gives knowledge about an organization. As Weick and Bougon put it: "The important thing to remember about a cause map is that it is the organization... The cause map contains the structure, the process, and the raw materials from which agreements and conflicts are built when people coordinate action" [43, p. 132]

The uses of cognitive maps are quite diverse, beginning with Axelrod [2] using cognitive mapping as a tool for understanding political decision making, and extending to Cropper, Eden and Ackerman [8] applying computer-based cognitive maps to examine and compare conflicting accounts of an event. Cognitive maps have been encoded into matrices to allow quantitative analysis of a decision maker's logic [41]. Uses such as information requirements analysis [28], knowledge engineering and expert knowledge analysis [29, 36], and medical technology assessment [38] provide further evidence of the representational adequacy of the cognitive map. Our work addresses the use of the cognitive map as a graphic representation tool to aid in the communication of understandings among decision makers.

ORGANIZATIONAL LEARNING

Work in organizations is profoundly social [26]. This is particularly true for that subset of work in organizations that is of interest to developmental efforts in computer supported cooperative work [35]. Distributed decision making, as a type of social interaction, will be effective to the extent that it is a social process of learning. In this process of learning, individuals first engage in a dialogue with their own representations, to help them self-reflect about their situation, developing improved understandings of it and of their role in effecting it. They also engage in dialogues with others in order to improve their self understandings, discover how others understand the situation, and understand how they interdepend in a larger organizational sense.

Our view of the process of learning in distributed decision making derives from the work of Argyris and Schon [1]. They characterize the behaviors-in-use by most managers as self-sealing and inhibitive to learning. Most managers, they observe, develop patterns of interaction with others that try to keep themselves in control, try to impose their will on others, and try to 'win' at the expense of others. As a result, valid data is not produced, assumptions are not tested, and important feelings and preferences are suppressed. They label this interaction pattern as model 1 behavior.

They propose their model 2 as an alternative set of behaviors, that is more likely to result in mutually beneficial learning. In model 2 behaviors, each manager is recognized as an origin of valid knowledge, inquiry is seen as jointly produced through open interaction, and decisions are the result of free, informed choice by each individual. The availability of valid data is the key difference between model 1 and model 2 behavior patterns. In model 1, managers communicate inferences without explicit reference to the particular incident(s) or facts which have led them to that conclusion. They also make inquiries of others without revealing their background understanding and ultimate intention. In both giving and receiving messages, therefore, managers instigate a chain reaction of withholding relevant data, failing to open themselves to being questioned, and inhibiting the possibility for learning.

Model 2 behavior, by contrast, emphasizes that inferences are always communicated along with the concrete incident(s) or particular facts on which they are based, and that inquiries of others are always accompanied by a statement of background understandings and preferences so that the intention of the inquiry can be more accurately apprehended and responded to. Overlaying the enriched contextual information that model 2 behavior includes in each interaction is an attitude of hypothesis testing and an openness to a challenge of the data, assumptions or interpretations that have led to a particular conclusion. Model 2 behavior, therefore, begins to resemble the type of learning process we associate with a scientific community. But instead of studying nature with a stance of objectivity, the managers are studying their organization and its environment with an explicit awareness of their own role as agents who transform both the organization and its environment through their actions. Conflict among perspectives leads to degenerative, self-sealing behavior under model 1, but leads to constructive problem resolution under model 2.

SPIDER, as a perspective sharing software, is designed to provide many of the features enabling a model 2 behavior pattern to emerge in an organization. First, unlike a group decision tool which might emphasize the construction of a single, common representation to be shared by all members of the group, SPIDER is designed so that each distributed decision maker is expected to have a representation of their own perspective. Each representation has an *owner* and only the owner can make changes to it. Other members of the distributed decision making set can mail reactions, questions or suggestions to the owner of a representation, but they may not unilaterally modify it.

Second, and following from the principle of ownership, it is expected that there will be a multiplicity of representations, each being a hypothesis, open for refinement through dialogue. Thus, SPIDER creates an environment of multiple, competing hypotheses and because each hypothesis represents the perspective of an autonomous sphere of concern, there is no expectation that they must be collapsed into a single, universal view. Conflicts, contradictions and paradoxes among perspectives are to be expected.

Third, the links in a representation are explicit recognition of the underlying assumptions, background facts, or prior beliefs that serve as the context for a decision maker's position. Following a link in a representation is a movement into the context of a factor in a cognitive map, or the numbers in a spreadsheet row.

Finally, it should be remembered that a SPIDER representation, unlike a report that may be filed and forgotten, is a live document that an author continues to work on over time. As long as a distributed decision maker is engaged in acting in a certain decision domain, the representation he or she makes is actively being updated, discussed and tested against emerging conditions. A decision, which would be the end point of a typical group support system, merely punctuates the process of developing a SPIDER representation. It is an occasion for reappraisal, refinement and further dialogue; the beginning of learning, not the end of it.

BUILDING MUTUAL TRUST

Trust is implied whenever two persons interact in any way. Trust enters our personal lives and our working lives. We trust others not to harm us, or else we would be paranoid, and we trust others to adhere to agreements and contracts, or else we would not be able to plan and conduct business. We believe that SPIDER has important implications for building mutual trust in a distributed decision setting through the revelation of formerly private or tacit understandings.

Trust is generated by and in turn leads to open, reciprocal communication. We argue that SPIDER, as an enabling tool for richer communication among distributed decision makers, can contribute to developing mutual trust. Beginning with a given, minimum level of trust and openness, SPIDER enables an increased realization of interdependence through perspective taking, associated with new possibilities for coordination of independent action and a resulting increase in trust and subsequent openness [17].

Trust is built slowly through repeated cycles of interaction. Trust increases vulnerability to loss, be it loss of reputation or money [17, 46]. So people economize on trust, and trust only when needed, to keep risks within acceptable limits [15]. Goffman [19], using a dramaturgical approach to everyday life, highlights that we act out roles in social situations. These roles are based on a cumulative set of shared expectations and understandings among social actors. These shared understanding are created and refined over repeated interactions. Every such interaction reinforces our trust in others. Trust, in the form of shared expectations and understanding, enables social interactions, and new social interactions produce more trust [47]. Trust therefore stands in a reflexive, reciprocal relationship with social interaction. 'Abnormal' behavior, where an actor appears ignorant of this shared context of expectations and understandings, leads to a breakdown in social communication [16].

Trust is manifest when a person is self-revealing without fear of being misinterpreted [17]. The motivation to trust is affected by the context of the situation where one has to make a decision to trust or not [44]. By supporting an environment conducive to model 2 behavior, we anticipate SPIDER will increase levels of trust among distributed decision makers. In our evaluation of SPIDER, we will explore its impacts on both the improved coordination of distributed decision making, and the increased levels of trust and openness among managers.

REPRESENTING AN UNDERSTANDING OF A SITUATION

The key to a robust communications environment is recognizing the tentative nature of the communicative hypotheses framing managerial dialogue. The impromptu, ad hoc nature of the understandings the decision makers wish to represent, requires flexibility in both the representational structures made available, and in the ways these structures can be created, shared, and modified. In creating an environment to foster richness of communication through the sharing of perspectives, there are two primary representational issues to be addressed: 1. What are the structures to be used in the formation of a perspective? 2. In what ways and through which tools should users be able to present their perspective for their own introspection and for the use of others?

Multimedia integrated document tools are beginning to proliferate, however we do not see these tools as appropriate for our task. Most of these applications focus on a text-based document that is enhanced through the inclusion of a picture, graph, table and even voice and video. Although appropriate for the creation of formal reports, documentation, and presentations, they do little to promote the communication of the fundamental underlying thoughts and concerns of the creator of the document. Even the expressive power of voice and video cannot be harnessed for the analysis and refinement of a decision rationale. Other more structured decision aid systems, such as Stella II, Sibyl [24] or Ibis [45], provide powerful representational tools but orient the user to a mathematical modelling paradigm that is neither conducive to flexible, impromptu thinking, nor amenable to the rich communication between colleagues that we seek. To support a rich and flexible form of communication, SPIDER allows an actor to easily build and modify a layered understanding of the situation he or she faces.

COGNITIVE MAPS, SPREADSHEETS AND NOTES LINKED AS A PERSPECTIVE

Understandings of a situation are developed in a linked set of documents that we refer to as a representation. A representation consists of cognitive maps, spreadsheets of supporting numeric data, and textual notes, linked as a multi-layered depiction of a complex understanding. Cognitive maps are structured representations of an understanding which can be depicted as a visual graph, or in any number of graph theoretic representations such as an adjacency matrix. We choose the former for human-computer interaction, and the latter for computer-intensive analysis. Arcs are labeled: + to indicate that a positive change in the evaluation of the source concept causes a positive change in the evaluation of the destination concept; or - to indicate that a positive change in the source node has a negative influence on the destination node. The extent and nature of the effect of one node on another is subjective and must be defined for each individual concept/node.

We begin by placing a cognitive map as the focal point of our representation, this being a guideline rather than a restriction. A graphically depicted cognitive map, consisting of factors and their causal relationships is drawn by a decision maker, using an interactive drawing tool developed specifically for cognitive mapping (see [42] for a more detailed description of the system). Each factor, or the map as a whole, can be linked to other maps, spreadsheets of supporting data, descriptive notes, or any combination of the above. Links are recursive in that a note can be linked to another note, map, spreadsheet, etc. It is these spreadsheets and notes that provide the background, explanation, and elaboration of the understanding of causal relations shown in an accompanying cognitive map.

The framework is both structured and fluid. The structure provided by a cognitive mapping framework as opposed to a general drawing tool, serves to focus the user on expressing the key factors in his or her model. The fluidity provided by the links to and from spreadsheets, notes, and other cognitive maps give rise to an ever changing picture of a decision scenario. What is seen by the reader of such a scenario depends on the perspective from which the web of documents is viewed. A document created with a cognitive map at its center, two supporting spreadsheets and a note, may be entered and viewed entirely from the spreadsheet rather than the originating map. This allows a quick shift of perspective from the overall decision rationale, as pictured by the cognitive map, to some important numeric details, as presented in the spreadsheet.

The links give rise to a web of ideas, assumptions, data, and supporting arguments, each appearing in the form most conducive to its clear expression, and assembled as layers of context easily reached by following the links. An example can be seen in figure 1.

COMMUNICATING RATIONALES

Manipulating an understanding of a situation to reveal the unique perspectives of the decision rationale being employed at a particular moment in time is of primary importance. Richness of information is found in the use, manipulation, and structure of information and not just in its quantity [37]. A manager's representation, including one or more documents, can be mailed to other managers who are system users. Such a mailing can include the complete representation or a subset of the documents in a representation along with their links.

To provide an overview of a potentially complex web of document links, we use a SPIDER *roadmap*. This roadmap gives a global perspective of the entire representation and allows the user to navigate through the document space. A roadmap is comprised of a set of labelled icons (one for each document in the representation) connected by lines (one for each document linkage) in a network-like diagram. Shifting from the global perspective to a local, or document-focused perspective is accomplished by selecting one of the documents from the roadmap, making it the current focus of attention.

ANALYZING A REPRESENTATION

The analysis of a representation by its author and readers is made possible by shifting perspectives in three levels of abstraction. 1. A global perspective is provided by the roadmap as described above. 2. At the document level, a user can display one or more documents at the same time to examine similar cognitive maps, understand a factor relationship in light of a descriptive note, or question the data underlying a relationship. 3. Within a cognitive map document, levels of detail can be hidden or revealed by applying special functions to portions of a displayed map. This quick shift of focus allows the user to concentrate on the currently relevant aspect of the representation.

Our future development plans include the use of graph theoretic techniques to automate the analysis of different cognitive maps, drawing on previous work mentioned above [8, 4, 1], as well as enhanced visual tools to depict characteristics such as preferences of outcome and action in a more robust cognitive representation [42].

CONCLUSION

Viewing distributed decision making as conflicting yet interdependent activities has helped identify the key issues of creating and sharing perspectives. The dynamic nature of these perspectives in a learning organization indicates the

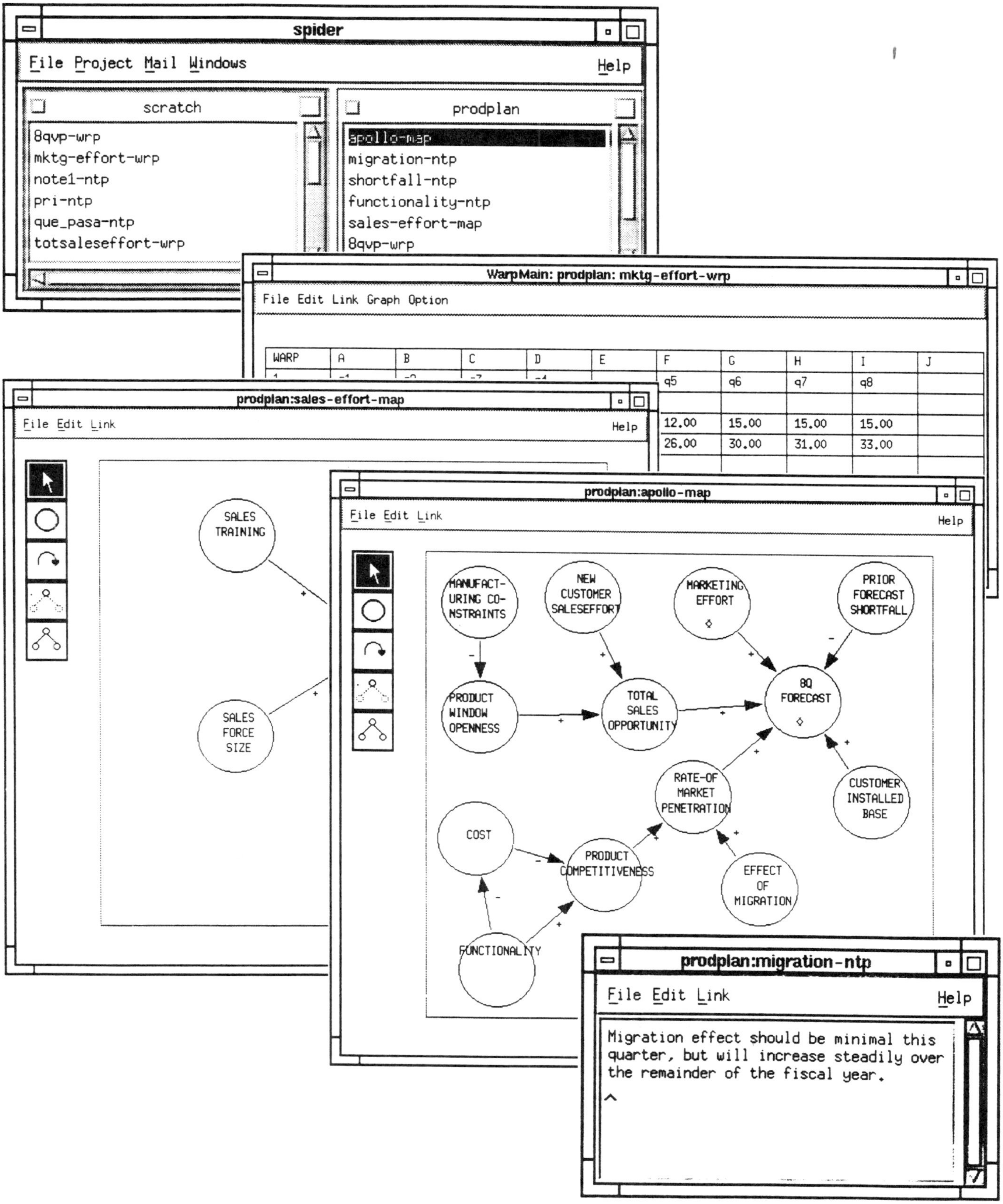

Figure 1. A sample screen from SPIDER showing multiple documents of a representation

importance of tools to support their development and exchange. Concrete results of such an effort will be seen in a deeper understanding, cooperation, and trust among decision makers. SPIDER and its underlying theory is a beginning in what we hope will be an extended effort to develop tools of self reflection and dialogue among managers in large, complex organizations. Environments such as SPIDER, through enriching perspective taking and communication offer a significant hope for moving beyond bureaucratic, procedural models of organizational control, and enabling the adaptive, learning types of organization structures needed for the future.

ACKNOWLEDGEMENTS

This research was funded by National Science Foundation Grant #9015526 and Digital Equipment Corporation External Research Grant #1111.

REFERENCES

1. Argyris, C., and Schon, D., *Organizational Learning*, Reading, MA: Addison-Wesley, 1978.

2. Axelrod, R., *Structure of Decision*, Princeton: Princeton University Press 1979.

3. Bakhtin, M.M., Discourse in the Novel, in M. Holquis (ed), *The Dialogic Imagination*, Austin, TX: University of Texas Press, 1981.

4. Brehmer, B., Distributed Decision Making: Some Notes on the Literature, in Rasmussen et al (ed), *Distributed Decision Making: Cognitive Models in Cooperative Work*, Blackwell, NY: John Wiley, 1991.

5. Brown, R., *Social Psychology*, New York: The Free Press, 1981

6. Clark, H.H., Language Use and Language Users, in G. Lindzey and E. Aronson (ed), *Handbook of Social Psychology*, New York: Random House, 1985.

7. Clark, H.H., and Marshall, C.E., Definite Reference and Mutual Knowledge, in A. Joshi, I. Sag and B. Webber (ed), *Elements of Discourse Understanding*, Cambridge: Cambridge University Press, 1981.

8. Cropper, S., Eden C., and Ackerman, F., Keeping Sense of Accounts Using Computer-Based Cognitive Maps, *Social Science Computer Review*, Vol. 8:3, pp. 345-367, Fall 1990.

9. Dawes, R.M., McTavish, J., and Shaklee, H., Behavior, Communication and Assumptions About Other People's Behavior in a Commons Dilemma Situation, *Journal of Personality and Social Psychology*, Vol. 35, pp. 1-11, 1977.

10. Dougherty, D., Interpretive barriers to successful product innovation in large firms, *Organization Science*, Vol. 3, pp. 179-202, 1992.

11. Eden, C., Jones, C., and Sims, D., *Thinking in Organizations* , Macmillan 1979.

12. Festinger, L., A Theory of Social Comparison Processes, *Human Relations*, Vol. 7, pp. 117-140, 1954.

13. Fulk, J., & Steinfeld, C.W., *Organizations and Communications Technology*, Newbury Park: Sage 1990.

14. Galegher, J., Kraut, R.E., & Egido, C., *Intellectual Teamwork: Social and Technological Foundations of Cooperative Work*, Hillsdale: Laurence Erlbaum 1990.

15. Gambetta, Diego, (ed.) *Trust: Making and Breaking Cooperative Relations*, New York: Basil Blackwell, 1988.

16. Garfinkel, H., A Conception of, and Experiments with, Trust as a Condition of Stable Concerted Actions, in O.J. Harvey (ed.) *Motivation and Social Interaction: Cognitive Determinants*, New York: Ronald Press, 1963.

17. Gibb., J.R., *Trust: A New View of Personal and Organizational Development*, California: Guild of Tutors Press, 1978

18. Giddens, A., *Central Problems in Social Theory*, Berkeley: University of California Press, 1979.

19. Goffman, E., *The Presentation of Self in Everyday Life*, Garden City, NY: Doubleday Anchor, 1959.

20. Huber, G.P., Organizational Learning: The Contributing Processes and the Literatures, *Organization Science* , 2, 1991, pp.88-115.

21. Kahneman, D., Slovic, P., and Tversky, A., *Judgement Under Uncertainty: Heuristics and Biases*, New York: Cambridge University Press, 1982.

22. Krauss, R.M., and Fussell, S. R., Perspective-Taking in Communication Representation of Others' Knowledge in Reference, *Social Cognition* Vol. 9 (1), p. 2-24, 1991.

23. Lawrence, P.R. and Lorsch, J.W., *Organization and Environment*, Cambridge, MA: Harvard University Press, 1967.

24. Lee, J., SIBYL, A Tool for Managing Group Design Rationals, in *Proceedings of the CSCW90*, Los Angeles, CA, 1990.

25. Malone, T. W., Yates, J., and Benjamin, R., Electronic Markets and Electronic Hierarchies, *Communications of the ACM* 30:6 1987, pp. 484-497.

26. March, J.G., and Simon, H.A., *Organizations*, New York: Wiley, 1958.

27. Mead, G.H., *Mind, Self and Society*, Chicago: University of Chicago Press, 1934.

28. Montazemi, A.R., and Conrath, D.W., The Use of Cognitive Mapping for Information Requirements Analysis, *MIS Quarterly*, pp. 45-53, March 1989.

29. Montazemi, A.R., and Chan, L., An Analysis of the Structure of Expert Knowledge, *European Journal of Operational Research*, Vol. 45, pp. 275-292, 1990.

30. Nisbett, R.E. and Ross, L.E., *Human Inference: Strategies and Shortcomings of Social Judgement*, Englewood Cliffs, NJ: Prentice-Hall, 1980.

31. Olson, M.H. (ed), *Technological Support for Work Group Collaboration*, Hillsdale, NJ: Laurence Erlbaum 1989.

32. Pondy, L.R., Boland, R.J., and Thomas, H., *Managing Ambiguity and Change*, John Wiley & sons, Chichester, 1987.

33. Rommetveit, R., On 'Meanings' of Acts and What is Meant By What is Said in a Pluralistic Social World, in M. Brenner (ed), *The Structure of Action*, Oxford: Blackwell and Mott, pp. 108-149, 1980.

34. Ross, L., Greene, D., and House, P., The False Consensus Phenomenon: An Attributional Bias in Self-Perception and Social Perception Processes, *Journal of Experimental Social Psychology*, Vol. 13, pp. 279-301, 1977.

35. Schmidt, K., Cooperative Work: A Conceptual Framework, in J. Rasmussen et. al (eds), *Distributed Decision Making: Cognitive Models in Cooperative Work*, Blackwell, NY: John Wiley, 1991.

36. Schwartz, D.G., Cognitive Mapping as a Knowledge Engineering Tool, *SPIE Conference on Applications of AI X:, Knowledge Based Systems*, Orlando, April 1992.

37. Sengupta, K. and Te'eni, D., Cognitive feedback in group decision support systems, *MIS Quarterly*, Forthcoming.

38. Shachter, R.D., Eddy, D.M., and Hasselblad, V., An Influence Diagram Approach to Medical Technology Assessment, in R.M. Oliver and J.Q. Smith (ed), *Influence Diagrams, Belief Nets and Decision Analysis*, pp. 321-350, John Wiley & Sons, 1990.

39. Simon, H.A., Bounded Rationality and Organizational Learning, *Organization Science*, 2, 1991, pp.125-139.

40. Steedman, M.J., and Johnson-Laird, P.N., The Productions of Sentences, Utterances and Speech Acts: Have Computers Anything to Say?, in B. Butterworth (ed), *Language Productions: Speech and Talk*, London: Academic Press, 1980.

41. Stubbart, C., and Ramaprasad, A., A Strategist's Cognitive Map of the Steel Industry: A case study of Mr. David Roderick (Chairman US Steel), Technical Report, University of Massachusetts, Department of Management, February 1987.

42. Te'eni, D., Schwartz, D. G., and Boland, R.J., Cognitive Maps for Communication: A Specification of Functionality and Usability, *Fourth Symposium on Human Factors in IS*, February 1992.

43. Weick, K. & Bougon, M.K., Organizations as Cognitive Maps: Charting Ways to Success and Failure in H.Sims & D.Goia (eds) *The Thinking Organization* San Francisco: Jossey-Bass, 1986.

44. Williams, B., Formal Structures and Social Reality" in Gambetta, Diego (ed) *Trust: Making and Breaking Cooperative Relations*, New York: Basil Blackwell, 1988.

45. Yakemovic, K.C.B., & E.J.Conklin, Report on a development project use of an issue-based information system in *Proceedings of CSCW'90 Conference* Los Angeles, 1990.

46. Zand, D., Trust and Managerial Problem-Solving, *Administrative Science Quarterly*, 1972.

47. Zucker, L.G., Production of Trust: Institutional Sources of Economic Structure, in Barry M. Staw and L.L. Cummings (eds.) *Research in Organizational Behavior*, Vol. 8, Greenwich, CT: JAI Press, 1986.

Distributed Facilitation: A Concept Whose Time Has Come?

Shelli Dubs

Alberta Research Council
6815 8th St. N.E.
Calgary, AB T2E 5Z6
(403) 297-7587 dubs@arcsun.arc.ab.ca

Stephen C. Hayne

Faculty of Management, MIS
University of Calgary
Calgary, AB T2N 1N4
(403)220-7161 schayne@acs.ucalgary.ca

ABSTRACT

Group facilitation is a dynamic process that involves managing relationships between people, tasks and technology, as well as structuring tasks and contributing to the effective accomplishment of the meetings outcomes. This is a difficult problem that becomes even more difficult as group work is geographically distributed. This paper provides a comprehensive framework, in the form of a meeting model, that defines the many activities that surround group work. We show that in existing systems support for facilitation is low and based on the level of facilitator control, we identify facilitation functions and suggest a rational for prioritizing them. With this in hand, we are designing and implementing a prototype facilitation system to support group activities in a distributed environment.

INTRODUCTION

Many, if not most, work processes require groups to meet and discuss concepts, ideas and plans. Information sharing, negotiation, argumentation and presentation form the kernel of this interaction. There is a growing recognition that computer support can enhance these meetings through individual group members working simultaneously and in parallel. An area of research which endeavors to support group work is Group Support Systems (GSS) [30]. GSS is simply technology which assist groups' working in real-time and in parallel. We believe that the DeSanctis and Gallupe definition for Group Decision Support Systems (GDSS), "an interactive computer-based system that facilitates the solution of unstructured problems by a set of decision-makers working together as a group" [8] is a subset of GSS. Not all group work results in a decision. We also believe that "the use of computer technology to enhance work group activity" [26] (CSCW) is another subset of GSS. Not all technologies require computers. The subsets may overlap as some systems can be used for both decision-making and collaborative work, depending on the task and the group process. Rather than split semantic hairs about the label which should be used, we will use the label GSS throughout this paper.

> **Facilitation:** to make easier or less difficult; help forward (an action, a process) [15].

The **art** of facilitating group work is still developing [19]. If we are to increase our understanding of the ways group problem solving and decision making can be enhanced by facilitating interaction processes, there are many critical issues to be addressed [14]. Yet, most researchers agree that facilitation is a dynamic process that involves managing relationships between people, tasks and technology, as well as structuring tasks and contributing to the effective accomplishment of the meetings outcomes [2]. Friedman suggests that proactive facilitation is necessary to assist problem-solving groups [12]. Alternatively, one could use an intervention strategy once problems arise [34]. Regardless of the approach, facilitation can be examined by first looking at a fundamental group activity, the meeting itself.

There are many different types of meetings. They can be categorized by size, frequency of occurrence, composition, motivation and decision process used [16]. The type of meeting affects the type of facilitation that is needed, i.e. a daily project meeting of three or four design engineers may require fairly unstructured facilitation while a quarterly departmental management meeting with twenty people may require more structured facilitation. Face-to-face meetings are not always possible or necessary. With the advances in computer and communication technology it is possible for individuals to meet as a group in their own locations by using either audio conference calls, video conferencing, or real-time computer conferencing. However, when we investigate the use of computers in a geographically distributed environment we find that there is a limited understanding of the meeting process itself and how it can be facilitated. It is important to remember that the "essential

Permission to copy without fee all or part of this material is granted provided that the copies are not made or distributed for direct commercial advantage, the ACM copyright notice and the title of the publication and its date appear, and notice is given that copying is by permission of the Association for Computing Machinery. To copy otherwise, or to republish, requires a fee and/or specific permission.

© 1992 ACM 0-89791-543-7/92/0010/0314...$1.50

characteristic of facilitation is to help make an activity or outcome easier to perform or achieve" [3].

PREVIOUS FACILITATION RESEARCH

Facilitation combines the disciplines of many diverse areas. As part of our investigation in distributed facilitation, we first examine the current research in the areas of meeting models, facilitator's roles, and meeting support systems.

Previous Meeting Models

An unproductive meeting is both frustrating and expensive. There are many reasons why meetings are unproductive (process losses) [25, 32]. For instance, process losses may occur through cognitive inertia, the difficulty of moving an entire group from a particular position to a new position, or from member domination. There are also many reasons why meetings perform better than other communication devices (process gains) [16, 25]. A process gain may occur such as stimulation, receiving feedback from other group members, or imitation, observing others and learning from them.

In order for all participants to benefit from the meeting process and avoid frustration, some amount of structure is required to ensure meeting success. It has been suggested [16, 18] that pre-meeting planning such as understanding the meeting objective, creating an agenda and informing the appropriate participants are steps in the right direction. The meeting process itself requires structure to ensure the group remains focused and accomplishes the necessary task with minimal interpersonal disruptions. Chilberg suggests that group process designs provide for effective and efficient group communication [3]. Maier et. al. provide evidence that shows meetings with explicit structured facilitation can have a positive influence on the quality of the group decision [22, 23]. And, when the meeting adjourns it should be followed-up with a summary of the discussions, decisions and action items.

It is important to ensure the meeting structure imposed on the group does not disrupt the groups' familiar meeting protocol and thereby impede their ability to be productive [11]. A balance must be struck between the restrictiveness which supports consistency/coordination, and flexibility which enables creativity/exploration [25]. The type of group (based on composition, size, etc.) and the type of meeting objective (e.g. design or management status) also assists in determining the appropriate balance.

Meetings are not static; a single meeting is usually one of many in the life cycle of a project, task force, or committee. Although it is possible to have a one-time meeting, most meetings are part of a larger process requiring group members to have many interactions. Bostrom et. al. explain this on-going activity in their Cycle Model (see Figure 1) [2]. A meeting moves from pre-meeting to

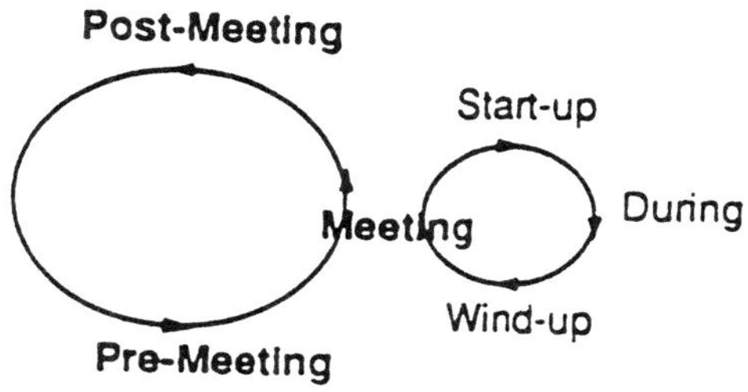

Figure 1: Meeting Cycle Model

meeting to post-meeting. The dynamic process then begins again with pre-meeting activities for the next step in the life cycle and this continues until the larger goal (e.g. project completion, or task force goal finalized) is met or continues indefinitely for those groups that are part of standing committees. With the cycle model as a basis, Bostrom et. al. present a meeting model which is outcome focused. They look at a meeting as a socio-technical change process, i.e. the meeting starts at a present state (problems) and uses resources (technology and people) through action steps to reach a desired state (outcomes - both task and relationship). In this model, sources (e.g. external facilitator, leader, member, GSS) provide structures (e.g. agenda, procedures, tools, etc.) and support (e.g. administer a procedure, handle disrupted participants, etc.) to the group. The structures and supports are used to positively influence the group's outcomes [2]. The Cycle Model provides a sound basis for any type of detailed meeting model. However, their detailed model is outcome focused and does not concentrate on the action steps which are needed to reach the desired outcomes. Our model concentrates on the process required to get to these outcomes.

The Role of the Facilitator

The facilitator can play an important role in all meetings. The facilitator can best assist the group by dealing with group process and structure and refraining from contributing to content [29]. In assisting the group, the facilitator has to deal with many different types of problems but they all can be categorized as [14]: 1) **substantive** - limitations in information available or use of information; 2) **procedural** - the best way to sequence group discussion; 3) **relational** - relationships among the group members. Throughout the process, the facilitator should be thought of as servant to the group rather than master [16]. There is evidence that shows that trained facilitators are more effective in producing higher quality group decisions [2, 23, 22, 29]. The activities of the facilitator have been summarized as [3, 19, 29]:

1. ensuring members identify and maintain a discussion focus and a procedure for that focus
2. ensuring everyone has an opportunity to contribute to the discussion and decisions regarding focus, procedures

and decision issues

3. creating situations conductive to learning
4. providing new values in process
5. confronting group regarding its process
6. providing structure to focus group limits and boundaries
7. establishing a model of behaviour
8. managing group creativity, anxiety and conflict
9. intervening when appropriate at level of group instead of individual
10. maintaining awareness of own feelings as an indicator

It is preferable to have a facilitator that is external to the group and one that is specifically trained for facilitation because it is easy for the facilitator to remain detached from the content and concentrate on the process and structure. However, an external facilitator is not always possible and a leader or member often becomes responsible for facilitation [20, 33]. Kerr and Jermier experimented with leadership substitutes based on characteristics of the subordinate, task and organization and found that there are alternate sources (e.g. intrinsically satisfying work, task-provided performance feedback, etc.) for guidance and good feelings in an organization than strictly hierarchical leadership. It is possible that some of these characteristics might also assist in the facilitation process. Aiken et al. suggest that expert systems can be used to assist facilitators and possibly relieve them of some of their tasks, such as process advisors (e.g. commitment coordinators, conflict managers, etc.), interaction tracers to identify patterns in discussions, or administration assistants to help novice facilitators with administration tasks such as logging in participants, changing tools, etc. [1]. Finally, it should be noted that the facilitation function can be shared by all participants even though one person usually has the formal responsibility [2]. This sharing of functions is most necessary with small groups when participant involvement in the content is critical to the success of the meeting. Given that groups are beginning to interact from geographically distributed sites, which facilitation functions are relevant, and how they can be applied?

Meeting Support Tools

To understand the current state of technology in terms of meeting and facilitation support, we examined the functionality of seven systems: GroupSystems [25, 5], VisionQuest [4], The Facilitator, rIBIS [7], GroupSketch [13], ObjectLens [21, 24], and The Coordinator [35]. There are many GSS in the literature, we present these as a representative sample of GSS. Three of these systems are from the GDSS domain and the remaining four from the CSCW domain. Each of the following systems span different types of meetings in the time and space continuum [17]. Although many of these tools have addressed functionality in the pre-meeting, meeting and post-meeting categories, as Table 1 shows, the major focus of these tools has **not** been to support the **facilitator** during the meeting activities. This omission represents an interesting area for research, especially when placed in the distributed meeting environment.

A MEETING MODEL

Johansen [18] suggests that a meeting process map is an effective and useful way to approach a meeting. We have developed the meeting process map in Figure 2. This is a descriptive model which represents an expansion of Bostrom et. al.'s Cycle model and the activities within each of its phases: pre-meeting, meeting and post-meeting. It demonstrates the big picture as well as the sequences of activities that can occur to enable the group to be as effective as possible before, during and after the meeting [1, 2, 16, 18, 25, 29, 33, 34]. The model does not place constraints on a time or place of the meeting and should be able to incorporate any combination.

The model represents a comprehensive list of the activities which could occur in any type of meeting. Although some activities are more critical than others, not all activities will be part of every meeting. The highly structured meeting is likely to explicitly incorporate all the activities. However, we believe that all meetings should **implicitly** incorporate most of the activities in order to ensure meeting success.

Pre-meeting Activities

Although these pre-meeting activities sometimes occur during the meeting, many are more effective if done in advance. These activities include: review previous meeting(s) to understand the status of the overall process, ensure the appropriate people attend and have the necessary background information; describe meeting goal which reflects the purpose of the meeting; develop roster which entails more than just listing the participants but also determining their familiarity with the tasks at hand; develop and gather documents which includes the key document, the agenda; select the tool/process most appropriate for the group and the meeting environment; handle logistics including arrangement of the facility and equipment; and inform participants of the meeting and provide them with the necessary material.

Meeting Activities

Similar to that of the overall meeting model the meeting activities can be divided into three phases: start-up, during and wind-up. Although there is a clear conceptual distinction between these phases, it is not necessary that they be apparent within the meeting.

- **Start-Up** phase is a direct follow-on from the pre-meeting activities. Since it is often the case that only a few individuals are involved in the pre-meeting activities, the other participants in the meeting may need to have a chance to comment and revise the meeting according to their personal needs.

	GroupSystems	VisionQuest	Facilitator	rIBIS	GroupSketch	ObjectLens	Coordinator
Pre-Meeting							
Agenda	⨀	⨀	⨀	–	–	⊙	⊙
Roster	⨀	⨀	–	⊙	–	–	⊙
Tool Selection	⨀	⨀	–	⊙	⊙	⊙	⊙
Meeting							
Monitor	⊙	⊙	⊙	⊙	⊙	–	–
Process	⊙	⊙	–	–	–	⊙	⊙
Record	⊙	⊙	⊙	⊙	⊙	⊙	⊙
Post-Meeting							
Documents	⨀	⨀	⨀	⨀	–	⨀	⨀

⨀ ⟶ Full Support
⊙ ⟶ Partial Support
– ⟶ No Support

Table 1: Facilitation Capabilities in Current GSS

- **During** phase activities are not sequential. Instead they happen concurrently and often interact with each other. These activities are the main emphasis of the meeting and of the longest duration:
  - *Monitoring* is used to observe and keep track of what is happening in a meeting, i.e. the time (keeping to the agenda), who is participating and how much, relationships between participants, the tools being used and the technology.
  - *Process* activities within the meeting surround and interact with the actual work or task activities; tasks are started and stopped, the flow of the meeting is maintained through adhering to or adjusting the time constraints, the participants, the tools used, the technology or the agenda. This activity is highly dependent on the monitoring activity which may point out potential problems to be dealt with.
  - *Task* activities are divided into three phases: stating the task objective, performing the task, and closing. At the beginning of each new task it is important that all the participants understand the expected outcome and how to perform the task. During closure, feedback should be generated as to whether the task was successfully addressed.
  - *Recording* can occur at all levels of activity within the meeting: at the monitor, task or process level. At the task level we may want to have a complete recording of the task (transaction based transcript), snapshots in time of the activity as well as a summary of the task activity. At the monitoring and process level we may want to record all of the activity or a just a summary of the highlights, e.g. recording the coming and going of participants so that it can be later determined who participated in the particular tasks [16]. For process, the changes to the tools used might be captured for preparing following meetings.
- **Wind-Up** phase attempts to ensure that the group members have a common understanding of what was accomplished at the meeting. This phase requires input from the participants. It is also another opportunity to get feedback on the meeting process and tasks themselves for improvement in the future.

Post-Meeting Activities

The output from the wind-up phase above can become the resources for input to the next meeting. The activities in this phase include: create and distribute documents to ensure all participants have a similar record of the meeting; review meeting through the feedback obtained and determine if any changes are necessary to forthcoming meetings; and communicate next steps so that all participants understand who is responsible for what.

Summary

The meeting is often only one step in a life cycle of a larger process. Thus each meeting should build on the past history to be most effective. The meeting model presented represents a comprehensive set of meeting activities that may take place at each of the meeting steps. Although the model seems highly structured it represents the extreme. Many meetings may have these activities more implicitly than explicitly as part of their process. It is important to remember that research shows that process **does** lead to more effective and efficient group communication [3] but that there needs to be a balance between restrictiveness and flexibility [25].

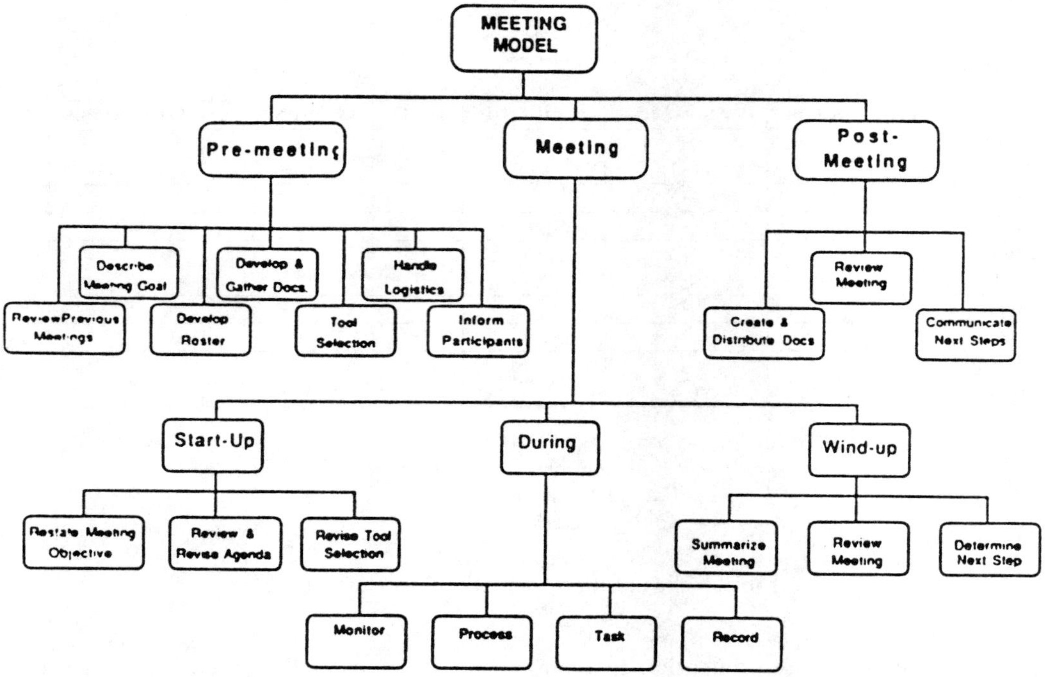

Figure 2: Meeting Model

CRITICAL FACILITATION FUNCTIONS

The Facilitation Control model (see Figure 3) is an overlay on the meeting model. Control is used to understand the facilitator's role in the meeting process. This perspective outlines the facilitator's control over the different meeting activities in order to identity those activities that are important to facilitation. Control within the model has been divided into the two dimensions of high and low control.

While the facilitator is often highly involved in many of the pre-meeting activities, a leader or sub-group makes most of the decisions (low control). The two exceptions are Tool Selection and Handle Logistics. Facilitators are trained to match the group goals with the available tools or processes at hand. The facilitator may determine that the best way to accomplish the group's objective is to use the Nominal Group Technique with an electronic meeting tool that supports it. The facilitator will then need control over the logistics so they can arrange for the most appropriate meeting environment. For the same reasons, the facilitator needs high control over Revise Tool Selection in the Meeting Start-Up Phase.

Within the meeting (During Phase), the facilitator has high control of three of the four activities. The task activity is highly content driven and thus is in the control of the group, however the other tasks are structure and process intensive and require control by the facilitator. Monitoring, process and recording are highly interrelated and require one source of control or at the least, access to information from the other activities in order to make decisions. For example, the act of recording enables the facilitator to monitor changes, which then enables the facilitator to determine if intervention is necessary.

It is important to note that although we would like each group to have a separate and distinct facilitator it is not always possible. It may be that the leader is playing that role or that several of the group members are performing different facilitator functions. Understanding where a facilitator requires the most control, assists us in determining how best to support these facilitation functions.

As our goal is to build a Distributed Facilitation System, we need to determine which components should be included within it and with what priority. Using the Facilitation Control model, the following section analyzes the potential facilitation functions and recommends an order of implementation.

Pre-meeting activities are performed to ensure that there is focus and direction to the meeting and ensure all participants can be as effective as possible. These activities take on an increased importance during computer-supported meetings [25]. We believe that in a distributed meeting environment the work involved to facilitate the pre-meeting activities is crucial to the meeting success. Supplying the facilitator with tools to manage the roster, agenda, or previous meeting work, etc. will not only be beneficial but vital. The post-meeting activities are also important but cannot be accomplished until the meeting has taken place and been recorded in some fashion. Although there may be a specific need to record information during post-meeting activities, the tools themselves during meeting activities should provide the facilities to do most of the recording. In the use of GSS at IBM,

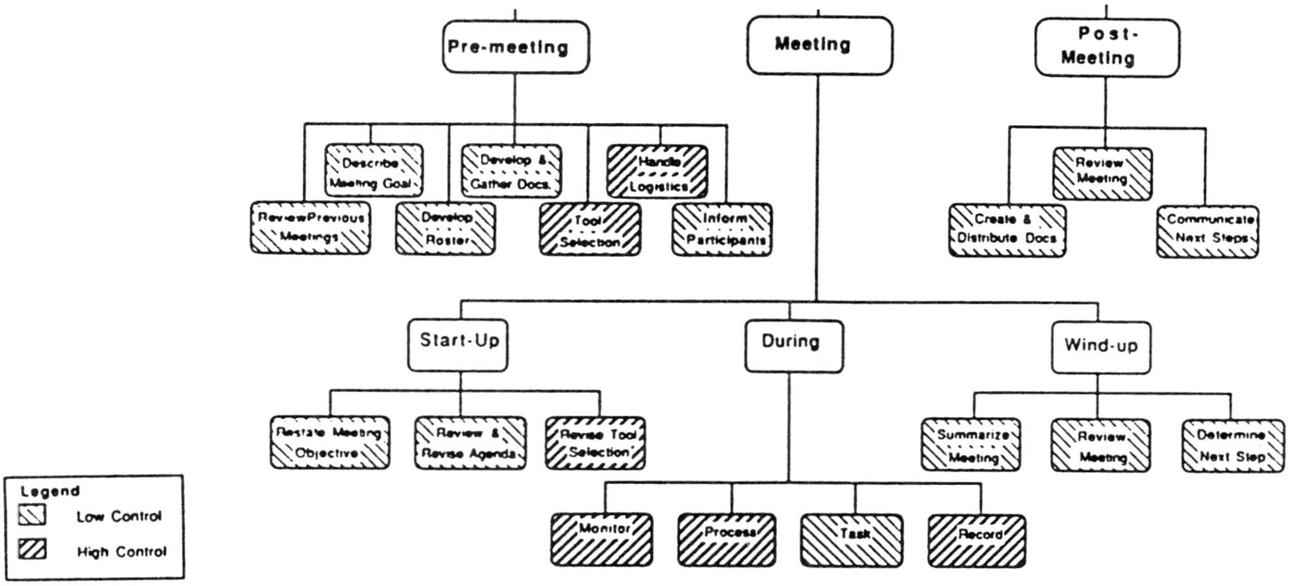

Figure 3: Facilitation Control Model

it was found that post-meeting distribution of the session data was crucial to the effectiveness of a long term process [25]. Although the support for pre- and post-meeting activities is indispensable for the facilitator, it will not be the focus of this research. It is clear from the face-to-face and distributed systems available today (see Table 2), that some research has already gone into developing these essential pre-meeting support components for the facilitator.

As shown in Figure 3, the focus for facilitation control is within the **During** meeting category. The during meeting activities include: monitor, process, task and record. Since the facilitator can best assist the group in process and structure and not in content [29], the facilitator needs little if any support for the task activities themselves. Thus, we have chosen to concentrate on the monitor, process and record activities.

The first step in assisting the facilitator during the meeting is to provide support for the recording of what went on. Without recording the events of the meeting or within the tasks, there would be nothing to monitor and little understanding of the process. Once recording has been implemented, the facilitator then needs support monitoring work. It is through monitoring that the facilitator determines whether the process needs changing. We believe that an effective facilitation system must support each of these three activities and we acknowledge that these components assume some pre-meeting and post-meeting functions will also be available.

Recording

We have identified three types of records which we feel capture enough information to assist the other components. These records will be stored in a database:

- **Transcripts** are the recordings of the activities within a particular task (tool). This recording is based on some predefined notion of action which we call unit of work. The units of work are determined by each individual tool, e.g. the unit of work for a discussion tool may be the sending and receiving of messages whereas in a drawing tool it may the creation, change or deletion of an object. In addition to recording the unit of work, which is merely a code, we attach content of the action as well. The content is dependent upon the unit of work, e.g. a discussion tool may record the content of the message, a drawing tool may record an object identifier. A filtered version of the complete transcript can be generated when querying the database.

- **Snapshots** are a complete capture of a particular task at a slice in time. For example, a snapshot of an brainstorming session would show the list of ideas created at the time of its capture, whereas a snapshot of a drawing activity would capture the graphical drawing created thus far. As it is often tedious to go through a complete transcript in order to understand what occurred during a meeting, we propose the use of change-tours [28]. Change-tours are composed of a time series of snapshots. By picking an appropriate time interval, the collection of snapshots can represent the general progress made within a meeting as well as the process used to accomplish the tasks. Combining the snapshots together provides the ability to replay, in time slices, the tasks within a meeting. This technique could be very useful in the wind-up or post-meeting activities such as summarize or review meeting. A change-tour could also be useful in the pre-meeting or start-up activities in order to review the previous meeting(s) or to bring people up to speed.

- **Summary** is also a useful record of what happened during the task, process or monitoring activities. Within the task itself, many tools already provide a summary of the conclusions of the meetings, i.e. the voting tool in GroupSystems records the details of who voted which way and how this translated into the aggregated outcome. However, in order to allow a summary to be created for each tool a separate function is required for the facilitator. The summary created could be simply a text file. The facilitator is responsible for the summaries, however if a facilitation module is available to all participants, they could create their own summaries.

Monitoring

We consider monitoring activities a major part of the facilitator's role. External facilitators may be more available for distributed meetings (no travel cost), but they still add to the cost of a meeting in additional personnel time and availability. Thus it is important that the participants be able take on facilitation roles by monitoring the necessary activities themselves. The monitoring of activities include watching the mood, time, participation, and relationships of the group. Keeping open channels with all participants through audio communication or a messaging tool is vital. "Without the affective signals, significant misunderstandings can occur, leading to unrealistic expectations and causing serious breakdowns in group process" [31].

Observation can take place by simply watching the group process within the particular task through the public display of information, by monitoring the audio channel, or by reviewing the recorded information. If the information the facilitator wants to monitor is not readily available, it may be appropriate to solicit information from the participants. The facilitator can use a messaging tool to get free text comments, or perhaps use a voting tool to produce a combined group result. It should not only be the facilitator who is able to request information, but also the participants who can submit comments at any time. Using a messaging tool the participants could submit comments to the facilitator or the rest of the group on their feelings about the task or process.

Process

The process activity within the meeting is what surrounds and interacts with the actual work or task activities. Thus within the process activity the tasks are started and stopped, and the flow of the meeting is maintained through adhering to or adjusting the time constraints. This activity is highly dependent on the monitoring activity which points out potential problems that need to be dealt with. For example, if the relationships among the group members are dysfunctional, relationship intervention or conflict management may be appropriate. Within the process activity adjustments to the tool selection, technology or agenda are also made. The particular process followed to support the group's tasks will be dependent on the group, their objectives, the tools available, and the familiarity with the process tecniques.

Summary

The record, monitor, and process components are not strictly sequential activities. Although the information from one may feed into another, at any point in the meeting the facilitator may be performing all functions independent of each other. For example, the facilitator may decide that it is time to take a snapshot of the group drawing being created while at the same time carefully observing the progress of the team to see if there is productive collaboration going on. The facilitator, with an ear on the conversation may decide to adjust the time available for the next agenda item if the group is determined to continue with the current drawing task until it is complete. In a distributed environment, a facilitator could drop in and out of several meetings, thereby spreading their expertise as far as possible.

CONCLUSIONS AND FUTURE RESEARCH

The study of group work has matured considerably in the past five years. Yet, it is an area of opportunity that is only beginning to demonstrate its vast potential. Automated support for distributed groups is becoming increasingly important. However, we believe that distributed facilitation for groups is very poorly understood - its time has not yet come. This paper provides a comprehensive framework, in the form of a meeting model, that defines the many activities that surround group work. We have shown that existing support for facilitation is low. Based on the level of facilitator control, we have identified facilitation functions and suggested a rational for prioritizing them. The model is applicable to both distributed and face-to-face environments.

We are currently developing a facilitation system for distributed meeting environments in order to validate our model and gain experience. Since face-to-face meetings seem to have more intense, richer interactions, it is important to provide as full an environment as possible in the distributed setting. For now, we assume that all participants have audio as well as data links for communication with each other. The use of the telephone is a low cost solution to produce a much richer environment for the participants and the facilitator. The audio channel could even be used to provide contextual cues for the group's activity by having participants announce their intents before taking action [10].

The Distributed Facilitation System is a separate process on all participant's workstations to make facilitator functions accessible to everyone. We are implementing this prototype on personal computers attached to local area networks. We have used the Actor object-oriented development environment under Microsoft Windows coupled with the Paradox database engine and an object-based secure session connection communication library [27]. When not in use, the system remains an icon in the workspace. Through use of the facilitation system, we can test further the concept of distributed facilitation.

REFERENCES

[1] M. Aiken, O. Sheng, and D. Vogel. Integrating expert systems with group decision support systems. *ACM Transactions on Information Systems*, 9(1):75–95, 1991.

[2] R. Bostrom, R. Anson, and V. Clawson. Group facilitation and group support systems. Department of Management, University of Georgia Working Paper, 1991.

[3] J. C. Chilberg. A review of group process designs for facilitating communication in problem-solving groups. *Management Communication Quarterly*, 3(1):51–71, 1989.

[4] Collaborative Technologies Co. Visionquest users guide. Suite 100, 8920 Business Park, Austin, TX 78759, 1991.

[5] Ventana Co. Groupsystems users guide. Tucson, Az, 1991.

[6] A.J. Cockburn and H. Thimbleby. A reflexive perspective of cscw. *SIGCHI Bulletin*, 23(3):63–68, 1991.

[7] J. Conklin and M.L. Begeman. gibis: A hypertext tool for exploratory policy discussion. *ACM Transactions on Office Information Systems*, pages 140–152, October 1988.

[8] G. DeSanctis and B.R. Gallupe. A foundation for the study of group decision support systems. *Management Science*, 33(5):589–609, May 1987.

[9] G. Easton, J.F. George, J.F. Nunamaker, and M.O. Pendergast. Using two different electronic meeting system tools for the same task: An experimental comparison. *Journal of Management Information Systems*, 7(1):85–100, 1990.

[10] C.A. Ellis, S.J. Gibbs, and G. L. Rein. Groupware: Some issues and experiences. *Communications of the ACM*, 34(1):38–58, 1991.

[11] M. Elwart-Keys, D. Halonen, M. Horton, R. Kass, and P. Scott. User interface requirements for face-to-face groupware. In *Proceedings of the CHI 1990 Conference*, pages 295–301, Seattle, WA, 1990.

[12] P. G. Friedman. Upstream facilitation: A proactive approach to managing problem-solving groups. *Management Communication Quarterly*, 3(1):33–50, 1989.

[13] S. Greenberg, M. Roseman, D. Webster, and R. Bohnet. Issues and experiences designing and implementing two group drawing tools. In *Proceedings of Hawaii International Conference on System Sciences*, volume 4. IEEE Press, January 1991.

[14] R. Y. Hirokawa and D. Gouran. Facilitation of group communication: A critique of prior research and an agenda for future research. *Management Communication Quarterly*, 3(1):71–92, 1989.

[15] Random House. *College Dictionary*. Random House, Inc., New York, NY, 1984.

[16] A. Jay. How to run a meeting. *Harvard Business Review*, pages 43–57, March 1976.

[17] R. Johansen. *Groupware: Computer Support for Business Teams*. Free Press, New York, 1988.

[18] R. Johansen, D. Sibbet, S. Benson, A. Martin, R. Mittman, and P. Saffo. What is a facilitator anyway? In E.H.Schein and R. Beckhard, editors, *Leading Business Teams: How Teams can use Technology and Group Process Tools to Enhance Performance*, pages 76–80. Addison-Wesley, Reading, Mass., 1991.

[19] J.S. Keltner. Facilitation: Catalyst for group problem-solving. *Management Communication Quarterly*, 3(1):8–31, 1989.

[20] S. Kerr and J. Jermier. Substitutes for leadership: Their meaning and measurement. *Organizational Behavior and Human Performance*, 22:375–403, 1978.

[21] K.Y. Lai and T.W. Malone. Object lens: A spreadsheet for cooperative work. In *Proceedings of the Conference on CSCW*, pages 115–124, 1988.

[22] N.R.F. Maier and L.R. Hoffman. Using trained developmental discussion leaders to improve further the quality of group decisions. *Journal of Applied Psychology*, 44:247–251, 1960.

[23] N.R.F. Maier and R.A. Maier. An experimental test of the effects of developmental vs. free discussions on the quality of group decisions. *Journal of Applied Psychology*, 41(5):320–323, 1957.

[24] T.W. Malone, K.R. Grant, K.Y. Lai, R. Rao, and D. Rosenblitt. Semistructured messages are surprisingly useful for computer-supported coordination. In *Proceedings of the Conference on Computer-Supported Cooperative Work*, 1986.

[25] J.F. Nunamaker, A. Dennis, J. Valacich, D. Vogel, and J. George. Electronic meeting systems to support group work. *Communications of the ACM*, 34(7):40–61, 1991.

[26] M.H. Olson. Computer supported cooperative work. *Office: Technology and People*, 3(2):77–81, 1987.

[27] M.O. Pendergast. Distributed object oriented environment for ems application development. In *Hawaii International Conference on System Sciences*, volume 1, pages 59–66, 1991.

[28] M.O. Pendergast and S.C. Hayne. Assisting groups during the merging process. In *Decision Sciences Conference*, November 1991.

[29] L.D Phillips and M.C. Phillips. Facilitating work groups: Theory and practice. Technical report, Decision Analysis Unit, London School of Economics and Political Science, Houghton Street. London NC2A 2AE, England, 1990. Working Paper.

[30] C. Pollard and D. Vogel. Group support system product comparisons. In *Hawaii International Conference on System Sciences*, pages 771–778, January 1991.

[31] G. Rein. A group mood meter. In *Proceedings of Twenty-Fourth Annual Hawaii International Conference on System Sciences*, pages 308–323, January 1991.

[32] J.S. Valacich, A.R. Dennis, J. George, and J.F. Nunamaker. Electronic support for group idea-generation: Shifting the balance of process gains and losses. Working Paper, University of Arizona, 1990.

[33] S. Viller. *Computer Support for Group Facilitators: An Investigation*. PhD thesis, University of Manchester, 1990. Unpublished M. Sc. Thesis.

[34] F. Westley and J. Waters. Group facilitation skills for managers. *Managment Education and Development*, 18(2):134–143, 1988.

[35] T. Winograd. A language/action perspective on the design of cooperative work. *Human-Computer Interaction*, 3(1):3–30, 1988.

Communication and Information Retrieval with a Pen-based Meeting Support Tool

Catherine G. Wolf, James R. Rhyne

IBM T. J. Watson Research Center
P. O. Box 704
Yorktown Heights, NY 10598
cwolf@.watson.ibm.com, jrhyne@.watson.ibm.com

Laura K. Briggs

Department of Psychology
Columbia University
New York, NY 10027

ABSTRACT

We-Met (Window Environment-Meeting Enhancement Tools) is a prototype pen-based tool designed to support both the communication and information retrieval needs of small group meetings. The first part of this paper describes We-Met and the rationale for its design, the second discusses findings from an empirical study of the use of We-Met for group communication, and the third discusses findings from a study of the search and retrieval of information from non-computer based meetings conducted to provide insight into how to facilitate these activities in We-Met. The paper identifies potential communication process gains due to the pen-based interface style, opportunities for the facilitation of information retrieval in a pen-based tool, and functionality/interface challenges in the design of a tool to support small group meetings.

KEYWORDS

Pen-based, meeting support, drawing

INTRODUCTION

In the late 1980's, researchers began to explore the use of conventional keyboard-based computers for the support of face-to-face [9, 15] and remote meetings [14]. These early systems served to elucidate important issues in the design of meeting support systems, and analyses of their shortcomings have contributed to our understanding of key requirements (see [18], for example). These keyboard-based systems did not enable users to communicate using sketches, a very common medium of communication in many meetings. Recognizing the importance of this mode of communication, several researchers have built shared drawing tools to support small group drawing activities by participants in different locations [1, 2, 6, 10, 17]. These systems were found to facilitate a style of interaction which was in many ways typical of face-to-face meetings.

The information generated in a meeting is typically used outside the meeting as well, and another line of research has sought to facilitate the use of collaboratively produced information. There is some evidence that the requirement to facilitate communication within a meeting may often conflict with the requirement to capture meeting information in a form which facilitates its review. Conklin [3] described a structured format for capturing design rationale that facilitates the later use of information. However, the cognitive overhead in using the method made it inappropriate for use during meetings. Videotape has been used to capture meeting information with little disruption of the meeting process (see [11], for example), but is very cumbersome to review.

We believe that an effective meeting support tool must facilitate both group communication and the capture and review of information. Over the past two years, we have been building We-Met (Window Environment- Meeting Enhancement Tools), a prototype pen-based system designed to meet both of these needs for small, informal work groups [19].

This paper is organized into three main parts. The first describes We-Met and the rationale for its design, the second describes a study of the use of We-Met for group communication, and the third describes a study

Permission to copy without fee all or part of this material is granted provided that the copies are not made or distributed for direct commercial advantage, the ACM copyright notice and the title of the publication and its date appear, and notice is given that copying is by permission of the Association for Computing Machinery. To copy otherwise, or to republish, requires a fee and/or specific permission.

© 1992 ACM 0-89791-543-7/92/0010/0322...$1.50

of the search and retrieval of information from non-computer based meetings which was conducted to give us insight into how to facilitate these activities in We-Met.

WE-MET

The We-Met user interface is shown in Figure 1. The We-Met prototype is under development and some of the features described here are not yet operational.

We-Met provides a shared drawing area in which several users can work at the same time. When one person writes, the other participants see each stroke as it is completed. Users have access to multiple shared drawing areas and can scroll within a drawing area. The displayed marks can be edited (see buttons in lower left of Figure 1). Additional features include writer identification, the importation of bit map images, and methods for joining and leaving a We-Met meeting.

Nunamaker and his colleagues [12] have distinguished features of a meeting system that support the communication process from features that structure it. Process support features enhance a meeting by facilitating communication among people (for example, a slide projector may serve this purpose). Process structure features affect the communication process by directing the "pattern, timing, or content" of communication (for example, following Roberts Rules of Order may have this effect). Because our goal was to facilitate the meetings of small, highly interactive, unpredictable groups, we deliberately chose to provide process support, rather than process structure. One consequence of this decision is that We-Met does not impose floor control on access to the drawing area or interface controls.

All meeting events are recorded and can be reviewed during or after the meeting. Our own observations as well as recent reports [1, 8] have suggested that the process by which information is created and used can be important for the understanding of the end product of the work group. The We-Met record preserves temporal information by creating a time-stamped history of meeting events (see [13] for a detailed description of the history mechanism). Users can travel backwards and forwards in the history and replay selected segments. Because the drawings and writings created in the shared work area have a temporal as well as spatial dimension, we refer to the shared work area as a "scene." In order to enable users to identify particular points (called "viewpoints") in a scene for later review, users may give these points a text name or mark them with a hand-drawn squiggle (such as a star). People make such marks in notebooks and whiteboards, and we expect that the ease of use of this technique will transfer to our computer-based tool.

We-Met runs on workstations with an attached LCD/digitizing tablet over a local area network. It can be used for face-to-face meetings, or remote meetings in conjunction with a telephone conference call. We envision the future use of We-Met on notepad computers connected by a wireless local area network.

USE OF WE-MET FOR GROUP COMMUNICATION

As the We-Met prototype has evolved, we have conducted informal experiments with our colleagues, visitors and ourselves. We plan to put it in the hands of existing groups to use in their work over extended periods of time. In order to get more detailed user feedback at an early stage of development, a pilot study was conducted using a prepared task. This study is described here.

The following features could be used by participants in the study:

- Shared scene for pen input
- New scene--To get a new, empty scene, a participant touched the **New** button (see Figure 1). All participants then saw the new scene on their displays.
- View another scene-- To view another, previously created scene, a participant touched the **Scenes** button. A selection box was presented and the user selected the desired scene from a numbered list. The selection box was presented only to the person who had initiated the dialog. After selection, all participants saw the selected scene.
- Scroll--To scroll spatially within the current scene, a participant used the scroll bars at the right and bottom of the application window. When an individual scrolled a scene, it did not scroll the scene presented to other participants.

All participants had equal access to the drawing area and controls, and could draw or operate a control at any time.

Study Procedure

The operation of the system was described and demonstrated to the group before they started the primary task.

The participants in the study consisted of 3 groups of 3 people and 1 group of 2. All members of a group were in the same room. The groups of 3 worked together and had frequent meetings. The group of 2 was recruited from a temporary employment agency; they had not met each other prior to the study.

The participants were seated in a U-shaped arrangement. In addition to their individual LCD/digitizing tablets, the output from one of the workstations was projected onto a wall for common viewing.

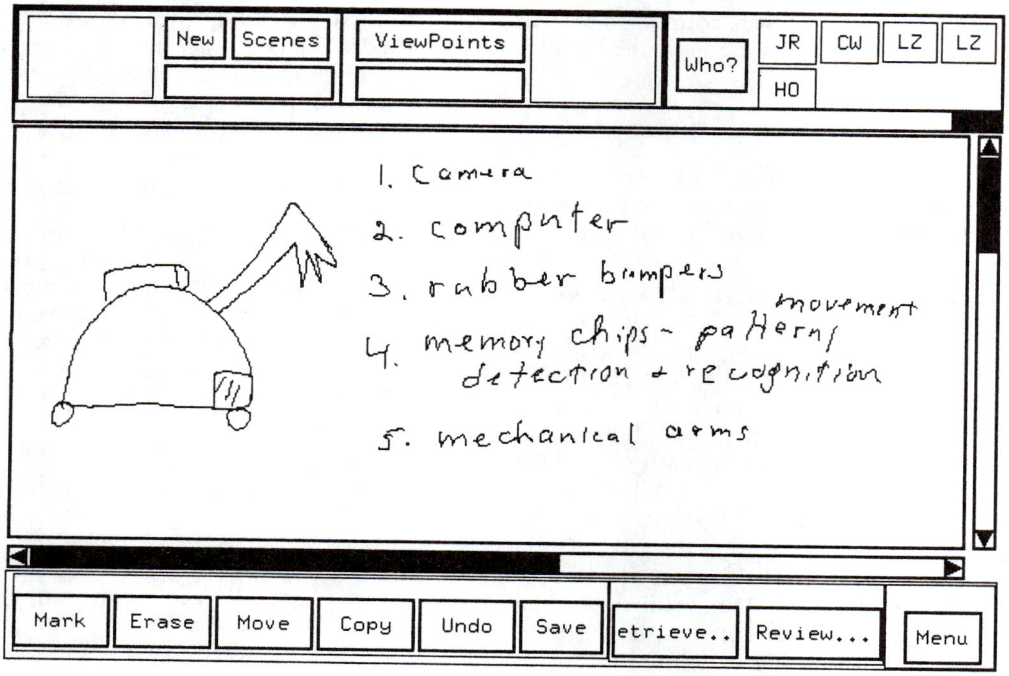

Figure 1. The We-Met Interface: Scene from the Clutter Collector Robot Task

The group was told that they were a committee assigned to work on the design of a Clutter Collector Robot which would pick up household clutter and put it in its proper place (a task created by one of the authors). They were told that they were not expected to reach a conclusion on the design, but to generate a number of ideas. The task was designed to encourage the production of sketches, diagrams and writing. The topic was chosen on the assumption that everyone was familiar with the problems of household clutter and, thus, had a basis for contributing to the discussion.

The groups worked on the task for about 30 minutes. They then filled out a brief questionnaire and discussed their reactions to the system.

One of the authors observed the meeting and took notes. In addition, the time stamped recording of meeting events was operational and used to create a log of the meeting for analysis. The participants and the We-Met screen were both videotaped.

Findings

The findings reported here are based on the participants' questionnaire responses, the post-task discussion, the observer's log, and preliminary analyses of the videotapes and We-Met log. The findings are discussed in terms of the apparent process gains or losses the We-Met meetings exhibited compared to face-to-face non-computer- based meetings or meetings supported by a keyboard-based system. We find it useful to characterize the findings in terms of process gains/losses even though this study did not include the two comparison conditions because it leads to the formulation of hypotheses that could be tested in future studies.

Ease of use of the pen-based interface

All participants found the pen-based interface easy to use. They found it easy to speak or listen and write or draw at the same time. For many people, the task of typing takes up too much cognitive capacity to allow them to simultaneously type and participate fully in the spoken discussion as listeners or speakers. Thus, the pen-based interface may produce a process gain compared to a keyboard interface because it permits parallel activity within individuals.

The pen-based interface facilitated the use of multiple channels of communication. As in a non-computer based meeting, participants spoke, drew, wrote, made hand gestures in the air, and made frequent eye contact (see [16] for a description of activities around a drawing pad in non-computer-based meetings). Because the pen could be used with equal facility for writing and drawing, unlike the case for a keyboard-mouse interface, there was no overhead for shifting between these activities. Transitions among the channels of communication were seamless and occurred frequently. The pen-based style of interaction and hardware seemed unobtrusive and did not interfere with interpersonal communication.

Interaction styles

Like [4], we also found that group interaction was characterized by a number of styles.

One group worked in a highly **collaborative** fashion throughout most of the session. One person might add to a list of requirements for the Clutter Collector Robot and another might expand that item. In two other groups, as well as this group, one person often took on the role of writer and another took on the role of sketcher. As the writer listed requirements for the robot, the sketcher drew it. Interestingly, the group of two who did not know each other prior to the study assumed this mode of interaction. All groups commented that it was much easier to make a contribution than in a conventional whiteboard meeting. In a conventional meeting, taking the floor often means standing up and taking the marker from the person at the board. In other words, taking the floor means taking it away from someone else. In the We-Met meeting, the floor could easily be shared. Thus, the threshold for making a contribution seemed to be lower than in a conventional whiteboard meeting. The resulting synergistic idea generation can be viewed as a process gain compared to conventional meetings.

Another style of interaction consisted of deliberately **separate parallel** activity. After some initial collaborative activity, one group decided to work independently for several minutes and then shared their individual creations sequentially. Another type of parallel activity occurred when one participant drew or wrote in an area of the scene not being viewed by others, while monitoring a conversation between the other two. In these instances, the individual was working on a topic different from the one under discussion by the other two. Typically, when the two finished their discussion, the third participant pointed out the new contribution. This separate parallel activity enables the generation of a greater number of ideas in a fixed period of time and represents a potential process gain over conventional meetings or computer-based systems which permit only person at a time to take the floor.

One group adopted a **moderator-led** style for the initial 15 minutes in which all three participated in the spoken conversation but one person did all the writing. This participant also controlled the discussion. This is the typical model for a conventional whiteboard meeting. As it happened, this participant's display was the one projected onto the wall for public viewing, and after a few minutes the other participants directed their attention to the wall as the moderator scrolled the scene. It is possible that control of the public display plus the knowledge that the others were looking at the display empowered this participant to control the floor (an interesting topic for future research).

Common work product

In response to the question, "What did you like about We-Met?" participants in each group commented that they liked the ability to produce a common work product. Compared to a conventional meeting, they thought that the "shared understanding" would help avoid misunderstanding and miscommunication among participants about the group's work.

Space management

The version of We-Met tested here did not enable participants to have a private scene for their own use. A number of participants commented on the need for a private scene for two purposes: private note-taking, and to work on ideas they were not ready to share with the group. For the latter purpose, people also wanted to be able to share the contents of the private scene with the group at will. In order to cope with the lack of a private drawing area, some users took advantage of the independent scrolling. They scrolled to an area of the screen not currently being used by others for their independent work. The group that decided to work in a separate parallel mode for a while actually drew lines across the scene to mark off a private area for each person. The lack of a private scene may produce a process loss if it inhibits the development of ideas which individuals are not yet ready to share with others, or causes users to forget ideas that they would have written down as personal notes.

Both display resolution and the size of the drawing area that could be viewed at one time were limited by current display technology, and were not sufficient for many of the participants. The resolution (VGA) limitations meant that writing had to be larger in size than on a sheet of paper in order to be legible. The size (7.5 inches by 3.38 inches) of the drawing area that could be viewed at one time is equivalent to about 1/3 of a sheet of paper. Users had two options for dealing with the lack of space: to scroll within the current scene, or to start a new scene. There seemed to be some individual differences concerning when to start a new scene vs. scroll for more space. In two groups, there were episodes in which one member suggested starting a new scene and another countered with the suggestion that they scroll within the existing scene. Compared to conventional whiteboard meetings, the lack of space is a process loss since it caused users to spend time trying to compensate for it, and may have curtailed their generation of ideas.

There is evidence that scenes were considered to be a means of organizing the logical structure of the meeting for some users. In one group, when the group ran out of space in a scene, a participant commented, "are we done now with this topic?" They did not continue with this topic after starting the new scene. In another group, a participant commented that changing scenes seemed to force closure on a topic. Thus, it seems that an interface characteristic, the amount of space available in a scene, may affect a characteristic of the meeting, the degree to which a topic is explored. Observations with groups meeting on real work topics where participants have more at stake are necessary to determine how the interface affects both the meeting process and eventual work product.

Coordination among participants

Participants had no problem coordinating written/drawn contributions with those of other participants. There was not a single instance of two people simultaneously trying to write in the same place, even in the collaborative style of interaction. Because they saw each other's marks on a stroke-by-stroke basis, an individual had almost instantaneous information about the writing of others. Even when all three participants contributed to a common list, social protocol seemed to coordinate their contributions.

There were two aspects of We-Met which caused some coordination problems: changing scenes and scrolling.

To start a new scene, a user simply touches the **New** button; the new scene is then displayed to all participants. To change scenes, a user touches the **Scenes** button and then selects the desired scene from a list presented in a selection box. The selection box is displayed only to the user who initiated the scene selection dialog.

There are three aspects of the scene change process which could potentially cause problems to users: agreeing on whether or not to change scenes, making the change, and realizing that the scene has just been changed. The first aspect was generally handled without problem by social protocols in this study. When a participant wanted to change scenes or start a new scene, he/she usually announced the intention with a comment such as, "should we go to a new scene now?".

The second, making the change, was occasionally a source of confusion. On at least two occasions, two people started a new scene after the group agreed to do so, each unaware of the other's action. This created one more scene than the group intended. When participants later tried to select a scene from the list, they were confused because there were more scenes than expected. In one case, a participant made five consecutive scene changes as he searched for the desired scene. This was followed by a scene change by another person as he independently tried to find the correct scene. The additional unexpected change caused the first participant some annoyance. Some possible means of control--locking out subsequent scene changes for an interval of time following a change or requiring confirmation of an impending change by all participants--have the unpleasant side effect of slowing the pace of interaction and burdening users with interface machinery. A combination of social protocol and improved feedback for in-progress scene changes are more appealing solutions.

The third aspect of a scene change, realizing that the scene had been changed, caused occasional difficulties. Although We-Met is designed so that the name of a scene (a number, by default, or a user-created text or drawing) is displayed above the drawing area, this feature was not implemented in the version tested. Thus, users did not always have adequate information for easy identification of scenes. Identification of scenes by names may make it easier to tell that a scene has been changed. Another, method of providing feedback for scene changes which is consistent with the scene metaphor would be to paint the screen with the new scene with a gradual "wipe".

Scrolling was a source of difficulty for some participants. Each participant could scroll the scene independently and that caused some problems coordinating the views of individual participants. Because all participants had the same view until one of them scrolled, and because a scene change initiated by one changed the view for all, some users initially assumed that scrolling was not independent (in spite of instructions to the contrary). They quickly learned that this was not the case.

Several people commented that they had difficulty keeping track of where others were writing, or when new information existed due to the independent scrolling. Unlike paper documents, in which the sights and sounds of page-turning inform a meeting participant that others are attending to a different part of the document, the physical cues for scrolling were few. This difficulty keeping track of where others were writing seemed to detract from the feeling of shared understanding. Others have also observed scroll coordination problems in shared drawing tools [6].

The most serious scrolling problem was finding the desired portion of the scene. Unlike a paper document, the LCDs of other participants were not easy to see; it was not easy to find the desired spot by looking at another's display. Although other participants frequently tried to help a member who was lost in space with advice such as "scroll down", they had no way of communicating the location information in an adequately precise way. On occasion, the person whose display was projected on the wall assumed the role of controlling the projected display for the benefit of all.

Scrolling is an interface technique developed for single-user applications to deal with the need for more screen space. Although users get lost when scrolling in single-user applications, the problem is perhaps more annoying in a shared application because the user must drop out of the ongoing discussion while searching for the desired position. Some obvious solutions to scroll coordination problems--such as scrolling all scenes in lock-step, or getting rid of the need for scrolling by limiting the size of a scene to the dimensions of the scene window--seem to have undesirable characteristics for a tool designed to support small, highly interactive groups in that they take control away from the user. Approaches that contribute to mutual awareness of location and scrolling actions by providing additional physical cues (see for example, [5]), or facilitate navigation to the desired location seem more promising.

Time lost in coordination confusion and the recovery from confusion constitute a process loss. However, time spent in proactive coordination, such as discussing whether the group should move to a new scene, may be more effective than any control mechanism or rule that could be built into a meeting support tool. As others have noted [7], developing effective CSCW tools means developing protocols and strategies for their use as well as developing technology.

Conclusion

This pilot study provided encouraging evidence for the ease of use of a pen-based meeting support tool, and suggested that We-Met supports a variety of interaction styles. It also alerted us to some potential process losses due to difficulties with available space and coordination of the use of interface controls across users. Finally, the study hints at some interesting interactions between technology and meeting process which should be explored in future studies.

SEARCH AND RETRIEVAL OF MEETING INFORMATION

In order to gain insight into how to facilitate the search and retrieval of information from We-Met meetings, we conducted a study of conventional meetings. The goals were two-fold: to identify methods of searching for meeting information which could be automated by a pen-based meeting tool and to identify difficulties in searching for this information which were amenable to computer support. This study was done before the system described in the previous section was operational.

Study Procedure

Ten meetings occurring at the IBM T. J. Watson Research Center were observed and videotaped. The groups consisted of both technical and non-technical staff. The meeting purposes included research design and planning, information gathering or presentation, project update, and project presentation. The modal number of people in a meeting was 3, with a range of 2 to 10 participants. A total of 23 participants from nine of these meetings were interviewed individually several days to two weeks later.

During the interview, a participant was first asked to recall the main points of the meeting, as well as the specific ideas, proposals, or plans discussed. In the second stage of the interview, participants were asked to search for one of these specific items in the videotape of the meeting. The participants searched the videotape by manipulating the play, reverse, fast forward, and slow speed search controls. They were told how long the meeting had been and could also use the time counter in their searches. As they searched the videotape, the experimenter encouraged the participants to describe how they were searching for the required information.

Findings

In considering the findings, one should keep in mind that the characteristics of videotape as a search medium constrain the possible search strategies. One cannot access semantic information directly, but must rely on more salient physical characteristics of the meeting. Furthermore, since videotape is a sequential medium, one must search the tape in time sequential order (backwards, forwards). However, since the drawings and writing in a We-Met scene are stored as strokes, rather than coded text or graphics, some of the difficulties of searching an analog medium apply to We-Met as well.

The study revealed that people search for meeting information using a number of characteristics.

- **Participant behavior**-- People looked for information based on the behavior of others ("I'm looking for times when the people (two other participants) were speaking"), or themselves ("I'm looking at myself taking notes").
- **Communication medium**-- People recalled the medium by which the information was presented (e.g. foil, whiteboard) and also searched for a particular communication medium to locate a spoken discussion ("I know it is around the chart presentation.")
- **Time**-- Several aspects of time were used to search for information: relative time ("it's probably midway into the meeting), duration (25 minutes into the discussion), and clock time ("we only got through item 1.2 by 5:00").
- **Relation to other events**-- As they played the videotape, people frequently remarked that the event they were looking for occurred before or after an event currently being viewed (e.g. when a person left the meeting). These events served as markers which guided the participant to move backwards or forwards in the videotape record.

Many of these search strategies can be automated with a computer, since these characteristics can be recorded as part of the meeting record. The We-Met record contains a time stamp for each event, so time could easily be used as a search strategy. Writer identification is recorded and this aspect of participant behavior could also be used. Much of the meeting information is contained in the spoken discussion, however, and the ability to search by speaker and play back speech in conjunction with the stroke-based record would be quite valuable. Communication medium could also be recorded and used for search. Characteristics such as these could be used in combination to limit the portion of the meeting searched.

In addition, participants used a strategy we call temporal sampling --viewing segments of the videotape, fast forwarding, and then viewing another segment of the videotape. This was a cumbersome process since the video could not be viewed in this mode of operation, and it was hard to control the distance moved with much precision. An interesting side effect of temporal sampling was that it occasionally caused people to revise their recollection of the meeting when they saw events they had forgotten or misremembered. We have implemented a simple version of temporal sampling in our current prototype. When the horizontal slider at the top of the drawing area is moved to the left, the meeting record is re-played in reverse temporal order and, as it is moved to the right, it is played in the forward direction. Our initial experience with this feature has been positive and we are eager to learn how users will employ this feature.

The search methods described above are a means to get to the desired semantic information. It would be quite desirable to enable the user to access this semantic information directly. Text-based databases typically use content or keyword searches for this purpose. Since the writing and drawings in the We-Met record are not recognized, a method analogous to content searching is not available to us. However, the ability to identify a viewpoint with a text name or hand-drawn squiggle may serve a purpose similar to searches based on explicitly defined keywords.

Conclusion

This study gave us insight into the methods people use to search for meeting information in a non-coded medium. We plan to explore some of these methods in future versions of We-Met. The research also suggested how the power of the computer could be used in new ways to facilitate searching of the meeting record. Finally, our observations have underscored the importance of dealing with the audio record, in addition to the stroke-based record, in future versions of We-Met.

SUMMARY

We have described We-Met, a pen-based prototype designed to explore the communication and information retrieval needs of small group meetings. The study of the use of We-Met suggests the pen-based interface style produces communication process gains, and supports a variety of participant interaction styles. This study also exposed some problems in the use of the limited display space and in the coordination of the use of interface controls across users. The study of strategies users employ when searching for meeting information on videotape identified a number of methods (such as searching by time or writer) which could be automated in a computer-based tool. Some of the problems encountered in searching videotape (such as the ability to directly access information) may be amenable to computer support in We-Met.

The empirical studies reported here have given us some early insights into the features required to support small group meetings. We look forward to reporting on our progress as we continue our development and evaluation efforts.

REFERENCES

1. S. A. Bly. A use of drawing surfaces in different collaborative settings. *CSCW 88: Proceedings of the Conference on Computer-Supported Cooperative Work, Portland, Oregon*, 250-256, 1988.

2. S. A. Bly. Commune: A shared drawing surface. *Proceedings of the Conference on Office Information Systems*, 184-192, 1990.

3. J. Conklin. Design rationale and maintainability. *Proceedings of the 22nd HICCS*, IEEE Computer Society Press, 1989.

4. C. A. Ellis, S. J. Gibbs, and G. L. Rein. Groupware: Some issues and experiences. *Communications of the ACM*, 34:39-58, 1991.

5. W. W. Gaver. Auditory icons, Using sound in computer interfaces. *Human-Computer Interaction*, 2:167-177, 1986.

6. S. Greenberg, M. Roseman, D. Webster, and R. Bohnet. Human and technical factors of distributed group drawing tools. *Interacting with Computers*, 1992. To appear.

7. P. Johnson-Lenz and T. Johnson-Lenz. Post-mechanistic groupware primitives: rhythms, boundaries and containers. *International Journal of Man-Machine Studies*, 34:395-417, 1991.

8. A. MacLean, R. M. Young, and T. P. Moran. Design rationale: The argument behind the artifact. *Proceedings of CHI '91*, 247-252, 1991.

9. M. Mantei. Capturing the Capture Lab concepts: A case study in the design of computer supported meeting environments. *CSCW 88: Proceedings of the Conference on Computer-Supported Cooperative Work, Portland, Oregon*, 257-270, 1988.

10. S. L. Minneman and S. A. Bly. Managing a trois: A study of a multi-user drawing tool in distributed design work. *CHI '91 Proceedings*, 217-224, 1991.

11. M. J. Muller. PICTIVE - An exppIoration in participatory design. *Proceedings of CHI '91*, 225-231, 1991.

12. J. F. Nunamaker, Jr., A. R. Dennis, J. S. Valacich, D. R. Vogel, and J. F. George. Electronic meetings systems to support group work. *Communications of the ACM*, 34:41-61, 1991.

13. J. R. Rhyne and C. G. Wolf. Collaboration process support toolkit. IBM Thomas J. Watson Research Center. 1992. Submitted to UIST 92.

14. S. Sarin and I. Greif. Computer-based real-time conferencing systems. In I. Greif, editor, *Computer-Supported Cooperative Work: A Book of Readings*, 397-420., Morgan Kaufmann, San Mateo, 1988.

15. M. Stefik, G. Foster, D. G. Bobrow, K. Kahn, S. Lanning, and L. Suchman. Beyond the chalkboard: Computer support for collaboration and problem solving in meetings. *Communications of the ACM*, 30:32-47, 1987.

16. J. C. Tang. Findings from observational studies of collaborative work. *International Journal of Man-Machine Studies*, 34:143-160, 1991.

17. J. C. Tang and S. Minneman. VideoWhiteBoard: Video shadows to support remote collaboration. *Proceedings of CHI '91*, 315-322, 1991.

18. D. G. Tatar, G. Foster, and D. G. Bobrow. Design for conversation: lessons from Cognoter. *International Journal of Man-Machine Studies*, 34:185-209, 1991.

19. C. G. Wolf, J. R. Rhyne, L. A. Zorman, and H. O. Ossher. WE-MET (Window Environment-Meeting Enhancement Tools). *CHI '91 Proceedings*, 441-442, 1991.

Looking at Ourselves: An Examination of the Social Organisation of Two Research Laboratories

Richard H. R. Harper

Rank Xerox Cambridge EuroPARC,
61 Regent Street,
Cambridge,
England, CB2 1AB
E-mail: harper@europarc.xerox.com
Phone: +44-223-341544
Fax: +44-223-341510

ABSTRACT

This paper reports findings from ongoing examinations into the social organisation of research laboratories. Two case studies are discussed, and it is suggested that although there are differences between the two sites, commonalities are shown in their hierarchical nature and in the status of researchers. It is argued that researchers form a professional group with all that entails in terms of rights and privileges. More generally it is argued that the social organisation of research laboratories is resistant to change. The consequences of this on the testing and development of systems that have the potential to transform hierarchical relations is briefly discussed and how this resistance and its causes differentiate research laboratories from other work places remarked.

KEYWORDS

Active badges, system design, ethnography.

RESEARCH LABORATORIES AS TOPICS OF RESEARCH

Collaborative work has been one of our primary concerns at EuroPARC. We are of the opinion that systems need to be designed with the *sociality* of work in mind to more effectively resonate with practical needs and requirements. We have used ourselves to test our ideas on sociality, seamless transitions, and more generally the relationship between systems and the individual, but we recognise that this is not without its problems. Crucially, we do not know how representative EuroPARC is of workplaces in general. It may be quite untypical, it may even be, as one discussant at EC-CSCW 91 put it, a "peculiar fish bowl". We are, of course, not alone in wanting to use ourselves to test out ideas. This is a common practice in (pure) research laboratories [7]. Yet, as far as we are aware, no-one has investigated what are the differences between research laboratories and other workplaces. There may be none; there may be many, but clearly it will be beneficial to know what they are. So, we have commenced such studies and are investigating the nature of work in research laboratories in Europe, England, and the USA. We believe that understanding the nature of working relations in research labs will provide a secure foundation for the development of systems supporting working relations in other workplaces.

In this paper I discuss findings from observations of two of eight laboratories currently under investigation. I select these two because a location information generating device in use in both labs provided a convenient methodological metric; and, moreover, attitudes and reactions to the system can be seen as encapsulating or being a prism for the social organisation of the two workplaces.

I have to admit from the start however, that there is no easy answer to the question of whether these two labs are representative of all laboratories. Both are relatively small, the largest having only 60 or so personnel; they are part of organisations that may be unlike other organisations. For these reasons, and doubtless others, the two labs may be unique. To some extent, it is simply not possible to answer the question of representativeness without examination of other labs, which, as I say, we are undertaking. But in any case, I believe that there are likely to be similarities or consistencies across labs, and that the evidence one can gather from just two will go some way toward indicating what those consistencies might be.

In particular I argue that if one looks at what I will call the "moral order" of the laboratories, that is at the inter-relation of formal and informal rules, obligations and interdependencies bound up with the various roles individuals have, then one will be able to uncover consistencies between the positions individuals have within

Permission to copy without fee all or part of this material is granted provided that the copies are not made or distributed for direct commercial advantage, the ACM copyright notice and the title of the publication and its date appear, and notice is given that copying is by permission of the Association for Computing Machinery. To copy otherwise, or to republish, requires a fee and/or specific permission.

© 1992 ACM 0-89791-543-7/92/0010/0330...$1.50

a workplace and their attitudes towards technology. Thus and for example one will find that research staff tend to form something like a *professional group*, with all that entails in terms of rights, privileges, control over work activities and so on. There is little hierarchy within this professional group on formal grounds, though extensive differentiation on the basis of personal esteem, regard and reputation. Research groups in different labs are distinguishable by the extent of their professional rights; some groups will have more autonomy, others less. Second, labs, as a whole and unlike the professional groups within them, are *hierarchical*, and this is shown both formally and informally, in procedures and protocols, and in the ways people in distinct positions within the hierarchy deal with each other. These features are likely to be consequential on the design and outcomes of trials, experiments and implementations of technologies within these environments. I shall briefly discuss these possible consequences once I have completed my attempt to characterise the two laboratories as *socially organised phenomena.*

THE RESEARCH

The methodological opportunity for the research was the existence of an *active badge* application, known as the *Locator*[1]. I do not report how the Locator was developed (see Want,[20]; Newman, *et al*, [17]; for an overview of active badge research see Pier, [18]; for the use of sociological reasoning in the design of Locator applications see Harper, *et al*, [11]) but instead, as I say, analyse attitudes towards badges and the Locator as a means of uncovering the social organisation of the two labs. These will be referred to as labs A and B.

Lab A consists of some 15 or so full time research staff, 10 or so associated and consulting researchers, and 5 administrators and technical staff. Researchers are able to pursue their own research interests as long as these are seen to fall within the overall remit. There are no receptionists, and individuals have their own answering machines. Lab B is larger than Lab A: there are just over 40 full time researchers, with some 15 affiliated or consulting personnel. They are supported by seven other individuals, including three receptionists. There are a handful of answering machines. Researchers are hired to work on prespecified projects.

The findings are primarily qualitative in nature and were gathered through informal interviews, poll counts of application usage and *ethnographic* observation of the individuals and the working contexts in which Locator applications are used and/or are available. Typically, the term ethnography is used to denote lengthy, non-intrusive observation of activities as they *naturally occur*. Optimally, the ethnographer participates in as many of the activities under examination as possible. In this case, I was able to observe activities over a two week period in lab B, and was a "member" and hence a participant in lab A[2]. As to the interviews, some thirty six were conducted. Topics discussed included the character of the work in which individuals were engaged, respective responsibilities and roles, the nature of working relations and their ideas about the Locator, badges and possible badge-based applications in the future. Some individuals had a lot to say about these matters and others very little; one person did not want to talk about badges, the Locator, or indeed anything to do with work: he just liked the idea of being interviewed. But whatever was discussed, the views elicited were treated by me as "instructions" as to how to perceive the respective labs. That is to say, not as objective descriptions, but as means whereby members of the labs expressed and attempted to validate their own views, attitudes and purposes. The particular version or perspective offered by each individual was responded to by way of reference to what, on the basis of my more general observations, I estimated to be the 'social role' of the individual in question. In some cases these responses were made in the initial interview, sometimes in subsequent ones. Interviewee's comments on these responses were then used to confirm or correct my emergent understanding of the laboratories[3]. Gradually, by combining information from the interviews with general observations, a conception of the two labs as socially organised phenomena was developed.

In condensed form the attitudes I want to deal with break down as follows. In Lab A, according to some researchers there is "no need" for the Locator while according to the administrators and support personnel there is. But there are

---

1 Active badges are location sensing devices designed to be worn during the course of work. Developed by Olivetti Research, they measure about 5cm square and are worn like normal security tags. Each badge has a different identity code, which it emits every 15 seconds or so using infra-red signalling similar to the method employed in TV remote controls. This code is picked up by receivers installed in the rooms, hallways and stairwells of the buildings. Roughly once per second, a polling computer interrogates each receiver for recently detected badge codes. When a badge is detected at a new location this event is stored in a record that includes date and time, the badge identity code and the old and new locations. A server makes these records available for applications like the Locator that provides a workstation window indicating the current whereabouts of badge wearers.

2 This means I was subject to the same kinds of pressures and influences as everyone else in the labs - perhaps more so given my involvement in the research reported here. For discussion of this see Harper [10].

3 The use of so-called informal interview techniques as part of the *modus operandi* of ethnographic observational studies has been subject to much debate in sociology. This is not the place to review these discussions. But it needs to be realised that sociology is very different from many of the other sciences that inquire into human action; so different, I suggest, that there are likely to be considerable difficulties in the achievement of interdisciplinarity in design, say in the CSCW area.

informal pressures that lead most researchers to wear badges (despite the lack of Locator use). These pressures are to do with not wanting to be "troublesome", a "spoil-sport", or with the wish to avoid drawing attention to oneself. There is a small contingent of researchers who have intense antipathy to badges. In Lab B there is, apparently, considerable need for the Locator recognised by all categories of staff. Researchers are still conscious of "informal pressures" but these have more to do with the *quid pro quo* of Locator use (i.e., "I get benefits from wearing a badge so I will wear the badge to give others the same benefits") rather than those pressures that exert themselves on researchers in Lab A (i.e., not wanting to "rock the boat" and the rest). No one objects to badges so strongly as to refuse to wear them. There is some concern amongst researchers about the social affects of badges "elsewhere".

It is my case that these differences in attitude can be explained and understood by reference to social organisation. My position is that a person's attitudes are intimately related to the role they have in an organisation[4]. An example will illustrate what I mean and allow me to begin to uncover the social organisation of the two labs. Explanation here consists of describing and evoking what a job means to those doing it[5]. Let us take receptionists in Lab B. The tasks of these people include, just to cite a few examples, finding people, relaying messages, and acting as the intermediary between the outside world and the lab. Their role consists of making contacts, of locating people. They know this; these are the matters that are of concern to them. We should not be surprised therefore that they perceive the Locator as a helpful, not to say essential, tool in their work. For them it makes practical sense given the nature of their work and the kinds of relations they have with others in the lab.

"For reception (the Locator) is wonderful. In this building we can't see anyone. They might be in the main lab, coffee lounge, corridors. Before, (the receptionist) would phone four or five places and in the mean time other calls would be coming in. This saves a lot of time and energy." (Receptionist, Lab B).

The fact that something is practical does not of course ensure that it is also acceptable. From some perspectives the Locator may seem to be a practical device but that does not mean it is also an acceptable one. I suggest that acceptability is partly a function of what can be thought of as the moral side of working life, that broader picture of working relations that includes more than just formal job specification. A particular manifestation of this moral side relates to entitlements over access to and rights to withhold information. Receptionists in Lab B have a "right" - though this is not expressed formally - to know more or less where everyone else in the lab is. Needless to say these rights have parameters, and there are limits of detail and particularity beyond which a receptionist's "right to know" are not acceptable. A light-hearted example will illustrate. There is some comment in lab B on receptionists' knowing by use of the locator whether someone has gone into the toilets or not. *"It was funny at first you know when I told callers that so and so had just gone into the toilet they used to get embarrassed and laugh. I don't say that anymore."* (Receptionist, lab B). This information crosses not only boundaries of propriety within work, but also ones that are to do with the relationship between society and the individual: going to the "loo" is for most of us a private affair at work as anywhere else[6]. The important issue however, is that receptionists are conscious, in varying degrees and capacities for articulation, of what these entitlements are, just as everyone else is. Given the nature of their relationship with others in lab B, the Locator then provides information that they already have rights to (albeit provided in different form). It does not alter this aspect of their working relations. Nor does the Locator alter what information others have about them. For the receptionists in lab B there is no opportunity to roam about like researchers in search of a colleague, a chat, or fresh air. The receptionists are tied to their desks: this they know when they take on the job, this again is part and parcel of what a receptionist's job entails. Everyone knows where the receptionists are, ought to be, and can be expected to stay. So, in terms of what information they have about others and what others know about them, the Locator makes no changes. The Locator preserves and reflects the already existing *status quo* of information distribution and use.

Individuals in different social roles will find the Locator alters the information they have available. An individual may need to pause a moment to decide whether these changes are acceptable to him or herself and to those they work with. Consider the example of administrators in Lab A. In one important respect these individuals have a similar social role to receptionists in the other lab: where they are is more or less certain: they have a place, an office, a desk where they can reasonably be expected to be. In other words, others in the research lab are entitled to know where the administrators are. Entitled in the sense that if

4 The notion of role has been extensively discussed in sociology. For a background see Biddle & Thomas [4]; for conflicts between roles see Merton [13]. For professionals and their roles see Moore [16]. I shall discuss later on how researchers may be thought of as incumbents of professional roles.

5 This is quite unlike the view on the specification of "jobs" and their constituent features relevant to design that one more often finds in, say, the expert system design literature. See for example, Downes [6].

6 Though in other societies it might not be: consider the communal lavatories of Imperial Rome, for instance and more generally, domestic arrangements historically. See Aries & Duby [1].

administrators are not at their desks others can ask "Where are they? Are they doing their job?" The Locator then makes no difference to this aspect of the relationship between administrators and everyone else in the lab. But in another respect the Locator does introduce a potential change. Administrators are not the primary medium of communication between the outside world and Lab A. Knowing where everyone is is not something administrators have a continuous entitlement to. It is only occasionally that they have such rights, only when, say, a caller does not have a name, a contact allowing a direct link with a member of the lab to be made. At those junctures they are entitled to find out, but for the rest of the time it is "none of the administrator's business". Yet the Locator provides them with information about other's whereabouts continuously. It thus alters what they have available to them and affects the character of their relations with everyone else. They are alert to the possible ramifications of this change. Although the Locator makes no difference to what information others have about them, it does provide information that may unsettle their relations with others. This is an issue that is a concern to them. They do not, for example, want to know when someone comes in to the lab since it is not a part of their job to "check up on people".

"I think it will be useful for emergencies. But I don't want (researchers) to think I know where they are and what time they come in. I don't want to be able to say they aren't in 'till 12pm." (Administrator Lab A).

THE MORAL ORDER

This contrast between receptionists and administrators in the two labs alludes then to how a role is a moral matter; that how someone behaves in an organisation - and indeed is expected to behave - is constituted by much more than mere formal job specification. It is important to recognise that incorporating the moral aspects of working life as part of the analytic conception I am developing allows one to understand a variety of attitudes and actions that would otherwise be opaque. From this view one can begin to comprehend why members of the labs feel so influenced by informal pressures. For their tasks - whether as administrators, support personnel, or researchers - consist of more than just what the "job's worth". They include, along with other things, getting on with everyone, being seen to be willing to participate and help out, and to avoid being unreasonable or obstructive. What I am saying is that work environments consist of a *moral order*[7]. This order will be reflected in attitudes towards and use of objects like active badges and associated applications, just as it will be with all the technologies devised and tested within these labs. Members of these settings are embedded in and wrapped up in criss-crossing sets of relations with one another, defined in part by formal hierarchies expressed in rule books and job descriptions and in part by tacit - and sometimes not so tacit - notions of mutual interdependency, obligation, respect and so on. The moral aspects of these environments are expressed in the delicate ways individuals try to preserve the order of their relations: they use a particular technology because it make sense to given what they do and how they work with others, they are worried about a technology because of how the using of it (whatever it might be) might infringe or be seen to infringe on the boundaries between and entitlements to information, for example.

I have made some remarks about the roles of administrators and receptionists and their respective location in the moral order of research labs and have thus begun to explain the differences in attitudes between these individuals. Space precludes analysis of all the various roles within the two labs, but what I have covered is sufficient to provide a background to understanding the role of researchers.

It seems to me that the character of relations between researchers and the consequent patterns of information distribution between them is not be easy to specify. Whereas the title for receptionists or administrators says much about their responsibilities, this is far from true with researchers. Consider, for instance, the comments of some of the researchers in Lab A as regards the reasons why they go along with the Locator.

"It's the kind of thing where you need a physical mass to make it useful. I don't want to upset (the lab). I don't mind." (Researcher, Lab A)

"I carry a badge now so as not to be a spoil-sport. But I don't like to carry it..." (Researcher, Lab A).

It would appear that relations between researchers in Lab A are delicate and easily unsettled. Researchers recognise that wearing a badge says something about their attitudes to other researchers and projects in the lab. There is a symbolism involved. They might not think the Locator project a good idea, but they do not want to be seen to be too negative; if nothing else this might jeopardise their own projects in the future.

Matters are made all the more complicated in lab A because a variety of active badge applications have been developed and are operational concurrent with our Locator inquiries. These applications mean that even though a researcher may

7 Numerous authors have looked at workplaces with an eye towards what they call its 'moral order'. I refer to the moral aspects of work in an attempt to capture accurately the way work is experienced. But for others, reference to the moral order serves different purposes. Woolgar [21] for instance uses the term moral order to refer to the symbolic boundaries of meaning, which are viewed as 'texts'. Chester Barnard [2, 3] uses the phrase the 'morality of the organisation' to refer to the benefits that organisations provide the individual and society. Goffman [9] uses the term 'moral careers' to refer to the fate of individuals in 'Total Institutions'.

agree to participate *only* in using and testing the Locator, other kinds of badge driven information are being provided for applications that they may not have agreed to be involved with. The reverse also holds true; i.e., some people are using badges for applications apart from the Locator. Wearing a badge means going along with, albeit tacitly, other developments. This makes it ambiguous what someone is implying when they wear a badge. Not rocking the boat is one thing, but getting involved in projects about which one knows next to nothing is altogether a different matter.

In Lab A preserving harmony is clearly something that some of the researchers concern themselves with. Wearing a badge in that lab is for some researchers the price to pay to avoid giving offence[8]. Why should these relations be so fragile? Why, on the other hand, is there little expression of fear about upsetting workmates in Lab B? Is it that working harmony in that lab is more robust and less vulnerable to the transformations that an information generating device can bring about?

The way in which the Locator is introduced into labs A and B draws attention to matters that are pertinent. In Lab B management decide that the wearing of badges for the Locator is compulsory for a two week period. Although many of those interviewed from this lab comment on the flat hierarchy and the trust between the managers and the researchers, that the Locator is introduced in this way suggests how closely knit this is as a workplace. Individuals here are subject to what one might refer to as the will of the corporate body. I am not thinking here in terms of the firm as a corporate entity but in terms of a social group and its ability to exert control over its members. This is not to say that researchers in Lab B are massively constrained but that the way the place is organised means that such things as the location of an individual can be treated as a matter that management are *entitled* to rule upon. To be sure, the fact that only a two week period is involved suggests how keen management are to be diplomatic, to preserve some kind of consensus and avoid being heavy handed. A short period can be defended as "reasonable" to try things out. If, after that period, it turns out that the Locator is of no benefit and upsets some individuals by intruding on what they perceive to be their rights to privacy, then management support can be withdrawn without loss of face or damage to management-researcher relations[9].

In Lab A no similar management sanction is offered or indeed sought, not simply because the developers of badges and the Locator do not want to ask, but because they know that the management will not get involved. The view of management in this lab is that researchers be given the opportunity to conduct research according to their own interests and expertise. Needless to say this has to relate to the goals of the lab and must in some way be seen to be productive, but on a day to day basis, it is a "hands off" policy. The Locator is not a development management feel entitled to adjudicate on. If researchers do not want to get involved with the Locator then, according to this philosophy, that is their concern.

"I don't want to get involved in this. I do not want this to cause any ( ) trouble. I do wear a badge as an emblem: I want to be seen to be even-handed." (Manager-researcher, Lab A).

Lab A is then highly individuated and the relationship between the organisation and the individual allows considerable autonomy. Lab B is organised differently. Researchers there are part of a unified body, one that 'exerts' - though this may be too strong a word - considerable control over its members.

The way research work is organised further underlines these differences. In Lab B researchers are hired to do particular tasks as part of the overall program of research set up by management. Each person has what is called one 'blue sky' day a week to conduct research on his or her chosen area, but for the rest they have to get on with 'lab work'. Typically these periods when researchers are given autonomy are insufficient to allow much research to be done.

"Well I have these blue sky days but to be honest with you I never actually get that time. I am nearly always doing my other work, lab stuff." (Researcher, Lab B).

The philosophy in Lab A, though requiring the building of some kind of consensus, is distinct in allowing individual researchers to pursue their own, sometimes unique, interests.

---

8 I do not want to imply that relations in the labs are and always have been happy, only that there is a tendency in all workplaces for relations to stabilise. There will be many factors causing this, including the work, whatever it is, becoming routine, orderly and unproblemmatic, and for people not to have the time or energy for strife.

9 There are, inevitably, tensions of one kind or another between researchers and their managers. These tensions are played out in the various forms of commitment of the individual researcher to their colleagues, to political groups or cabals within their organisation, to the company at large and so on. In the case of researchers, these tensions are exacerbated by their commitment to "the intellectual community," that small grouping of individuals transcending organisational, institutional and even national boundaries. See Merton [14] for analysis of the relationship between intellectuals and bureaucracy; Burns and Stalker [5] for relations between research scientists, engineers and managers in industrial organisations.

"No. I am hired to research and that's up to me. I mean what research I do is my responsibility." (Researcher, Lab A).

As workplaces, then, the two labs are dissimilar in terms of the autonomy given individual researchers. For much of the time, this difference may be negligible, and something research members of the labs do not give a second thought to. At other times, and the introduction and use of the Locator is one, this autonomy and its manifestation in the boundary between what researchers can call their own private business and what is public, may be highlighted. It is my view that the Locator compromises this boundary, shifting what individuals are entitled to know about each other. The acceptability of this, whether such a compromise affronts rights that people are not prepared to forsake, depends upon a melange of factors that I have gradually been uncovering. My point is that in Lab B researchers have a smaller domain that they can call their own affair; in Lab A, they have a larger one. Consequently the Locator is more of an issue for the latter since researchers in that lab have, in a sense, more to lose[10].

CONCLUSION

There are a variety of ways that analysis of social organisation can be incorporated in to the design process. There are too, many methods deployed to generate data about social processes: video and audio tape analysis is one, ethnography another. Each of these methods provides distinct orders of materials but each is intended to prize open social organisation as a phenomenon in its own right[11]. Here the purpose has been to describe elements of the working environments of research labs as they are lived and experienced. This has involved using the term social organisation in a broad sense to include such things as how relations between people are as much political matters as organisational ones, bound up with values of good and bad, of things done well and things done badly, since this is how they are experienced. It is this extended conception of the relations between people that has led me to say of the workplace that it consists of a moral order.

It is my case that these research labs consist of a distribution of work roles within a formally specified hierarchy; this is located within a broader network of relations and interdependencies where notions of favours owed, of mutual support and helpfulness, of respect, trust, and of course, dislike and unwillingness to 'help out' are involved. Individuals are required to make information about their location available or choose not to do so - it can work either way - as a function of their formally defined work role, their consequent position within the hierarchy, and the character of their working relationships - be they good or bad, temporary or long lasting; in short as a function of their *social role within the moral order of their workplace*. Put another way, and bearing in mind the technology referred to in this study, how the Locator is used, what it represents to individuals, is determined by what they do, their formal position, and their state of relations - meant here in the broadest sense - with others in the labs. From this view, wearing a badge, viewing the Locator as acceptable or not as the case may be, symbolically represents one's job, one's status, one's location within the moral order.

An important finding is that one role within the moral order has a considerable amount of autonomy associated with it - the role of researcher. For these individuals, wearing a badge can mean a variety of things - interest in badge research, a keenness to help out those in other subordinate roles, administrators, support staff, and others. But, apart from the two week period in lab B, one could not say they wear a badge because they are obliged to. Researchers in both labs have a role and a position which provides them with what might be thought of as a *professional's* right to choose. Though, clearly, in many ways, computer scientists, programmers, designers and all the other specialists that fall into the catch all role 'researchers in IT labs' are not professional in the exactly the same way that one thinks of lawyers, doctors, accountants with all their administrative bodies, rituals and powers[12], but the term professional does draw attention to the considerable difference between the role of researcher and that of, say, administrator. The researchers in the two labs are treated as if they were professionals; that is as able to choose for themselves such things as when they come to

10 The particular 'expertise' of the researcher may also be a factor in determining how much is at stake. At one time, programmers had an almost craftsman-like status but, as software activities have become increasingly a matter of software engineering, so has the expertise of these people become a kind of commodity bought and sold like so many other 'non professional' skills. Research programmers may be resistant to changes in their rights in research labs for fear of becoming like their colleagues in industrial settings. This may differentiate them from those with other skills. My findings do not allow me to investigate this matter however. But for discussion of this possibility see Stinchcombe & Heimer [19]. For an analysis of the impact of Taylorist management practices on 'Data-Processing' professionals see Greenbaum [8].

11 Here I do not want to deliberate on which of these is better, or the particular advantages any one might have. Choice between them will be based on what is pertinent to any design program and practical considerations like what is available in terms of access, funds, and expertise.

12 These one might think of as the formally defined professions. Amongst the characteristics pertinent here are controls over access to the education and experience requisite for membership; a certain amount of arcane knowledge and expertise that is judged and evaluated from within the profession (i.e, by the profession's ruling bodies etc), and privileges and rights bestowed by society, as represented by the state [12].

work and how long they should work; as individuals who are judged by their peers and not say, through crude quantitative measures and so on. In short, researchers are given a large amount of *control over their jobs*.

Moreover, and closely related to their status, researchers have considerable rights over information, in particular information about themselves. There is a boundary between what others in research labs are entitled to know about researchers and what they are not entitled to. Although the position of this boundary may differ between the two labs, the important issue is that researchers become concerned when this boundary is interfered with. Researchers will only accept such interference or changes when they perceive that advantages will come of it. Researchers in lab B were accepting of the loss of some degree of privacy because of the advantages the locator provided; in lab A, where there were not perceived to be so many benefits, some individuals were far less willing to "pay the cost" of losing some control over information.

This has numerous implications relating to the character of the artifacts designed, built and tested in research laboratories, in particular those which are intended to affect the character of working relations in deep and radical ways - one possible goal of CSCW technology. When I say deep and radical I am alluding to the possibility of transforming the character of relations not just between individuals in similar social roles but between individuals in very different roles: say, between administrators and researchers, between receptionists and managers, in other words, between people who have, at any particular moment in time, different status. If the evidence provided here is anything to go by, then these relations are complex and delicate, with hierarchical differentials manifest in entitlements to such things as information distribution and control. Individuals in a whole variety of roles - not just those with the most privilege - will be ill at ease when attempts are made to change patterns of entitlement, obligation, respect, informal and formal hierarchy, and more. In short, the social organisation of these workplaces is *resistant* to change. Consequently it may not be appropriate to use research labs to test systems designed to alter social relations since these places may simply be too static to make it worthwhile - and that is not to mention the turmoil doing so can create.

Moreover, that this is so alludes to how research labs may be different from other workplaces. The resistance to change and *hierarchical stasis* may be specific to the forms of role relations one finds in them. In particular the high proportion of individuals who have what I have called "professional rights". In workplaces were there are fewer individuals with these rights, in relation to the overall numbers of staff, changes may be more acceptable. Less people will "loose out" in such changes, and those unaffected will feel less worried about how change will affect their general working relations and, in particular, those with "professional" colleagues. In short, what makes Information Technology research labs *peculiar fish bowls* is not the technology, the active badges, the Locator, and other "widgets", but the forms of working relationships one finds therein.

REFERENCES

1. Aries,P. & Duby,G. (Eds.) (1985-87), *Histoire de la vie privee*, Editions du Soleuil, five volumes. Paris.

2. Barnard,C. (1948) *Organisations and Management*, Harvard University Press, Cambridge.

3. Barnard,C. (1968) *The Functions of the Executive*, Harvard University Press, Harvard.

4. Biddle, B. & Thomas, E. (1966). *Role theory: Concepts and research*. Wiley: New York.

5. Burns,T. & Stalker,G.M. (1966) *The Management of Innovation*, Tavistock, London.

6. Downes,C.G. (1988) Representing the Structure of jobs in job analysis. *Journal of Man-Machine Studies*, Vol 28, pp363-390.

7. Friedman,A.L. (with Cornford,D.S.) (1989) *Computer Systems Development: History, organisation and implementation*, John Wiley, Chichester.

8. Greenbaum,J.M. (1979) *In the Name of Efficiency: Management Theory and Shopfloor Practice in Data-Processing Work*, Temple University Press, Philidelphia.

9. Goffman,E. (1961) *Asylums*, Aldine, Chicago.

10. Harper, R.H.R. (1990). *The social organisation of invention: Preliminary comments on an ongoing ethnography*. Paper presented to the Sociology Dept., Manchester University, Dec. 12th.

11. Harper, R.H.R., Lamming, M.G., & Newman, W.N. (1992). Locating Systems at Work. *EuroPARC Technical Report* and *Interacting With Computers*, (in press) .

12. Johnson,T. (1981) *Professions and Power*, Macmillan, London.

13. Merton,R.K. (1957a) The Role Set: Problems in Sociological Theory. *British Journal of Sociology*, Vol 8, pp. 110-120.

14. Merton,R.K. (1957b). *Social Theory and Social Structure*, (revised edition), Free Press, New York.

15. Moore,W.E. (1970). *The Professions: Roles and Rules*, Russell Sage Foundation, New York.

16. Newman, W.N. Eldridge, M. & Lamming, M.G. (1991). Pepys: Generating Autobiographies by Automatic Tracking. *Proceedings of E-CSCW 91*, Amsterdam, Kluwer, Amsterdam.

17. Pier,K. (Ed.) (1991). Active Badge Panel. *Proceedings, Conference on Organizational Computing Systems,* November 5-8, Atlanta, Georgia.

18. Stinchcombe,A. & Heimer,C.A. (1988) Interorganisational Relations and Careers in Computer Software Firms. *Research in the Sociology of Work,* Vol. 4, pp. 179-204.

19. Want,R. (in press) The Active Badge Locator System. *ACM Transactions on Office Information Systems.*

20. Woolgar,S. (1989) Representation, cognition, self: what prospects for an integration of the sociology and psychology of science? In Fuller,S. de May,M. and Woolgar,S. (Eds.) *The Cognitive Turn: sociological and psychological perspectives on science,* Kluwer, Dordrecht, pp. 201-224.

CSCW challenges in large-scale technical projects - a case study

Kaj Grønbæk, Morten Kyng, Preben Mogensen

Computer Science Department, Aarhus University,
Ny Munkegade 116, DK 8000 Aarhus C, Denmark.
kgronbak@daimi.aau.dk, mkyng@daimi.aau.dk, pmogensen@daimi.aau.dk
+45 86 12 71 88.

ABSTRACT

This paper investigates CSCW aspects of large-scale technical projects based on a case study of a specific Danish engineering company and uncovers challenges to CSCW applications in this setting. The company is responsible for management and supervision of one of the worlds largest tunnel/bridge construction projects. Our primary aim is to determine requirements on CSCW as they unfold in this concrete setting as opposed to survey and laboratory investigations. The requirements provide feedback to product development both on specific functionality and as a long term vision for CSCW in such settings.

The initial qualitative analysis identified a number of bottlenecks in daily work, where support for cooperation is needed. Examples of bottlenecks are: sharing materials, issuing tasks, and keeping track of task status. Grounded in the analysis, cooperative design workshops based on scenarios of future work situations were established to investigate the potential of different CSCW technologies in this setting. In the workshops, mock-ups and prototypes were used to support end-users in assessing CSCW technologies based on concrete, hands-on experiences. The workshops uncovered several challenges. First, support for sharing materials would require a huge body of diverse materials to be integrated, for example into a hypermedia network. Second, daily work tasks are event driven and plans change too rapidly for people to register them on a computer. Finally, tasks are closely coupled to materials being processed thus a coordination tool should integrate facilities for managing materials.

KEYWORDS

Cooperative design, hypermedia, coordination, evaluation, case study.

1. INTRODUCTION

Since the first CSCW workshop in 1984 interest in the area has grown rapidly, yet successful products are relatively few. Grudin [11] point to explanations such as: those who do the work don't get the benefit; and difficulties in evaluating CSCW applications. From our perspective of cooperative design one could add: insufficient involvement of end-users. Cooperative design, as developed in Scandinavia over the last decades, stresses the importance of creative participation of potential end-users in design processes in general [4,10,5]. Kyng [16] argues that for CSCW applications the problems created by lack of user involvement are particularly severe. This paper describes an attempt to take a step towards greater user participation in the design of CSCW applications. Such participation requires techniques that enable end-users to understand the possibilities for computer support and to envision work with a proposed system. Traditional requirement specifications are not suited for this purpose since most users are not able to bridge the gap between dry descriptions and their professional knowledge and skills. Instead we apply tools and techniques developed specifically for cooperative design. These include cooperative design workshops with end-users, where future work situations are envisioned by simulation of possible computer support using mock-ups and prototypes thus allowing end-users to get hands-on experiences. However, the focus of this paper is on developing CSCW requirements in a concrete setting using cooperative techniques, not on the techniques themselves. We refer readers interested in cooperative design to the papers listed above.

The work described in this paper is part of a multinational, EC Esprit II project, EuroCoOp, developing systems supporting distributed collaborative work. The primary goal of the analysis presented and discussed here is to provide feedback to product development in the EuroCoOp project, both on specific functionality and as a long term vision for CSCW in such settings. A secondary goal is to function as facilitator for the ongoing development of the user organization in question.

The paper includes excerpts from a project report [13], and it is organized as follows. Section 2 describes the case being studied. Section 3 discusses bottlenecks in daily work, particularly with respect to cooperation in the user organization. Section 4 discusses challenges in overcoming the identified bottlenecks. Section 5 concludes the paper.

Permission to copy without fee all or part of this material is granted provided that the copies are not made or distributed for direct commercial advantage, the ACM copyright notice and the title of the publication and its date appear, and notice is given that copying is by permission of the Association for Computing Machinery. To copy otherwise, or to republish, requires a fee and/or specific permission.

© 1992 ACM 0-89791-543-7/92/0010/0338...$1.50

2. THE CASE: A LARGE-SCALE TECHNICAL PROJECT

The domain considered is large-scale technical project management, in our case, the Great Belt bridge/tunnel project. The bridge/tunnel over The Great Belt consists of a railway tunnel and a roadway bridge from Halsskov, Zealand to Sprogø (8 km) and a combined bridge from Sprogø to Knudshoved, Funen – the West Bridge (7 km). The company has offices in Copenhagen, Halsskov, Knudshoved and Sprogø.

When the decision to build a bridge/tunnel was agreed upon, Great Belt Link Ltd. (GBL) was established. Early work centred around creating the organization and producing the material for the invitation of tenders. Later GBL managed the selection of contractors and formation of contracts. In the third phase GBL is supervising the construction activities. In this phase the organization has changed again by establishing site-offices. When the bridges and tunnel are completed in the late '90's, the organization will be responsible for operation and maintenance.

2.1. Supervision

In this section we focus on GBL's supervision of the construction of the West Bridge. The major part of this work is done by the GBL site-office in Knudshoved (Figure 1). The construction of the West Bridge is done by an international consortium. The construction is specified in thousands of pages. During construction these specifications evolve and progress is monitored. In turn, this process involves thousands of pages of progress reports, change requests and nonconformance reports. The supervision involves three perspectives: *time , economy, and quality.*

Handling of information according to the three perspectives is carried out primarily by the functions Time Planning, Economy, and Documentation respectively, cf. Figure 1, the bottom rectangles, center and right.

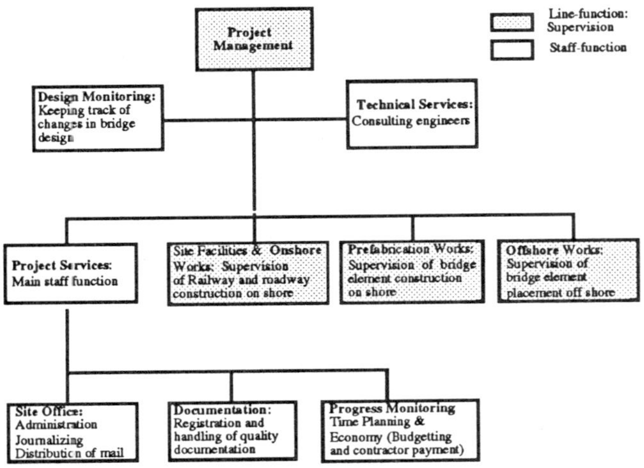

Figure 1: Overview of the organizational structure of the site-office in Knudshoved.

2.2 Computer support

GBL has a comprehensive computer installation based on local area networks with 2 Mb connections between offices. Approximately 80% of the personnel have their own PCs. We briefly describe the computer systems, beginning with three systems respectively handling information according to the perspectives: time, economy, and quality.

Time & Artemis

GBL reviews the contractors' workplans and monitors their progress. The workplans are divided into three groups: 1) main activities (hundreds) 2) contract activities (one or two thousands), and 3) subactivities (several thousands).

The computer support in Time Planning consists mainly of the Artemis system. This system supports: 1) analyzing estimates, for example, the consequences of an altered duration of a contract activity with respect to milestones and the activity network of the whole construction project, 2) maintenance of time plans, 3) several standard outputs: barcharts, critical paths, resource scheduling, etc., 4) programming the system to produce special reports.

Economy & SØS

GBL manages all economic transactions with contractors. Prices are specified in contracts, but the amount being paid depend on the quality and status of the deliverables. Payments are calculated on a monthly basis.

The main computer support consists of the financial management system, SØS. The functionality of SØS includes: accounting, project economy (planning, budgeting, registration), contracts (balance, obligations, suppliers). SØS supports monitoring of main activities, contract activities, and work items, which corresponds to subactivities in the time perspective. To ease the daily work, work items are further decomposed, and spread-sheet applications are used to monitor at this level.

Quality & KIS

Traditionally, in the construction business, supervisors check delivered products on site. Due to the complexity in building the bridge/tunnel, GBL has chosen another approach. Following the new ISO 9000 standards, the contract specifies requirements for both construction and quality assurance. The idea is that the contractor should document that specified requirements are met. In contrast to traditional supervision, supervisors at GBL inspect contractor documentation as well as spot check products and procedures.

For each check performed by the contractor, a Quality Control form (QC-form) is prepared and sent to GBL. Typically a QC-form has a large number of paper based addenda. The QC-forms are handled by a special-purpose quality assurance system, KIS. This system contains information about planned quality checks and produces a monthly Document Plan Status showing accepted, missing and rejected forms, respectively.

For handling exceptional situations, two additional document types are used: *Non-conformance* reports, retrospectively reporting deviations from prescribed procedures; and *Change requests* for advance assessment of deviations from a planned procedure/design. Processing these documents requires frequent examination of a handbook, describing the work procedures for construction, quality control, and supervision. This handbook is referred to as the SAB.

Drawings & DMS
In order to manage approximately 35.000 drawings GBL has developed a computer based Drawing Management System, DMS. Essentially, the system is a database with online access. DMS lets supervisors retrieve, view, and plot drawings. Before plotting a drawing, annotations to appear on the plot can be made. However, the annotations cannot be linked to the drawing in DMS.

Journal system
All correspondence is logged centrally in the journal system SCAN-JOUR with the following keys: ID number, category number, date, sender/receiver and keywords. All managers can, via secretaries, inspect the correspondence lists for the whole organization and decide whether they want to request hard-copies of any of the letters.

Office software
Standard software packages (from WordPerfect Corporation) is used to support e-mail, calendar, word-processing, and spread-sheets.

3. PROBLEMS AND BOTTLENECKS IN DAILY WORK AND COLLABORATION

A particularly striking aspect of work at GBL is the discrepancy between large monolithic, vertical systems and daily work. Numerous cumbersome procedures have been developed using ad hoc computer support in order to provide the "glue" to connect these vertical systems, and to tie them to actual supervision activities.

KIS, Artemis and SØS are primarily used to produce monthly reports. But much work in Time Planning and Economy concerns gathering data and validating data through negotiations. To this end, e.g. Economy makes use of spread-sheet-applications, and the supervisors have built special applications to monitor the construction process. The Quality Information System, KIS, organizes information according to a hierarchy facilitating traceability when the link is finished and in use. There is no support for using quality information in the construction phase concerning, for example, tracing information about who handled a case, what was the problem, and any relevant or similar cases. Thus KIS is currently used for registration of standard data and production of monthly reports, whereas e.g. the registration of non-conformances and change-requests is done in Artemis, and a separate database program is used to create an overview of all the documents (e.g. statistics).

In the following we discuss problems and bottlenecks related to sharing materials and to coordination. We also briefly mention some related to communication. Related distinctions were proposed by Sørgaard [18].

3.1 Sharing materials

Archiving
Processing of correspondence is largely based on standard procedures, supported by computers. These procedures make manual sharing of this material in departmental archives feasible. In contrast, internal basic information such as casting reports, supervision diaries, supervision notes, pictorial documentation, and video is handled manually and with word processors in an ad hoc fashion by the supervisors. This implies the existence of a considerable number of different, non-integrated archives, some of which contain redundant information. Thus, sharing materials, in particular for writing joint reports or updating the SAB, is difficult.

Retrieval
The ease of retrieving materials depends on the archive in question: in the Journal system one can search by key; retrieval of drawings in DMS can be done by name and number; materials archived locally are often personal and only organized by date. Furthermore, keys are static and either extremely standardized or so personal that they are useless to all but their creator.

A typical task for a supervisor includes assessing a QC-form, handling a non-conformance report, or handling a change-request. The information needed includes: similar cases from the past, previous correspondence concerning this issue, and pictures of this or similar parts of the bridge. In these cases, retrieval of materials is not easy. The proper key to an archive is seldom present. And, if the keys are present, it is cumbersome to find the material in the non-integrated archives in different locations. In many cases material has to be obtained directly from the people organizing a local archive.

3.2 Coordination

Coordination in Prefab: Action lists
The area manager in Prefab (Prefabrication Work, cf. Figure 1) analyses incoming letters and decides on their urgency, who should have copies, and who should be responsible for taking action. The letters are registered in an "action list" together with a deadline and initials of the person responsible. Actions are categorized by three types of deadlines: two days (ASAP), one week, and two weeks. The only reminders provided for the responsible engineers, are weekly copies of the most recent action list. When an item on the action list is completed it is moved to a "done-list."

Although there are no facilities for automatic alerting or for searching actions on special criteria, the supervisors explained that the existing facilities have worked reasonably well. But as document flow increases due to progress in the construction activities, they anticipate that the current approach will become insufficient.

Coordination in Progress Monitoring: Reporting
Each month the contractor delivers drafts of their progress reports to GBL in order to get payment for completed work. GBL needs to assess whether the drafts reflect the reality on site. To undertake this assessment parts of the contractor's reports are distributed to supervisors within GBL in order to get their responses one or two days later. Responses need to be collected before the progress reports can be negotiated with the contractor. Progress Monitoring is responsible for coordinating these responses and for making the final version of the progress report.

Currently there is no support for coordination in progress assessment, for retrieval of material related to current and previous assessments, or for the supervisor's comments and changes to the materials.

3.3 Communication

In the analysis, several problems concerning explicit communication were identified. One concerns synchronous interaction when situations on site demand quick, mutual, decision making by personnel situated in different locations (Copenhagen, Knudshoved, Lindholm, etc.). Other types of problems are concerned with asynchronous aspects such as: how to share knowledge possessed by another department; and how to trace personnel in the workplace. Addressing these problems was outside the scope of the design workshops undertaken so far, hence we do not elaborate further on these problems.

4. CHALLENGES TO CSCW TECHNOLOGY FOR LARGE-SCALE TECHNICAL PROJECTS

In this section we assess the potentials of two evolving CSCW technologies, hypermedia and coordination technology, in supporting sharing of materials and task administration. This assessment is based on the cooperative design workshops carried out at GBL.

4.1 Hypermedia support for sharing materials

Several bottlenecks have been identified with respect to sharing materials at GBL: lack of support for tracing specific subsets of related materials, and lack of support for groups of people collaboratively writing and annotating reports, e.g. progress reports. Hypermedia technology [6] has shown promise in supporting groups working on shared materials [2,9,19,20]. We explored ways hypermedia technology could be introduced to overcome the bottlenecks and problems related to sharing of materials.

4.1.1 A possible GBL hypermedia architecture
We envision a hypermedia based architecture (Figure 2) where a link server is plugged into the LAN to support interlinking of materials [12]. A similar link server approach has been proposed by Pearl [17]. The hypermedia supplements a traditional database organization of the materials rather than replacing it. For instance, it should be possible to sort and index some material types to support traditional database query facilities.

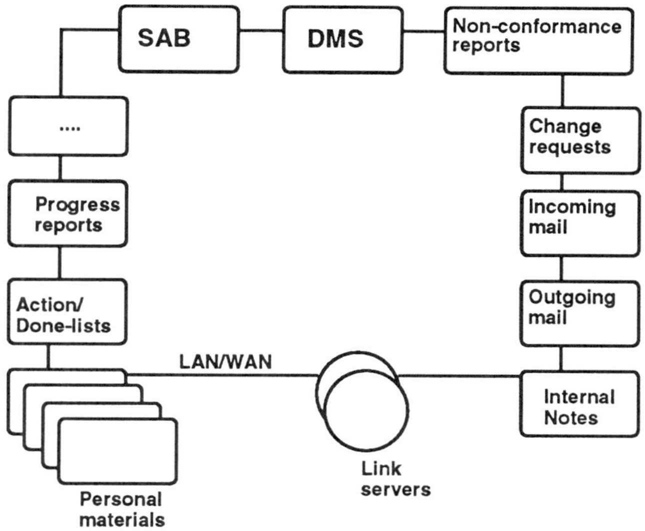

Figure 2: A possible hypermedia architecture for interlinking of materials at GBL. Rounded rectangles represent archives of specific node types. Circles represent link databases (servers).

To support daily work at GBL, at least the following kinds of materials should be accessible as node types in the hypermedia:

- The SAB handbook. The chapters should be nodes in the hypermedia while sections/paragraphs/words can serve as link anchors.
- DMS drawings should be included via a CAD node type. Arbitrary drawing objects should ideally be anchorable.
- Non-conformance reports and Change requests should be stored and indexed as separate nodes.
- Incoming mail/fax should be scanned or otherwise entered as nodes in the hypermedia. Anchoring of regions in letters should be provided regardless of whether letters have been converted via Character Recognition (OCR).
- Outgoing mail/fax and internal notes already in computer-based form should be stored as nodes.
- Action/Done-lists should be available as nodes. Action descriptions should be anchorable units.
- Progress reports should be included in the hypermedia. Addenda should be nodes and the report itself needs to be broken into several nodes to allow simultaneous user annotations.
- The supervisors' materials: supervision diaries, notes, pictures, videos, etc., should be accessible in the hypermedia to support internal cross references and external access.

The tools: CAD systems, word processors, etc., are responsible for defining the types of anchorable units in the specific material. Links between anchors in materials are stored in one or more link databases, servers, in the network. This allows the whole organization, a department, or a smaller group of people to share materials and networks of links.

4.1.2 A use scenario for hypermedia technology
The hypermedia services should be available to all GBL personnel in the WAN subject to suitable access restrictions. Due to performance requirements, separate link servers for each LAN is needed, but it should be possible to link across LANs.

A Journal system (cf. Section 2.2) is an integrated part of the hypermedia. The secretaries currently responsible for registering correspondence become responsible for entering letters, faxes, change requests, and non-conformance reports into the hypermedia network. As a supplement and partly a substitute for registering keywords, they establish initial sets of public links between new and existing materials in the hypermedia. When, for example, an incoming letter is a response to a letter already stored in the network, a "Refer-to"- link is established between them.

Instead of having secretaries photocopy incoming materials for manual distribution and filing in several local archives, the entry of material into the hypermedia should imply automatic notifications to personnel subscribing to that type of material (cf. [20]). This procedure requires less photocopying, but more printers for enabling people to get hardcopies quickly. Photocopies of certain materials may be made for a few persons who have to print anyway.

Other personnel can immediately inspect materials in the system. They can follow links made during "journalization," add links to existing materials, and annotate materials, thus sharing their reactions with others.

For instance, when a supervisor gets the responsibility for carrying out an action, he may want to find all earlier correspondence and notes regarding this matter. Assuming existing materials were entered and interlinked during earlier work on the case, the relevant materials could be accessed directly by following links. Semi-automatic gathering of materials from the hypermedia is supported by browsers of nodes and links with certain characteristics. Specifying a linearization of subsets of nodes for making printouts should also be supported.

4.1.3 Challenges in supporting shared materials
The above scenario was developed in conjunction with evaluation of a prototype illustrating hypermedia potentials in the GBL context. This subsection summarises the important issues uncovered by GBL personnel's reactions to the hypermedia prototype and use scenario.

Making a diversity of shared materials accessible
Supporting efficient on-line access to all shared materials would greatly reduce the need for multiple archiving, reduce the workload on the secretaries responsible for archiving, and finally support the engineers in sharing materials needed for their work. But the materials also need to be stored on paper for legal reasons.

The materials used for daily work represent giga-bytes of text, scanned letters, CAD drawings, spreadsheets, Artemis diagrams, videos, and still pictures. To make such a diversity of materials electronically accessible, it is necessary to be able to interlink the heterogeneous materials with a homogeneous linking mechanism across the tools, as e.g. proposed by Pearl [17].

Finally, providing on-line access to all relevant materials, requires support for scanning and storing a large body of incoming paper mail. Similar challenges are identified by DeYoung [8] in supporting auditing with hypertext. It is also important that letters preserve their formatting, hence OCR should only be applied when letters received are drafts to be used for further revision.

Supporting collaborative writing
Today several documents (progress reports, SAB and meeting minutes) include contributions from many persons. Currently, however, one person is responsible for collecting paper proposals and materials to edit into final documents. The hypermedia should support electronic collection and commenting of documents in progress, but the main editing responsibility may still be assigned to one person. Private sets of nodes and links both for shared and individual materials should also be supported, similar to "separate contexts" proposed in [9].

Supporting link attributes
It should be easy to see who has established a certain link, since the competencies of the individuals who make annotations are important to assess the status of a document or a case being worked on.

Different categories of links such as "Comment-", "See-", "Refers-to-", and "Follow-Up-" links, are needed. For instance, it should be possible to get a browser view of all "See-" references without including annotations in the view. Supporting such categorization could be provided by a flexible attribute mechanism as proposed in [14].

Combining linking and keyword search for information retrieval
Currently the only way to find a document in the Journal system is via key-based search. This is insufficient even if key-assignment is highly standardized in the group. In contrast marked links in materials support immediate access without having to guess, e.g. a date or which keywords another person assigned to the document being looked for. The hypermedia should also allow query search to find root documents which can be used for further link following.

The existing materials are manually interlinked with cross-references; e.g. half of the letters refer to sections or paragraphs in the SAB, and the SAB is often examined to check the actual wording. Links would increase efficiency in SAB access from other documents. Moreover, an accepted change request implies the addition of variation notes to the SAB. Variation notes should be linked to relevant sections of the SAB and to the instigating change request.

Dynamic journalization via distributed link creation
The secretaries should maintain standard sets of public links between documents. For instance, the "Master File" of contract activity contains a standard set of documents that need to be interlinked in a standard way to ease navigation among them.

The obvious links (e.g. "Refers-to") between incoming mail and existing materials should also be established by the secretaries responsible for entering mail into the hypermedia. In contrast to the current static key encoding, the engineers become responsible for establishing public links that support later tracking of the materials with respect to contents.

For documents under modification, a reasonable procedure would be to assign a maintainer for modifications of contents that may affect links to and from the document.

Introducing hypermedia
Developing a hypermedia architecture should not require reprogramming all existing applications. Instead a hypermedia architecture should be bootstrapped by installing a kernel supporting linking and the most fundamental text nodes and then making "wrappers" for other applications like CAD systems. A wrapper is an object in the hypermedia architecture that encapsulates a non-hypermedia application and provides linking to and from the basic unit of material supported by the application. Such a minimal architecture might support linking from, say, a word in a report to a CAD drawing, but not to parts of the drawing, because the wrapped CAD system does not support anchoring.

Finally, a huge effort is required to integrate old materials into a hypermedia. Probably it is only realistic to enter new incoming materials in the hypermedia. Links to old materials could be entered incrementally in conjunction with work on a case. Alternatively a hypermedia needs to be in place at (sub-) project start.

4.2 Support for Coordination
The CSCW literature contains many proposals for coordination technology (e.g. [1,3,7,15]). Several of these proposals are based on rather formal models of human communication and people's roles in cooperation. In contrast to coordination based on communication models, our analysis showed that the majority of coordination activities were closely coupled to materials being processed, and tasks being assigned to people were triggered by events on site or receival documents. At GBL short action descriptions maintained in lists with references to documents and people responsible play an important role in coordination of daily work.

4.2.1 Possible coordination technology for GBL
We envision computer support for the coordination of document flow from the area manager and progress monitoring respectively to the supervisors and back. The idea is that, for example, the area manager receives scanned documents to be assessed from the contractor. These are then dealt with by means of an action list appearing in a window as sketched in the Area Manager's View in Figure 3.

Each line consists of a folder icon linking to the relevant material, a name identifying the document(s) in question, the due-date, and the responsible supervisor. Parts of the list are then issued, resulting in appropriate lines popping up in the local ToDo lists of the responsible supervisors (as illustrated in the Supervisors View in Figure 3). The supervisor can then select an icon and read the documents on screen (or print them out) and add comments. When the supervisor is finished (e.g. pressing a done-button), the folder icon on the area manager's screen is highlighted (probably in two different ways according to whether the action requires further action or not).

This way, actions and relevant material are coupled, and systematic distribution of tasks to people takes place when needed instead of today's weekly action list; a continuously updated overview of the state of the tasks is provided; and access to documents as well as coordination of the tasks concerning specific documents could be direct and visible to all participants. Seen from the area manager's point of view, tasks are handled based on the type of the documents and the type of bridge/tunnel components, because the concern of the area manager is recurrent problems rather than specific ones.

Another example of using the coordination facilities is illustrated in Progress Monitoring's View in Figure 3. In this view progress of the construction of specific elements is essential. To support this, progress reports should be organized according to contract activities and work items. In contrast, supervisors accessing documents need access according to different technical criteria. A central feature of a coordination tool is that it should allow everybody to organize their own view of the materials without having to store multiple copies.

A reminder facility should be provided to monitor different time limits: the area manager should be notified as to whether the different tasks are carried out on time, and the supervisors as deadlines approach. The three views should be integrated as shown in Figure 3.

4.2.2 Challenges with respect to coordination
The scenario above was developed in conjunction with a paper-based mock-up illustrating coordination and communication technology potentials in the GBL context. This subsection discusses a sample of GBL personnel's reactions to the mock-up and use scenario.

Task management is closely coupled to materials being processed
The majority of supervision tasks at GBL are initiated by documents sent by the contractor. Thus, a manual approach to coordination, coupling action lists and (references to) materials important for the actions, was chosen. However, due to the large body of materials and implied actions, computer support is needed. In addition, support for structuring and

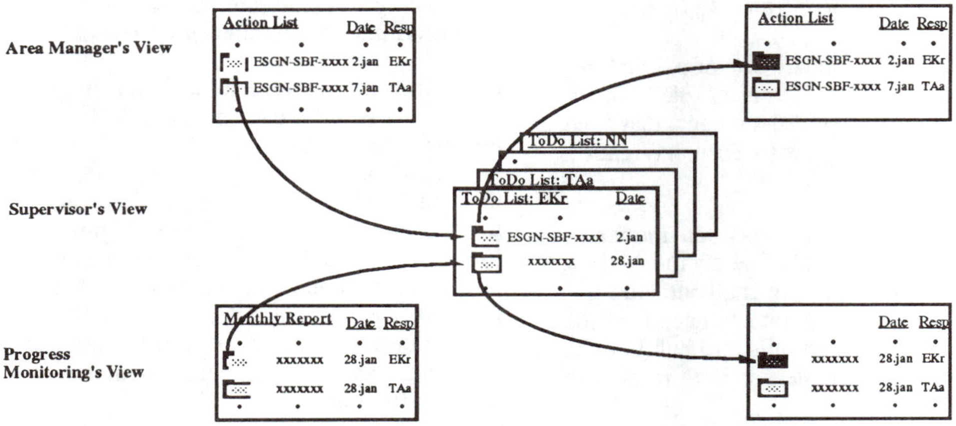

Figure 3: Possible support for coordination

monitoring ongoing activities is needed. But it is crucial that a coordination tool monitoring tasks also support retrieval of materials related to the tasks.

Task assignment is event driven

Often, letters or phone calls from the contractor or construction site initiate tasks needing immediate attention. This implies that it is hard to plan in advance; personnel often cancel other appointments to take action in these cases. Such reactions to the use scenario challenge the usefulness of detailed task registration on an hour-to-hour basis. However, administering longer term tasks, as the action lists and progress reporting represents, could be supported as in the above scenario.

Recurrent task assignments

Support for issuing recurrent tasks to people is needed. For instance, the monthly progress reporting requires the same types of material to be assessed by nearly the same subset of engineers/managers by a certain deadline. Today a manual template is used for distributing these tasks, and the Progress Monitoring engineer has to follow up on the tasks by calling people who do not respond in time. Hence, having computer support to handle a recurrent set of tasks and issuing them periodically by editing a template would be useful. The template should support inclusion of references to materials to be assessed by the person responsible for the task.

Coordination support without overhead

Another issue of great concern to the users is overhead. Coordination support should not appear as yet another system requesting input, because of management needs to monitor status. Similar observations are discussed in [11]. One way to reduce overhead is to integrate the 'administration' of tasks with handling of materials for the tasks as proposed above.

A related problem with a separate coordination tool is that area managers and Progress Monitoring would hesitate in using it to issue tasks, fearing that people would not notice the tasks they are assigned to.

5. CONCLUDING REMARKS

The investigation described here was part of the EuroCoOp Esprit project aimed at developing CSCW tools for domains such as large scale technical projects. Due to recognized difficulties in designing CSCW applications [11, 16], we undertook a cooperative design process together with users from the GBL organisation.

Information systems in use at GBL are mainly vertical and aimed at producing periodical reports for management. The daily cooperation around supervision activities including processing a large body of documents is not supported, leading to several bottlenecks in the cooperation, which currently is based on ad hoc combinations of manual procedures and office applications.

In the cooperative design workshops assessing hypermedia and coordination technology it was seen that a *combination* of the technologies would help overcome a number of the identified bottlenecks and open new possibilities for supervision and management of tasks. However, the investigation also uncovered a number of challenges for CSCW tools in such domains:

- Most current hypermedia systems exist as closed entities based on a set of special purpose editors. In contrast, the technical project domain needs a homogeneous linking mechanism to loosely couple a heterogeneous set of applications. This should support both navigation in gigabytes of information and collaborative writing
- Most proposals for coordination technology are based on formal models of communication and roles. In contrast, our domain requires coordination support closely coupled to the materials processed and flexible enough to support a dynamic, event driven environment evolving via the tasks to be monitored.

The results of the investigation described in this paper are providing input for the ongoing development of hypermedia and coordination technology as well as the overall CSCW architecture in the EuroCoOp project and a follow up Esprit III project called EuroCODE.

ACKNOWLEDGEMENTS

We thank GBL personnel for their enthusiastic participation in our workshops. We thank our Esprit II colleagues at Triumph Adler and GMD, Bonn Germany for their contributions to the coordination technology parts of the analysis. We thank Jens Hem and Lennart Sloth for their contributions to the initial analysis. We thank Randall Trigg for his comments on an earlier version of the paper. Finally we acknowledge Esprit II and The Danish Natural Science Research Council, grant no. 11-8385 for funding this work.

REFERENCES

1. Benford, S. Requirements of Activity Management. In J. Bowers & S. Benford (eds.), *Studies in Computer Supported Cooperative Work: Theory, Practice and Design.* Elsevier Science Publishers/North Holland, Amsterdam, 1991, pp. 285-298.

2. Berlin, L.M., and O'Day, V.L. Platform and Application Issues in Multi-user Hypertext. *In proceedings of IFIP TC8/WG8.4 Conference on Multi-User Interfaces and Applications* (Crete, Greece, 1990).

3. Bignoli, C. and Simone, C. AI techniques for supporting human to human communication in CHAOS. In J. Bowers & S. Benford (eds.), *Studies in Computer Supported Cooperative Work: Theory, Practice and Design,* Elsevier Science Publishers/North Holland. Amsterdam, 1991, pp. 103-118.

4. Bjerknes, G., Ehn, P., and Kyng, M. (eds.) *Computers and Democracy - A Scandinavian Challenge,* Avebury, Aldershot, England, 1987.

5. Bødker, S., Grønbæk, K. & Kyng, M. Cooperative Design: Techniques and Experiences from the Scandinavian Scene. In Namioka & Schuler (eds.) *Participatory Design: Perspectives of Systems Design.* Lawrence Erlbaum Associates, New Jersey, USA, forthcoming.

6. Conklin, J. Hypertext: An Introduction and Survey. *IEEE Computer, 20(9),* (1987), pp. 17-41.

7. de Cindio, F., Michelis, G. De, Simone, C. Vassallo, R. and Zanaboni, A. CHAOS as a Coordination Technology. In *Proceedings of the CSCW '86 Conference..* (Austin, Texas, December 1986), pp 325-342.

8. DeYoung, Laura. Hypertext challenges in the auditing domain. In *Proceedings of the Hypertext '89 Conference,* (Pittsburgh, Pa., November 1989), pp. 169-180.

9. Garrett, L., Smith, K., and Meyrowitz, N. Intermedia: Issues, strategies, and tactics in the design of a hypermedia document system. In *Proceedings of the CSCW '86 Conference.* (Austin, Texas, December, 1986), pp. 163-174.

10. Greenbaum, J. and Kyng, M. (eds.). *Design at Work: Cooperative Design of Computer Systems.* Lawrence Erlbaum Associates, Hillsdale, NJ, 1991.

11. Grudin, J. Why CSCW Applications Fail: Problems in the Design and Evaluation of Organizational Interfaces. In Tater, D.(ed.) *Proceedings of Conference on CSCW,* (Portland, Oregon, September 1988), New York: ACM, pp. 85-93.

12. Grønbæk, K. and Knudsen, J. L. Tools and Techniques for Experimental System Development. In Systä, K., Kellomäki, P., and Mäkinen, R.(eds.) *Proceedings of the Nordic Workshop on Programming Environment Research,* (Tampere, Finland, January 8-10, 1992).

13. Grønbæk, K., Kyng, M., and Mogensen, P. Euro-CoOp Workpackage WP1 Task T1.1 report: *On cooperation, computers and the organization of work at A/S Storebæltsforbindelsen* (Great Belt Link Ltd.),. September 1991.

14. Halasz, F., and Schwartz, M. The Dexter hypertext reference. *Proceedings of the Hypertext Standardization Workshop,* (Gaithersburg, Md., January, 1990), pp. 95-133.

15. Kreifelts, T., Pankoke-Babatz, U., and Victor, F. A model for the coordination of cooperative activities. In Gorlin, K. & Sattler, C. (eds.) *Proceedings of the International workshop on CSCW* (Berlin April, 1991), Institut für Informatik und Rechentechnik, Berlin.

16. Kyng, M. Designing for cooperation: Cooperating in design. *Communications of the ACM, 34,* 12 (December 1991), 65-73.

17. Pearl, Amy. Sun's link service: A protocol for open linking. In *Proceedings of the Hypertext '89 Conference,* (Pittsburgh, Pa., November, 1989), pp. 137-146.

18. Sørgaard, Pål. A Cooperative Work Perspective on Use and Development of Computer Artifacts. In Järvinen, P. (ed.) *Report of the 10th IRIS* (Information Research Seminar In Scandinavia) *Seminar,* University of Tampere, November 1987, pp. 719–734.

19. Trigg, R., Suchman, L., and Halasz, F. Supporting collaboration in NoteCards. In *Proceedings of the CSCW '86 Conference,* (Austin, Texas, December, 1986), pp. 153-162.

20. Wiil, U.K. Using events as Support for Data Sharing In Collaborative Work. In Gorlin, K. & Sattler, C. (eds.) *Proceedings of the International workshop on CSCW,* (Berlin April, 1991), Institut für Informatik und Rechentechnik, Berlin.

Ghosts in the Network: Distributed Troubleshooting in a Shared Working Environment

Yvonne Rogers

School of Cognitive and Computing Sciences
The University of Sussex
Brighton
BN1 9QH
UK
(+44-0273-606755) yvonner@cogs.susx.ac.uk

ABSTRACT

The implementation of networking technology in work settings offers numerous opportunities for improving the transmission of information and the sharing of resources within and between organizations. Its success in integrating distributed working activities, however, rests on how well the users of a network can coordinate their activities with respect to each other. This paper examines the communicative and interactive processes that take place when a typical breakdown occurs in a networked environment. A detailed analysis is presented which interprets the events that unfold in relation to the socio-cognitive issues of shared understanding, the transmission of knowledge and distributed problem-solving.

KEYWORDS

Distributed problem-solving, networked technologies, ethnographic analysis, breakdowns.

INTRODUCTION

The introduction of distributed computer systems within commercial organizations is becoming widespread [11]. The linking up of remote workstations, file servers and plotters together with the use of networking software means that information previously stored in separate systems can be automatically transferred between different locations. Such a capability obviously has the potential for improving the efficiency of information flow within and between organizations and facilitating coordination between inter-dependent activities [9]. Moreover, where networking has been incorporated in professions where much distributed working[1] takes place, it offers the opportunity of integrating formerly separate stages of the design process and enabling the co-authored objects of production to flow more freely between the different parties involved. For example, networking technology enables the same files to be displayed simultaneously on different terminals, allowing the users connected to the network to be constantly updated of the progress of each other's work. Such capabilities also provide the means by which innovative CSCW applications (e.g. shared editing, co-authoring) can be put into practice.

The implementation of networking technology in a work setting is obviously going to have a significant effect on the working practices of an organization. The transition from a set-up of single user systems, to a network of interconnected users and computer systems, will inevitably bring about changes in how tasks are carried out (e.g. synchronously or asynchronously), when activities are performed and who performs them. Moreover, the sharing of files and system components (e.g. plotters) will require additional methods of managing the flow of work through the organization. A key issue, therefore, is how well organizations will adapt to these changes; will it be a smooth transition or will it be fraught with difficulties? If the latter is true, how can the kinds of problems that are likely to arise be identified and characterized such that they can inform the development and implementation of future network systems in organizations?

Chandrasekaran [2] comments on how a contemporary organization is itself a distributed system of subdivisions which, "when successful, mesh together in a miracle of purposefulness, but when the overall structure strays too far from the changing environment, it resembles a maladaptive dinosaur" (p3). Appending another distributed system, in the form of a computer network, to a complex human network already in existence, likewise, could either clog up the arteries or facilitate the flow of blood in that organization. The success of introducing networking for the purpose of integrating inter-independent activities in and across organizations, therefore, will depend largely on supporting a flexible relationship between the two distributed systems. To this end, it is important to examine current patterns of the social organization of inter-dependent activities and how groups of people working together adapt to changing socio-technological set-ups.

The development of distributed computer systems, however, has largely been concerned with specifying the requirements for platforms on which applications for sharing information and communication are to be built [6]. While being concerned with various user issues such as access, privacy and availability of objects there has been very little consideration of the social, cultural and cognitive aspects of changing the way information is transmitted, constructed and manipulated throughout an organization. In particular, there has been little research into the processes of coordination (e.g. control, management, negotiation,

Permission to copy without fee all or part of this material is granted provided that the copies are not made or distributed for direct commercial advantage, the ACM copyright notice and the title of the publication and its date appear, and notice is given that copying is by permission of the Association for Computing Machinery. To copy otherwise, or to republish, requires a fee and/or specific permission.

© 1992 ACM 0-89791-543-7/92/0010/0346...$1.50

delegation of responsibility and exchange), which are so integral to the successful cohesion of a group.

The aim of this paper is to examine the means by which a group of inter-dependent workers interact with each other and a computer network. In particular, it focuses on the communication process that takes place when breakdowns occur between the interconnected networks of people and technology. An analysis is presented which interprets the events as they unfold in relation to the socio-cognitive issues of shared understanding, transmission of knowledge and distributed problem-solving. From an applied perspective, it considers the need to develop 'coordination software' in combination with 'preventative software' to facilitate the mediation of interactions between users and the computer network.

ANALYSING INTER-INDEPENDENT ACTIVITIES

There is a growing concern in CSCW research that attempts to model the working activities of organizations for the purpose of using them as the basis for developing CSCW systems is misguided. Robinson and Bannon [24], for example, discuss the problems of assuming that a model can somehow capture the objective reality of work organizations. In the introductory chapter of the ECSCW'91 proceedings, Schmidt [26] describes such attempts as "reckless as a daredevel mounting a Bengal tiger" (p1). Simply, the reality of work settings is that they are continuously evolving in response to the ever-changing demands of the situation. Hence, distributed work inevitably involves the vagaries of negotiation and re-negotiation. For example, in an empirical study of how spreadsheets are used in a work setting, Nardi and Miller [22] comment on how their construction and use flow in fluid, informal ways and how cooperation among spreadsheet users has a spontaneous self-directed character.

But if distributed work activity is so variable and complex, how is it possible to carry out any sensible research that can lead to a better understanding of it and which can also inform the design of better or more useful CSCW systems? One approach that is currently receiving considerable interest is to examine the design process itself [20, 24]. Another approach is to observe the actual goings on in a work setting using various ethnographic and microgenetic methods [1, 18]. Whilst not being application-driven, such research can be highly informative insofar as it can provide very detailed accounts of important qualitative structures of activities that are critical to the coordination of distributed work activity, which it is argued could go unnoticed through the use of modelling techniques. This is achieved by examining the intricate details of seemingly, simple phenomena and rendering the invisible and subtle changes in the interactions and actions that take place as explicit.

The recognition of the importance of analysing activities in situ has resulted in a number of studies that have examined the details of the communicative and collaborative processes that take place in work settings, where new technological artefacts have been or are in the process of being introduced [7, 8, 10, 13, 25, 27]. A number of recurring themes have emerged from these studies. In particular, a general observation is the instrumental role played by cultural and technological artefacts in mediating distributed activities. In a study of an airline operations room, Suchman and Trigg [27] discuss the multiple roles played by both paper documents and on-line computer information displays in coordinating the work of the operators. Rogers [25], also discusses the important social role played by a shared information display, in the form of a whiteboard, to coordinate the activities of a group of engineers working closely together.

Another major finding from the empirically-based studies of work-in-setting is the flexibility of groups to adapt the division of labour to the dynamic exigencies of the environment. Hutchins [14] notes how a ship's navigation team were able to restructure their collective activities in a systematic way in response to an unexpected change in the informational environment, when a piece of the navigational equipment failed. Moreover, the participants solved the problem initially without any conscious reflection, suggesting that the solution was discovered by 'the organization itself' before being learned or discovered by any of the individuals. Similarly, in a study of a London Underground control room, Heath and Luff [10] found that when a crisis arose the controllers were able to manage the difficulties through an emergence of a flexible division of labour. They adapted their working practices to the fluctuating local task needs without any explicit recognition of a new strategy emerging. Specifically, the controllers developed the practice of overhearing each other's conversations in conjunction with overseeing each other's actions, while simultaneously engaged in distinct and apparently unrelated tasks.

A NEW THEORETICAL FRAMEWORK

The studies described above indicate the importance of having technological systems that provide mechanisms which support flexible social interactions and work practices. In particular, they suggest that work settings need to provide a variety of mediating mechanisms that allow the workers to organize and coordinate their working activities in relation to one another. From a theoretical perspective, they have raised a number of questions concerning the adequacy of existing conceptual frameworks to account for the types of organizational change and collaboration which have been observed [14]. In particular, the finding that working groups discover new solutions to unexpected changes in the local environment, largely through implicit and intersubjectively constructed processes, begs for accounts that explain the nature of these processes, how they emerge and continue to adapt. This is especially so, in view of the fact that current organizational [see 12], social and cognitive accounts often have failed to recognize the dynamic and intersubjective processes by which the members of the group organize their work and develop informal codes of practice.

In response to the lack of theoretical treatment of local adaptation to organizational and technological change, several researchers have begun developing new analytic frameworks by utilizing a diversity of theoretical constructs. These include the application of activity theory [7, 16], conversational analysis [10], distributed cognition [14], anthropological theories of culture [19] and organizational/community memory [23].

A main concern of the new framework building is determining the nature of the social interactions and cultural mechanisms by which knowledge about activities and tasks is communicated in a group setting. Krauss and Fusell [15], for example, point out how the dynamic process of knowledge transfer between different individuals, who share mutual knowledge, beliefs and assumptions, is highly complex, entailing several interwoven levels of intersubjectivity. Drawing from Clark and his colleagues theory of *common ground* [3, 4] they describe how in order for some item of information to be mutually known by A and B, it is necessary but not sufficient that A and B know X. A must also know that B knows X, that B knows A knows X, that B knows that A knows that B knows that A knows X and so forth. Obviously when more than two individuals are involved, the layering of who knows what and how this is transmitted becomes considerably more complex. To ground the process by which knowledge is mutually transmitted, the theory assumes that when communicating, participants try to establish that what has been said has been understood. How this is achieved, however, varies considerably from one situation to the next [5].

The major problem of grounding communication in a shared arena where much knowledge and many beliefs are mutually assumed between the participants, is that numerous misunderstandings can arise. In particular, in collaborative situations where many inter-dependent interactions take place between members of the group, it is possible for the confounding of expectations to occur, having repercussions for subsequent interactions and actions. While one individual might assume that the other/s know what is meant by a particular speech act or action – in terms of the actions which the other person/s should carry out in response – the other/s may interpret the situation quite differently and carry out a different set of actions (or not perform any action) than what the first individual assumed they would do.

Although, in general, it may be the case that the context of the particular social interaction can provide sufficient grounding from which the other individuals of the group can interpret correctly the intentions of each other, when much is left *unsaid* the ongoing situation can often be interpreted quite differently by the various individuals. Hence breakdowns in the coordination of distributed activities can arise, because of a failure of the participants to effectively co-construct a compatible meaning of the particular situation. For example, Rogers [25] found how informally established mechanisms of coordination easily broke down, because the various individuals often had different expectations of which mediating mechanism was currently active.

When a group of people work together, via a computer network, it is highly probable that misunderstandings of the ongoing situation be exacerbated. One reason is because of the changes in the way users interact with the networked technology. In particular, the need to constantly negotiate, monitor and check with each other when sharing files, printers, etc., is highly vulnerable to coordination breakdowns [25]. For example, the occurence of file corruption, missing data and printer blockages can be attributed to misunderstandings between the users of the network. Moreover, on discovering such problems, attempts by the users to resolve them are likely to be further hampered by misconceptions and faulty transmission of knowledge of the on-going situation.

Besides considering the nature of social interactions that facilitate the coordination of a groups' inter-independent activities, therefore, it is necessary to analyse the extent to which multiple misunderstandings can percolate in collaborative work settings. As the following case-study illustrates, slippages in the shared understanding of which remedial actions are required to solve a breakdown in the computer network, are common and very time-consuming.

THE ETHNOGRAPHIC STUDY: THE CIVIL ENGINEERING PRACTICE

Details concerning the nature of the engineering practice that was observed in this study are described elsewhere [25]. Briefly, the type of work that the civil engineering group carry out, includes producing sets of design plans such as street designs and improvement grading plans. This requires much iterative design, with different engineers working on the same drawing plans at different stages of the design. The introduction of a networking system, comprising of workstations, PC's, file servers and plotters was intended to support this process. Specifically, it has enabled files of the drawing plans to be transferred automatically between the various designers and drafters. The networking software that has been installed also allows the same files to be accessed simultaneously at different locations. This means that the engineers can open up any file at any time, for referencing purposes, but not be able to work on the same file simultaneously, because of the problem of potential data clashes. The introduction of the computer network also has enabled an expensive electrostatic plotter to be shared between the different design groups within the practice.

The engineering company is divided into a number of semi-autonomous design groups; each comprising of a core group, who continuously utilize the networking facilities, and an attached support group consisting of management, administrative staff and non-CAD designers The core groups usually consist of six engineers (two project managers, two designers and two drafters) who work very closely together. Each core group is located in an open plan working area with a particular network configuration. This is linked up with a central workstation (R7), that is located in another part of the building. It is the most powerful machine and is directly connected to the electrostatic plotter. The local network that was set up for the design group, that was observed in this study, comprised of three powerful workstations, two PC's, a file server and an ink plotter. The various components had been configured so that one of the workstations (R5) acted as the main communication centre, that connected to R7. Thus to send a file from one of the PC's or workstations to the electrostatic plotter, required transmitting it via R5 and R7.

A problem of printing files through the network, from either the ink plotter or the electrostatic plotter, is that they have to be sent in a suitable format that is acceptable by the different plotters. This requires the creation of plotfiles that specify the correct parameters for the particular kind of plot requested. A blockage in the network can arise if the commands are not correctly put in. Files can also get 'stuck' in the network for no apparent reason.

The detailed analysis presented below, describes how the design group dealt with a network blockage incident that occurred during a typical morning's working activities. Given that this type of problem is an emergent property of the networking environment, there were no written procedures available which the group could follow to remedy it. Instead they have had to first discover the problem, then identify the possible causes and finally develop ways of dealing with it. Of interest here, is how that process has been established and the extent to which it has been maintained, in the context of the problem of mutual knowledge transmission in an ever-changing environment.

Detailed analysis of distributed troubleshooting

As mentioned above, the plotter problem is caused by various conditions and can be resolved by carrying out certain actions. Through having successively dealt with this type of breakdown over a period of many months, the group have developed a shared understanding of an informal troubleshooting schema (see Figure 1). Primarily, the schema consists of various working hypotheses about the nature of the problem and a set of remedial actions that should be followed on detecting various symptoms. An important difference between the various remedial actions that can be carried out, is the extent to which they disrupt the other processes that are currently active on the network. This can range from having no effect, to disrupting all processes that are connected to the central workstation, R7.

Symptom:	Electrostatic plotter not printing
Default condition:	R7 is blocked
Default cause:	*One plotfile is not able to be printed preventing any others being printed*
Default action:	**Kill the guilty plotfile and resend** (localised, no effect on other processes)
	If symptom persists: **Redo primary action** If still continues to fail then take:
Secondary actions:	**i) Publicise the problem and inform group of intended action**
	ii) Reboot R5 (requires anyone in the design group linked to R5 to stop working on process)
Possible cause:	*Bad communication between workstations and PC's*
	iii) Recreate plotfile
Possible cause:	*Bad element in plotfile*
	iv) Ask system manager to reboot R7 (requires every one from all the design groups linked to R7 to stop working on process)
Possible cause:	*Overloading of R7*

Figure 1. The troubleshooting schema.

What appears on the surface as a fairly straight forward routine, that should be relatively easy to implement and maintain (especially, since the problem has arisen and been dealt with, previously, on numerous occasions), however, has not been established. While the engineers are all familiar with the various aspects of the schema, it appears that they have immense difficulty in coordinating their activities and expectations of what each other knows about the network problem. Alternatively, 'ontological drift' [24] can arise whereby the various members of the group develop differing interpretations of the state of the problem. Moreover, such discrepancies can often go undetected for long periods of time.

Stage 1. Identification of the plotter problem.

Mark[2] (a drafter) initially recognizes that there is a problem in the network, having failed to print plotfiles off the electrostatic plotter. He associates it with the default condition of the troubleshooting schema and subsequently adopts the default action of resending the plotfiles (see Figure 1). After resending the plotfile, he brings up the plot monitor queue (qstat[3]) on his PC monitor. This shows its status, as represented in the plot queue, as having arrived at R7. This should mean that it has been accepted for printing and hence should be coming off the plotter. To determine if the plotfile actually is being printed, Mark goes downstairs to where the electrostatic plotter is located. He discovers that the plotfile has not been printed and so tries again. But, after thirty minutes of repeating several times the cycle of resending plotfiles, checking qstat and going downstairs, it becomes blatantly clear to him that the default action has not worked and that the plotfiles are still getting stuck in the network.

The problem Mark is confronted with is a discrepancy between the physical evidence (the plot is not being printed off) and the information displayed on qstat (stating that the plotfile has arrived and, therefore, should be printing). The mismatch of external representations eventually leads Mark re-consider his model of the likely cause of the problem. This triggers the decision to take a secondary action, which is to reboot R5. However, unlike the default action, which simply removes the guilty plotfile, rebooting will kill everyone else's processes that are connected to R5. Taking such action, therefore, requires Mark to inform the others of his intended remedial action.

Stage 2. Making public the problem.

Mark transmits his discovery of the plotter breakdown by first informing Gary (a designer), who is the only other person sitting in the shared working area at the time (see Figure 2). Without waiting for any acknowledgement from Gary, he continues by stating that he is going to reboot R5. Gary responds in amazement, that Mark is not following the implicitly accepted code of practice which is to *ask* everyone else connected to R5 if it is OK to reboot R5. However, Mark does not concede to Gary's rebuttal. This could be because he considers it unnecessary to inform anyone else as Gary is currently the only other person in the shared working area (and hence connected to R5).

This dialogue indicates a mismatch of expectations between two members of the group as to what constitutes the 'correct' way of transmitting knowledge of how to take control of a shared object. On the one hand, it appears that one interpretation of the situation is that a communicative act is required to inform, while on the other, it is assumed that a negotiative process be set up whereby permission to execute the action is first requested. However, the two participants do not seem to take any notice of each other's interpretation of the situation. Indeed, the ensuing discourse appears more like two parallel streams of talk, which occasionally interact with each other, and whereby the context of the problem is continuously re-interpreted with respect to each other's concerns (see Figure 2). Mark's stream of talk is largely mediated by the information that is displayed on his monitor, while Gary's contributions are oriented towards prescribing the correct practice.

(10.05)
Mark: We got trouble here. <looks at monitor>
Gary: (laugh) Why's that?
Mark: Sent out. There it's [
Gary: [won't go?
Mark: It won't go. (...)We need to reboot this one.
Gary: Reboot this one?
Mark: Yeh!
Gary: No, no, no, no, no, no,[
Mark: [yes, because
Gary: [yes, because right now all of us are hooked up. You reboot you kill me.
Mark: (laugh)
Gary: You have to check, make sure no-one else is on Rick 5.
Mark: No reply. (...) Sent. Trouble at end. It arrives and then not comes out. <brings up qstat again> (...)
Gary: <moves over to Mark's PC and peers at his monitor> Check it, make sure what the problem is first.

Figure 2. Making the problem public.

Following the dialogue with Gary, Mark elaborates his working hypothesis to me as to what he perceives the problem to be (see Figure 3). The reason why he has decided that it is necessary to reboot R5 is because he thinks there must be a communication problem between his PC and R5. Even so, he is still not certain what is preventing his plotfiles from reaching R7.

(10.10)
Mark: The plot is stuck and not going. It's somewhere.
Y: So [
Mark: [So we send it over there. It goes over there <points to R5> and it stay in there and not go down there.
Y: Oh, it's not going downstairs?
Mark: No, it sometime happen like that. It should be queuing here. <points to plot queue monitor> We cannot queue it.
Y: So you don't know where the problem is?
Mark: <shakes his head>

Figure 3. Enumeration of working hypothesis.

Stage 3. Wider transmission of the problem.
At this point Phil (the project manager) walks into the shared working area. Mark immediately shouts out to him that the plotter is 'not going'. Phil responds by asking him for how long this has been a problem. Mark answers by saying about half an hour. Phil then asks if Kate (another drafter) is downstairs, to which Mark simply shrugs his shoulders and the conversation ends. There is no explicit communication between the two as to the possible cause. Furthermore, Mark, does not volunteer further information about his working hypothesis of the problem being a communication problem between his PC and R5.

Here, we see the beginning of a mismatch of 'local' knowledge between the two. Instead of trying to co-construct a mutual understanding of the current state of the problem through learning more about Mark's experience, Phil decides to seek more information from the system manager (Brian), whose job it is to oversee the running of R7. He calls Brian, who is physically located next to R7, and begins to explain to him the problem in the wider context of the design group's activities – the need to get a set of plots off for checking (see Figure 4). Brian replies and Phil's immediate response is confrontational. There is no negotiation between the two about the cause of the problem or the remedial action required at that stage. Instead, Phil ends the conversation abruptly, not having got any closer to resolving the problem.

(10.15)
Phil: Hey Brian, do you know if the plotter's all blocked up? (...) We're all doing electrostatics for one last check. We send em [
Brian: <replies over phone>
Phil: Don't you ever get your plot queue thing to roll?
Brian: <replies again over the phone>
Phil: No? Hang on, I'll call back later.

Figure 4. Telephone call between project manager and system manager.

In the meantime Kate has returned from downstairs, after waiting for her plotfiles to come off the plotter. Phil asks her if she has had any success and for an update of her situation. She begins to explain how many plotfiles she has created and what has happened to them but is interrupted in mid-sentence by Phil. Whilst listening to Kate, he has simultaneously brought up qstat on R5. At a glance he has been able to deduce the same information that Kate is verbally communicating to him; that the files have been sent and are showing up as having arrived and therefore should be printing. Here, again is another example of a technological artefact mediating the communication. By 'reading' off the screen, Mark is able to confirm his interpretation of the situation as represented by the network, with Kate's explanation.

At this point all the members of the group collaborate, by sharing their acknowledgement of the problem (see Figure 5). They spend considerable time informing each other of the status of the various plotfiles that have been submitted and compare this with the information displayed on the screen. There is much verbal repetition of the events that have occurred. The outcome allows Phil to become aware of the discrepancy between the network's representation of the plotfile and its actual state, which Mark had experienced earlier but which had not been communicated between the two. The difference between their understanding, however, is that Phil's knowledge of the problem is constituted through a combined interpretation of the system's representation of the plotfiles and his understanding of the information obtained from the other engineers' problems, while Mark and Kate's understanding, also is based on their direct interaction with the network – in terms of sending plotfiles. As a consequence, it appears that Phil's interpretation of the situation is at odds with Mark's and Kate's. Rather than assuming it to be a communication problem between the terminals on the network, Phil initially attributes the disappearance of the plotfiles to the possibility of another person inadvertently walking off with the printed files. Hence, at this stage he is inclined to believe the network and consider the problem as a human error. Such a possibility is not even considered by Kate or Mark since they 'know' the local situation at the plotter, having made frequent visits downstairs.

(10.25)
Phil: On the computer it just says 'waiting in line', so you got trouble on that computer too?
Kate <nods>
Phil: You got trouble, too?
Gary: About half an hour ago.
Mark: Me too.
(...)

(10.35)
Phil: OK, we're going to re-submit them and see what happens. (...) Someone may have walked off with it or something. (...) Check that one <pointing to filename on screen> (...) it's not that big a file, either. (...) Yes, you see something isn't right. (...) Rick 5. (...) Can't do it. (...) Oh yes, I got a couple stuck here.
Kate: Oh?
Phil: One says routing and the other says queuing. {muttering to himself}. I'm going to reboot this machine. We could try that, try that first and I'll get back to you. {in loud voice} OK everyone off. I'll reboot this one[
Mark: [So it's going?
Gary: Nothing really good[
Mark: [It's gone away?
Phil: Everybody off, Gary. Are you on Rick5, there? Anyone?
Gary: Yes! (...) What a mess eh? Can't believe it. <starts to whistle>

Figure 5. Acknowledgement of each other's problems and collaborative troubleshooting.

On finding that the default action initially has not worked, Phil, like Mark, repeats the cycle of killing the plotfiles and resending them. However, each time he repeats the remedial action he requests Kate or Mark to act as relays for him – whereby they go downstairs to see if the plotfiles are being printed. Mark complies, even though he has been through the same process before and has as a result established a different working hypothesis. Neither, does he say anything about his current hypothesis. Consequently, the shifting of the responsibility of the problem from being one individual's to becoming the group's – but with a different person taking up the main role of troubleshooter – causes it to go back a stage in its resolution.

Stage 4. Taking up secondary action.
Having gone through the motions of the first stage of identifying the problem, Phil decides to take up the secondary action of rebooting R5 – which is what Mark had wanted to do in the first place. The manner in which Phil decides to carry out the action is similar to Mark's, but even more abrupt (see Figure 5). Rather than asking if the others linked to R5 mind being booted off the network, he categorically demands that everyone just get off it. Gary, who happens to be connected, responds by shouting out 'yes'. In contrast with the previous conversation with Mark in the same situation, however, he does not try to point out the 'correct' code of practice to Phil. Alternatively, he makes a jocular comment on the whole state of affairs. The different organizational roles of Mark and Phil result in different discourses. Whereas Mark is a drafter, and hence of lower status than Gary, Phil is of higher status as a manager, and thus cannot be reprimanded in the same manner.

On another level, the discourse between Mark, Phil and Gary is remarkably similar to the previous interaction between Mark and Gary. But this time it appears as if three streams of conversation are taking place, with each participant ignoring the contributions of the others. This is most evident when on hearing Phil mention that one plotfile is routing and another queuing, Mark asks if Phil has succeeded in sending the plotfiles. On not receiving a response from Phil, he repeats the question. But again Phil does not respond and so Mark is not able to determine what Phil meant by his earlier comment. Here again, is another example of a lack of communication preventing the participants from updating each other about the knowledge and understanding of the problem.

Stage 5. The critical shift in working hypothesis.
Whilst Phil is rebooting R5, the others have started working on other tasks. Other engineers from the design group also enter into the working area requesting information and sets of files from Phil. Phil switches between the various demands, while continuing to focus on the network problem. The effect of rebooting R5 should be to unblock the connections between the peripheral terminals and R7. However, the information provided by qstat suggests that this secondary action has also failed (see Figure 6). At this point, Phil is still interpreting the anomaly with respect to his original hypothesis.

(10.40)
Phil: I don't understand. I think if I reboot {mutter}. There should be something down there. (...) S9 was backed up, S8 was just sent down there.
Kate: Yer.
Mark: No Rick5 got some trouble routing. I mean stuck forever. I do it Saturday and it come back Monday, still in there.
Phil: You reboot, yer?
Mark: I reboot it.
Phil: Where?
Mark: Gone {inaudible mumble}.
Phil: You did that on Saturday?
Mark: I did it on Saturday. Yer only one sheet {inaudible as mumbles last part to himself}.
(...)

(10.45)
Y: What do you think the problem is now?
Phil: Oh, a queuing problem, one machine not talking to another. (...) Carry on and then the signal get crushed.
Y: And you loose the file?
Phil: No, just the plotfile. They can recreate them.

Figure 6. Shift of working hypothesis.

There is then a critical turning point when Mark boldly volunteers his secondary working hypothesis that the problem is a communication failure between the peripheral terminals and R5. He backs his case with evidence of having had similar problems when rebooting R5 three days earlier. Such a disclosure enables Phil to consider the problem in a different context and as a result he shifts his hypothesis to match up with Mark's current working hypothesis. Transmission of knowledge is explicit at this point. There is, however, no explicit confirmation between the two or the others, who are listening in on the conversation, of what the new information that has been disclosed means with respect to what action should be taken next. Instead the dialogue simply tapers off and the engineers continue with their respective activities. After several minutes, Phil resumes the conversation but on a different topic.

Phil reboots R5 three more times. However, each time the same discrepant information appears on qstat. At this point, he changes his current working hypothesis (i.e. a bad connection between the workstations and R5) to the other secondary cause of the troubleshooting schema (i.e. a fault with the elements in the plotfiles). He mutters this to himself twice and the necessary remedial action. Meanwhile, the others are talking with each other about another issue and so do not overhear him. His change in working hypothesis, therefore, is not transmitted.

After rebooting R5, Phil informs the group that they can start working on the network again. Although there has not been any explicit confirmation with the others, there is an implicit expectation by Phil now for the others to adopt the secondary action of recreating plotfiles[4] instead of resending them. However, the assumption is grounded only through Phil's interactions with the network. Kate 'picks up' the new expectation and, accordingly, recreates her plotfile. On the other hand, Mark continues to follow the remedial action of killing his stuck plotfile and simply resending it. Based on his earlier question to Phil, as to whether the routing problem had 'gone', his not 'picking up' the new course of remedial action, could be because he is still assuming the problem had been due to communication failures at R5 but which he assumed has now been rectified by Phil.

The mismatch in expectations, as to which remedial action should be taken, continues undetected for some time. As a result the routing problem persists and still no plotfiles are printed. After about ten minutes, Mark asks Kate whether she is re-sending to the plotter the plotfile for file S9 again (see Figure 7). Whilst acknowledging Kate's reply that she is now recreating her plotfiles, Mark still does not 'pick up' on the expectation that he, too, is expected to recreate his plotfiles. It could be that Mark interprets Kate's comments to mean that only the plotfile S9 was bad and needed recreating.

(10.55)
Mark: Kate, are you sending this one downstairs?
Kate: Not yet. I'm {waiting to see if BOZO[5] get's stuck}
Mark: Create BOZO?
Kate: Yer we have to recreate it.
Mark: No?
Kate: Yer!
Mark: Again?
Kate: Yer, Phil reckons there was a lot of bad elements in that file.
Mark: Oh.
Kate: And wanted us to recreate it.

Figure 7. Explicit communication of new working hypothesis.

Even though Kate has recreated her plotfile for S9, she still finds that it is getting stuck in the network. She points this out to Phil who confirms with her that she has actually sent a recreated plotfile. However, throughout their conversation it does not occur to either of them that Mark might still be re-sending a 'bad' plotfile. Such an omission seems perfectly reasonable, given Kates previous conversation with Mark about Phil's expectation that they adopt the new course of action to recreate plotfiles.

Another ten minutes passes, during which there is no interaction between any of the engineers. Kate returns again, from being downstairs at the plotter. She says aloud that the plotfile for S9 did not go. Phil returns and Mark, Phil and Kate talk in unison. At this point it occurs to Kate that Mark may not actually be following the alternative remedial action. On asking Mark if he has been continuing to re-send his plotfile (see Figure 8), Mark admits to not having done so. Phil, on overhearing this admission, severely reprimands him. Mark, however, is not given an opportunity to justify his actions, even though there may have been a legitimate reason for him not recreating his plotfiles.

(11.05)
Kate: Is this the same plotfile?
{Kate, Mark and Phil begin talking at the same time}
Mark: We resend the plot?
Kate: The old one?
Phil: 9 and 8. (...) You resend the old one?
Mark: <All heads turned towards Mark> Yeh.
Phil: No, no, no, no, no, no, no! Shouldn't do that. If it doesn't go, it's bad. Is probably why it was screwing up. You have to recreate it. Did you recreate it?
Mark: No.
Phil: Don't do that. <brings up qstat and types in various commands> When you realize something screw up, recreate it.
(...)
Kate: Happens every time.
Gary: Never fail
Mark: (laugh)
Gary: Never fail.

Figure 8. Public disclosure and reprimand of Mark's misconduct.

The public reprimanding of Mark, enables the group to explicitly reify the secondary action of needing to recreate a plotfile if a networking problem persists. Hence Mark's admission to not adopting the alternative action of recreating plotfiles, at the undeclared time when Phil had decided that it should be the new procedure, provides grounding for the heuristic to become explicitly established as an appropriate code of conduct.

The four of them continue interacting, with Phil once again taking central control. On his orders, Mark recreates S9 and, likewise, Kate recreates S8. Phil brings up qstat to check whether the plotfiles have been queued for plotting. But still the plotfiles are not being printed off. Phil can not quite believe this and attributes the blockage to the bad elements in S9 again, even though the file has been recreated at this point. Gary also shares this view with him.

There is, though, a crucial difference between the information represented by qstat insofar as the plotfiles are displayed as queuing on the monitor rather than arriving. This should mean that they are actually at the plotter. Phil, however, is still reluctant to change his working hypothesis of S9 being the guilty plotfile – although he does acknowledge the change in the locus of the problem in the network from R5 to R7. Before embarking on another remedial action, however, he requests actual physical evidence of whether the files have been plotted. Once again, Mark is sent downstairs to check the status of the plotter. On returning empty handed, Phil decides that the final measure – rebooting R7 – needs to be taken. He can not do this himself, however, as this is the system manager's responsibility.

Phil calls up the system manager in charge of the running of R7 (who is more senior than the one he talked to earlier) and asks him if he will reboot it. The response is favourable and Phil thanks him profusely. On putting the phone down he announces to everyone that R7 is about to rebooted. But there is no acknowledgement from any of the others. Instead, they continue working on other tasks not requiring the use of the network. Phil disappears and then returns ten minutes later. He asks Mark to check qstat. Both Mark and Gary bring up qstat and comment that S8 has disappeared from the monitor, S9 is queuing and S10 is still running. The fact that S8 has disappeared from qstat implies that it has finally run off the plotter. However, there are no shared signs of relief. Phil simply asks Mark to go and collect the printed copy of S8 so that he can start the checking process. The production process recommences and the files start to print off in an orderly fashion. No one mentions that the problem is resolved or what is finally accepted as the cause. The incident passes as a new set of demands takes it place.

But the next day the same problem recurs; this time it is Phil who discovers and first makes public that a file he has sent to the plotter has got stuck in the network. And this time, it is Mark who dares to ask him if he has recreated the plotfile. And the cycle of events repeats itself, taking a couple of hours to sort out, but with the engineers playing different roles with a different pattern of misunderstandings, regressions, mutual sharing of knowledge and confirmations.

IMPLICATIONS AND CONCLUSIONS

The analysis has shown how a relatively simple network problem can disrupt distributed work activities quite considerably. Furthermore, even though this type of breakdown has been identified and resolved on numerous other occasions by the group, it has not been possible for a routine solution to be established, akin to following the procedures in the troubleshooting schema outlined in Figure 1. Alternatively, the 'ghosts in the machine' problem emerges in differing contexts, with a different pattern of actions and interactions taking place. Each time, a complex web of communication pathways have to be set up, maintained and coordinated in order to resolve the problem. However, this type of self-organizing appears to be very resistant to being transformed into a crystallized set of working procedures. Instead, the dynamics of the moment-to-moment demands of the multitude of activities taking place in the work setting need to be dealt with in a flexible and reactive manner.

An advantage of this form of local adaptation is that whenever new 'teething' problems arise (which is inevitable given that systems are regularly being reconfigured, with new components being added or replaced and new versions of software being updated), the group are able to modify their ways of working without having to radically restructure their set of working practices. In addition, contrary to the common assumption that increasingly sophisticated technology results in more alienation, the networking technology has brought about more social interaction in the work place[6]. The analysis showed how the engineers need to know what each other is doing on the network. This knowledge is communicated quite freely and often reiterated, enabling all members of the group to be updated of each others progress. However, the transcription also showed, that even though the level of communication may have increased, misunderstandings still frequently occur between members of the group. Critical knowledge which one or more of the group possesses, may fail to be transmitted at the 'window of opportunity' to the other/s engaged in the distributed problem solving. Consequently, a tremendous amount of time is wasted managing the network breakdowns.

Clearly, such a situation is undesirable and counter to the expectation that networking can improve efficiency within and across organizations. The important research issue, therefore, is to determine what types of communicative and informational support are needed to help the group manage networking and communicative problems when they arise. This entails developing resources which can facilitate collaboration and also to seek ways of detecting and recognizing misunderstandings and misinterpretations of situations between members of the group.

As was pointed out in the analysis, a contributing factor to the misunderstandings that arose between the engineers was the discrepant representational states of the files. Specifically, the information provided by the network did not match up with the physical reality of the situation. As a consequence, the engineers had difficulties in diagnosing the cause of the problem, which led to the emergence of differing working hypotheses. An obvious solution to reducing such anomalies would be to develop more informative monitoring systems that reflect more accurately the current status of files in the network. A problem with this solution, though, is the level of 'intelligence' that would need to be programmed into the network, to provide a more transparent interface.

Other kinds of 'coordination' software which could be beneficial include an on-line update of the activities of each of the users and a CSCW-type communication facility, where local negotiations could take place. For example, if a user needed to reboot a communal system it would be useful if they could alert all the other users of their intended action via some form of electronic mail or, perhaps, even set up a negotiating space by which the other users could accept or request that the user wait until they are ready to quit the network.

Another solution could be to provide more 'preventative' software, whereby the system is programmed to have increasing responsibility [see 25]. One potential advantage of delegating the network as manager and organizer, is that it could prevent some of the undesirable situations arising through misunderstandings or miscommunication. For example, file clashes could be prevented by implementing file-locking mechanisms; printer blockages could be reduced by restricting access to certain file types or users or through automatic rebooting and so on. But in giving the network increasing power and authority, it raises the question of what the resulting relationship will be between the users and the system. In particular, will such a set-up constrain the flexible working practices that exist in an organization to the extent that the communication processes in the group begin to break down? Or will the current trend of facilitating social interaction continue by drawing the users together against the network?

Future research and developments in networking environments will need to consider carefully the nature of the relationships between users, artefacts and mediating mechanisms. The implications of introducing more preventative measures or allowing greater flexibility of user control will need to be analysed with respect to the social functions that come to be served by the network, as more or less responsibility is delegated to it, and how in doing so the network is able (or not) to prescribe certain behaviours in the users [cf. 17]. Conversely, in the social context of their use, set-ups of networks will need to be analysed from the perspective of participants in the pursuits of their users [cf. 23].

ACKNOWLEDGEMENTS
The study was carried out whilst visiting the Cognitive Science Department, UCSD. The research was supported, in part, by grant NCC 2-591 awarded to Donald Norman and Edwin Hutchins from the Ames Research Center of the National Aeronautics and Space Agency in the Aviation Safety/Automation Program.

The paper has developed from the ideas that were being explored in the Distributed Cognition Group led at the time by Ed Hutchins. Thanks to Tim DeWitt of Rick Engineering, San Diego, for allowing me to carry out an ethnographic study of his design group.

REFERENCES

1. Agre, P.E. and Shrager, J. Routine evolution as the microgenetic basis of skill acquisition. In *Proc. of the 12th Annual Conference of the Cognitive Science Society* (1991), LEA: Hillsdale, NJ.

2. Chandrasekaran, B. Natural and social system metaphors for distributed problem solving: Introduction to the issue. *SMC-11*, (1981), 1-5.

3. Clark, H.H. and Marshall, C.E. Definitive reference and mutual knowledge. In *Elements of Discourse Understanding,* A. K. Joshi, I. Sag and B. Webber, Eds., CUP: Cambridge, 1981, pp. 10-63.

4. Clark, H.H. and Shaefer, E.F. Concealing one's meanings from overhearers. *Journal of Memory and Language,* 26, (1987), pp. 209-255.

5. Clark, H.H. and Brennan, S.E. Grounding in communication. In *Perspectives on Socially Shared Cognition,* L.B. Resnick, J.M. Levine and S.D. Teasley, Eds, American Psychological Association: Washington DC, 1991, pp. 127-149.

6. Dollimore, J., Miranda, E. and Xu, W. The design of a system for distributing shared objects. *The Computer Journal,* 34, (1991), 514-527.

7. Engeström, Y. *Learning, Working and Imaging: Twelve Studies in Activity Theory.* Orienta-Konsultit Oy: Helsinki, 1990.

8. Goodwin, C. and Goodwin, M.J. Formulating planes: seeing as a situated activity. To appear in *Cognition and Communication at Work,* D. Middleton, and Y. Engeström, Eds., Sage: London (in press).

9. Hart, P. and Estrin, D. Computer integration: a co-requirement for effective inter-organization computer network implementation. In *CSCW'90 Proc.* (7th-10th October, 1990, Los Angeles), ACM: New York, 131-142.

10. Heath, C. and Luff, P. Collaborative activity and technological design: task coordination in London underground control rooms. In *Proc. of the Second European Conference on Computer-Supported Cooperative Work: ECSCW'91,* L. Bannon, M. Robinson, and K. Schmidt, Eds, Kluwer: Dordrecht (September 25th-27th, 1991, Amsterdam), pp. 65-80.

11. Herbert, A. Editorial: Distributed Systems. *The Computer Journal*, 1991, 34, 481.

12. Hewitt, B., Gilbert, N., Jirkota, M. and Wilbur, S. *Theories of Multi Party Interaction.* TMPI End of Year Report. British Telecom, Queen Mary and Westfield Colleges and the University of Surrey, 1990.

13. Hutchins, E. The technology of team navigation. In *Intellectual Teamwork: Social and Technical Bases of Collaborative Work*, J. Galegher, R.E., Kraut and C. Egido, Eds, Hillsdale, NJ: LEA., 1990, pp. 191-220.

14. Hutchins, E. Organizing work by adaptation. *Organizational Science*, 2, (1991), 14-39.

15. Krauss, R.M. and Fussell, S.R. Constructing shared communicative environments. In *Perspectives on Socially Shared Cognition,* L.B. Resnick, J.M. Levine and S.D. Teasley, Eds, American Psychological Association: Washington DC, 1991, pp. 172-200.

16. Kuutii, K. The concept of activity as a basic unit of analysis for CSCW research. In *Proc. of the Second European Conference on Computer-Supported Cooperative Work: ECSCW'91,* L. Bannon, M. Robinson, and K. Schmidt, Eds, Kluwer: Dordrecht, 1991, pp. 249-264.

17. Latour, B. Where are the missing masses? Sociology of a few mundane artifacts. To appear in *Shaping Technology-Building Society,* W. Bijker, and J. Law, Eds, MIT Press, (in press).

18. Lave, J. *Cognition in Practice,* CUP: Cambridge, 1988.

19. Levine, J.M. and Moreland, R.L. Culture and socialization in work groups. In *Perspectives on Socially Shared Cognition,* L.B. Resnick, J.M. Levine and S.D. Teasley, Eds, American Psychological Association: Washington DC, 1991, pp. 257-279.

20. MacLean, A. Bellotti, V., Young, R. and Moran, T. Reaching through analogy: design rationale perspective on roles of analogy. In *CHI'91 Proc.,* (April 27th-May 2nd, 1991), S.P. Robertson, G.M. Olson and J.S. Olson, Eds, Addison Wesley: New York, pp. 167-172.

21. Middleton, D. and Edwards D. (Eds), *Collective Remembering*. Sage: London, 1990.

22. Nardi, B.A. and Miller, J.R. An ethnographic study of distributed problem solving in spreadsheet development. In *CSCW'90 Proc.* (7th-10th October, 1990, Los Angeles), ACM: New York, pp.197-208.

23. Orr, J.E. (1990). Sharing knowledge, celebrating identity: community memory in a service culture. In *Collective Remembering*, D. Middleton and D. Edwards , Eds, Sage: London, 1990, pp. 169-189.

24. Robinson, M. and Bannon, L. Questioning representations. In *Proc. of the Second European Conference on Computer-Supported Cooperative Work: ECSCW'91,* L. Bannon, M. Robinson, and K. Schmidt, Eds, Kluwer: Dordrecht, (September 25th-27th, 1991, Amsterdam), pp. 219-234.

25. Rogers, Y. Mediating mechanisms in distributed work actvities. *CSCW* (accepted for publication).

26. Schmidt, K. Riding a tiger, or computer supported cooperative work. In *Proc. of the Second European Conference on Computer-Supported Cooperative Work: ECSCW'91,* L. Bannon, M. Robinson, and K. Schmidt, Eds, Kluwer: Dordrecht, (September 25th-27th, 1991, Amsterdam) pp.1-16.

27. Suchman, L.A. and Trigg, R.H., Understanding practice: video as a medium for reflection and design. In *Design at Work,* J. Greenbaum and M. Kyng, Eds, LEA: Hillsdale, NJ, 1991, pp.65-90.

APPENDIX: NOTATION USED IN TRANSCRIPTIONS

[current speaker's talk overlapped by the talk of another
(...) untimed pause
< > activity
{ } comment on activity
( ) transcriber's uncertainty over verbatim

NOTES

[1]Distributed activities are defined as activities which are carried out individually or jointly in a group, as part of an iterative process. The sense of distributed refers to the notion that the activities are inter-dependent; an individual or joint activity has consequences for, or is contingent upon another activity, which is currently or will be carried out by another individual or sub-set of individuals in the group. For example, a design may be initially created by one person which is then passed on to other people to review and make their comments. The document is then returned to the first person or is given to someone else to make the proposed changes and so on.

[2]All names have been changed.

[3] The qstat provides information on the status of files sent over the network; they can be either on route, queuing, waiting, on hold or arriving.

[4]Recreating a plotfile requires setting a whole set of formatting parameters which takes much more time and effort than resending a plotfile.

[5]BOZO is the name given when first creating a plotfile.

[6]This was pointed out to me by Geoff Cooper.

Hardwiring Weak Ties: Individual and Institutional Issues in Computer Mediated Communication

Jeanne M. Pickering and John Leslie King
Information and Computer Science
University of California, Irvine
Irvine, CA 92717
pickerin@ics.uci.edu 714-856-6388
king@ics.uci.edu 714-854-6388

ABSTRACT

Recent accounts of computer-mediated communication (CMC) systems in organizations are mixed about the success of CMC. While some organizations eagerly embrace CMC systems for their employees, and support systems with thousands of users and multiple uses, other organizations have refused their employees access to CMC systems, or removed such systems after they have become established in use. Why the wide disparity in organizational support of CMC? We show the importance of differences in institutional dependencies on CMC support of individuals' "weak-tie" relationships for explaining differences in willingness to support CMC infrastructure. We then examine the downstream implications of maintenance of weak ties via CMC infrastructure for individuals and institutions.

KEYWORDS

Computer-mediated communication, organizational issues, weak ties

INTRODUCTION

It is generally held that computers make interpersonal communication easier. Computer-mediated communication (CMC) reduces the constraints of space and time among communicators, and in so doing reduces the transactions costs of initiating and maintaining interpersonal ties. The reduction in individual-level transaction costs of communication through CMC does not constitute a real reduction in the costs of communication, however. Rather, individual costs are generally transformed into the CMC-supporting computer infrastructure (equipment, people and processes) costs. These costs, at least thus far in the history of CMC, have been paid for largely by organizations and institutions, and not by the individuals who use the systems. For example, the widely used Internet system that ties together many communities from the academic, government, military and corporate worlds, has been supported mainly through sizeable federal funding and institutional investments in infrastructure at the organizational level of university campuses, military contractors, government agencies, and military installations. The willingness of these institutions to support the infrastructure of CMC over the long run will be determined by whether the institutions receive a reasonable return on the investment required to establish and maintain the infrastructure.

Our interest in this paper is the question of when, and under what circumstances, institutional investments that provide communications benefits for individuals will be initiated and maintained over time without restrictions on individual use. We raise the question for two reasons. First, it seems likely that the long "experimental" period of networking represented by the ARPANet, Bitnet, EARN, and other such systems must eventually come to a close. The concepts these experimental systems were designed to prove have been proven conclusively. Eventually, the "public good" rationale for underwriting these networks must weaken in the face of widespread use by private individuals for private purposes. And since communications generally and telephone communications in particular have long been regulated and managed by organizations in a way that restricts personal use of the communication infrastructure, we would expect that use of the CMC infrastructure will eventually be similarly restricted. Second, the fundamental question of institutional benefit from individual use of CMC infrastructure is cloudy. It is very unlikely that institutions will continue to support systems that are of primary benefit to individuals unless such uses accrue to the benefit of the institutions themselves.

In the discussion that follows, we explore the use of CMC infrastructure in the establishment and maintenance of social ties, concentrating particularly on the effects of CMC on so-called "weak ties" between individuals. We argue that some institutional settings are highly dependent on maintenance of weak interpersonal ties across broad geographic or social distances, and in such settings the CMC infrastructure will continue to be provided by institutions even if there are substantial benefits to the private individuals using that infrastructure. However, in other institutional settings where maintenance of weak ties is not important to institutional welfare, or where structural and organizational characteristics of the setting facilitate weak tie maintenance without the need for CMC infrastructure, the institutional incentive to provide such infrastructure will be weak. As we shall show, empirical research on the use of electronic mail systems supports these conjec-

Permission to copy without fee all or part of this material is granted provided that the copies are not made or distributed for direct commercial advantage, the ACM copyright notice and the title of the publication and its date appear, and notice is given that copying is by permission of the Association for Computing Machinery. To copy otherwise, or to republish, requires a fee and/or specific permission.

© 1992 ACM 0-89791-543-7/92/0010/0356...$1.50

tures. Finally, we shall examine the broader question of the downstream implications from maintenance of weak ties via CMC infrastructure.

WEAK TIES AND COMPUTER-MEDIATED COMMUNICATION

Individuals who use CMC systems express a variety of reasons for their use of these systems. Generally, they claim the benefits of asynchronous communication, rapid and felicitous response and forwarding capabilities, ease of "broadcast" distribution, and so on. These features of CMC systems are somewhat superficial, however, because they do not address the issue of the fundamental personal benefits provided by CMC systems. We posit that the primary benefit from CMC systems to individuals is the increased number of interpersonal ties that an individual can maintain through use of such systems. These ties have been classified in social network theory as either "strong" or "weak." [7] Granovetter [8] characterizes the differences between strong and weak ties via four definitional dimensions: time, emotional intensity, mutual confidence and reciprocity.

Strong ties are maintained through frequent and emotionally intense communication. They usually entail the sharing of confidences among the communicating parties, and over time, the establishment of reciprocity between the parties. People maintain strong ties with their spouses, children and friends. They sometimes maintain strong ties with co-workers with whom they share mutual dependencies in the execution of work-related tasks.

Weak ties are maintained through less frequent communication, and although such communications can be peppered with strong feelings (e.g., "flaming"), they generally lack the emotional intensity of strong-tie communications. Perhaps most important, weak ties usually do not require or encourage sharing of confidences or establishment of strong reciprocities. Weak ties are maintained among extended family members, coworkers not central to an individual's task domain, and everyday acquaintances made in connection with work, social activities, and mutual friendships.

Given the intensity of strong-tie communications, it is not likely that CMC systems play a central and indispensable role in maintenance of strong ties. The fact that such ties have been part of social life long before CMC was ever imagined suggests that at best CMC systems will serve an important supplemental role in strong-tie communications. And in such cases, the supplementary effects are likely to be limited to subsets of strong-tie networks, and particularly those related to an individual's work life. This is because CMC systems are usually limited in scope to individuals who work in a particular organization, or in another organization with CMC ties to the first. Thus, strong ties among spouses and family members are unlikely to be affected by CMC until access to CMC systems is extended to include these people. Nevertheless, no one seriously believes such strong ties will be weakened due to lack of CMC access. This illustrates the general fact that new communication technologies supplement but do not supplant earlier communication technologies.

The effects of CMC systems on weak ties is another matter altogether. In an insightful piece of research, Feldman [5] examined the role of a key CMC technology, electronic mail, in establishment of weak ties. She argues that the use of distributed lists (DL) in email systems greatly reduces the costs to the individual of discovering others with common interests. The key is the ease with which one can "post" a message to a large number of individuals, and the ease with which others can respond. If posting and responding become trivially easy, one would expect a proliferation of such "postings", and indeed, this is precisely what has occurred with USENET. USENET is a conglomeration of so-called "newsgroups" or electronic bulletin boards accessible from the Internet community. In just five years USENET has grown from a small enterprise to a huge network of more than 500 newsgroups accessed regularly by more than a million users. Feldman's argument seems to be supported by this example alone.

We should be careful in drawing too much from this insight or its impressive support in the USENET community. One must ask what specific weak-tie value individuals derive from this use of CMC systems. Many of the "connections" to USENET are strictly one-way. No one knows how many so-called "lurkers" the system supports. These are individuals who never post anything to the network, but who read the messages posted there. Lurkers are no more "tied" to the network than viewers of broadcast television are "tied" to the stations they view. It would seem that that a small fraction of those who access given news groups on USENET post to those groups regularly. It has been shown in studies of email and distributed lists that a minority of those who have access to CMC actively post to it [3] [6]. Thus, it is fair to conclude that a large fraction of CMC traffic is not in support of "ties" of any kind, but rather is a form of limited-access mass media broadcast. Most users of electronic mail systems have been placed as addressees on such lists, and have found that much of the communication they receive is "junk email" that elicits no confidences or reciprocity of any kind. [11], [2]

Nevertheless, we can see in the networks like USENET and the DL's the germ of something important. In both cases those individuals who read the newsgroups and mail from DL's are probably maintaining their minimal level of contact with a particular community of interest simply because it is so inexpensive for them to do so. Note here that the "tie", to the extent that the label is fair, is not between individuals as much as it is between individuals and an amorphous community of interests.

Why do people maintain weak ties? Granovetter theorized (and subsequent research showed [7]) that weak ties served as links between strong tie networks, expanding the channels of information sources for the individual. It is not merely that there is more information available, but that there is a *potential* for strong ties available over weak tie communication lines. For example, the maintenance of weak ties can play a crucial role for an individual when he or she is forced to change jobs. Such a situation is a classic case where current job ties are likely to be useless, but ties to individuals in other employment settings might be very valuable indeed. In this case, weak ties provide the means of shifting oneself into a new network of strong ties. This is the case with CMC services such as newsgroups and distributed lists. The readers and recipients can maintain weak ties passively by simply checking in on the newsgroups or keeping their names on DL's. But by doing so, they retain the option of engaging in communication that could lead to stronger ties. It is this low-cost maintenance of options for social ties that signals a powerful role for CMC systems, particularly with respect to weak ties.

CMC supported weak ties are often maintained in order to gather information and facilitate problem solving. Feldman posits that the increase in information diffusion via electronic distribution lists might improve problem solving when the problems are not well-structured or do not align well with the organization's problem-solving structures. Many of the messages posted to USENET newsgroups are requests for information and help with problem-solving, to the extent that the more popular groups maintain lists of FAQs - frequently asked questions.

Weak ties can be said to preserve the option of shifting oneself into new strong-tie networks (e.g., via job change), or to facilitate access to locally unavailable but important information. In either case, the immediate value to the individual for maintaining such ties is evident. The institutional value of such ties is less obvious. Naturally, one can make a general welfare argument in either case. For example, exchange of employment information facilitates a free labor market, which benefits all organizations. Likewise, the organization benefits when its employees obtain needed information for organizational problem solving from outside the organization. But such general welfare arguments are not particularly strong given the obvious counter examples available: that a free labor market can facilitate employees "bidding up" the price of labor in tight labor markets, and the competitive advantage organizations gain from special information is greatest when the information is captive within the organization.

Herein lies an interesting dilemma regarding the value of CMC systems for organizations. On one hand is the widely accepted proposition that greater knowledge empowers workers to do a better job for their employers. On the other hand, however, is the fact that newly empowered workers do not necessarily apply their new powers to the goals of their employers. The empowering of lower-level workers can exacerbate endemic problems of goal incongruence that most organizations harbor. Moreover, placing in the hands of lower-level workers the authority to go outside the organization to seek task-related information is risky, because information exchange in the "net" is not a one-way street. Information is *exchanged,* not merely passed along to those who ask. The employee who seeks information on a regular basis is likely to find it necessary to begin providing information in order to maintain a balanced negotiated order of exchange.

There is no doubt that some organizations do find genuine value in giving their employees access to CMC systems, but it is not clear that many organizations are in this situation. Sproull and Kiesler note that the connection between increased employee communications or better informed employees and benefit to the employing organization may not exist in the short-run and is unclear in the long run. [14] The case for institutional welfare from individual weak-tie maintenance through CMC systems is not obvious, particularly in cases where the institutional investment in the CMC infrastructure is costly. In fact, evidence suggests that CMC systems are likely targets for cutting when organizations get into financial trouble [4]. When fiances are tight, "cost-benefit" analysis in the absence of clear benefits reduces quickly to cost counting, and expensive CMC systems easily stand out as luxuries.

Where does organizational management see value in CMC supported weak ties? A key enabling factor is that management must recognize a value associated with workers' weak ties even without the computer support. We emphasize that this is a necessary but not sufficient condition. In addition, management must believe that the the additional power employees gain from use of the networks will accrue to the net advantage of the organization. This is by no means guaranteed. Weak tie networks are not completely under management's control — they can be used to spread information about sensitive issues such as salaries, or to generate group actions that threaten management control. CMC-supported weak-tie networks are open channels, particularly when the networks go outside the organization. Internal electronic communication networks can be monitored – Sproull and Kiesler cite several examples of this. [14] External networks often cannot. In this case, management may decide to restrict or even eliminate the problem altogether by eliminating the network..

Where management does perceive a value to weak-tie networks, CMC is not necessarily the least costly or more efficient alternative. For example, an organization whose labor force primarily consists of one or two similar occupations all working in the same physical location, will already have in place much less expensive and more controllable media to support occupational community activities. But where the organization is already paying a high price to keep employees in touch with their occupational colleagues, CMC is an attractive alternative.

WEAK TIES AND OCCUPATIONAL COMMUNITIES

There are institutional settings that depend to a great extent on the maintenance of weak, extra-organizational ties among their members. The most common form of this is dispersed occupational communities (OC). [10]. OCs are groups of people who see themselves as engaged in work with such a high professional content that the norms of the profession transcend the norms of the actual organization where they work. In most cases this work is key to the self-identity of individuals – a "central life interest." OC's are communities because they share values, norms and perspectives and their contacts frequently extend beyond their work life. Some occupational communities are composed of members who are all situated in one organization or in close proximity to each other. The ties in these communities can become very strong – members not only work together but also socialize together, live near each other and, in some cases, are related to each other. But physical proximity is not a necessary condition for an occupational community. Members may be widely separated geographically and still identify with the community.

We are particularly interested in OC's characterized by wide geographical separation among the members of the OC. Such separation raises barriers to the processes that develop and maintain shared values. To overcome these barriers community members find various ways of getting together and various technologies for staying in contact. An OC will often hold conferences and conventions, publish newsletters and journals, and maintain a formal institutional infrastructure separate from the organizations for which its members work. Professional associations are a good example of this. In some cases these professional associations exert great social influence, accrediting educational programs in their profession, barring from practice individuals not sanctioned by the association, and disciplining their members for misconduct or malpractice. Professional associations are embodiments of OC's, but not all OC's are as formal or organized as professional associations. Some are very loosely coupled, as with the "invisible colleges" of academics engaged in common research pursuits. Whether formalized or loosely coupled, the individuals in a geographically dispersed OC are likely to find CMC systems of considerable value in maintaining ties with fellow members.

The academic research community provides a useful example of an arena where weak-tie maintenance is important to organizations and where CMC reduces the cost of weak ties. The academic research world is organized into occupational communities whose members are widely dispersed throughout many organizations separated geographically. [1] The need for an individual researcher to maintain ties with other members in the discipline is great. Traditionally, these ties are kept via journal publications, conference attendance and activities in the formal institutions of their discipline. But these are high cost activities. Much of the work of these activities can be shifted to the CMC medium. In an interesting study of oceanographers, Hesse, Sproull, Kiesler and Walsh found that the researchers used an electronic communication network for working on papers together, reviewing manuscripts, committee work and other organizational activities in addition to making new contacts within their discipline [9]. The exponential growth in electronic network connections between universities may be explained in part by the opportunity that the networks provide academicians to increase their ties to their communities at low cost to them individually.

The universities have been bearing most of the costs of CMC infrastructure, at least locally. And they are surely a part of the community of interest that has built the large national networks that connect universities. In this, we could argue that the institutional setting of the university is no different from that of a private company when it comes to gaining value from CMC infrastructure. But a quick glance at the peculiar character of the academic world shows this is not so. Universities have traditionally borne the cost incurred by their faculty in the maintenance of weak ties within respective disciplines. This has occurred because universities, and particularly those engaged with research, are serving multiple missions that create practical conflicts. For example, a strong research program in a particular field might require the hiring of numerous faculty to provide "critical mass." But this is costly, and the greatest expense comes from failure to provide adequate coverage of all the academic disciplines required to form a solid instructional program. In some fields, particularly those with broad scope but few students (e.g., classics), an academic department will be made up of one specialist in each of N areas. This provides coverage for the instructional programs, but it does not create critical mass for research work. [13]. Universities have handled this problem by underwriting the maintenance of weak ties among faculty in their disciplines through mechanisms such as conference trips, research visits, sabbaticals and leaves of absence.

The academy is not the only institutional setting in which support of weak ties among employees benefits the institution. Large corporations frequently have employees in many dispersed locations, sometimes throughout the world. Although the corporation may hire many members of a profession, it may have only a few (or even just one) in any given location. Such corporations often spend considerable sums each year for travel as these professionals visit one another or attend professional meetings together. The performance of its professional members is an important matter for most organizations, and some concession to the needs of the individual professionals in particular OC's is usually required if a company wishes to remain competitive.

Management support of these distributed OCs is not a foregone conclusion, however. It is often unclear whether the investment in an employee's social networks yields value to the organization. [4] Also, occupational communities are potential rivals to managerial control. [12] They direct employees loyalties outside the organization, they are sources of values and norms in which management may have little influence, they provide information about job opportunities and salaries that employees can use as leverage with management. On the other hand, occupational communities can demand support for and freedom to use an electronic communications network for several reasons. [10]. Members of occupational communities may provide scarce expertise or have skills that are in high demand. They may hold a critical position in the organization's work flow. Management may perceive the cost of supporting CMC as a necessary cost for retaining the skills of their employees.

As more OC processes and relationships are maintained via the electronic medium, the OC's dependence on management provision of infrastructure grows. This provides opportunities for conflict between the institutional forces of organizations and the OC's to which their employees belong. Such conflicts arise quickly when management attempts to exercise control over issues that the members of the OC consider their domain. The recent controversies in universities about the posting of what some view as sexually and racially biased material to university-owned electronic communication networks provides a good example of the dilemma. Universities are subject to pressures to allow the use of their resources in only socially and politically acceptable ways. But university professors and students hold freedom of expression as a critically important value to their ability to do their work. The university may want to suppress certain opinions and activities from being conducted on the electronic equipment that the university owns. Such restrictions the professors may view as direct attacks on the autonomy of their community.

Our objective in this discussion has been to show that different institutional arrangements create different rationales and incentives for institutional support of CMC infrastructure in support of weak tie maintenance. In institutional settings where weak ties between employees within and outside the organization are not necessary for organizational welfare we expect to see little sustained institutional investment in CMC infrastructure. The same conclusion holds in institutional settings where weak ties between employees are important, but where physical proximity or other means of communication provide adequate channels for maintenance of weak ties. We expect to see serious institutional investments in CMC infrastructure for weak tie maintenance only in those organizations where essential aspects of organizational welfare are served by maintaining the weak ties among distributed members of occupational communities. The use of electronic mail among faculty researchers in universities provides an excellent example of such a case. But it is unwise to generalize from this institutional setting to all institutional settings. And even in this setting, the desires and aspirations of occupational communities can be at odds with the welfare of the institution as perceived by institutional leadership. Concerns about liability and cost of maintaining the networks must eventually force a consideration of institutional welfare in the support of CMC networks, even in those organizations most dependent on maintenance of weak ties among employees.

LONG-TERM IMPLICATIONS OF CMC EFFECTS ON WEAK TIES

Most studies of CMC are conducted in organizations where computing is well established and strategically important occupational communities are geographically dispersed. We argue that it is precisely in these situations where CMC is going to be perceived as valuable to both the individual users and to organizational management and where its use is likely to grow. Here we must ask what difference CMC support of weak tie maintenance will make in the long run.

We suggest that the consequences will be mixed, and contrary to conventional expectations. To the extent that CMC systems facilitate the maintenance of occupational communities, they are merely supplementing the well developed and long used mechanisms for occupational community support. In fact, the rise of CMC systems appears not to have altered the relative frequency or attendance rates at professional conferences or conventions, or the publication rates of professional journals. If anything, CMC systems have been used to help coordinate conferences and conventions, and they are beginning to be used as media for publication of professional journals. While these systems might alter some of the ways in which weak ties are maintained in occupational communities, we doubt very much that use of the systems will fundamentally alter the character or behavior of the communities substantially.

On the other hand, subtle but important effects from extensive use of of CMC systems for weak tie maintenance are possible. These effects are not so much due to structural changes in occupational communities themselves as in the processes by which individuals with different points of view become dominant in the communities. We imagine that there could be changes in the ways in which points of view are formed and in the kinds of pressures brought to bear on the activities of institutions and occupational communities. The rapid mobilization of bias against the marketing of the Lotus Households product via electronic mail provides an example of how a highly distributed community of interest brought great pressure on a powerful business interest, resulting in the cancellation of the product. Similarly, very detailed examinations of distributed communities of scholars using CMC suggest that subtle changes in community norms and expectations are underway because the CMC technologies have given voice to interests not previously heard in the traditional channels of communication. [13] These are the changes that bear watching as experience with CMC grows.

ACKNOWLEDGMENTS

We appreciate the helpful comments we received from Mark Granovetter, the anonymous reviewers, as well as Rob Kling, Jonathan Grudin and others in the Computers, Organizations, Policy and Society (CORPS) area at UCI.

REFERENCES

[1] D. Crane. *Invisible Colleges: diffusion of knowledge in scientific communities.* University of Chicago Press, Chicago, 1972.

[2] P. Denning. Electronic junk. *Commun. ACM*, 23(3):163–165, March 1982.

[3] J. D. Eveland and T. K. Bikson. Evolving electronic communication networks: An empirical assessment. *Office: Technology and People*, 3:103–128, 1987.

[4] T. Fanning and B. Raphael. Computer teleconferencing: Experience at hewlett packard. In *Proceedings of CSCW'86*, pages 291–306, 1986.

[5] M. S. Feldman. Electronic mail and weak ties in organizations. *Office, Technology and People*, 3:83–101, 1987.

[6] T. Finholt and L. S. Sproull. Electronic groups at work. *Organization Science*, 1(1):41–64, 1990.

[7] M. Granovetter. The strength of weak ties: A network theory revisited. In R. Collins, editor, *Sociological Theory 1983*, pages 210–233. Jossey-Bass Publishers, 1983.

[8] M. S. Granovetter. The strength of weak ties. *American Journal of Sociology*, 78(6):1360–1380, 1973.

[9] B. W. Hesse, L. Sproull, S. Kiesler, and J. P. Walsh. Computer network support for science: The case of oceanography. Paper in progress, 1990.

[10] J. Van Maanen and S. R. Barley. Occupational communities: Culture and control in organizatihons. *Research in Organizational Behaviour*, 6:287–365, 1984.

[11] W. E. Mackay. Diversity in the use of electronic mail: A preliminary inquiry. *ACM Trans. on Office Information Systems*, 6(7):380–397, October 1988.

[12] C. Perin. Electronic social fields in bureaucracies. *Communications of the ACM*, 34(12):75–82, December 1991.

[13] K. Ruhleder. *Information Technologies as Instruments of Social Transformation: The Computerization of Classical Scholarship*. PhD thesis, University of California, Irvine, Irvine, CA, May 1991.

[14] L. Sproull and S. Kiesler. *Connections: New Ways of Working in the Networked Organization*. The MIT Press, Cambridge, Mass., 1991.

LEARNING FROM NOTES: Organizational Issues in Groupware Implementation

Wanda J. Orlikowski

Sloan School of Management
Massachusetts Institute of Technology
50 Memorial Drive (E53-329)
Cambridge, MA 02139
(617) 253-0443 wanda@eagle.mit.edu

ABSTRACT
This paper explores the introduction of groupware into an organization to understand the changes in work practices and social interaction facilitated by the technology. The results suggest that people's mental models and organizations' structure and culture significantly influence how groupware is implemented and used. Specifically, in the absence of mental models that stressed its collaborative nature, groupware was intepreted in terms of familiar personal, stand-alone technologies such as spreadsheets. Further, the culture and structure provided few incentives or norms for cooperating or sharing expertise, hence the groupware on its own was unlikely to engender collaboration. Recognizing the central influence of these cognitive and organizational elements is critical to developers, researchers, and practitioners of groupware.

KEYWORDS
Groupware, Implementation, Lotus Notes, Organizational Factors, Technological Frames

INTRODUCTION
Computer-supported cooperative work, collaborative computing, and groupware have become common labels in our contemporary technological vocabulary. While some have discussed the potential for such technologies to enhance organizational effectiveness [3, 8, 9, 15], others have suggested that the implementation of such technologies is more difficult and yields more unintended consequences than is typically acknowledged [2, 10, 11, 12, 16]. Empirical studies of groupware usage in organizations are clearly needed to shed light on these diverse expectations. While there have been many field studies of electronic mail usage [1, 4, 5, 6, 13, 14, 17], groupware (that includes more collaborative features than electronic mail) has been studied less frequently.

Permission to copy without fee all or part of this material is granted provided that the copies are not made or distributed for direct commercial advantage, the ACM copyright notice and the title of the publication and its date appear, and notice is given that copying is by permission of the Association for Computing Machinery. To copy otherwise, or to republish, requires a fee and/or specific permission.

© 1992 ACM 0-89791-543-7/92/0010/0362...$1.50

In this paper I describe the findings of an exploratory field study which examined the implementation of the groupware product *Notes®* (from Lotus Development Corporation)[1] into one office of a large organization. My interest in studying the implementation and use of this product was to investigate whether and how the use of a collaborative tool changes the nature of work and the pattern of social interactions in the office, and with what intended and unintended consequences. The findings suggest that two organizational elements seem especially relevant in influencing the effective utilization of groupware: people's *cognitions* or mental models about technology and their work, and the *structural properties* of the organization such as policies, norms, and reward systems. The findings suggest that where people's mental models do not understand or appreciate the collaborative nature of groupware, such technologies will be intepreted and used as if they were more familiar technologies, such as personal, stand-alone software (e.g., a spreadsheet or word processing program). The findings further suggest, that where the premises underlying the groupware technology (shared effort, cooperation, collaboration) are counter-cultural to an organization's structural properties (competitive and individualistic culture, rigid hierarchy, etc.), the technology will be unlikely to facilitate collective use and value. That is, where there are few incentives or norms for cooperating or sharing expertise, goupware technology alone cannot engender these. Conversely, where the structural properties do support shared effort, cooperation, and collaboration, it is likely that the technology will be used collaboratively, that is, it will be another medium within which those values and norms are expressed. Recognizing the significant influence of these organizational elements appears critical to groupware developers, users, and researchers.

[1] Notes is an application development environment that can support communication, coordination, and collaboration within groups or organizations. While some features such as electronic mail are built-in, others need to be built by the adopting organization, e.g. discussion forums and customized views of shared databases. See Marshak (1990) for more details.

RESEARCH SITE AND METHODS

Field work was conducted within a large services firm, Alpha Corporation (a pseudonym), which provides consulting services to clients around the world. The career structure within Alpha is hierarchical with four primary milestones--staff consultant, senior consultant, manager, and principal. In contrast to the pyramidal career structure, the firm operates through a matrix form, with client work being executed and managed in a decentralized fashion out of local offices, while being coordinated through consulting practice management centralized in the headquarters office.

A few years ago, Alpha purchased and distributed Notes to all their consultants and support staff as part of a strategy, described by a senior principal as an attempt to "leverage the expertise of our firm." My research study examined the implementation of Notes in one large office of Alpha over a period of five months.[2] Detailed data collection was conducted through unstructured interviews, review of office documents, and observation of meetings, work sessions, and training classes. Over ninety interviews were conducted, each about an hour in length, with some participants being interviewed more than once over the period of study. In addition to the office where the study was conducted, I interviewed key players from Alpha's headquarters and technology group. Participants spanned various hierarchical levels and were either consultants in active practice, administrators supporting practice activities, or members of the centralized technology support function (see Table 1).

	Practice	Technology	Total
Principals	13	4	17
Managers	26	15	41
Seniors	12	13	25
Admin.	8	--	8
Total	59	32	91

Table 1: Number and Type of Interviews in Alpha

The research study was designed to examine how the groupware technology is adopted and used by individuals, and how work and social relations change as a consequence. The research study began in February 1991 before the Notes system was due to be installed within the office and continued through the implementation and early use of the Notes system (June 1991). The findings reflect participants' anticipations of as well as their early exposure to the Notes system.[3] These findings need to be interpreted cautiously as they only reflect the adoption and early use experiences of a sample of individuals within a specific office in what is a larger implementation process continuing over time in Alpha. While early, the findings to date are interesting as they reflect people's initial experiences and assessments of Notes in light of their current work practices and assumptions about technology. The initial period following the implementation of a technology is typically a brief and rare opportunity for users to examine and think about the technology as a discrete artifact, before it is assimilated into cognitive habits and work practices, and disappears from view [18]. It is possible that with time, greater use, and appropriate circumstances, these early experiences will change.

[2] henceforth referred to simply as "the office."

[3] This research study represents the first of a series of studies that are being conducted within Alpha over time. Further analyses and observations are thus anticipated.

RESEARCH RESULTS

Background to the Notes Acquisition

In the late eighties, a few senior principals realized that Alpha, relative to its competitors and clients' expectations, was not utilizing information technology as effectively as they could. In response, they commissioned an internal study of the firm's technological capabilities, weaknesses, and requirements. On the basis of this study's recommendations, a new and powerful position--akin to that of a Chief Information Officer (CIO)--was created within Alpha with responsibility for the firm's internal use of information technology. One of the first tasks the new CIO took on was the creation of firm-wide standards for the personal computing environments utilized in Alpha offices. It was while reviewing communication software that the CIO was introduced to the Notes groupware system. As he remarked later, after a few days of "playing with Notes," he quickly realized that it was "a breakthrough technology," with the potential to create "a revolution" in how members of Alpha communicated and coordinated their activities. Shortly thereafter the CIO acquired a site license to install Notes throughout the firm, and announced that the product would be Alpha's communications standard.

The CIO began to market Notes energetically within various arenas of the firm. He gave numerous talks to principals and managers, both at national meetings and in local offices, during which he promoted his vision of how Notes "can help us manage our expertise and transform our practice." Through interest and persuasion, demand for Notes grew, and the physical deployment of the technology proceeded rapidly throughout the firm. The actual use of Notes within the office I studied, however, appeared to be advancing more slowly. While electronic mail usage had been adopted widely and enthusiastically, the use of Notes to share expertise, and the integration of Notes into work practices and policies had not yet been accomplished. The data I collected and analyzed during my field study of one office suggests that at least two organizational elements--cognitive and structural--influenced the participants' adoption, understanding, and early use of Notes.

Cognitive Elements

Cognitive elements are the mental models or frames of references that individuals have about the world, their organization, work, technology, and so on. While these frames are held by individuals, many assumptions and values constituting the frames tend to be shared with others. Such sharing of cognitions is facilitated by common educational and professional backgrounds, work experiences, and regular interaction. In the context of groupware, those cognitive elements that have to do with information technology become particularly salient. Elsewhere, I have termed these *technological frames,* and described how they shape the way information technology is designed and used in organizations [7].

When confronted with a new technology, individuals try to understand it in terms of their existing technological frames, often augmenting these frames to accommodate special aspects of the technology. If the technology is sufficiently different, however, these existing frames may be inappropriate, and individuals will need to significantly modify their technological frames in order to understand or interact effectively with the new technology. How users change their technological frames in response to a new technology is influenced by (i) the kind and amount of product information communicated to them, and (ii) the nature and form of training they receive on the product.

(i) Communication about Notes

Employees in the office I studied received relatively little communication about Notes. Many of them first heard about the CIO's decision to standardize on Notes through the trade press. Others encountered it during Alpha's annual management seminars that form part of consultants' continuing education program. Most encountered it for the first time when it was installed on their computers. Without explicit information about what Notes is and why Alpha had purchased it, these individuals were left to make their own assumptions about the technology and why it was being distributed. This contributed to weakly developed technological frames around Notes in the office. Consider, for example, these remarks made by individuals a few weeks before Notes was to be installed on their computers:

> *I know absolutely nothing about Notes. I don't know what it is supposed to do.*
>
> *All I know is the firm bought it, but I don't know why.*
>
> *I first heard that the firm had bought Notes through the Wall Street Journal. Then your study was the next mention of it. That's all I know about it.*
>
> *I heard about Notes at the [management seminars] about eight months ago. I still don't know what it is.*
>
> *It has something to do with communications.*
>
> *It's big email.*
>
> *I've heard that it's hard copy of email ... but I am not very clear about what it is exactly.*
>
> *Is it a new version of 1-2-3?*
>
> *I believe Notes is putting word processing power into spreadsheets.*
>
> *It's a network... I don't know how the network works. Where does all this information go after I switch my machine off?*
>
> *It's a database housed somewhere in the center of the universe.*

Weakly developed technological frames of a new and different technology are a significant problem in technology transfer because people act towards technology on the basis of the meaning it has for them. If people have a poor or inappropriate understanding of the unique and different features of a new technology they may resist using it, or may not integrate it appropriately into their work practices. In the office, one consequence of such poor understanding was a skepticism towards Notes and its capabilities. For example, principals and managers in the office commented:

> *I first heard about Notes when I read in the Wall Street Journal that Alpha had purchased a revolutionary new piece of software. My first thought was -- how much is this costing me personally? ... [T]his kind of implementation affects all of our pocketbooks. ... I have [heard that] there is no value in information technology -- so you can imagine how I feel!*
>
> *When I first heard about it, I thought "Oh yech! First hook me up to the network, and then I'll listen." Right now I still can't see the benefit.*
>
> *I don't believe that Notes will help our business that much, unless all of our business is information transfer. It's not. Business is based on relationships. Ideas are created in non-work situations, socially, over lunch, etc.*

Poor circulation of information about Notes was a consequence of the rapid installation of Notes that Alpha had pursued. The CIO had delegated responsibility for Notes deployment to the firm's technology group. Because demand for Notes was growing quickly, the technologists did not have an opportunity to plan the Notes rollout, and did not develop or pursue a formal implementation plan or information dissemination strategy. Two technology managers commented:

> *We tried to stay one step ahead of the firm's demand and [the CIO's] evangelism. We were swamped with requests. Every time [the CIO] gave a talk, we'd be deluged with requests for Notes. ... We had no time to do a formal plan or a grand strategy because [the CIO] had raised the level of enthusiasm in the firm, and there was no way we could say to the principals "wait while we get our act together."*
>
> *[The CIO] set the tone for the deployment strategy by generating interest in the product at the top. He was pushing a top-down approach, getting to all the principals first. So our deployment was driven by a lot of user pull and a little push from us. ... We were constantly struggling to keep up with demand.*

This rapid, demand-driven rollout was consistent with the CIO's assumption about how technologies such as Notes should be implemented. He commented that:

> *Our strategy was to blast Notes through our organization as quickly as possible, with no prototypes, no pilots, no lengthy technical evaluation. We want to transform the way we deliver service to clients.*

He believed that an "empowering" technology such as Notes should be put in the hands of as many people as possible, and that if the technology is compelling enough "they will drift into new ways of doing things." That is,

> *[I]f you believe that Notes is a competitive technology you have to deploy it quickly, and put it in the hands of the users as fast as possible. Critical mass is key.*

In particular, the CIO focused on convincing the key "opinion leaders" in the firm of the value of the technology, as he believed that these individuals would lead the charge in defining and spreading the uses of Notes throughout the firm.

(ii) Training on Notes

Training users on new technology is central to their understanding of its capabilities and appreciating how it differs from other technologies with which they are familiar. It also significantly influences the augmentation of existing technological frames or the development of new ones. Because the technologists were extremely busy deploying Notes and keeping it up and running, they did not have the resources to pay much attention to the education of users. Their first priority was to physically install hundreds of copies of Notes in multiple offices around the country and keep them operational. As one technology manager noted, it was a matter of priorities:

> *We made a conscious decision between whether we should throw it [Notes] to the users versus spending a lot of time training. We decided on the former.*

The under-emphasis on training was consistent with the CIO's general view that Notes does not require formal end-user training, and that it is through experimentation and use, not formal education programs that people begin to appreciate a technology's potential and learn to use it in different and interesting ways. This user-driven diffusion strategy, however, typically takes time, particularly in a busy services firm with considerable production pressures. Because this study did not detect any new user initiatives around the use of Notes in the office, it is possible that the timing of the research is simply too early in the implementation process. The following experiences thus represent the first encounters consultants had with Notes and how they initially appropriated it.

The training that was made available to users in the office I studied came in two forms, self-study and classroom training. The former provided users with a videotape and work-book, and covered Notes' basic functions and interfaces. The latter offered up to four hours of instruction and hands-on exercises by local computer support personnel. None of these training options emphasized its collaborative nature or possible business value. The training materials were relatively technical, individual-oriented, and non-specific in content. Trainees were exposed to the basic Notes functions such as electronic mail, editing, and database browsing. While facilitating the accessibility of the material to all individuals, from secretaries to principals, this "one size fits all" training strategy had the effect--at least initially--of not conveying the power of Notes to support specific consulting applications or group coordination.

This training on Notes resembled that of the training conducted on personal productivity tools. While useful for teaching the mechanics of Notes, it does not give users a new way of thinking differently about their work in terms of groupware. While Alpha was less concerned with collaborative or group work than with sharing expertise across the firm, the effect of the initial training was that participants in my study attempted to understand Notes through their existing frame of personal computing software. Such interpretations encouraged thinking about Notes as an individual productivity tool rather than as a collaborative technology or a forum for sharing ideas. For example, one manager noted:

> *I see Notes as a personal communication tool. That is, with a modem and fax applications I can do work at home or at a client site and use Notes to transfer work back and forth. In the office, instead of getting my secretary to make twenty copies of a memo she can just push a button.*

Further, the applications built for users by the technology group tended to automate existing information flows rather than creating new ones through the cooperative features of Notes. This reinforced the message that users received in their training, that Notes is an incremental rather than a transforming technology, and that new technological frames or new work practices around it are not required. Thus, in contrast to the technologists' vision of Notes as a technology that can "fundamentally change the way we do business," consultants in the office appeared to expect, at most, incremental improvements in operations. A manager noted:

> *The general perception of Notes is that it is an efficient tool, making what we do now better, but it is not viewed by the organization as a major change. Remember we're ... a management consulting firm and management consultants stick to management issues. We don't get into technology issues.*

Another said:

> *I think it will reduce the time of gathering information. I think it will cut down on frustration in transferring information. But it is not a radical change.*

As a result of the lack of resources that technologists had for communication and training, users of Notes in the office developed technological frames that either had weakly developed notions of Notes, or that interpreted Notes as a personal rather than a group or firm productivity tool. Because technological frames may change over time and with changing contexts, it is possible that the frames developed by the office participants will change over time. For example, if individuals are exposed to other applications of Notes developed elsewhere in the firm or in other firms, or if their increased use of Notes helps them understand how they can change the way they work, new understandings and uses of Notes may result. Our ongoing study of this implementation will monitor such possible developments.

Structural Elements

Structural properties of organizations encompass the reward systems, policies, work practices, and norms that shape and are shaped by the everyday action of organizational members. In the office, three such structural properties significantly influenced individuals' perceptions and early use of Notes.

(i) Reward Systems

Within Alpha there is an expectation--shared by many services firms--that all or most employee hours should be "billable," that is, charged to clients. This is a major evaluation criterion on which employees are assessed, and employees studiously avoid "non-billable hours." Because most of the participants did not initially perceive using Notes as a client-related activity (and hence as "not chargeable"), they were disinclined to spend time on it. Further, given their lack of understanding and skepticism of Notes, they were unwilling to give up personal time to learn or use it. Consider these comments from senior consultants and managers:

> *One of the problems is time. Given my billing rate, it makes no sense for me to take the time to learn the technology. In Alpha we put so much emphasis on chargeable hours and that puts a lot of pressure on managers. ... And now we've made an enormous commitment to Notes and Hardware, and LANs, but we haven't given people the time and opportunity to learn it. For them to do classes they have to work extra on weekends to meet deadlines.*

> *I think it is going to be a real issue to find time to use Notes. We don't have the time to read or enter information in Notes. What would I charge it to? We already complain that we can't charge our reading of our mail to anything. We end up having to charge it to ourselves [he reads his mail on the train going home].*

> *I don't think that Notes will ever be used in Alpha as effectively as it could be. We're not going to make sure everyone in the office has fifteen hours over the next year to spend time learning it. And if they expect us to take it out of our own time I'm not going to invest that time. I have another life too.*

> *The opportunity costs for me to take training in the office are very high. At my level, every week is a deadline, every week is a crisis. No accommodations are made in our schedules or workload to allow us to train on technology. So I won't learn it unless it's mandatory.*

Thus, one significant inhibitor of learning and using Notes was the office's reward system with its accompanying incentive schemes and evaluation criteria. Because the reward system had not changed since the implementation of Notes, consultants in the office perceived time spent on Notes as less legitimate than client work. While many used Notes for electronic mail or database browsing, these activities amounted to a few minutes a day, and hence were easily subsumed into client or personal time. However, any more extensive use of Notes was seen as potentially disrupting the balance between billable hours and personal time, and hence to be avoided. These concerns, however, varied by position in the office. Not surprisingly, principals were willing to take a longer-term and firm-wide perspective on Notes, being less preoccupied than were managers and senior consultants with time constraints, "billable hours," personal performance, and their own careers.

(ii) Policies and Procedures

Along with the few resources dedicated to Notes training and communication, the office--at the time of my study--had not formulated new work procedures or set new policies around data quality, confidentiality, and access control. Many participants indicated that their use of Notes was inhibited by their lack of knowledge about these issues, particularly concerns about liability (their own and Alpha's). Principals for example, worried about data security:

> *Security is a concern for me. ... We need to worry about who is seeing the data. ... Managers should not be able to access all the information even if it is useful, [such as] financial information to clients, because they leave and may go and work for competitors. So there should be prohibitions on information access.*

> *I am not sure how secure Notes is. Many times we have run into difficulties and things have got lost in never-never land.*

> *I have concerns about what goes into the databases and who has access to them and what access they have. ... But we haven't thought that through yet.*

Managers and senior consultants in the office were more anxious about personal liability or embarrassment:

> *I would be careful what I put out on Notes though. I like to retain personal control so that when people call me I can tell them not to use it for such and such. But there is no such control within Notes.*

> *My other concern is that information changes a lot. So if I put out a memo saying X today and then have a new memo two weeks later, the person accessing the information may not know about the second memo which had canceled the first. Also if you had a personal discussion you could explain the caveats and the interpretations and how they should and shouldn't use the information.*

> *I'd be more fearful that I'd put something out there and it was wrong and somebody would catch it.*

I would be concerned in using Notes that I would come to the wrong conclusion and others would see it. What would make me worry is that it was public information and people were using it and what if it was wrong? I would not want to be cited by someone who hasn't talked to me first. I'm worried that my information would be misconstrued and it would end up in Wichita, Kansas "as per J. Brown in New York" being used and relied on. You should be able to limit what access people have to what information, particularly if is your information. I would definitely want to know who was looking at it.

There is a hesitancy here because you don't want to put everything into public information as people may rely on that information and screw up, and it may reflect badly on you.

The lack of explicit procedures and policies around Notes highlights the difficulty of enforcing firm-wide policies in a decentralized firm. While the CIO has been able to institute standards around certain technology platforms--clearly a technical domain, instituting standard procedures and policies about data quality, control, and liability begins to encroach on the organizational domain--an arena where the CIO's authority is less established. As a result, the technologists have been careful about setting policies that would require organizational changes and that might invoke turf issues. Managers of local offices, however, had not devoted any attention to this issue, at least in the early adoption phase. As a result, there was some ambiguity about the locus and nature of responsibility and liability with respect to the intellectual content of Notes databases. This may have inhibited the application of Notes to a broader range of work practices in the early phase of implementation.

(iii) Firm Culture and Work Norms

Alpha shares with many other consulting firms a relatively competitive culture--at least at the levels below principal. The pyramidal structure and the hierarchical "up or out" career path promote and reinforce an individualistic culture among consultants, where those who have not yet attained principal status vie with each other to get the relatively few promotions handed out each year. In such a competitive culture, there are few norms around cooperating or sharing knowledge with peers. These comments by consultants in the office are illustrative:

This is definitely a competitive culture--it's an up or out atmosphere.

Usually managers work alone because of the competitiveness among the managers. There is a lot of one-upmanship against each other. Their life dream is to become a principal in Alpha, and they'll do anything to get there.

The atmosphere is competitive and cut-throat; all they want is to get ahead as individuals.

Interestingly, there was some evidence that there is much more collegiality at the highest levels of the firm, where principals--having attained tenure and the highest career rank--enact more of a "fraternal culture" than the competitive individualism evident at lower levels. This is also evident in service organizations with similar organizational structures, such as firms providing legal, accounting, or medical services. Below the principal level, however, managers and senior consultants in my study indicated that there was generally little precedent for sharing or cooperating with colleagues, and little incentive to do so as they needed to differentiate themselves from their peers. For example:

The corporate psychology makes the use of Notes difficult. Particularly the consultant career path which creates a back-stabbing and aggressive environment. People aren't backstabbing consciously, it's just that the environment makes people maximize opportunities for themselves.

I'm trying to develop an area of expertise that makes me stand out. If I shared that with you you'd get the credit not me.... It's really a cut-throat environment.

Power in this firm is your client base and technical ability. ... It is definitely a function of consulting firms. Now if you put all this information in a Notes database you lose power. There will be nothing that's privy to you, so you will lose power. It's important that I am selling something that no one else has. When I hear people talk about the importance of sharing expertise in the firm, I say "Reality is a nice construct."

The competitive individualism--which reinforces individual effort and ability, and does not support cooperation or sharing of expertise--is counter-cultural to the underlying premise of groupware technologies. It is thus not surprising that, at all but the highest career level, Notes is being used largely as an individual productivity tool in the office. Senior consultants and managers within this office feel little incentive to share their ideas for fear that they may lose status, power, and distinctive competence. Principals, on the other hand, do not share this fear and are more focused on the interests of the office and the firm than on their individual careers. An interesting contrast to this point, which further supports it, is that Notes is being used by Alpha technologists to exchange technical expertise. Not being subject to the competitive culture, individual-focused reward systems, "up-or-out" career pressures, and "chargeable hours" constraints of the consultants, the technologists appear to have been able to use the technology to conduct their work, that is, solving technical problems.

DISCUSSION

The results of this research suggest that the organizational introduction of groupware will interact with cognitive and structural elements, and that these elements will have significant implications for the adoption, understanding, and early use of the technology. Because people act towards technology on the basis of their understanding of it, people's technological frames often need to be changed to accommodate a new technology. Where people do not appreciate the premises and purposes of a technology they may use it in less effective ways. A major premise underlying groupware is the coordination of activities and people across time and space. For many users, such a premise may represent a radically different understanding of technology than they have experienced before. This suggests that a particularly central aspect of implementing groupware is ensuring that prospective users have an appropriate understanding of the technology, that is, that their technological frames reflect a perception of the technology as a collective rather than a personal tool.

At the time I conducted my study, many of the participants in the office did not have a good conception of what Notes was and how they could use it. Their technological frames around Notes were weakly developed and relied heavily on their knowledge and experience of other individually-used technologies. Given such cognitions, it is not surprising that in their early use of the technology, these participants had not generated new patterns of social interaction, nor had they developed fundamentally different work practices around Notes. Instead, they had either chosen not to use Notes, or had subsumed it within prior technological frames and were using it primarily to enhance personal productivity through electronic mail, file transfer, or accessing news services. As indicated above, however, these findings reflect an early phase of the participants' experiences with Notes. It is possible that these experiences will change over time as they get more accustomed to using Notes, and these are expected to change over time depending on their ongoing experiences with the technology.

Where a new technological frame is desirable because the technology is sufficiently unprecedented to require new assumptions and meanings, communication and education are central in fostering the development of new technological frames. Such communication and education should stress the required shift in technological frame, as well as provide technical and logistic information on use. A training approach that resembles that used for personal computing software is unlikely to help individuals develop an appreciation of groupware. For individuals used to personal computing environments and individual applications, shared technology use and cooperative applications are difficult to grasp. In these cases, concrete demonstrations of group applications can help to provide insight. Further, learning groupware collectively may foster joint understanding and expectations. Where individuals learn a shared technology in isolation, they may form their own assumptions, expectations, and procedures which may differ from those of the people they will interact with through the technology.

In situations where the premises underlying groupware are incongruent with those of the organization's culture, policies, and reward systems, it is unlikely that effective cooperative computing will result without a change in structural properties. Such changes are difficult to accomplish, and usually meet with resistance. Without such changes, however, the existing structural elements of the firm will likely serve as significant barriers to the desired use of the technology. For example, in the study described above, the existing norms, policies, and rewards appear to be in conflict with the premises of Notes. Because incentive schemes and evaluation criteria in the office had not been modified to encourage or accommodate cooperation and expertise sharing through Notes, members feared loss of power, control, prestige, and promotion opportunities if they shared their ideas, or if their lack of knowledge or misinterpretations were made visible. Thus, in a relatively competitive culture where members are evaluated and rewarded as individuals, there will be few norms for sharing and cooperating. If groupware is to be used cooperatively in such cultures, these norms need to be changed--either inculcated top-down through training, communication, leadership, and structural legitimation, or bottom-up through support for local opportunities and experimentation around cooperation. Without some such grounding in shared norms, groupware will likely be used primarily for advancing individual productivity.

In addition to norms, resources are a further important facilitator of shared technology use. Whether formally ear-marked from some firm-wide R&D budget, or provided informally through local slack resources, occasions for experimenting with shared applications are needed to generate interest and use around cooperative computing. In the office, for example, there had been no change in the allocation of resources following the implementation of Notes, and members had not been given time to use and experiment with Notes. There was thus a tension between the structural requirement that all work be production-oriented, and the adoption of an infrastructure technology such as Notes which was perceived to be only indirectly related to production work. Where individuals are not given resources to learn and experiment with the new technology, or not given specific applications that help them accomplish their production work within the technology, the immediate pressures of daily production tasks and deadlines will tend to dominate their decisions around how they allocate their time.

This research study suggests that in the early adoption of a technology, cognitive and structural elements play an important role in influencing how people think about and assess the value of the technology. And these significantly influence how they choose to use the technology. When an organization deploys a new technology with an intent to make substantial changes in business processes, people's technological frames and the organization's work practices will likely require substantial change. An interesting issue raised by this requirement is how to anticipate the required structural and cognitive changes when the technology is brand new. That is, how do you devise a game plan if you have never played the game before? This is particularly likely in the case of an unprecedented technology such as groupware. One strategy would be to deploy the technology widely in the belief that through experimentation and use over time creative ideas and innovations will flourish. Another strategy would prototype the technology in a representative group of the organization--on a pilot basis--and then deploy it to the rest of the organization once the technology's capabilities and implications are understood. This way the required structural and cognitive changes learned through the pilot can be transferred. Viewed in terms of these two strategies, aspects of Alpha's adoption activites now appear to resemble the former strategy. Our future studies should indicate how successful this strategy has been.

It is worth noting that while the early use of Notes in the office has proved more valuable for facilitating individual productivity than for collective productivity, the implementation of Notes has resulted in the installation of an advanced and standardized technology infrastructure. As one technology manager put it: "A side-benefit of Notes is that it got people into a more sophisticated environment of computing than we could have done otherwise." Most of the office members--from principals to senior consultants--now have ready and easy access to a network of personal computers and laser printers. Thus, while the initial experiences with Notes in the office may not have significantly changed work practices or policies, the office appears to be relatively well-positioned to use this platform to take advantage of any future technological or work-related initiatives.

In general, the findings presented here provide insight for future research into the structural and cognitive organizational elements that interact with and shape the adoption and early use of groupware in organizations. They also have practical implications, indicating how and where such organizational elements might be managed to more effectively implement groupware in various organizational circumstances.

ACKNOWLEDGMENTS

Support from MIT's Center for Coordination Science is gratefully acknowledged. Jolene Galegher, Bob Halperin, Tom Malone, and Judith Quillard provided helpful comments on an earlier version of the paper. Thanks are also due to the participants from Alpha Corporation.

REFERENCES

1. Bair, J.H. and Gale, S. An Investigation of the COORDINATOR as an Example of CSCW, *Proc. CSCW* (Portland, September 1988).

2. Bullen, C. and Bennett, J. Groupware in Practice: An Interpretation of Work Experience, *Proc. CSCW* (Los Angeles, October 1990), 291-302.

3. Dyson, Esther Why Groupware is gaining Ground, *Datamation* (March 1, 1990), 52-56.

4. Eveland, J.D. and Bikson, T.K. "Evolving Electronic Communication Networks: An Empirical Assessment," *Proc. CSCW* (Austin, August 1986), 91-101.

5. Feldman, M.S. Electronic Mail and Weak Ties in Organizations, *Office: Technology and People*, 3 (1987), 83-101.

6. Finholt, T. and Sproull, L.S. Electronic Groups at Work, *Organization Science*, 1:1 (1990), 41-64.

7. Gash, D.C. and Orlikowski, W.J. Changing Frames: Towards an Understanding of Information Technology and Organizational Change, *Academy of Management Best Papers Proc.*, 51st Annual Meeting (Miami Beach, August 1991), 189-193.

8. Govani, Stephen J. License to Kill, *Information Week* (January 6, 1992), 22-28.

9. Groupware: The Teamwork Approach, Supplement to *PC Week*, 8, 41 (October 14, 1991).

10. Grudin, J. Why CSCW applications fail: Problems in design and evaluation of Organization Interfaces, *Proc. CSCW* (Portland, September 1990), 85-93.

11. Kiesler, S. The Hidden Messages in Computer Networks, *Harvard Business Review* (January-February 1986), 46-59.

12. Kling, R. Cooperation, Coordination, and Control in Computer-Supported Work, *Comm. of the ACM*, 34, 2 (1991), 83-88.

13. Mackay, W.E. Diversity in the Use of Electronic Mail, *ACM Transactions on Office Information Systems*, 6:4 (1988), 380-397.

14. Markus, M. L.. Toward a 'Critical Mass' Theory of Interactive Media, *Communication Research*, 14:5 (October 1987), 491-511.

15. Marshak, David S. Lotus Notes: A Platform for Developing Workgroup Applications, *Patricia Seybold's Office Computing Report*, (July 1990).

16. Perin, C. Electronic Social Fields in Bureaucracies *Comm. of the ACM*, 34, 2 (1991), 75-82.

17. Sproull, L.S. and Kiesler, S. Reducing Social Context Cues: Electronic Mail in Organizational Communication, *Management Science*, 32, 11 (1986), 1492-1512.

18. Tyre, M.J. and Orlikowski, W.J. Windows of Opportunity: Creating Occasions for Technological Adaptation in Organizations, Sloan School of Management #3309, MIT (Cambridge, July 1992).

The CSCW Implementation Process: An Interpretative Model and Case Study of the Implementation of a Videoconference System.

Duncan Sanderson

Canadian Workplace Automation Research Centre
1575 Chomedey Blvd.,
Laval, Québec, Canada H7V 2X2
(514) 682-3400 DSanderson@ccrit.doc.ca

ABSTRACT

An understanding of the implementation process of CSCW in organizations can contribute to the design, testing, evaluation, and effective use of this technology. A dynamic, interconnected model is presented which is sensitive to the user, organizational, and technological context of the implementation process. The model is then used to structure observations of the implementation of a videoconference system for regular meetings among senior managers in a large decentralized organization. Knowledge of the context of the implementation was essential in order to interpret the observations, outcome of the implementation, and pertinence of the videoconference terminal design.

KEYWORDS

implementation process, videoconference, case study

INTRODUCTION

An increasing number of authors are investigating the technology implementation process, not only to better understand the factors that lead to failure, but also to identify ways of improving the effectiveness of technology implementation [2, 4, 6, 8, 9, 11, 12, 13]. In this paper, our efforts are not so much oriented towards suggesting immediate ways for better managing this process, although some suggestions are discussed in the conclusion, as to identifying the complex relationships that need to be considered if better understanding of the process is to emerge. We will first suggest that attention to the implementation process, defined as "the sequence of activities undertaken to embed new technologies in organizations" [12], will contribute to the continuing development of the field of CSCW. This is followed by the presentation of a general model of the implementation process. Finally, a case study of the implementation of a videoconference system will be presented in order to illustrate both the model and the complexity of the process. The particular contribution of this study is that it suggests a comprehensive and interpretative approach to the analysis of the CSCW implementation process.

Permission to copy without fee all or part of this material is granted provided that the copies are not made or distributed for direct commercial advantage, the ACM copyright notice and the title of the publication and its date appear, and notice is given that copying is by permission of the Association for Computing Machinery. To copy otherwise, or to republish, requires a fee and/or specific permission.

© 1992 ACM 0-89791-543-7/92/0010/0370...$1.50

THE IMPLEMENTATION PROCESS AND CSCW RESEARCH

An initial example should help to suggest the importance of observations of the CSCW implementation process. Imagine that two organizations agree to test the same prototype of a technology for CSCW. The researchers that designed the technology find that in one organization, the users are satisfied with the technology, and identify certain productivity benefits. In the other, users dislike the technology, and suggest that it be removed. What are the researchers to do? Especially if a manufacturing company offers to market the technology only to organizations with characteristics similar to those where the technology was a success?

However, let's say that the researchers had been collecting regular observations in relation to the way in which the organizations were implementing the technology, and were monitoring user reactions to it. In this case, the researchers would then have been able to determine if there were design problems with the technology (that could be changed to everyone's satisfaction), or if the failure of the technology was more directly related to user characteristics or the different ways in which the organization implemented the technology. It may then have been possible to make certain changes to the technology, or to make recommendations to the host organization that could eventually have lead to a positive outcome of the trial. The point of this hypothetical example is that even studies of initial field trials of prototype CSCW technology need to observe and take into account the way in which the technology was introduced into its organizational setting.

Several other observations suggest the importance of including the study of the implementation process in the field of CSCW:

- problems with CSCW technology implementation could be observed similar to those for mainframe and micro-computer systems [6, 9, 12, 13]. However, the often distributed nature of the technology, users, and organizational coordination, could exacerbate these problems.
- the technical infrastructure of CSCW, usually based on a network, often requires that multiple actors, potentially in different organizations, coordinate their actions. An effective technical infrastructure may in turn depend on an effective social network.
- CSCW usually requires group adoption, which may be a process quite different from single-user adoption. Attaining a critical mass of users can be a more complex process than simply offering an application to an individual, or requiring him or her to use it.
- several CSCW technologies are still mostly experimental (multi-media desktop conferencing, co-authoring technologies). However, the ultimate objective for these technologies must not only be successful design, but effective use in the workplace. Implementation issues need to be addressed in order to meet this ultimate objective.
- because of their potential role in group and organizational communication, CSCW technologies may have different requirements or a more significant impact on the organization than "individualized" technologies. Thus it is important to study the planning, installation, and long-term use of these technologies.

The preceding observations underline the importance of acquiring better understanding of the implementation process of CSCW technologies.

A MODEL OF THE IMPLEMENTATION PROCESS

Much of the existing literature tends to approach the analysis of the implementation of technology in the organization from the perspective of the impact of particular factors [7]. For example, various authors have noted the impact of top management support and user-designer interaction.

However, interest has also been shown for a more comprehensive and dynamic conceptualization [2, 7], what Kwon and Zmud call process and political research. In this research, the way in which commitment to change is sought, the project definition and planning process, the appearance and management of conflict, the integration of stakeholder interests [8], and the securing of power and personal interests [5, 11] become key analytical dimensions. The model that we propose here, which could provide a framework for approaching the analysis of the implementation of CSCW technology, is mainly derived from this latter research approach.

The implementation process must first be conceptualized in broad terms, to include the organizational and user dynamics, the implementation related activities and outcomes, and the possible recurrent links between these [2]. The process spans and includes such activities as the creation of awareness of a need for a technical system (or need to solve problems due to existing technology), formalized planning activities, formulation and justification of courses of action, installation, user training and reactions, technical changes, the integration of the technology into daily work, studies of the technology and its impacts on the organization, changes in work and the organization, and incremental modifications that follow after installation [12]. Thus a first desirable characteristic of a model of the implementation process is that it is comprehensive enough to encompass the various actors, discourses, actions, and outcomes that are significant in this process.

A second desirable characteristic of a model is that it allow for repetition in activities (recursiveness), and not assume that activities will necessarily follow an idealized set of stages. For example, an organization may effectuate recurring analyses of its information and communication needs. Or organizational inertia [6] may even stall the implementation before any technology is put in place.

A final desirable characteristic of a model of the implementation process is that it help point to the influence of the organizational context on the process, and reciprocally, to changes in the organization that may result from the implementation process. Several authors emphasize the utility of documenting the history of the organization and observing the context of the development and use of a technology [2, 4, 6, 11, 12]. Four main areas appear to be of potential significance in this regard: the political and communication structures of the organization (and their evolution), the technology, the users, and the work (or task) for which the technology is used. The model that appears in the accompanying schematic, modified from that of Cooper and Zmud [2], identifies both the implementation activities, the contextual forces associated with the organization, and the reciprocal relationships that may exist within and between the two.

This model could be a valuable methodological tool for orienting and structuring observations. It provides a detailed checklist of observable actions and suggests ways of situating these in the context of the organization, the technology, and the work for which the technology is used.

The model was formalized subsequent to the following case study. It would have been useful before conducting the study, however, as it suggests areas where other observations could have been sought. For its part, the case study approach appears to be particularly useful for

A Model of the Implementation Process

Classes of Activities	Activities and Outcomes
Initiation	- technology watch - technology acquisition planning - coordination of technology acquisition - user requests for technologies, features - trials or visits to sites with a technology - emulation or comparison with peer organizations
Definition of Technology	- analysis of funding options - feasibility studies; cost/benefit analysis - possible consultation of stakeholders - definition of technology, functions, tasks - prototyping and observations of users - definition of the management of the implementation
Decision-making	- involvement of senior management - possible initiation of evaluation activities - building support for implementation - acceptance or resistance by stakeholders - possible plan for implementation
Installation	- installation of hardware/software - definitions of technical support roles - negotiation with other support groups - possible support staff training - possible training of end-users
User Reactions	- initial user reactions - possible support activities by end-users - possible formation of support network - solicitation of user reactions
Modifications	- technology may be modified, redesigned - end-users may participate in modifications - possible changes in responsibilities
Use & Impacts	- use of technology (amount and types) - changes in general use, or use of functions - motivation or coercion of users - possible unforeseen use; - non-use of certain functions - possible changes in work, communication structures - creation of user and organizational norms concerning access or use of technology
Evaluation	- possible assessment of impacts - search of ways of improving technology - promised and actual improvements - may be ongoing through implementation
Re-initiation	- initiatives to build on existing technology, expertise

Contextual Forces	
Organization	- strategic orientations (and environment) - organizational culture - role of technology in organization - expertise, representations of managers - division of responsibilities - political processes in the organization (control, influence, use of power; [5]) - history of organization, technological implementation
Technology	- existing hardware, software, expertise - complexity and nature of technology - the social organization of support and maintenance of the technology - organizational readiness for problems - characteristics of the technology that allow it to mesh with or adapt to work
Users	- attitudes towards the technology - experience with technology - representations of how they could use the technology, be affected by it - possible pressures on the users to adopt, adapt to, or learn to use the technology
Work (Task)	- the nature of work to be done via the technology - the social organization of work, division of labour

developing the richness of detail that is necessary to illustrate or substantiate such a model.

A CASE STUDY OF THE IMPLEMENTATION OF A VIDEO CONFERENCE SYSTEM

In order to illustrate the preceding model, we will describe and interpret the implementation process of a particular videoconference system. There is increasing interest in integrating videoconference technology into other CSCW technology, particularly in the form of multi-media desktop units. The videoconference unit that was used during the study was a roll-about terminal, but it is still relevant to the field of CSCW, as it was installed in order to facilitate mediated meetings among executive officers in a large, dispersed organization. Other research into videoconferencing will be noted first, then the methodology will be described, followed by a summary presentation of the observed activities. After this, the activities will be interpreted and analyzed in light of the contextual forces.

Although some studies of videoconferencing examine certain aspects of the implementation process, we have been unable to identify any that take a detailed interpretative approach to describing or analyzing the implementation of a videoconference system in a particular organization. Some authors discuss the evaluation issues related to the implementation of the technology [10, 14]. Still others discuss user training and ways of improving the conduct of meetings [1,3]. The current study will suggest the usefulness of attempting broader analyses of the overall implementation process.

The methodology of the study consisted of direct observation of meetings, a video recording of one of the meetings, and repeated, semi-structured interviews with meeting participants, technical personnel, and the project manager.[1] The present analysis of the implementation process was part of a more general formative evaluation study.

A minimum of contextual information should be provided first. The organization that installed the videoconference system was a large regionally-oriented organization, with a center of operations in one city. The audioconference was often used in the organization for mediated meetings. The organization already had several years of experience with videoconferencing, having installed two private rooms, one in the central city, and a second facility in a city where a regional executive officer was based. A telephone company provided the transmission services between the two sites for the videoconference. Although various technical problems were experienced more or less frequently during those years, both the regional executive officer and the chief executive officer were relatively satisfied with the technology. Thus it would appear appropriate to qualify the particular videoconference installation that we are discussing as a "second round" in the implementation process.

[1] A questionnaire was also designed, although it was not distributed for various reasons. The ongoing observations were communicated to the project manager on a monthly basis, and to a stakeholder's committee.

The Implementation Activities and Outcomes

The implementation activities will be presented in terms of the classes of activities that are identified in the implementation model. Although this means of presentation should add clarity, it does not, however, completely depict the actual sequence of activities. The activities are summarized for presentation purposes.

Initiation

- a computer systems engineer was asked to plan the expansion of the videoconference to all five regional offices in the spring, 1990; the proposal did not address the eventual use of the network (aside from facilitating weekly executive officer meetings).
- a videoconference terminal designer asked the chief executive officer if he would try his new roll-about system. The design had certain innovations[2] (three cameras as compared to the existing system's single camera; a hand held control unit). He was also installing a room in a city where another regional executive officer was located.

Definition of the Technology

- the engineer's proposal recommended purchase of a videoconference system, and the use of land-based transmission lines. Desirable characteristics for the room or a terminal were not defined.

Decision-making

- consultation and decision-making activities mostly unknown; however, it was decided to rent a system for the central office on a trial basis, and the regional executive officer agreed to pay for the videoconference room rental on a usage basis.
- internal telecommunications personnel not consulted.
- the computer engineer was appointed project manager (he had no experience with videoconferencing).
- the trial would run for 3 months, then be extended to all regions.
- 2 regional executive officers would participate in the videoconference, 3 others in the audioconference, and the officers at the central site in both.

Installation

- acoustics and lighting modified in the board room, and the unit installed.
- one or two tests conducted in August 1990, then working conferences began.

[2] This innovation is relative: various private and commercial systems have incorporated such a feature.

- telecommunications support personnel (who were responsible for the operation of the videoconference facility) received some training, none for the users.
- aside from the officers (and eventually the researchers) no other personnel were allowed to attend the conferences (confidentiality). The project manager never observed any of the conferences, and the terminal designer's direct experience was limited to the occasional test period before the conference began (in the videoconference room and not on the audioconference).

User Reactions

- various sound problems were experienced (clipping, echo, inaudible speech), irritating audioconference users in particular.
- user reaction eventually worked its way to the project manager, terminal designer.
- researchers sent written observations to the project manager each month.

Modifications

- During the fall 1990, the project manager organized the occasional meeting that included various technical personnel.
- various technical experiments and adjustments continued during the fall. These changes or their results were not documented by the technical personnel.
- in November 1990, responsibility for establishing the videoconference was contracted out to the terminal designer.

More User Reaction, Decisions, and Modifications

- early December 1990, a multi-site videoconference with all five regions was announced for January 1991.
- in Jan. 1991, the project manager announced (due to suggestions from his superior), that the audioconference had to be improved before expanding the videoconference trial.
- the researchers noted again that the participants in the audioconference had significant difficulties in hearing the videoconference participants.
- it was decided that the terminal designer would install specialized audioconference equipment in the three audioconference sites (although one of the regional executive officers eventually bought his own equipment).[3]
- the project manager began to hold weekly technical meetings.
- by March 1991, the quality and reliability of the sound in the conferences had improved.

Use and Impacts

- the conferencing technology allowed the regional executive officers to participate in the meetings, and they were pleased to do so.
- the new videoconference terminal was used exclusively for the officers' meetings (twice weekly), and no attempt was made to encourage use of the facilities.
- the 2 regional executive officers who had access to the videoconference were sometimes included instead on the audioconference (due to reservation errors, or because the participant preferred to not travel to the video conference room). Only 3 multi-point conferences were held.
- the office of a regional executive officer often failed to cancel a scheduled videoconference (resulting in charges for non-existant videoconferences).
- the users at the central site rarely used the hand held control[4], rendering the three cameras concept irrelevant[5].
- the roll-about unit was never moved to another room (and this would have been difficult, given the acoustical and lighting modifications).
- the unit's audioconference integration feature was used frequently.
- the users at the regional sites learned to (and did) use the camera control, although those at the central site did not.
- the videoconference allowed some communication of body language, and better indication of appropriate moments to make comments.
- a regional participant found the single conference during which the cameras were used, to be "more dynamic."

Evaluation

- the formative evaluation activities continued throughout the implementation.
- the study became a formal feedback mechanism that complemented informal communication of users' reactions.
- the researchers' observations concerning the poor sound quality for the audioconference participants, may have helped to focus the project manager's and terminal designer's attention on this.
- interim recommendations about the social and organizational issues (training of users, reservation

---

3 Few systematic subjective observations were made for the audioconferencing equipment, and no objective measurements were ever made.

4 There were 48 buttons on this control, with little obvious pattern to the layout.

5 In theory, the design allows rapid switching of camera shots in order to frame a speaker (or subgroup) in a group of speakers. This facility allows for close-ups, and an occasional contextual image of the full group. The design principle augments the flexibility of the images that can be captured of a group, given the transmission of only one image, while allowing for multiple images if the transmission technology and economics permits.

procedures, further testing of a full multi-point videoconference) were not implemented.

- the evaluation study may have contributed to a decision to continue the trial (rather than purchase the terminal, or permanent expansion to other sites).

Re-initiation

- an informal scan is continuing of videoconferencing technologies, with a desire to extend the technology to other sites.

Interpretation and Analysis of the Contextual Forces

The previous skeleton account of the activities and outcomes associated with the implementation process cannot be adequately explained without recourse to observations of the context of the implementation. Knowledge of the organization, technology, users, and task, is needed in order to provide a framework that can help situate and explain the observations. Here, we will illustrate only some of the major links that can be established. Many of these links became readily apparent because of the problems that were experienced, but it is likely that these relationships can also be observed with a technology implementation that is relatively problem free.

The Organization

During the spring of 1990, the organization had continued to implement a strategic policy of decentralization. The regional executive officers were asked to assume a greater responsibility for the management of the organization, to report directly to the chief executive officer, and to participate in the weekly executive officer meetings. In fact, even before the installation of the new videoconference terminals, the regional executive officers participated in these meetings via audioconference. The important point here is that the organization had first decided to attribute a more significant role to the regional executive officers. This could have taken place with only the audioconference: the videoconference was perceived as an enhanced audioconference and as a possible means of facilitating these meetings. Thus the videoconference did not have a structural impact *per se*, but was rather an instrument for facilitating an organizational design decision.

Another relevant observation is that the organization had a history of encouraging the development of promising technologies. The terminal designer presented his design as an innovation that had a reasonable chance of being adopted by organizations using or considering the use of videoconferencing. The senior officers were willing to risk time and money on an unproved terminal, considering the project a means for developing the technology and its market.

It is also possible to interpret the observations in terms of the political processes in the organization, although, in this case[6], perhaps not to the extent suggested by other authors [5]. To some extent, the senior executive officers likely considered themselves knowledgeable about videoconference technology, because of the years that they had been using it, and may have been reluctant to consult staff who were under them. The use of the expression of "trial" itself also defines a situation of short duration, wherein risk is acknowledged, and possible negative outcomes are implied to be acceptable. Although unconfirmed, these hypotheses point to possible explanations of an apparent lack of consultation prior to the decision to test the technology.

As well, the apparent difficulties that the organization had in mastering the technology may have been interpreted by some as an embarrassment for the organization. The ongoing technical problems appeared to have had direct political consequences in the sense that the executive officer who was responsible for new technologies, became concerned by these problems. He indicated to the project manager that the problems with the sound had to be fixed. It is also likely that this officer played an important role in postponing the expansion of the trial.

The lack of cancellations of conferences that were not attended is also significant in that they suggest various structures and relationships in the organization. The manager noted that he felt ill at ease discussing this issue with the officers. The executive officers or their assistants may not have been aware of the issue and the financial implications of the lack of cancellations. If this were the case, then it suggests weaknesses in the management and communication structures within the organization.

Some blame was also directed at the "technology" (the telephone company) because of the perceived inflexibility of reservation procedures. The two-way interaction between the organizational structure and the implementation process can be recognized here : the additional costs failed to be addressed within the existing organizational structure, and these may have contributed to the postponement of the projected expansion.

The project manager appeared to define his role in terms of the technical installation of the technology, since he was reluctant to address the human and organizational issues that appeared with the implementation. This observation also suggests how actors' own definition of their role (and the organization's action or inaction in relation to it) can have an impact on the implementation process.

Thus the organizational context, the history, structure, political processes, evolving strategic orientation, management approach, and representations of responsibilities, had close links with the implementation process. The organization conditioned and oriented that process (for example through the choice of a project

---

[6] It could be noted that the videoconference system was more of a "peripheral" technology than is often the case for computer systems in large organizations.

manager, or through the definition of the implementation as a "trial"), while at the same time responding to the implementation activities (for example, when the senior executive officer asked the project manager to solve the sound problems).

Technological Context
The terminal, telecommunications, and the technical support group's knowledge of the equipment played a key role in the observed activities. For example, the persistence of the sound problems[7] were not attributable to any one actor or even solely to the terminal itself. Rather, an assortment of contributing factors may be cited: the inexperience of the terminal designer and project manager in relation to videoconference technology, the fact that the terminal had not been fully tested before installation, the particular room conditions (several participants in a relatively untreated acoustical environment), a possible lack of clarity in the specifications by the telephone company, the absence of a consistent approach to calibrating the conference, the lack of direct observation by the designer and manager, and finally, the services provided by two different phone companies. Although not a direct part of the technology, the absence of specifications for a videoconference system also contributed to ambiguity in terms of what the organization required and what the terminal designer was required to provide. All these factors contributed directly to the technical performance of the system.

Users
A variation in individual attitudes towards the technology and the trial was also noted. At the central site, some of the participants were interested in experimenting with the technology, whereas others were critical of it. These attitudes were partially influenced by the organizational changes that had lead to the inclusion of the regional executive officers in the senior executive group. Some of these participants had reacted negatively to this change. Their perception of the videoconference technology was thus perhaps negatively coloured by the broader organizational context.

On the other hand, the regional participants were the users that acquired the greatest mastery of the videoconference control. They also had generally favourable attitudes towards the videoconference, and were interested in its communication potential. However, the regional officers did not enjoy having to drive to the videoconference room, and did not mind when errors in reservation procedures allowed them to join the audioconference from their own office. All the regional officers (including the ones in the audioconference) appreciated the opportunity to participate in the senior management meetings (which offered them more opportunity to understand and influence the activities of the organization, and conferred greater status on themselves). Thus it is important to take into account the experience and attitudes of the users in order to situate the different outcomes at the various sites.

The characteristics and behavior of the users had a part to play in the implementation process. For example, there was a very wide range in the loudness of the participants' voices, creating particularly difficult technical conditions. Much effort was subsequently deployed to render the microphones more sensitive to participants who spoke softly. This again suggests the interconnecting links that existed between the technology, the users, and the implementation activities.

Work (Task)
The particular work or task in relation to which the videoconference was tested was limited to the relatively formal management meetings. There were two ways in which the work, particularly at the central site, did not provide a conducive setting for experimentation and operation of the system. First, participants either did not feel at ease in trying the control or in operating it or they were too busy following the discussion to operate it. Second, the large group was used to conducting the meeting with a certain amount of "hustle and bustle," which added a significant amount of extra noise. All of this contributed to the problems experienced by the audioconference participants.

In another kind of communication situation, or with a smaller group, the videoconference system may have required much less or different "fine-tuning." This suggests once again the connecting relationships: the work that was conducted by means of the technology revealed limitations in that technology, and thus indirectly contributed to the activities that were initiated in the implementation process.

CONCLUSION
We have suggested that analysis of the implementation process is an essential part of CSCW research. A dynamic model was proposed in order to better understand implementation activities. This model was used to present and interpret a case study of the implementation of a videoconference system. Relatively few case studies of this type exist, and most of these are based on the implementation of computer technology [6, 13].

The study has implications for the design process and management of CSCW technology, as well as for the analysis of CSCW technology implementation. In the case study that was presented, it appeared that the videoconference control needed redesign. However even if the control had been more user-friendly, it is doubtful that it would have been used at the central site, given the particular context of the conferences. A sophisticated voice-activated intelligent system, participant-activated button, or human operator was needed for effective camera switching. Thus prototypes of technologies need to be tested as early as possible, by various kinds of users, in various organizations, and for varying work, with an understanding

---

[7] Various participants cited this as a critical and recurring problem.

of the implementation process and contextual factors being used to improve the design process.

Several management issues also surfaced: 1) the distributed nature of the technology and its management contributed to the observed problems, 2) the implementation required the coordination of several actors with varying and sometimes imprecise responsibilities, 3) technological and organizational factors contributed to the limited use of the technology, although it may have been possible to influence these in a positive manner, and 4) it became apparent that designers and managers require prolonged, direct experience with the technology that is being implemented, and that they need to seek out and respond to user reactions. The effective participation of stakeholders in the implementation process, as real decision-makers, appears to be one way of facilitating this.

The study also has implications for the analysis of the CSCW implementation process: 1) it is not necessarily a linear process that follows exactly plans and hypothetical stages, and 2) the context and activities of the organization and users have to be assessed in order to understand the implementation. Future directions for research could include the use of the model in describing and analyzing more comprehensive installations of technology, and the exploration of ways to encourage managers to become aware of and to use practical implementation guidelines [1, 3, 14].

ACKNOWLEDGMENTS

Richard Lavoie and Chantal Aurousseau contributed to the observations, and Richard Lavoie helped to shape our understanding of the contextual forces. The author would like to acknowledge the contributions of his colleagues at CWARC to the model. The fieldwork was undertaken while the author was a visiting NSERC research fellow at CWARC, although the opinions expressed here are his alone.

REFERENCES

1. Bell, B., Cukier, W. Human and Organizational Factors in Implementing Teleconferencing, in *Proceedings of the International Teleconference Symposium*, 1984, 299-306.

2. Cooper, R., Zmud, R. Information Technology Implementation Research: A Technological Diffusion Approach. *Management Science*, 36, 2, Feb. 1990, 123-139.

3. Earon, A., Douglas, S. Seven Steps to Successful Teleconferencing, in Steinfield, C., Breaugh, S. (ed.) *ITCA Teleconferencing Yearbook 1990*, Washington: International Teleconferencing Association, 1990, 106-117.

4. Grote, G., Baitsch, C. Reciprocal Effects Between Organizational Culture and the Implementation of an Office Communication System: A Case Study. *Behavior and Information Technology*, 10 (3) 1991, 207-218.

5. Kling, R., Iacono, S. The Control of Information Systems Developments After Implementation, in *Communications of the ACM*, 27, 12, 1984, 1218-1226.

6. Kling, R., Iacono, S. The Institutional Character of Computerized Information Systems. *Office: Technology and People*, 5, 1, 1989, 7-27.

7. Kwon, T., Zmud, R. Unifying the Fragmented Models of Information Systems Implementation, in Boland and Hirschheim (ed.) *Critical Issues in Information Systems Research*. New York: John Wiley, 1987.

8. Légaré, J. L'évaluation d'implantations technologiques: une approche naturaliste centrée sur l'utilisateur. Canadian Workplace Automation Research Centre, 1990.

9. Lyytinen K., Hirschheim, R. Information Systems Failures: A Survey and Classification of the Empirical Literature, in *Oxford Surveys in Information Technology*, 4, 1987, 257-309.

10. Mitsugi, M., Okamoto, T. Implementation and User Evaluation of a Teleconference System in Fujitsu Limited, in *Proceedings of the International Teleconference Symposium*, International Telecommunications Satellite Organization, 1984, 128-134.

11. Smith, H., McKeen, J. Computerization and Management: A Study of Conflict and Change. *Information & Management* 22, 1992, 53-64.

12. Stasz, C., Bikson, T., Eveland, J., Mittman, B. *Information Technology in the U.S. Forest Service.* RAND publication R 3908-USDAFS, 1990.

13. Walsham, G. Problèmes d'implémentation dans l'évaluation des systèmes d'information. *Technologies de l'information et société*, 3, 2/3, 1991, 69-83.

14. Young, I., Birrell, J., Derbyshire, A. The Implementation of Teleconferencing: Some Lessons Learned, in Parker, L., Olgren, C. ed. *Teleconferencing and Electronic Communications: Applications, Technologies and Human Factors.* Madison: University of Wisconsin-Extension, 1982, 431-438.

Flexible, Active Support for Collaborative Work with ConversationBuilder

Simon M. Kaplan, William J. Tolone, Douglas P. Bogia and Celsina Bignoli

Human-Computer Interaction Laboratory
Department of Computer Science
University of Illinois at Urbana-Champaign
Urbana, IL 61801, USA
(217) 244 0392 {kaplan,tolone,bogia,bignoli}@cs.uiuc.edu

ABSTRACT

Work activities have a highly *situated* nature. As a result, it is not possible to classify activities exactly, since they tend to evolve as they progress. This raises a significant problem for work support tools: how to address the trade off between *active support*, which requires knowledge of the activity at hand, and *flexibility*, which is a measure of how well a system can respond to changes in activities. We have been developing the ConversationBuilder, a support tool that is intended to provide flexible, active support for (collaborative) work activities. This paper overviews the Conversation-Builder, discusses both the kinds of support it provides and its architecture, and illustrates its use through an example.

KEYWORDS

Toolkits, CSCW Environments, Active/Flexible Support.

INTRODUCTION

This paper reports on our investigations into the development of environments that provide *flexible, active* support for CSCW. The *situated* [16] nature of work activities is by now well-known. From the point of view of providing tool support for collaborative work[1], this raises the difficult problem of how to support work when the tasks that we are trying to support can be continuously changing[2]. For a work support tool to be *flexible*, it must be able to deal with such changes. Further, if we provide computerized support for work, it is reasonable for the system to aid its users in varying degrees, depending on the particular task at hand. An *active* support environment would provide such facilities.

One of the primary challenges of this research is to find a way to maximize both flexibility and active support. Unfortunately, these requirements tend to oppose each other. Increasing flexibility can mean sacrificing knowledge about what the users of the system are doing, which reduces the handle we can get on providing active support. On the other hand, increasing the amount of knowledge we have about user actions, and thereby increasing the potential for active support, tends to decrease the room for users to maneuver. We believe that our environment, the ConversationBuilder (CB) [10, 9], makes significant strides in dealing with this problem, both through the mechanism of *protocols*, which allows different activity types and policies to be defined to the system, and through the mechanism of *obligations* which allows us dynamically to weave individual activities together.

A critical element of successful work support tools is the melding of appropriate theory with innovative approaches to tool development. Our project therefore stands on five legs:

• A theoretical vision which can be used to drive our approach to building a very elegant and simple tool kernel. Our vision is based on the work of Winograd and Flores concerning the equivalence of language and action [17].

• A theoretical vision of the situated nature of work motivating both the need for great flexibility which is

[1]We see almost all work situations as being potentially collaborative; thus collaborative work support must include support for individual work as well. We will simply use the term 'work' in this paper to cover both cases.

[2]By this we mean both that the task itself can be changing, and that relationships among tasks or subtasks can change.

Permission to copy without fee all or part of this material is granted provided that the copies are not made or distributed for direct commercial advantage, the ACM copyright notice and the title of the publication and its date appear, and notice is given that copying is by permission of the Association for Computing Machinery. To copy otherwise, or to republish, requires a fee and/or specific permission.

© 1992 ACM 0-89791-543-7/92/0010/0378...$1.50

used to drive our approach to our descriptions of work activities (which we call protocols) and the need for both flexibility and active support. Our vision is strongly influenced by work concerning situated action and ethnomethodology, and is also justified by many studies which are not intentionally related to these fields [16, 8].

- The development of a simple yet extremely powerful kernel of an active support tool. This kernel allows us to specify activities and interconnections among activities in a dynamic way, moving us simultaneously towards flexibility and active support. Users are allowed to work on as many activities of different types simultaneously as they find useful, to context-switch among activities, and to relate activities together in arbitrary ways.
- The development of an *open* architecture into which the kernel and collections of other tools can be integrated. This architecture also adds to the flexibility of the system by allowing users control over the tools they use to interact with the system.
- The development of user interface models that allow the development and generation of the dynamic interfaces that next-generation work support tools such as CB appear to need.

The body of the paper discusses the problem we are tackling in more detail, the facilities a CSCW system should provide, the architecture of our tool, and an example.

CONTRIBUTIONS

Unlike other active support tools, such as Coordinator [17], Chaos [5]or gIBIS [4], CB allows the specification of multiple protocols, and allows users the ability to work with arbitrary numbers of instantiations of any of these protocols as suitable to the situation at hand.

CB supports the idea of shared data models which can be worked into a hypertext. This makes CB closer to many hypertext systems, but distinguishes it from systems such as Strudel [15], which support an analogous concept of protocol specification but provide no shared data model. We believe the ability to access and manipulate shared data is vital to the successful support of work as the data provides a focal point around which the activities of collaborating workers can coalesce.

The Obligation facility of CB allows users to dynamically weave webs of interconnections among activities, and to model the flexible way in which we naturally build up and break down such dependency structures.

CB aids the user to a degree by enabling her or him to be aware of the activities in which s/he is engaged, the relations among these activities, the legal actions that can be performed in each activity, the structure of the hypertext, and the relevant actions of other workers.

From a systems architecture and tools point of view, CB provides advances in the communications facilities for use in CSCW applications and in the construction of advanced user interfaces.

CHARACTERIZATION OF PROBLEM AND REQUIREMENTS FOR SOLUTIONS

In order to support work on the computer, we need to have some characterizations of the problem, some view of how characterizing the problem enables us to approach a solution, and some goals which we would like a work support tool to meet. This section of the paper addresses these issues.

Problem Characterization

The nature of cooperative work, and work in general, has been much investigated both by social scientists and by those interested in providing computerized support for work activities (see, e.g. [17, 16, 8, 14]). The *situated* nature of work activities emerges strongly from all of these investigations: work activities shape themselves as they evolve, often in unexpected ways. A practical consequence of this is that it is nearly impossible to characterize most work activities exactly enough to be able to contemplate 'writing a computer program' that directly supports them, as it is not possible to articulate exactly what comprises the activities[3]. In particular, we usually cannot precisely characterize:

Control Structures. We do not know exactly what steps make up the work activity, in what order they are performed, when backtracking is and is not permissible, and so forth.

Data. We do not know exactly what data is to be manipulated during the course of the activity, and/or how associated access capabilities may evolve.

Who. It may not be clear exactly who will participate in the activity, or what roles participants will play. Additionally, this information may change over time.

Relationships among activities. Activities that seem independent may turn out to be related, and vice versa, over time.

Figure 1 outlines some continuua along which one could characterize work situations. It follows from the discussion above that one can never characterize an activity exactly along many of these continuua, but rather, we have to recognize that over time the positioning of an activity can change. For our purposes, these characterizations allow us to determine strategies for providing flexible, active computerized support for various tasks.

[3]Space in this paper is extremely limited; we therefore make little effort to justify these contentions here, as we believe that they are widely held within the CSCW community at this time. If the reviewers feel that additional justification is necessary we will gladly expand on these arguments in the final version.

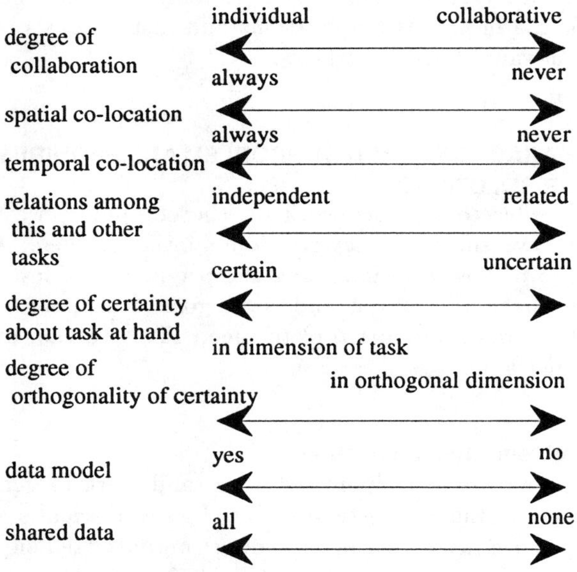

Figure 1: Continuua of Collaborative Work Situations

Degree of Collaboration determines how much of the task is carried out by an individual versus a group.
Spatial Co-Location represents whether or not the participant(s) must be spatially co-located[4] for successful completion of the task.
Temporal Co-Location specifies the degree to which participants must be available at the same time versus being able to work on their own.
Relations among Tasks refers to the dependence of this task upon the completion of other tasks or vice versa. Such dependencies are dynamic.
Degree of Certainty about the Task at Hand refers to our understanding of and ability to articulate the process of completing a task. Having a high degree of certainty about tasks is definitely a desirable characteristic; unfortunately, due to the situated nature of work activities, this is seldom the case. For example, in an office automation problem, we might be concerned with what steps the office workers go through when performing a task, in what order the steps are performed, and where backtracking is permitted. In a software engineering support environments, we are interested both in the steps the software development group goes through when developing software *and* in the actions the group performs when manipulating the artifacts that make up the end result (e.g., documents, designs and program modules).
Degree of Orthogonality of Certainty describes how much the degree of certainty is *orthogonal* to the task. There are times when we know the procedure for performing some task and, thus, can either automate the task or provide a semi-rigid set of guidelines to accomplish the task. Other times we may have little knowledge which relates directly to the task and therefore can provide little direct support unless we provide support which is flexible in the face of the large degree of uncertainty present. However, many times we have knowledge about things that are *orthogonal* to the task itself, but which, when supported, provide support for the task. An excellent illustration of this is the support of various *document manipulation* activities necessary for such tasks as code development and technical design or documentation development in software development situations. In these situations, teams of software developers evolve strong cultural conventions for the *manipulation of the artifacts* making up the total software system. These conventions specify how to control access to information, allow team members to create, edit and version modules of a document, place these modules into configurations of various kinds, and so forth; but, the conventions do not specify how to generate the information in a document and are, therefore, orthogonal to the document generation task.
Data Model refers to the amount of data available to the participants in the task. As mentioned, if there is a data model, sometimes supporting manipulations of the data rather than the activities around the data, will support the collaborative work without overly restricting the workers [7].
Shared Data determines the degree to which data are shared among the participants versus being private to a participant or group. This raises the critical issue of determining the proper conventions and mechanisms for sharing data.

[4]Technology can be used to allow participants to appear co-located when they are not (video, audio, etc.).

Taxonomy of Work Activities

Experience with CB suggests strongly that we can classify the various work activities into three broad categories. We outline these, and discuss their relationship to our continuua, in this section of the paper.

To understand the following taxonomy, we must explain what we mean by a *protocol*. Protocols are context-sensitive specifications of the actions that can be performed in an activity, and their effects. The concept of being able to tailor the CB system to the culture of its intended users via protocol modification is extremely important as it means that users can adapt the system to their models of work rather than the other way around.

Conferences are activities in which the participants are spatially and/or temporally co-located, and with little certainty about the task at hand, reducing the handle on which to hang active support. As a result the only support one tends to find in conference protocols are administrative facilities (such as controlling who is in the conference) and facilities for imposing or dealing with obligation structures. Examples include free-form discussion, meetings of various kinds, and structured discussions. In the case of many meeting and free-form discussion situations, it's very difficult to know what participants will want to do in advance, and therefore it seems better to simply provide very generic facilities and let the active part of the system 'get out of the way'. In the case of structured discussions, models such as those found in Coordinator or Chaos can be deployed if appropriate[5].

Free-form discussion support has been investigated by many projects, including the EuroPARC RAVE project [2], Sun MicroSystems' COCO [6] and the AT&T Bell Labs Rapport project [1]. Each of these focuses on the problems of providing virtual co-location and realtime access to shared information, and does little work on the problem of active support for collaboration, with which we are interested here. Our investigations in this area have focused on emulating protocols such as Coordinator or Chaos, or simple free-form talk, and have avoided such high-tech investigations simply because we have not had adequate resources. However, discussions with researchers working on these projects have led us to believe that integration of advanced video and audio capabilities will not be conceptually difficult.

Document Manipulations are activities where the focus is on manipulating families of artifacts (which we call documents). Thus, these activities tend to require low degrees of spatial or temporal co-location, do not necessarily require that the activity at hand be undertaken collaboratively, and have a very strong notion of a shared data model, parts of which are public. This occurs naturally, for example, in paper writing, programming, and technical documentation activities. Examples are protocols such as the IBIS protocol used in gIBIS [4] or the Castle protocol developed as part of the CB project [3]. These two protocols are very different; IBIS is used to build a shared hypertext of Issues, Positions and Arguments, while Castle is used for building up complex 'documents' such as this paper or the source code for each of the components of the CB implementation, and provides versioning, configuration management and other standard facilities of this type.

What makes IBIS and Castle document manipulation protocols is that, in both cases, the actions in the protocol are concerned *not* with the activity at hand but instead with the rules by which artifacts can be manipulated while undertaking that activity. In other words, these activities demonstrate a high degree of certainty about these artifact manipulation rules without demonstrating a high degree of certainty about the activity itself. Document protocols are thus a prime example of how we use orthogonal information to provide useful, flexible and active support for users.

Jobs are activities where we have varying degrees of certainty in the dimension of the task. Examples include document routing, purchase ordering, other bureaucratic activities [12], and software process modeling. The major function of a job activity is to be able to create a flow-structure of obligations which represent the steps of the activity, and be able to edit this in an *ad-hoc* way to reflect dynamically changing situations. Additionally, participants in a job will need to manipulate documents, parts of documents, or families of documents as part of the job activity; they will also need to talk to one another, and create and pass around obligations. Last, there is a need for a concept of *environment*, which is a way of associating users with roles, creating collections of users and so forth, to be referenced within job activities.

Job activities are a mix of all the continuua mentioned above, but there is a definite focus on using the ability to edit obligation structures to provide a way of getting into the control dimension in spite of the fact that we know that any knowledge we have been given about that dimension may turn out to be false.

Active Environments Support Requirements

This section of the paper outlines three sets of facilities that we believe a CSCW support tool must provide in order to meet our goals of flexibility and active support. The first set includes those facilities allowing users to work on, and relate among, arbitrary sets of activities:

- Provide the ability to allow new kinds of activities to be specified to the system. We call the specifications of such situations *protocols*.
- Allow the user to have as many activities running (we call each a *conversation*) simultaneously as useful.
- Allow the user to relate activities to one another as s/he sees fit, i.e. to make an activity subordinate to another, or group of other, activities.
- Be able to impose obligations on other users, or other contexts, from any context, at will, and be able to manipulate one's own obligations, including handing them off, changing their context, declaring them complete and refusing offered obligations.
- Allow the user to switch among activities at will and as painlessly as possible.

The second set of facilities concerns with helping the

[5]We simply dodge the question of whether these kinds of models are actually appropriate for negotiation. The role of CB is to provide rich mechanisms for collaboration, and particular approaches represent policies. For our purposes, we must be able to support such policies, if user communities find them appropriate.

user to find out where s/he is in the CB system, and what can be done there.
• Help the user determine how s/he got into a particular context (conversation).
• Indicate what legal actions can now be performed in a given context.
• Perform any of these actions.
• Indicate to the user his or her obligations which must be met before an activity is complete.
• Enable the user to understand the relationships (if any) that exist among the data that are present in the system.
• Enable the user to understand the relationships among all the contexts in which s/he is involved.
• Allow members of a group to be 'aware' of what other group members are doing.

The third set of facilities are miscellaneous, but necessary.
• Allow the construction of arbitrary networks (hypertext systems) of data, in which both nodes and links can be typed, so that both shared and private data of various types can be modeled within the system.
• Continue to provide 'traditional' support facilities, such as compilation, version control, editing and mail.
• Allow the incorporation of new tools as required by users.

CB meets all of these requirements to some degree. This should not be interpreted as meaning that CB is in any way a perfect system, or even close to it; indeed, many of our solutions are rather crude, and significantly more work is needed to make CB more sophisticated.

THE ARCHITECTURE OF THE CONVERSATIONBUILDER

Our architecture, as we indicated in the introduction, is based on the theoretical orientation we derive from the work of Winograd and Flores on the equivalence of language and action. Following this model, we view each 'activity' in which the user is engaged as a 'conversation' in which the user make 'utterances' or, equivalently, 'perform actions'. Also, the performing of an action modifies the space for action of other participants.

All actions a user can perform in CB are viewed as utterances in a conversation. This has allowed us to keep the kernel of CB very small and clean, which we believe has a direct and positive impact on the ease of writing protocols and the flexibility of the system as a whole.

The CB system is easily extensible through submitting new protocols to the kernel. The protocols must specify:
• The *new features of data structures* to be manipulated by the protocol. A running protocol (a conversation) requires a *shared conversation space* which holds information shared by all participants, and an *individual action space* for each participant, holding information unique to that participant in that conversation. Most of the information in these structures is specified by inheritance.
• The *legal utterances in the protocol.* Utterances specify when they can be applied (thus making the protocol context-sensitive), the ways in which shared and individual conversation spaces are affected, any changes to the hypertext system, and the generation of subconversations where appropriate. Many utterances in conversations are obtained by inheritance (e.g., all the administrative utterances controlling joining/leaving conversations, listing information about conversations, controlling obligation structures, and controlling relationships among conversations).
• *New hypertext node and link types, and associated display methods*, are sometimes needed if new data types are introduced into the hypertext. For example, changing a feature of text nodes is unlikely to require much work, but introducing synchronized video and audio nodes would be more complicated.

Figure 2 shows a schematic representation of the CB architecture.

USER ENVIRONMENT AND EXAMPLE

In this section of the paper, to give the reader a feel for the user's view of the system, we illustrate CB in action through an example based on a situation from a software development protocol. Before proceeding with the example, however, a brief description of some of the user interface components is necessary[6].

A user's view of CB is comprised of several components which include ActionSpace windows, Node Display windows, obligation windows, and graphical browsers. An ActionSpace is a user's view into a conversation and contains both shared and user specific information. Figure 3(a) depicts a typical Castle ActionSpace. Across the top of this window there are several of menus (i.e. Actions, Operations, Administration and Controls). Actions and Administration provide protocol-specific actions, while Operations and Controls provide generic actions for manipulation of ActionSpaces. The Obligations and Tasks lists show the users obligations, and the obligations he has placed on others, respectively. The Configuration list shows all the artifacts in this configuration, and the InBox shows active subconversations.

Figure 3(b) is an example of a typical Node Display window. One can see that this particular node is version 1.0.1.1 and is currently checked out by user 'tolone'.

[6] Because of space limitations many details have been omitted.

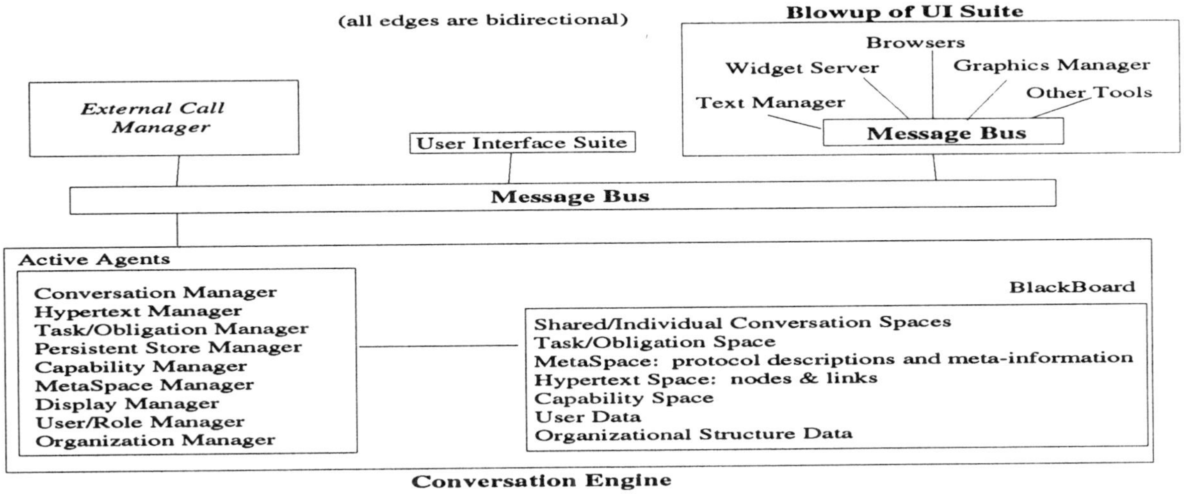

Figure 2: Architectural Schematic of ConversationBuilder

We now proceed with our example. Consider a situation in which Bill, Elsa, Simon, Alan and Doug are working on the development of a new version of the CB kernel. Each has responsibility for a portion of the new system; when they are done, Bill has been detailed to test the new code. The project is, in this case, being jointly managed by all five participants, i.e. any one of them can control the obligation model they build up (this is not a requirement; a subset of the users could have been made the manager, or someone else could be managing the group).

The job ActionSpace for Bill is shown in Figure 4(a). Within Bill's job ActionSpace, the obligation structure is shown. In our example, the merge and test obligation is waiting on completion of four active code development tasks. When these obligations have been met, the merging/testing obligation will become active and appear in Bill's obligation list. Any user with appropriate permissions can modify the obligation structure shown in the window. In order to complete their work the five programmers must talk to one another; thus, there are several conferences ongoing. Each portion of the CB system is represented as a document, which is being manipulated using our Castle protocol.

Relatively little work is actually done in the job context; the evolution of the code is taken care of in the document contexts, discussion takes place in the conference contexts, and the obligation mechanism is used to glue all this together. For example, consider a situation in which Doug finds that he needs a function that is Elsa's responsibility to provide. He creates an obligation and fills it in as shown in Figure 4(b) before handing it off to Elsa. Elsa can inspect the obligation, and perform whatever actions she wants before declaring it fulfilled, as shown in Figure 4(d).

To illustrate obligation dependency modification, if the situation of the job changes the dependency structure can be modified. Figure 4(c) shows a set of changes to the initial dependency structure. This in turn causes a change in the order in which obligations are created and passed around.

EXPERIENCE AND IMPLEMENTATION

The CB system outlined in this paper is implemented and in daily use at the University of Illinois. It is used for its own development and maintenance, thesis and paper writing activities (including this paper and the theses of students in the group) and for experimentation with new protocols, tools and facilities. For example, we are developing, or working with our sponsors to develop, several new protocols, including inspection and review meeting support, Design Rationale support [13], Software Process support, and several applications in the traditional office automation and document routing domain. CB is also installed at several of our sponsors, and at several universities.

While we have run no formal 'usability studies', we could argue that CB's daily use for its own development and maintenance is one of the best possible kinds of usability study. Certainly the system has evolved extensively under this regime, and is now remarkably stable.

CB is implemented in a mixture of CLOS [11] and C,

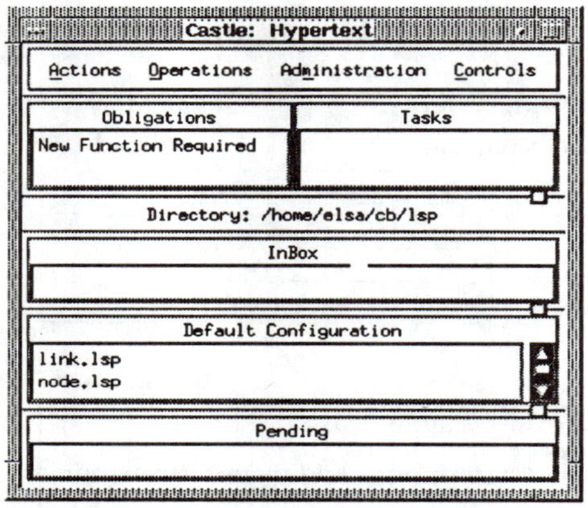

(a) ActionSpace

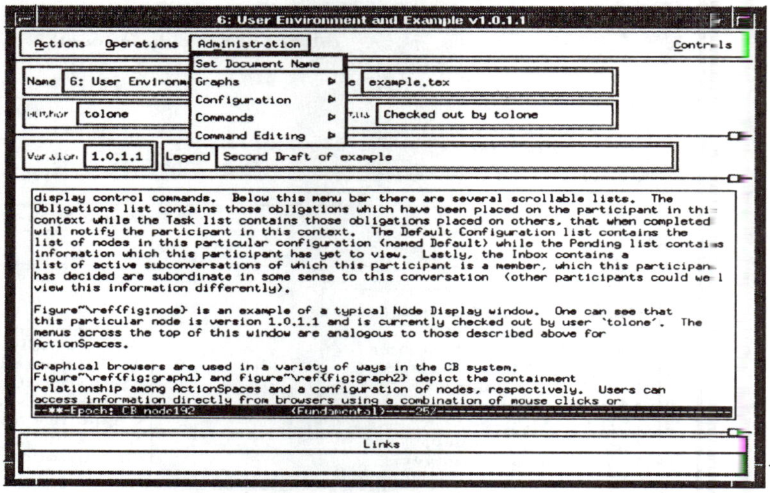

(b) Node Display

Figure 3: CB Snapshots

and runs on a wide variety of Un*x platforms, including Sun, HP, IBM RS6000, and NeXT. The User Interface part of CB will also run on just about any Un*x machine with X11R4 and Motif.

Acknowledgements

The authors would like to thank Alan Carroll for his work in the development of CB. This work is supported in part by the National Science Foundation/DARPA under grant CCR-9007195 and by Intel, Bull, Open Systems Solutions Inc., and Hewlett-Packard. Celsina Bignoli is supported in part by a scholarship from the Universita' degli Studi di Milano.

References

[1] S. R. Ahuja, J. Ensor, and D. Horn. The rapport multimedia conferencing system. In *Proceedings Conference on Office Information Systems (COIS) 88*, pages 1–8, Palo Alto, CA, March 1988.

[2] W. Buxton and T. Moran. Europarc's integrated interactive intermedia facility (iiif): Early experiences. In *Proceedings of IFIP WG8.4 Conference on Multi-User Interfaces and Applications*, Heraklion, Greece, September 1990.

[3] Alan M. Carroll. *The ConversationBuilder Kernel and Applications.* PhD thesis, University of Illinois, 1992.

[4] Jeff Conklin and Michael L. Begeman. gIBIS: A hypertext tool for exploratory policy discussion. *ACM Transactions on Office Information Systems*, 6(4):303–331, October 1988.

[5] F. DeCindio, C. Simone, A. Vassallo, and A. Zanaboni. Chaos: A knowledge-based system for conversing within offices. In W. Lamersdorf, editor, *Office Knowledge: Representation, Management and Utilization*, pages 257–276. Elsevier Science Publishers B.V. (North-Holland), 1988.

[6] David Gedye, Greg McLaughlin, Amy Pearl, and John Tang. Conferencing and collaboration project. In *Record of the ECSCW-91 Developers Workshop, SIGOIS Bulletin*, to appear, 1992.

[7] Christian Heath and Paul Luff. Collaborative activity and technological design: Task coordination in london underground control rooms. In Mike Robinson Liam Bannon and Kjeld Schmidt, editors, *Proceedings 2nd European Conference on Computer Supported Cooperative Work (ECSCW) 91*, pages 65–80. Kluwer Academic, September 1991.

[8] John Heritage. *Garfinkel and Ethnomethodology.* Polity Press, 1984.

[9] Simon M. Kaplan and Alan M. Carroll. Supporting collaborative processes with conversationbuilder. *Computers and Communications*, To appear, 1992.

[10] Simon M. Kaplan, Alan M. Carroll, and Kenneth J. MacGregor. Supporting collaborative processes with conversationbuilder. In Peter de Jong, editor, *Proceedings ACM 1991 Conference on Organizational Computer Systems (COCS)*, pages 69–79. ACM Press, 1991.

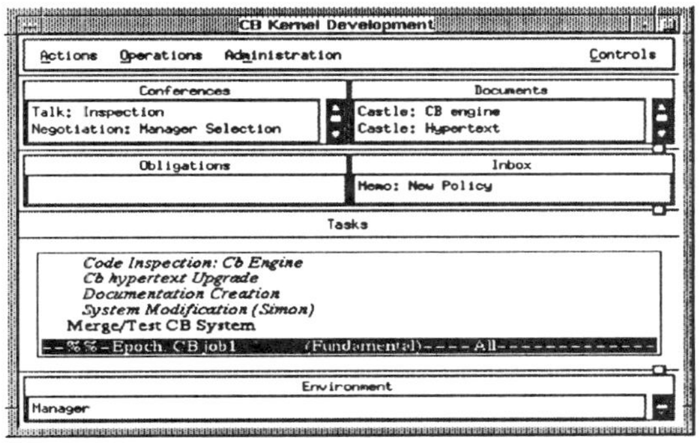

(a) ActionSpace I

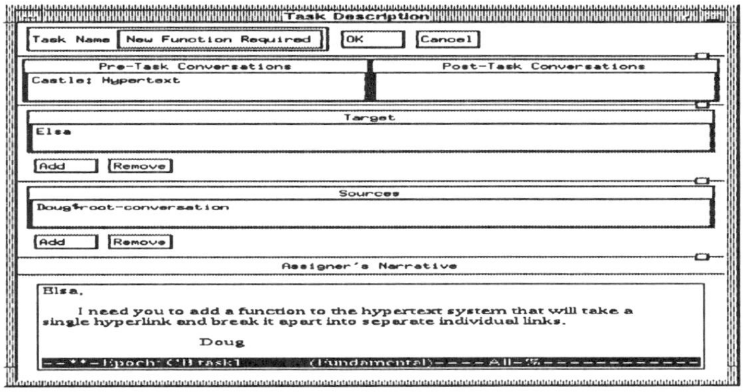

(b) Obligation Request

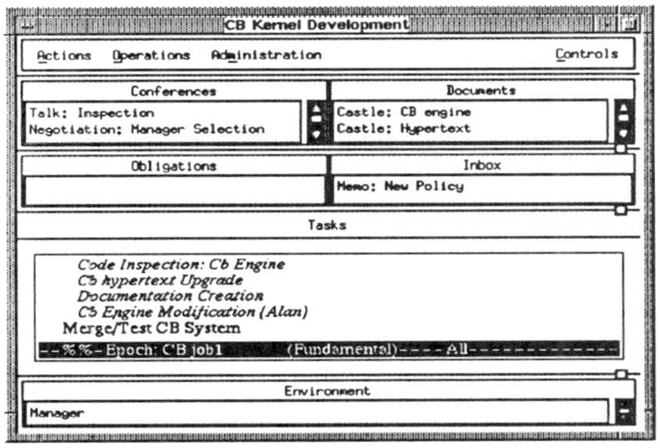

(c) ActionSpace II

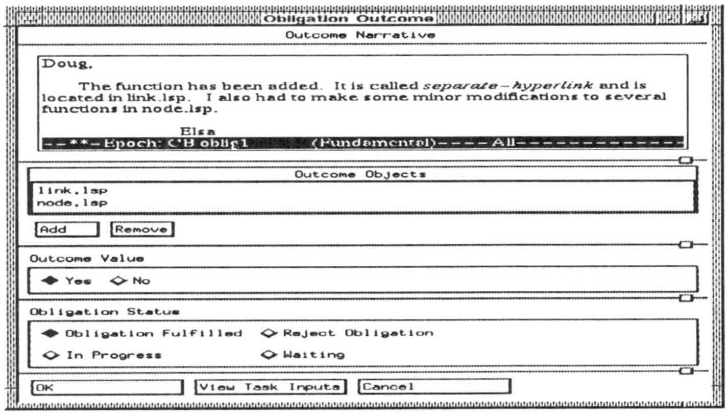

(d) Obligation Outcome

Figure 4: CB Snapshots

[11] Sonya Keene. *Object-Oriented Programming in Common Lisp.* Addison-Wesley, Reading, Massachusetts, 1989.

[12] Thomas Kreifelts, E. Hinrichs, K.-H. Klein, P. Seuffert, and G. Woetzel. Experience with the domino office procedures system. In Mike Robinson Liam Bannon and Kjeld Schmidt, editors, *Proceedings 2nd European Conference on Computer Supported Cooperative Work (ECSCW) 91*, pages 117–130. Kluwer Academic, September 1991.

[13] Alan MacLean, Victoria Bellotti, and Richard Young. What rationale is there in design. In G. Cockton D. Diaper, D. Gilmore and B. Shackel, editors, *Proceedings IFIP Human-Computer Interaction INTERACT 90*, pages 207–212. North-Holland, 1990.

[14] David A. Marca. Specifying groupware requirements from direct experience. In *Proceedings of the 6th International Workshop on Software Specification and Design*, pages 224–232, Como, Italy, October 1991.

[15] Allan Shepherd, Neils Mayer, and Allan Kuchinsky. Strudel: An extensibleelectronic conversation toolkit. In *Proceedings ACM Conference on Computer-Supported Cooperative Work (CSCW) 90*, pages 93–104. ACM Press, October 1990.

[16] Lucy Suchman. *Plans and Situated Actions.* Cambridge University Press, 1987.

[17] Terry Winograd and Fernando Flores. *Understanding Computers and Cognition.* Addison-Wesley, Reading, Mass., 1987.

BibDb: A Bibliographic Database for Collaboration

David J. Musliner **James W. Dolter** **Kang G. Shin**

Computer Science and Engineering Division
Department of Electrical Engineering and Computer Science
The University of Michigan
Ann Arbor, Michigan 48109-2122
(313) 936–2495 {djm, jdolter, kgshin}@eecs.umich.edu

ABSTRACT

While researchers strive to develop new systems to enhance the cooperative document editing process, many authors already collaborate, using *existing* text processing systems to produce papers and reports. Using these tools, one of the most time-consuming and error-prone collaboration tasks is maintaining a consistent shared bibliography. We have designed and implemented the BibDb system to simplify collaborative authoring by providing a shared, cooperatively maintained bibliographic database. BibDb uses existing networking technology and merges seamlessly into the LaTeX/BibTeX text processing system [5]. The contributions of BibDb include a set of user interface policies and software implementation techniques that support cooperative database maintenance.

KEYWORDS

Bibliographic databases, collaborative writing, distributed & replicated databases, partial locking, relaxed consistency, incremental indexing.

INTRODUCTION

Despite their overwhelming popularity in the scientific community, computerized text formatting systems have remained quite primitive, and do not yet take advantage of the potential for sharing and cooperation which is embodied in local-area networks (LANs) and the nationwide Internet. For instance, every formatting system has some technique for constructing a bibliography of references automatically, but each user must type the bibliographic reference material into his/her own database file. In addition to a tremendous amount of replicated effort, this isolation of personal databases leads to pervasive inconsistency in reference formats (especially in abbreviations of journal and proceedings titles) and incompatible citation keys. As a result, collaborating authors find it nearly impossible to smoothly merge their individual databases and reference styles. A few user groups have cooperated to form larger, shared databases of references, but the performance of programs which access these databases does not scale well, because the databases are simply large text lists of bibliographic entries.

Permission to copy without fee all or part of this material is granted provided that the copies are not made or distributed for direct commercial advantage, the ACM copyright notice and the title of the publication and its date appear, and notice is given that copying is by permission of the Association for Computing Machinery. To copy otherwise, or to republish, requires a fee and/or specific permission.

© 1992 ACM 0-89791-543-7/92/0010/0386...$1.50

To address the deficiencies of current bibliographic systems within the context of existing text processing and networking technology, we have designed and implemented the BibDb bibliographic database system. The BibDb system is designed to maintain a single vast bibliographic database, shared by all users and accessible to any UNIX machine on the Internet. The database is not stored or accessed linearly, so search and access performance does not depend linearly on the size of the database. Local copies of the database are maintained at each installation (perhaps one installation per university or LAN), so that most accesses to the database are done over LANs rather than the nationwide network. Additions to the database are incremental and global, and data is never removed from the system: once an entry is added at one installation, it is available (and will not be added again) at all installations.

Our work on BibDb has been carefully focused on developing practical mechanisms to allow cooperative database maintenance and to enhance collaborative authoring capabilities. We have developed a set of user interface policies that encourage harmonious cooperative efforts. We have also developed several unique software mechanisms useful for implementing this shared distributed database. These implementation details include a uniquely powerful client/server organization, a relaxed database consistency criterion, a partial database locking method, and a dynamic overload scheme leading to graceful degradation.

The remainder of this paper is organized into six sections. The next section presents an overview of the BibDb system goals and organization. The following three sections describe the server and access programs which make up the system. The last two sections compare BibDb to competing bibliographic systems, and describe the current status and future extensions of the system.

THE BibDb SYSTEM

Design goals

We designed the BibDb system to address the variety of problems perceived in existing bibliographic systems. The primary goal was to create a system which takes advantage of cooperative efforts at database maintenance and eases collaborative authoring, within the context of currently popular text processing packages. Based on personal experience and discussions with other users, we designed BIBDB with the following specific aims:

- Data sharing. BIBDB maintains a very large database of bibliographic information entered, maintained, and shared by all users and accessible over LANs and the Internet. Sharing the database avoids redundant data entry.
- A one-to-one mapping of keys to references. BIBDB goes to great lengths to prevent duplicate entries, and will never issue the same citation key for two different references. Thus there is never any confusion about what information a citation points to, and collaborating authors can exchange simple citation keys, rather than extensive bibliographic data.
- Citation permanence. Once a citation key has been issued for a new entry, it will always point to that entry. Documents produced using the BIBDB system will never be invalidated by changes to the database.
- Consistent referencing. BIBDB encourages users to employ standard string aliases, so that references to similar works are formatted similarly.
- Powerful searching. BIBDB includes an associative cross-indexing mechanism, so users can perform keyword searches for articles. These searching facilities make the database a major resource both for finding specific references and for blind literature searches.
- Speed and scalability. BIBDB stores references in a hashed database format which makes retrieval extremely fast. The database is never processed entirely or searched linearly.
- Incremental growth. As users add new entries, BIBDB does not re-process the entire database in any way.

The BIBDB system is intended to merge seamlessly into the LaTeX/BibTeX formatting system [5]. In the LaTeX system, text formatting commands are included in a document to control its eventual printed form. The companion BibTeX system provides bibliographic reference indexing and formatting. BibTeX bibliographic entries are typed in a fixed format, with each entry assigned a unique key by which it is cited. Figure 1 shows an example BibTeX entry for a (mythical) journal article, as well as the use of *strings* (or aliases) to abbreviate commonly used journal names and other text items. The "@article" portion specifies that the entry's *type* is article, which the `bibtex` program knows how to format. The entry type can also be "@inproceedings", "@book", etc. After the type specification, the entry's unique key is specified (here, "musliner:92"). Then a series of "*field* = *value*" pairs specifies the bibliographic data.

```
@string{CCJ = "The Cool Computing Journal"}
@article{musliner:92,
author = "D. J. Musliner and J. W. Dolter",
title = "A Cool Bibliographic System",
journal = CCJ,
year = 1992 }
```

Figure 1: An example BibTeX entry.

System overview

Figure 2 shows the organization of the entire BIBDB system, which is composed of database files, server programs, and client programs. A copy of the entire database exists at each installation, where installations are allocated to LANs with fairly large groups of users (e.g., universities, research companies). Each installation runs the `bibdb-server` program, which provides database maintenance and access services to users. Users connect to the `bibdb-server` by running client programs on their own computer. The client programs usually connect to the closest installation's server, but may connect to a server at any installation. The database copies at each installation are kept consistent by their connection to the central `keymaster`. The `keymaster` coordinates all updates to the database, systemwide, and ensures that different users do not simultaneously add the same entry.

All of the BIBDB programs are written in *perl* [9], a commonly available and freely-licensed interpreted language which contains nearly all of the features of awk, sed, c-shell and C. Like Lisp, perl has an 'eval' function which runs the interpreter on a perl expression. A perl program can write its own code by assigning valid perl code to a string variable and then eval-ing the variable.

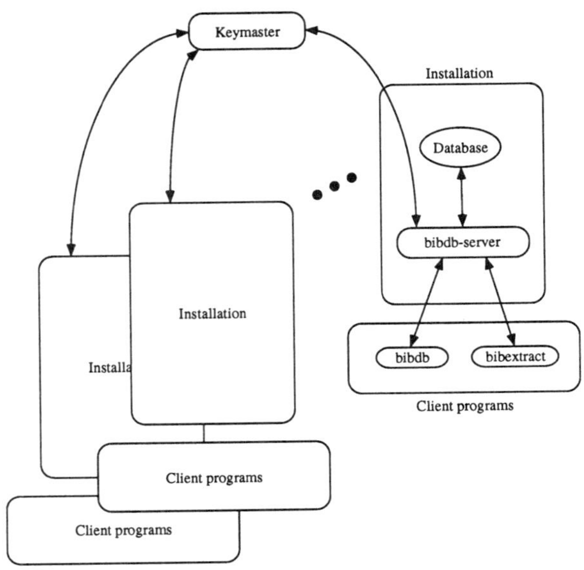

Figure 2: Overview of the BIBDB system.

The server programs

The `bibdb-server` provides all database services to the user. This program embodies the various administrative policies of the BIBDB system, which are described in the next section. Each installation's server program opens a "well-known" socket to which the client programs connect. The server forks copies of itself for each connecting client, so that multiple clients may access the database simultaneously.

The `bibdb-server` connects to the `keymaster` via a well-known socket, and tells the `keymaster` about all changes to the database. The `keymaster` forks copies of itself for each connecting `bibdb-server`, and tells each `bibdb-server` about changes that others have made to the database. These programs and their interactions will be described in more detail in the following sections.

The client programs

The client programs `bibdb` and `bibextract` are actually very small perl scripts that simply connect to the appropriate server and act as a "programmable conduit" for information. Aside from a single routine to connect to the appropriate server program, the entire body of the client programs is shown in Figure 3. The client programs connect to a server and then read lines from the connected socket, either printing them out or eval-ing them. Thus the server program can send executable code to the client program, causing the client to, for instance, open a file and send its contents back to the server. All file operations, prompting, and data manipulation are actually controlled by the server program, and the client programs just provide a channel over which information can flow to and from the user's computer. This organization has several beneficial aspects:

- Security. Since the data operations are all completely controlled from the server program, there is virtually no way a user can interfere with or alter the database in an unacceptable manner. The `bibdb-server` gives users a limited ability to modify or delete information from the database, and malicious users cannot expand upon that ability because the information exchange protocol is dynamically downloaded from the server. The server even has to tell the client program when to prompt the user for input.
- Speed. Since the client programs are very small perl programs, they start very quickly. The high cost of parsing the complex database management routines is paid only when the server program is started, not each time a user wishes to access the database.
- Optional distribution. The server program can download subroutine definitions to the client programs and then send invocations of those subroutines, thus offloading computations from the server computer to the user's computer. This feature is most useful for I/O routines which can be offloaded without compromising security.
- Protocol locality. Because the entire interaction protocol is contained within the server program, it is much easier to recognize errors in the protocol when writing these programs. While debugging, we do not need to constantly switch between the client and server programs to understand how information is being exchanged, and what the response to various inputs will be. The `keymaster/bibdb-server` interface, which does not share this feature, has been much more difficult to develop and debug.
- Easy code updates. Making changes to the BIBDB implementation is extremely easy, because there are relatively few copies of the server program (one per installation). There may be many thousands of copies of the trivial client programs, but these need never be changed, because the actual interface is contained solely in the server. In fact, since the client programs were first developed in this form, we have made hundreds of changes to the server program, but not one to the client programs.

The fact that the client programs are such minimalist shells is not visible to the user. The user simply starts one of the client programs, which then appears to prompt and interact with the user in a normal fashion. Thus we describe the behavior of the client programs as though they actually define those interaction patterns, when in fact the server program does.

BIBDB

The `bibdb` program is the database maintenance program, allowing the user to add and modify entries and strings, and communicating with the keymaster to keep the local database copy up-to-date with the other installations. The program also provides a powerful user interface to the database's searching mechanisms, including an associative cross-index which allows keyword search without linear scanning.

Policy-directed functions

The `bibdb` program implements many of the policies with which the BIBDB system addresses the shortcomings of other bibliographic databases. For instance, each user of a referencing program tends to develop his/her own style of citations. This means that combining or exchanging databases or even single citations can be difficult, because citation keys may conflict, or duplicate entries may not be detected. To avoid these problems, `bibdb` automatically generates the citation keys for all entries when they are added to the database. All authors then use the same key to cite the same entry in the shared BIBDB database. Keys are formed from the last name of the first author, a colon, the last 2 digits of the year, and a suffixed 'a', 'b', 'c', etc, to distinguish otherwise identical entries (e.g., musliner:92a). No two entries may have the same key. When entries are added, if entries with the same *key-root* (all but suffix character) exist, the system queries the user to make sure a duplicate entry is not being introduced, as illustrated in Figure 4. Barring typographic errors in the first author's last name or the year, this technique detects all possible duplicate entries. A title comparison heuristic then

```
while (<SERVER>)                # While (get a line of input from the server)
  {
      chop;                     # Strip newline from input.
      if (s/^\001//)            # If input starts with CTRL-A,
          { eval; }             # it is executable perl code, so execute it.
      else                      # Else,
          { print "$_\n"; }     # just print the input to the user.
  }
```

Figure 3: Main body of client programs (in perl).

makes continue/abort recommendations to the user. Unfortunately, differing interpretations and typographic errors are much more common in the titles of papers, and thus human intervention is still required to make the final decision to abort an addition. Fortunately, bibliographic systems are not so critical that we need to worry too much about errors. The inevitable typographic errors [1] are easily fixed, since `bibdb` allows users to modify any entry in the database.

Since BIBDB depends on users to add its entries in the first place, we must explicitly trust the user when necessary. Despite the best heuristic efforts, some duplicate entries will undoubtedly be introduced. In that case, two different citation keys will point to (potentially) different data for the same real reference. This violates one of our fundamental goals, since there is no longer a one-to-one mapping of unique keys to unique references. However, we cannot allow a user to fix this problem by simple deleting a citation key and its corresponding reference, because that key would no longer be valid. Some other user who cited that key in a document would then have an invalid document, violating the citation permanence design goal. Once a document is successfully generated, changes to the bibliographic database should not alter the citation structure such that the document's citations are no longer valid. Therefore, we allow a user to fix duplicate entries by "redirecting" one of the keys to the other key for the same reference. The redirected key is still a valid citation key, but now it points to the data associated with the other key. Changes made to the data will be visible to citations using either key.

BIBTEX provides the string alias mechanism both to save typing effort and to lend consistency to references. For example, good bibliographic style dictates a consistent format for the titles of conferences and workshops. A bibliography which cites "The Proceedings of the Third International Conference on Widgets" and also "Proc. 3rd Int'l Conf. Widgets" is inconsistent and undesirable. Thus `bibdb` provides a powerful automatic string substitution mechanism which encourages users to employ string aliases, leading to more compact references and consistent formatting. The program examines the fields of each entry, heuristically checking to see if they resemble strings which are defined. If so, the program offers those substitutions to the user, as illustrated near the bottom of Figure 4.

Finally, since one of the major goals of BIBDB is to conveniently share the bibliographic data, multiple users may run `bibdb` in parallel, concurrently accessing and modifying an installation's database. This is a particularly tricky feature, since UNIX does not strongly support multiple-writer files. In fact, all changes to the database files must be serialized, but `bibdb` restricts the serialized sections of code (monitors) to very short operations, thus allowing most `bibdb`s to carry on interactions with their users while one `bibdb` has the database briefly locked. Locks on the database are only acquired once a final decision has been made to modify the database. When any `bibdb` user is modifying the database, all `bibdb` accesses to the same installation are preceded by cache flushes and reloads, so that the data which the `bibdb` user sees is as up-to-date as possible.

The bibliographic database

The BIBDB database is optimized for access by the unique key which must be associated with each BIBTEX entry. The bibliographic data is stored in "gdbm" format, which is a freely-licensed database format based on the "ndbm" system supplied with most UNIX installations. Perl can access these database files as though they were associative arrays (that is, arrays indexed by arbitrary strings). So, bibliographic entries are stored in a huge associative array, indexed by their unique citation key.

```
key --> [database] --> entry
```

The cross-index

To allow the user to find an entry whose key is unknown, all words in each entry are used as indices into an associative cross-index, which maps arbitrary words to the keys of entries which contain those words.

```
word --> [cross-index] --> list of keys
```

The `bibdb` program gives the user a powerful set of searching primitives which locate references based on boolean combinations of keywords, as listed in the cross-index. For example, the command "`find author musliner and title database`" specifies a search for entries in which the author field contains "musliner" and the title field contains "database". These searches are always case-insensitive. The cross-index database maps each field/value pair in the search

Print out the file of new data.

```
unix% cat new.bib
@article{ignored-key,
        author = "D. J. Musliner and J. W. Dolter",
        title = "A Cool Bibliographic System",
        journal = "J. of Cool Computing",
        year = 1992 }
```

Start the database maintenance program.

Add the new data file.

Bibdb detects a similar entry.

```
unix% bibdb
Connected to bibdb-server at [huron.eecs.umich.edu]
bibdb> add new.bib
WARNING: a key collision has occurred.
The key for the existing entry :
   @inproceedings{musliner:92,
                 author = "D. J. Musliner and J. W. Dolter",
                 title = "Another Neat Bibliographic System",
                 booktitle = "Proc.  Conf.  on Important Things",
                 year = 1992 }
Conflicts with the proposed key for the new entry :
   @article{musliner:92,
                 author = "D. J. Musliner and J. W. Dolter",
                 title = "A Cool Bibliographic System",
                 journal = "J. of Cool Computing",
                 year = 1992 }
```

Bibdb lists options.

```
Enter one of the following options:
   (c)autiously continue:  try the next lexical key
   (a)bort the addition
   (r)eplace existing entry with new entry
```

And provides advice based on heuristics.

User agrees entries are different, so bibdb tries new key and finds no conflict.

```
Title comparison suggests the entries are NOT the same
and you should choose the (c)autious option
key-collision-action> cautious
Continuing addition attempt:  generating new key
Adding new entry with key [musliner:92a]
```

Bibdb detects a common string.

User chooses the suggested alias.

```
The following strings are similar to the
original journal ["J. of Cool Computing"]:
        1 :  CCJ = "The Cool Computing Journal"
Please choose a number, or <Return> for the original value
string choice> 1
bibdb>
```

Figure 4: Showing how the `bibdb` interface tries to prevent duplicate entries and encourages common string usage when a new data file is added. Note the new entry's citation key in the data file is ignored, and `bibdb` creates the key itself.

command to a list of citation keys. The "and" indicates that the result of the whole search command should be the intersection of the two intermediate lists. Replacing "and" with "or" yields the union of the intermediate lists.

Finding the intersection or union of lists involves a linear scan of the lists, and thus can have relatively high cost. To limit the maximum time which a search can take, and also to restrict the size of the cross-index entries, words which map to too many[1] entry keys are declared "overloaded," and are not allowed as cross-index indices. However, they may still be used in searches: as long as a non-overloaded keyword is specified, the search routines return a list of keys[2] which is then scanned by a post-processing step for the overloaded search terms.

THE KEYMASTER

The `keymaster` is responsible for ensuring that each of the installation databases is "consistent." Essentially, the `keymaster` must make sure that every valid citation key is assigned to exactly one entry (hence the name). No installation must be able to assign a key that has already been used,

[1] N = "too many" is a constant on the order of 500-1000.

[2] of length $\leq N$.

and all installations must agree on which entry a particular key points to. However, since our bibliographic database does not have the temporal consistency requirements of a banking database, the installations need not be identical at all times. In fact, the only time it is important for an installation to be completely up-to-date is when a user is trying to modify the database: `bibdb` must have access to all the existing entries, so it can issue an unused key and make sure the user is not creating a duplicate entry. Therefore, we have implemented a type of "relaxed consistency" in which installations can become outdated if they have not been changed recently.

Relaxed consistency

The `keymaster` assigns a unique, monotonically increasing *update-id* to each database change sent from a `bibdb-server`. When a `bibdb-server` initiates a modification to the database by contacting the `keymaster`, it first requests all the updates since its last contact (as identified by its most recent update-id). The `keymaster` sends all the more recent updates back to the `bibdb-server`, thus ensuring that the installation's database is up-to-date before the change.

This approach has the advantage that installations only need to be connected to the `keymaster` when the user tries to change the database. Periods of Internet downtime do not completely incapacitate the BIBDB system: installations which cannot connect to the `keymaster` essentially become read-only, so users can still extract entries which they have used before. Documents which were successfully produced in the past are not suddenly crippled by network problems.

Despite the relaxed consistency technique, the `keymaster` is the bottleneck of the BIBDB system. All changes to the database must eventually be serialized at the `keymaster` (because UNIX does not support multiple-writer files). The `keymaster` does not actually have a gdbm copy of the database: it only maintains a file containing all of the modifications to the database (the *updates-file*). The updates-file is the single-writer bottleneck, since database changes must be recorded serially in the file. Although a `keymaster` is forked for each `bibdb-server` which is trying to change the database, these `keymasters` cannot all write to the updates-file at the same time. We have minimized the cost of this restriction through a technique we call "key-root locking."

Key-root locking

If a user is going to add a new entry, the addition may take as much as a minute or two, because the user may have to resolve key conflicts and string-substitutions. We do not wish to have the updates-file locked for that entire time. So, we allow the `bibdb-server` to request an exclusive key-root lock, disallowing all other changes which involve database entries with the same key-root (author name and year). The key-root lock is held for the duration of the bibdb/user interaction dealing with the new entry. But the updates-file is locked only briefly, once the user has confirmed the addition. The `bibdb-server` sends the confirmation to the `keymaster`, which locks the updates-file, writes out the update information, and immediately releases the lock on the updates-file. Thus, the time during which the forked `keymasters` must be serialized (essentially, the monitor section of the `keymaster`) is extremely short. Multiple users can simultaneously interact with `bibdb` to arrange changes to the database, as long as the key-root locks do not conflict.

In fact, the forked `keymasters` are also serialized when they issue a new update-id, since that number must be unique and monotonically increasing. The key-root locks and update-id locks are implemented through *flock*, the UNIX file locking facility.

BIBEXTRACT

The `bibextract` program interfaces the BIBDB database system into the normal LaTeX/BibTeX system. `Bibextract` finds the citations in a LaTeX document and retrieves the corresponding entries (and all necessary string definitions) from the BIBDB database, building a reference file tailored to the exact needs of the document.

Normally, the "\cite{}" commands in a LaTeX document will specify the exact BIBDB citation key, so that `bibextract` can use a simple lookup in the BIBDB database. The time required for this extraction process does not grow linearly with the size of the database, because the database is indexed associatively.

`Bibextract` also allows users to pass the "\cite{}" command an "imprecise citation," consisting of a set of semicolon-separated words which appear in the desired bibliographic entry (i.e., an imprecise citation for this paper might have the form "\cite{musliner;bibdb;1992}"). `Bibextract` will attempt to resolve imprecise citations to unique entries using the BIBDB associative cross-index.

COMPETING DATABASES

This section compares BIBDB to a variety of competing bibliographic database systems, both commercial and public domain. We demonstrate that BIBDB provides a unique set of features, combining the best aspects of many other systems while largely avoiding their disadvantages.

Refer

The *refer* system mentioned in the introduction is an older reference-maintenance system which was developed to work with *troff*. Since *refer* has been around so long, many people have very large *refer* databases, and there are various modifications available to make the system usable with other text processing systems. *Refer* is the most popular competitor to BibTeX.

Aside from minor formatting differences, the primary difference between the BibTeX and *refer* systems is that *refer* allows imprecise citations. *Refer*'s `indxbib` program examines a *refer* text database and creates a cross-index similar to the BIBDB cross-index. The `refer` program uses this cross-index to attempt to resolve imprecise citations to unique articles. If the citation is not sufficiently precise, so that it matches more than one database entry, `refer` prints an error message. The citation must then be enhanced to specify a unique reference.

During the design of BIBDB, we carefully considered the strengths and weaknesses of *refer*-style imprecise citations. The main advantage of the technique is that a user need not remember some (possibly cryptic) unique key to cite a paper. There are several significant disadvantages. Primarily, imprecise citations do not permit the "citation permanence" guarantees we desire. Consider the case when a user has cited a reference and generated a paper, but the next day the paper is no longer properly generated because another user has added an entry which also matches the imprecise citation, and thus the citation is no longer sufficient. We consider this an unacceptable failure, especially since we intend BIBDB to facilitate collaboration and incremental expansion. Confusion and annoyance could only result if a co-author found that another co-author's imprecise citation suddenly did not indicate a unique entry.

However, since we already have a fully developed cross-index to allow nonlinear searches of the database, there is no reason we can not also allow imprecise citations in the *refer* manner. Thus, `bibextract` does attempt to resolve imprecise citations, as described earlier. In fact, BIBDB implements imprecise citations with lower cost and greater flexibility than *refer*. If a *refer* user does not run `indxbib` on the entire database, `refer` must use a linear scan to resolve citations. Each change to a *refer* database requires that the entire database be re-indexed by an `indxbib` linear scan. BIBDB, on the other hand, performs its cross-indexing incrementally, as each entry is added, so once an entry has been cross-indexed it need never be done again. The `bibextract` operation never involves processing the entire database.

The `indxbib` program itself has a number of limitations which the BIBDB cross-index does not share. `Indxbib` truncates all words to six characters and discards words shorter than 3 characters, numbers less than 1900 or greater than 2000, and the 100 most common English words. The BIBDB overloaded-word mechanism is a far more flexible, dynamic implementation of the same attempt to reduce the size of the cross-index. And, since overloaded words can still be used in imprecise citations as long as at least one non-overloaded word is used, BIBDB provides more powerful and less costly imprecise citations than *refer*.

Mail-servers

A number of bibliographic database projects have recently made their databases available through mail-servers [2, 4]. In these systems, users email specially formatted queries to a public address, where an automated mail server processes the requests, usually overnight. The main disadvantage of these systems is that they are not on-line. Users must wait for unpredictable electronic mail to transmit their data, and they cannot find out if their queries were even properly formatted until at least the next day. Our queries to the LIDO mail-server [4], for instance, took over 2 days to return.

Mail-servers have the advantage that, since their processing can be batched to run when other demands on the host system are low, they can provide computationally expensive services. In particular, all of the mail-servers we have encountered use a simple linear scan of a text database. Since they are already doing linear scanning, the mail-servers can afford to allow regular expressions in the queries. Thus, mail servers can easily be implemented as front-ends to UNIX filters of the "grep" family. While regular expressions provide a more powerful mechanism for blind searching when the desired reference is not known, we consider the delays associated with mail-servers to be unacceptably long. Essentially, these services can be useful for literature searches, but are not integrated with text formatting systems and provide no way for users to add or modify entries.

However, mail-servers do not require Internet access: any user who can send and receive email can access the mail-servers. This vastly increases the number of people who can use these services. Fortunately, nothing in the nature of BIBDB prevents us from implementing a simple mail-server interface to accommodate those users. While the interactions required to verify changes to the database could become complex and slow, the retrieval functions could certainly be on par with any existing mail-server.

Other BIBTEX systems

Bibliographic database managers are a recurrent theme on the electronic newsgroups related to text formatting. A number of users have made their systems available to the Internet community [3, 7]. Most of these systems essentially provide front-end interfaces to textual BIBTEX databases, usually including regular-expression matching. While these systems are useful for maintaining small, personal databases, they have no provisions for sharing data or avoiding linear scanning. BIBDB is a far more powerful and wider-scope database management system.

Commercial systems

Most modern research libraries have electronic card catalogs which maintain records of bound publications. There are also a few services which list not just bound publications, but the separate articles within those publications. For example, the University of Michigan library provides network access to the Wilson Indexes to Journal Articles, a commercial database listing references from the Applied Science and Technology Index, Art Index, Social Sciences Index, and others. This resource provides exactly the sort of on-line keyword searching which BIBDB provides, over a much larger database than BIBDB currently controls. While the system is not interfaced to any bibliographic system, it probably could be. However, this may never occur, because the commercial systems all copyright their data. Using their data to directly create a document might violate that copyright.

The main advantage of these systems is that they can achieve complete coverage of the contents of periodicals, because the licensing fees are used to hire people whose sole responsibility is to input data. By relying on users for input, BIBDB grows slowly and provides only spotty coverage of publications. On the other hand, it also necessarily includes exactly the articles which users find useful, and thus it may be considered a pre-filtered source for literature searches, less complete than commercial systems, but more convenient when it comes time to write a paper or report.

Aside from copyright limitations, nothing prevents us from integrating the data from larger databases into the BIBDB database. We hope that in the future, major periodical publishers like the IEEE and ACM will send bibliographic information on their new publications directly into the BIBDB database, eliminating most user additions and improving coverage.

CURRENT STATUS & FUTURE WORK

The prototype BIBDB system operates as described in this paper. The initial release is confined to the University of Michigan, so only a single `bibdb-server` is kept running. The system is currently managing a database of over 15,000 bibliographic entries and over 250 string abbreviations. The associative retrieval of entries from known keys is essentially instantaneous. Searches that require computing the union and/or intersection of lists of entries take no more than a few seconds. This version and a previous, single-user version have been in use for over two years, helping members of the Real-Time Computing Laboratory (RTCL) at the University of Michigan produce dozens of papers. Several users outside of RTCL have also recognized the advantages of the system, and now use BIBDB full-time. The database has proven quite useful for blind searches, yielding dozens of useful references in our experience.

We intend to improve several aspects of the implementation, as outlined below.

Locking

Because BIBDB shares several kinds of writable data among multiple users, it makes extensive use of locking. We currently use the UNIX *flock* mechanism to implement locking. This method requires file system accesses which make locking fairly slow, thus increasing the severity of the `keymaster` bottleneck. Since all the `keymaster` copies run on the same machine, we could use shared-memory semaphores to implement locking, speeding the `keymaster`'s response time and increasing the number of `bibdb-servers` which could be served without significant performance degradation. Similarly, all the `bibdb-servers` at an installation run on the same machine, and could do their own locking via semaphores.

Data compression

Not surprisingly, the BIBDB database occupies large amounts of disk space. While the programs are quite small, the database is huge: the current bibliographic database occupies over 4.6 megabytes of disk space, and the cross-index consumes 31.7 megabytes. Obviously, using data compression techniques to reduce this excessive space requirement would be a desirable feature. We have examined several mechanisms for compressing the bibliographic data.

In order to maintain the incremental nature of BIBDB, we cannot compress the entire database at once: each entry must be stored in the gdbm file in its compressed form, independent of the other entries. Thus, so-called "universal" coding algorithms [10] which optimize themselves to their input are inappropriate, because the bibliographic entries do not supply enough data to establish valid statistical features. Tests with the UNIX universal coding `compress` utility confirm that strings of 300 bytes[3] can be compressed as little as 11%.

Coding algorithms which do not require lengthy input streams are more appropriate. Huffman coding provides high compression rates (on the order of 45–65%) when given a fixed set of input probabilities [6, 8]. We have written a utility which computes these probabilities from a BIBDB database. The existing database contains a very large sample of the expected BIBDB data, and thus provides input probabilities which will be representative of most new entries. All that remains is to integrate Huffman encoding and decoding routines with the gdbm library.

REFERENCES

[1] C. P. Bourne, "Frequency and Impact of Spelling Errors in Bibliographic Databases," *Information Processing Management*, vol. 13, no. 1, pp. 1–12, 1977.

[2] K. Ginther-Webster. *A New Resource for AAAI Members: Project Mercury: An Electronic Library.* in letter from AAAI, 1990.

[3] P. King. *Bibtex Database Management Programs.* USENET news article 4070 on comp.text.tex, December 1990.

[4] A. Kobsa. *The LIDO Mailserver for AI Literature.* USENET news article 7513 on comp.ai, November 1990.

[5] L. Lamport, *LaTeX : A Document Preparation System*, Addison Wesley, 1986.

[6] D. Severance, "A Practitioner's Guide to Database Compression," *Information Systems*, vol. 8, no. 1, , 1983.

[7] A. Shah. *Bibliography Management Tools, Take 2.* USENET news article 4089 on comp.text.tex, December 1990.

[8] J. D. Ullman, *Principles of Database Systems, Second Edition*, Computer Science Press, 1982.

[9] L. Wall and R. L. Schwartz, *Programming perl*, O'Reilly & Associates, Inc., 1991.

[10] J. Ziv and A. Lempel, "A Universal Algorithm for Sequential Data Compression," *IEEE Trans. Information Theory*, vol. IT-23, no. 3, pp. 337–343, May 1977.

[3] The current database averages 280 bytes per entry.

Supporting Communication between Designers with Artifact-Centered Evolving Information Spaces

Brent Reeves and Frank Shipman

Department of Computer Science and Institute of Cognitive Science
Campus Box 430
University of Colorado, Boulder, Colorado 80309
{brentr,shipman}@cs.colorado.edu

ABSTRACT

The interaction of various design decisions and the communication of the rationale for decisions between designers are two problems that have not been solved by current systems supporting design. Through the observation of computer network designers we have developed a framework, system architecture, and prototype implementation for supporting this type of communication within an evolving information space centered around the artifact being designed. The importance of our approach is in the integration of the design of the artifact and the communication between the designers. XNETWORK, a knowledge-based design environment for computer network design, incorporates this artifact-centered communication as a method for the easy addition of network designers' understanding about the design task.

KEYWORDS

Artifact based communication, information spaces, asynchronous collaboration, design environments

INTRODUCTION

Though ''collaboration happens'', it is not understood well enough for computer systems to help more than hinder in the process. Our work focuses on the central role that design artifacts play in the design process. We argue that supporting intermediate representations and design discussions is not enough. Discussions *about* the design must be embedded *in* the design [16]. Furthermore, this support must be integrated in a way that provides a seamless environment for both individual and group work [7, 5].

Permission to copy without fee all or part of this material is granted provided that the copies are not made or distributed for direct commercial advantage, the ACM copyright notice and the title of the publication and its date appear, and notice is given that copying is by permission of the Association for Computing Machinery. To copy otherwise, or to republish, requires a fee and/or specific permission.

© 1992 ACM 0-89791-543-7/92/0010/0394...$1.50

Two technical difficulties to embedding the discussion in the design have been providing support for different perspectives and different levels of abstraction. This paper describes extensions to a framework for design environments [4] and their instantiation in XNETWORK, a prototype design environment for supporting the collaborative design of computer networks.

We first give a theoretical framework for the context of our work. Next is an analysis of the tasks network designers face and the artifacts used to support those tasks. The related work section shows how this work differs from similar research. Next we describe in more detail the mechanisms of our prototype system. A scenario provides a concrete example of how our system supports network designers. Finally, we analyze the current weaknesses of this approach and point to future work.

THEORETICAL FRAMEWORK

Two factors combine to motivate the present focus on artifact-centered communication. First, individuals arrive at solutions by iteratively reframing the problem [11, 13]. This view of problem solving places more emphasis on the context of ill-defined problems and less on specific problem-solving techniques which might be applicable to well-defined problems. Second, most design work is done in teams [6] [8] [3]. This is hardly controversial; however it presents special difficulties for system designers who are trying to provide design environments that will be used to solve real-world problems.

Research has shown that problems and solutions often co-evolve, sometimes described as ''situated cognition.'' In a study done to understand how people learn and use mathematics in everyday problem solving, Lave discovered that solving problems is not just matching predefined techniques to problems found in the world, but that the problems themselves become defined as solutions are explored:

> People do not have a math problem unless they have a resolution shape — a sense of an answer and a process for bringing it together with its parts [11 ,p 19].

Furthermore, discussion among designers is crucial in framing the problem. A system for design teams should provide embedded communication facilities that are flexible enough to allow discussion at various levels: from specific design unit placement to more global issues.

> But with this emphasis on problem solving, we ignore problem *setting,* the process by which we define the decision to be made, the ends to be achieved, the means which may be chosen. In real-world practice, problems do not present themselves to the practitioner as givens. They must be constructed from the materials of problematic situations which are puzzling, troubling, and uncertain [15 ,p39,40].

This intertwining of problem and solution presents difficulties for group work situations. As group members bring differing perspectives to the problem solving process, each begins to understand the problem differently. After a while team members are no longer working on the same problem. The challenge is to coordinate the various evolving problem understandings. A designer working alone has the freedom to reframe a problem as deemed useful, but designers working as part of a team must continually consider others' understanding of the problem.

In recognition of the crucial role discussions and rationale play in the design of complex systems, computer systems have been built that attempt to capture design rationale. As will be seen later in the Related Work section, most computer supported cooperative work (CSCW) systems that focus on design rationale are written such that the design rationale evolves separately from the design artifact. This leads to several problems:

- It is difficult to establish the exact correspondence between a given feature of the evolving artifact and the discussion (design rationale) that motivated that feature.
- It is easy to overlook design decisions, to forget to "implement" in the artifact a design decision arrived at during discussions.
- It is easy to waste time making decisions that have already been made, since changing the design artifact space does not necessarily cause relevant aspects of the design discussions to be brought to the foreground.

Much of the time that designers work they work individually. When designers are working individually, on a divisible aspect of a design task, they should not be bothered with extra effort required by a system designed to support collaborative work. Artifact-centered information spaces support communication during collaborative work as well as individual work. Integrating group work and individual work is one difficulty of providing a tool that will be accepted by designers.

TASK ANALYSIS

On their own, designers in various domains of expertise have evolved certain representations to meet the above needs. The domain of interest to us is that of local-area network design. Over time, the logical map has evolved to serve as a key design document. It abstracts away many physical characteristics of the network but preserves connectedness. Types of devices are represented by icons that were agreed on by consensus of the community of network designers. Our approach to tools and artifacts currently in use by network designers might best be described as "respect." Respecting the tradition, yet still seeking ways to transcend everyday work practices [9].

Figure 1 shows an example of a logical map, used to ground discussions about changes to the (real) network. This map is a portion of a MacDraw document created by a network designer. This artifact was used to focus issues that arose during design meetings. One can write on it directly, annotating and arguing. It is easy to do ''end-user modification'': one just adds a symbol in the lower right-hand side box and then does a cut-and-paste onto the document. This representation has the same limitation that any domain-independent tool has: changes to this document have no semantic meaning beyond the interpretation given to them by the users.

Figure 2 shows another logical map produced by a computer tool, the MIT LCS Interactive Map program. This tool goes beyond the static document depicted in Figure 1 by adding domain-specific support and active components, e.g. an SNMP (simple network management protocol) component that allows the user to select a node and query the network to see its current state. The downside is that the system is not easily changed to accommodate new devices: one cannot just "add a new icon" and start placing it in the network, as in the case with the MacDraw document.

Both types of design artifacts shown in these figures influenced our work on a network design environment. These diagrams are similar to those used extensively by network designers in videotaped sessions to explain the history and rationale behind previous decisions and to discuss possible revisions when given ''what if'' scenarios. The videos illustrated the importance of grounding one's interactions in an appropriate representation of the artifact being designed and interpreted.

An ideal design artifact should have the following attributes: first, it should support the semantics of the domain; second, it should be modifiable by the designers; and third, the artifact should allow discussions to be embedded, rather than stored separately.

Schoen [1983] described design as:

> Designing is not primarily a form of problem solving, information processing, or search, but a kind of making. On this view, design knowledge and reasoning are expressed in designers' transactions with materials, artifacts made, conditions under which they are made, and manner of making.

Our goal was to address the above shortcomings and

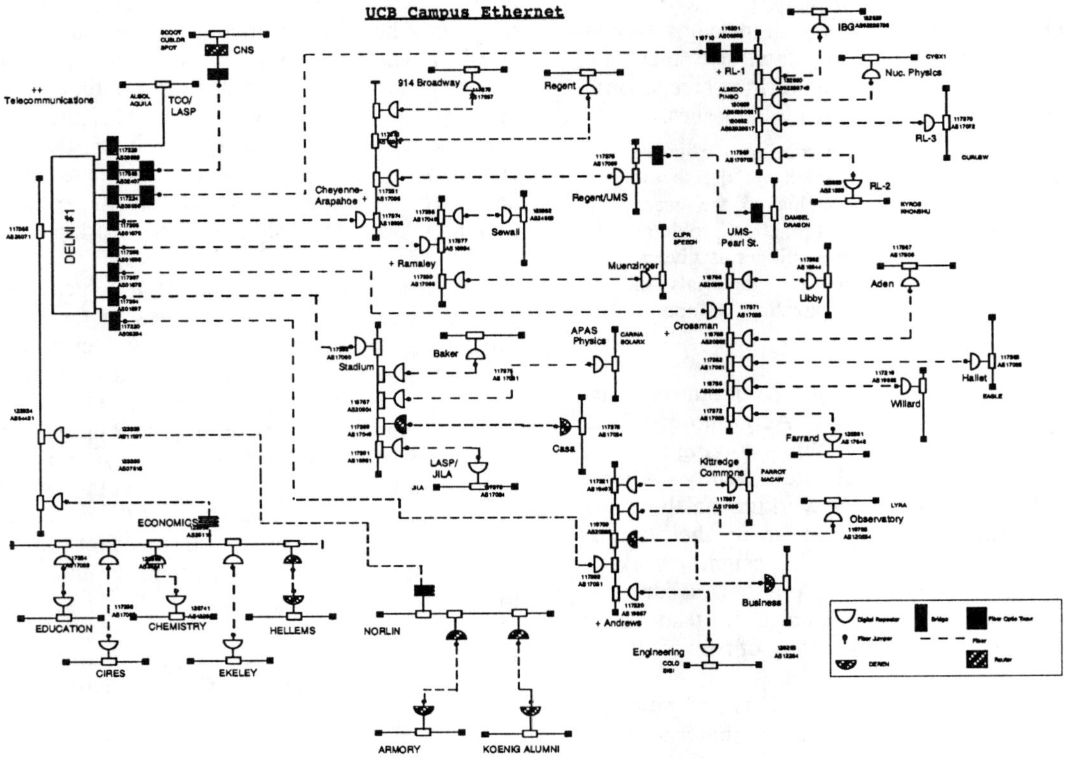

Figure 1: A portion of a logical map from a network designer

attempt to ground more of the designers ''transactions'' in the computer-mediated design artifact. The "making" and the "discussions about the making" were to be integrated. The logical map was chosen as the central design artifact. Other issues important to the design process would be placed in its context. Besides various technical details necessary to provide a good design tool, the next requirement that surfaced was that designers be able to deliberate decisions and document those deliberations in the form of design rationale. In design meetings (videotaped for analysis), those discussions were not divorced from the design artifact, but grounded in it.

Collaborating designers prefer to ground discussions in design representations. In video-taped sessions, we observed network designers as they explained previous design decisions and solved theoretical and upcoming expansion problems. The logical maps served to:

- point out inconsistencies between an appealing idea and its difficulty of implementation,
- remind participants of important constraints,
- and describe network states before and after changes.

Integrating the discussion with the design artifact is an obvious thing to do, but several difficulties have hampered progress. Most often researchers' interests are so specialized that one may study design rationale completely apart from any real design artifact. Another difficulty is that group members need to view the evolving artifact from different perspectives. Supporting multiple perspectives on a complex design artifact is not something that can be easily added later as a separate component. Knowledge representation also presents problems in embedding discussions in the design artifact. A computer-based system must support the whole spectrum of unstructured to structured data.

The difficulty of multiple perspectives in network design can be seen from the two most apparent views:

- Physical: this includes the physical attributes of all the devices, such as disk space and physical location.
- Logical: this is a higher level view that abstracts away many of the details in order to provide a global picture.

These viewpoints are supported by similar data namely formal representations of physical placement, devices, and connectivity. These viewpoints are not separable from the social context. Information about which group uses a set of machines and the type of work they do is important to the network design. This information involves formal information about which machines are used in which rooms by the group as well the implications of the network requirements for the type of work this group does.

An example mentioned in design sessions was that of a work group with one physically distant (though still in the same building) member. This caused wiring to be run so the work-group could be supported on a separate sub-net.

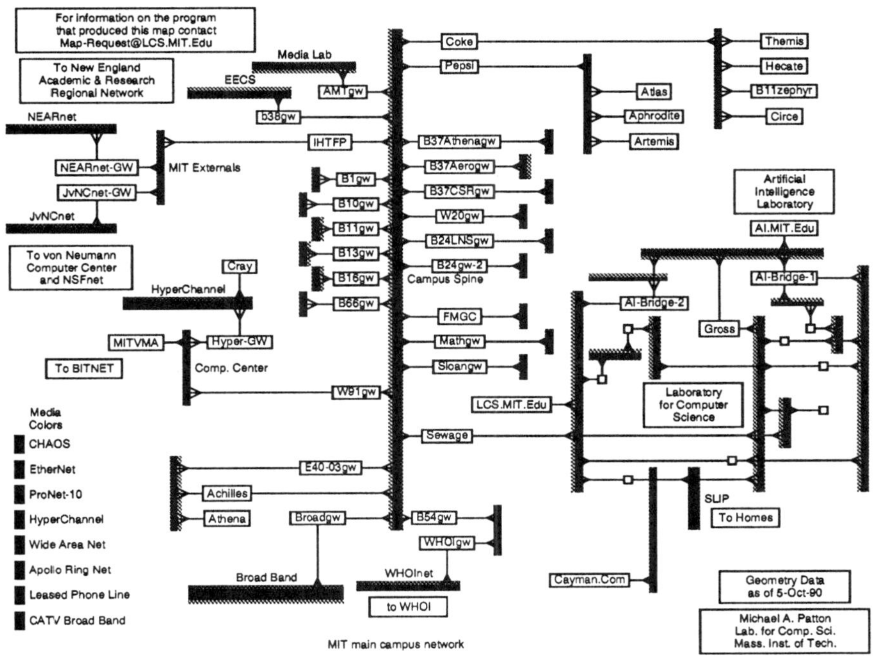

Figure 2: Output of computer tool used by network designers

This person moved several times, and each time, physical wires had to be routed. Network designers cannot dictate where work-groups are located and must adjust to the members' changing locations.

RELATED WORK

In supporting communication between designers in an artifact-centered way we have two classes of systems that are closely related to our work. Design rationale systems provide a framework in which discussions about design decisions can occur and be recorded, and we have included techniques from this approach. Annotation systems allow discussions to occur in a domain independent way. Our work combines these approaches to address difficulties encountered when used separately.

Design Rationale

Systems were built that support the capture of design rationale because most often design is a collaborative process and argument over various design trade-offs plays a central role. Issue-Based Information System (IBIS) is a methodology for documenting and structuring design deliberations [10]. Issues, positions, and arguments document the structure of the discussions. In response to perceived shortcomings of IBIS, PHI was developed [12]. It builds on IBIS by adding dependency relationships between issue resolutions, and adding support for documenting questions that, though they are not deliberated, are nevertheless important.

The gIBIS [2] system incorporates the IBIS methodology supports group communication in the form of issue-based design rationale through a graphical interface. In one observational study [17] the recording of design rationale was found to provide long term rewards if the initial work of recording the design rationale could be accomplished. It is unclear how well the current generation of design rationale systems work in practice without strong support internal to a project for the approach.

One emphasis of our work is to integrate the design rationale into the construction situation to make its use provide more obvious benefits for the designers. Design rationale should not exist as a separate entity from the design but should be able to exist in the design it is discussing. It is important that examples, as partial or whole designs, can be added into the design rationale.

Annotation

FREESTYLE is a commercial product that supports annotation of MS-DOS screen images combined with electronic and voice mail. The idea is that a person using an MS-DOS machine can "grab" any screen, say of a Lotus spreadsheet, and mail it electronically. In addition to mailing any screen, one can also annotate it in two ways: 1) by use of a stylus, e.g. drawing circles around "important" items, and 2) by voice mail. The receiver of the message gets the application screen, a dynamic replay of the voice mail and the stylus gestures that the sender made.

PREP supports asynchronously collaborating authors [1]. The document is organized by columns, which can be used for different grouping purposes, such as the text itself, plans, outlines, or various author's comments. This comes closest to our approach of integrating artifact and discussion since users can alter the original or comment in separate columns. It differs in that it serves as a tool and does not provide knowledge-based support.

The key difference between these kinds of annotation products and our approach is that we integrate the annotation- and construction-component. Integrating the annotation and the graphical design environment will help sharing substantive as well as procedural and annotative activities [16]. Substantive refers to the design artifact, the "substance" of discussion. Annotative activities are about the work, such as commenting and questioning; here the focus of critiquing support. Procedural activity pertains to discussions about the conventions for using the medium, for example turn-taking and recording discussions.

APPROACH

Our approach to solving the problems described in the last sections is based on experience with writing cooperative problem solving systems and builds on the framework described elsewhere [4]. As a result, we describe here only briefly the components of this architecture that are relevant to the current discussion. The primary focus has been on asynchronous communication and work on synchronous collaboration is in progress.

Mechanisms

The system described here (XNETWORK) supports the construction task, the capture of design rationale, and communication among designers. Previous work on design environments has integrated the construction of form with the argumentation about decisions through the combination of a construction component with a hypermedia argumentation component [4].

XNETWORK goes beyond this framework of connecting components that deal with a particular type of knowledge in isolation. XNETWORK allows for the integration of partial or whole design artifacts, PHI-style argumentation, and textual post-it notes within a single view. While separate components may and still do exist to support different tasks, the need for designers to use a particular component to access a certain type of knowledge has been greatly reduced. All the knowledge in the system is available to all the components.

As in other design environments XNETWORK includes a workspace where the design of form will most often occur. This construction kit represents domain specific building blocks which the designer uses to build graphical representations of the design [4]. Figure 3 shows a construction kit with a palette of network devices and cables that can be selected in the workspace to the left of the palette. The items in this palette were chosen by examining existing network design artifacts. The construction overview, an addition to previous construction kits used in design environments, provides the designer with a context for the part of the design shown in the workspace. This is needed in network design because of the size and complexity of designs. Previous design environments have dealt with domains where designs contain at most tens of objects, while a departmental network will often include many hundreds of devices.

One aspect of this architecture relevant to the discussion of artifact-centered communication is the annotation component that is embedded in the construction space. This allows designers to attach comments to the design artifacts. By integrating the construction and the discussion about the construction, the most crucial aspects of an argument are placed where they are most influential.

When a discussion is no longer needed in the workspace it can be moved to another view, or perhaps into an argumentation page. In previous design environments the argumentation component captures design rationale and evolves over time to reflect changes in technology and policy. Generic as well as project-specific information is contained. XNETWORK extends the argumentation component by providing generic argumentation pages that can be used as in previous design environments but also can contain pieces of designs and the textual discussion of the design. There is no loss of functionality in moving a piece of a design or discussion to an argumentation page except the absence of the palette and overview. Figure 4 shows an argumentation page containing PHI structured argumentation which, in turn, contains a piece of the design seen in figure 3, along with its discussion.

The integration of these components is possible because of a homogeneous underlying knowledge representation. One cannot simply tack on an annotation system and achieve the integration necessary to support the evolution of the design artifact and the discussion about that artifact. The system must be designed from the ground up to support the diverse types of knowledge that must be represented in a system. From formal knowledge about domain-specific data types, through semi-formal argumentation and to free-text notes: all are part of an evolving artifact.

XNETWORK supports the use of different views of the same network. Different views can be created and manipulated about the same network by copying a design into a new page and modifying it as desired. Changes to the graphical layout of a view (other than changes to devices graphical display primitives or to text) do not affect other views of the network. Changes made to a design's underlying knowledge (such as attributes of an object, graphical display primitives, and text) will also change this information for other views of the design.

Besides creating other views of a design the designers may create copies of a design or part of a design. Copies are different from views in that changes made to the underlying knowledge of a copy of a design does not affect the underlying knowledge of the original design.

Views and copies were motivated by the videotape sessions with network designers. The designers often referred to the state of a design at a particular time ("Before the CAPP lab

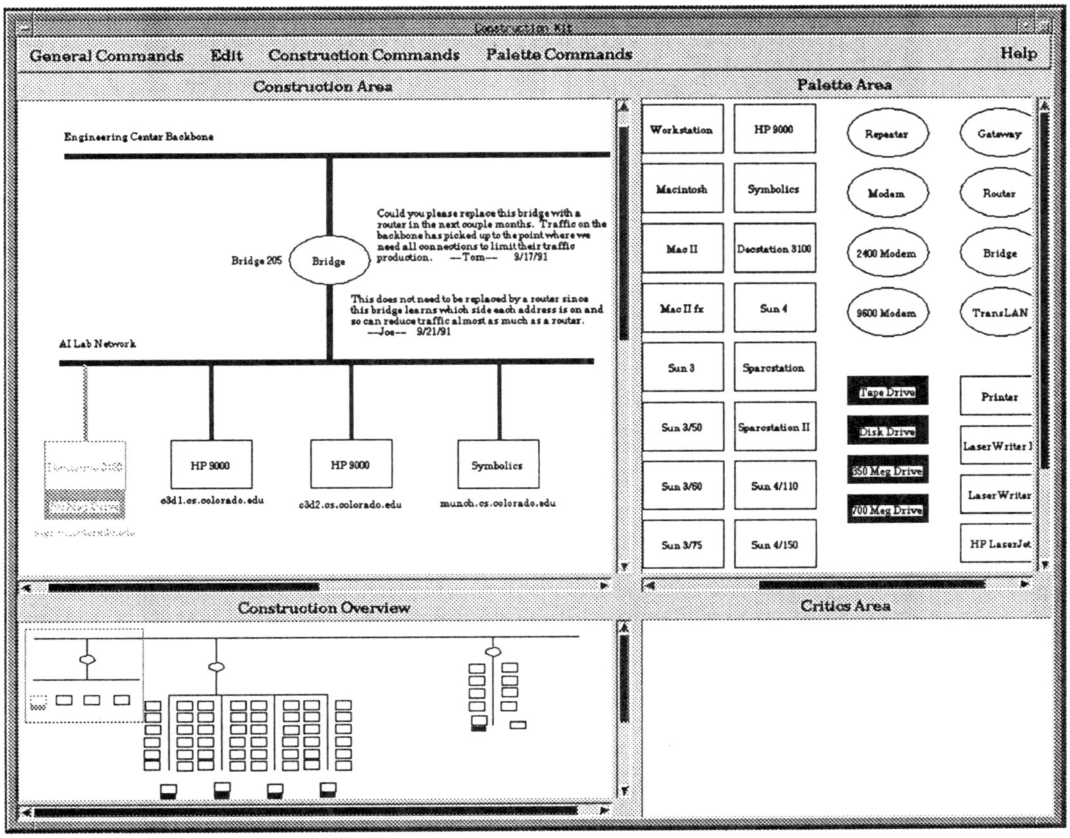

Figure 3: The Construction Kit for XNETWORK, a Prototype Network Design Environment

move ...") Copies can be used to record previous states of a design that can later provide a context for an old discussion or as examples in an argumentation structure. The designers also redrew parts of the design depending on what point they were trying to make or what decision they were discussing. XNETWORK's support for multiple views of an evolving design allows for views representing different perspectives of a design.

Scenario

Now that we have described the features of XNETWORK that are new to design environments we will present a scenario that illustrates some of the benefits of these features. The scenario describes what we consider to be ordinary usage of the system. Though designers have used the system to help us in task analysis and all of the functionality described here is implemented, this scenario was first written to serve as a design requirements document and did not happen in real use.

This scenario describes the use of XNETWORK, as it currently exists, by three network administrators: Pat, Joe, and Tom. These three designers have different responsibilities for a departmental network. Pat is in charge of the network segments in the classroom wing of the building, Joe is in charge of the network segments in the office tower part of the building, and Tom is in charge of the overall design of the network.

Because of the global concern for increasing traffic on the departmental backbone cable Tom has decided that backbone connections should be done only with routers. Tom locates the devices connected to the backbone and finds that Joe and Pat use bridges for connections to the backbone cable in their sections of the network. Tom leaves a note for Joe and Pat next to the bridges in the design artifact that should be changed and asks that they be replaced by a certain date.

Joe reads Tom's note and wants to look up rationale for bridges and routers. By browsing the topics related to bridges and selecting the issue shown in Figure 4, Joe finds that Tom has added the rationale for routers to the argumentation base.

After evaluating the argumentation and Tom's comment, Joe replies by adding a note next to the bridge in this section of the network arguing that the present configuration achieves Tom's intent. Figure 3 shows the part of the design in the location of this bridge.

Pat's view of the network abstracts out most of the details on the office tower segments, instead focusing on classroom computation. Notice that in Pat's view the AI Lab Network, shown in detail in Joe's view, is represented by one cable in Pat's view. If Pat asks to see the system's knowledge on the bridge to the AI Lab Network the system

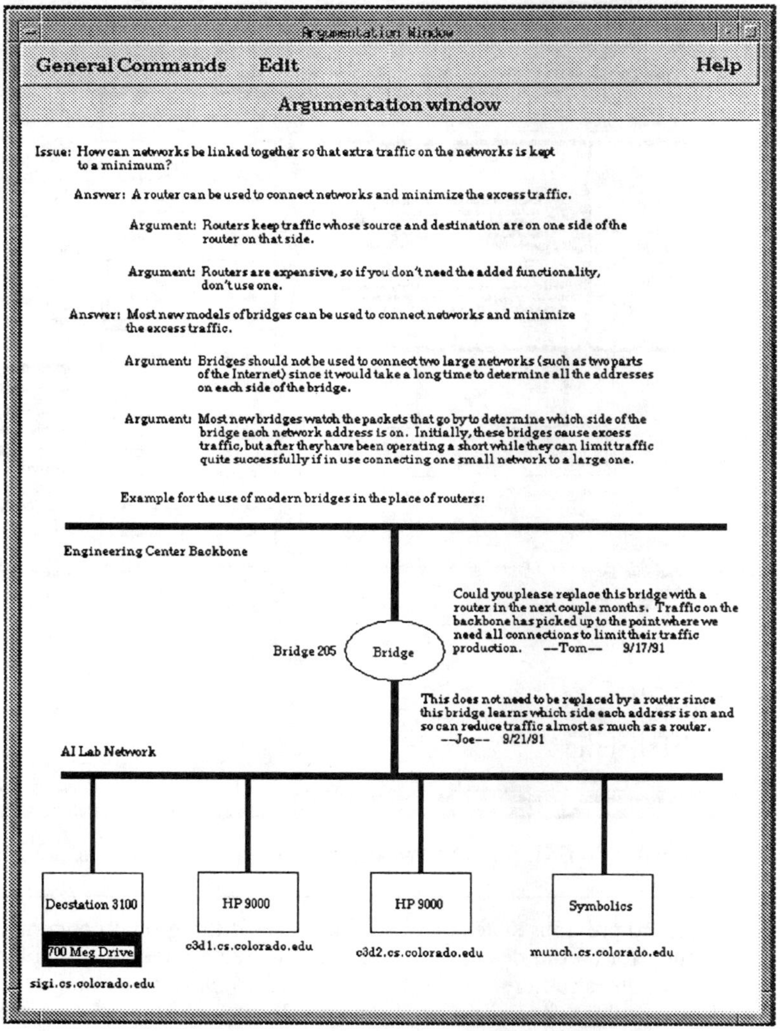

Figure 4: Argumentation Page with an Example in XNETWORK

will display the same information that is available in Joe's view, i.e. the data is there and can be reached even though it may not be visible from a particular view.

In another section of the network, Pat needs to address Tom's request to replace a bridge. By looking at other connections to the backbone cable, Pat learns of the similar request of Joe. Pat is interested in how Joe is addressing the request and reads the conversation around the bridge in Joe's section of the network and in the argumentation.

After reading the discussion Pat decides this would make a good example to show the use of a bridge in resolving the issue about how networks should be connected. Pat makes a copy of the appropriate subpart of the design and places it as an example in the argumentation page discussing how to connect networks using smart traffic control bridges, a new answer to an issue that already existed in the argumentation. The result of this addition can be seen in figure 4. Pat decides that this situation is not like Joe's but to replace the older bridge with a newer bridge, citing the new argumentation as an explanation for this decision.

This scenario provides an example of how we see XNETWORK being used. It shows the need to support multiple views and the need for representations of varying degrees of formality.

DISCUSSION/CONCLUSIONS

Limitations

Certain limitations are directly related to network design. Our approach focuses on domains that can be graphically represented, especially network design. Designers in this domain distinguish between logical and physical design and the correspondence is well understood. Also, our approach has so far focused on a class of users that is homogeneous, namely logical designers. However the approach appears to hold the most promise for groups of designers that are from varied backgrounds.

Other limitations are aspects of the prototype system. One

problem with carrying out discussions in the construction space is that it quickly becomes cluttered. It does not take many notes to obscure the design artifact. One factor that helps the situation is that over time, text notes will become integrated with the argumentation structure. They will still be accessible through the artifact, but may be hidden in the artifact itself to help with the clutter. One can select linked objects from a menu reachable from any object.

One solution we provide to address this problem of clutter is a filter. Different perspectives can be used to filter out the notes. For example, in Figure 3 the Global Construction View filters out labels and annotations. Currently there is no general-purpose filter facility to remove all objects of a given item type, but allowing the users to suppress notes and labels handles the bulk of the problem.

Though we think that unstructured textual notes combined with the argumentation component are a step towards capturing important influences at the social/political level, we realize that these issues will always resist formalization. Until we know how to better help designers represent these concepts without the disadvantages of making them explicit, we will continue to make incremental and experimental strides. As the system is now, people decide just how much information to submit and track, choosing what information to represent and how formal to make it.

Summary

Designers have always preferred working on the design artifact itself: evaluating various options by direct manipulation. When this becomes impossible (architecture, networks) representations are constructed that ground the design discussion. Domain-dependent annotation is required to ground the discussion and allow knowledge-based systems to leverage human expertise. Tools must be provided to support the merging of these notes into the existing argumentation space. In this way, the system uses an evolving information space to support communication among collaborating designers.

ACKNOWLEDGEMENTS

We thank Skip Ellis, Gerhard Fischer, Jonathan Grudin, the network designers at CU Boulder, and the anonymous reviewers for helping in various ways with this work and paper. This research was supported in part by grant No. IRI-9015441 from the National Science Foundation.

REFERENCES

1. Cavalier, T., Chandhok, R., Morris, J., Kaufer, D. and Neuwirth, C. A visual design for collaborative work: Columns for commenting and annotation. The 24th Hawaii International Conference on System Sciences, January, 1991, pp. 729-738.

2. Conklin, J. and Begeman M. "gIBIS: A Hypertext Tool for Exploratory Policy Discussion". *Transactions of Office Information Systems 6*, 4 (October 1988), 303-331.

3. DeMarco, T. and Lister, T. *Peopleware: Productive Projects and Teams.* Dorset House Publishing, New York, 1987.

4. Fischer, G., Grudin, J., Lemke, A.C., McCall, R., Ostwald, J., Reeves, B.N. and Shipman, F. "Supporting Indirect, Collaborative Design with Integrated Knowledge-Based Design Environments". *Human Computer Interaction 7*, 3 (1992). (in press).

5. Foster, G. and Tatar, D. Experiments in computer support for teamwork - Colab (Video).

6. Hackman, J.R. and Kaplan, R.E. "Interventions into group process: An approach to improving the effectiveness of groups". *Decision Sciences 5* (1974), 459-480.

7. Ishii, H. and Miyake, N. "Toward an open shared workspace: Computer and Video Fusion Approach of Teamworkstation". *Communications of the ACM 34*, 12 (December 1991), 37-50.

8. Johansen, R. *Groupware: Computer Support for Business Teams.* The Free Press, New York, 1988.

9. Kling, R. "Cooperation, Coordination and Control in Comptuer Supported Work". *Communications of the ACM 34*, 12 (December 1991), 83-88.

10. Kunz, W. and Rittel, H.W.J. Issues as Elements of Information Systems. Working Paper 131, Center for Planning and Development Research, University of California, Berkeley, CA, 1970.

11. Lave, J. *Cognition in Practice.* Cambridge University Press, Cambridge, UK, 1988.

12. McCall, R. On the Structure and Use of Issue Systems in Design. University Microfilms, 1979.

13. Rittel, H.W.J. Second-Generation Design Methods. In N. Cross, Ed., *Developments in Design Methodology*, John Wiley & Sons, New York, 1984, pp. 317-327.

14. Schoen, D.A. *The Reflective Practitioner: How Professionals Think in Action.* Basic Books, New York, 1983.

15. Schoen, D.A. *Educating the Reflective Practitioner.* Jossey-Bass Publishers, San Francisco, CA, 1987.

16. Trigg, R.H., Suchman, L.A. and Halasz F.G. Supporting Collaboration in NoteCards. Proceedings of the Conference on Computer-Supported Cooperative Work (CSCW'86), MCC, Austin, TX, December, 1986, pp. 153-162.

17. Yakemovic, K.C. and Conklin, E.J. Report of a Development Project Use of an Issue-Based Information System. Proceedings of the Conference on Computer-Supported Cooperative Work (CSCW'90), 1990, pp. 105-118.

Index of Authors

~ Notes ~